ESSAYS ON
Freedom and Power

By

John Emerich Edward Dalberg-Acton
FIRST BARON ACTON

Selected, and with an introduction by
Gertrude Himmelfarb

Preface by
Herman Finer

1949

Trade Edition: THE BEACON PRESS, *Boston, Mass.*
Text and Library Edition: THE FREE PRESS, *Glencoe, Ill.*

Copyright, 1948
THE FREE PRESS
Second printing, November, 1949

PRINTED IN U.S.A.

ACKNOWLEDGMENT

Grateful acknowledgment is made to the Macmillan Company for permission to reprint material from the following books: *The History of Freedom and Other Essays, Historical Essays and Studies, Lectures on the French Revolution, Lectures on Modern History* and *Letters of Lord Acton to Mary Gladstone.*

PREFACE

Those who read Acton today will treble Lord Morley's praise of him and affirm that they would undertake to find on every page of Acton at the very least one pregnant, pithy, luminous, suggestive saying. For Acton's is the splendid voice of charity and informed wisdom heard from above the merciless and warring extremists of a sorely perplexed time. His reputation as a master historian, elevated as a mountain of constancy above the flat wastelands, attests that the greatness of a soul is measurable by the duration — the undefeatable vitality — of its moral force.

To what is the perennial appeal of Acton due? Above all, to Acton's moral integrity. Firm, steady, dispassionate, self-controlled, unbelievably erudite, he does not yield his ethical principles one iota. In devotion to the supremacy of the Sermon on the Mount, he said "no surrender" to iniquity. His studies command a persistent, ever-recurring esteem for his own precious, sacrificial devotion to truth. Though men may be errant, they are brought back again to Acton's vindication of the supreme human truths as they shine forth from the course of history: religion, veracity, justice, the hatred of lies and cruelty.

Acton was no mystic, though like all men his mind reposed upon a faith. He was an intellectual who wrote of men's gravest concerns, earnestly and scrupulously, with brilliant illumination, following the discoverable evidence. He was a powerful, indefatigable explorer of human nature and human events, rich in ideas, deep in thought, highly practiced in reflection. He believed in the capacity and the right of man's intellect to investigate and to discriminate between good and evil, not that man's mind must suffer defeat. For Acton, historical exploration was the true demonstration and sovereign guidance of private and public conscience.

I compute that he read some twenty thousand books. What appears here is a representative portion of what he wrote or spoke on the path to what he never succeeded in writing, a *History of Liberty*. Greater integrity hath no man than this, that he abandoneth his unwritten book when intellect hath declared the materials imperfect.

In time of affliction it becomes compulsive in mankind to rake over the ashes to identify at what point — virtue, character, fate, knowledge or environment — the course might have been differently ordered. Acton is an oracle today because he is a "universal" historian, that is to say, his range is immense in time and terrestrial area. He is sophisticated enough to include the making of history, as he said, by events "on the political backstairs." Acton's history is a steady majestic voyage of the mind and soul in a vast and comprehensible path and design, not merely mundane, concrete. It has spiritual meaning: gushes lessons on the nature, capacities, and destiny of man, the relationship of individual conscience to the movement of society and of the rights of man to the power of government. It promises to enable us to make political science and political judgments effective. The standing attraction of this kind of history is its assured offer of something like the full formula of human nature in politics.

If the design were something horrible, Acton's history might still be left in its little black boxes used by the author as his storehouse of notes. Acton's history vindicates human freedom, which he sets above any other human interest. "Liberty," says Acton, "is not a means to a higher political end. It is itself the highest political end." Now everybody is a devotee of freedom — for what particular good is another matter. And whether one can bestow it on all, without denying a proportion of it to each, is also another matter, as we shall see. But the prayer to liberty must find eager admirers in an age chastised by total war, diabolically ingenious torture, thorny economic and social perplexities; in an age in which a developing democratic conscience is at odds with almighty economic entrepreneurs and hereditary vested interests, of conscious extensive state economic planning, and of intransigent, despotic and murderous politicians of extreme left and right, who have contemptuously discarded charity and banished truth, virtue and mercy.

Arnold J. Toynbee's *A Study of History* is not formally a history of liberty; but, in so far as it is a significant history of civilizations it is bound to be a valuable history of liberty. It is just possible that Acton did not so succeed because he became prophetic enough to realize that success meant failure. Toynbee's success (which he did not purpose) consists in almost completely revealing the gaps in a full and final account of man in society; and not only this, but the dreadful inevitability of gaps, the fatality of the necessary escape of facts and understanding which the historian tries to domesticate. The pattern the historian discovers is seen to be an approximation, after all. Acton must have looked back on the essays of his earlier days — for example, the two on the "civil war" in the United States — and surely have learned that if man can err on a contemporary event of world magnitude, how hesitant must a man of conscience (which Acton was above all else) be about events of a remoter past?

People seek a broad sweeping historical induction which shall be the truth, the whole truth, and nothing but the truth — wide in its compass, profound in its insight, and utterly convincing in its finish and definition — but such revelation cannot be won once and for all, at any one time by a single man, or a sect, school, church or nation, or even by an international band of scholars. Acton deplores the imperfection of historical materials. His efforts furnish a grand practical dual lesson in history: what we must add to historical induction to reach valid social conclusions, and with what a qualifying spirit the historians' conclusions must be read if their account of human nature is to be helpful to those who are governed and those who govern. How foolish it would be not to listen to so earnest, learned and wise a man, speaking on the grandest of human concerns in grave and noble accents, simply because it is given to no man to be capable of uttering any more than a warning!

However scrupulous Acton was to assimilate and write all his facts, as Ranke desired — letting them speak for themselves without personal interference — his conception of the role of history is provocative. His rule was:

> The inflexible integrity of the moral code is, to me, the secret of the authority, the dignity, the utility of History. If we may debase the currency for the sake of genius, or success, or rank, or reputation, we may debase it for the sake of a man's influence, of his religion, of his disgrace. Then History ceases to be a science, an arbiter of controversy, a guide of the wanderer, the upholder of that moral standard which the powers of the earth, and religion itself, tend constantly to depress.

Whoever holds the view that he is a moral censor must begin with a principle of censure; and we, who read to learn, can be sure rather of his iterated principle than confident that we have been told all. When Acton declares that "all history is the true demonstration of religion," or postulates that "the full exposition of truth is the great object for which the existence of mankind is prolonged on earth," or that "liberty is the highest political end," we are so dazzled that we suspect that many phenomena may still lurk unexamined in the shadow. He has judged well for us, and yet has not brought into our own court the alternatives, the facts presented to him. Our judgment is usurped, and our right of moral choice annexed. When history is a tool of morality, it can enlighten us as much as the moralist can, but no more; for we are likely to end the study of history exactly where we began, except that immorality (with Acton) has illustrations to adorn the tale, and morality shines in picturesque raiment.

Acton had a very resolute standard of judgment, and a standard kills some of life. Acton's standard was less clear-cut and monistic than he himself thought proper. In the actual blended plurality of his own values against his own will and logic, there is a lesson he never consciously used about the understanding of human nature in politics and society. It is that no single solitary unmixed idea has ever ruled or satisfied man, nor can it do so; all social science, like all motivation, is an affair of degree; and universal histories are not capable of revealing exact degree to us. The air of certitude imported into judgment is ill-adapted to inquiry. Acton quotes with approval from the theologian Mozeley:

A Christian is bound by his very creed to suspect evil, and cannot release himself. . . . He owns the doctrine of original sin; that doctrine necessarily puts him on his guard against appearances, sustains his apprehension under perplexity, and prepares him for recognizing anywhere what he knows to be everywhere.

This kind of certitude can have a very bad influence on bad men. More valuable by far are Acton's dicta regarding the stern obligation of the historian to make out the other side's case even better than the other side could make it out for itself. This method has to be balanced against the threat of the overfervent moral criterion.

Acton's value to the student of history, and still more to the student of politics and society, is his perennial concern with the grand themes of Power, Democracy, Equality, Liberty, Nationality and Religion. People are less interested in mere narration than in social judgment. It will be seen that all of Acton's teaching is conditioned by, if it does not issue from, his disavowal of Power. This is most acutely encountered in two of his own sayings: "Power tends to corrupt and absolute power corrupts absolutely. Great men are almost always bad men, even when they exercise influence not authority." And the second is: "The greatest crime is Homicide. The accomplice is no better than the assassin; the theorist is worse."

It is this which puts a limiting perimeter on his admiration for Democracy, Liberty, and Equality, and even, it must be said, for Religion, for he certainly and abundantly recorded it of his own Church. He appreciates the values in the various liberties. He gladly acknowledges that they constituted human progress. He joyously applauds the movements in history which overthrew the many varieties of despotism. He welcomes the men and the doctrines that established the principles and the institutions of the triumphant liberal and representative states. But he sees also that if any single, untempered idea, should attain the exclusive dominion over the mind of man, however good it were, the power needed to establish its victory and cement its reign — thus Equality, or Democracy, or Nationality — must limit and debase Liberty. Though he did not quote Montesquieu, their minds move together: "Virtue itself hath need of limits," for freedom and tranquillity lie in self-restraint. To demand all is to lose all by very excess.

Yet, though these are indispensable truths, they ought not to obscure the equally indispensable truth that Power is beneficent. Pascal spoke concerning this, once and for all: "Without Power, Justice is unavailing." For the kingdom of politics is of this world. And Power, as the biographies of so many statesmen reveal (for example, that of Sir Thomas More), heightens sensitiveness, stimulates the imagination of purposes and expedients, generates invention, develops compassion when it places men where they confront the sorrows which government exists to assuage and the trials which must be visited on some in order that others may have a more abundant life; and power develops humility and fortitude. These are precious qualities in the service of mankind, and inseverable from power. Together they will one day enable humanity to progress, as Acton recommended, from nationalism to an embracing state that shall include the whole world.

The study of Acton in this volume, in a sympathetic and alert spirit, cannot fail to multiply the number of truly democratic citizens, or to enhance their abilities and their acknowledgment of obligation to their fellow men.

HERMAN FINER

The University of Chicago
April, 1948

CONTENTS

ACKNOWLEDGMENTS	v
PREFACE	vii
INTRODUCTION	xv
CHAPTER I—Inaugural Lecture on the Study of History	3
CHAPTER II—The History of Freedom in Antiquity .	30
CHAPTER III—The History of Freedom in Christianity	58
CHAPTER IV—The Protestant Theory of Persecution .	88
CHAPTER V—Sir Erskine May's "Democracy in Europe"	128
CHAPTER VI—Nationality	166
CHAPTER VII—Political Causes of the American Revolution	196
CHAPTER VIII—The Background of the French Revolution	251
CHAPTER IX—Conflicts with Rome	269
CHAPTER X—The Vatican Council	299
ACTON-CREIGHTON CORRESPONDENCE	357
BIBLIOGRAPHY	374
APPENDIX—Notes to Chapter I	399
INDEX	429

INTRODUCTION

I

WHEN LORD ACTON died in 1902 his name was unfamiliar to the general public. The assiduous reader of the London *Times* might have identified him as reputedly the most erudite man of his era He might have remembered the rumors, some thirty years before, of Acton's possible excommunication from the Catholic church. He might have recalled occasional items in the society, court and literary columns in which Acton had figured as the week-end guest of Mr. Gladstone at Hawarden, as Lord-in-Waiting to Her late Majesty at Windsor Castle, as professor at Cambridge University and editor of a grand, new, encyclopedic venture, the *Cambridge Modern History*. It would have been a miscellaneous assortment of facts, likely to confirm Acton's own sense of the futility of his life.

The current fortune of his reputation would have been more agreeable to Acton. It would have gratified him to know that his maxim, "Power tends to corrupt and absolute power corrupts absolutely," has become commonplace enough to serve as the text for editorials in daily newspapers, and that he has been awarded the titles of prophet of liberalism and magistrate of history. If he could claim no particular distinction for his own life, he could claim to have given distinction to the two ideas he valued most, the ideas of liberty and morality.

Now that Acton has attained the status of a minor prophet, it is difficult to reconstruct his life in Victorian England. Not only do his ideas transcend the period in which they were conceived, but the details of his life and background often jar with the familiar picture of that period. Related to a variety of nationalities and aristocracies, he was as far removed as possible from the insularity and even provincialism that seemed to be settling over England by the middle of the nineteenth century.

John Emerich Edward Dalberg-Acton was born in Naples in 1834. His paternal ancestors are recorded as having occupied the family estate of Aldenham in Shropshire as far back as the beginning of the fourteenth century. In the eighteenth century an adventurous junior branch of the family had transferred its allegiance to France and then to Italy. Acton's grandfather, Sir John Acton, having won the affections of the Queen of Naples, converted the role of adventurer into that of prime minister of Naples. With the extinction of the older branch of the family in 1791, Sir John succeeded to the baronetcy and estate. His grandson, born forty-three years later, disapproved of the unconventional life and career of his grandfather (which included a period as head of a reign of terror in Palermo), and refused to accept money due him from the Italian fortune.

His maternal ancestors were more respectable and more congenial to Acton's temperament. The Dalbergs had been the first nobles under the emperor in the Holy Roman Empire, and claimed the further and less verifiable distinction of descent from a relative of Jesus Christ himself. (The story of the relationship to Jesus is no doubt apocryphal, but if it does not establish glorious antiquity, it does suggest religious piety.) Like the Actons, the Dalbergs were nationally uprooted and shared the uncertain fate of the Empire. It has been said that a treatise on the law of nationality and domicile could be based on the frequent migrations and changes of position of the dukes of Dalberg who finally threw in their lot with France during the Restoration and were created peers. The family estate continued to be maintained at Herrnsheim on the Rhine.

Acton's father, Sir Richard, died prematurely, and in his stepfather the family circle acquired yet another illustrious name, that of Lord Leveson, later the second Earl Granville. The Leveson-Gowers had long been prominent in the Whig aristocracy and in English diplomacy and politics, and Acton's stepfather continued the tradition as foreign minister in the Liberal cabinets of Lord John Russell and William Gladstone. Acton's cosmopolitanism was more than a matter of principle or training; it was the substance of all his life. His early youth was passed, alternately, at the family residences at Naples, Paris, Herrnsheim, Aldenham and London. He soon spoke and wrote Italian, French, German and English with almost equal fluency. Later in life the conversation at his dinner table was multilingual to accommodate all the members of the family: he chatted in English with his children, in German with his Bavarian-born wife (a daughter of Count Arco-Valley and a first cousin to Acton), in French with his sister-in-law, and in Italian with his mother-in-law.

The Dalbergs, like the great majority of the Bavarian aristocracy, had always been Catholic, and the Actons had been reconverted to Catholicism in the eighteenth century. One of the stipulations in the marriage agreement between Lady Acton and Lord Leveson was that her son should be brought up in her faith. At no time does his stepfather's Anglicanism seem to have affected the Catholic piety and orthodoxy of Acton's childhood, although it was important in giving him entrance into the great Protestant houses of England.

His education, in fact, highlights the main personalities and schools of Catholic thought in the last half of the century. He studied for a short time under Monsignor Félix Dupanloup in Paris,[1] for a long period at the Catholic college, Oscott, in England, of which Bishop Nicholas Wiseman was president, and he completed his education at the university level under Professor Johann Ignaz von Döllinger in Munich. Dupanloup was involved for a while in one of the most interesting Catholic experiments in modern times,

---
[1] Archbishop David Mathew, in his recent biography, *Acton: The Formative Years* (London, 1946), doubts that Acton was a student at Dupanloup's seminary of Saint Nicolas. "If Acton was ever taught by Dupanloup, he does not seem to have referred to it" (p 54). There are, in fact, several references by Acton, in his personal notes left to the Cambridge University Library (for example, in Additional MSS, 4975), to the period spent at the seminary in 1842-43 These confirm the testimony of several of his friends.

the attempt to restate the relations of church and state so as to satisfy the requirements of political liberalism. Wiseman was the guiding spirit of a new ecclesiastical offensive, Ultramontanism, directed against the liberal state and intended to revive some of the dormant authority of the church. Döllinger was a distinguished scholar who despised the principles Wiseman stood for, and sacrificed his communion in the church by leading the opposition to the papal pretensions asserted by Pius IX.

Acton arrived in Munich in 1850, a decisive date, for the shadow of Döllinger was to hover behind him the rest of his life.[2] Had Cambridge agreed to admit him (he had applied to three colleges and had been rejected by all, probably because of the strong prejudice against Catholics), his future career might have been very different. Cambridge at the time prided itself on its prosaic, matter-of-fact common sense. Leslie Stephen recalled that Cambridge men "did not deny the existence of the soul, but they knew that it should be kept in its proper place." Cambridge might have fashioned Acton in the model of Lord Granville, the practical, urbane and good-humored politician, whose enthusiasm never extended to the point of committing a breach of taste. Instead, Acton came under the influence of Döllinger, the earnest and scrupulous historian and moralist. It was Döllinger who originally inspired him with his respect for learning and scholarship, a respect that later involved both master and disciple in conflict with those in the church who arrogated to themselves the right to pass upon the findings of scholarship and to judge

---
[2] This date is almost always given as 1848. The editors of Acton's correspondence, J N. Figgis and R V. Laurence, were probably originally responsible for the error. In one of his first letters from Munich to his family, Acton mentioned Döllinger's attendance at the meetings of the Assembly. Assuming that the reference was to the Frankfurt Assembly, to which Dollinger had been a delegate, the editors dated the letter as 1848. The *Dictionary of National Biography* and almost all subsequent biographers, including Archbishop Mathew, commit the same error Acton's personal notes and the three-volume biography of Dollinger by Johann Friedrich establish the fact of Acton's arrival at Munich in the summer of 1850, when Dollinger was present at the sessions of the Bavarian Assembly, of which he was a member. Professor Herbert Butterfield makes this point in his review of Mathew's book in the *English Historical Review*, Vol. LXI (1946).

the propriety of making them known. The principle of the autonomy of science, the cardinal point of Döllinger's teaching, was the core of Acton's entire philosophy of political liberalism.

It was said of Acton that he knew everyone worth knowing and had read everything worth reading, and both distinctions date from this period. He read voluminously in history, philosophy, literature and theology, started to collect the library which was to grow to such huge proportions, and travelled extensively — vacation trips with Döllinger on the continent, a visit to the United States in 1853 in the company of his relative, the Earl of Ellesmere, and a visit to Russia in 1856 as secretary to Lord Granville. He became personally acquainted with almost every important theologian, historian and Catholic layman in England, on the continent, and even in the United States, and with many prominent statesmen and diplomats. Born into the social aristocracy, he early acquired a similar status in the intellectual, religious and political elite.

In 1859, when he was twenty-five, he assumed the editorship of the Catholic periodical, the *Rambler,* and proposed, with more enthusiasm than discretion, to instruct his countrymen in the ways of the true learning (in which only the Germans were initiated), and to enlighten them as to their real political interests. The ecclesiastical authorities had long been provoked by what they considered to be the irreverent manner of the *Rambler,* and just before Acton became associated with the journal, John Henry Newman, England's most famous convert, had served as editor in the futile hope of placating the authorities. Almost every issue under Acton's editorship found occasion to point the moral: faith and knowledge, religion and science, were necessarily in harmony and had nothing to fear from each other; the temporal interests of the church must not be confused with its ultimate purpose, and the authorities must resist the temptation to deny unsavory historical truths or to conceal discoveries that might be of comfort to unbelievers; scientific truth could not but vindicate the true religion.

With the journal's change from a bimonthly to a quarterly in 1862, it appeared under the title of the *Home and Foreign Review*. Its message, however, remained unchanged, and its very first issue brought down the censure of Wiseman. "Biblical criticism," Darwinism, frank appraisals of church history and contemporary Catholic governments — the review took them all in its stride. The English Ultramontanes, particularly Cardinal Wiseman, Bishop Manning and W. G. Ward, naturally regarded it as a threat to their authority and teaching. Their task was, as Manning put it, to overcome "the anti-Roman and anti-papal spirit of the English Catholics." The *Home and Foreign Review* seemed bent upon aggravating the condition they wished to remedy. Acton himself chose to interpret the quarrels between the *Review* and the hierarchy as a struggle between Italy and Germany for the soul of England — Italy representing the ecclesiastical organization superstitiously confounding its own will with that of God, and Germany representing the pure spirit of scholarship and truth:

> The German writers were engaged in an arduous struggle, in which their antagonists [the Protestants] were sustained by intellectual power, solid learning, and deep thought, such as the defenders of the Church in Catholic countries have never had to encounter. In this conflict the Italian divines could render no assistance. They had shown themselves altogether incompetent to cope with modern science.[3]

At a Catholic congress in Munich in 1863, Döllinger appealed to the church to bring to an end its hostility towards historical criticism. The pope's response took the form of a brief to the Archbishop of Munich declaring the opinions of Catholic writers subject to Rome. The *Home and Foreign Review*, which had enthusiastically reported Dollinger's speech, could no longer disregard the strictures of the church. "Conflicts with Rome" appeared in the *Review* in April, 1864, announcing Acton's decision to suspend publication. He could not change his views, but neither would he continue to flout the hierarchy. That same year Pius IX issued his

---
[3] "Conflicts with Rome," p. 283 of this volume.

famous Syllabus of Errors, a list of the heresies disseminated by liberalism; the final heresy reads like a declaration of Acton's principles: "The Roman Pontiff can and ought to reconcile himself to, and agree with, progress, liberalism and recent civilization."

During this time, Lord Granville had tried to introduce Acton into the conventional stream of Liberal party politics. In 1859 he obtained for him the seat of an Irish borough, Carlow. Acton confined his public addresses in the House of Commons to three questions concerning Catholic affairs, and the electorate of Carlow, unimpressed by this record, did not renominate him. Instead, in 1865 he stood for an English borough, Bridgnorth, near Aldenham, and was elected, only to be unseated early the next year on a recount. (Almost a dozen members of parliament were unseated after the general elections of 1859 and 1865 on charges of corruption and bribery by their agents. It is ironic that Acton, so concerned with the problem of public morality, should have been one of them.) Three years later he again stood unsuccessfully for Bridgnorth; this was his last half-hearted attempt to discharge the parliamentary obligation he felt.[4] The next year, upon Gladstone's recommendation, he was created a baron. There had been some talk at this time of the desirability of giving representation in the nobility to the Jews and Catholics, and Acton was raised to the peerage in the same New Year's announcement that gave the title of baron to Nathaniel Rothschild.

The conflicts with Rome gained in weight and momentum. The plea for intellectual freedom, sponsored by the liberal Catholics, jostled first with the program of the English Ultramontanes and then with the will of the pope. It had long been known that Pius considered himself the infallible instrument of God, and there had been indications that he would attempt to have the dogma of infallibility decreed by a general council of the church. In 1854 he had proclaimed the dogma of the immaculate conception of the Virgin Mary,

---
[4] Acton's parliamentary career is discussed in detail by James J. Auchmuty in "Acton's Election as an Irish Member of Parliament," *English Historical Review*, Vol. LXI (1946).

and it was because he saw himself under the special providence of Mary that he felt called upon to proclaim his own infallibility. The move was also, perhaps, intended to compensate for the actual loss of authority then impending, as the new Italian national government prepared to deprive him of his temporal power in Italy.

In December, 1869, the first ecumenical council since the Council of Trent, held more than three centuries earlier, assembled in Rome. In 1867, when the council was first announced, Acton, Döllinger, and liberal Catholics generally, hoped, without much conviction, that it would be a genuine council of reform. It was a magnificent opportunity, they felt, to erase the "stamp of an intolerant age," as Acton put it, which Trent had impressed upon Catholicism, and to reform the organization of the church by distributing among the episcopacy and laity many of the powers concentrated in Rome. However, the Roman court proved to be unrepentant; it was recalcitrant in matters of reform and belligerent in advancing claims even more extreme than those of Trent.

Acton made his position public in the *North British Review* of October, 1869, when he discussed a book, *The Pope and the Council,* recently published in Germany under the pseudonym of Janus, who was quickly and rightly identified as Döllinger. The argument of the book, and of Acton's article, was that the Christian fathers had held the pope to be fallible, and had decided that dogmatic questions could be settled only by a general council of the church. If the doctrine of infallibility, Acton continued, had gained such general adherence, it was because "the passage from the Catholicism of the Fathers to that of the modern Popes was accomplished by willful falsehood; and the whole structure of traditions, laws, and doctrines that supports the theory of infallibility, and the practical despotism of the Popes, stands on a basis of fraud."[5]

---

[5] "The Pope and the Council," *North British Review,* CI (1869), 130.

Acton was in Rome during all but the final six weeks of the council, which lasted until July, 1870, to the discomfort of the pope who had anticipated a speedy decision by acclamation. Although Döllinger was popularly supposed to be the spearhead of the opposition, he remained in Germany all of the time, and Acton was credited with being the source of much of the information that found its way into the press, and the organizer of the "Minority," as the bishops opposed to infallibility were soon dubbed. The legend has it that Acton walked the streets of Rome in disguise, fearing assassination, and it may have been true that he did, on occasion, try to avoid public recognition. Certainly the feeling against him was bitter enough; the pope even refused to extend his blessing to Acton's children. It was no secret that Acton had been in correspondence with Gladstone, decrying the activity of the council, although it was not so well known that he had urged Gladstone to appeal to the states of Europe to issue a joint protest against the impending decrees. At the time, too, a series of letters, over the name of "Quirinus," appeared in the *Augsburger Allgemeine Zeitung* which revealed an intimate knowledge of the most private sessions of the council. It was suspected that Döllinger was the author and that one of his informants was Acton, a suspicion that today seems well founded.[6]

The *Letters from Rome on the Council* are a fascinating study of the techniques used by Rome to impose her will. They were based on daily, personal observations, and because the details are so sharp and unmarred by retrospection, they are a valuable source of material for a sociological study of the institutions and forms of power that can be pressed into the service of a supposedly religious cause. Even in comparison with the exposés available today of more familiar events

---

[6] Quirinus, *Letters from Rome on the Council*, authorized translation (London, 1870) Regarding their authorship see Johann Friedrich, *Ignaz von Döllinger* (Munich, 1899-1901), III, 520, 703-4; Georges Goyau, *L'Allemagne religieuse le Catholicisme* (Paris, 1905-09), IV, 361; Ferdinand Gregorovius, *Roman Journals*, ed. F. Althaus (London, 1911), p. 356.

— the struggles for power within the Communist parties and the techniques by which dissident factions are suppressed — the *Letters from Rome* are shockingly astute and frank, and were it not for the established integrity of the author and his informants, and the corroboration of most of the more scandalous details by independent authorities, the volume would certainly be suspect. The methods of absolutism, as Acton was fond of pointing out, are the same everywhere — an assertion amply confirmed by the letters. The pope and his entourage, they charge, did not hesitate to apply the most subtle as well as the most open pressure upon the assembly: bishops were threatened with imprisonment and in some cases were deliberately subjected to physical discomfort; they were told that resistance to the dogma of papal infallibility was a blasphemy against the Holy Ghost; the whole stock of papal privileges — the bestowal of sees and titles, special rights, benedictions and dispensations — was tossed into the battle, and fifteen empty cardinal's hats were dangled over many more vacillating heads. Nine-tenths of the prelates were silenced because they could not speak Latin readily, others by the choice of a hall in which the acoustics were notoriously bad but which provided a regal backdrop for the papal throne. The procedure and the entire order of business were decided upon by commissions appointed by the pope himself. Meetings composed of more than twenty bishops were forbidden and strict secrecy was enjoined, except in the case of Manning and three other infallibilists who enjoyed special papal dispensations to divulge appropriate information to selected confidants. The details of machinations and intrigues crowd upon each other in a dismal spectacle.

In July, 1870, the decrees were formally promulgated: the pope cannot err when he alone defines, *ex cathedra* and in virtue of his apostolic authority, any doctrine of faith and morals. After much probing of consciences, most of the Minority bishops submitted to the decrees. Others, including Döllinger, who refused to submit, were excommunicated and founded the Old Catholic churches. Acton, as a layman, was not automatically called upon to subscribe to the decrees. In August he addressed an open letter to one of the Minority bishops who had yielded, accusing him of failing to keep faith with his principles. In October he wrote an article on the council for the *North British Review* (included in this volume), in which he repeated his criticisms in their harshest form. As late as the spring of 1871 his article, "The Pope and the Council," appeared in his own translation in Germany. Yet when the Old Catholics were formed in September of that year, Acton did not join them.

Döllinger, Acton explained in one of his notes, received the decree of excommunication "as a deliverance," because he "held very strongly that nobody should voluntarily sever himself from the Roman Communion."[7] Acton, too, felt strongly on this point, and he criticized the French historian, Eugène Michaud, who "did not wait till his archbishop put the knife at his throat but took the initiative of that operation on himself."[8] To leave the church voluntarily at this time, he felt, was to exonerate implicitly the behavior of Rome in all the centuries before the new dogma, because such an act assumed that until the promulgation of infallibility, Rome had been untainted by heresy.

Two years later Acton had occasion to use this argument again, but in a different context. Gladstone had published a pamphlet attacking the Vatican decrees as having altered the status of English Catholics, who, he argued, had received emancipation in 1826 on the assumption that they were loyal citizens of the realm, and who were now obliged to transfer their primary allegiance to Rome. In a letter in the *Times* Acton replied that the decrees actually assigned to the papacy no greater temporal power than it had always claimed, and that the practical conditions that had previously made those claims ineffectual continued to exist — the "pre-July" church, in other words, had been no better than its "post-July" successor. An editorial statement in the *Times* described him as

---
[7] Add. MSS, 4912
[8] *Selections from the Correspondence of the First Lord Acton*, ed J N Figgis and R. V. Laurence (London, 1908), p 117

having treated the decrees as a nullity. Thereupon Archbishop Manning intervened, calling for Acton's interpretation of the decrees and for his assurance that he had no heretical intent. Acton responded that he had no private interpretation, intended no heresy, and did not feel obliged or qualified to engage in theological discussion. This did not conciliate Manning, although Acton had already satisfied the bishop of his own diocese as to his orthodoxy. Manning was furious and threatened to take the matter to Rome, but nothing came of it. It has been suggested that Acton was too important a layman to be sacrificed by Rome, and that his excommunication would have played into the hands of the church's critics.

The reluctance of the church to press the charges against Acton is understandable; what is not so easy to understand is Acton's submission to the church. The central fact appears to be that he was a pious and practising Catholic for whom separation from the church would have been extremely painful. And in support of his religious instincts, he could call upon two doctrines that gave sanction to both his dissent and his compliance: the doctrine distinguishing between the mortal and fallible ecclesiastical organization and the eternal and true church; and the doctrine of development, adopted from Döllinger and Newman, which maintained that just as organization and dogma changed and developed in the course of time, so whatever was immoral and unchristian would eventually be eliminated. He might also have taken comfort in the thought that the submission of a layman does not have the same meaning as that of a priest. As a priest, Döllinger, for example, would have had to teach a doctrine that he considered false and immoral, and thus risk corrupting the souls of others; Acton was responsible for his own soul alone. He himself deserves the final word on a very delicate personal decision. One of his notes tersely explains: "I could not defend the Council or its action; but I always professed that the acceptance of either by the Church would supply its deficiency. The act was one of pure obedience, and was not grounded on the removal of my motives of opposition to the decrees." [9]

Although his opposition to what he termed ecclesiastical crimes continued, the climax had passed. He devoted himself to his books and research and planned the composition of his *chef d'oeuvre*, the History of Liberty — the greatest book, it has been suggested, that never was written. (Two essays, "History of Liberty in Antiquity" and "History of Liberty in Christianity," were delivered as lectures in 1877, and they may be considered a prologue to the monumental study that was to have followed.) Hundreds of files of notes, a fine collection of manuscripts, and the thousands of annotated volumes in his library are evidence of the care, devotion and imagination that he brought to the task. As early as 1880, however, he began to suspect that his life work might go unwritten. Mary Gladstone (later Mrs. Mary Drew) had called his attention to a story by Henry James, "The Madonna of the Future," about an artist who had dedicated his life to the vision of a magnificent picture he was to paint; after his death, when his studio was entered, a blank canvas was discovered upon the easel. Acton thereupon baptized his History of Liberty, "the Madonna of the Future."

Many have speculated on the reasons for Acton's apparent unproductivity. One theory has it that the History of Liberty would certainly have provoked papal censure, and this knowledge persuaded him to abandon the project. Yet his published essays in no way truckled to ecclesiastical prejudices and well merited a place on the Index. According to another theory, he felt that the truth about the French Revolution was not yet available, and the History could not be constructed without an evaluation of one of its central events. The lectures on the French Revolution, however, reveal a reasonable amount of confidence and no great qualms about dealing with the subject. A more popular and satisfactory explanation refers to the grandiose nature of his ambitions. For even if one person could assimilate the vast stock of ideas

---
[9] Add. MSS, 4905.

and facts that Acton considered relevant, it was improbable that he could manipulate them. "He knew too much to write," Acton once said of Döllinger,[10] a judgment that might stand for his own epitaph. Nor was comprehensiveness the only difficulty. To take all history, philosophy, theology, law — in short all of culture — for his province, and then to saddle himself further with the most exacting historical method, was inevitably to invite frustration. Another of Acton's comments on Döllinger (who did, as a matter of fact, produce a number of sustained works) is revealing: "He would not write with imperfect materials, and to him the materials were always imperfect." [11]

Döllinger himself contributed, unintentionally but in no small measure, to Acton's reluctance to write. He had been Acton's patron and ally in all of the early disputes with Rome, had taken a firm stand regarding the Vatican council and had been excommunicated as a result. Acton, whose behavior seems to have been not quite so uncompromising, nevertheless soon began to feel that Döllinger's moral principles were lax. He had become slack, Acton charged, in pressing the claims of morality: he offered explanations in extenuation of crimes, spoke of the understandable pressures of time and place, and failed to realize fully the urgency of the moral issues. The indictment is certainly excessive, both in tone and content, and is made even more singular by the circumstance of what was probably the first major incident in the estrangement of the two men — the contribution by Döllinger of a preface to a paper written upon the death of Dupanloup, a contribution made in a spirit of generosity to the memory of an opponent. Dupanloup, like other French "Liberal Catholics," had shed most of his liberal principles early in his career, and had supported both the Syllabus of 1864 and the decree of infallibility (although he considered its declaration to have been inopportune.) Acton considered him an Ultramontane, hence "a common rogue and

---

[10] "Döllinger's Historical Work," *English Historical Review*, Vol V (1890), reprinted in *History of Freedom*, ed. J. N. Figgis and R. V. Laurence (London, 1907), p. 434.
[11] *Ibid.*, p. 432.

imposter,"[12] and anyone tolerant of Ultramontanism, as he now thought Döllinger was, was implicated in its sins. In a pathetic letter, a draft of which is contained among his manuscripts, he described his sense of despair when he became aware of what he felt to be Döllinger's defection and when he realized the enormity of his isolation. Döllinger, he said, had been in a better position than anyone else to appreciate his ethical ideals, and if he could not accept them, surely no one else would:

I am absolutely alone in my essential ethical position, and therefore useless. . . . The probability of doing good by writings so isolated and repulsive, of obtaining influence for [my] views, etc., is so small that I have no right to sacrifice to it my own tranquillity and my duty of educating my children. My time can be better employed than in waging a hopeless war. And the more my life has been thrown away, the more necessary to turn now, and employ better what remains.[13]

It may be difficult to see the scandal in Döllinger's attitude, but it is impossible to ignore the desperation in Acton's. The disagreement, while a matter of regret for Döllinger, was one of almost neurotic anxiety and disquiet for Acton. It was not a temper conducive to the writing of a History of Liberty.

After 1879 Acton spent most of his time in London, Bavaria, and on the Riviera, drawing upon his books at Aldenham as he needed them. He maintained a close association with Gladstone and a lively interest in liberal politics. In 1873 he was seriously considered for the post of ambassador to Germany. Between 1878 and 1885, although he published nothing, his reputation as a historian increased. An article on George Eliot appeared in the *Nineteenth Century* in 1885, and the following year he was one of a small group of men who helped found the *English Historical Review*. Mandell Creighton, later Bishop Creighton (of the Church of England), editor of the *Review,* wrote of his association with Acton: "[He] especially is most helpful through his learning,

---
[12] Add. MSS, 5403.
[13] *Ibid.*

which is probably greater than that of any other Englishman now alive"; and of his contribution to the first issue of the new journal, "German Schools of History": "I have just received the proof of an excellent article by Lord Acton — the sort of thing that takes your breath away, a philosophical criticism of all German historians of the century, most brilliant."[14] The conventional honors of the scholar also came his way: in 1873 he was awarded an honorary degree of Doctor of Philosophy by the University of Munich and three years later he was elected a member of the Royal Academy of Munich; in 1888 he received the honorary degree of Doctor of Laws from Cambridge, and in 1889 the degree of Doctor of Civil Law from Oxford; in 1890 he was elected an honorary fellow of All Souls, Oxford, a distinction he shared only with Gladstone.

The year 1890 also brought a financial crisis for Acton, who had already sold or rented most of his estates. One of his tenants was Joseph Chamberlain, the great enemy of Gladstone, who, the story goes, declared himself quite unimpressed with Acton's library because it contained no works of reference! When that library, with its invaluable manuscript collections and source materials, was announced for sale in an auctioneer's advertisement, Gladstone, a better judge in these matters than Chamberlain, conveyed his distress to Andrew Carnegie, the American millionaire and philanthropist. Carnegie purchased the library outright and assigned its custodianship to Acton, who was never told the name of his benefactor. Since Acton's affairs were in a thorough muddle, it was found impossible to reinstate him as legal owner. Carnegie's biographer, B. J. Hendrick, sententiously comments: "The story was the familiar one of the man of ideas unfit to cope with the realities of a sordid world."

Among the many ironies of Acton's career was his appointment in 1892 as Lord-in-Waiting to Queen Victoria, a strange office for the historian. Actually his duties were neither

---

[14] *Life and Letters of Mandell Creighton* (London, 1904), I, 334, 339.

cumbersome nor disagreeable; he was able to explore new libraries and collections of court documents and to mingle with the people he knew so well. Three years later, Lord Rosebery, then prime minister, recommended him to fill the vacancy of the Regius Professorship in History at Cambridge, assuring the Queen that the duties of the position would not interfere with the discharge of his functions in Her Majesty's household. This too had its minor ironies, for it was Rosebery rather than Acton's life-long friend Gladstone who was responsible for the appointment, and it was at Cambridge, where he had been denied admission as a student, that he was now greeted as a professor. The appointment came as a surprise to the public and the university; Creighton referred to him as a "dark horse."

Acton realized, regretfully, that the position of Regius Professor was more a public platform than a chair of research. His inaugural lecture, "The Study of History," delivered in June, 1895, was in the dense, elliptical style of all his writings, weighted with unidentified names and references, terse in its exposition of ideas, generous in its subtleties and innuendoes. Some of his audience welcomed it as the product of a mature and sophisticated mind. The *Saturday Review*, however, saw it only as a kind of "mental gymnastics," full of "pretensions and confused fancies" and the "Batavian splutterings" of an awkward pen. In the lectures that followed, a series on modern history and another on the French Revolution, delivered between 1895 and 1901, Acton mended his ways, at least in the opinion of such critics. Except for his sharp and colorful phrasing, occasional lapses into ellipticism, and a greater insistence upon ideas, the lectures were not very different from others intended for undergraduates. Even so he made more demands upon the intelligence of his audience than was customary, which perhaps flattered the throngs of women who, attracted by his reputation and social standing, attended faithfully.

To Arnold Toynbee, a contemporary historian who shares none of Acton's inhibitions against writing, Acton is a grotesque sacrifice to the spirit of the age. The sterilizing influence of industrialism, with its constant compulsion to exploit new materials and its faith in the division of labor, thwarted the historian of liberty and made of "one of the greatest minds among modern Western historians" an editor of a compilation unworthy of his talents. The *Cambridge Modern History,* planned and edited by Acton at the request of the syndics of the University from 1896 until his final illness, has been widely criticized. "Lord Acton's Encyclical" it was christened by those who resented the idea of issuing a universal history prepared by specialists with a final word to say on every subject. Others complained that the specialists were not specialized enough; there were errors in the history and defects of organization. Whether he undertook the editing of the project because he despaired of doing any further significant work by himself, or whether he undertook it as an obligation associated with the Regius Professorship, it is difficult to determine. In any event, he devoted an enormous amount of thought and time to it, as is revealed by his voluminous notes and correspondence on subjects and contributors. But for good or bad, he cannot be saddled with sole responsibility for the finished work. He became ill in April, 1901, and resigned soon afterwards. At that time only part of the first volume was in type, and it did not appear until the autumn of 1902, four months after his death. He had intended to contribute the first chapter, "The Legacy of the Middle Ages," but the tasks of editing and teaching left little time for writing and the chapter was absent from the published work. The titles and general subject matter of the twelve volumes were plotted by Acton, but the chapters do not always conform to the original plan and there were many changes in contributors.

When he died in June, 1902, Acton left behind a body of essays, a magnificent library (now in the north wing of the Cambridge University Library), and a mass of notes, transcriptions, drafts of lectures, articles and letters, and personal reflections that he hoped might be useful to others in writing the history he had failed to write. John Morley, who respected him enormously, thought of him as a "standing riddle." Certainly a later generation, knowing him only by his written work and from casual remarks dropped by his contemporaries, must confess its bewilderment. He was not the scholar so overawed by a multiplicity of facts that he could not deliver judgment; he was, on the contrary, as ready in pronouncing judgment as he was in dispensing fact, and if his essays are luxuriant in detail, they are also copious in superlatives. He could confidently refer to "the greatest man born of a Jewish mother since Titus" (the German statesman and philosopher, Stahl), and could declare without hesitation who had "the most prodigal imagination ever possessed by man" (the Renaissance poet, Ariosto). "When was London in the greatest danger?" someone casually wondered. "In 1803," came Acton's prompt reply, "when Fulton proposed to put the French army across the channel in steamboats, and Napoleon rejected the scheme." His imagination did not balk at the most excessive demands. If his talents went unfulfilled, it was possibly because his will was not as fearless as his imagination.

II

It is customary to relate a thinker to the spirit of his age. With Lord Acton, however intimately he was involved in the affairs of his time, it would be more pertinent to relate him to the spirit of ours. He was fond of saying that he agreed with no one. In the only sense in which he recognized contemporaries, the sense of ideological confrères, there is some truth in his lament. He invites identification with none of the dominant currents of thought in Victorian England: the utilitarian gospel of the greatest happiness of the greatest number, the humanitarian campaign for improved social conditions, the rationalist crusade against religious obscurantism and superstition, the imperialist mission to spread Christianity and English civilization, the working class protest against exploitation, or the laissez-faire individualism of the traditional liberal philosophy. All of these were aggressively this-worldly and man-centered in a spirit foreign to Acton. The Victorian period has been called the age of hope, but it was confidence, more precisely than hope, that distinguished it. If only man continued in the self-sufficient and self-inspired path he had already marked out for himself, his fate was assured — in this tenet the diverse creeds were united.

Such was the dominant tone of the age, the tone imposed upon it by the major movements and schools of thought. And it is this tone that gives rise to the familiar charges leveled against Victorianism — the charges of complacency, materialism and philistinism. Even the restlessness of the social reformers and socialist revolutionaries failed to violate the conventional boundaries of interests and values, for it was within the framework of profits, progress and physical well-being that their criticism was formulated.

Yet almost every great thinker of the age despised it — with the notable exception of Thomas Macaulay. His more sophisticated colleagues agreed that he represented all that was vulgar and superficial in the thought of the period. The fact that he was worshiped by the literate public made him only more odious to the select, for it was clear that Macaulay was Victorianism come of age, proud of its accomplishments and humble before no one. As the talented artist of the anonymous middle class, he fashioned history in the image of the early Victorian Whig, representing the contours of British industrial civilization as the essential features of society, and the movement of history as a glorious surge of progress that would bring to materialization the divine will of God. He celebrated material greatness, confident that moral excellence would follow in its wake.

In his diary John Stuart Mill confessed his fears that posterity would remember his age as one that had exulted over the writings of Macaulay. Shallowness and aggressive self-satisfaction repelled Mill, and he sought to replace Macaulay's ideal of material progress with one of moral and spiritual progress. But the temper of the time exacted its price. Mill found that he could introduce the moral and spiritual only by withdrawing the sanction of divinity from the works of men, and by locating morality and spirit within the empirical methods of science, the secular structure of society and the realm of nature — a more complete capitulation to materialism, in one sense, than even Macaulay had achieved.

From the superior perspective of Matthew Arnold, Mill and Macaulay were together responsible for the "hopeless tangle" of the times. If Mill feared that Macaulay's name would prejudice the judgment of posterity, Arnold feared that the method of Mill was prejudicing the spiritual condition of the present. He deplored the effort of the scientists and scholars to release men from the commitments of religion in order to make them receptive to the unhindered operations of the intelligence. Devoted as he was to the "sweetness and light" of reason, he did not put his entire trust in reason — at least not in the kind of reason Mill extolled. "The whole work of again cementing the alliance between the imagination and conduct remains to be effected," he said. Once the useless lumber of dogma and superstition were cleared away, a basic religious faith would remain to give conviction to morality. Without that faith, and without the culture of the historical past, there would be no personality, no sense of connection with one's own personal past. And along with personality would be surrendered personal, responsible thinking — that is, morality.

In the "high seriousness" of Arnold there is a suggestion of the spirit of Acton. Yet Arnold, the religious humanist and liberal Protestant, the fanatic of moderation as G. K. Chesterton has described him, was not really the sympathetic contemporary Acton sought. Nor were any of the great rebels of the age. Carlyle with his extravagant worship of Frederick the Great and loathing of Catholicism, Ruskin and Morris idealizing the culture of the Middle Ages without being moved to repudiate the Protestantism that overthrew that culture, Newman who sought the cure for religious indifferentism in the dogmas and rites of Roman Catholicism and developed on his own part, at least in the opinion of

Acton, a form of moral indifferentism — none of these could appease Acton's sense of alienation.

His alienation, as he saw it, was the result of his dual allegiance to Catholicism on the one hand and liberalism on the other. He once wrote to Mandell Creighton, then editor of the *English Historical Review:*

> It is a real comfort to know that you suffer from my complaint of not getting people to agree with you. And one likes to be told that one has a philosophy of history. If I have one, there is no secret about it, and no compact with the Evil one. I find that people disagree with me either because they hold that Liberalism is not true, or that Catholicism is not true, or that both cannot be true together. If I could discover anyone who is not included in these categories, I fancy we should get on very well together.[15]

"Liberal Catholicism" was a familiar enough label in the nineteenth century. In France the school of Lamennais and Montalembert had pushed Liberal Catholicism to the brink of papal excommunication. But theirs was the liberalism of the French state of Louis Philippe and Napoleon III. It was less a devotion to the moral ideals of liberalism than an admission of the autonomy and rights of the supposedly popular and democratic secular state. Acton's was a different synthesis of liberalism and Catholicism. His liberalism breathed a religious fervor which can only be described as dogmatic and doctrinaire. Yet his religion was neither dogmatic nor doctrinaire in the conventional sense. He accepted the mysteries and dogmas of Catholicism, particularly those of the primitive church, tranquilly and as a matter of fact, but his missionary zeal was not directed in their defense, still less in the defense of the church or of the ecclesiastical hierarchy. On the contrary, it was diverted to an attack upon the existing church, exposing its deplorable politics and history, its Machiavellian tactics and its unscientific, uncritical habits of mind. His politics were a form of religion and his religion a form of politics, and both were conceived in the likeness of an austere and absolute morality:

---
[15] Add. MSS, 6871.

Have you not discovered, have I never betrayed, what a narrow doctrinaire I am, under a thin disguise of levity? .... Politics come nearer religion with me, a party is more like a church, error more like heresy, prejudice more like sin, than I find it to be with better men.[16]

The liberalism of the nineteenth century clearly had little in common with the liberalism that was Acton's passion. It was not informed by the high moral seriousness, the uncompromising principles, of Acton's faith. Neither Macaulay nor Mill, the ideological spokesmen for the prevailing mood of liberalism, could have had absolute moral principles, according to Acton, because they did not have absolute religious principles. Among the notes that were to have been the basis of his History of Liberty are a number of cards headed "Enemies of Conscience," under which Mill's name is prominent, with occasionally an explanatory phrase such as "Christianity is but a word."[17] Sometimes Mill himself was the target of Acton's attack, but more often it was an earlier figure, Edmund Burke, whom Acton in his youth had regarded as his political mentor and whom he disowned in his maturity, or John Morley, Mill's most eminent disciple, with whom Acton entered into a somewhat uneasy friendship. Against Burke and Morley the charge was that they treated political questions "experimentally, by the Baconian methods." "They think that politics teach what is likely to do good or harm, not what is right and wrong, innocent or sinful."[18] For Acton politics was a science, the application of the principles of morality. For Burke and Morley it was, as Morley once quipped, something like logic — neither a science nor an art but a dodge. Politics for them was a series of expediencies and compromises. True to their empiricism, Acton complained, they could not see the presence of eternal and absolute moral principles because they had no sense of the religious sanctity of those principles. "As

---
[16] *Letters of Lord Acton to Mary Gladstone*, ed Herbert Paul (1st ed.; New York, 1905), p. 314.
[17] Add. MSS, 4901.
[18] *Letters to Mary Gladstone* (2nd ed ; London, 1913), p. 180.

there are, for him [Morley], no rights of God, there are no rights of man — the consequence, on earth, of obligation in Heaven. Therefore he never tries to adjust his view to many conditions and times and circumstances, but approaches each with a mind uncommitted to doctrines and untrammelled by analogies."[19]

Of the hundred definitions of liberty that Acton amassed, his favorites spoke of the rights of conscience. Of the hundred books that he selected as the greatest of all time, well over half dealt with matters of religion. The connection was obvious to Acton: if liberty is the right of conscience, the first agent in the perfection of conscience is religion. The corollary was equally obvious: if religious faiths should continue to crumble, liberty, dependent upon law and morality, would collapse with it. His description of the decline of Athenian liberty might be taken as a parable of the situation in his own day:

An unparalleled activity of intellect was shaking the credit of the gods, and the gods were the givers of the law. It was a very short step from the suspicion of Protagoras, that there were no gods, to the assertion of Critias that there is no sanction for laws. If nothing was certain in theology, there was no certainty in ethics and no moral obligation.[20]

It is here perhaps that Acton speaks to our age more than to his own. At a time when most of his contemporaries were acclaiming their emancipation from religion and the wonderful vistas of progress open to them, Acton saw that "progress [is] the religion of those who have none."[21] His was not the only voice to question the new "religion" of progress, the new exaltation of human capabilities. Matthew Arnold, for one, shared his fears that no intelligence patterned upon the cold reasoning of logic could be a satisfactory substitute for religion. But for the most part the champions of religion were timid minds reluctant to alter a line in the traditional world-picture of the Bible; in their fixed scheme

---

[19] *Ibid.*, p. 179.
[20] "May's Democracy in Europe," p. 136 of this volume.
[21] Add. MSS, 5648.

of things, biblical criticism was heresy, and the truths of Christianity stood or fell with the truth of every miracle in its texts. Acton, on the other hand, had mastered the methods of biblical criticism and welcomed the findings of science. He was as "enlightened" as Mill or Morley, who were obliged to respect him even though they disagreed with him. Had it not been for the more commanding authority of the Wisemans and Mannings, Acton might have had some influence in his day. As it was, science and philosophy were ranged against religion, and the voice of Acton was drowned out in the noisy tussle between "enlightenment" and "bigotry."

Now that the warfare between science and religion has subsided somewhat, Acton's voice is more audible and carries more assurance. Clerics are not alone in carrying the banner of religion; they have been joined by a multitude of those who, in Acton's own time, would almost certainly have been in the camp of the opposition. It was not until well into the twentieth century, with its shattering experience of two world wars, its nihilistic political doctrines and barbarous political practices, that a score of volumes clamorously discovered the "crisis of our age." The anticipated progress has become a rout; the traditional scheme of values has disintegrated, and we are importuned to revitalize old faiths and old authorities to halt the plunge into moral anarchy. The secular hopes of the preceding period have vanished as surely as the religious fears of an earlier one. Conscience has become insensible or irresponsible. In despair, some have called for a self-conscious revival of religious belief, the deliberate resolve to act as though one believed the truths that were once actually and implicitly believed. Others have sought salvation in forms of authority that do not wait upon the individual's erratic intelligence or dubious good will. Of the organized churches, Catholicism has probably had most success in attracting penitents.

The reaction, indeed, may have gone further than Acton would have liked. For Acton was always careful to keep both adversaries in sight and to enlist in the service of neither. If he thought that the secular liberals were undermining the sanctions of morality, he was also certain that the ecclesiastical hierarchy had committed grave moral offences. A series of unsettling personal experiences in the Catholic church and a careful reading of a score of disagreeable episodes in its history deprived him of the comfort and security of the Catholic *Weltanschauung*. Although he was not taken in by those who saw an easy way of divorcing the institution of the church from the convictions and practices of morality, he shared the sophistication of those who saw no necessary correlation between the two. Describing the dilemma of the Anglican who was attracted to the Catholic church, Acton once offered the following as a "possible" argument to deter his conversion:

Roman Catholic divines hold that the Thirty-nine Articles may be understood in a favourable sense. Anglicans hold that they are not literally binding on the clergy. Still less on the laity. Therefore his position in the English Church does not involve this layman in any error. It may involve him in certain dangers and difficulties. But these are not greater than the dangers and difficulties which would follow his conversion. For there are many opinions, not only sanctioned but enforced by the authorities of the Church of Rome, which none can adhere to without peril to the soul. The moral risk on one side is greater than the dogmatic risk on the other. He can escape heresy in Anglicanism more easily than he can escape the ungodly ethics of the papacy, the Inquisition, the Casuists, in the Roman Communion. The solicitation, the compulsion, will be more irresistible in the latter. A man who thought it wrong to murder a Protestant King would be left for hell by half the Confessors on the Continent. [The Anglicans] Montagu, Bramhall will not sap this man's Catholic faith so surely as the Spanish and Italian moralists will corrupt his soul.[22]

In an essay on George Eliot, he described the fascination he felt for this atheist and iconoclast who had violated the most peremptory social conventions of her day. Eliot, he

---
[22] *Letters to Mary Gladstone* (1st ed.), pp. 233-34.

said, was a "consummate expert in the pathology of conscience." "It was the problem of her age to reconcile the practical ethics of unbelief and of belief, to save virtue and happiness when dogmas and authorities decay." Her novels were "the emblem of a generation distracted between the intense need of believing and the difficulty of belief."[23] Forfeiting the appeal to the theology and mythology of the Scriptures and the idea of divine retribution, she managed to cull out of atheism a profound sense of morality. Philosophically, he found, it was not as sound as Christianity because it failed to secure the sanctions of morality on unyielding ground. Ethically it was less satisfactory because it ran the risk of being satisfied with the obvious effects of man's actions rather than seeking out the symptoms of their subtle and hidden effects. But spiritually the doctrine of earthly retribution was a noble attempt to define vice and virtue in uncompromising terms. Indeed its very paganism might be deemed an advantage. "It had no weak places, no evil champions, no bad purpose, to screen or to excuse, unlike almost all forms of Christianity."[24]

Renan said that what drove him out of the church was not its philosophy but its history and historians. And so it very nearly was with Acton. The church might have used the social prestige and authority of a believing age to guide men through an unbelieving age; instead it seemed to use what remained of its authority for purposes of a low ambition. The original significance of the church, Acton held, was its doctrine of a higher law prescribing rights and duties transcending those of men and governments. The new dispensation, announced by Jesus, "Render unto Caesar the things that are Caesar's, and unto God the things that are God's," gave the individual conscience a vantage point from which it might resist the encroachments of political authority. In the age of martyrdom, the church maintained the purity

---
[23] "George Eliot's Life," *Nineteenth Century*, Vol. XVII (1885), reprinted in *Historical Essays and Studies*, ed. J. N. Figgis and R. V. Laurence (London, 1908), pp. 277, 283, 303.
[24] *Correspondence of Lord Acton*, p. 292.

of its ideal, only to pervert it after attaining recognition and respectability. In the late Roman era and the early Middle Ages the church served as the "gilded crutch of absolutism." With the advance of feudalism, the ambitions of the ecclesiastical hierarchy collided with those of the feudal hierarchy, and this clash gave birth to the first liberal institutions of the modern world. The towns of Italy and Germany won their franchise and self-government; the beginnings of responsible and constitutional authority were to be seen in France's States-General and England's parliament; the principles of taxation by representation, trial by jury and ecclesiastical independence were proclaimed. To be sure, the aim of both parties, church and state, was absolute authority, but fortunately both were thwarted, and the long struggle had as its by-product liberty. This period, which saw the development of a kind of adventitious liberalism, was succeeded by open absolutism; the absolute monarchy of France was created by cardinals of the church, while the kings of Spain appropriated the terrors of the Inquisition to establish their despotism.

The *Catholic World* once charged that it was common knowledge at Cambridge that Acton had "Inquisition on the brain." The charge is true, although the petulance of the Catholic critic is undeserved. Scrupulous in all matters relating to the history of liberty, and convinced that the church must occupy a central role in that history, Acton was naturally obsessed with the fact of the Inquisition. At most he could ascribe to the Catholic Inquisitors the diabolical dignity of Dostoyevsky's Grand Inquisitor: "We shall triumph and shall be Caesars, and then we shall plan the universal happiness of man." Of the Jesuits he once said: "It is this combination of an eager sense of duty, zeal for sacrifice, and love of virtue, with the deadly taint of a conscience perverted by authority, that makes them so odious to touch and so curious to study."[25] But this was in an unusually contemplative mood. More often he experienced a revulsion that carried him far beyond the dispassionate curiosity of the historian:

[25] *Letters to Mary Gladstone* (1st ed.), p. 251.

The Inquisition is peculiarly the weapon and peculiarly the work of the Popes. It stands out from all those things in which they co-operated, followed, or assented as the distinctive feature of papal Rome. It was set up, renewed, and perfected by a long series of acts emanating from the supreme authority in the Church. No other institution, no doctrine, no ceremony, is so distinctly the individual creation of the papacy, except the Dispensing power. It is the principal thing with which the papacy is identified, and by which it must be judged.

. . . . The principle of the Inquisition is murderous, and a man's opinion of the papacy is regulated and determined by his opinion about religious assassination.

If he honestly looks on it as an abomination, he can only accept the Primacy with a drawback, with precaution, suspicion, and aversion for its acts.

If he accepts the Primacy with confidence, admiration, unconditional obedience, he must have made terms with murder.

. . . . That blot [the Inquisition] is so large and foul that it precedes and eclipses the rest, and claims the first attention.[26]

Acton assumed the office of historian in a serious spirit. History was a trust to be carefully tended, for it was the repository of the moral life of man. The historian, keeper of the conscience of all men, was obliged to mete out rewards and punishments — few rewards and many punishments, because "the uncounted majority of those who get a place in its [history's] pages are bad."[27] Acton prided himself on being a "hanging judge," and was disappointed to find, for example, that Tocqueville, in his *Memoirs* and letters, did not appear in the same light. It was urged upon Acton that he should take into account the moral climate prevalent in a particular age and among a particular people, and the special influences to which men in public affairs — the popes, notably — are subject. He replied that if any indulgence was forthcoming, it should be reserved for those who were not educated to the level of moral comprehension and who were remote from the centers of civilization or Christian culture. Applying this

---
[26] *Ibid.*, pp. 298-300.
[27] *Ibid.*, p. 228.

test, Catholics should be judged more severely than non-Catholics, priests more severely than laymen, and prelates more severely than priests.[28]

If Acton's judgment was frequently so much more harsh than that of others, it was not, he insisted, because his code was esoteric or idiosyncratic. "It supposes nothing and implies nothing but what is universally current and familiar. It is the common, even the vulgar, code I appeal to." [29] Murder is the "low-water mark," the "scientific zero," of the conventional code of morality and the legal code of the courtroom. If that is not uniformly maintained, there is no standard of measurement for all other deviations from morality: corruption, mendacity, treason. Those who admit extenuating pleas "debase the currency"[30] and convert history into a monument of sin.

The natural tendency of the historian is to set the seal of approval on the past. Professor Herbert Butterfield, in the *Whig Interpretation of History,* has brilliantly exposed this temptation. He illustrates the theme in the case of the English historian who was Protestant, progressive and Whig, who glorified revolutions when they were successful, ratified the past, and read into the future the principles of progress by which the past had become the present. It is in the nature of historical study to be, in this sense, Whig. All abridgments of the past necessarily select those features that are relevant to the present. Whether the historian wills it or not, the moral bias in favor of the Whig emerges; the Whig's success seems to vindicate his ideals and establish them as eternally true and right. The only corrective to "Whig history" is the detailed study of a specialized period or problem, restoring in all of its complexity and fullness the context of the past with its many unspent possibilities, and explaining each event in terms of the specific peculiarities that determined it. It is only very special and limited truths that historians can properly deduce, not the universal truths to which the philosophers of history have pretensions.

---

[28] Add. MSS, 4863.
[29] Add. MSS, 6871, p. 363 of this volume.
[30] *Ibid.,* p. 365.

Macaulay is a good example of the Whig historian, for he combined a sense of satisfaction towards the course of past affairs with a feeling of moral righteousness that permitted him to project the past into the ideal of the future. Acton was like Macaulay in refusing to observe the past dispassionately. But unlike Macaulay, he tended to judge the past adversely, rather than favorably. Macaulay's standard was actually derived from history, from its successes and failures; Acton's was derived from a supra-historical moral code, the code of primitive Christianity, which was in constant conflict with history and could be imposed upon it only by the eternal vigilance and constant intervention of the moralist-historian. Acton repudiated the "canonization of the past" because it would "perpetuate the reign of sin." He conceived it "the part of real greatness to know how to stand and fall alone, stemming, for a lifetime, the contemporary flood." [31] His interpretation of history, then, is once removed from that of the Whig historian by virtue of its absolute rather than its pragmatic moral judgments — and is at least twice removed from the objectivity and neutrality that Professor Butterfield considers the proper temper of the historian.

Acton belonged rather to the tradition of religious propheticism than to that of English Whiggism. He saw sin where others saw only error because he was constantly confronted by the apparition of original sin, and felt called upon to expose it at every turn. His view of human nature was profoundly pessimistic, in that haunted, tormented spirit generally associated with Calvinism rather than Catholicism. In the Inaugural Lecture, he cited in his behalf James Mozley, the Oxford theologian:

A Christian is bound by his very creed to suspect evil, and cannot release himself. His religion has brought evil to light in a way in which it never was before; it has shown its depth, subtlety, ubiquity; and a revelation, full of mercy on the one hand, is terrible in its exposure of the world's real state on the other. The Gospel fastens the sense of evil upon the mind; a Christian

---
[31] "Study of History," p. 27 of this volume.

is enlightened, hardened, sharpened, as to evil; he sees it where others do not. . . . . He owns the doctrine of original sin; that doctrine puts him necessarily on his guard against all appearances, sustains his apprehension under perplexity, and prepares him for recognizing anywhere what he knows to be everywhere.[32]

The priest in the confessional, Acton remarks repeatedly in his notes, has the widest and most intimate knowledge of man; and he seems to wonder how the priest can so placidly bear it.

It was not that he naturally thought ill of people, he hastened to assure a correspondent. On the contrary, it was right to think well of them until forced to think ill. Certainly the majority of "little people" deserve to be thought well of. Those who have no conspicuous role in history escape the temptations in which history abounds. But of those who are prominent, we must be prepared for the obligation to think the worst: "Most assuredly, now as heretofore, the Men of the Time are, in most cases, unprincipled, and act from motives of interest, of passion, of prejudice cherished and unchecked, of selfish hope or unworthy fear." [33]

The malignant force that converts "Great Men" into bad men is Power. Two of Acton's contemporaries, an American and a Swiss, both self-confessed "failures" in the competitive struggle of modern society, agreed that power was the root of the evil. The favorite dictum of Henry Adams was, "Power is poison." Jacob Burckhardt wrote: "Power is of its nature evil, whoever wields it. It is not a stability but a lust, and *ipso facto* insatiable, therefore unhappy in itself and doomed to make others unhappy." The emphasis upon power has a long and respectable genealogy, but in the history of political thought its paternity is often fixed upon either Machiavelli or Hobbes. Perhaps that is because both philosophers scandalized the consciences of men when they candidly described the omnivorousness of power and at the same time proposed to base their philosophies upon the desire for it. Machiavelli took for granted the aggressive and acquisitive instincts of men and went on to analyze the best course for the ruler determined to consolidate his power. Hobbes slightly

---
[32] *Ibid.*, p. 28.
[33] *Letters to Mary Gladstone* (1st ed.), p. 228.

altered the form of the argument, making it more acceptable to those who distrust generalizations about human instincts. Man seeks power, he said, in order to secure his own preservation, but that security being a precarious affair, he must acquire more power to secure that which he has already won. And so proceeds the "perpetual and restless desire of power after power, that ceaseth only in death." Neither Machiavelli nor Hobbes adopted a censorious tone in speaking of what they considered to be a perfectly natural drive common to all men. But the sensibilities of men like Adams, Burckhardt and Acton were less resilient and could not withstand the shock administered by their study of history. Aware of the universality of the evil they described, they were nevertheless outraged; they retreated and withdrew from its presence so as not to be defiled by the moral guilt emanating from it.

The usual modern assumption of naturalistic philosophies is that power is in itself morally neutral; it acquires moral content only in the context of its performance. To Acton this assumption would have meant a surrender to evil incarnate. "History is not a web woven with innocent hands. Among all the causes which degrade and demoralize men, power is the most constant and the most active." [34] If pope and king are judged more severely than other men, it is partly because the presumption of evil is upon them, and that presumption increases as their effective power increases.

The remark of Goethe, "The man of action is essentially conscienceless," is endorsed by most observers of political affairs. Henry Maine, a contemporary of Acton, used to say that a leader of a party, however virtuous his private conduct, could not, in his political position, exercise the common virtues of the honest man. Truth, justice and moral intrepidity came into play only when they were of service to the party. Gladstone, leader of the Liberal party during most of the second half of the century, had the reputation of being a man of stubborn principles; his enemies called him doctrinaire, and Acton lauded his "science of statesmanship." Yet in his correspondence with Gladstone's daughter, Acton had oc-

---
[34] Add. MSS, 5011.

casion to take the prime minister to task for actions that suggested "opportunism." When his great political opponent, Disraeli, died, Gladstone, in the convention of political magnanimity, delivered a tribute to his memory. Acton, who shared Gladstone's private sentiments and regarded Disraeli as a demagogue and hypocrite who had stimulated the lowest passions of men and had demoralized public opinion in order to maintain his political power, felt that it was inexcusable of Gladstone to mouth praise that he obviously did not believe. This was a trivial incident, but it is an example of the more or less serious moral predicaments with which the ordinary, even the conscientious, politician casually comes to terms. For Acton each situation of this kind would have assumed the proportions of a moral crisis.

Acton's attitude toward power might be dismissed as hopelessly utopian, and there is no doubt that he was often naïve in vilifying the personalities of history and contemporary politics. Yet he was brilliantly perceptive and just in describing the moral degeneration that power sets in motion. His celebrated aphorism, "Power tends to corrupt and absolute power corrupts absolutely," [35] is more realistic than either of two other popular philosophies parading under the guise of *realpolitik*—naturalistic liberalism and Marxism. Liberalism seeks the specific historical causes of social evils and moral corruption without allowing for a general, more basic and more radical evil. Not only does it repudiate the metaphysical doctrine of original sin, it also shies from empirical generalizations on the corrupting effects of political power. It sometimes even assumes that there can come a time when a mature mass intelligence and the systematic cultivation of the scientific temper will eliminate the problems plaguing politics and morality today. Statesmen, imbued with the proper devotion to the methods of science, would then be rid of the distracting temptations that now besiege them; social policies would be executed exactly as they were planned and would have exactly the consequences they were intended to have. Thus liberalism spurns the metaphysics of pessimism only to embrace the even more chimerical metaphysics of optimism,

---

[35] P. 364 of this volume.

Marxism, priding itself on its hard-headedness, takes the problem of power more seriously. For the Marxist all social power is the power of social classes. Power relations can be said to be "distorted" when governmental power is wielded by a class that has lost effective social power — when the unproductive aristocracy in nineteenth century England, for example, attempted to maintain political power in defiance of the economically dominant new bourgeoisie. When the impotent dare to defy history in this way, they are before long put in their place by a corrective revolution, violent or not. Power, then, must conform to the realities of the economic situation; it is a reflection of the economic situation, and the only time it can be said to be distorted is when it fails to reflect that situation truly.

If the moral drama of history tends to be too rich and highly colored in Acton's hands, it is entirely too impoverished and drab in the Marxist's. The problems of power that are most crucial today are those in which power seems to generate its own rationale, and produces, at least as much as it mirrors, the social scene outside it. Fascism and communism seem to create, in large measure, the conditions under which they thrive. Power, in these systems of government, has emerged unmistakably as an autonomous and primary factor; it will no longer consent to be treated as a mere reflection of other factors. The apparatus of power is no negligible rival to the means of production in determining the character of a society. The brutalizing, corrupting and degrading effects of the Nazi power have fixed for some time the psychological tone of the world, and have set in motion forces that no amount of economic juggling can immobilize. Fascism is "irrational," people protest, thus testifying to their inability to subsume it under the traditional, rational categories of sociology. Liberals and socialists, unwilling to grant to fascism the possibility of popular consent, predicted its collapse as soon as the last desperate measures of brutal force were spent. They failed to see that power may create the popular consent it desires, and that brutal force may be the character of a new kind of society whose conventions are accepted as the norms of moral and physical life. Optimistic liberalism, vigorous in the nineteenth century and in our own day up to the recent revelations of the horrors of Nazism, had little appreciation of the possible depths of organized human depravity. It was deluded by an excessive faith in the potentialities of social reorganization. If Acton seems to speak to us with peculiar relevancy, it is because we are today more receptive to the idea that neither human intelligence nor material progress can be relied upon to usher in the millennium.

Acton's criticism of secular liberalism derived from the religious tradition of the prophets; it depended upon the paradoxical insight that men are sinful creatures, not to be confused with God, and that, created in the likeness of God, they have spiritual needs that no amount of material well-being can satisfy. Conversely, his criticism of religion had its source in the principles of political liberalism. One of his contributions to the *Rambler,* "The Protestant Theory of Persecution," set the tone for his subsequent criticism of the church. It was an attack upon Protestantism, to be sure, but the weapons were just as effective against Catholicism, and the guns were turned as soon as the Catholic Church exposed itself in a vulnerable position.

To most non-Catholic historians, the Protestant Reformation appears as a major event in the liberation of the human spirit. "The Protestant Theory of Persecution" is a brilliant argument against this conventional view. The identification of Protestantism and toleration, it declares, was a temporary expedient of the reformers. As long as the secular authorities were behind the Catholic church, the reformers had to assert the theory of religious toleration. "Every religious party, however exclusive or servile its theory may be, if it is in contradiction with a system generally accepted and protected by law, must necessarily, at its first appearance, assume the protection of the idea that the conscience is free." [36] With the growth of dissension in his own ranks — the Zwinglian schism

---

[36] P. 91 of this volume.

INTRODUCTION   li

and the rise of the Anabaptists — and the hated Peasants' War, Luther turned to the princes for support, and the doctrine of obedience to the state was pronounced in its most rigorous form. No injustice could warrant revolt against secular authority, he preached. "The princes of this world are gods." "Disobedience is a greater sin than murder, unchastity, theft, and dishonesty, and all that these may include." He also yielded to the state in all religious matters, and it is as a result of this that the Protestants developed a theory of persecution more noxious than the older Catholic theory.

Catholic persecution, Acton argued, had had a practical motive; it had been based on the idea that dissent threatened the moral fabric of Christian society. The state was based upon religious unity, and that unity was incorporated into its laws and administration. The authority of the church and the orthodoxy of her doctrine could not be impaired, said Catholic casuists, because they were the cornerstone of the social and political order. Those who held schismatic views were sometimes tolerated, being allowed to enjoy personal freedom and property rights, but they were not admitted to political rights because they did not profess the religious beliefs and duties upon which political rights were conditional.

The Protestant theory of persecution had a different rationale. It simply asserted the right of the state to suppress religious error — to suppress, not the practical immorality of blasphemy or crime, but a purely speculative, dogmatic error:

Catholic intolerance is handed down from an age when unity subsisted, and when its preservation, being essential for that of society, became a necessity of State as well as a result of circumstances. Protestant intolerance, on the contrary, was the peculiar fruit of a dogmatic system in contradiction with the facts and principles on which the intolerance actually existing among Catholics was founded.[37]

This is a bald sketch of the argument, which is so cleverly

---
[37] *Ibid.*, pp. 108-09.

constructed and manipulates ideas so dexterously that one can savor it without giving assent. Acton himself was not entirely taken in by his argument, for he proceeded to point out that the Catholic position was, in fact, untenable. The Protestants might have claimed, as the Catholics did on so many occasions, that speculative differences involved blasphemy and blasphemy obviously undermined the social order, or that a sect was fanatical and consequently subversive. If Catholics and Protestants are judged in terms of their theories alone and in terms of the dangers of false ideologies, the Catholics fare better than the Protestants. On other counts, Acton admitted, there was not much to choose from between them, and if Protestants are reproached for their illiberal theories, Catholics are guilty of the no less grave charge of having perpetrated the more numerous and cruel persecutions. "Those who — in agreement with the principle of the early Church, that men are free in matters of conscience — condemn all intolerance, will censure Catholics and Protestants alike." [38]

"The Protestant Theory of Persecution" appeared in 1862, when Acton was twenty-eight. In the course of time his views of Catholic persecution became more harsh and his judgment of Protestantism less harsh. He never condoned Lutheranism and Calvinism as systems of thought, but he did learn to respect the original motives that inspired the Reformation and the philosophies developed by the sects of the seventeenth century. The exchange of letters between Bishop Creighton and Lord Acton, published in this volume, contains a remarkable discussion of the pre-Reformation church, in which the Anglican finds circumstances extenuating the Catholic hierarchy, and the Catholic finds "the authority of tradition and the spiritual interests of man" on the side of the reformers. Even in his early articles, however, his views were far more liberal than those of most liberal Catholics. Compared with the most eminent liberal Catholic today, Jacques Maritain, Acton appears almost heretical.

[38] *Ibid.*, p. 125.

For political liberals who are also Catholics, one of the most delicate and awkward problems is the relation of church and state. If Catholicism is the true religion, it should be reflected in all features of human existence. As Maritain puts it:

The Catholic Church insists upon the principle that truth must have precedence over error and that the true religion, when it is known, should be aided in its spiritual mission in preference to religions whose message is more or less faltering and in which error is mingled with truth. This is but a simple consequence of what man owes to truth.[89]

In this respect Maritain is in complete agreement with a typical nineteenth century Ultramontane, Archbishop Maning. Acton, with his strong religious and ethical conscience, was not insensible to the seductiveness of this argument. He granted in two early articles ("Political Thoughts on the Church," 1859, and "Goldwin Smith's Irish History," 1862) that Catholicism had the duty, and therefore the right, of impressing its image upon society. Just as the likeness of God is reflected in man, so the divine order must be made manifest in the world. But this did not necessarily imply the unity of church and state. While Maritain is the more orthodox Catholic, Acton is the more orthodox liberal. For Acton, the unity of church and state in the Middle Ages was justified by the exigencies of a barbarous and lawless society where only the spiritual authority of the church, exercised in close association with the state, could introduce the elementary forms of civilization, let alone the forms of Christianity. Moreover, at that time the acquiescence of the entire nation testified to the rightness of Catholic establishments. The entire nation was Catholic, the church having preceded the state and then having helped sustain it, and the connection between church and state was natural and not arbitrary. But in the nineteenth century the exigencies that once required unity, and the natural conditions that made unity tolerable, were happily absent,

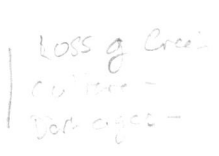

---

[89] Jacques Maritain, *The Rights of Man and Natural Law,* trans. D. C. Anson (New York, 1943), pp. 25-26.

and the church could "revert to a policy more suited to her nature."[40] The principle of religious toleration was truer to her oldest traditions and to her present situation. Where the shift from unity to toleration did not occur, the church was caught up in spiritual disaster. It became associated with absolutism and was reduced to a fatal condition of dependence:

In modern times the absolute monarchy in Catholic countries has been, next to the Reformation, the greatest and most formidable enemy of the church. . . . . The church is at this day more free under Protestant than under Catholic governments — in Prussia or England than in France or Piedmont, Naples or Bavaria. . . . .

It is absurd to pretend that at the present day France, or Spain, or Naples, are better governed than England, Holland or Prussia. A country entirely Protestant may have more Catholic elements in its government than one where the population is wholly Catholic. The State which is Catholic *par excellence* is a by-word for misgovernment, because the orthodoxy and piety of its administrators are deemed a substitute for a better system. The demand for a really Catholic system of government falls with the greatest weight of reproach on the Catholic States. . . . . [The remains of the medieval system and the true idea of the Christian state] will be found in the country [England] which, in the midst of its apostasy, and in spite of so much guilt towards religion, has preserved the Catholic spirit in her political institutions more than any Catholic nation.[41]

Maritain's philosophy is, of course, more abstract and systematic than Acton's. For him the principle of the relationship of church and state is decided in terms of a religious dogma to which the confusions of empirical politics must be accommodated. In effect, therefore, he reverses Acton's formula. Acton had assigned priority to the principle of religious toleration, to the political principle, that is, of the separation of church and state; the unity of the Middle Ages was a departure from this principle justified by the unusual

---
[40] "Goldwin Smith's Irish History," *Rambler* (new series), Vol. VI (1862), reprinted in *History of Freedom*, p. 255.
[41] "Political Thoughts on the Church," *Rambler*, Vol. XI (1859), reprinted in *History of Freedom*, pp. 206-11.

exigencies of that time. Maritain assigns priority to the principle of religious unity, and it is only the unusual exigencies of our time that prevent the fulfillment of this religious principle. He bases himself upon the medieval theory of the "indirect power" of the church in the temporal sphere — indirect as compared with its direct power in the spiritual. This indirect power is prescribed wherever spiritual interests are involved. And since the state is directed to a temporal good that is also moral and spiritual, it may properly come under the jurisdiction of the church. "One sword is under the other," this theory holds, and the church's is the upper sword. Moreover, since "there are in the concrete no morally indifferent human acts," this indirect power has infinite scope:

Any sort of temporal work — not only a public decree or legislative enactment, the raising of taxes, the declaration of war or a treaty of peace, but also the activity of a professional or syndical or political group, the exercise of some particular civic right — may come into special connection with the good of souls, once it becomes for instance the occasion of some spiritual aberration or happens to affect sufficiently seriously the rights and liberty of the Church or the orientation of the faithful towards eternal salvation. Who is to be the judge of such a connection and the gravity of the spiritual interests involved? Clearly the Church alone.[42]

Nor does Maritain permit the power to be diluted or made ineffectual; he deplores the error of some modern thinkers who exaggerate the distinction between authority and power, and concede to the church its proper authority in temporal affairs but refuse it a corresponding power.

Up to this point Maritain's argument is identical with Manning's: "The spiritual power knows, with divine certainty, the limits of its own jurisdiction." Manning differed from Maritain only on the practical question — whether the church should attempt to exercise its rightful power. Manning insisted upon the full plenitude of its power; Maritain urges a voluntary and partial abdication. Religious conform-

[42] Maritain, *The Things that Are Not Caesar's*, trans. J. F. Scanlan (New York, 1931), pp. 22-23.

ity today, Maritain says, is not practicable, and to insist upon it might jeopardize the civil peace of the community. As a concession, then, to the spirit of the age, "the state can and ought in the actual circumstances of our time to tolerate within it modes of worship that diverge to a greater or lesser extent from the true worship." [43]

The differences between Acton and the conventional Catholic liberal like Maritain — to say nothing of the Ultramontane Manning — are significant even on the basis of Acton's early articles. In his later work the differences are much sharper and the points of contact between the two are fewer. Acton considered that he had "renounced everything in Catholicism which was not compatible with Liberty, and everything in Politics which was not compatible with Catholicity." [44] The sentiment is pious but unpersuasive. Another of his maxims may be cited against him: "We may pursue several objects, we may weave many principles, but we cannot have two courts of final appeal." [45] In fact, when the two conflicted, Acton set liberalism above Catholicism, and this was more and more true as time went on.

Acton's political ideas have been compared with those of Burke and Tocqueville. All three were concerned with the practical conditions favoring liberty, and were suspicious of the rationalist frame of mind which desired to impose liberty, as a ready-made set of doctrines, upon a supposedly compliant and reasonable society. They feared men's power more than they trusted men's ideals. They anticipated no miracle of happiness on earth, no "heavenly city" such as the eighteenth century philosophers dreamt of. Instead they distrusted these dreams. For if the heavenly city was a utopian vision, a hell on earth was not, and in the excesses of the French Revolution and the Reign of Terror, they saw the inevitable judgment on

---

[43] Maritain, *Freedom in the Modern World*, trans. R. O'Sullivan (New York, 1936), p. 65.
[44] *Correspondence of Lord Acton*, p. 54.
[45] *Ibid.*, p. 185.

the sin of pride. They appreciated the enormous complexity of society, feared the destructive and despotic temper of impatient reformers, and preferred instead the multiplicity of forces and ideas represented in the existing constitutions — the distinctions of class, the distribution of political power, personal loyalty divided among family, province and nation, the traditions and idiosyncracies perpetuated by history.[46]

A phrase has gained currency in recent years, "totalitarian liberalism," to describe the habit liberals have fallen into of calling upon the state to undertake all the reforms they desire — to protect the rights of labor, enforce the rights of suffrage, extend the privilege of education, provide insurance and social relief, prohibit the dissemination of racist doctrines and bigoted opinions—to control, in short, the welfare of society. However urgent each of these reforms is, it is nevertheless true that the tendency to look upon the state as a vast social-work agency has its dangers, for it invests the state with a formidable power, and makes liberty dependent not upon the rights of autonomous groups and corporations but upon the generosity of an omnipotent government.

In a very early article on "Contemporary Events" written for the *Rambler,* Acton took the measure of the totalitarian liberal of his day: "No despotism is more complete than that which is the aim of modern liberals. . . . The liberal doctrine subjects the desire of freedom to the desire of power, and the more it demands a share of power, the more it is averse to exemptions from it." [47] This theme runs through all of his work. It determined his judgment of the classical state in antiquity, Protestantism, democracy and nationalism, the French Revolution, nineteenth century Prussia, the

---

[46] There was another strain in Burke's thought that places him outside the political tradition with which he is usually identified Burke believed, as firmly as his enemy Rousseau, that the state should be "a moral person," "absolute, sacred and inviolable," and he confused, just as disastrously, the concept of government, state and society The state, or society, he said, "is a partnership in all science, a partnership in all art; a partnership in every virtue and in all perfection."

[47] *Rambler* (new series), II (1860), 265.

Italian struggle for independence, and the American Civil War. All, he said, were tarred by the same brush. All destroyed every authority except the state, and made the state the custodian of all values and all powers. In religion, nationality and political power, the state became a single unit and the independent authorities that formerly mediated between the individual and the state — churches, local and national loyalties and class affiliations — were swept away.

It has been said that the true liberal reveres God but respects the devil. Acton revered the ideals over which the state might preside, but respected the temptations to which it would be subject and the infinite possibilities of corruption and tyranny to which it would inevitably fall victim. Liberty, he insisted, does not reside in the power of the majority to identify its will with that of the state, but in the security of a minority not to be encroached upon by the state:

The true democratic principle, that none shall have power over the people, is taken to mean that none shall be able to restrain or to elude its power. The true democratic principle, that the people shall not be made to do what it does not like, is taken to mean that it shall never be required to tolerate what it does not like. The true democratic principle, that every man's free will shall be as unfettered as possible, is taken to mean that the free will of the collective people shall be fettered in nothing.[48]

It is bad to be oppressed by a minority, but it is worse to be oppressed by a majority. For there is a reserve of latent power in the masses which, if it is called into play, the minority can seldom resist. But from the absolute will of an entire people there is no appeal, no redemption, no refuge but treason.[49]

That democracy — in the sense of the unfettered rule of the majority — might be inimical to liberty is an idea prominent enough in the nineteenth century. Many feared what Gerald Massey, a contemporary of Acton, spoke of proudly as "the tramp of Democracy's earthquake feet." Matthew Arnold

---
[48] "May's Democracy in Europe," p. 159 of this volume.
[49] "History of Freedom in Antiquity," p. 40 of this volume.

expressed a typical anxiety: "Great qualities are trodden down . . . and littleness united . . . is become invincible." Tocqueville said that the modern idea of leveling the population to a single class would have been pleasing to Richelieu: "This level surface facilitates the exercise of power." The lesson commonly drawn was that the extension of the suffrage was an evil to be resisted. The English historian Lecky, for example, violently attacked the reform acts enfranchising the urban and rural workers. Yet Acton vigorously, not apologetically, supported them.

The conservatives were apprehensive because they were convinced of the political superiority of "the educated class." Acton had no such faith. On the contrary, he was certain that if the masses were not divinely inspired, neither was any particular class. It was because Gladstone feared democracy and yet favored universal suffrage that Acton so admired him. Two letters, written in appreciation of Gladstone's support of the reform acts, deserve to be included among the great documents of modern democratic thought:

The decisive test of his greatness will be the gap he will leave. Among those who come after him there will be none who understand that the men who pay wages ought not to be the political masters of those who earn them (because laws should be adapted to those who have the heaviest stake in the country, for whom misgovernment means not mortified pride or stinted luxury, but want and pain, and degradation and risk to their own lives and to their children's souls), and who yet can understand and feel sympathy for institutions that incorporate tradition and prolong the reign of the dead.[50]

As to Democracy, it is true that [the] masses of new electors are utterly ignorant, that they are easily deceived by appeals to prejudice and passion, and are consequently unstable, and that the difficulty of explaining economic questions to them, and of linking their interests with those of the State, may become a danger to the public credit, if not to the security of private property. A true Liberal, as distinguished from a Democrat, keeps this peril always before him.

---
[50] *Letters to Mary Gladstone* (1st ed.), p. 147.

The answer is, that you cannot make an omelette without breaking eggs — that politics are not made up of artifices only, but of truths, and that truths have to be told.

We are forced, in equity, to share the government with the working class by considerations which were made supreme by the awakening of political economy. Adam Smith set up two propositions — that contracts ought to be free between capital and labour, and that labour is the source, he sometimes says the only source, of wealth. If the last sentence, in its exclusive form, was true, it was difficult to resist the conclusion that the class on which national prosperity depends ought to control the wealth it supplies, that is, ought to govern instead of the useless unproductive class, and that the class which earns the increment ought to enjoy it. That is the foreign effect of Adam Smith — French Revolution and Socialism. We, who reject the extreme proposition, cannot resist the logical pressure of the other. If there is a free contract, in open market, between capital and labour, it cannot be right that one of the two contracting parties should have the making of the laws, the management of the conditions, the keeping of the peace, the administration of justice, the distribution of taxes, the control of expenditure, in its own hands exclusively. It is unjust that all these securities, all these advantages, should be on the same side. It is monstrous that they should be all on the side that has least urgent need of them, that has least to lose. Before this argument, the ancient dogma, that power attends on property, broke down. Justice required that property should — not abdicate, but — share its political supremacy. Without this partition, free contract was as illusory as a fair duel in which one man supplies seconds, arms, and ammunition. . . . .

They [the opponents of reform] will admit much of my theory, but then they will say, like practical men, that the ignorant classes cannot understand affairs of state, and are sure to go wrong. But the odd thing is that the most prosperous nations in the world are both governed by the masses — France and America. So there must be a flaw in the argument somewhere. The fact is that education, intelligence, wealth, are a security against certain faults of conduct, not against errors of policy. There is no error so monstrous that it fails to find defenders among the ablest men. . . . . The danger is not that a particular class is unfit to govern. Every class is unfit to govern.[51]

[51] *Ibid.*, pp. 193-96.

These citations are from letters written in 1880 and 1881. They represent a decided advance upon his earlier position. If by democracy is meant the participation of the people in the affairs of government, rather than the unlimited power of the people in the affairs of society, Acton may be said to have progressed in the direction of democracy in his later writings.

Earlier in his career, as editor of the *Rambler* and *Home and Foreign Review,* his political views had been considerably more conservative. He admired Austrian conservatism, denied that representative institutions and constitutionalism were essential for either good government or liberty, uncritically praised feudalism, and commended England for her alacrity in assuming "the glorious mission of representing in Asia the civilization of Christianity."[52] Austria, he said, was a valuable asset to Europe because she boasted the only real nobility on the continent, and the Old Regime of France with its privileged classes and provincial rights was preferable to the equality and centralization that were the fruit of the revolution. The common denominator of these judgments was the desire to see political power distributed among a host of social groups, to multiply the sources of authority so as to break down the identity of state and society. It was the equivalent for society of the principle of checks and balances in government. A political institution, attitude or doctrine, Acton seemed to imply, must be tested by its practical effect upon the conditions in which liberty prospers. The judgment was not an abstract one: it was not the moral superiority *per se* of the aristocracy in Austria or France that endeared it to Acton, but its utility as a political force.

"Political Causes of the American Revolution," reprinted here from the *Rambler* of 1861, illustrates the attitude of the young Acton. The "American Revolution" to which the title refers is the American Civil War, a revolution, according to Acton, promoted by the northern abolitionists. The essay is interesting not because it is a particularly good account of a contemporary event (its interpretation is sometimes ex-

---
[52] "The Count de Montalembert," *Rambler,* X (1858), 425.

tremely naïve), but because it is a penetrating revelation of Acton's political thought at the time. It was not the South, he argued, with its threat of secession that destroyed the American union, but the North with its appeal to a law and moral obligation superior to the constitution. The Catholic, Orestes Brownson, is cited in support of the doctrine represented by the South that no one may set up his own conscience as superior to the laws of the state. The South had the law in its favor, Acton found; therefore it was in the right morally as well. Moreover, by defending the institution of slavery, the South took its stand against democracy and the pernicious democratic doctrine of the equal rights of man. Neither on moral nor on political grounds did Acton admit the justice of a categorical prohibition of slavery:

> In this, as in all other things, they [the abolitionists] exhibit the same abstract, ideal absolutism, which is equally hostile with the Catholic and with the English spirit. Their democratic system poisons everything it touches. All constitutional questions are referred to the one fundamental principle of popular sovereignty, without consideration of policy or expediency. .... Very different is the mode in which the Church labours to reform mankind by assimilating realities with ideals, and accommodating herself to times and circumstances.[53]

Gradually Acton's ideas shifted, so that the resemblance to Burke ("Political Causes of the American Revolution" reads like an adaptation of Burke's "Reflections on the French Revolution") is blurred and even at times effaced. "Considerations of policy or expediency" became anathema to him. He became less conservative, more critical of Austria and Spain and less favorably disposed to feudalism. He was converted to the view that representative institutions were the prerequisites of good government and liberty, and one of the prominent themes in his later correspondence is the immorality of imperialism. In a journal of 1857 he had spoken proudly of the English Catholics as "the only permanently conservative element in the state." [54] Later, "conservatism,"

---

[53] "Political Causes of the American Revolution," p. 246 of this volume.

like "Toryism" (except when it was used casually and loosely), became a term of derogation in his vocabulary, synonymous with immorality, opportunism, and ethical and political depravity. And Burke, whose writings he had once worshipped as "the law and the prophets," [55] was remembered kindly only as the champion of America's noble revolution; more often, particularly in Acton's personal notes and letters, he was remembered with bitterness and contempt: "To a Liberal, all the stages between Burke and Nero are little more than the phases of forgotten moons." [56]

Yet Acton did not entirely discard his early views. If it is difficult to place him within a recognizable tradition of political liberalism, it is not, as he seemed to have thought, because he was creating a new synthesis of liberalism and Catholicism. It was rather because he failed to create such a synthesis. His insights were brilliant but they were not systematically sustained, and his thought was torn between the claims of a practical political liberalism and a dogmatic religious morality. Upon his early views was imposed an alien, even a contradictory, set of political principles and attitudes which, although dominant in the last twenty years of his life, never succeeded in suppressing the earlier ones. The empirical attitude that he had acquired by studying Burke — the disregard for the metaphysical abstractions of right and justice, the exclusive concern with the practical test of political principles and institutions — yielded more and more to a doctrinaire attitude: an unwillingness to deviate from the absolute ideals of right and justice, and a profound distaste for traffic with the expediencies and compromises of practical politics.

If the essay on the American Civil War illustrates the political thinking of Acton's youth, his views on the American Revolution illustrate the dominant temper of his thought in maturity. In an extravagant tribute to the American Revolution he ranked 1776 as the first date in the history

---
[54] Add. MSS, 5751.
[55] *Lord Acton and His Circle*, ed. Abbot Gasquet (London, 1906), p. 60.
[56] Add. MSS, 4973.

of liberty. It was then that America demonstrated her faith in liberty as a matter of pure principle and pure idea, and flouted the ignoble solicitations of material interests, practical caution, and the security of life and property. (Acton's unconventional reading of history may be quarreled with here too, but that is not now the issue.) The American Revolution was significant as "the supreme manifestation of the law of resistance, as the abstract revolution in its purest and most perfect shape." [57] The revolutionists jeopardized their lives, fortunes and even their country; they created a "lake of blood" in their determination to resist their monarch and parliament, the legally constituted authorities, and they erected their commonwealth on a principle subversive of all law and tradition. "Here or nowhere we have the broken chain, the rejected past, precedent and statute superseded by unwritten law, sons wiser than their fathers, ideas rooted in the future, reason cutting as clean as Atropos." [58]

Acton's rupture with Burke and with his own early views could not have been more defiant, it would seem, for he was now identifying morality with the principle of the "abstract revolution." He even declared himself willing to take the risks of that revolution and all the evils that might attend it. At least he was willing to do so in the case of the American Revolution. In other cases he quite obviously was not. His lectures on the French Revolution, for example, seem to derive, in the main, from his earlier thinking, when he was still under the spell of Burke's attack on the revolution. Yet even in these lectures there is a noticeable contradiction. For he was attempting to straddle two incompatible principles: the pure, ethical principle that provided the initial incentive for the revolution and its moral justification, and the principle of the liberal society that should have been the outcome of the revolution, with its checks and balances, restrictions

---
[57] Review of James Bryce, *The American Commonwealth*, *English Historical Review*, IV (1889), reprinted in *History of Freedom*, p. 586.
[58] *Ibid.*

INTRODUCTION lxv

on power, corporations independent of the state, and practical securities for liberty.

Burke, more logical and consistent than Acton in this respect, had said that revolution in the service of an absolute idea must necessarily give way to the state in the service of an absolute power. If the laws, traditions and irrationalities of history are subjected to the discretions of men, if they are judged by conscience and higher law, the course of rationalism would lead fatally to absolutism, because there would no longer be any room for the multiplicity of social forces upon which real liberty depends. Acton himself was not unaware of this. One of his notes reads: "Government by Idea tends to take in everything, to make the whole of society obedient to the idea. Spaces not so governed are unconquered, beyond the border, unconverted, unconvinced, a future danger." [59] More often, however, he ignored Burke's warnings, dismissing him as an unprincipled opportunist who substituted the expediencies of politics for the precepts of morality.

It is perhaps unfair to insist on the contradictions in Acton's thought. He was not, after all, a systematic philosopher. It would undoubtedly be more generous to accept his separate insights for what they are worth, without seeking to impose a general structure upon his work. It would be generous, but hardly to Acton's liking. For Acton was, more than a historian, a political theorist. The actual events of politics and history were for him merely the occasions for the appearance of their true meanings, their ideas, which it was the task of the historian to relate to a universe of discourse consisting of the basic and eternal principles of morality.

So perhaps it is more generous, after all, not to dismiss the contradictions as verbal or minor. Perhaps it might be best to take them in the grand and serious style in which Acton approached all problems. In that case, they must be seen as a profound ambivalence eating away at the very heart of his work. For whatever temporary reconciliations may be

[59] Add. MSS, 4941.

effected between an absolute morality and a pragmatic, temporizing liberalism, the tension between them persists.

Matthew Arnold, also obsessed by the antagonism between the actual and the ideal, found in criticism the means of their reconciliation:

> Criticism must maintain its independence of the practical spirit and its aims. Even with well-meant efforts of the practical spirit it must express dissatisfaction, if in the sphere of the ideal they seem impoverishing and limiting. It must not hurry on to the goal because of its practical importance. It must be patient, and know how to wait; and flexible, and know how to attach itself to things and how to withdraw from them. It must be apt to study and praise elements that for the fullness of spiritual perfection are wanted, even though they belong to a power which in the practical sphere may be maleficent. It must be apt to discern the spiritual shortcomings or illusions of powers that in the practical sphere may be beneficent.

"Praise elements that for the fullness of spiritual perfection are wanted. . . ." — praise the spiritual grandeur of pure abstract idealism, even though in practice it generates a hateful absolutism; "Discern the spiritual shortcomings. . . ." — discern the spiritual suicide of a system, however liberal, tolerant and satisfactory in practice, which rests content with an ethics of prudence and a politics of interest. It was this double-edged instrument of criticism that cleaved through Acton's philosophy.

GERTRUDE HIMMELFARB

New York City
January, 1948

ESSAYS ON
FREEDOM AND POWER

Chapter I

INAUGURAL LECTURE ON THE STUDY OF HISTORY

Fellow Students—I look back to-day to a time before the middle of the century, when I was reading at Edinburgh and fervently wishing to come to this University. At three colleges I applied for admission, and, as things then were, I was refused by all. Here, from the first, I vainly fixed my hopes, and here, in a happier hour, after five-and-forty years, they are at last fulfilled.

I desire, first, to speak to you of that which I may reasonably call the Unity of Modern History, as an easy approach to questions necessary to be met on the threshold by anyone occupying this place, which my predecessor has made so formidable to me by the reflected lustre of his name.

You have often heard it said that modern history is a subject to which neither beginning nor end can be assigned. No beginning, because the dense web of the fortunes of man is woven without a void; because, in society as in nature, the structure is continuous, and we can trace things back uninterruptedly, until we dimly descry the Declaration of Independence in the forests of Germany. No end, because, on the same principle, history made and history making are scientifically inseparable and separately unmeaning.

"Politics," said Sir John Seeley, "are vulgar when they are not liberalised by history, and history fades into mere litera-

---
Note· This lecture was delivered at Cambridge, June 11, 1895 (London, 1895): reprinted in *Lectures on Modern History* (London· Macmillan Co., 1906), pp. 1-30 and 319-342.

ture when it loses sight of its relation to practical politics." Everybody perceives the sense in which this is true. For the science of politics is the one science that is deposited by the stream of history, like grains of gold in the sand of a river; and the knowledge of the past, the record of truths revealed by experience, is eminently practical, as an instrument of action and a power that goes to the making of the future.[1] In France, such is the weight attached to the study of our own time, that there is an appointed course of contemporary history, with appropriate textbooks.[2] That is a chair which, in the progressive division of labour by which both science and government prosper,[3] may some day be founded in this country. Meantime, we do well to acknowledge the points at which the two epochs diverge. For the contemporary differs from the modern in this, that many of its facts cannot by us be definitely ascertained. The living do not give up their secrets with the candour of the dead; one key is always excepted, and a generation passes before we can ensure accuracy. Common report and outward seeming are bad copies of the reality, as the initiated know it. Even of a thing so memorable as the war of 1870, the true cause is still obscure; much that we believed has been scattered to the winds in the last six months, and further revelations by important witnesses are about to appear. The use of history turns far more on certainty than on abundance of acquired information.

Beyond the question of certainty is the question of detachment. The process by which principles are discovered and appropriated is other than that by which, in practice, they are applied; and our most sacred and disinterested convictions ought to take shape in the tranquil regions of the air, above the tumult and the tempest of active life.[4] For a man is justly despised who has one opinion in history and another in politics, one for abroad and another at home, one for opposition and another for office. History compels us to fasten on abiding issues, and rescues us from the temporary and transient. Politics and history are interwoven, but are not commen-

---

[1] The notes to this chapter will be found in the Appendix, pp. 399-428.

INAUGURAL LECTURE ON THE STUDY OF HISTORY 5

surate. Ours is a domain that reaches farther than affairs of state, and is not subject to the jurisdiction of governments. It is our function to keep in view and to command the movement of ideas, which are not the effect but the cause of public events; [5] and even to allow some priority to ecclesiastical history over civil, since, by reason of the graver issues concerned, and the vital consequences of error, it opened the way in research, and was the first to be treated by close reasoners and scholars of the higher rank.[6]

In the same manner, there is wisdom and depth in the philosophy which always considers the origin and the germ, and glories in history as one consistent epic.[7] Yet every student ought to know that mastery is acquired by resolved limitation. And confusion ensues from the theory of Montesquieu and of his school, who, adapting the same term to things unlike, insist that freedom is the primitive condition of the race from which we are sprung.[8] If we are to account mind not matter, ideas not force, the spiritual property that gives dignity and grace and intellectual value to history, and its action on the ascending life of man, then we shall not be prone to explain the universal by the national, and civilization by custom.[9] A speech of Antigone, a single sentence of Socrates, a few lines that were inscribed on an Indian rock before the Second Punic War, the footsteps of a silent yet prophetic people who dwelt by the Dead Sea, and perished in the fall of Jerusalem, come nearer to our lives than the ancestral wisdom of barbarians who fed their swine on the Hercynian acorns.

For our present purpose, then, I describe as modern history that which begins four hundred years ago, which is marked off by an evident and intelligible line from the time immediately preceding, and displays in its course specific and distinctive characteristics of its own.[10] The modern age did not proceed from mediæval by normal succession, with outward tokens of legitimate descent. Unheralded, it founded a new order of things, under a law of innovation, sapping the ancient reign of continuity. In those days Columbus subverted the notions of the world, and reversed the conditions of production, wealth, and power; in those days Machiavelli released government from the restraint of law; Erasmus diverted the current of ancient learning from profane into Christian channels; Luther broke the chain of authority and tradition at the strongest link; and Copernicus erected an invincible power that set forever the mark of progress upon the time that was to come. There is the same unbound originality and disregard for inherited sanctions in the rare philosophers as in the discovery of Divine Right, and the intruding Imperialism of Rome. The like effects are visible everywhere, and one generation beheld them all. It was an awakening of new life; the world revolved in a different orbit, determined by influences unknown before. After many ages persuaded of the headlong decline and impending dissolution of society,[11] and governed by usage and the will of masters who were in their graves, the sixteenth century went forth armed for untried experience, and ready to watch with hopefulness a prospect of incalculable change.

That forward movement divides it broadly from the older world; and the unity of the new is manifest in the universal spirit of investigation and discovery which did not cease to operate, and withstood the recurring efforts of reaction, until, by the advent of the reign of general ideas which we call the Revolution, it at length prevailed.[12] This successive deliverance and gradual passage, for good and evil, from subordination to independence is a phenomenon of primary import to us, because historical science has been one of its instruments.[13] If the Past has been an obstacle and a burden, knowledge of the Past is the safest and the surest emancipation. And the earnest search for it is one of the signs that distinguish the four centuries of which I speak from those that went before. The Middle Ages, which possessed good writers of contemporary narrative, were careless and impatient of older fact. They became content to be deceived, to live in a twilight of fiction, under clouds of false witness, inventing according to convenience, and glad to welcome the forger and the cheat.[14] As time went on, the atmosphere of accredited mendacity thickened, until in the Renaissance, the art of exposing falsehood dawned upon keen Italian minds. It was then that history as we understand it began to be understood, and the illustrious dynasty of scholars arose to whom we still look both for method and material. Unlike the dreaming prehistoric world, ours knows the need and the duty to make itself master of the earlier times, and to forfeit nothing of their wisdom or their warnings,[15] and has devoted its best energy and treasure to the sovereign purpose of detecting error and vindicating entrusted truth.[16]

In this epoch of full-grown history men have not acquiesced in the given conditions of their lives. Taking little for granted they have sought to know the ground they stand on, and the road they travel, and the reason why. Over them, therefore, the historian has obtained an increasing ascendancy.[17] The law of stability was overcome by the power of ideas, constantly varied and rapidly renewed;[18] ideas that give life and motion, that take wing and traverse seas and frontiers, making it futile to pursue the consecutive order of events in the seclusion of a separate nationality.[19] They compel us to share the existence of societies wider than our own, to be familiar with distant and exotic types, to hold our march upon the loftier summits, along the central range, to live in the company of heroes, and saints, and men of genius, that no single country could produce. We cannot afford wantonly to lose sight of great men and memorable lives, and are bound to store up objects for admiration as far as may be;[20] for the effect of implacable research is constantly to reduce their number. No intellectual exercise, for instance, can be more invigorating than to watch the working of the mind of Napoleon, the most entirely known as well as the ablest of historic men. In another sphere, it is the vision of a higher world to be intimate with the character of Fénelon, the cherished model of politicians, ecclesiastics, and men of letters, the witness against one century and precursor of another, the advocate of the poor against oppression, of liberty in an age of arbitrary power, of tolerance in an age of persecution, of the humane virtues among men accustomed to sacrifice them to authority, the man of whom one enemy says that his cleverness was enough to strike terror, and another, that genius poured in torrents from his eyes. For the minds that are greatest and best alone furnish the instructive examples. A man of ordinary proportion or inferior metal knows not how to think out the rounded circle of his thought, how to divest his will of its surroundings and to rise above the pressure of time and race and circumstances,[21] to choose the star that guides his course, to correct and test, and assay his convictions by the light within,[22] and, with a resolute conscience and ideal courage, to remodel and reconstitute the character which birth and education gave him.[23]

For ourselves, if it were not the quest of the higher level and the extended horizon, international history would be imposed by the exclusive and insular reason that parliamentary reporting is younger than parliaments. The foreigner has no mystic fabric in his government, and no *arcanum imperii*. For him the foundations have been laid bare; every motive and function of the mechanism is accounted for as distinctly as the works of a watch. But with our indigenous constitution, not made with hands or written upon paper, but claiming to develop by a law of organic growth; with our disbelief in the virtue of definitions and general principles and our reliance on relative truths, we can have nothing equivalent to the vivid and prolonged debates in which other communities have displayed the inmost secrets of political science to every man who can read. And the discussions of constituent assemblies, at Philadelphia, Versailles and Paris, at Cadiz and Brussels, at Geneva, Frankfort and Berlin, above nearly all, those of the most enlightened States in the American Union, when they have recast their institutions, are paramount in the literature of politics, and proffer treasures which at home we have never enjoyed.

To historians the later part of their enormous subject is precious because it is inexhaustible. It is the best to know because it is the best known and the most explicit. Earlier scenes stand out from a background of obscurity. We soon reach the sphere of hopeless ignorance and unprofitable doubt. But hundreds and even thousands of the moderns have borne testimony against themselves, and may be studied in their private correspondence and sentenced on their own confession. Their deeds are done in the daylight. Every country opens its archives and invites us to penetrate the mysteries of State. When Hallam wrote his chapter on James II, France was the only Power whose reports were available. Rome followed, and the Hague; and then came the stores of the Italian States, and at last the Prussian and the Austrian papers, and partly those of Spain. Where Hallam and Lingard were dependent on Barillon, their successors consult the diplomacy of ten governments. The topics, indeed, are few on which the resources have been so employed that we can be content with the work done for us and never wish it to be done over again. Part of the lives of Luther and Frederic, a little of the Thirty Years' War, much of the American Revolution and the French Restoration, the early years of Richelieu and Mazarin, and a few volumes of Mr. Gardiner, show here and there like Pacific islands in the ocean. I should not even venture to claim for Ranke, the real originator of the heroic study of records, and the most prompt and fortunate of European pathfinders, that there is one of his seventy volumes that has not been overtaken and in part surpassed. It is through his accelerating influence mainly that our branch of study has become progressive, so that the best master is quickly distanced by the better pupil.[24] The Vatican archives alone, now made accessible to the world, filled 3,239 cases when they were sent to France; and they are not the richest. We are still at the beginning of the documentary age, which will tend to make history independent of historians, to develop learning at the expense of writing, and to accomplish a revolution in other sciences as well.[25]

To men in general I would justify the stress I am laying on modern history, neither by urging its varied wealth, nor the rupture with precedent, nor the perpetuity of change and increase of pace, nor the growing predominance of opinion over belief, and of knowledge over opinion, but by the argument that it is a narrative told of ourselves, the record of a life which is our own, of efforts not yet abandoned to repose, of problems that still entangle the feet and vex the hearts of men. Every part of it is weighty with inestimable lessons that we must learn by experience and at a great price, if we know not how to profit by the example and teaching of those who have gone before us, in a society largely resembling the one we live in.[26] Its study fulfills its purpose even if it only makes us wiser, without producing books, and gives us the gift of historical thinking, which is better than historical learning.[27] It is a most powerful ingredient in the formation of character and the training of talent, and our historical judgments have as much to do with hopes of heaven as public or private conduct. Convictions that have been strained through the instances and the comparisons of modern times differ immeasurably in solidity and force from those which every new fact perturbs, and which are often little better than illusions or unsifted prejudice.[28]

The first of human concerns is religion, and it is the salient feature of modern centuries. They are signalised as the scene of Protestant developments. Starting from a time of extreme indifference, ignorance, and decline, they were at once occupied with that conflict which was to rage so long, and of which no man could imagine the infinite consequences. Dogmatic conviction — for I shun to speak of faith in connection with many characters of those days — dogmatic conviction rose to be the centre of universal interest, and remained down to Cromwell the supreme influence and motive of public policy. A time came when the intensity of prolonged conflict, when even the energy of antagonistic assurance abated somewhat, and the controversial spirit began to make room for the scientific; and as the storm subsided, and the area of settled questions emerged, much of the dispute was abandoned to the serene and soothing touch of historians, invested as they are with the prerogative of redeeming the cause of religion from many unjust reproaches, and from the graver evil of reproaches that are just. Ranke used to say that Church interests prevailed in politics until the Seven Years' War, and marked a phase of society that ended when the hosts of Brandenburg went into action at Leuthen, chaunting their

Lutheran hymns.[29] That bold proposition would be disputed even if applied to the present age. After Sir Robert Peel had broken up his party, the leaders who followed him declared that no popery was the only basis on which it could be reconstructed.[30] On the other side may be urged that, in July 1870, at the outbreak of the French war, the only government that insisted on the abolition of the temporal power was Austria; and since then we have witnessed the fall of Castelar, because he attempted to reconcile Spain with Rome.

Soon after 1850 several of the most intelligent men in France, struck by the arrested increase of their own population and by the telling statistics from Further Britain, foretold the coming preponderance of the English race. They did not foretell, what none could then foresee, the still more sudden growth of Prussia, or that the three most important countries of the globe would, by the end of the century, be those that chiefly belonged to the conquests of the Reformation. So that in Religion, as in so many things, the product of these centuries has favoured the new elements; and the centre of gravity, moving from the Mediterranean nations to the Oceanic, from the Latin to the Teuton, has also passed from the Catholic to the Protestant.[31]

Out of these controversies proceeded political as well as historical science. It was in the Puritan phase, before the restoration of the Stuarts, that theology, blending with politics, effected a fundamental change. The essentially English reformation of the seventeenth century was less a struggle between churches than between sects, often subdivided by questions of discipline and self-regulation rather than by dogma. The sectaries cherished no purpose or prospect of prevailing over the nations; and they were concerned with the individual more than with the congregation, with conventicles, not with State churches. Their view was narrowed, but their sight was sharpened. It appeared to them that governments and institutions are made to pass away, like things of earth, whilst souls are immortal; that there is no more proportion between liberty and power than between eternity and time; that, therefore, the sphere of enforced command ought to be restricted within fixed limits, and that which had been done by authority, and outward discipline, and organised violence, should be attempted by division of power, and committed to the intellect and the conscience of free men.[32] Thus was exchanged the dominion of will over will for the dominion of reason over reason. The true apostles of toleration are not those who sought protection for their own beliefs, or who had none to protect; but men to whom, irrespective of their cause, it was a political, a moral, and a theological dogma, a question of conscience involving both religion and policy.[33] Such a man was Socinus; and others arose in the smaller sects, — the Independent founder of the colony of Rhode Island, and the Quaker patriarch of Pennsylvania. Much of the energy and zeal which had laboured for authority of doctrine was employed for liberty of prophesying. The air was filled with the enthusiasm of a new cry; but the cause was still the same. It became a boast that religion was the mother of freedom, that freedom was the lawful offspring of religion; and this transmutation, this subversion of established forms of political life by the development of religious thought, brings us to the heart of my subject, to the significant and central feature of the historical cycles before us. Beginning with the strongest religious movement and the most refined despotism ever known, it has led to the superiority of politics over divinity in the life of nations, and terminates in the equal claim of every man to be unhindered by man in the fulfillment of duty to God [34] — a doctrine laden with storm and havoc, which is the secret essence of the Rights of Man, and indestructible soul of Revolution.

When we consider what the adverse forces were, their sustained resistance, their frequent recovery, the critical moments when the struggle seemed for ever desperate, in 1685, in 1772, in 1808, it is no hyperbole to say that the progress of the world towards self-government would have been arrested but for the strength afforded by the religious motive in the seventeenth century. And this constancy of progress, of progress in the direction of organised and assured freedom, is the characteristic fact of modern history, and its tribute to the theory of Providence.[35] Many persons, I am well assured, would detect that this is a very old story, and a trivial commonplace, and would challenge proof that the world is making progress in aught but intellect, that it is gaining in freedom, or that increase in freedom is either a progress or a gain. Ranke, who was my own master, rejected the view that I have stated;[36] Comte, the master of better men, believed that we drag a lengthening chain under the gathered weight of the dead hand;[37] and many of our recent classics — Carlyle, Newman, Froude — were persuaded that there is no progress justifying the ways of God to man, and that the mere consolidation of liberty is like the motion of creatures whose advance is in the direction of their tails. They deem that anxious precaution against bad government is an obstruction to good, and degrades morality and mind by placing the capable at the mercy of the incapable, dethroning enlightened virtue for the benefit of the average man. They hold that great and salutary things are done for mankind by power concentrated, not by power balanced and cancelled and dispersed, and that the whig theory, sprung from decomposing sects, the theory that authority is legitimate only by virtue of its checks, and that the sovereign is dependent on the subject, is rebellion against the divine will manifested all down the stream of time.

I state the objection not that we may plunge into the crucial controversy of a science that is not identical with ours, but in order to make my drift clear by the defining aid of express contradiction. No political dogma is as serviceable to my purpose here as the historian's maxim to do the best he can for the other side, and to avoid pertinacity or emphasis on his own. Like the economic precept *laissez faire*,[38] which the eighteenth century derived from Colbert, it has been an important, if not a final step in the making of method. The strongest and most impressive personalities, it is true, like Macaulay, Thiers, and the two greatest of living writers, Mommsen and Treitschke, project their own broad shadow upon their pages. This is a practice proper to great men, and a great man may be worth several immaculate historians.

Otherwise there is virtue in the saying that a historian is seen at his best when he does not appear.[39] Better for us is the example of the Bishop of Oxford, who never lets us know what he thinks of anything but the matter before him; and of his illustrious French rival, Fustel de Coulanges, who said to an excited audience: "Do not imagine you are listening to me; it is history itself that speaks."[40] We can found no philosophy on the observation of four hundred years, excluding three thousand. It would be an imperfect and a fallacious induction. But I hope that even this narrow and disedifying section of history will aid you to see that the action of Christ who is risen on mankind whom he redeemed fails not, but increases;[41] that the wisdom of divine rule appears not in the perfection but in the improvement of the world[42] and that achieved liberty is the one ethical result that rests on the converging and combined conditions of advancing civilisation.[43] Then you will understand what a famous philosopher said, that history is the true demonstration of religion.[44]

But what do people mean who proclaim that liberty is the palm, and the prize, and the crown, seeing that it is an idea of which there are two hundred definitions, and that this wealth of interpretation has caused more bloodshed than anything, except theology? Is it Democracy as in France, or Federalism as in America, or the national independence which bounds the Italian view, or the reign of the fittest, which is the ideal of Germans?[45] I know not whether it will ever fall within my sphere of duty to trace the slow progress of that idea through the chequered scenes of our history, and to describe how subtle speculations touching the nature of conscience promoted a nobler and more spiritual conception of the liberty that protects it,[46] until the guardian of rights developed into the guardian of duties which are the cause of rights,[47] and that which had been prized as the material safeguard for treasures of earth became sacred as security for things that are divine. All that we require is a work-day key to history, and our present need can be supplied without pausing to satisfy philosophers. Without inquiring how far Sarasa or Butler, Kant or Vinet, is right as to the infallible voice of God in man, we may easily agree in this, that where absolutism reigned, by irresistible arms, concentrated possessions, auxiliary churches, and inhuman laws, it reigns no more; that commerce having risen against land, labour against wealth, the State against the forces dominant in society,[48] the division of power against the State, the thought of individuals against the practice of ages, neither authorities, nor minorities, nor majorities can command implicit obedience; and, where there has been long and arduous experience, a rampart of tried conviction and accumulated knowledge,[49] where there is a fair level of general morality, education, courage, and self-restraint, there, if there only, a society may be found that exhibits the condition of life towards which, by elimination of failures, the world has been moving through the allotted space.[50] You will know it by outward signs: Representation, the extinction of slavery, the reign of opinion, and the like; better still by less apparent evidences: the security of the weaker groups[51] and the liberty of conscience, which, effectually secured, secures the rest.

Here we reach a point at which my argument threatens to abut on a contradiction. If the supreme conquests of society are won more often by violence than by lenient arts, if the trend and drift of things is towards convulsions and catastrophes,[52] if the world owes religious liberty to the Dutch Revolution, constitutional government to the English, federal republicanism to the American, political equality to the French and its successors,[53] what is to become of us, docile and attentive students of the absorbing past? The triumph of the Revolutionist annuls the historian.[54] By its authentic exponents, Jefferson and Siéyès, the Revolution of the last century repudiates history. Their followers renounced acquaintance with it, and were ready to destroy its records and to abolish its inoffensive professors. But the unexpected truth, stranger than fiction, is that this was not the ruin but the renovation of history. Directly and indirectly, by process of development and by process of reaction, an impulse was given which made it infinitely more effectual as a factor of civilisation than ever before, and a movement began in the world of minds which was deeper and more serious than the revival of ancient learning.[55] The dispensation under which we live and labour consists first in the recoil from the negative spirit that rejected the law of growth, and partly in the endeavour to classify and adjust the Revolution, and to account for it by the natural working of historic causes. The Conservative line of writers, under the name of the Romantic or Historical School, had its seat in Germany, looked upon the Revolution as an alien episode, the error of an age, a disease to be treated by the investigation of its origin, and strove to unite the broken threads and to restore the normal conditions of organic evolution. The Liberal School, whose home was France, explained and justified the Revolution as a true development, and the ripened fruit of all history.[56] These are the two main arguments of the generation to which we owe the notion and the scientific methods that make history so unlike what it was to the survivors of the last century. Severally, the innovators were not superior to the men of old. Muratori was as widely read, Tillemont as accurate, Leibniz as able, Freret as acute, Gibbon as masterly in the craft of composite construction. Nevertheless, in the second quarter of this century, a new era began for historians.

I would point to three things in particular, out of many, which constitute the amended order. Of the incessant deluge of new and unsuspected matter I need say little. For some years, the secret archives of the papacy were accessible at Paris; but the time was not ripe, and almost the only man whom they availed was the archivist himself.[57] Towards 1830 the documentary studies began on a large scale, Austria leading the way. Michelet, who claims, towards 1836, to have been the pioneer,[58] was preceded by such rivals as Mackintosh, Bucholtz, and Mignet. A new and more productive period began thirty years later, when the war of 1859 laid open the spoils of Italy. Every country in succession has now allowed the exploration of its records, and there is more fear of drowning than of drought. The result has been that a lifetime spent in the largest collection of printed books would not suffice to train a real master of modern history. After he had turned from literature to sources, from Burnet to Pocock, from Macaulay to Madame Campana, from Thiers to the interminable correspondence of the Bonapartes, he would still feel instant need of inquiry at Venice or Naples, in the Ossuna library or at the Hermitage.[59]

These matters do not now concern us. For our purpose, the main thing to learn is not the art of accumulating material, but the sublimer art of investigating it, of discerning truth from falsehood and certainty from doubt. It is by solidity of criticism more than by the plenitude of erudition, that the study of history strengthens, and straightens, and extends the mind.[60] And the accession of the critic in the place of the indefatigable compiler, of the artist in coloured narrative, the skilled limner of character, the persuasive advocate of good, or other, causes, amounts to a transfer of government, to a change of dynasty, in the historic realm. For the critic is one who, when he lights on an interesting statement, begins by suspecting it. He remains in suspense until he has subjected his authority to three operations. First, he asks whether he has read the passage as the author wrote it. For the transcriber, and the editor, and the official or officious censor on the top of the editor, have played strange tricks, and have much to answer for. And if they are not to blame, it may turn out that the author wrote his book twice over, that you can discover the first jet, the progressive variations, things added, and things struck out. Next is the question where the writer got his information. If from a previous writer, it can be ascertained, and the inquiry has to be repeated. If from unpublished papers, they must be traced, and when the fountainhead is reached, or the track disappears, the question of veracity arises. The responsible writer's character, his position, antecedents, and probable motives have to be examined into; and this is what, in a different and adapted sense of the word, may be called the higher criticism, in comparison with the servile and often mechanical work of pursuing statements to their root. For a historian has to be treated as a witness, and not believed unless his sincerity is established.[61] The maxim that a man must be presumed to be innocent until his guilt is proved, was not made for him.

For us, then, the estimate of authorities, the weighing of testimony, is more meritorious than the potential discovery of new matter.[62] And modern history, which is the widest field of application, is not the best to learn our business in; for it is too wide, and the harvest has not been winnowed as in antiquity, and further on to the Crusades. It is better to examine what has been done for questions that are compact and circumscribed, such as the sources of Plutarch's *Pericles*, the two tracts on *Athenian Government*, the origin of the *Epistle to Diognetus*, the date of the *Life of St. Antony;* and to learn from Schwegler how this analytical work began. More satisfying because more decisive has been the critical treatment of the mediæval writers, parallel with the new editions, on which incredible labour has been lavished, and of which we have no better examples than the prefaces of Bishop Stubbs. An important event in this series was the attack on Dino Compagni, which, for the sake of Dante, roused the best Italian scholars to a not unequal contest. When we are told that England is behind the Continent in critical faculty, we must admit that this is true as to quantity, not as to quality of work. As they are no longer living, I will say of two Cambridge professors, Lightfoot and Hort, that they were critical scholars whom neither Frenchman nor German has surpassed.

The third distinctive note of the generation of writers who dug so deep a trench between history as known to our grandfathers and as it appears to us is their dogma of impartiality. To an ordinary man the word means no more than justice. He considers that he may proclaim the merits of his own religion, of his prosperous and enlightened country, of his political persuasion, whether democracy, or liberal monarchy, or historical conservatism, without transgression or offense, so long as he is fair to the relative, though inferior, merits of others, and never treats men as saints or as rogues for the side they take. There is no impartiality, he would say, like that of a hanging judge. The men who, with the compass of criticism in their hands, sailed the unchartered sea of original research proposed a different view. History, to be above evasion or dispute, must stand on documents, not on opinions. They had their own notion of truthfulness, based on the exceeding difficulty of finding truth, and the still greater difficulty of impressing it when found. They thought it possible to write, with so much scruple, and simplicity, and insight, as to carry along with them every man of good will, and, whatever his feelings, to compel his assent. Ideas which, in religion and in politics, are truths, in history are forces. They must be respected; they must not be affirmed. By dint of a supreme reserve, by much self-control, by a timely and discreet indifference, by secrecy in the matter of the black cap, history might be lifted above contention, and made an accepted tribunal, and the same for all.[63] If men were truly sincere, and delivered judgment by no canons but those of evident morality, then Julian would be described in the same terms by Christian and pagan, Luther by Catholic and Protestant, Washington by Whig and Tory, Napoleon by patriotic Frenchman and patriotic German.[64]

I speak of this school with reverence, for the good it has done, by the assertion of historic truth and of its legitimate authority over the minds of men. It provides a discipline which every one of us does well to undergo, and perhaps also well to relinquish. For it is not the whole truth. Lanfrey's essay on Carnot, Chuquet's wars of the Revolution, Ropes' military histories, Roget's Geneva in the time of Calvin, will supply you with examples of a more robust impartiality than I have described. Renan calls it the luxury of an opulent and aristocratic society, doomed to vanish in an age of fierce and sordid striving. In our universities it has a magnificent and appointed refuge; and to serve its cause, which is sacred, because it is the cause of truth and honour, we may import a profitable lesson from the highly unscientific region of public life. There a man does not take long to find out that he is opposed by some who are abler and better than himself. And, in order to understand the cosmic force and the true connection of ideas, it is a source of power, and an excellent school of principle, not to rest until, by excluding the fallacies, the prejudices, the exaggerations which perpetual contention and the consequent precautions breed, we have made out for our opponents a stronger and more impressive case than they present themselves.[65] Excepting one to which we are coming before I release you, there is no precept less faithfully observed by historians.

Ranke is the representative of the age which instituted the modern study of history. He taught it to be critical, to be colourless, and to be new. We meet him at every step, and he has done more for us than any other man. There are stronger books than any one of his, and some may have surpassed him in political, religious, philosophic insight, in vividness of the creative imagination, in originality, elevation, and depth of thought; but by the extent of important work well executed, by his influence on able men, and by the amount of knowledge which mankind receives and employs with the stamp of his mind upon it, he stands without a rival. I saw him last in 1877, when he was feeble, sunken, and almost blind, and scarcely able to read or write. He uttered his farewell with a kindly emotion, and I feared that the next I should hear of him would be the news of his death. Two years later he began a Universal History, which is not without traces of weakness, but which, composed after the age of eighty-three, and carried, in seventeen volumes, far into the Middle Ages, brings to a close the most astonishing career in literature.

His course had been determined, in early life, by *Quentin Durward*. The shock of the discovery that Scott's Lewis the Eleventh was inconsistent with the original in Commynes made him resolve that his object thenceforth should be above all things to follow, without swerving, and in stern subordination and surrender, the lead of his authorities. He decided effectually to repress the poet, the patriot, the religious or political partisan, to sustain no cause, to vanish himself from his books, and to write nothing that would gratify his own feelings or disclose his private convictions.[66] When a strenuous divine, who, like him, had written on the Reformation, hailed him as a comrade, Ranke repelled his advances. "You," he said, "are in the first place a Christian: I am in the first place a historian. There is a gulf between us."[67] He was the first eminent writer who exhibited what Michelet calls *le désintéressement des morts*. It was a moral triumph for him when he could refrain from judging, show that much might be said on both sides, and leave the rest to Providence.[68] He would have felt sympathy with the two famous London physicians of our day, of whom it is told that they could not make up their minds on a case and reported dubiously. The head of the family insisted on a positive opinion. They answered that they were unable to give one, but he might easily find fifty doctors who could.

Niebuhr had pointed out that chroniclers who wrote before the invention of printing generally copied one predecessor at a time, and knew little about sifting or combining authorities. The suggestion became luminous in Ranke's hands, and with his light and dexterous touch he scrutinised and dissected the principal historians, from Machiavelli to the *Mémoires d'un Homme d'État*, with a rigour never before applied to moderns. But whilst Niebuhr dismissed the traditional story, replacing it with a construction of his own, it was Ranke's mission to preserve, not to undermine, and to set up masters whom, in their proper sphere, he could obey. The many excellent dissertations in which he displayed this art, though his successors in the next generation matched his skill and did still more thorough work, are the best introduction from which we can learn the technical process by which within living memory the study of modern history has been renewed. Ranke's contemporaries, weary of his neutrality and suspense, and of the useful but subordinate work that was done by beginners who borrowed his wand, thought that too much was made of these obscure preliminaries which a man may accomplish for himself, in the silence of his chamber, with less demand on the attention of the public.[69] That may be reasonable in men who are practised in these fundamental technicalities. We who have to learn them must immerse ourselves in the study of the great examples.

Apart from what is technical, method is only the reduplication of common sense, and is best acquired by observing its use by the ablest men in every variety of intellectual employment.[70] Bentham acknowledged that he learned less from his own profession than from writers like Linnæus and Cullen; and Brougham advised the student of Law to begin with Dante. Liebig described his *Organic Chemistry* as an application of ideas found in Mill's *Logic,* and a distinguished physician, not to be named lest he should overhear me, read three books to enlarge his medical mind; and they were Gibbon, Grote, and Mill. He goes on to say, "An educated man cannot become so on one study alone, but must be brought under the influence of natural, civil, and moral modes of thought."[71] I quote my colleague's golden words in order to reciprocate them. If men of science owe anything to us, we may learn much from them that is essential.[72] For they can show how to test proof, how to secure fulness and soundness in induction, how to restrain and to employ with safety hypothesis and analogy. It is they who hold the secret of the mysterious property of the mind by which error ministers to truth, and truth slowly but irrevocably prevails.[73] Theirs is the logic of discovery,[74] the demonstration of the advance of knowledge and the development of ideas, which as the earthly wants and passions of men remain almost unchanged, are the charter of progress and the vital spark in history. And they often give us invaluable counsel when they attend to their own subjects and address their own people. Remember Darwin taking note only of those passages that raised difficulties in his way; the French philosopher complaining that his work stood still, because he found no more contradicting facts; Baer, who thinks error treated thoroughly nearly as remunerative as truth, by the discovery of new objections; for, as Sir Robert Ball warns us, it is by considering objections that we often learn.[75] Faraday declared that "in knowledge, that man only is to be condemned and despised who is not in a state of transition." And John Hunter spoke for all of us when he said: "Never ask me what I have said or what I have written; but if you will ask me what my present opinions are, I will tell you."

From the first years of the century we have been quickened and enriched by contributors from every quarter. The jurists brought us that law of continuous growth which has transformed history from a chronicle of casual occurrences into the likeness of something organic.[76] Towards 1820 divines began to recast their doctrines on the lines of development, of which Newman said, long after that evolution had come to confirm it.[77] Even the economists, who were practical men, dissolved their science into liquid history, affirming that it is not an auxiliary, but the actual subject-matter of their inquiry.[78] Philosophers claim that, as early as 1804, they began to bow the metaphysical neck beneath the historical yoke. They taught that philosophy is only the amended sum of all philosophies, that systems pass with the age whose impress they bear,[79] that the problem is to focus the rays of wandering but extant truth, and that history is the source of philosophy, if not quite a substitute for it.[80] Comte begins a volume with the words that the preponderance of history over philosophy was the characteristic of the time he lived in.[81] Since Cuvier first recognized the conjunction between the course of inductive discovery and the course of civilisation,[82] science had its share in saturating the age with historic ways of thought, and subjecting all things to that influence for which the depressing names historicism and historical-mindedness have been devised.

There are certain faults which are corrigible mental defects on which I ought to say a few denouncing words, because they are common to us all. First: the want of an energetic understanding of the sequence and real significance of events, which would be fatal to a practical politician, is ruin to a student of history, who is the politician with his face turned backwards.[83] It is playing at study, to see nothing but the unmeaning and unsuggestive surface, as we generally do. Then we have a curious proclivity to neglect, and by degrees to forget, what has been certainly known. An instance or two will explain my idea. The most popular English writer relates how it happened in his presence that the title of Tory was conferred upon the Conservative party. For it was an opprobrious name at the time, applied to men for whom the Irish Government offered head-money; so that if I have made too sure of progress, I may at least complacently point to this instance of our mended manners. One day, Titus Oates lost his temper with the men who refused to believe him, and, after looking about for a scorching imprecation, he began to call them Tories.[84] The name remained; but its origin, attested by Defoe, dropped out of common memory, as if one party were ashamed of their godfather, and the other did not care to be identified with his cause and character. You all know, I am sure, the story of the news of Trafalgar, and how, two days after it had arrived, Mr. Pitt, drawn by an enthusiastic crowd, went to dine in the city. When they drank the health of the minister who had saved his country, he declined the praise. "England," he said, "has saved herself by her own energy; and I hope that after having saved herself by her energy, she will save Europe by her example." In 1814, when this hope had been realised, the last speech of the great orator was remembered, and a medal was struck upon which the whole sentence was engraved, in four words of compressed Latin: *Seipsam virtute, Europam exemplo.* Now it was just at the time of his last appearance in public that Mr. Pitt heard of the overwhelming success of the French in Germany, and of the Austrian surrender at Ulm. His friends concluded that the contest on land was hopeless, and that it was time to abandon the Continent to the conqueror, and to fall back upon our new empire of the sea. Pitt did not agree with them. He said that Napoleon would meet with a check whenever he encountered a national resistance; and he declared that Spain was the place for it, and that then England would intervene.[85] General Wellesley, fresh from India, was present. Ten years later, when he had accomplished that which Pitt had seen in the lucid prescience of his last days, he related at Paris what I scarcely hesitate to call the most astounding and profound prediction in all political history, where such things have not been rare.

I shall never again enjoy the opportunity of speaking my thoughts to such an audience as this, and on so privileged an occasion a lecturer may well be tempted to bethink himself

INAUGURAL LECTURE ON THE STUDY OF HISTORY 25

whether he knows of any neglected truth, any cardinal proposition, that might serve as his selected epigraph, as a last signal, perhaps even as a target. I am not thinking of those shining precepts which are the registered property of every school; that is to say — Learn as much by writing as by reading; be not content with the best book; seek sidelights from the others; have no favourites; keep men and things apart; guard against the prestige of great names;[86] see that your judgments are your own, and do not shrink from disagreement; no trusting without testing; be more severe to ideas than to actions;[87] do not overlook the strength of the bad cause or the weakness of the good;[88] never be surprised by the crumbling of an idol or the disclosure of a skeleton; judge talent at its best and character at its worst; suspect power more than vice,[89] and study problems in preference to periods; for instance: the derivation of Luther, the scientific influence of Bacon, the predecessors of Adam Smith, the mediæval masters of Rousseau, the consistency of Burke, the identity of the first Whig. Most of this, I suppose, is undisputed, and calls for no enlargement. But the weight of opinion is against me when I exhort you never to debase the moral currency or to lower the standard of rectitude, but to try others by the final maxim that governs your own lives, and to suffer no man and no cause to escape the undying penalty which history has the power to inflict on wrong.[90] The plea in extenuation of guilt and mitigation of punishment is perpetual. At every step we are met by arguments which go to excuse, to palliate, to confound right and wrong, and reduce the just man to the level of the reprobate. The men who plot to baffle and resist us are, first of all, those who made history what it has become. They set up the principle that only a foolish Conservative judges the present time with the ideas of the past; that only a foolish Liberal judges the past with the ideas of the present.[91]

The mission of that school was to make distant times, and especially the Middle Ages, then most distant of all, intelligible and acceptable to a society issuing from the eighteenth century. There were difficulties in the way; and among others this, that, in the first fervour of the Crusades, the men who took the Cross, after receiving communion, heartily devoted the day to the extermination of Jews. To judge them by a fixed standard, to call them sacrilegious fanatics or furious hypocrites, was to yield a gratuitous victory to Voltaire. It became a rule of policy to praise the spirit when you could not defend the deed. So that we have no common code; our moral notions are always fluid; and you must consider the times, the class from which men sprang, the surrounding influences, the masters in their schools, the preachers in their pulpits, the movement they obscurely obeyed, and so on, until responsibility is merged in numbers, and not a culprit is left for execution.[92] A murderer was no criminal if he followed local custom, if neighbours approved, if he was encouraged by official advisers or prompted by just authority, if he acted for the reason of state or the pure love of religion, or if he sheltered himself behind the complicity of the Law. The depression of morality was flagrant; but the motives were those which have enabled us to contemplate with distressing complacency the secret of unhallowed lives. The code that is greatly modified by time and place will vary according to the cause. The amnesty is an artifice that enables us to make exceptions, to tamper with weights and measures, to deal unequal justice to friends and enemies.

It is associated with that philosophy which Cato attributes to the gods. For we have a theory which justifies Providence by the event, and holds nothing so deserving as success, to which there can be no victory in a bad cause; prescription and duration legitimate;[93] and whatever exists is right and reasonable; and as God manifests His will by that which He tolerates, we must conform to the divine decree by living to shape the future after the ratified image of the past.[94] Another theory, less confidently urged, regards history as our guide, as much by showing errors to evade as examples to pursue. It is suspicious of illusions in success, and, though there may be hope of ultimate triumph for what is true, if not by its own attraction, by the gradual exhaustion of error, it admits no corresponding promise for what is ethically right.

It deems the canonisation of the historic past more perilous than ignorance or denial, because it would perpetuate the reign of sin and acknowledge the sovereignty of wrong, and conceives it the part of real greatness to know how to stand and fall alone, stemming, for a lifetime, the contemporary flood.[95]

Ranke relates, without adornment, that William III ordered the extirpation of a Catholic clan, and scouts the faltering excuse of his defenders. But when he comes to the death and character of the international deliverer, Glencoe is forgotten, the imputation of murder drops, like a thing unworthy of notice.[96] Johannes Müller, a great Swiss celebrity, writes that the British Constitution occurred to somebody, perhaps to Halifax. This artless statement might not be approved by rigid lawyers as a faithful and felicitous indication of the manner of that mysterious growth of ages, from occult beginnings, that was never profaned by the invading wit of man;[97] but it is less grotesque than it appears. Lord Halifax was the most original writer of political tracts in the pamphleteering crowd between Harrington and Bolingbroke; and in the Exclusion struggle he produced a scheme of limitations which, in substance, if not in form, foreshadowed the position of the monarchy in the later Hanoverian reigns. Although Halifax did not believe in the plot,[98] he insisted that innocent victims should be sacrificed to content the multitude. Sir William Temple writes: "We only disagreed in one point, which was the leaving some priests to the law upon the accusation of being priests only, as the House of Commons had desired; which I thought wholly unjust. Upon this point Lord Halifax and I had so sharp a debate at Lord Sunderland's lodgings, that he told me, if I would not concur in points which were so necessary for the people's satisfaction, he would tell everybody I was a Papist. And upon his affirming that the plot must be handled as if it were true, whether it were so or no, in those points that were so generally believed." In spite of this accusing passage, Macaulay, who prefers Halifax to all the statesmen of his age, praises him for his mercy: "His dislike of extremes, and a forgiving and compassionate temper which seems to have been natural to him, preserved him from all participation in the worst crimes of his time."

If, in our uncertainty, we must often err, it may be sometimes better to risk excess in rigour than in indulgence, for then at least we do no injury by loss of principle. As Bayle has said, it is more probable that the secret motives of an indifferent action are bad than good;[99] and this discouraging conclusion does not depend upon theology, for James Mozley supports the sceptic from the other flank, with all the artillery of Tractarian Oxford. "A Christian," he says, "is bound by his very creed to suspect evil, and cannot release himself. . . . He sees it where others do not; his instinct is divinely strengthened; his eye is supernaturally keen; he has a spiritual insight, and senses exercised to discern. . . . He owns the doctrine of original sin; that doctrine puts him necessarily on his guard against appearances, sustains his apprehension under perplexity, and prepares him for recognising anywhere what he knows to be everywhere."[100] There is a popular saying of Madame de Staël, that we forgive whatever we really understand. The paradox has been judiciously pruned by her descendant, the Duke de Broglie, in the words: "Beware of too much explaining, lest we end by too much excusing."[101] History, says Froude, does teach that right and wrong are real distinctions. Opinions alter, manners change, creeds rise and fall, but the moral law is written on the tablets of eternity.[102] And if there are moments when we may resist the teaching of Froude, we have seldom the chance of resisting when he is supported by Mr. Goldwin Smith: "A sound historical morality will sanction strong measures in evil times; selfish ambition, treachery, murder, perjury, it will never sanction in the worst of times, for these are the things that make times evil — Justice has been justice, mercy has been mercy, honour has been honour, good faith has been good faith, truthfulness has been truthfulness from the beginning." The doctrine that, as Sir Thomas Browne says, morality is not ambulatory,[103] is expressed as follows by Burke, who, when true to himself, is the most intelligent of our instructors: "My principles enable me to form my judgment upon men and actions in history, just as they do in common life; and are not formed out of events and characters, either present or past. History is a preceptor of prudence, not of principles. The principles of true politics are those of morality enlarged; and I neither now do, nor ever will admit of any other."[104]

Whatever a man's notions of these later centuries are, such, in the main, the man himself will be. Under the name of History, they cover the articles of his philosophic, his religious, and his political creed.[105] They give his measure; they denote his character: and, as praise is the shipwreck of historians, his preferences betray him more than his aversions. Modern history touches us so nearly, it is so deep a question of life and death, that we are bound to find our own way through it, and to owe our insight to ourselves. The historians of former ages, unapproachable for us in knowledge and in talent, cannot be our limit. We have the power to be more rigidly impersonal, disinterested and just than they; and to learn from undisguised and genuine records to look with remorse upon the past, and to the future with assured hope of better things; bearing this in mind, that if we lower our standard in history, we cannot uphold it in Church or State.

Chapter II

THE HISTORY OF FREEDOM IN ANTIQUITY

LIBERTY, NEXT TO religion, has been the motive of good deeds and the common pretext of crime, from the sowing of the seed at Athens, two thousand four hundred and sixty years ago, until the ripened harvest was gathered by men of our race. It is the delicate fruit of a mature civilisation; and scarcely a century has passed since nations, that knew the meaning of the term, resolved to be free. In every age its progress has been beset by its natural enemies, by ignorance and superstition, by lust of conquest and by love of ease, by the strong man's craving for power, and the poor man's craving for food. During long intervals it has been utterly arrested, when nations were being rescued from barbarism and from the grasp of strangers, and when the perpetual struggle for existence, depriving men of all interest and understanding in politics, has made them eager to sell their birthright for a mess of pottage, and ignorant of the treasure they resigned. At all times sincere friends of freedom have been rare, and its triumphs have been due to minorities, that have prevailed by associating themselves with auxiliaries whose objects often differed from their own; and this association, which is always dangerous, has been sometimes disastrous, by giving to opponents just grounds of opposition, and by kindling dispute over the spoils in the hour of success. No obstacle has been so constant, or so difficult to overcome,

---

NOTE: This address was delivered to the members of the Bridgnorth Institution at the Agricultural Hall, February 26, 1877 (Bridgnorth, 1877): reprinted in *The History of Freedom and Other Essays* (London: Macmillan Co., 1907), pp. 1-29.

as uncertainty and confusion touching the nature of true liberty. If hostile interests have wrought much injury, false ideas have wrought still more; and its advance is recorded in the increase of knowledge, as much as in the improvement of laws. The history of institutions is often a history of deception and illusions; for their virtue depends on the ideas that produce and on the spirit that preserves them, and the form may remain unaltered when the substance has passed away.

A few familiar examples from modern politics will explain why it is that the burden of my argument will lie outside the domain of legislation. It is often said that our Constitution attained its formal perfection in 1679, when the Habeas Corpus Act was passed. Yet Charles II succeeded, only two years later, in making himself independent of Parliament. In 1789, while the States-General assembled at Versailles, the Spanish Cortes, older than Magna Charta and more venerable than our House of Commons, were summoned after an interval of generations, but they immediately prayed the King to abstain from consulting them, and to make his reforms of his own wisdom and authority. According to the common opinion, indirect elections are a safeguard of conservatism. But all the Assemblies of the French Revolution issued from indirect elections. A restricted suffrage is another reputed security for monarchy. But the Parliament of Charles X, which was returned by 90,000 electors, resisted and overthrew the throne; while the Parliament of Louis Philippe, chosen by a Constitution of 250,000, obsequiously promoted the reactionary policy of his Ministers, and in the fatal division which, by rejecting reform, laid the monarchy in the dust, Guizot's majority was obtained by the votes of 129 public functionaries. An unpaid legislature is, for obvious reasons, more independent than most of the Continental legislatures which receive pay. But it would be unreasonable in America to send a member as far as from here to Constantinople to live for twelve months at his own expense in the dearest of capital cities. Legally and to outward seeming the American President is the successor of Washington, and still enjoys powers devised and limited by the Convention of Philadelphia. In reality the new President differs from the Magistrate imagined by the Fathers of the Republic as widely as Monarchy from Democracy, for he is expected to make 70,000 changes in the public service; fifty years ago John Quincy Adams dismissed only two men. The purchase of judicial appointments is manifestly indefensible; yet in the old French monarchy that monstrous practice created the only corporation able to resist the king. Official corruption, which would ruin a commonwealth, serves in Russia as a salutary relief from the pressure of absolutism. There are conditions in which it is scarcely a hyperbole to say that slavery itself is a stage on the road to freedom. Therefore we are not so much concerned this evening with the dead letter of edicts and of statutes as with the living thoughts of men. A century ago it was perfectly well known that whoever had one audience of a Master in Chancery was made to pay for three, but no man heeded the enormity until it suggested to a young lawyer that it might be well to question and examine with rigorous suspicion every part of a system in which such things were done. The day on which that gleam lighted up the clear, hard mind of Jeremy Bentham is memorable in the political calendar beyond the entire administration of many statesmen. It would be easy to point out a paragraph in St. Augustine, or a sentence of Grotius that outweighs in influence the Acts of fifty Parliaments, and our cause owes more to Cicero and Seneca, to Vinet and Tocqueville, than to the laws of Lycurgus or the Five Codes of France.

By liberty I mean the assurance that every man shall be protected in doing what he believes his duty against the influence of authority and majorities, custom and opinion. The State is competent to assign duties and draw the line between good and evil only in its immediate sphere. Beyond the limits of things necessary for its well-being, it can only give indirect help to fight the battle of life by promoting the influences which prevail against temptation, — religion, education, and the distribution of wealth. In ancient times the State absorbed authorities not its own, and intruded on the domain of personal freedom. In the Middle Ages it possessed too little authority, and suffered others to intrude. Modern States fall habitually into both excesses. The most certain test by which we judge whether a country is really free is the amount of security enjoyed by minorities. Liberty, by this definition, is the essential condition and guardian of religion; and it is in the history of the Chosen People, accordingly, that the first illustrations of my subject are obtained. The government of the Israelites was a federation, held together by no political authority, but by the unity of race and faith, and founded, not on physical force, but on a voluntary covenant. The principle of self-government was carried out not only in each tribe, but in every group of at least 120 families; and there was neither privilege of rank nor inequality before the law. Monarchy was so alien to the primitive spirit of the community that it was resisted by Samuel in that momentous protestation and warning which all the kingdoms of Asia and many of the kingdoms of Europe have unceasingly confirmed. The throne was erected on a compact; and the king was deprived of the right of legislation among a people that recognized no lawgiver but God, whose highest aim in politics was to restore the original purity of the constitution, and to make its government conform to the ideal type that was hallowed by the sanctions of heaven. The inspired men who rose in unfailing succession to prophesy against the usurper and the tyrant, constantly proclaimed that the laws, which were divine, were paramount over sinful rulers, and appealed from the established authorities, from the king, the priests, and the princes of the people, to the healing forces that slept in the uncorrupted consciences of the masses. Thus the example of the Hebrew nation laid down the parallel lines on which all freedom has been won — the doctrine of national tradition and the doctrine of the higher law; the principle that a constitution grows from a root, by process of development, and not of essential change; and the principle that all political authorities must be tested and reformed according to a code which was not made by man. The operation of these principles, in unison, or in antagonism, occupies the whole of the space we are going over together.

The conflict between liberty under divine authority and the absolutism of human authorities ended disastrously. In the year 622 a supreme effort was made at Jerusalem to reform and preserve the State. The High Priest produced from the temple of Jehovah the book of the deserted and forgotten law, and both king and people bound themselves by solemn oaths to observe it. But that early example of limited monarchy and of the supremacy of law neither lasted nor spread; and the forces by which freedom has conquered must be sought elsewhere. In the very year 586, in which the flood of Asiatic despotism closed over the city which had been, and was destined again to be, the sanctuary of freedom in the East, a new home was prepared for it in the West, where, guarded by the sea and the mountains, and by valiant hearts, that stately plant was reared under whose shade we dwell, and which is extending its invincible arms so slowly and yet so surely over the civilised world.

According to a famous saying of the most famous authoress of the Continent, liberty is ancient, and it is despotism that is new. It has been the pride of recent historians to vindicate the truth of that maxim. The heroic age of Greece confirms it, and it is still more conspicuously true of Teutonic Europe. Wherever we can trace the earlier life of the Aryan nations we discover germs which favouring circumstances and assiduous culture might have developed into free societies. They exhibit some sense of common interest in common concerns, little reverence for external authority, and an imperfect sense of the function and supremacy of the State. Where the division of property and labour is incomplete there is little division of classes and of power. Until societies are tried by the complex problems of civilisation they may escape despotism, as societies that are undisturbed by religious diversity avoid persecution. In general, the forms of the patriarchal age failed to resist the growth of absolute States when the difficulties and temptations of advancing life began to tell; and with one sovereign exception, which is not within my scope to-day, it is scarcely possible to trace their survival in the institutions of later times. Six hundred years before the birth of Christ absolutism held unbounded sway. Throughout the East it was propped by the unchanging influence of priests and armies. In the West, where there were no sacred books requiring trained interpreters, the priesthood acquired no preponderance, and when the kings were overthrown their powers passed to aristocracies of birth. What followed, during many generations, was the cruel domination of class over class, the oppression of the poor by the rich, and of the ignorant by the wise. The spirit of that domination found passionate utterance in the verses of the aristocratic poet Theognis, a man of genius and refinement, who avows that he longed to drink the blood of his political adversaries. From these oppressors the people of many cities sought deliverance in the less intolerable tyranny of revolutionary usurpers. The remedy gave new shape and energy to the evil. The tyrants were often men of surprising capacity and merit, like some of those who, in the fourteenth century, made themselves lords of Italian cities; but rights secured by equal laws and by sharing power existed nowhere.

From this universal degradation the world was rescued by the most gifted of the nations. Athens, which like other cities was distracted and oppressed by a privileged class, avoided violence and appointed Solon to revise its laws. It was the happiest choice that history records. Solon was not only the wisest man to be found in Athens, but the most profound political genius of antiquity; and the easy, bloodless, and pacific revolution by which he accomplished the deliverance of his country was the first step in a career which our age glories in pursuing, and instituted a power which has done more than anything, except revealed religion, for the regeneration of society. The upper class had possessed the right of making and administering the laws, and he left them in possession, only transferring to wealth what had been the privilege of birth. To the rich, who alone had the means of sustaining the burden of public service in taxation and war, Solon gave a share of power proportioned to the demands made on their resources. The poorest classes were exempt from direct taxes, but were excluded from office.

Solon gave them a voice in electing magistrates from the classes above them, and the right of calling them to account. This concession, apparently so slender, was the beginning of a mighty change. It introduced the idea that a man ought to have a voice in selecting those to whose rectitude and wisdom he is compelled to trust his fortune, his family, and his life. And this idea completely inverted the notion of human authority, for it inaugurated the reign of moral influence where all political power had depended on moral force. Government by consent superseded government by compulsion, and the pyramid which had stood on a point was made to stand upon its base. By making every citizen the guardian of his own interest Solon admitted the element of democracy into the State. The greatest glory of a ruler, he said, is to create a popular government. Believing that no man can be entirely trusted, he subjected all who exercised power to the vigilant control of those for whom they acted.

The only resource against political disorders that had been known till then was the concentration of power. Solon undertook to effect the same object by the distribution of power. He gave to the common people as much influence as he thought them able to employ, that the State might be exempt from arbitrary government. It is the essence of democracy, he said, to obey no master but the law. Solon recognised the principle that political forms are not final or inviolable, and must adapt themselves to facts; and he provided so well for the revision of his constitution, without breach of continuity or loss of stability, that for centuries after his death the Attic orators attributed to him, and quoted by his name, the whole structure of Athenian law. The direction of its growth was determined by the fundamental doctrine of Solon, that political power ought to be commensurate with public service. In the Persian war the services of the democracy eclipsed those of the Patrician orders, for the fleet that swept the Asiatics from the Aegean Sea was manned by the poorer Athenians. That class, whose valour had saved the State and had preserved European civilisation, had gained a title to increase of influence and privilege. The offices of State, which had been a monopoly of the rich, were thrown open to the poor, and in order to make sure that they should obtain their share, all but the highest commands were distributed by lot.

Whilst the ancient authorities were decaying, there was no accepted standard of moral and political right to make the framework of society fast in the midst of change. The instability that had seized on the forms threatened the very principles of government. The national beliefs were yielding to doubt, and doubt was not yet making way for knowledge. There had been a time when the obligations of public as well as private life were identified with the will of the gods. But that time had passed. Pallas, the ethereal goddess of the Athenians, and the Sun God whose oracles, delivered from the temple between the twin summits of Parnassus, did so much for the Greek nationality, aided in keeping up a lofty ideal of religion; but when the enlightened men of Greece learnt to apply their keen faculty of reasoning to the system of their inherited belief, they became quickly conscious that the conceptions of the gods corrupted the life and degraded the minds of the public. Popular morality could not be sustained by the popular religion. The moral instruction which was no longer supplied by the gods could not yet be found in books. There was no venerable code expounded by experts, no doctrine proclaimed by men of reputed sanctity like those teachers of the far East whose words still rule the fate of nearly half mankind. The effort to account for things by close observation and exact reasoning began by destroying. There came a time when the philosophers of the Porch and the Academy wrought the dictates of wisdom and virtue into a system so consistent and profound that it has vastly shortened the task of the Christian divines. But that time had not yet come.

The epoch of doubt and transition during which the Greeks passed from the dim fancies of mythology to the fierce light of science was the age of Pericles, and the endeavour to substitute certain truth for the prescriptions of impaired authorities, which was then beginning to absorb the energies of the Greek intellect, is the grandest movement in the profane annals of mankind, for to it we owe, even after the immeasurable progress accomplished by Christianity, much of our philosophy and far the better part of the political knowledge we possess. Pericles, who was at the head of the Athenian government, was the first statesman who encountered the problem which the rapid weakening of traditions forced on the political world. No authority in morals or in politics remained unshaken by the motion that was in the air. No guide could be confidently trusted; there was no available criterion to appeal to, for the means of controlling or denying convictions that prevailed among the people. The popular sentiment as to what was right might be mistaken, but it was subject to no test. The people were, for practical purposes, the seat of the knowledge of good and evil. The people, therefore, were the seat of power.

The political philosophy of Pericles consisted of this conclusion. He resolutely struck away all the props that still sustained the artificial preponderance of wealth. For the ancient doctrine that power goes with land, he introduced the idea that power ought to be so equitably diffused as to afford equal security to all. That one part of the community should govern the whole, or that one class should make laws for another, he declared to be tyrannical. The abolition of privilege would have served only to transfer the supremacy from the rich to the poor, if Pericles had not redressed the balance by restricting the right of citizenship to Athenians of pure descent. By this measure the class which formed what we should call the third estate was brought down to 14,000 citizens, and became about equal in numbers with the higher ranks. Pericles held that every Athenian who neglected to take his part in the public business inflicted an injury on the commonwealth. That none might be excluded by poverty, he caused the poor to be paid for their attendance out of the funds of the State; for his administration of the federal tribute had brought together a treasure of more than two million sterling. The instrument of his sway was the art of speaking. He governed by persuasion. Everything was decided by argument in open deliberation, and every influence bowed before the ascendancy of mind. The idea that the object of constitutions is not to confirm the predominance of any interest, but to prevent it; to preserve with equal care the independence of labour and the security of property; to make the rich safe against envy, and the poor against oppression, marks the highest level attained by the statesmanship of Greece. It hardly survived the great patriot who conceived it; and all history has been occupied with the endeavour to upset the balance of power by giving the advantage to money, land, or numbers. A generation followed that has never been equalled in talent — a generation of men whose works, in poetry and eloquence, are still the envy of the world, and in history, philosophy, and politics remain unsurpassed. But it produced no successor to Pericles, and no man was able to wield the sceptre that fell from his hand.

It was a momentous step in the progress of nations when the principle that every interest should have the right and the means of asserting itself was adopted by the Athenian Constitution. But for those who were beaten in the vote there was no redress. The law did not check the triumph of majorities or rescue the minority from the dire penalty of having been outnumbered. When the overwhelming influence of Pericles was removed, the conflict between classes raged without restraint, and the slaughter that befell the higher ranks in the Peloponnesian war gave an irresistible preponderance to the lower. The restless and inquiring spirit of the Athenians was prompt to unfold the reason of every institution and the consequences of every principle, and their Constitution ran its course from infancy to decrepitude with unexampled speed.

Two men's lives span the interval from the first admission of popular influence, under Solon, to the downfall of the State. Their history furnishes the classic example of the peril of democracy under conditions singularly favourable. For the Athenians were not only brave and patriotic and capable of generous sacrifice, but they were the most religious of the Greeks. They venerated the Constitution which had given them prosperity, and equality, and freedom, and never questioned the fundamental laws which regulated the enormous power of the Assembly. They tolerated considerable variety of opinion and great licence of speech; and their humanity towards their slaves roused the indignation even of the most intelligent partisan of aristocracy. Thus they became the only people of antiquity that grew great by democratic institutions. But the possession of unlimited power, which corrodes the conscience, hardens the heart, and confounds the understanding of monarchs, exercised its demoralising influence on the illustrious democracy of Athens. It is bad to be oppressed by a minority, but it is worse to be oppressed by a majority. For there is a reserve of latent power in the masses which, if it is called into play, the minority can seldom resist. But from the absolute will of an entire people there is no appeal, no redemption, no refuge but treason. The humblest and most numerous class of the Athenians united the legislative, the judicial, and, in part, the executive power. The philosophy that was then in the ascendant taught them that there is no law superior to that of the State — the lawgiver is above the law.

It followed that the sovereign people had a right to do whatever was within its power, and was bound by no rule of right or wrong but its own judgment of expediency. On a memorable occasion the assembled Athenians declared it monstrous that they should be prevented from doing whatever they chose. No force that existed could restrain them; and they resolved that no duty should restrain them, and that they would be bound by no laws that were not of their own making. In this way the emancipated people of Athens became a tyrant; and their government, the pioneer of European freedom, stands condemned with a terrible unanimity by all the wisest of the ancients. They ruined their city by attempting to conduct war by debate in the marketplace. Like the French Republic, they put their unsuccessful commanders to death. They treated their dependencies with such injustice that they lost their maritime Empire. They plundered the rich until the rich conspired with the public enemy, and they crowned their guilt by the martyrdom of Socrates.

When the absolute sway of numbers had endured for near a quarter of a century, nothing but bare existence was left for the State to lose; and the Athenians, wearied and despondent, confessed the true cause of their ruin. They understood that for liberty, justice, and equal laws, it is as necessary that democracy should restrain itself as it had been that it should restrain the oligarchy. They resolved to take their stand once more upon the ancient ways, and to restore the order of things which had subsisted when the monopoly of power had been taken from the rich and had not been acquired by the poor. After a first restoration had failed, which is only memorable because Thucydides, whose judgment in politics is never at fault, pronounced it the best government Athens had enjoyed, the attempt was renewed with more experience and greater singleness of purpose. The hostile parties were reconciled, and proclaimed an amnesty, the first in history. They resolved to govern by concurrence. The laws, which had the sanction of tradition, were reduced to a code; and no act of the sovereign assembly was valid with which they might be found to disagree. Between the sacred lines of the Constitution which were to remain inviolate, and the decrees which met from time to time the needs and notions of the day, a broad distinction was drawn; and the fabric of a law which had been the work of generations was made independent of momentary variations in the popular will. The repentance of the Athenians came too late to save the Republic. But the lesson of their experience endures for all times, for it teaches that government by the whole people, being the government of the most numerous and most powerful class, is an evil of the same nature as unmixed monarchy, and requires, for nearly the same reasons, institutions that shall protect it against itself, and shall uphold the permanent reign of law against arbitrary revolutions of opinion.

Parallel with the rise and fall of Athenian freedom, Rome was employed in working out the same problems, with greater constructive sense, and greater temporary success, but ending at last in a far more terrible catastrophe. That which among the ingenious Athenians had been a development carried forward by the spell of plausible argument, was in Rome a conflict between rival forces. Speculative politics had no attraction for the grim and practical genius of the Romans. They did not consider what would be the cleverest way of getting over a difficulty, but what way was indicated by analogous cases; and they assigned less influence to the impulse and spirit of the moment, than to precedent and example. Their peculiar character prompted them to ascribe the origin of their laws to early times, and in their desire to justify the continuity of their institutions, and to get rid of the reproach of innovation, they imagined the legendary history of the kings of Rome. The energy of their adherence to traditions made their progress slow, they advanced only under compulsion of almost unavoidable necessity, and the same questions recurred often, before they were settled. The constitutional history of the Republic turns on the endeavours of the aristocracy, who claimed to be the only true Romans, to retain in their hands the power they had wrested from the kings, and of the plebeians to get an equal share in it. And this controversy, which the eager and restless Athenians went through in one generation, lasted for more than two centuries, from a time when the *plebs* were excluded from the government of the city, and were taxed, and made to serve without pay, until, in the year 286, they were admitted to political equality. Then followed one hundred and fifty years of unexampled prosperity and glory; and then, out of the original conflict which had been compromised, if not theoretically settled, a new struggle arose which was without an issue.

The mass of poorer families, impoverished by incessant service in war, were reduced to dependence on an aristocracy of about two thousand wealthy men, who divided among themselves the immense domain of the State. When the need became intense the Gracchi tried to relieve it by inducing the richer classes to allot some share in the public lands to the common people. The old and famous aristocracy of birth and rank had made a stubborn resistance, but it knew the art of yielding. The later and more selfish aristocracy was unable to learn it. The character of the people was changed by the sterner motives of dispute. The fight for political power had been carried on with the moderation which is so honourable a quality of party contests in England. But the struggle for the objects of material existence grew to be as ferocious as civil controversies in France. Repulsed by the rich, after a struggle of twenty-two years, the people, three hundred and twenty thousand of whom depended on public rations for food, were ready to follow any man who promised to obtain for them by revolution what they could not obtain by law.

For a time the Senate, representing the ancient and threatened order of things, was strong enough to overcome every popular leader that arose, until Julius Cæsar, supported by an army which he had led in an unparalleled career of conquest, and by the famished masses which he won by his lavish liberality, and skilled beyond all other men in the art of governing, converted the Republic into a monarchy by a series of measures that were neither violent nor injurious.

The Empire preserved the Republican forms until the reign of Diocletian; but the will of the Emperors was as uncontrolled as that of the people had been after the victory of the Tribunes. Their power was arbitrary even when it was most widely employed, and yet the Roman Empire rendered greater services to the cause of liberty than the Roman Republic. I do not mean by reason of the temporary accident that there were emperors who made good use of their immense opportunities, such as Nerva, of whom Tacitus says that he combined monarchy and liberty, things otherwise incompatible; or that the Empire was what its panegyrists declared it, the perfection of democracy. In truth, it was at best an ill-disguised and odious despotism. But Frederic the Great was a despot; yet he was a friend to toleration and free discussion. The Bonapartes were despotic; yet no liberal ruler was ever more acceptable to the masses of the people than the First Napoleon, after he had destroyed the Republic, in 1805, and the Third Napoleon at the height of his power in 1859. In the same way, the Roman Empire possessed merits which, at a distance, and especially at a great distance of time, concern men more deeply than the tragic tyranny which was felt in the neighbourhood of the Palace. The poor had what they had demanded in vain of the Republic. The rich fared better than during the Triumvirate. The rights of Roman citizens were extended to the people of the provinces. To the imperial epoch belong the better part of Roman literature and nearly the entire Civil Law; and it was the Empire that mitigated slavery, instituted religious toleration, made a beginning of the law of nations, and created a perfect system of the law of property. The Republic which Cæsar overthrew had been anything but a free State. It provided admirable securities for the rights of citizens; it treated with savage disregard the rights of men; and allowed the free Roman to inflict atrocious wrongs on his children, on debtors and dependants, on prisoners and slaves. Those deeper ideas of right and duty, which are not found on the tables of municipal law, but with which the generous minds of Greece were conversant, were held of little account, and the philosophy which dealt with such speculations was repeatedly proscribed, as a teacher of sedition and impiety.

At length, in the year 155, the Athenian philosopher Carneades appeared at Rome on a political mission. During an interval of official business he delivered two public orations, to give the unlettered conquerors of his country a taste of the disputations that flourished in the Attic schools. On the first day he discoursed of natural justice. On the next, he denied its existence, arguing that all our notions of good and evil are derived from positive enactment. From the time of that memorable display, the genius of the vanquished held its conquerors in thrall. The most eminent of the public men of Rome, such as Scipio and Cicero, formed

THE HISTORY OF FREEDOM IN ANTIQUITY 45

their minds on Grecian models, and her jurists underwent the rigorous discipline of Zeno and Chrysippus.

If, drawing the limit in the second century, when the influence of Christianity becomes perceptible, we should form our judgment of the politics of antiquity by its actual legislation, our estimate would be low. The prevailing notions of freedom were imperfect, and the endeavours to realise them were wide of the mark. The ancients understood the regulation of power better than the regulation of liberty. They concentrated so many prerogatives in the State as to leave no footing from which a man could deny its jurisdiction or assign bounds to its activity. If I may employ an expressive anachronism, the vice of the classic State was that it was both Church and State in one. Morality was undistinguished from religion and politics from morals; and in religion, morality, and politics there was only one legislator and one authority. The State, while it did deplorably little for education, for practical science, for the indigent and helpless, or for the spiritual needs of man, nevertheless claimed the use of all his faculties and the determination of all his duties. Individuals and families, associations and dependencies were so much material that the sovereign power consumed for its own purposes. What the slave was in the hands of his master, the citizen was in the hands of the community. The most sacred obligations vanished before the public advantage. The passengers existed for the sake of the ship. By their disregard for private interests, and for the moral welfare and improvement of the people, both Greece and Rome destroyed the vital elements on which the prosperity of nations rests, and perished by the decay of families and the depopulation of the country. They survive not in their institutions, but in their ideas, and by their ideas, especially on the art of government, they are —

> The dead, but sceptred sovereigns who still rule
> Our spirits from their urns.

To them, indeed, may be tracked nearly all the errors that are undermining political society — communism, utilitarianism, the confusion between tyranny and authority, and between lawlessness and freedom.

The notion that men lived originally in a state of nature, by violence and without laws, is due to Critias. Communism in its grossest form was recommended by Diogenes of Sinope. According to the Sophists, there is no duty above expediency and no virtue apart from pleasure. Laws are an invention of weak men to rob their betters of the reasonable enjoyment of their superiority. It is better to inflict than to suffer wrong; and as there is no greater good than to do evil without fear of retribution, so there is no worse evil than to suffer without the consolation of revenge. Justice is the mask of a craven spirit; injustice is worldly wisdom; and duty, obedience, self-denial are the impostures of hypocrisy. Government is absolute, and may ordain what it pleases, and no subject can complain that it does him wrong, but as long as he can escape compulsion and punishment, he is always free to disobey. Happiness consists in obtaining power and in eluding the necessity of obedience; and he that gains a throne by perfidy and murder, deserves to be truly envied.

Epicurus differed but little from the propounders of the code of revolutionary despotism. All societies, he said, are founded on contract for mutual protection. Good and evil are conventional terms, for the thunderbolts of heaven fall alike on the just and the unjust. The objection to wrongdoing is not the act, but in its consequences to the wrongdoer. Wise men contrive laws, not to bind, but to protect themselves; and when they prove to be unprofitable they cease to be valid. The illiberal sentiments of even the most illustrious metaphysicians are disclosed in the saying of Aristotle, that the mark of the worst governments is that they leave men free to live as they please.

If you will bear in mind that Socrates, the best of the pagans, knew of no higher criterion for men, of no better guide of conduct, than the laws of each country; that Plato, whose sublime doctrine was so near an anticipation of Christianity that celebrated theologians wished his works to be forbidden, lest men should be content with them, and indifferent to any higher dogma — to whom was granted that prophetic vision of the Just Man, accused, condemned and scourged, and dying on a Cross — nevertheless employed the most splendid intellect ever bestowed on man to advocate the abolition of the family and the exposure of infants; that Aristotle, the ablest moralist of antiquity, saw no harm in making raids upon a neighbouring people, for the sake of reducing them to slavery — still more, if you will consider that, among the moderns, men of genius equal to these have held political doctrines not less criminal or absurd — it will be apparent to you how stubborn a phalanx of error blocks the paths of truth; that pure reason is as powerless as custom to solve the problem of free government; that it can only be the fruit of long, manifold, and painful experience; and that the tracing of the methods by which divine wisdom has educated the nations to appreciate and to assume the duties of freedom, is not the least part of that true philosophy that studies to

Assert eternal Providence,
And justify the ways of God to men.

But, having sounded the depth of their errors, I should give you a very inadequate idea of the wisdom of the ancients if I allowed it to appear that their precepts were no better than their practice. While statesmen and senates and popular assemblies supplied examples of every description of blunder, a noble literature arose, in which a priceless treasure of political knowledge was stored, and in which the defects of the existing institutions were exposed with unsparing sagacity. The point on which the ancients were most nearly unanimous is the right of the people to govern, and their inability to govern alone. To meet this difficulty, to give to the popular element a full share without a monopoly of power, they adopted very generally the theory of a mixed Constitution. They differed from our notion of the same thing, because modern Constitutions have been a device for limiting monarchy; with them they were invented to curb democracy. The idea arose in the time of Plato — though he repelled it — when the early monarchies and oligarchies had vanished, and it continued to be cherished long after all democracies had been absorbed in the Roman Empire. But whereas a sovereign prince who surrenders part of his authority yields to the argument of superior force, a sovereign people relinquishing its own prerogative succumbs to the influence of reason. And it has in all times proved more easy to create limitations by the use of force than by persuasion.

The ancient writers saw very clearly that each principle of government standing alone is carried to excess and provokes a reaction. Monarchy hardens into despotism. Aristocracy contracts into oligarchy. Democracy expands into the supremacy of numbers. They therefore imagined that to restrain each element by combining it with the others would avert the natural process of self-destruction, and endow the State with perpetual youth. But this harmony of monarchy, aristocracy, and democracy blended together, which was the ideal of many writers, and which they supposed to be exhibited by Sparta, by Carthage, and by Rome, was a chimera of philosophers never realised by antiquity. At last Tacitus, wiser than the rest, confessed that the mixed Constitution, however admirable in theory, was difficult to establish and impossible to maintain. His disheartening avowal is not disowned by later experience.

The experiment has been tried more often than I can tell, with a combination of resources that were unknown to the ancients — with Christianity, parliamentary government, and a free press. Yet there is no example of such a balanced Constitution having lasted a century. If it has succeeded anywhere it has been in our favoured country and in our time; and we know not yet how long the wisdom of the nation will preserve the equipoise. The Federal check was as familiar to the ancients as the Constitutional. For the type of all their Republics was the government of a city by its own inhabitants meeting in the public place. An administration embracing many cities was known to them only in the form of the oppression which Sparta exercised over the Messenians, Athens over her Confederates, and Rome over Italy. The resources which, in modern times, enabled a great people to govern itself through a single centre did not exist. Equality could be preserved only by federalism; and it occurs more often amongst them than in the modern world. If the distribution of power among the several parts of the State is the most efficient restraint on monarchy, the distribution of power among several States is the best check on democracy. By multiplying centres of government and discussion it promotes the diffusion of political knowledge and the maintenance of healthy and independent opinion. It is the protectorate of minorities, and the consecration of self-government. But although it must be enumerated among the better achievements of practical genius in antiquity, it arose from necessity, and its properties were imperfectly investigated in theory.

When the Greeks began to reflect on the problems of society, they first of all accepted things as they were, and did their best to explain and defend them. Inquiry, which with us is stimulated by doubt, began with them in wonder. The most illustrious of the early philosophers, Pythagoras, promulgated a theory for the preservation of political power in the educated class, and ennobled a form of government which was generally founded on popular ignorance and on strong class interests. He preached authority and subordination, and dwelt more on duties than on rights, on religion than on policy; and his system perished in the revolution by which oligarchies were swept away. The revolution afterwards developed its own philosophy, whose excesses I have described.

But between the two eras, between the rigid didactics of the early Pythagoreans and the dissolving theories of Protagoras, a philosopher arose who stood aloof from both extremes, and whose difficult sayings were never really understood or valued until our time. Heraclitus, of Ephesus, deposited his book in the temple of Diana. The book has perished, like the temple and the worship, but its fragments have been collected and interpreted with incredible ardour, by the scholars, the divines, the philosophers, and politicians who have been engaged the most intensely in the toil and stress of this century. The most renowned logician of the last century adopted every one of his propositions; and the most brilliant agitator among Continental Socialists composed a work of eight hundred and forty pages to celebrate his memory.

Heraclitus complained that the masses were deaf to truth, and knew not that one good man counts for more than thousands; but he held the existing order in no superstitious reverence. Strife, he says, is the source and the master of all things. Life is perpetual motion, and repose is death. No man can plunge twice into the same current, for it is always flowing and passing, and is never the same. The only thing fixed and certain in the midst of change is the universal and sovereign reason, which all men may not perceive, but which is common to all. Laws are sustained by no human authority, but by virtue of their derivation from the one law that is divine. These sayings, which recall the grand outlines of political truth which we have found in the Sacred Books, and carry us forward to the latest teaching of our most enlightened contemporaries, would bear a good deal of elucidation and comment. Heraclitus is, unfortunately, so obscure that Socrates could not understand him, and I won't pretend to have succeeded better.

If the topic of my address was the history of political science, the highest and the largest place would belong to Plato and Aristotle. The *Laws* of the one, the *Politics* of the other, are, if I may trust my own experience, the books from which we may learn the most about the principles of politics. The penetration with which those great masters of thought analysed the institutions of Greece, and exposed their vices, is not surpassed by anything in later literature; by Burke or Hamilton, the best political writers of the last century; by Tocqueville or Roscher, the most eminent of our own. But Plato and Aristotle were philosophers, studious not of unguided freedom, but of intelligent government. They saw the disastrous effects of ill-directed striving for liberty; and they resolved that it was better not to strive for it, but to be content with a strong administration, prudently adapted to make men prosperous and happy.

Now liberty and good government do not exclude each other; and there are excellent reasons why they should go together. Liberty is not a means to a higher political end. It is itself the highest political end. It is not for the sake of a good public administration that it is required, but for security in the pursuit of the highest objects of civil society, and of private life. Increase of freedom in the State may sometimes promote mediocrity, and give vitality to prejudice; it may even retard useful legislation, diminish the capacity for war, and restrict the boundaries of Empire. It might be plausibly argued that, if many things would be worse in England or Ireland under an intelligent despotism, some things would be managed better; that the Roman government was more enlightened under Augustus and Antoninus than under the Senate, in the days of Marius or of Pompey. A generous spirit prefers that his country should be poor, and weak, and of no account, but free, rather than powerful, prosperous, and enslaved. It is better to be the citizen of a humble commonwealth in the Alps, without a prospect of influence beyond the narrow frontier, than a subject of the superb autocracy that overshadows half of Asia and of Europe. But it may be urged, on the other side, that liberty is not the sum or the substitute of all the things men ought to live for; that to be real it must be circumscribed, and that the limits of circumscription vary; that advancing civilisation invests the State with increased rights and duties, and imposes increased burdens and constraint on the subject; that a highly instructed and intelligent community may perceive the benefit of compulsory obligations which, at a lower stage, would be thought unbearable; that liberal progress is not vague or indefinite, but aims at a point where the public is subject to no restrictions but those of which it feels the advantage; that a free country may be less capable of doing much for the advancement of religion, the prevention of vice, or the relief of suffering, than one that does not shrink from confronting great emergencies by some sacrifice of individual rights, and some concentration of power; and that the supreme political object ought to be sometimes postponed to still higher moral objects. My argument involves no collision with these qualifying reflections. We are dealing, not with the effects of freedom, but with its causes. We are seeking out the influences which brought arbitrary government under control, either by the diffusion of power, or by the appeal to an authority which transcends all government, and among those influences the greatest philosophers of Greece have no claim to be reckoned.

It is the Stoics who emancipated mankind from its subjugation to despotic rule, and whose enlightened and elevated views of life bridged the chasm that separates the ancient from the Christian state, and led the way to freedom. Seeing how little security there is that the laws of any land shall be wise or just, and that the unanimous will of a people and the assent of nations are liable to err, the Stoics looked beyond those narrow barriers, and above those inferior sanctions, for the principles that ought to regulate the lives of men and the existence of society. They made it known that there is a will superior to the collective will of man, and a law that overrules those of Solon and Lycurgus. Their test of good government is its conformity to principles that can be traced to a higher legislator. That which we must obey, that to which we are bound to reduce all civil authorities, and to sacrifice every earthly interest, is that immutable law which is perfect and eternal as God Himself, which proceeds from His nature, and reigns over heaven and earth and over all the nations.

The great question is to discover, not what governments prescribe, but what they ought to prescribe; for no prescription is valid against the conscience of mankind. Before God, there is neither Greek nor barbarian, neither rich nor poor, and the slave is as good as his master, for by birth all men are free; they are citizens of that universal commonwealth which embraces all the world, brethren of one family, and children of God. The true guide of our conduct is no outward authority, but the voice of God, who comes down to dwell in our souls, who knows all our thoughts, to whom are owing all the truth we know, and all the good we do; for vice is voluntary, and virtue comes from the grace of the heavenly spirit within.

What the teaching of that divine voice is, the philosophers who had imbibed the sublime ethics of the Porch went on to expound: It is not enough to act up to the written law, or to give all men their due; we ought to give them more than their due, to be generous and beneficent, to devote ourselves for the good of others, seeking our reward in self-denial and sacrifice, acting from the motive of sympathy and not of personal advantage. Therefore we must treat others as we wish to be treated by them, and must persist until death in doing good to our enemies, regardless of unworthiness and ingratitude. For we must be at war with evil, but at peace with men, and it is better to suffer than to commit injustice. True freedom, says the most eloquent of the Stoics, consists in obeying God. A State governed by such principles as these would have been free far beyond the measure of Greek or Roman freedom; for they open a door to religious toleration, and close it against slavery. Neither conquest nor purchase, said Zeno, can make one man the property of another.

These doctrines were adopted and applied by the great jurists of the Empire. The law of nature, they said, is superior to the written law, and slavery contradicts the law of nature. Men have no right to do what they please with their own, or to make profit out of another's loss. Such is the political wisdom of the ancients, touching the foundations of liberty, as we find it in its highest development, in Cicero, and Seneca, and Philo, a Jew of Alexandria. Their writings impress upon us the greatness of the work of preparation for the Gospel which had been accomplished among men on the eve of the mission of the Apostles. St. Augustine, after quoting Seneca, exclaims: "What more could a Christian say than this Pagan has said?" The enlightened pagans had reached nearly the last point attainable without a new dispensation, when the fulness of time was come. We have seen the breadth and the splendour of the domain of Hellenic thought, and it has brought us to the threshold of a greater kingdom. The best of the later classics speak almost the language of Christianity, and they border on its spirit.

But in all that I have been able to cite from classical literature, three things are wanting, — representative government, the emancipation of the slaves, and liberty of conscience. There were, it is true, deliberative assemblies, chosen by the people; and confederate cities, of which, both in Asia and Africa, there were so many leagues, sent their delegates to sit in Federal Councils. But government by an elected Parliament was even in theory a thing unknown. It is congruous with the nature of Polytheism to admit some measure of toleration. And Socrates, when he avowed that he must obey God rather than the Athenians, and the Stoics, when they set the wise man above the law, were very near giving utterance to the principle. But it was first proclaimed and established by enactment, not in polytheistic and philosophical Greece, but in India, by Asoka, the earliest of the Buddhist kings, two hundred and fifty years before the birth of Christ.

Slavery has been, far more than intolerance, the perpetual curse and reproach of ancient civilisation, and although its rightfulness was disputed as early as the days of Aristotle, and was implicitly, if not definitely, denied by several Stoics, the moral philosophy of the Greeks and Romans, as well as their practice, pronounced decidedly in its favour. But there was one extraordinary people who, in this as in other things, anticipated the purer precept that was to come. Philo of Alexandria is one of the writers whose views on society were most advanced. He applauds not only liberty but equality in the enjoyment of wealth. He believes that a limited democracy, purged of its grosser elements, is the most perfect government, and will extend itself gradually over all the world. By freedom he understood the following of God. Philo, though he required that the condition of the slave should be made compatible with the wants and claims of his higher nature, did not absolutely condemn slavery. But he has put on record the customs of the Essenes of Palestine, a people who, uniting the wisdom of the Gentiles with the faith of the Jews, led lives which were uncontaminated by the surrounding civilisation, and were the first to reject slavery both in principle and practice. They formed a religious community rather than a State, and their numbers did not exceed 4,000. But their example testifies to how great a height religious men were able to raise their conception of society even without the succour of the New Testament, and affords the strongest condemnation of their contemporaries.

This, then, is the conclusion to which our survey brings us: there is hardly a truth in politics or in the system of the rights of man that was not grasped by the wisest of the Gentiles and the Jews, or that they did not declare with a refinement of thought and a nobleness of expression that later writers could never surpass. I might go on for hours, reciting to you passages on the law of nature and the duties of man, so solemn and religious that though they come from the profane theatre on the Acropolis, and from the Roman forum, you would deem that you were listening to the hymns of Christian churches and the discourse of ordained divines. But although the maxims of the great classic teachers, of Sophocles, and Plato, and Seneca, and the glorious examples of public virtue were in the mouths of all men, there was no power in them to avert the doom of that civilisation for which the blood of so many patriots and the genius of such incomparable writers had been wasted in vain. The liberties of the ancient nations were crushed beneath a hopeless and inevitable despotism, and their vitality was spent, when the new power came forth from Galilee, giving what was wanting to the efficacy of human knowledge to redeem societies as well as men.

It would be presumptuous if I attempted to indicate the numberless channels by which Christian influence gradually penetrated the State. The first striking phenomenon is the slowness with which an action destined to be so prodigious became manifest. Going forth to all nations, in many stages of civilisation and under almost every form of government, Christianity had none of the character of a political apostolate, and in its absorbing mission to individuals did not challenge public authority. The early Christians avoided contact with the State, abstained from the responsibilities of office, and were even reluctant to serve in the army. Cherishing their citizenship of a kingdom not of this world, they despaired of an empire which seemed too powerful to be resisted and too corrupt to be converted, whose institutions, the work and the pride of untold centuries of paganism, drew their sanctions from the gods whom the Christians accounted devils, which plunged its hands from age to age in the blood of martyrs, and was beyond the hope of regeneration and foredoomed to perish. They were so much overawed as to imagine that the fall of the State would be the end of the Church and of the world, and no man dreamed of the boundless future of spiritual and social influence that awaited their religion among the race of destroyers that were bringing the empire of Augustus and of Constantine to humiliation and ruin. The duties of government were less in their thoughts than the private virtues and duties of subjects; and it was long before they became aware of the burden of power in their faith. Down almost to the time of Chrysostom, they shrank from contemplating the obligation to emancipate the slaves.

Although the doctrine of self-reliance and self-denial, which is the foundation of political economy, was written as legibly in the New Testament as in the *Wealth of Nations,* it was not recognised until our age. Tertullian boasts of the passive obedience of the Christians. Melito writes to a pagan Emperor as if he were incapable of giving an unjust command; and in Christian times Optatus thought that whoever presumed to find fault with his sovereign exalted himself almost to the level of a god. But this political quietism was not universal. Origen, the ablest writer of early times, spoke with approval of conspiring for the destruction of tyranny.

After the fourth century the declarations against slavery are earnest and continual. And in a theological but yet pregnant sense, divines of the second century insist on liberty, and divines of the fourth century on equality. There was one essential and inevitable transformation in politics. Popular governments had existed, and also mixed and federal governments, but there had been no limited government, no State the circumference of whose authority had been defined by a force external to its own. That was the great problem which philosophy had raised, and which no statesmanship had been able to solve. Those who proclaimed the assistance of a higher authority had indeed drawn a metaphysical barrier before the governments, but they had not known how to make it real. All that Socrates could effect by way of protest against the tyranny of the reformed democracy was to die for his convictions. The Stoics could only advise the wise man to hold aloof from politics, keeping the unwritten law in his heart. But when Christ said: "Render unto Cæsar the things that are Cæsar's, and unto God the things that are God's," those words, spoken on His last visit to the Temple, three days before His death, gave to the civil power, under the protection of conscience, a sacredness it had never enjoyed, and bounds it had never acknowledged; and they were the repudiation of absolutism and the inauguration of freedom. For our Lord not only delivered the precept, but created the force to execute it. To maintain the necessary immunity in one supreme sphere, to reduce all political authority within defined limits, ceased to be an aspiration of patient reasoners, and was made the perpetual charge and care of the most energetic institution and the most universal association in the world. The new law, the new spirit, the new authority, gave to liberty a meaning and a value it had not possessed in the philosophy or in the constitution of Greece or Rome before the knowledge of the truth that makes us free.

Chapter III

THE HISTORY OF FREEDOM IN CHRISTIANITY

When Constantine the Great carried the seat of empire from Rome to Constantinople he set up in the marketplace of the new capital a porphyry pillar which had come from Egypt, and of which a strange tale is told. In a vault beneath he secretly buried the seven sacred emblems of the Roman state, which were guarded by the virgins in the temple of Vesta, with the fire that might never be quenched. On the summit he raised a statue of Apollo, representing himself, and enclosing a fragment of the Cross; and he crowned it with a diadem of rays consisting of the nails employed at the Crucifixion, which his mother was believed to have found at Jerusalem.

The pillar still stands, the most significant monument that exists of the converted Empire; for the notion that the nails which had pierced the body of Christ became a fit ornament for a heathen idol as soon as it was called by the name of a living emperor indicates the position designed for Christianity in the imperial structure of Constantine. Diocletian's attempt to transform the Roman government into a despotism of the Eastern type had brought on the last and most serious persecution of the Christians; and Constantine, in adopting their faith, intended neither to abandon his predecessor's scheme of policy nor to renounce the fascinations of

---

Note: This address was delivered to the members of the Bridgnorth Institution at the Agricultural Hall, May 28, 1877 (Bridgnorth, 1877) reprinted in *The History of Freedom and Other Essays* (London, Macmillan Co., 1907), pp. 30-60.

arbitrary authority, but to strengthen his throne with the support of a religion which had astonished the world by its power of resistance, and to obtain that support absolutely and without a drawback he fixed the seat of his government in the East, with a patriarch of his own creation.

Nobody warned him that by promoting the Christian religion he was tying one of his hands, and surrendering the prerogative of the Cæsars. As the acknowledged author of the liberty and superiority of the Church, he was appealed to as the guardian of her unity. He admitted the obligation; he accepted the trust; and the divisions that prevailed among the Christians supplied his successors with many opportunities of extending that protectorate, and preventing any reduction of the claims or of the resources of imperialism.

Constantine declared his own will equivalent to a canon of the Church. According to Justinian, the Roman people had formally transferred to the employers the entire plenitude of its authority, and, therefore, the Emperor's pleasure, expressed by edict or by letter, had force of law. Even in the fervent age of its conversion the Empire employed its refined civilisation, the accumulated wisdom of ancient sages, the reasonableness and sublety of Roman law, and the entire inheritance of the Jewish, the Pagan, and the Christian world, to make the Church serve as a gilded crutch of absolutism. Neither an enlightened philosophy, nor all the political wisdom of Rome, nor even the faith and virtue of the Christians availed against the incorrigible tradition of antiquity. Something was wanted beyond all the gifts of reflection and experience — a faculty of self-government and self-control, developed like its language in the fibre of a nation, and growing with its growth. This vital element, which many centuries of warfare, of anarchy, of oppression had extinguished in the countries that were still draped in the pomp of ancient civilisation, was deposited on the soil of Christendom by the fertilising stream of migration that overthrew the empire of the West.

In the height of their power the Romans became aware of a race of men that had not abdicated freedom in the hands of a monarch; and the ablest writer of the empire pointed to them with a vague and bitter feeling that, to the institutions of these barbarians, not yet crushed by despotism, the future of the world belonged. Their kings, when they had kings, did not preside at their councils; they were sometimes elective; they were sometimes deposed; and they were bound by oath to act in obedience with the general wish. They enjoyed real authority only in war. This primitive Republicanism, which admits monarchy as an occasional incident, but holds fast to the collective supremacy of all free men, of the constituent authority over all constituted authorities, is the remote germ of parliamentary government. The action of the State was confined to narrow limits; but, besides his position as head of the State, the king was surrounded by a body of followers attached to him by personal or political ties. In these, his immediate dependants, disobedience or resistance to orders was no more tolerated than in a wife, a child, or a soldier; and a man was expected to murder his own father if his chieftain required it. Thus these Teutonic communities admitted an independence of government that threatened to dissolve society; and a dependence on persons that was dangerous to freedom. It was a system very favourable to corporations, but offering no security to individuals. The State was not likely to oppress its subjects; and was not able to protect them.

The first effect of the great Teutonic migration into the regions civilised by Rome was to throw back Europe many centuries to a condition scarcely more advanced than that from which the institutions of Solon had rescued Athens. Whilst the Greeks preserved the literature, the arts, and the science of antiquity and all the sacred monuments of early Christianity with a completeness of which the rended fragments that have come down to us give no commensurate idea, and even the peasants of Bulgaria knew the New Testament by heart, Western Europe lay under the grasp of masters the ablest of whom could not write their names. The faculty of exact reasoning, of accurate observation, became extinct for five hundred years, and even the sciences most needful to society, medicine and geometry, fell into decay, until the teachers of the West went to school at the feet of Arabian masters. To bring order out of chaotic ruin, to rear a new civilisation and blend hostile and unequal races into a nation, the thing wanted was not liberty but force. And for centuries all progress is attached to the action of men like Clovis, Charlemagne, and William the Norman, who were resolute and peremptory, and prompt to be obeyed.

The spirit of immemorial paganism which had saturated ancient society could not be exorcised except by the combined influence of Church and State; and the universal sense that their union was necessary created the Byzantine despotism. The divines of the Empire who could not fancy Christianity flourishing beyond its borders, insisted that the State is not in the Church, but the Church in the State. This doctrine had scarcely been uttered when the rapid collapse of the Western Empire opened a wider horizon; and Salvianus, a priest at Marseilles, proclaimed that the social virtues, which were decaying amid the civilised Romans, existed in greater purity and promise among the Pagan invaders. They were converted with ease and rapidity; and their conversion was generally brought about by their kings.

Christianity, which in earlier times had addressed itself to the masses, and relied on the principle of liberty, now made its appeal to the rulers, and threw its mighty influence into the scale of authority. The barbarians, who possessed no books, no secular knowledge, no education, except in the schools of the clergy, and who had scarcely acquired the rudiments of religious instruction, turned with childlike attachment to men whose minds were stored with the knowledge of Scripture, of Cicero, of St. Augustine; and in the scanty world of their ideas, the Church was felt to be something infinitely vaster, stronger, holier than their newly founded States. The clergy supplied the means of conducting the new governments, and were made exempt from taxation, from the jurisdiction of the civil magistrate, and of the political administrator. They taught that power ought to be conferred by election; and the Councils of Toledo furnished the framework of the parliamentary system of Spain, which is, by a long interval, the oldest in the world. But the monarchy of the Goths in Spain, as well as that of the Saxons in England, in both of which the nobles and the prelates surrounded the throne with the semblance of free institutions, passed away; and the people that prospered and overshadowed the rest were the Franks, who had no native nobility, whose law of succession to the Crown became for one thousand years the fixed object of an unchanging superstition, and under whom the feudal system was developed to excess.

Feudalism made land the measure and the master of all things. Having no other source of wealth than the produce of the soil, men depended on the landlord for the means of escaping starvation; and thus his power became paramount over the liberty of the subject and the authority of the State. Every baron, said the French maxim, is sovereign in his own domain. The nations of the West lay between the competing tyrannies of local magnates and of absolute monarchs, when a force was brought upon the scene which proved for a time superior alike to the vassal and his lord.

In the days of the Conquest, when the Normans destroyed the liberties of England, the rude institutions which had come with the Saxons, the Goths, and the Franks from the forests of Germany were suffering decay, and the new element of popular government afterwards supplied by the rise of towns and the formation of a middle class was not yet active. The only influence capable of resisting the feudal hierarchy was the ecclesiastical hierarchy; and they came into collision, when the process of feudalism threatened the independence of the Church by subjecting the prelates severally to that form of personal dependence on the kings which was peculiar to the Teutonic state.

To that conflict of four hundred years we owe the rise of civil liberty. If the Church had continued to buttress the thrones of the kings whom it anointed, or if the struggle had terminated speedily in an undivided victory, all Europe would have sunk down under a Byzantine or Muscovite despotism. For the aim of both contending parties was absolute authority. But although liberty was not the end for which they strove, it was the means by which the temporal and the spiritual power called the nations to their aid. The towns of Italy and Germany won their franchises, France got her States-General, and England her Parliament out of the alternate phases of the contest; and as long as it lasted it prevented the rise of divine right. A disposition existed to regard the crown as an estate descending under the law of real property in the family that possessed it. But the authority of religion, and especially of the papacy, was thrown on the side that denied the indefeasible title of kings. In France what was afterwards called the Gallican theory maintained that the reigning house was above the law, and that the sceptre was not to pass away from it as long as there should be princes of the royal blood of St. Louis. But in other countries the oath of fidelity itself attested that it was conditional, and should be kept only during good behaviour; and it was in conformity with the public law to which all monarchs were held subject, that King John was declared a rebel against the barons, and that the men who raised Edward III to the throne from which they had deposed his father invoked the maxim *Vox populi Vox Dei.*

And this doctrine of the divine right of the people to raise up and pull down princes, after obtaining the sanctions of religion, was made to stand on broader grounds, and was strong enough to resist both Church and king. In the struggle between the House of Bruce and the House of Plantagenet for the possession of Scotland and Ireland, the English claim was backed by the censures of Rome. But the Irish and the Scots refused it, and the address in which the Scottish Parliament informed the Pope of their resolution shows how firmly the popular doctrine had taken root. Speaking of Robert Bruce, they say: "Divine Providence, the laws and customs of the country, which we will defend till death, and the choice of the people, have made him our king. If he should ever betray his principles, and consent that we should be subjects of the English king, then we shall treat him as an enemy, as the subverter of our rights and his own, and shall elect another in his place. We care not for glory or for wealth, but for that liberty which no true man will give up but with his life." This estimate of royalty was natural among men accustomed to see those whom they most respected in constant strife with their rulers. Gregory VII had begun the disparagement of civil authorities by saying that they are the work of the devil; and already in his time both parties were driven to acknowledge the sovereignty of the people, and appealed to it as the immediate source of power.

Two centuries later this political theory had gained both in definiteness and in force among the Guelphs, who were the Church party, and among the Ghibellines, or Imperialists. Here are the sentiments of the most celebrated of all the Guelphic writers: "A king who is unfaithful to his duty forfeits his claim to obedience. It is not rebellion to depose him, for he is himself a rebel whom the nation has a right to put down. But it is better to abridge his power, that he may be unable to abuse it. For this purpose, the whole nation ought to have a share in governing itself; the Constitution ought to combine a limited and elective monarchy, with an aristocracy of merit, and such an admixture of democracy as shall admit all classes to office, by popular election. No government has a right to levy taxes beyond the limit determined by the people. All political authority is derived from popular suffrage, and all laws must be made by the people or their representatives. There is no security for us as long as we depend on the will of another man." This language, which contains the earliest exposition of the Whig theory of the revolution, is taken from the works of St. Thomas Aquinas, of whom Lord Bacon says that he had the largest heart of the school divines. And it is worth while to observe that he wrote at the very moment when Simon de Montfort summoned the Commons; and that the politics of the Neapolitan friar are centuries in advance of the English statesman's.

The ablest writer of the Ghibelline party was Marsilius of Padua. "Laws," he said, "derive their authority from the nation, and are invalid without its assent. As the whole is greater than any part, it is wrong that any part should legislate for the whole; and as men are equal, it is wrong that one should be bound by laws made by another. But in obeying laws to which all men have agreed, all men, in reality, govern themselves. The monarch, who is instituted by the legislature to execute its will, ought to be armed with a force sufficient to coerce individuals, but not sufficient to control the majority of the people. He is responsible to the nation, and subject to the law; and the nation that appoints him, and assigns him his duties, has to see that he obeys the Constitution, and has to dismiss him if he breaks it. The rights of citizens are independent of the faith they profess; and no man may be punished for his religion." This writer, who saw in some respects farther than Locke or Montesquieu, who, in regard to the sovereignty of the nation, representative government, the superiority of the legislature over the executive, and the liberty of conscience, had so firm a grasp of the principles that were to sway the modern world, lived in the reign of Edward II, five hundred and fifty years ago.

It is significant that these two writers should agree on so many of the fundamental points which have been, ever since, the topic of controversy; for they belonged to hostile schools, and one of them would have thought the other worthy of death. St. Thomas would have made the papacy control all Christian governments. Marsilius would have had the clergy submit to the law of the land; and would have put them under restrictions both as to property and numbers. As the great debate went on, many things gradually made themselves clear, and grew into settled convictions. For these were not only the thoughts of prophetic minds that surpassed the level of contemporaries; there was some prospect that they would master the practical world. The ancient reign of the barons was seriously threatened. The opening of the East by the Crusades had imparted a great stimulus to industry. A stream set in from the country to the towns, and there was no room for the government of towns in the feudal machinery. When men found a way of earning a livelihood without depending for it on the good will of the class that owned the land, the landowner lost much of his importance, and it began to pass to the possessors of moveable wealth. The townspeople not only made themselves free from the control of prelates and barons, but endeavoured to obtain for their own class and interest the command of the State.

The fourteenth century was filled with the tumult of this struggle between democracy and chivalry. The Italian towns, foremost in intelligence and civilisation, led the way with democratic constitutions of an ideal and generally an impracticable type. The Swiss cast off the yoke of Austria. Two long chains of free cities arose, along the valley of the Rhine, and across the heart of Germany. The citizens of Paris got possession of the king, reformed the State, and began their tremendous career of experiments to govern France. But the most healthy and vigorous growth of municipal liberties was in Belgium, of all countries on the Continent, that which has been from immemorial ages the most stubborn in its fidelity to the principle of self-government. So vast were the resources concentrated in the Flemish towns, so widespread was the movement of democracy, that it was long doubtful whether the new interest would not prevail, and whether the ascendancy of the military aristocracy would not pass over to the wealth and intelligence of the men that lived by trade. But Rienzi, Marcel, Artevelde, and the other champions of the unripe democracy of those days, lived and died in vain. The upheaval of the middle class had disclosed the need, the passions, the aspirations of the suffering poor below; ferocious insurrections in France and England caused a reaction that retarded for centuries the readjustment of power, and the red spectre of social revolution arose in the track of democracy. The armed citizens of Ghent were crushed by the French chivalry; and monarchy alone reaped the fruit of the change that was going on in the position of classes, and stirred the minds of men.

Looking back over the space of a thousand years, which we call the Middle Ages, to get an estimate of the work they had done, if not towards perfection in their institutions, at least towards attaining the knowledge of political truth, this is what we find: Representative government, which was unknown to the ancients, was almost universal. The methods of election were crude; but the principle that no tax was lawful that was not granted by the class that paid it — that is, that taxation was inseparable from representation — was recognised, not as the privilege of certain countries, but as the right of all. Not a prince in the world, said Philip de Commines, can levy a penny without the consent of the people. Slavery was almost everywhere extinct; and absolute power was deemed more intolerable and more criminal than slavery. The right of insurrection was not only admitted but defined, as a duty sanctioned by religion. Even the principles of the Habeas Corpus Act, and the method of the income tax, were already known. The issue of ancient politics was an absolute state planted on slavery. The political produce of the Middle Ages was a system of states in which authority was restricted by the representation of powerful classes, by privileged associations, and by the acknowledgment of duties superior to those which are imposed by man.

As regards the realisation in practice of what was seen to be good, there was almost everything to do. But the great problems of principle had been solved, and we come to the question, How did the sixteenth century husband the treasure which the Middle Ages had stored up? The most visible sign of the times was the decline of the religious influence that had reigned so long. Sixty years passed after the invention of printing, and thirty thousand books had issued from European presses, before anybody undertook to print the Greek Testament. In the days when every State made the unity of faith its first care, it came to be thought that the rights of men, and the duties of neighbours and of rulers towards them, varied according to their religion; and society did not acknowledge the same obligations to a Turk or a Jew, a pagan or a heretic, or a devil worshipper, as to an orthodox Christian. As the ascendency of religion grew weaker, this privilege of treating its enemies on exceptional principles was claimed by the State for its own benefit; and the idea that the ends of government justify the means employed was worked into system by Machiavelli. He was an acute politician, sincerely anxious that the obstacles to the intelligent government of Italy should be swept away. It appeared to him that the most vexatious obstacle to intellect is conscience, and that the vigorous use of statecraft necessary for the success of difficult schemes would never be made if governments allowed themselves to be hampered by the precepts of the copy-book.

His audacious doctrine was avowed in the succeeding age by men whose personal character stood high. They saw that in critical times good men have seldom strength for their goodness, and yield to those who have grasped the meaning of the maxim that you cannot make an omelette if you are afraid to break the eggs. They saw that public morality differs from private, because no government can turn the other cheek, or can admit that mercy is better than justice. And they could not define the difference or draw the limits of exception; or tell what other standard for a nation's acts there is than the judgment which Heaven pronounces in this world by success.

Machiavelli's teaching would hardly have stood the test of parliamentary government, for public discussion demands at least the profession of good faith. But it gave an immense impulse to absolutism by silencing the consciences of very religious kings, and made the good and the bad very much alike. Charles V offered 5,000 crowns for the murder of an enemy. Ferdinand I and Ferdinand II, Henry III and Louis XIII each caused his most powerful subject to be treacherously despatched. Elizabeth and Mary Stuart tried to do the same to each other. The way was paved for absolute monarchy to triumph over the spirit and institutions of a better age, not by isolated acts of wickedness, but by a studied philosophy of crime and so thorough a perversion of the moral sense that the like of it had not been since the Stoics reformed the morality of paganism.

The clergy, who had in so many ways served the cause of freedom during the prolonged strife against feudalism and slavery, were associated now with the interest of royalty. Attempts had been made to reform the Church on the Constitutional model; they had failed, but they had united the hierarchy and the crown against the system of divided power as against a common enemy. Strong kings were able to bring the spirituality under subjection in France and Spain, in Sicily and in England. The absolute monarchy of France was built up in the two following centuries by twelve political cardinals. The kings of Spain obtained the same effect almost at a single stroke by reviving and appropriating to their own use the tribunal of the Inquisition, which had been growing obsolete, but now served to arm them with terrors which effectually made them despotic. One generation beheld the change all over Europe, from the anarchy of the days of the Roses to the passionate submission, the gratified acquiescence in tyranny that marks the reign of Henry VIII and the kings of his time.

The tide was running fast when the Reformation began at Wittenberg, and it was to be expected that Luther's influence would stem the flood of absolutism. For he was confronted everywhere by the compact alliance of the Church with the State; and a great part of his country was governed by hostile potentates who were prelates of the Court of Rome. He had, indeed, more to fear from temporal than from spiritual foes. The leading German bishops wished that the Protestant demands should be conceded; and the Pope himself vainly urged on the Emperor a conciliatory policy. But Charles V had outlawed Luther, and attempted to waylay him; and the Dukes of Bavaria were active in beheading and burning his disciples, whilst the democracy of the towns generally took his side. But the dread of revolution was the deepest of his political sentiments; and the gloss by which the Guelphic divines had got over the passive obedience of the apostolic age was characteristic of that mediæval method of interpretation which he rejected. He swerved for a moment in his later years; but the substance of his political teaching was eminently conservative, the Lutheran States became the stronghold of rigid immobility, and Lutheran writers constantly condemned the democratic literature that arose in the second age of the Reformation. For the Swiss reformers were bolder than the Germans in mixing up their cause with politics. Zürich and Geneva were Republics, and the spirit of their governments influenced both Zwingli and Calvin.

Zwingli indeed did not shrink from the mediæval doctrine that evil magistrates must be cashiered; but he was killed too early to act either deeply or permanently on the political character of Protestantism. Calvin, although a Republican, judged that the people are unfit to govern themselves, and declared the popular assembly an abuse that ought to be abolished. He desired an aristocracy of the elect, armed with the means of punishing not only crime but vice and error. For he thought that the severity of the mediæval laws was insufficient for the need of the times; and he favoured the most irresistible weapon which the inquisitorial procedure put into the hand of the Government, the right of subjecting prisoners to intolerable torture, not because they were guilty, but because their guilt could not be proved. His teaching, though not calculated to promote popular institutions, was so adverse to the authority of the surrounding monarchs, that he softened down the expression of his political views in the French edition of his *Institutes*.

The direct political influence of the Reformation effected less than has been supposed. Most States were strong enough to control it. Some, by intense exertion, shut out the pouring flood. Others, with consummate skill, diverted it to their own uses. The Polish government alone at that time left it to its course. Scotland was the only kingdom in which the Reformation triumphed over the resistance of the State; and Ireland was the only instance where it failed, in spite of government support. But in almost every other case, both the princes that spread their canvas to the gale and those that faced it, employed the zeal, the alarm, the passions it aroused as instruments for the increase of power. Nations eagerly invested their rulers with every prerogative needed to preserve their faith, and all the care to keep Church and State asunder, and to prevent the confusion of their powers, which had been the work of ages, was renounced in the intensity of the crisis. Atrocious deeds were done, in which religious passion was often the instrument, but policy was the motive.

Fanaticism displays itself in the masses, but the masses were rarely fanaticised, and the crimes ascribed to it were commonly due to the calculations of dispassionate politicians. When the King of France undertook to kill all the Protestants, he was obliged to do it by his own agents. It was nowhere the spontaneous act of the population, and in many towns and in entire provinces the magistrates refused to obey. The motive of the Court was so far from mere fanaticism that the Queen immediately challenged Elizabeth to do the like to the English Catholics. Francis I and Henry II sent nearly a hundred Huguenots to the stake, but they were cordial and assiduous promoters of the Protestant religion in Germany. Sir Nicholas Bacon was one of the ministers who suppressed the mass in England. Yet when the Huguenot refugees came over he liked them so little that he reminded Parliament of the summary way in which Henry V at Agincourt dealt with the Frenchmen who fell into his hands. John Knox thought that every Catholic in Scotland ought to be put to death, and no man ever had disciples of a sterner or more relentless temper. But his counsel was not followed.

All through the religious conflict policy kept the upper hand. When the last of the Reformers died, religion, instead of emancipating the nations, had become an excuse for the criminal art of despots. Calvin preached and Bellarmine lectured, but Machiavelli reigned. Before the close of the century three events occurred which mark the beginning of a momentous change. The massacre of St. Bartholomew convinced the bulk of Calvinists of the lawfulness of rebellion against tyrants, and they became advocates of that doctrine in which the Bishop of Winchester had led the way,[1] and which Knox and Buchanan had received, through their master at Paris, straight from the mediæval schools. Adopted out of aversion to the King of France, it was soon put in practice against the King of Spain. The revolted Netherlands, by a

---
[1] Poynet, in his *Treatise on Political Power*.

solemn Act, deposed Philip II, and made themselves independent under the Prince of Orange, who had been, and continued to be, styled his Lieutenant. Their example was important, not only because subjects of one religion deposed a monarch of another, for that had been seen in Scotland, but because, moreover, it put a republic in the place of a monarchy, and forced the public law of Europe to recognise the accomplished revolution. At the same time, the French Catholics, rising against Henry III, who was the most contemptible of tyrants, and against his heir, Henry of Navarre, who, as a Protestant, repelled the majority of the nation, fought for the same principles with sword and pen.

Many shelves might be filled with the books which came out in their defence during half a century, and they include the most comprehensive treatises on laws ever written. Nearly all are vitiated by the defect which disfigured political literature in the Middle Ages. That literature, as I have tried to show, is extremely remarkable, and its services in aiding human progress are very great. But from the death of St. Bernard until the appearance of Sir Thomas More's *Utopia*, there was hardly a writer who did not make his politics subservient to the interest of either Pope or King. And those who came after the Reformation were always thinking of laws as they might affect Catholics or Protestants. Knox thundered against what he called *the Monstrous Regiment of Women*, because the Queen went to mass, and Mariana praised the assassin of Henry III because the King was in league with Huguenots. For the belief that it is right to murder tyrants, first taught among Christians, I believe, by John of Salisbury, the most distinguished English writer of the twelfth century, and confirmed by Roger Bacon, the most celebrated Englishman of the thirteenth, had acquired this time a fatal significance. Nobody sincerely thought of politics as a law for the just and the unjust, or tried to find out a set of principles that should hold good alike under all changes of religion. Hooker's *Ecclesiastical Polity* stands almost alone among the works I am speaking of, and is still read with admiration by every thoughtful man as the earliest and one of the finest prose classics in our language. But though few of the others have survived, they contributed to hand down masculine notions of limited authority and conditional obedience from the epoch of theory to generations of free men. Even the coarse violence of Buchanan and Boucher was a link in the chain of tradition that connects the Hildebrandine controversy with the Long Parliament, and St. Thomas with Edmund Burke.

That men should understand that governments do not exist by divine right, and that arbitrary government is the violation of divine right, was no doubt the medicine suited to the malady under which Europe languished. But although the knowledge of this truth might become an element of salutary destruction, it could give little aid to progress and reform. Resistance to tyranny implied no faculty of constructing a legal government in its place. Tyburn tree may be a useful thing, but it is better still that the offender should live for repentance and reformation. The principles which discriminate in politics between good and evil, and make States worthy to last, were not yet found.

The French philosopher Charron was one of the men least demoralised by party spirit, and least blinded by zeal for a cause. In a passage almost literally taken from St. Thomas, he describes our subordination under a law of nature, to which all legislation must conform; and he ascertains it not by the light of revealed religion, but by the voice of universal reason, through which God enlightens the consciences of men. Upon this foundation Grotius drew the lines of real political science. In gathering the materials of international law, he had to go beyond national treaties and denominational interests for a principle embracing all mankind. The principles of law must stand, he said, even if we suppose that there is no God. By these inaccurate terms he meant that they must be found independently of revelation. From that time it became possible to make politics a matter of principle and of conscience, so that men and nations differing in all other things could live in peace together, under the sanctions of a common law. Grotius himself used his discovery to little purpose, as he deprived it of immediate effect by admitting that the right to reign may be enjoyed as a freehold, subject to no conditions.

When Cumberland and Pufendorf unfolded the true significance of his doctrine, every settled authority, every triumphant interest recoiled aghast. None were willing to surrender advantages won by force or skill, because they might be in contradiction, not with the Ten Commandments, but with an unknown code, which Grotius himself had not attempted to draw up, and touching which no two philosophers agreed. It was manifest that all persons who had learned that political science is an affair of conscience rather than of might or expediency, must regard their adversaries as men without principle, that the controversy between them would perpetually involve morality, and could not be governed by the plea of good intentions, which softens down the asperities of religious strife. Nearly all the greatest men of the seventeenth century repudiated the innovation. In the eighteenth, the two ideas of Grotius, that there are certain political truths, by which every State and every interest must stand or fall, and that society is knit together by a series of real and hypothetical contracts, became, in other hands, the lever that displaced the world. When, by what seemed the operation of an irresistible and constant law, royalty had prevailed over all enemies and all competitors, it became a religion. Its ancient rivals, the baron and the prelate, figured as supporters by its side. Year after year, the assemblies that represented the self-government of provinces and of privileged classes, all over the Continent, met for the last time and passed away, to the satisfaction of the people, who had learned to venerate the throne as the constructor of their unity, the promoter of prosperity and power, the defender of orthodoxy, and the employer of talent.

The Bourbons, who had snatched the crown from a rebellious democracy, the Stuarts, who had come in as usurpers, set up the doctrine that States are formed by the valour, the policy, and the appropriate marriages of the royal family; that the king is consequently anterior to the people, that he is its maker rather than its handiwork, and reigns independently of consent. Theology followed up divine right with passive obedience. In the golden age of religious science, Archbishop Ussher, the most learned of Anglican prelates, and Bossuet, the ablest of the French, declared that resistance to kings is a crime and that they may lawfully employ compulsion against the faith of their subjects. The philosophers heartily supported the divines. Bacon fixed his hope of all human progress on the strong hand of kings. Descartes advised them to crush all those who might be able to resist their power. Hobbes taught that authority is always in the right. Pascal considered it absurd to reform laws, or to set up an ideal justice against actual force. Even Spinoza, who was a Republican and a Jew, assigned to the State the absolute control of religion.

Monarchy exerted a charm over the imagination, so unlike the unceremonious spirit of the Middle Ages, that, on learning the execution of Charles I, men died of the shock; and the same thing occurred at the death of Louis XVI and of the Duke of Enghein. The classic land of absolute monarchy was France. Richelieu held that it would be impossible to keep the people down if they were suffered to be well off. The Chancellor affirmed that France could not be governed without the right of arbitrary arrest and exile; and that in case of danger to the State it may be well that a hundred innocent men should perish. The Minister of Finance called it sedition to demand that the Crown should keep faith. One who lived on intimate terms with Louis XIV says that even the slightest disobedience to the royal will is a crime to be punished with death. Louis employed these precepts to their fullest extent. He candidly avows that kings are no more bound by the terms of a treaty than by the words of a compliment; and that there is nothing in the possession of their subjects which they may not lawfully take from them. In obedience to this principle, when Marshal Vauban, appalled by the misery of the people, proposed that all existing imposts should be repealed for a single tax that would be less onerous, the King took his advice, but retained all the old taxes whilst he imposed the new. With half the present population, he maintained an army of 450,000 men; nearly twice as large as that which the late Emperor Napoleon assembled to attack Germany. Meanwhile the people starved on grass. France, said Fénelon, is one enormous hospital. French historians believe that in a single generation six millions of people died of want. It would be easy to find tyrants more violent, more malignant, more odious than Louis XIV, but there was not one who ever used his power to inflict greater suffering or greater wrong; and the admiration with which he inspired the most illustrious men of his time denotes the lowest depth to which the turpitude of absolutism has ever degraded the conscience of Europe.

The Republics of that day were, for the most part, so governed as to reconcile men with the less opprobrious vices of monarchy. Poland was a State made up of centrifugal forces. What the nobles called liberty was the right of each of them to veto the acts of the Diet, and to persecute the peasants on his estates — rights which they refused to surrender up to the time of the partition, and thus verified the warning of a preacher spoken long ago: "You will perish, not by invasion or war, but by your infernal liberties." Venice suffered from the opposite evil of excessive concentration. It was the most sagacious of governments, and would rarely have made mistakes if it had not imputed to others motives as wise as its own, and had taken account of passions and follies of which it had little cognisance. But the supreme power of the nobility had passed to a committee, from the committee to a Council of Ten, from the Ten to three Inquisitors of State; and in this intensely centralised form it became, about the year 1600, a frightful despotism. I have shown you how Machiavelli supplied the immoral theory needful for the consummation of royal absolutism; the absolute oligarchy of Venice required the same assurance against the revolt of conscience. It was provided by a writer as able as Machiavelli, who analysed the wants and resources of aristocracy, and made known that its best security is poison. As late as a century ago, Venetian senators of honourable and even religious lives employed assassins for the public good with no more compunction than Philip II or Charles IX.

The Swiss Cantons, especially Geneva, profoundly influenced opinion in the days preceding the French Revolution, but they had had no part in the earlier movement to inaugurate the reign of law. That honour belongs to the Netherlands alone among the Commonwealths. They earned it, not by their form of government, which was defective and precarious, for the Orange party perpetually plotted against it, and slew the two most eminent of the Republican statesmen, and William III himself intrigued for English aid to set the crown upon his head; but by the freedom of the press, which made Holland the vantage-ground from which, in the darkest hour of oppression, the victims of the oppressors obtained the ear of Europe.

The ordinance of Louis XIV, that every French Protestant should immediately renounce his religion, went out in the year in which James II became king. The Protestant refugees did what their ancestors had done a century before. They asserted the deposing power of subjects over rulers who had broken the original contract between them, and all the Powers, excepting France, countenanced their argument, and sent forth William of Orange on that expedition which was the faint dawn of a brighter day.

It is to this unexampled combination of things on the Continent, more than to her own energy, that England owes her deliverance. The efforts made by the Scots, by the Irish, and at last by the Long Parliament to get rid of the misrule of the Stuarts had been foiled, not by the resistance of Monarchy, but by the helplessness of the Republic. State and Church were swept away; new institutions were raised up under the ablest ruler that had ever sprung from a revolution; and England, seething with the toil of political thought, had produced at least two writers who in many directions saw as far and as clearly as we do now. But Cromwell's Constitution was rolled up like a scroll; Harrington and Lilburne were laughed at for a time and forgotten; the country confessed the failure of its striving, disavowed its aims, and flung itself with enthusiasm, and without any effective stipulations, at the feet of a worthless king.

If the people of England had accomplished no more than this to relieve mankind from the pervading pressure of unlimited monarchy, they would have done more harm than good. By the fanatical treachery with which, violating the Parliament and the law, they contrived the death of King Charles, by the ribaldry of the Latin pamphlet with which Milton justified the act before the world, by persuading the world that the Republicans were hostile alike to liberty and to authority, and did not believe in themselves, they gave strength and reason to the current of Royalism, which, at the Restoration, overwhelmed their work. If there had been nothing to make up for this defect of certainty and of constancy in politics England would have gone the way of other nations.

At that time there was some truth in the old joke which describes the English dislike of speculation by saying that all our philosophy consists of a short catechism in two questions: "What is mind? No matter. What is matter? Never mind." The only accepted appeal was to tradition. Patriots were in the habit of saying that they took their stand upon the ancient ways, and would not have the laws of England changed. To enforce their argument they invented a story that the constitution had come from Troy, and that the Romans had allowed it to subsist untouched. Such fables did not avail against Strafford; and the oracle of precedent sometimes gave responses adverse to the popular cause. In the sovereign question of religion, this was decisive, for the practice of the sixteenth century, as well as of the fifteenth, testified in favour of intolerance. By royal command, the nation had passed four times in one generation from one faith to another, with a facility that made a fatal impression on Laud. In a country that had proscribed every religion in turn, and had submitted to such a variety of penal measures against Lollard and Arian, against Augsburg and Rome, it seemed there could be no danger in cropping the ears of a Puritan.

But an age of stronger conviction had arrived; and men

resolved to abandon the ancient ways that led to the scaffold and the rack, and to make the wisdom of their ancestors and the statutes of the land bow before an unwritten law. Religious liberty had been the dream of great Christian writers in the age of Constantine and Valentinian, a dream never wholly realised in the Empire, and rudely dispelled when the barbarians found that it exceeded the resources of their art to govern civilised populations of another religion, and unity of worship was imposed by laws of blood and by theories more cruel than the laws. But from St. Athanasius and St. Ambrose down to Erasmus and More, each age heard the protest of earnest men in behalf of the liberty of conscience, and the peaceful days before the Reformation were full of promise that it would prevail.

In the commotion that followed, men were glad to get tolerated themselves by way of privilege and compromise, and willingly renounced the wider application of the principle. Socinus was the first who, on the ground that Church and State ought to be separated, required universal toleration. But Socinus disarmed his own theory, for he was a strict advocate of passive obedience.

The idea that religious liberty is the generating principle of civil, and that civil liberty is the necessary condition of religious, was a discovery reserved for the seventeenth century. Many years before the names of Milton and Taylor, of Baxter and Locke were made illustrious by their partial condemnation of intolerance, there were men among the Independent congregations who grasped with vigour and sincerity the principle that it is only by abridging the authority of States that the liberty of Churches can be assured. That great political idea, sanctifying freedom and consecrating it to God, teaching men to treasure the liberties of others as their own, and to defend them for the love of justice and charity more than as a claim of right, has been the soul of what is great and good in the progress of the last two hundred years. The cause of religion, even under the unregenerate influence of worldly passion, had as much to do as any clear notions of policy in making this country the foremost of the free. It had been the deepest current in the movement of 1641, and it remained the strongest motive that survived the reaction of 1660.

The greatest writers of the Whig party, Burke and Macaulay, constantly represented the statesmen of the Revolution as the legitimate ancestors of modern liberty. It is humiliating to trace a political lineage to Algernon Sidney, who was the paid agent of the French king; to Lord Russell, who opposed religious toleration at least as much as absolute monarchy; to Shaftesbury, who dipped his hands in the innocent blood shed by the perjury of Titus Oates; to Halifax, who insisted that the plot must be supported even if untrue; to Marlborough, who sent his comrades to perish on an expedition which he had betrayed to the French; to Locke, whose notion of liberty involves nothing more spiritual than the security of property, and is consistent with slavery and persecution; or even to Addison, who conceived that the right of voting taxes belonged to no country but his own. Defoe affirms that from the time of Charles II to that of George I he never knew a politician who truly held the faith of either party; and the perversity of the statesmen who led the assault against the later Stuarts threw back the cause of progress for a century.

When the purport of the secret treaty became suspected by which Louis XIV pledged himself to support Charles II with an army for the destruction of Parliament, if Charles would overthrow the Anglican Church, it was found necessary to make concession to the popular alarm. It was proposed that whenever James should succeed, great part of the royal prerogative and patronage should be transferred to Parliament. At the same time, the disabilities of Nonconformists and Catholics would have been removed. If the Limitation Bill, which Halifax supported with signal ability, had passed, the monarchical constitution would have advanced, in the seventeenth century, farther than it was destined to do until the second quarter of the nineteenth. But the enemies of James, guided by the Prince of Orange, preferred a Protestant king who should be nearly absolute, to a constitutional king who should be a Catholic. The scheme failed. James succeeded to a power which, in more cautious hands, would have been practically uncontrolled, and the storm that cast him down gathered beyond the sea.

By arresting the preponderance of France, the Revolution of 1688 struck the first real blow at Continental despotism. At home it relieved dissent, purified justice, developed the national energies and resources, and ultimately, by the Act of Settlement, placed the crown in the gift of the people. But it neither introduced nor determined any important principle, and, that both parties might be able to work together, it left untouched the fundamental question between Whig and Tory. For the divine right of kings it established, in the words of Defoe, the divine right of freeholders; and their domination extended for seventy years, under the authority of John Locke, the philosopher of government by the gentry. Even Hume did not enlarge the bounds of his ideas; and his narrow materialistic belief in the connection between liberty and property captivated even the bolder mind of Fox.

By his idea that the powers of government ought to be divided according to their nature, and not according to the division of classes, which Montesquieu took up and developed with consummate talent, Locke is the originator of the long reign of English institutions in foreign lands. And his doctrine of resistance, or, as he finally termed it, the appeal to Heaven, ruled the judgment of Chatham at a moment of solemn transition in the history of the world. Our parliamentary system, managed by the great revolution families, was a contrivance by which electors were compelled, and legislators were induced to vote against their convictions; and the intimidation of the constituencies was rewarded by the corruption of their representatives. About the year 1770 things had been brought back, by indirect ways, nearly to the condition which the Revolution had been designed to remedy for ever. Europe seemed incapable of becoming the home of free States. It was from America that the plain ideas that men ought to mind their own business, and that the nation is responsible to Heaven for the acts of the State, — ideas long locked in the breast of solitary thinkers, and hidden among Latin folios, — burst forth like a conqueror upon the world they were destined to transform, under the title of the Rights of Man. Whether the British legislature had a constitutional right to tax a subject colony was hard to say, by the letter of the law. The general presumption was immense on the side of authority; and the world believed that the will of the constituted ruler ought to be supreme, and not the will of the subject people. Very few bold writers went so far as to say that lawful power may be resisted in cases of extreme necessity. But the colonisers of America, who had gone forth not in search of gain, but to escape from laws under which other Englishmen were content to live, were so sensitive even to appearances that the Blue Laws of Connecticut forbade men to walk to church within ten feet of their wives. And the proposed tax, of only £12,000 a year, might have been easily borne. But the reasons why Edward I and his Council were not allowed to tax England were reasons why George III and his Parliament should not tax America. The dispute involved a principle, namely, the right of controlling government. Furthermore, it involved the conclusion that the Parliament brought together by a derisive election had no just right over the unrepresented nation, and it called on the people of England to take back its power. Our best statesmen saw that whatever might be the law, the rights of the nation were at stake. Chatham, in speeches better remembered than any that have been delivered in Parliament, exhorted America to be firm. Lord Camden, the late Chancellor, said: "Taxation and representation are inseparably united. God hath joined them. No British Parliament can separate them."

From the elements of that crisis Burke built up the noblest political philosophy in the world. "I do not know the method," said he, "of drawing up an indictment against a whole people. The natural rights of mankind are indeed sacred things, and if any public measure is proved mischievously to affect them, the objection ought to be fatal to that measure, even if no charter at all could be set up against it. Only a sovereign reason, paramount to all forms of legislation and administration, should dictate." In this way, just a hundred years ago, the opportune reticence, the politic hesitancy of European statesmanship, was at last broken down; and the principle gained ground, that a nation can never abandon its fate to an authority it cannot control. The Americans placed it at the foundation of their new government. They did more; for having subjected all civil authorities to the popular will, they surrounded the popular will with restrictions that the British legislature would not endure.

During the revolution in France the example of England, which had been held up so long, could not for a moment compete with the influence of a country whose institutions were so wisely framed to protect freedom even against the perils of democracy. When Louis Philippe became king, he assured the old Republican, Lafayette, that what he had seen in the United States had convinced him that no government can be so good as a Republic. There was a time in the Presidency of Monroe, about fifty-five years ago, which men still speak of as "the era of good feeling," when most of the incongruities that had come down from the Stuarts had been reformed, and the motives of later divisions were yet inactive. The causes of old-world trouble,—popular ignorance, pauperism, the glaring contrast between rich and poor, religious strife, public debts, standing armies and war, — were almost unknown. No other age or country had solved so successfully the problems that attend the growth of free societies, and time was to bring no further progress.

But I have reached the end of my time, and have hardly come to the beginning of my task. In the ages of which I have spoken, the history of freedom was the history of the thing that was not. But since the Declaration of Independence, or, to speak more justly, since the Spaniards, deprived of their king, made a new government for themselves, the only known forms of liberty, Republics and Constitutional Monarchy, have made their way over the world. It would have been interesting to trace the reaction of America on the

Monarchies that achieved its independence; to see how the sudden rise of political economy suggested the idea of applying the methods of science to the art of government; how Louis XVI, after confessing that despotism was useless, even to make men happy by compulsion, appealed to the nation to do what was beyond his skill, and thereby resigned his sceptre to the middle class, and the intelligent men of France, shuddering at the awful recollections of their own experience, struggled to shut out the past, that they might deliver their children from the prince of the world and rescue the living from the clutch of the dead, until the finest opportunity ever given to the world was thrown away, because the passion for equality made vain the hope of freedom.

And I should have wished to show you that the same deliberate rejection of the moral code which smoothed the paths of absolute monarchy and of oligarchy, signalised the advent of the democratic claim to unlimited power, — that one of its leading champions avowed the design of corrupting the moral sense of men, in order to destroy the influence of religion, and a famous apostle of enlightenment and toleration wished that the last king might be strangled with the entrails of the last priest. I would have tried to explain the connection between the doctrine of Adam Smith, that labour is the original source of all wealth, and the conclusion that the producers of wealth virtually compose the nation, by which Siéyès subverted historic France; and to show that Rousseau's definition of the social compact as a voluntary association of equal partners conducted Marat, by short and unavoidable stages, to declare that the poorer classes were absolved, by the law of self-preservation, from the conditions of a contract which awarded to them misery and death; that they were at war with society, and had a right to all they could get by exterminating the rich, and that their inflexible theory of equality, the chief legacy of the Revolution, together with the avowed inadequacy of economic science to grapple with problems of the poor, revived the idea of renovating society on the principle of self-sacrifice, which had been the generous aspiration of the Essenes and the early Christians,

THE HISTORY OF FREEDOM IN CHRISTIANITY

of Fathers and Canonists and Friars, of Erasmus, the most celebrated precursor of the Reformation, of Sir Thomas More, its most illustrious victim, and of Fénelon, the most popular of bishops, but which, during the forty years of its revival, has been associated with envy and hatred and bloodshed, and is now the most dangerous enemy lurking in our path.

Last, and most of all, having told so much of the unwisdom of our ancestors, having exposed the sterility of the convulsion that burned what they adored, and made the sins of the Republic mount up as high as those of the monarchy, having shown that Legitimacy, which repudiated the Revolution, and Imperialism, which crowned it, were but disguises of the same element of violence and wrong, I should have wished, in order that my address might not break off without a meaning or a moral, to relate by whom, and in what connection, the true law of the formation of free States was recognised, and how that discovery, closely akin to those which, under the names of development, evolution, and continuity, have given a new and deeper method to other sciences, solved the ancient problem between stability and change, and determined the authority of tradition on the progress of thought; how that theory, which Sir James Mackintosh expressed by saying that constitutions are not made, but grow; the theory that custom and the national qualities of the governed, and not the will of the government, are the makers of the law; and therefore that the nation, which is the source of its own organic institutions, should be charged with the perpetual custody of their integrity, and with the duty of bringing the form into harmony with the spirit, was made, by the singular co-operation of the purest conservative intellect with red-handed revolution, of Niebuhr with Mazzini, to yield the idea of nationality, which, far more than the idea of liberty, has governed the movement of the present age.

I do not like to conclude without inviting attention to the impressive fact that so much of the hard fighting, the thinking, the enduring that has contributed to the deliverance of man from the power of man, has been the work of our countrymen, and of their descendants in other lands. We have had to contend, as much as any people, against monarchs of strong will and of resources secured by their foreign possession, against men of rare capacity, against whole dynasties of born tyrants. And yet that proud prerogative stands out on the background of our history. Within a generation of the Conquest, the Normans were compelled to recognise, in some grudging measure, the claims of the English people. When the struggle between Church and State extended to England, our Churchmen learned to associate themselves with the popular cause; and, with few exceptions, neither the hierarchical spirit of the foreign divines, nor the monarchical bias peculiar to the French, characterised the writers of the English school. The Civil Law, transmitted from the degenerate Empire to be the common prop of absolute power, was excluded from England. The Canon Law was restrained, and this country never admitted the Inquisition, nor fully accepted the use of torture which invested Continental royalty with so many terrors. At the end of the Middle Ages foreign writers acknowledged our superiority, and pointed to these causes. After that, our gentry maintained the means of local self-government such as no other country possessed. Divisions in religion forced toleration. The confusion of the common law taught the people that their best safeguard was the independence and the integrity of the judges.

All these explanations lie on the surface, and are as visible as the protecting ocean; but they can only be successive effects of a constant cause which must lie in the same native qualities of perseverance, moderation, individuality, and the manly sense of duty, which give to the English race its supremacy in the stern art of labour, which has enabled it to thrive as no other can on inhospitable shores, and which (although no great people has less of the bloodthirsty craving for glory and an army of 50,000 English soldiers has never been seen in battle) caused Napoleon to exclaim, as he rode away from Waterloo, "It has always been the same since Crécy."

Therefore, if there is reason for pride in the past, there is more for hope in the time to come. Our advantages increase, while other nations fear their neighbours or covet their neighbours' goods. Anomalies and defects there are, fewer and less intolerable, if not less flagrant than of old.

But I have fixed my eyes on the spaces that Heaven's light illuminates, that I may not lay too heavy a strain on the indulgence with which you have accompanied me over the dreary and heart-breaking course by which men have passed to freedom; and because the light that has guided us is still unquenched, and the causes that have carried us so far in the van of free nations have not spent their power; because the story of the future is written in the past, and that which hath been is the same thing that shall be.

Chapter IV

THE PROTESTANT THEORY OF PERSECUTION

The manner in which Religion influences State policy is more easily ascertained in the case of Protestantism than in that of the Catholic Church: for whilst the expression of Catholic doctrines is authoritative and unvarying, the great social problems did not all arise at once, and have at various times received different solutions. The reformers failed to construct a complete and harmonious code of doctrine; but

---

Note: This essay first appeared in *The Rambler*, New Series, I (July, 1862), 1-25; reprinted in *The History of Freedom and Other Essays* (London, Macmillan Co., 1907), pp. 150-87.

There has been some controversy about the authorship of this article. In a footnote to a letter written by Acton to Simpson, the editor of *The Rambler*, Gasquet, interprets the words, "your article," as referring to "Protestant Theory of Persecution," thus attributing the article to Simpson. The editors of *History of Freedom*, Figgis and Laurence, declare in their preface that this was an error and they include the article in their edition of Acton's writings. The late G. G. Coulton revived the dispute in the *English Historical Review* of July, 1931. According to Coulton, Laurence and Figgis admitted the essay on the testimony of Wetherell, who had been associated with the journal but whose memory was not entirely trustworthy. Because the article does not impress him as "Actonian" (in style and content), Coulton agreed with Gasquet and assigned it to Simpson. The author of the introduction to the present volume maintains that the article, both in style and content, is entirely typical of the young Acton, and that many of its ideas, in embryonic form, may be found in his early journals and notebooks. Even if it could be shown, however, that the article was not actually composed by Acton, it is certain that Acton agreed with its sentiments, particularly if it is assumed that the author was Simpson. Acton and Simpson worked in close collaboration, so that it is sometimes difficult to assign exact responsibility for each contribution. (For example, the theme, development of the argument, and most of the illustrations for "Philosopher's Stone" (*Rambler*, July 1860), originated with Acton, although the article in its final form was composed by Simpson.)

they were compelled to supplement the new theology by a body of new rules for the guidance of their followers in those innumerable questions with regard to which the practice of the Church had grown out of the experience of ages. And although the dogmatic system of Protestantism was not completed in their time, yet the Protestant spirit animated them in greater purity and force than it did any later generation. Now, when a religion is applied to the social and political sphere, its general spirit must be considered, rather than its particular precepts. So that in studying the points of this application in the case of Protestantism, we may consult the writings of the reformers with greater confidence than we could do for an exposition of Protestant theology; and accept them as a greater authority, because they agree more entirely among themselves. We can be more sure that we have the true Protestant opinion in a political or social question on which all the reformers are agreed, than in a theological question on which they differ; for the concurrent opinion must be founded on an element common to all, and therefore essential. If it should further appear that this opinion was injurious to their actual interests, and maintained at a sacrifice to themselves, we should then have an additional security for its necessary connection with their fundamental views.

The most important example of this law is the Protestant theory of toleration. The views of the reformers on religious liberty are not fragmentary, accidental opinions, unconnected with their doctrines, or suggested by the circumstances amidst which they lived; but the product of their theological system, and of their ideas of political and ecclesiastical government. Civil and religious liberty are so commonly associated in people's mouths, and are so rare in fact, that their definition is evidently as little understood as the principle of their connection. The point at which they unite, the common root from which they derive their sustenance, is the right of self-government. The modern theory, which has swept away every authority except that of the State, and has made the sovereign power irresistible by multiplying those who share it, is the enemy of that common freedom in which religious freedom is included. It condemns, as a State within the State, every inner group and community, class or corporation, administering its own affairs; and, by proclaiming the abolition of privileges, it emancipates the subjects of every such authority in order to transfer them exclusively to its own. It recognises liberty only in the individual, because it is only in the individual that liberty can be separated from authority, and the right of conditional obedience deprived of the security of a limited command. Under its sway, therefore, every man may profess his own religion more or less freely; but his religion is not free to administer its own laws. In other words, religious profession is free, but Church government is controlled. And where ecclesiastical authority is restricted, religious liberty is virtually denied.

For religious liberty is not the negative right of being without any particular religion, just as self-government is not anarchy. It is the right of religious communities to the practice of their own duties, the enjoyment of their own constitution, and the protection of the law, which equally secures to all the possession of their own independence. Far from implying a general toleration, it is best secured by a limited one. In an indifferent State, that is, in a State without any definite religious character (if such a thing is conceivable), no ecclesiastical authority could exist. A hierarchical organisation would not be tolerated by the sects that have none, or by the enemies of all definite religion; for it would be in contradiction to the prevailing theory of atomic freedom. Nor can a religion be free when it is alone, unless it makes the State subject to it. For governments restrict the liberty of the favoured Church, by way of remunerating themselves for their service in preserving her unity. The most violent and prolonged conflicts for religious freedom occurred in the Middle Ages between a Church which was not threatened by rivals and States which were most attentive to preserve her exclusive predominance. Frederic II, the most tyrannical oppressor of the Church among the German emperors, was the author of those sanguinary laws against heresy which prevailed so long in many parts of Europe. The Inquisition,

THE PROTESTANT THEORY OF PERSECUTION 91

which upheld the religious unity of the Spanish nation, imposed the severest restrictions on the Spanish Church; and in England conformity has been most rigorously exacted by those sovereigns who have most completely tyrannised over the Established Church. Religious liberty, therefore, is possible only where the coexistence of different religions is admitted, with an equal right to govern themselves according to their own several principles. Tolerance of error is requisite for freedom; but freedom will be most complete where there is no actual diversity to be resisted, and no theoretical unity to be maintained, but where unity exists as the triumph of truth, not of force, through the victory of the Church, not through the enactment of the State.

This freedom is attainable only in communities where rights are sacred, and where law is supreme. If the first duty is held to be obedience to authority and the preservation of order, as in the case of aristocracies and monarchies of the patriarchal type, there is no safety for the liberties either of individuals or of religion. Where the highest consideration is the public good and the popular will, as in democracies, and in constitutional monarchies after the French pattern, majority takes the place of authority; an irresistible power is substituted for an idolatrous principle, and all private rights are equally insecure. The true theory of freedom excludes all absolute power and arbitrary action, and requires that a tyrannical or revolutionary government shall be coerced by the people; but it teaches that insurrection is criminal, except as a corrective of revolution and tyranny. In order to understand the views of the Protestant reformers on toleration, they must be considered with reference to these points.

While the Reformation was an act of individual resistance and not a system, and when the secular powers were engaged in supporting the authority of the Church, the authors of the movement were compelled to claim impunity for their opinions, and they held language regarding the right of governments to interfere with religious belief which resembles that of friends of toleration. Every religious party, however exclusive or servile its theory may be, if it is in contradiction with a system generally accepted and protected by law, must necessarily, at its first appearance, assume the protection of the idea that the conscience is free.[1] Before a new authority can be set up in the place of one that exists, there is an interval when the right of dissent must be proclaimed. At the beginning of Luther's contest with the Holy See there was no rival authority for him to appeal to. No ecclesiastical organism existed, the civil power was not on his side, and not even a definite system had yet been evolved by controversy out of his original doctrine of justification. His first efforts were acts of hostility, his exhortations were entirely aggressive, and his appeal was to the masses. When the prohibition of his New Testament confirmed him in the belief that no favour was to be expected from the princes, he published his book on the civil power, which he judged superior to everything that had been written on government since the days of the Apostles, and in which he asserts that authority is given to the State only against the wicked, and that it cannot coerce the godly. "Princes," he says, "are not to be obeyed when they command submission to superstitious errors, but their aid is not to be invoked in support of the Word of God."[2] Heretics must be converted by the Scriptures, and not by fire,

---

[1] "Le vrai principe de Luther est celui-ci: La volonté est esclave par nature. . . . Le libre examen a été pour Luther un moyen et non un principe. Il s'en est servi, et était contraint de s'en servir pour établir son vrai principe, qui était le toute-puissance de la foi de la grâce. . . . C'est ainsi que le libre examen s'imposa au Protestantisme. L'accessoire devint le principal, et la forme dévora plus ou moins le fond." — Janet, *Histoire de la Philosophie Morale*, II, 38, 39.

[2] "If they prohibit true doctrine, and punish their subjects for receiving the entire sacrament, as Christ ordained it, compel the people to idolatrous practices, with masses for the dead, indulgences, invocation of saints, and the like, in these things they exceed their office, and seek to deprive God of the obedience due to Him. For God requires from us this above all, that we hear His Word, and follow it; but where the Government desires to prevent this, the subjects must know that they are not bound to obey it." — Luther's *Werke*, XIII, 2244. "Non est, mi Spalatine, principum et istius saeculi Pontificum tueri verbum Dei, nec ea gratia ullorum peto praesidium." — Luther's *Briefe*, ed. De Wette, I, 521, Nov. 4, 1520. "I will compel and urge by force no man: for the faith must be voluntary and not compulsory, and must be adopted without violence." — "Sermonen an Carlstadt," *Werke*, XX, 24, 1522.

otherwise the hangman would be the greatest doctor.[3] At the time when this was written Luther was expecting the bull of excommunication and the ban of the empire, and for several years it appeared doubtful whether he would escape the treatment he condemned. He lived in constant fear of assassination, and his friends amused themselves with his terrors. At one time he believed that a Jew had been hired by the Polish bishops to despatch him; that an invisible physician was on his way to Wittenberg to murder him; that the pulpit from which he preached was impregnated with a subtle poison.[4] These alarms dictated his language during those early years. It was not the true expression of his views, which he was not yet strong enough openly to put forth.[5]

The Zwinglian schism, the rise of the Anabaptists, and the Peasants' War altered the aspect of affairs. Luther recognised in them the fruits of his theory of the right of private

---

[3] "Schrift an den christlichen Adel " — *Werke,* X, 574, June, 1520. His proposition, *Haereticos comburi esse contra voluntatem spiritus,* was one of those condemned by Leo X as pestilent, scandalous, and contrary to Christian charity.

[4] "Nihil non tentabunt Romanenses, nec protest satis Huttenus me monere, adeo mihi de veneno timet " — De Wette, I, 487. "Etiam inimici mei quidam miserti per amicos ex Halberstadio fecerunt moneri me· esse quemdam doctorem medicinae, qui arte magica factus pro libito invisibilis, quemdam occidit, mandatum habentem et occidendi Lutheri, venturumque ad futuram Dominicam ostensionis reliquiarum: valde hoc constanter narratur." — De Wette, I, 441. "Est hic apud nos Judaeus Polonus, missus sub pretio 2000 aureorum, ut me veneno perdat, ab amicis per literas mihi proditus Doctor est medicinae, et nihil non audere et facere paratus incredibili astutia et agilitate." — De Wette, II, 616. See also Jarcke, *Studien zur Geschichte der Reformation,* p. 176.

[5] "Multa ego premo et causa principis et universitatis nostrae cohibeo, quae (si alibi essem) evomerem in vastatricem Scripturae et Ecclesiae Romanae. . . . Timeo miser, ne forte non sim dignus pati et occidi pro tali causa· erit ista felicitas meliorum hominum, non tam foedi peccatoris. Dixi tibi semper me paratum esse cedere loco, si qua ego principi ill viderer periculo hic vivere. Aliquando certe moriendum est, quanquam jam edita vernacula quadam apologia satis aduler Romanae Ecclesiae et Pontifici, si quid forte id prosit." — De Wette, I, 260, 261. "Ubi periculum est, ne iis protectoribus tutus saevius in Romanenses sim grassaturus, quam si sub principis imperio publicis militarem officiis docendi. . . . Ego vicissim, nisi ignem habere nequeam damnabo, publiceque concremabo jus pontificium totum, id est, lernam illam haeresium; et finem habebit humilitatis exhibitae hactenusque frustratae observantia qua nolo amplius inflari hostes Evangelii." — *Ibid.* pp. 465, 466, July 10, 1520.

judgment and of dissent,[6] and the moment had arrived to secure his Church against the application of the same dissolving principles which had served him to break off from his allegiance to Rome.[7] The excesses of the social war threatened to deprive the movement of the sympathy of the higher classes, especially of the governments; and with the defeat of the peasants the popular phase of the Reformation came to an end on the Continent. "The devil," Luther said, "having failed to put him down by the help of the Pope, was seeking his destruction through the preachers of treason and blood."[8] He instantly turned from the people to the princes;[9] impressed on his party that character of political dependence, and that habit of passive obedience to the State, which it has ever since retained, and gave it a stability it could never otherwise have acquired. In thus taking refuge in the arms of the civil power, purchasing the safety of his doctrine by the sacrifice of its freedom, and conferring on the State, together with the right of control, the duty of imposing it at the point of the sword, Luther in reality reverted to his original teaching.[10] The notion of liberty, whether civil or religious, was hateful to his despotic nature, and contrary to his interpretation of Scripture. As early as 1519 he had said that even the Turk was to be reverenced as an authority.[11] The de-

---

[6] "Out of the Gospel and divine truth come devilish lies; . . . from the blood in our body comes corruption; out of Luther come Muntzer, and rebels, Anabaptists, Sacramentarians, and false brethren." — *Werke,* I, 75.

[7] "Habemus," wrote Erasmus, "fructum tui spiritus . . non agnoscis hosce seditiosos, opinor, sed illi te agnoscunt . . . nec tamen efficis quominus credant homines per tuos libellos . . . pro libertate evangelica, contra tyrannidem humanam, hisce tumultibus fuisse datam occasionem." "And who will deny," adds a Protestant classic, "that the fault was partly owing to them?" — Planck, *Geschichte der protestantischen Kirche,* II, 183.

[8] "Ich sehe das wohl, dass der Teufel, so er mich bisher nicht hat mogen umbringen durch den Pabst, sucht er mich durch die blutdurstigen Mordpropheten und Rottengeisten, so unter euch sind, zu vertilgen und auffressen." — *Werke,* XVI, 77.

[9] Schenkel, *Wesen des Protestantismus,* III, 348, 351; Hagen, *Geist der Reformation,* II, 146, 151; Menzel, *Neuere Geschichte der Deutschen,* I, 115.

[10] See the best of his biographies, Jürgens, *Luther's Leben,* III, 601.

[11] "Quid hoc ad me? qui sciam etiam Turcam honorandum et ferendum potestatis gratia. Quia certus sum non nisi volente Deo ullam potestatem consistere." — De Wette, I, 236.

moralising servitude and lawless oppression which the peasants endured, gave them, in his eyes, no right to relief; and when they rushed to arms, invoking his name as their deliverer he exhorted the nobles to take a merciless revenge.[12] Their crime was, that they were animated by the sectarian spirit, which it was the most important interest of Luther to suppress.

The Protestant authorities throughout Southern Germany were perplexed by their victory over the Anabaptists. It was not easy to show that their political tenets were revolutionary, and the only subversive portion of their doctrine was that they held, with the Catholics, that the State is not responsible for religion.[13] They were punished, therefore, because they taught that no man ought to suffer for his faith. At Nuremberg the magistrates did not know how to proceed against them. They seemed no worse than the Catholics, whom there was no question at that time of exterminating. The celebrated Osiander deemed these scruples inconsistent. The Papists, he said, ought also to be suppressed; and so long as this was not done, it was impossible to proceed to extremities against the Anabaptists, who were no worse than they. Luther also was consulted, and he decided that they ought not to be

---

[12] "I beg first of all that you will not help to mollify Count Albert in these matters, but let him go on as he has begun . . . Encourage him to go on briskly, to leave things in the hands of God, and obey His divine command to wield the sword as long as he can." "Do not allow yourselves to be much disturbed, for it will redound to the advantage of many souls that will be terrified by it, and preserved." "If there are innocent persons amongst them, God will surely save and preserve them, as He did with Lot and Jeremiah. If He does not, then they are certainly not innocent. . . . We must pray for them that they obey, otherwise this is no time for compassion; just let the guns deal with them " "Sentio melius esse omnes rusticos caedi quam principes et magistratus, eo quod rustici sine autoritate Dei gladium accipiunt. Quam nequitiam Satanae sequi non potest nisi mera Satanica vastitas regni Dei, et mundi principes etsi excedunt, tamen gladium autoritate Dei gerunt. Ibi utrumque regnum consistere potest, quare nulla misericordia, nulla patientia rusticis debetur, sed ira et indignatio Dei et hominum " — De Wette, II, 653, 655, 666, 669, 671.

[13] "Wir lehren die christlich Obrigkeit moge nicht nur, sondern solle auch sich der Religion und Glaubenssachen mit Ernst annehmen; davon halten die Wiedertaufer steif das Widerspiel, welches sie auch zum Theil gemein haben mit den Pralaten der romischen Kirche." — Declaration of the Protestants, quoted in Jörg, *Deutschland von* 1522 *bis* 1526, p. 709.

punished unless they refused to conform at the command of the Government.[14] The Margrave of Brandenburg was also advised by the divines that a heretic who could not be converted out of Scripture might be condemned; but that in his sentence nothing should be said about heresy, but only about sedition and murderous intent, though he should be guiltless of these.[15] With the aid of this artifice great numbers were put to death.

Luther's proud and ardent spirit despised such pretences. He had cast off all reserve, and spoke his mind openly on the rights and duties of the State towards the Church and the people. His first step was to proclaim it the office of the civil power to prevent abominations.[16] He provided no security that, in discharging this duty, the sovereign should be guided by the advice of orthodox divines;[17] but he held the duty itself to be imperative. In obedience to the fundamental principle, that the Bible is the sole guide in all things, he defined the office and justified it by scriptural precedents. The Mosaic code, he argued, awarded to false prophets the punishment of death, and the majesty of God is not to be less deeply reverenced or less rigorously vindicated under the New Testament than under the Old; in a more perfect revelation the obligation is stronger. Those who will not hear the Church must be excluded from the communion; but the civil power is to intervene when the ecclesiastical excommuni-

---

[14] "As to your question, how they are to be punished, I do not consider them blasphemers, but regard them in the light of the Turks, or deluded Christians, whom the civil power has not to punish, at least bodily. But if they refuse to acknowledge and to obey the civil authority, then they forfeit all they have and are, for then sedition and murder are certainly in their hearts " — De Wette, II, 622; Osiander's opinion in Jorg, p 706.

[15] "Dass in dem Urtheil und desselben offentlicher Verkundigung Keines Irrthums oder Ketzereien . . . sondern allein der Aufruhr and furgenommenen Morderei, die ihm doch laut seiner Urgicht nie lieb gewesen, gedacht werde." — Jorg, p. 708.

[16] "Principes nostri non cogunt ad fidem et Evangelion, sed cohibent externas abominationes." — De Wette, III, 50. "Wenn die weltliche Obrigkeit die Verbrechen wider die zweite Gesetzestafel bestrafen, und aus der menschlichen Gesellschaft tilgen solle, wie vielmehr denn die Verbrechen wider die erste?" — Luther, *apud* Bucholtz, *Geschichte Ferdinands I*, III, 571.

[17] Planck, IV, 61, explains why this was not thought of.

cation has been pronounced, and men must be compelled to come in. For, according to the more accurate definition of the Church which is given in the Confession of Schmalkald, and in the Apology of the Confession of Augsburg, excommunication involves damnation. There is no salvation to be hoped for out of the Church, and the test of orthodoxy against the Pope, the devil, and all the world, is the dogma of justification by faith.[18]

The defence of religion became, on this theory, not only the duty of the civil power, but the object of its institution. Its business was solely the coercion of those who were out of the Church. The faithful could not be the objects of its action; they did of their own accord more than any laws required. "A good tree," says Luther, "brings forth good fruit by nature, without compulsion; is it not madness to prescribe laws to an apple-tree that it shall bear apples and not thorns?"[19] This view naturally proceeded from the axiom of the certainty of the salvation of all who believe in the Confession of Augsburg.[20] It is the most important element in Luther's political system, because, while it made all Protestant governments despotic, it led to the rejection of the authority of Catholic governments. This is the point where Protestant and Catholic intolerance meet. If the State were instituted to promote the faith, no obedience could be due to a State of a different faith. Protestants could not conscientiously be faithful subjects of Catholic Powers, and they could not, therefore, be tolerated. Misbelievers would have no rights under an orthodox State, and a misbelieving prince would have no authority over orthodox subjects. The more, therefore, Luther expounded the guilt of resistance and the Divine sanction of authority, the more subversive his influence became in Catholic countries. His system was alike revolutionary, whether he defied the Catholic powers or promoted a Protestant tyranny. He had no notion of political right.

---

[18] Linde, *Staatskirche,* p. 23. "Der Papst sammt seinem Haufen glaubt nicht; darum bekennen wir, er werde nicht selig, das ist verdammt werden."— *Table-Talk,* II, 350.
[19] Kaltenborn, *Vorlaufer des Grotius,* 208.
[20] Möhler, *Symbolik,* 428.

He found no authority for such a claim in the New Testament, and he held that righteousness does not need to exhibit itself in works.

It was the same helpless dependence on the letter of Scripture which led the reformers to consequences more subversive of Christian morality than their views on questions of polity. When Carlstadt cited the Mosaic law in defence of polygamy, Luther was indignant. If the Mosaic law is to govern everything, he said, we should be compelled to adopt circumcision.[21] Nevertheless, as there is no prohibition of polygamy in the New Testament, the reformers were unable to condemn it. They did not forbid it as a matter of Divine law, and referred it entirely to the decision of the civil legislator.[22] This, accordingly, was the view which guided Luther and Melanchthon in treating the problem, the ultimate solution of which was the separation of England from the Church.[23] When the Landgrave Philip afterwards appealed to this opinion, and to the earlier commentaries of Luther,

---

[21] "Quodsi unam legem Mosi cogimur servare, eadem ratione et circumcidemur, et totam legem servare oportebit. . . . Nunc vero non sumus amplius sub lege Mosi, sed subjecti legibus civilibus in talibus rebus." — Luther to Barnes, Sept. 5, 1531; De Wette, IV, 296.

[22] All things that we find done by the patriarchs in the Old Testament ought to be free and not forbidden. Circumcision is abolished, but not so that it would be a sin to perform it, but optional, neither sinful nor acceptable. . . . In like manner it is not forbidden that a man should have more than one wife. Even at the present day I could not prohibit it; but I would not recommend it." — Commentary on Genesis, 1528; see Jarcke, *Studien*, p. 108. "Ego sane fateor, me non posse prohibere, siquis plures velit uxores ducere, nec repugnat sacris literis: verum tamen apud Christianos id exempli nollem primo introduci, apud quos decet etiam ea intermittere, quae licita sunt, pro vitando scandalo, et pro honestate vitae." — De Wette, II, 459, Jan. 13, 1524. "From these instances of bigamy (Lamech, Jacob) no rule can be drawn for our times; and such examples have no power with us Christians, for we live under our authorities, and are subject to our civil laws." — *Table-Talk*, V, 64.

[23] "Antequam tale repudium, probarem potius regi permitterem alteram reginam quoque ducere, et exemplo patrum et regum duas simul uxores seu reginas habere. . . . Si peccavit ducendo uxorem fratris mortui, peccavit in legem humanam seu civilem; si autem repudiaverit, peccabit in legem mere divinam." — De Wette, IV, 296. "Haud dubio rex Angliae uxorem fratris mortui ductam retinere potest . . . docendus quod has res politicas commiserit Deus magistratibus, neque nos alligaverit ad Moisen. . . . Si vult rex successioni prospicere, quanto satius est, id facere sine infamia prioris conjugii. Ac

the reformers were compelled to approve his having two wives. Melanchthon was a witness at the wedding of the second, and the only reservation was a request that the matter should not be allowed to get abroad.[24] It was the same portion of Luther's theology, and the same opposition to the spirit of the Church in the treatment of Scripture, that induced him to believe in astrology and to ridicule the Copernican system.[25]

His view of the authority of Scripture and his theory of justification both precluded him from appreciating freedom. "Christian freedom," he said, "consists in the belief that we require no works to attain piety and salvation." [26] Thus he became the inventor of the theory of passive obedience, ac-

---

potest id fieri sine ullo periculo conscientiae cujuscunque aut famae per polygamian. Etsi enim non velim concedere polygamiam vulgo, dixi enim supra, nos non ferre leges, tamen in hoc casu propter magnam utilitatem regni, fortassis etiam propter conscientiam regis, ita pronuncio: tutissimum esse regi, si ducat secundam uxorem, priore non abjecta, quia certum est polygamiam non esse prohibitam jure divino, nec res est omnino inusitata "—*Melanchthonis Opera*, ed. Bretschneider, II, 524, 526. "Nolumus esse auctores divortii, cum conjugium cum jure divino non pugnet. Hi, qui diversum pronunciant, terribiliter exaggerant et exasperant jus divinum. Nos contra exaggeramus in rebus politicis auctoritatem magistratus, quae profecto non est levis, multaque justa sunt propter magistratus auctoritatem, quae alioqui in dubium vocantur." — Melanchthon to Bucer, Bretschneider, II, 552.

[24] "Suadere non possumus ut introducatur publice et velut lege sanciatur permissio, plures quam unam uxores ducendi. . . . Primum ante omnia cavendum, ne haec res inducatur in orbem ad modum legis, quam sequendi libera omnibus sit potestas Deinde considerare dignetur vestra celsitudo scandalum, nimirum quod Evangelio hostes exclamaturi sint, nos similes esse Anabaptistis, qui plures simul duxerunt uxores." — De Wette, V, 236. Signed by Luther, Melanchthon, and Bucer.

[25] "He that would appear wise will not be satisfied with anything that others do; he must do something for himself, and that must be better than anything This fool (Copernicus) wants to overturn the whole science of astronomy. But, as the holy Scriptures tell us, Joshua told the sun to stand still, and not the earth." — *Table-Talk*, IV, 575.

[26] "Das ist die christliche Freiheit, der einige Glaube, der da macht, nicht dass wir mussig gehen oder ubel thun mogen, sondern dass wir keines Werks bedurfen, die Frommigkeit und Seligkeit zu erlangen." — *Sermon von der Freiheit*. A Protestant historian, who quotes this passage, goes on to say "On the other hand, the body must be brought under discipline by every means, in order that it may obey and not burden the inner man. Outward servitude, therefore, assists the progress towards internal freedom." — Bensen, *Geschichte des Bauernkriegs*, 269.

cording to which no motives or provocation can justify a revolt; and the party against whom the revolt is directed, whatever its guilt may be, is to be preferred to the party revolting, however just its cause.[27] In 1530 he therefore declared that the German princes had no right to resist the Emperor in defence of their religion. "It was the duty of a Christian," he said, "to suffer wrong, and no breach of oath or of duty could deprive the Emperor of his right to the unconditional obedience of his subjects."[28] Even the empire seemed to him a despotism, from his scriptural belief that it was a continuation of the last of the four monarchies.[29] He preferred submission, in the hope of seeing a future Protestant Emperor, to a resistance which might have dismembered the empire if it had succeeded, and in which failure would have been fatal to the Protestants; and he was always afraid to draw the logical consequences of his theory of the duty of Protestants towards Catholic sovereigns. In consequence of this fact, Ranke affirms that the great reformer was also one of the greatest conservatives that ever lived; and his biographer, Jurgens, makes the more discriminating remark that history knows of no man who was at once so great an insurgent and so great an upholder of order as he.[30] Neither of these writers understood that the same principle lies at the root both of revolution and of passive obedience, and that the difference is only in the temper of the person who applies it, and in the outward circumstances.

Luther's theory is apparently in opposition to Protestant interests, for it entitles Catholicism to the protection of Catholic Powers. He disguised from himself this inconsistency, and

---

[27] *Werke*, X, 413.

[28] "According to Scripture, it is by no means proper that one who would be a Christian should set himself against his superiors, whether by God's permission they act justly or unjustly. But a Christian must suffer violence and wrong, especially from his superiors. . . . As the emperor continues emperor, and princes princes, though they transgress all God's commandments, yea, even if they be heathen, so they do even when they do not observe their oath and duty. . . . Sin does not suspend authority and allegiance." — De Wette, III, 560.

[29] Ranke, *Reformation*, III, 183.

[30] Ranke, IV, 7; Jurgens, III, 601.

reconciled theory with expediency by the calculation that the immense advantages which his system offered to the princes would induce them all to adopt it. For, besides the consolatory doctrine of justification, — "a doctrine original, specious, persuasive, powerful against Rome, and wonderfully adapted, as if prophetically, to the genius of the times which were to follow,"[31] — he bribed the princes with the wealth of the Church, independence of ecclesiastical authority, facilities for polygamy, and absolute power. He told the peasants not to take arms against the Church unless they could persuade the Government to give the order; but thinking it probable, in 1522, that the Catholic clergy would, in spite of his advice, be exterminated by the fury of the people, he urged the Government to suppress them, because what was done by the constituted authority could not be wrong.[32] Persuaded that the sovereign power would be on his side, he allowed no limits to its extent. It is absurd, he says, to imagine that, even with the best intentions, kings can avoid committing occasional injustice; they stand, therefore, particularly in need — not of safeguards against the abuse of power, but — of the forgiveness of sins.[33] The power thus concentrated in the hands of the rulers for the guardianship of the faith, he wished to be used with the utmost severity against unregenerate men, in whom there was neither moral virtue nor civil rights, and from whom no good could come until they were converted. He therefore required that all crimes should be most cruelly punished and that the secular arm should be employed to convert where it did not destroy. The idea of mercy tempering justice he denounced as a Popish superstition.[34]

The chief object of the severity thus recommended was,

---

[31] Newman, *Lectures on Justification*, p 386.

[32] "Was durch ordentliche Gewalt geschieht, ist nicht fur Aufruhr zu halten." — Bensen, p. 269; Jarcke, *Studien*, p 312, Janet, II, 40

[33] "Princes, and all rulers and governments, however pious and God-fearing they may be, cannot be without sin in their office and temporal administration. . . . They cannot always be so exactly just and successful as some wiseacres suppose; therefore they are above all in need of the forgiveness of sins " — See Kaltenborn, p 209

[34] "Of old, under the Papacy, princes and lords, and all judges, were very

of course, efficaciously to promote the end for which Government itself was held to be instituted. The clergy had authority over the conscience, but it was thought necessary that they should be supported by the State with the absolute penalties of outlawry, in order that error might be exterminated, although it was impossible to banish sin.[35] No Government, it was maintained, could tolerate heresy without being responsible for the souls that were seduced by it;[36] and as Ezechiel destroyed the brazen serpent to prevent idolatry, the mass must be suppressed, for the mass was the worst kind of idolatry.[37] In 1530, when it was proposed to leave the matters in dispute to the decision of the future Council, Luther declared that the mass and monastic life could not be tolerated in the meantime, because it was unlawful to connive at error.[38] "It will lie heavy on your conscience," he writes to the Duke of Saxony, "if you tolerate the Catholic worship; for no secular prince can permit his subjects to be divided by the preaching of opposite doctrines. The Catholics have no right to complain, for they do not prove the truth of their doctrine from Scripture, and therefore do not conscientiously believe it.[39] He would tolerate them only if they acknowl-

---

timid in shedding blood, and punishing robbers, murderers, thieves, and all manner of evil-doers; for they knew not how to distinguish a private individual who is not in office from one in office, charged with the duty of punishing. . . . The executioner had always to do penance, and to apologise beforehand to the convicted criminal for what he was going to do to him, just as if it was sinful and wrong." "Thus they were persuaded by monks to be gracious, indulgent, and peaceable. But authorities, princes and lords ought not to be merciful " — *Table-Talk,* IV, 159, 160.

[35] "Den weltlichen Bann sollten Konige und Kaiser wieder aufrichten, denn wir konnen ihn jetzt nicht anrichten. . . . Aber so wir nicht konnen die Sunde des Lebens bannen und strafen, so bannen wir doch die Sunde der Lehre." — Brans, *Luther's Predigten,* 63.

[36] "Wo sie solche Rottengeister wurden zulassen und leiden, so sie es doch wehren und vorkommen konnen, wurden sie ihre Gewissen graulich beschweren, und vielleicht nimmermehr widder stillen konnen, nicht allein der Seelen halben, die dadurch verfuhrt und verdammt werden . . . sondern auch der ganzen heiligen Kirchen halben." — De Wette, IV, 355.

[37] "Nu ist alle Abgotterey gegen die Messe ein geringes " — De Wette, V, 191; sec. IV, 307.

[38] Bucholtz, III, 570.

[39] "Sie aber verachten die Schrift muthwilliglich, darum waren sie billig aus der einigen Ursach zu stillen, oder nicht zu leiden." — De Wette, III, 90.

edged themselves, like the Jews, enemies of Christ and of the Emperor, and consented to exist as outcasts of society.[40] "Heretics," he said, "are not to be disputed with, but to be condemned unheard, and whilst they perish by fire, the faithful ought to pursue the evil to its source, and bathe their hands in the blood of the Catholic bishops, and of the Pope, who is a devil in disguise." [41]

The persecuting principles which were involved in Luther's system, but which he cared neither to develop, to apply, nor to defend, were formed into a definite theory by the colder genius of Melanchthon. Destitute of Luther's confidence in his own strength, and in the infallible success of his doctrine, he clung more eagerly to the hope of achieving victory by the use of physical force. Like his master he too hesitated at first, and opposed the use of severe measures against the Zwickau prophets; but when he saw the development of that early germ of dissent, and the gradual dissolution of Lutheran unity, he repented of his ill-timed clemency.[42] He was not deterred from asserting the duty of persecution by the risk of putting arms into the hands of the enemies of the Reformation. He acknowledged the danger, but he denied the right. Catholic powers, he deemed, might justly persecute, but they could only persecute error. They must apply the same criterion which the Lutherans applied, and then they were justified in persecuting those whom the Lutherans also proscribed. For the civil power had no right to proscribe a religion in order to save itself from the dangers

---

[40] "Wollen sie aber wie die Juden seyn, nicht Christen heissen, noch Kaisers Glieder, sondern sich lassen Christus und Kaisers Feinde nennen, wie die Juden; wohlan, so wollen wir's auch leiden, dass sie in ihren Synagogen, wie die Juden, verschlossen lästern, so lang sie wollen." — De Wette, IV, 94.

[41] Riffel, *Kirchengeschichte*, II, 9; *Table-Talk*, III, 175.

[42] "Ego ab initio, cum primum caepi nosse Ciconiam et Ciconiae factionem, unde hoc totum genus Anabaptistarum exortum est, fui stulte clemens. Sentiebant enim et alii haereticos non esse ferro opprimendos Et tunc dux Fridericus vehementer iratus erat Ciconiae· ac nisi a nobis tectus esset, fuisset de homine furioso et perdite malo sumtum supplicium Nunc me ejus clementiae non parum poenitet. . . . Brentius nimis clemens est." — Bretschneider, II, 17. Feb. 1530.

of a distracted and divided population. The judge of the fact and of the danger must be, not the magistrate, but the clergy.[43] The crime lay, not in dissent, but in error. Here, therefore, Melanchthon repudiated the theory and practice of the Catholics, whose aid he invoked; for all the intolerance in the Catholic times was founded on the combination of two ideas — the criminality of apostasy, and the inability of the State to maintain its authority where the moral sense of a part of the community was in opposition to it. The reformers, therefore, approved the Catholic practice of intolerance, and even encouraged it, although their own principles of persecution were destitute not only of connection, but even of analogy, with it. By simply accepting the inheritance of the mediæval theory of the religious unity of the empire, they would have been its victims. By asserting that persecution was justifiable only against error, that is, only when purely religious, they set up a shield for themselves, and a sword against those sects for whose destruction they were more eager than the Catholics. Whether we refer the origin of Protestant intolerance to the doctrines or to the interests of the Reformation, it appears totally unconnected with the tradition of Catholic ages, or the atmosphere of Catholicism. All severities exercised by Catholics before that time had a practical motive; but Protestant persecution was based on a purely speculative foundation, and was due partly to the influence of Scripture examples, partly to the supposed interests of the Protestant party. It never admitted the exclusion of dissent to be a political right of the State, but maintained the suppression of error to be its political duty. To say, therefore, that the Protestants learnt persecution from the Catholics, is

---

[43] "Sed objiciunt exemplum nobis periculosum: si haec pertinent ad magistratus, quoties igitur magistratus judicabit aliquos errare, saeviet in eos. Caesar igitur debet nos opprimere, quoniam ita judicat nos errare. Respondeo: certe debet errores et prohibere et punire. . . . Non est enim solius Caesaris cognitio, sicut in urbibus haec cognitio non est tantum magistratus prophani, sed est doctorum. Viderit igitur magistratus ut recte judicet." — Bretschneider, II, 712. "Deliberent igitur principes, non cum tyrannis, non cum pontificibus, non cum hypocritis, monachis aut aliis, sed cum ipsa Evangelii voce, cum probatis scriptoribus." — Bretschneider, III, 254.

as false as to say that they used it by way of revenge. For they founded it on very different and contradictory grounds, and they admitted the right of the Catholics to persecute even the Protestant sects.

Melanchthon taught that the sects ought to be put down by the sword, and that any individual who started new opinions ought to be punished with death.[44] He carefully laid down that these severities were requisite, not in consideration of the danger to the State, nor of immoral teaching, nor even of such differences as would weaken the authority or arrest the action of the ecclesiastical organisation, but simply on account of a difference, however slight, in the theologumena of Protestantism.[45] Thamer, who held the possibility

---

[44] "Quare ita sentias, magistratum debere uti summa severitate in coercendis hujusmodi spiritibus. . . . Sines igitur novis exemplis timorem incuti multitudini . . . ad haec notae tibi sint causae seditionum, quas gladio prohiberi oportet. . . . Propterea sentio de his qui etiamsi non defendunt seditiosos articulos, habent manifeste blasphemos, quod interfici a magistratu debeant." — II, 17, 18. "De Anabaptistis tulimus hic in genere sententiam: quia constat sectam diabolicam esse, non esse tolerandam: dissipari enim ecclesias per eos, cum ipsi nullam habeant certam doctrinam. . . . Ideo in capita factionum in singulis locis ultima supplicia constituenda esse judicavimus." — II, 549. "It is clear that it is the duty of secular government to punish blasphemy, false doctrine, and heresy, on the bodies of those who are guilty of them . . . Since it is evident that there are gross errors in the articles of the Anabaptist sect, we conclude that in this case the obstinate ought to be punished with death." — III, 199. "Propter hanc causam Deus ordinavit politias ut Evangelium propagari possit . . . nec revocamus politiam Moysi, sed lex moralis perpetua est omnium aetatum . . . quandocumque constat doctrinam esse impiam, nihil dubium est quin sanior pars Ecclesiae debeat malos pastores removere et abolere impios cultus. Et hanc emendationem praecipue adjuvare debent magistratus, tanquam potiora membra Ecclesiae." — III, 242, 244. "Thammerus, qui Mahometicas seu Ethnicas opiniones spargit, vagatur in dioecesi Mindensi, quem publicis suppliciis adficere debebant. . . . Evomuit blasphemias, quae refutandae sunt non tantum disputatione aut scriptis, sed etiam justo officio pii magistratus " — IX, 125, 131.

[45] "Voco autem blasphemos qui articulos habent, qui proprie non pertinent ad civilem statum, sed continent θεωρίας ut de divinitate Christi et similes. Etsi enim gradus quidam sunt, tamen huc etiam refero baptismum infantum. . . . Quia magistratui commissa est tutela totius legis, quod attinet ad externam disciplinam et externa facta. Quare delicta externa contra primam tabulam prohibere ac punire debet. . . . Quare non solum concessum est, sed etiam mandatum est magistratui, impias doctrinas abolere, et tueri pias in suis ditionibus." — II, 711. "Ecclesiastica potestas tantum judicat et excommunicat

of salvation among the heathen; Schwenkfeld, who taught that not the written Word, but the internal illumination of grace in the soul was the channel of God's influence on man; the Zwinglians, with their error on the Eucharist, all these met with no more favour than the fanatical Anabaptists.[46] The State was held bound to vindicate the first table of the law with the same severity as those commandments on which civil society depends for its existence. The government of the Church being administered by the civil magistrates, it was their office also to enforce the ordinances of religion; and the same power whose voice proclaimed religious orthodoxy and law held in its hand the sword by which they were enforced. No religious authority existed except through the civil power.[47] The Church was merged in the State; but the laws of the State, in return, were identified with the commandments of religion.[48]

In accordance with these principles, the condemnation of Servetus by a civil tribunal, which had no authority over him, and no jurisdiction over his crime — the most aggressive and revolutionary act, therefore, that is conceivable in the casuistry of persecution — was highly approved by Melanchthon.

haereticos, non occidit. Sed potestas civilis debet constituere poenas et supplicia in haereticos, sicut in blasphemos constituit supplicia. . . . Non enim plectitur fides, sed haeresis." — XII, 697.

[46] "Notum est etiam, quosdam tetra et δύσφημα dixisse de sanguine Christi, quos puniri oportuit et propter gloriam Christi, et exempli causa." — VIII, 553. "Argumentatur ille praestigiator (Schwenkfeld), verbum externum non esse medium, quo Deus est efficax. Talis sophistica principum severitate compescenda erat." — IX, 579.

[47] "The office of preacher is distinct from that of governor, yet both have to contribute to the praise of God. Princes are not only to protect the goods and bodily life of their subjects, but the principal function is to promote the honour of God, and to prevent idolatry and blasphemy." — III, 199. "Errant igitur magistratus, qui divellunt gubernationem a fine, et se tantum pacis ac ventris custodes esse existimant. . . . At si tantum venter curandus esset, quid differrent principes ab armentariis? Nam longe aliter sentiendum est. Politias divinitus admirabili sapientia et bonitate constitutas esse, non tantum ad quaerenda et fruenda ventris bona, sed multo magis, ut Deus in societate innotescat, ut aeterna bona quaerantur " — III, 246

[48] "Neque illa barbarica excusatio audienda est, leges illas pertinere ad politiam Mosaicam, non ad nostram. Ut Decalogus ipse ad omnes pertinet, ita judex ubique omnia Decalogi officia in externa disciplina tueatur." — VIII, 520.

He declared it a most useful example for all future ages, and could not understand that there should be any who did not regard it in the same favourable light.[49] It is true that Servetus, by denying the divinity of Christ, was open to the charge of blasphemy in a stricter sense than that in which the reformers generally applied it. But this was not the case with the Catholics. They did not represent, like the sects, an element of dissolution in Protestantism, and the bulk of their doctrine was admitted by the reformers. They were not in revolt against existing authority; they required no special innovations for their protection; they demanded only that the change of religion should not be compulsory. Yet Melanchthon held that they too were to be proscribed, because their worship was idolatrous.[50] In doing this he adopted the principle of aggressive intolerance, which was at that time new to the Christian world; and which the Popes and Councils of the Catholic Church had condemned when the zeal of laymen had gone beyond the lawful measure. In the Middle Ages there had been persecution far more sanguinary than any that has been inflicted by Protestants. Various motives had occasioned it and various arguments had been used in its defence. But the principle on which the Protestants oppressed the Catholics was new. The Catholics had never admitted the theory of absolute toleration, as it was defined

---

[49] "Legi scriptum tuum, in quo refutasti luculenter horrendas Serveti blasphemias, ac filio Dei gratias ago, qui fuit βραβευτής hujus tui agonis, Tibi quoque Ecclesia et nunc et ad posteros gratitudinem debet et debebit Tuo judicio prorsus adsentior Affirmo etiam, vestros magistratus juste fecisse, quod hominem blasphemum, re ordine judicata, interfecerunt."—Melanchthon to Calvin, Bretschneider, VIII, 362. "Judico etiam Senatum Genevensem recte fecisse, quod hominem pertinacem et non omissurum blasphemias sustulit. Ac miratus sum, esse, qui severitatem illam improbent "— VIII, 523. "Dedit vero et Genevensis reip. magistratus ante annos quatuor punitae insanabilis blasphemiae adversus filium Dei, sublato Serveto Arragone pium et memorabile ad omnem posteritatem exemplum " — IX, 133

[50] "Abusus missae per magistratus debet tolli Non aliter, atque sustulit aeneum serpentem Ezechias, aut excelsa demolitus est Josias."— I, 480. "Politicis magistratibus severissime mandatum est, ut suo quisque loco manibus et armis tollant statuas, ad quas fiunt hominum concursus et invocationes, et puniant suppliciis corporum insanabiles, qui idolorum cultum pertinaciter retinent, aut blasphemias serunt." — IX, 77.

at first by Luther, and afterwards by some of the sects. In principle, their tolerance differed from that of the Protestants as widely as their intolerance. They had exterminated sects which, like the Albigenses, threatened to overturn the fabric of Christian society. They had proscribed different religions where the State was founded on religious unity, and where this unity formed an integral part of its laws and administration. They had gone one step further, and punished those whom the Church condemned as apostates; thereby vindicating, not, as in the first case, the moral basis of society, nor, as in the second, the religious foundation of the State, but the authority of the Church and the purity of her doctrine, on which they relied as the pillar and bulwark of the social and political order. Where a portion of the inhabitants of any country preferred a different creed, Jew, Mohammedan, heathen, or schismatic, they had been generally tolerated, with enjoyment of property and personal freedom, but not with that of political power or autonomy. But political freedom had been denied them because they did not admit the common ideas of duty which were its basis. This position, however, was not tenable, and was the source of great disorders. The Protestants, in like manner, could give reasons for several kinds of persecution. They could bring the Socinians under the category of blasphemers; and blasphemy, like the ridicule of sacred things, destroys reverence and awe, and tends to the destruction of society. The Anabaptists, they might argue, were revolutionary fanatics, whose doctrines were subversive of the civil order; and the dogmatic sects threatened the ruin of ecclesiastical unity within the Protestant community itself. But by placing the necessity of intolerance on the simple ground of religious error, and in directing it against the Church which they themselves had abandoned, they introduced a purely subjective test, and a purely revolutionary system. It is on this account that the *tu quoque*, or retaliatory argument, is inadmissible between Catholics and Protestants. Catholic intolerance is handed down from an age when unity subsisted, and when its preservation, being essential for that of society, became a necessity of State as well as a result of circumstances. Protestant intolerance, on the contrary was the peculiar fruit of a dogmatic system in contradiction with the facts and principles on which the intolerance actually existing among Catholics was founded. Spanish intolerance has been infinitely more sanguinary than Swedish; but in Spain, independently of the interests of religion, there were strong political and social reasons to justify persecution without seeking any theory to prop it up; whilst in Sweden all those practical considerations have either been wanting, or have been opposed to persecution, which has consequently had no justification except the theory of the Reformation. The only instance in which the Protestant theory has been adopted by Catholics is the revocation of the Edict of Nantes.

Towards the end of his life, Melanchthon, having ceased to be a strict Lutheran, receded somewhat from his former uncompromising position, and was adverse to a strict scrutiny into minor theological differences. He drew a distinction between errors that required punishment and variations that were not of practical importance.[51] The English Calvinists who took refuge in Germany in the reign of Mary Tudor were ungraciously received by those who were stricter Lutherans than Melanchthon. He was consulted concerning the course to be adopted towards the refugees, and he recommended toleration. But both at Wesel and at Frankfort his advice was, to his great disgust, overruled.[52]

---

[51] "If the French and English community at Frankfort shared the errors of Servetus or Thamer, or other enemies of the Symbols, or the errors of the Anabaptists on infant baptism, against the authority of the State, etc., I should faithfully advise and strongly recommend that they should be soon driven away; for the civil power is bound to prevent and to punish proved blasphemy and sedition. But I find that this community is orthodox in the symbolical articles on the Son of God, and in other articles of the Symbol. . . . If the faith of the citizens in every town were inquired into, what trouble and confusion would not arise in many countries and towns!" — IX, 179.

[52] Schmidt, *Philipp Melanchthon*, p. 640. His exhortations to the Landgrave to put down the Zwinglians are characteristic: "The Zwinglians, without waiting for the Council, persecute the Papists and the Anabaptists; why must it be wrong for others to prohibit their indefensible doctrine independent of the Council?" Philip replied: "Forcibly, to prohibit a doctrine which neither contradicts the articles of faith nor encourages sedition, I do not think

The severities of the Protestants were chiefly provoked by the Anabaptists, who denied the lawfulness of civil government, and strove to realise the kingdom of God on earth by absorbing the State in the Church.[53] None protested more loudly than they against the Lutheran intolerance, or suffered from it more severely. But while denying the spiritual authority of the State, they claimed for their religious community a still more absolute right of punishing error by death. Though they sacrificed government to religion, the effect was the same as that of absorbing the Church in the State. In 1524 Münzer published a sermon, in which he besought the Lutheran princes to extirpate Catholicism. "Have no remorse," he says; "for He to whom all power is given in heaven and on earth means to govern alone." [54] He demanded the punishment of all heretics, the destruction of all who were not of his faith, and the institution of religious unity. "Do not pretend," he says, "that the power of God will accomplish it without the use of your sword, or it will grow rusty in the scabbard. The tree that bringeth not forth good fruit must be cut down and cast into the fire." And elsewhere, "the ungodly have no right to live, except so far as the elect choose to grant it them." [55] When the Anabaptists were supreme at Münster, they exhibited the same intolerance. At seven in the morning of Friday, 27th February 1534, they ran

---

right . . . When Luther began to write and to preach, he admonished and instructed the Government that it had no right to forbid books or to prevent preaching, and that its office did not extend so far, but that it had only to govern the body and goods. . . . I had not heard before that the Zwinglians persecute the Papists; but if they abolish abuses, it is not unjust, for the Papists wish to deserve heaven by their works, and so blaspheme the Son of God That they should persecute the Anabaptists is also not wrong, for their doctrine is in part seditious " The divines answered: "If by God's grace our true and necessary doctrine is tolerated as it has hitherto been by the emperor, though reluctantly, we think that we ought not to prevent it by undertaking the defence of the Zwinglian doctrine, if that should not be tolerated. . . . As to the argument that we ought to spare the people while persecuting the leaders, our answer is, that it is not a question of persons, but only of doctrine, whether it be true or false " — Correspondence of Brenz and Melanchthon with Landgrave Philip of Hesse, Bretschneider, II, 95, 98, 101.

[53] Hardwicke, *Reformation*, p. 274.
[54] Seidemann, *Thomas Munzer*, p. 35.
[55] Heinrich Grosbeck's *Bericht*, ed. Cornelius, 19.

through the streets crying, "Away with the ungodly!" Breaking into the houses of those who refused their baptism, they drove the men out of the town, and forcibly rebaptized the women who remained behind.[56] Whilst, therefore, the Anabaptists were punished for questioning the authority of the Lutherans in religious matters, they practically justified their persecution by their own intolerant doctrines. In fact, they carried the Protestant principles of persecution to an extreme. For whereas the Lutherans regarded the defence of truth and punishment of error as being, in part, the object of the institution of civil government, they recognised it as an advantage by which the State was rewarded for its pains; but the Anabaptists repudiated the political element altogether, and held that error should be exterminated solely for the sake of truth, and at the expense of all existing States.

Bucer, whose position in the history of the Reformation is so peculiar, and who differed in important points from the Saxon leaders, agreed with them on the necessity of persecuting. He was so anxious for the success of Protestantism, that he was ready to sacrifice and renounce important doctrines, in order to save the appearance of unity;[57] but those opinions in which he took so little dogmatic interest, he was resolved to defend by force. He was very much dissatisfied with the reluctance of the Senate of Strasburg to adopt severe measures against the Catholics. His colleague Capito was singularly tolerant; for the feeling of the inhabitants was not decidedly in favour of the change.[58] But Bucer, his biographer tells us, was, in spite of his inclination to mediate, not friendly to this temporising system; partly because he had an organising intellect, which relied greatly on practical discipline to preserve what had been conquered, and on restriction of liberty to be the most certain security for its preservation; partly because he had a deep insight into the nature of various religious tendencies, and was justly alarmed at their consequences for Church and State.[59] This point in the char-

---
[56] Schenkel, III, 381.
[57] Herzog, *Encyclopädie für protestantische Theologie*, II, 418.
[58] Bussierre, *Etablissement du Protestantisme en Alsace*, p. 429.
[59] Baum, *Capito und Butzer*, p. 489.

acter of Bucer provoked a powerful resistance to his system of ecclesiastical discipline, for it was feared that he would give to the clergy a tyrannical power.[60] It is true that the demoralisation which ensued on the destruction of the old ecclesiastical authority rendered a strict attention on the part of the State to the affairs of religion highly necessary.[61] The private and confidential communications of the German reformers give a more hideous picture of the moral condition of the generation which followed the Reformation than they draw in their published writings of that which preceded it. It is on this account that Bucer so strongly insisted on the necessity of the interference of the civil power in support of the discipline of the Church.

The Swiss reformers, between whom and the Saxons Bucer forms a connecting link, differ from them in one respect, which greatly influenced their notions of government. Luther lived under a monarchy which was almost absolute, and in which the common people, who were of Slavonic origin, were in the position of the most abject servitude; but the divines of Zürich and Bern were republicans. They did not therefore entertain his exalted views as to the irresistible might of the State; and instead of requiring as absolute a theory of the indefectibility of the civil power as he did, they were satisfied with obtaining a preponderating influence for themselves. Where the power was in hands less favourable to their cause, they had less inducement to exaggerate its rights.

Zwingli abolished both the distinction between Church and State and the notion of ecclesiastical authority. In his system the civil rulers possess the spiritual functions; and, as their foremost duty is the preservation and promotion of the true religion, it is their business to preach. As magistrates are too much occupied with other things, they must delegate the

---

[60] Baum, p. 492; Erbkam, *Protestantische Sekten*, p. 581.

[61] Ursinus writes to Bullinger: "Liberavit nos Deus ab idolatria: succedit licentia infinita et horribilis divini nominis, ecclesiae doctrinae purioris et sacramentorum prophanatio et sub pedibus porcorum et canum, conniventibus atque utinam non defendentibus iis qui prohibere suo loco debebant, conculcatio." — Sudhoff, *Olevianus und Ursinus*, p. 340.

ministry of the word to preachers, for whose orthodoxy they have to provide. They are bound to establish uniformity of doctrine, and to defend it against Papists and heretics. This is not only their right, but their duty; and not only their duty, but the condition on which they retain office.[62] Rulers who do not act in accordance with it are to be dismissed. Thus Zwingli combined persecution and revolution in the same doctrine. But he was not a fanatical persecutor, and his severity was directed less against the Catholics than against the Anabaptists,[63] whose prohibition of all civil offices was more subversive of order in a republic than in a monarchy. Even, however, in the case of the Anabaptists the special provocation was — not the peril to the State, nor the scandal of their errors, but — the schism which weakened the Church.[64] The punishment of heresy for the glory of God was almost inconsistent with the theory that there is no ecclesiastical power. It was not so much provoked in Zürich as elsewhere, because in a small republican community, where the governing body was supreme over both civil and religious affairs, religious unity was a matter of course. The practical necessity of maintaining unity put out of sight the speculative question of the guilt and penalty of error.

Soon after Zwingli's death, Leo Judæ called for severer measures against the Catholics, expressly stating, however, that they did not deserve death. "Excommunication," he said, "was too light a punishment to be inflicted by the State which wields the sword, and the faults in question were not great enough to involve the danger of death." [65] Afterwards he fell into doubts as to the propriety of severe measures against dissenters, but his friends Bullinger and Capito succeeded in removing his scruples, and in obtaining his ac-

---

[62] "Adserere audemus, neminem magistratum recte gerere ne posse quidem, nisi Christianus sit." — Zwingli, *Opera*, III, 296. "If they shall proceed in an unbrotherly way, and against the ordinance of Christ, then let them be deposed, in God's name." — Schenkel, III, 362.

[63] Christoffel, *Huldreich Zwingli*, p. 251.

[64] Zwingli's advice to the Protestants of St. Gall, in Pressel, *Joachim Vadian*, p. 45.

[65] Pestalozzi, *Heinrich Bullinger*, p. 95.

quiescence in that intolerance, which was, says his biographer, a question of life and death for the Protestant Church.[66] Bullinger took, like Zwingli, a more practical view of the question than was common in Germany. He thought it safer strictly to exclude religious differences than to put them down with fire and sword; "for in this case," he says, "the victims compare themselves to the early martyrs, and make their punishment a weapon of defence." [67] He did not, however, forbid capital punishment in cases of heresy. In the year 1535 he drew up an opinion on the treatment of religious error, which is written in a tone of great moderation. In this document he says "that all sects which introduce division into the Church must be put down, and not only such as, like the Anabaptists, threaten to subvert society, for the destruction of order and unity often begins in an apparently harmless or imperceptible way. The culprit should be examined with gentleness. If his disposition is good he will not refuse instruction; if not, still patience must be shown until there is no hope of converting him. Then he must be treated like other malefactors, and handed over to the torturer and the executioner." [68] After this time there were no executions for religion in Zurich, and the number, even in the lifetime of Zwingli, was less considerable than in many other places. But it was still understood that confirmed heretics would be put to death. In 1546, in answer to the Pope's invitation to the Council of Trent, Bullinger indignantly repudiates the insinuation that the Protestant cantons were heretical, "for, by the grace of God, we have always punished the vices of heresy and sodomy with fire, and have looked upon them, and still look upon them, with horror." [69] This accusation of heresy inflamed the zeal of the reformers against heretics, in order to prove to the Catholics that they had no sympathy with them. On these grounds Bullinger recommended the execution of Servetus. "If the high Council inflicts on him the fate

---

[66] *Ibid.*, Leo Juda, p. 50.
[67] Pestalozzi, *Heinrich Bullinger*, p. 146.
[68] *Ibid.*, p. 149.
[69] *Ibid.*, p. 270.

due to a worthless blasphemer, all the world will see that the people of Geneva hate blasphemers, and that they punish with the sword of justice heretics who are obstinate in their heresy. . . . Strict fidelity and vigilance are needed, because our churches are in ill repute abroad, as if we were heretics and friends of heresy. Now God's holy providence has furnished an opportunity of clearing ourselves of this evil suspicion." [70] After the event he advised Calvin to justify it, as there were some who were taken aback. "Everywhere," he says, "there are excellent men who are convinced that godless and blaspheming men ought not only to be rebuked and imprisoned, but also to be put to death. . . . How Servetus could have been spared I cannot see." [71]

The position of Œcolampadius in reference to these questions was altogether singular and exceptional. He dreaded the absorption of the ecclesiastical functions by the State, and sought to avoid it by the introduction of a council of twelve elders, partly magistrates, partly clergy, to direct ecclesiastical affairs. "Many things," he said, "are punished by the secular power less severely than the dignity of the Church demands. On the other hand, it punishes the repentant, to whom the Church shows mercy. Either it blunts the edge of its sword by not punishing the guilty, or it brings some hatred on the Gospel by severity." [72] But the people of Basel were deaf to the arguments of the reformer, and here, as elsewhere, the civil power usurped the office of the Church. In harmony with this jealousy of political interference, Œcolampadius was very merciful to the Anabaptists. "Severe penalties," he said, "were likely to aggravate the evil; forgiveness would hasten

---

[70] Pestalozzi, *Heinrich Bullinger*, p. 426.

[71] In the year 1555 he writes to Socinus: "I too am of opinion that heretical men must be cut off with the spiritual sword. . . . The Lutherans at first did not understand that sectaries must be restrained and punished, but after the fall of Munster, when thousands of poor misguided men, many of them orthodox, had perished, they were compelled to admit that it is wiser and better for the Government not only to restrain wrong-headed men, but also, by putting to death a few that deserve it, to protect thousands of inhabitants." — *Ibid.*, p. 428.

[72] Herzog, *Leben Oekolampads*, II, 197.

the cure."[73] A few months later, however, he regretted this leniency. "We perceive," he writes to a friend, "that we have sometimes shown too much indulgence; but this is better than to proceed tyrannically, or to surrender the keys of the Church."[74] Whilst, on the other hand, he rejoiced at the expulsion of the Catholics, he ingeniously justified the practice of the Catholic persecutors. "In the early ages of the Church, when the divinity of Christ manifested itself to the world by miracles, God incited the Apostles to treat the ungodly with severity. When the miracles ceased, and the faith was universally adopted, He gained the hearts of princes and rulers, so that they undertook to protect with the sword the gentleness and patience of the Church. They rigorously resisted, in fulfillment of the duties of their office, the contemners of the Church."[75] "The clergy," he goes on to say, "became tyrannical because they usurped to themselves a power which they ought to have shared with others; and as the people dread the return of this tyranny of ecclesiastical authority, it is wiser for the Protestant clergy to make no use of the similar power of excommunication which is intrusted to them."

Calvin, as the subject of an absolute monarch, and the ruling spirit in a republic, differed both from the German and the Swiss reformers in his idea of the State both in its object and in its duty towards the Church. An exile from his own country, he had lost the associations and habits of monarchy, and his views of discipline as well as doctrine were matured before he took up his abode in Switzerland.[76] His system was not founded on existing facts; it had no roots in history, but was purely ideal, speculative, and therefore more consistent and inflexible than any other. Luther's political ideas were bounded by the horizon of the monarchical abso-

---

[73] *Ibid.*, p. 189.
[74] *Ibid.*, p. 206.
[75] Herzog, *Leben Oekolampads*, II, 195. Herzog finds an excuse for the harsh treatment of the Lutherans at Basel in the still greater severity of the Lutheran Churches against the followers of the Swiss reformation. — *Ibid.*, 213.
[76] Hundeshagen, *Conflikte des Zwinglianismus und Calvinismus*, 41.

lutism under which he lived. Zwingli's were influenced by the democratic forms of his native country, which gave to the whole community the right of appointing the governing body. Calvin, independent of all such considerations, studied only how his doctrine could best be realised, whether through the instrumentality of existing authorities, or at their expense. In his eyes its interests were paramount, their promotion the supreme duty, opposition to them an unpardonable crime. There was nothing in the institutions of men, no authority, no right, no liberty, that he cared to preserve, or towards which he entertained any feelings of reverence or obligation.

His theory made the support of religious truth the end and office of the State,[77] which was bound therefore to protect, and consequently to obey, the Church, and had no control over it. In religion the first and highest thing was the dogma: the preservation of morals was one important office of government; but the maintenance of the purity of doctrine was the highest. The result of this theory is the institution of a pure theocracy. If the elect were alone upon the earth, Calvin taught, there would be no need of the political order, and the Anabaptists would be right in rejecting it; [78] but the elect are in a minority; and there is the mass of reprobates who must be coerced by the sword, in order that all the world

---

[77] "Huc spectat (politia) . . . ne idololatria, ne in Dei nomen sacrilegia, ne adversus ejus veritatem blasphemiae aliaeque religionis offensiones publice emergant ac in populum spargantur   Politicam ordinationem probo, quae in hoc incumbit, ne vera religio, quae Dei lege continetur, palam, publicisque sacrilegiis impune violetur." — *Institutio Christianae Religionis*, ed. Tholuck, II, 477. "Hoc ergo summopere requiritur a regibus, ut gladio quo praediti sunt utantur ad cultum Dei asserendum." — *Praelectiones in Prophetas, Opera*, V, 233, ed. 1667.

[78] "Huic etiam colligere promptum est, quam stulta fuerit imaginatio eorum qui volebant usum gladii tollere e mundo, Evangelii praetextu. Scimus Anabaptistas fuisse tumultuatos, quasi totus ordo politicus repugnaret Christi regno, quia regnum Christi continetur sola doctrina; deinde nulla futura sit vis. Hoc quidem verum esset, si essemus in hoc mundo angeli   sed quemadmodum jam dixi, exiguus est piorum numerus: ideo necesse est reliquam turbam cohiberi violento freno: quia permixti sunt filii Dei vel saevis belluis, vel vulpibus et fraudulentis hominibus." — *Pr in Michaeam*, V, 310. "In quo non suam modo inscitiam, sed diabolicum fastum produnt, dum perfectionem sibi arrogant; cujus ne centesima quidem pars in illis conspicitur." — *Institutio*, II, 478.

may be made subject to the truth, by the conquerors imposing their faith upon the vanquished.[79] He wished to extend religion by the sword, but to reserve death as the punishment of apostasy; and as this law would include the Catholics, who were in Calvin's eyes apostates from the truth, he narrowed it further to those who were apostates from the community. In this way, he said, there was no pretext given to the Catholics to retaliate.[80] They, as well as the Jews and Mohammedans, must be allowed to live: death was only the penalty of Protestants who relapsed into error; but to them it applied equally whether they were converted to the Church or joined the sects and fell into unbelief. Only in cases where there was no danger of his words being used against the Protestants, and in letters not intended for publication, he required that Catholics should suffer the same penalties as those who were guilty of sedition, on the ground that the majesty of God must be as strictly avenged as the throne of the king.[81]

If the defence of the truth was the purpose for which power was intrusted to princes, it was natural that it should be also the condition on which they held it. Long before the revolution of 1688, Calvin had decided that princes who deny the true faith, "abdicate" their crowns, and are no longer to be obeyed; [82] and that no oaths are binding which are in contra-

---

[79] "Tota igitur excellentia, tota dignitas, tota potentia Ecclesiae debet huc referri, ut omnia subjaceant Deo, et quicquid erit in gentibus hoc totum sit sacrum, ut scilicet cultus Dei tam apud victores quam apud victos vigeat." — *Pr. in Michaeam*, V, 317.

[80] "Ita tollitur offensio, quae multos imperitos fallit, dum metuunt ne hoc praetextu ad saeviendum armentur Papae carnifices " Calvin was warned by experience of the imprudence of Luther's language. "In Gallis proceres in excusanda saevitia immani allegant autoritatem Lutheri." — Melanchthon, *Opera*, V, 176.

[81] "Vous avez deux espèces de mutins qui se sont eslevez entre le roy et l'estat du royaume: Les uns sont gens fantastiques, qui soubs couleur de l'évangile vouldroient mettre tout en confusion Les aultres sont gens obstinés aux superstitions de l'Antéchrist de Rome. Tous ensemble méritent bien d'estre réprimés par le glayve qui vous est commis, veu qu'ils s'attaschent non seulement au roy, mais à Dieu qui l'a assis au siège royal." — Calvin to Somerset, Oct. 22, 1540; *Lettres de Calvin*, ed. Bonnet, I, 267. See also Henry, *Leben Calvins*, II, Append. 30.

[82] "Abdicant enim se potestate terreni principes dum insurgunt contra

THE PROTESTANT THEORY OF PERSECUTION   119

diction to the interests of Protestantism.[83] He painted the princes of his age in the blackest colours,[84] and prayed to God for their destruction;[85] though at the same time he condemned all rebellion on the part of his friends, so long as there were great doubts of their success.[86] His principles, however, were often stronger than his exhortations, and he had difficulty in preventing murders and seditious movements in France.[87] When he was dead, nobody prevented them, and it became clear that his system, by subjecting the civil

---

Deum: imo indigni sunt qui censeantur in hominum numero. Potius ergo conspuere oportet in ipsorum capita, quam illis parere, ubi ita protervium ut velint etiam spoliare Deum jure suo, et quasi occupare solium ejus, acsi possent eum a coelo detrahere." — *Pr. in Danielem*, V, 91.

[83] "Quant au serment qu'on vous a contraincte de faire, comme vous avez failli et offensé Dieu en le faisant, aussi n'estes-vous tenue de le garder." — Calvin to the Duchess of Ferrara, *Bonnet*, II, 338. She had taken an oath, at her husband's death, that she would not correspond with Calvin.

[84] "In aulis regum videmus primas teneri a bestiis. Nam hodie, ne repetamus veteres historias, ut reges fere omnes fatui sunt ac bruti, ita etiam sunt quasi equi et asini brutorum animalium . . . Reges sunt hodie fere mancipia." — *Pr. in Danielem*, V, 82. "Videmus enim ut hodie quoque pro sua libidine commoveant totum orbem principes; quia produnt alii aliis innoxios populos, et exercent foedam nundinationem, dum quisque commodum suum venatur, et sine ullo pudore, tantum ut augeat suam potentiam, alios tradit in manum inimici." — *Pr. in Nahum*, V, 363. "Hodie pudet reges aliquid prae se ferre humanum, sed omnes gestus accommodant ad tyrannidem." — *Pr. in Jeremiam*, V, 257.

[85] "Sur ce que je vous avais allégué, que David nous instruict par son exemple de haïr des ennemis de Dieu, vous respondez que c'estoit pour ce temps-là duquel sous la loi de rigueur il estoit permis de haïr les ennemis. Or, madame, ceste glose seroit pour renverser toute l'Escriture, et partant il la fault fuir comme une peste mortelle . . . Combien que j'aye toujours prié Dieu de luy faire mercy, si est-ce que j'ay souvent désiré que Dieu mist la main sur luy (Guise) pour en deslivrer son Eglise, s'il ne le vouloit convertir." — Calvin to the Duchess of Ferrara, *Bonnet*, II, 551. Luther was in this respect equally unscrupulous: "This year we must pray Duke Maurice to death, we must kill him with our prayers; for he will be an evil man." — MS. quoted in Dollinger, *Reformation*, III, 266.

[86] "Quod de praepostero nostrorum fervore scribis, verissimum est, neque tamen ulla occurrit moderandi ratio, quia sanis consiliis non obtemperant. Passim denuntio, si judex essem me non minus severe in rabioso, istos impetus vindicaturum, quam rex suis edictis mandat. Pergendum nihilominus, quando nos Deus voluit stultis esse debitores." — Calvin to Beza; Henry, *Leben Calvins*, III, Append. 164.

[87] "Il n'a tenu qu'à moi que, devant la guerre, gens de faict et d'exécution ne se soyent efforcez de l'exterminer du monde (Guise) lesquels ont esté retenus par ma seule exhortation." — *Bonnet*, II, 553.

power to the service of religion, was more dangerous to toleration than Luther's plan of giving to the State supremacy over the Church.

Calvin was as positive as Luther in asserting the duty of obedience to rulers irrespective of their mode of government.[88] He constantly declared that tyranny was not to be resisted on political grounds; that no civil rights could outweigh the divine sanction of government; except in cases where a special office was appointed for the purpose. Where there was no such office — where, for instance, the estates of the realm had lost their independence — there was no protection. This is one of the most important and essential characteristics of the politics of the reformers. By making the protection of their religion the principal business of government, they put out of sight its more immediate and universal duties, and made the political objects of the State disappear behind its religious end. A government was to be judged, in their eyes, only by its fidelity to the Protestant Church. If it fulfilled those requirements, no other complaints against it could be entertained. A tyrannical prince could not be resisted if he was orthodox; a just prince could be dethroned if he failed in the more essential condition of faith. In this way Protestantism became favourable at once to despotism and to revolution, and was ever ready to sacrifice good government to its own interests. It subverted monarchies, and, at the same time, denounced those who, for political causes, sought their subversion; but though the monarchies it subverted were sometimes tyrannical, and the seditions it prevented sometimes revolutionary the order it defended or sought to establish was never legitimate and free, for it was

---

[88] "Hoc nobis si assidue ob animos et oculos obversetur, eodem decreto constitui etiam nequissimos reges, quo regum auctoritas statuitur; nunquam in animum nobis seditiosae illae cogitationes venient, tractandum esse pro meritis regem nec aequum esse, ut subditos ei nos praestemus, qui vicissim regem nobis se non praestet. . . . De privatis hominibus semper loquor. Nam si qui nunc sint populares magistratus ad moderandam regum libidinem constituti (quales olim erant . . ephori . . tribuni . . . demarchi: et qua etiam forte potestate, ut nunc res habent, funguntur in singulis regnis tres ordines, quum primarios conventus peragunt) . . . illos ferocienti regum licentiae pro officio intercedere non veto." — *Institutio*, II, 493, 495.

THE PROTESTANT THEORY OF PERSECUTION 121

always invested with the function of religious proselytism,[89] and with the obligation of removing every traditional, social, or political right or power which could oppose the discharge of that essential duty.

The part Calvin had taken in the death of Servetus obliged him to develop more fully his views on the punishment of heresy. He wrote a short account of the trial,[90] and argued that governments are bound to suppress heresy, and that those who deny the justice of the punishment, themselves deserve it.[91] The book was signed by all the clergy of Geneva, as Calvin's compurgators. It was generally considered a failure; and a refutation appeared, which was so skilful as to produce a great sensation in the Protestant world.[92] This famous tract, now of extreme rarity, did not, as has been said, "contain the pith of those arguments which have ultimately triumphed in almost every part of Europe"; nor did it preach an unconditional toleration.[93] But it struck hard at Calvin

---

[89] "Quum ergo ita licentiose omnia sibi permittent (Donatistae), volebant tamen impune manere sua scelera· et in primis tenebant hoc principium: non esse poenas sumendas, si quis ab aliis dissideret in religionis doctrina: quemadmodum hodie videmus quosdam de hac re nimis cupide contendere. Certum est quid cupiant. Nam si quis ipsos respiciat, sunt impii Dei contemptores· saltem vellent nihil certum esse in religione; ideo labefactare, et quantum in se est etiam convellere nituntur omnia pietatis principia Ut ergo liceat ipsis evomere virus suum, ideo tantopere litigant pro impunitate, et negant poenas de haereticis et blasphemis sumendas esse."—*Pr. in Danielem*, V, 51

[90] "Defensio Orthodoxae Fidei . . . ubi ostenditur Haereticos jure gladii coercendos esse," 1554.

[91] "Non modo liberum esse magistratibus poenas sumere de coelestis doctrinae corruptoribus, sed divinitus esse mandatum, ut pestiferis erroribus impunitatem dare nequeant, quin desciscant ab officii sui fide. . . . Nunc vero quisquis haereticis et blasphemis injuste paenam infligi contenderet, sciens et volens se obstringet blasphemiae reatu. . . . Ubi a suis fundamentis convellitur religio, detestandae in Deum blasphemiae proferuntur, impiis et pestiferis dogmatibus in exitium rapiuntur animae, denique ubi palam defectio ab unico Deo puraque doctrina tentatur, ad extremum illud remedium descendere necesse "— See Schenkel, III, 389, Dyer, *Life of Calvin*, p. 354; Henry, III, 234.

[92] *De Haereticis an sint persequendi*, Magdeburgi, 1554. Chataillon, to whom it is generally attributed, was not the author.— See Heppe, *Theodor Beza*, p 37.

[93] Hallam, *Literature of Europe*, II, 81; Schlosser, *Leben des Beza*, p. 55. This is proved by the following passage from the dedication: "This I say not

by quoting a passage from the first edition of his *Institutes*, afterwards omitted, in which he spoke for toleration. "Some of those," says the author, "whom we quote have subsequently written in a different spirit. Nevertheless, we have cited the earlier opinion as the true one, as it was expressed under the pressure of persecution." [94] The first edition, we are informed by Calvin himself, was written for the purpose of vindicating the Protestants who were put to death, and of putting a stop to the persecution. It was anonymous, and naturally dwelt on the principles of toleration.

Although this book did not denounce all intolerance, and although it was extremely moderate, Calvin and his friends were filled with horror. "What remains of Christianity," exclaimed Beza, "if we silently admit what this man has expectorated in his preface? . . . Since the beginning of Christianity no such blasphemy was ever heard." [95] Beza undertook to defend Calvin in an elaborate work,[96] in which it was easy for him to cite the authority of all the leading reformers in favour of the practice of putting heretics to death, and in which he reproduced all the arguments of those who had

---

to favour the heretics, whom I abhor, but because there are here two dangerous rocks to be avoided. In the first place, that no man should be deemed a heretic when he is not, . . and that the real rebel be distinguished from the Christian who, by following the teaching and example of his Master, necessarily causes separation from the wicked and unbelieving. The other danger is, lest the real heretics be not more severely punished than the discipline of the Church requires." — Baum, *Theodor Beza*, I, 215.

[94] "Multis piis hominibus in Gallia exustis grave passim apud Germanos odium ignes illi excitaverant, sparsi sunt, ejus restinguendi causa, improbi ac mendaces libelli, non alios tam crudeliter tractari, quam Anabaptistas ac turbulentos homines, qui perversis deliriis non religionem modo sed totum ordinem politicum convellerent . . . Haec mihi edendae Institutionis causa fuit, primum ut ab injusta contumelia vindicarem fratres meos, quorum mors pretiosa erat in conspectu Domini; deinde quum multis miseris eadem visitarent supplicia, pro illis dolor saltem aliquis et sollicitudo exteras gentes tangeret." — *Praefatio in Psalmos.* See "Historia Litteraria de Calvini Institutione," in *Scrinium Antiquarium*, II, 452.

[95] Baum, I, 206. "Telles gens," says Calvin, "seroient contents qu'il n'y eust ne loy, ne bride au monde. Voilà pourquoy ils ont basti ce beau libvre *De non comburendis Haereticis*, où ils ont falsifié les noms tant des villes que des personnes, non pour aultre cause sinon pource que le dit livre est farcy de blasphèmes insupportables." — Bonnet, II, 18.

[96] *De Haereticis a civili Magistratu puniendis*, 1554.

THE PROTESTANT THEORY OF PERSECUTION 123

written on the subjects before him. More systematic than Calvin, he first of all excludes those who are not Christians — the Jews, Turks, and heathen — whom his inquiry does not touch; "among Christians," he proceeds to say, "some are schismatics, who sin against the peace of the Church, or disbelievers, who reject her doctrine. Among these, some err in all simplicity; and if their error is not very grave, and if they do not seduce others, they need not be punished." [97] "But obstinate heretics are far worse than parricides, and deserve death, even if they repent." [98] "It is the duty of the State to punish them, for the whole ecclesiastical order is upheld by the political." [99] In early ages this power was exercised by the temporal sovereigns; they convoked councils, punished heretics, promulgated dogmas. The Papacy afterwards arose, in evil times, and was a great calamity; but it was preferable a hundred times to the anarchy which was defended under the name of merciful toleration.

The circumstances of the condemnation of Servetus make it the most perfect and characteristic example of the abstract intolerance of the reformers. Servetus was guilty of no political crime; he was not an inhabitant of Geneva, and was on the point of leaving it, and nothing immoral could be attributed to him. He was not even an advocate of absolute toleration.[100] The occasion of his apprehension was a dispute be-

---

[97] "Absit autem a nobis, ut in eos, qui vel simplicitate peccant, sine aliorum pernicie et insigni blasphemia, vel in explicando quopiam Scripturae loco dissident a recepta opinione, magistratum armemus." — *Tractatus Theologici*, I, 95.

[98] This was sometimes the practice in Catholic countries, where heresy was equivalent to treason. Duke William of Bavaria ordered obstinate Anabaptists to be burnt; those who recanted to be beheaded. "Welcher revocir, den soll man köpfen; welcher nicht revocir, den soll man brennen." — Jorg, p. 717.

[99] "Ex quibus omnibus una conjunctio efficitur, istos quibus haeretici videntur non esse puniendi, opinionem in Ecclesiam Dei conari longe omnium pestilentissimam invehere et ex diametro repugnantem doctrinae primum a Deo Patre proditae, deinde a Christo instauratae, ab universa denique Ecclesia orthodoxa perpetuo consensu usurpatae, ut mihi quidem magis absurde facere videantur quam si sacrilegas aut parricidas puniendos negarent, quum sint istis omnibus haeretici infinitis partibus deteriores." — *Tract. Theol.*, I, 143.

[100] "Verum est quod correctione non exspectata Ananiam et Sapphiram occidit Petrus. Quia Spiritus Sanctus tunc maxime vigens, quem spreverant, docebat

tween a Catholic and a Protestant, as to which party was most zealous in suppressing egregious errors. Calvin, who had long before declared that if Servetus came to Geneva he should never leave it alive,[101] did all he could to obtain his condemnation by the Inquisition at Vienne. At Geneva he was anxious that the sentence should be death,[102] and in this he was encouraged by the Swiss churches, but especially by Beza, Farel, Bullinger, and Peter Martyr.[103] All the Protestant

---

esse incorrigibiles, in malitia obstinatos. Hoc crimen est morte simpliciter dignum et apud Deum et apud homines. In aliis autem criminibus, ubi Spiritus Sanctus speciale quid non docet, ubi non est inveterata malitia, aut obstinatio certa non apparet aut atrocitas magna, correctionem per alias castigationes sperare potius debemus." — Servetus, *Restitutio Christianismi*, 656; Henry, III, 235.

[101] "Nam si venerit, modo valeat mea authoritas, vivum exire nunquam patiar." — Calvin to Farel, in Henry, III, Append , 65; Audin, *Vie de Calvin*, II, 314; Dyer, 544

[102] "Spero capitale saltem fore judicium poenae vero atrocitatem remitti cupio." — Calvin to Farel, Henry, III, 189 Dr Henry makes no attempt to clear Calvin of the imputation of having caused the death of Servetus. Nevertheless he proposed, some years later, that the three-hundredth anniversary of the execution should be celebrated in the Church of Geneva by a demonstration "It ought to declare itself in a body, in a manner worthy of our principles, admitting that in past times the authorities of Geneva were mistaken, loudly proclaiming toleration, which is truly the crown of our Church, and paying due honour to Calvin, because he had no hand in the business (parcequ'il n'a pas trempé dans cette affaire), of which he has unjustly borne the whole burden." The impudence of this declaration is surpassed by the editor of the French periodical from which we extract it. He appends to the words in our parenthesis the following note "We underline in order to call attention to this opinion of Dr. Henry, who is so thoroughly acquainted with the whole question." — *Bulletin de la Société de l'Histoire du Protestantisme Français*, II, 114.

[103] "Qui scripserunt de non plectendis haereticis, semper mihi visi sunt non parum errare " — Farel to Blaarer, Henry, III, 202 During the trial he wrote to Calvin· "If you desire to diminish the horrible punishment, you will act as a friend towards your most dangerous enemy If I were to seduce anybody from the true faith, I should consider myself worthy of death; I cannot judge differently of another than of myself." — Schmidt, *Farel und Viret*, p. 33.

Before sentence was pronounced Bullinger wrote to Beza: "Quid vero amplissimus Senatus Genevensis ageret cum blasphemo illo nebulone Serveto Si sapit et officium suum facit, caedit, ut totus orbis videat Genevam Christi gloriam cupere servatam." — Baum, I, 204. With reference to Socinus he wrote: "Sentio ego spirituali gladio abscindendos esse homines haereticos " — Henry, III, 225.

Peter Martyr Vermili also gave in his adhesion to Calvin's policy: "De Serveto Hispano, quid aliud dicam non habeo, nisi eum fuisse genuinum

THE PROTESTANT THEORY OF PERSECUTION 125

authorities, therefore, agreed in the justice of putting a writer to death in whose case all the secondary motives of intolerance were wanting. Servetus was not a party leader. He had no followers who threatened to upset the peace and unity of the Church. His doctrine was speculative, without power or attraction for the masses, like Lutheranism; and without consequences subversive of morality, or affecting in any direct way the existence of society, like Anabaptism.[104] He had nothing to do with Geneva, and his persecutors would have rejoiced if he had been put to death elsewhere. "Bayle," says Hallam,[105] "has an excellent remark on this controversy." Bayle's remark is as follows: "Whenever Protestants complain, they are answered by the right which Calvin and Beza recognised in magistrates; and to this day there has been nobody who has not failed pitiably against this *argumentum ad hominem.*"

No question of the merits of the Reformation or of persecution is involved in an inquiry as to the source and connection of the opinions on toleration held by the Protestant reformers. No man's sentiments on the rightfulness of religious persecution will be affected by the theories we have described, and they have no bearing whatever on doctrinal controversy. Those who — in agreement with the principle of the early Church, that men are free in matters of conscience — condemn all intolerance, will censure Catholics and Protestants alike.

Diaboli filium, cujus pestifera et detestanda doctrina undique profliganda est, neque magistratus, qui de illo supplicium extremum sumpsit, accusandus est, cum emendationis nulla indicia in eo possent deprehendi, illiusque blasphemiae omnino intolerabiles essent " — *Loci Communes,* 1114 See Schlosser, *Leben des Beza und des Peter Martyr Vermili,* 512.

Zanchi, who at the instigation of Bullinger also published a treatise, *De Haereticis Coercendis,* says of Beza's work: "Non poterit non probari summopere piis omnibus. Satis superque respondit quidem ille novis istis academicis, ita ut supervacanea et inutilis omnino videatur mea tractatio." — Baum, I, 232.

[104] "The trial of Servetus," says a very ardent Calvinist, "is illegal only in one point—the crime if crime there be, had not been committed at Geneva; but long before the Councils had usurped the unjust privilege of judging strangers stopping at Geneva, although the crimes they were accused of had not been committed there." — Haag, *La France Protestante,* III, 129.

[105] *Literature of Europe,* II, 82.

Those who pursue the same principle one step farther and practically invert it, by insisting on the right and duty not only of professing but of extending the truth, must, as it seems to us, approve the conduct both of Protestants and Catholics, unless they make the justice of the persecution depend on the truth of the doctrine defended, in which case they will divide on both sides. Such persons, again, as are more strongly impressed with the cruelty of actual executions than with the danger of false theories, may concentrate their indignation on the Catholics of Languedoc and Spain; while those who judge principles, not by the accidental details attending their practical realisation, but by the reasoning on which they are founded, will arrive at a verdict adverse to the Protestants. These comparative inquiries, however, have little serious interest. If we give our admiration to tolerance, we must remember that the Spanish Moors and the Turks in Europe have been more tolerant than the Christians; and if we admit the principle of intolerance, and judge its application by particular conditions, we are bound to acknowledge that the Romans had better reason for persecution than any modern State, since their empire was involved in the decline of the old religion, with which it was bound up, whereas no Christian polity has been subverted by the mere presence of religious dissent. The comparison is, moreover, entirely unreasonable, for there is nothing in common between Catholic and Protestant intolerance. The Church began with the principle of liberty, both as her claim and as her rule; and external circumstances forced intolerance upon her, after her spirit of unity had triumphed, in spite both of the freedom she proclaimed and of the persecutions she suffered. Protestantism set up intolerance as an imperative precept and as a part of its doctrine, and it was forced to admit toleration by the necessities of its position, after the rigorous penalties it imposed had failed to arrest the process of internal dissolution.[106]

---

[106] This is the ground taken by two Dutch divines in answer to the consultation of John of Nassau in 1579: "Neque in imperio, neque in Galliis, neque in Belgio speranda esset unquam libertas in externo religionis exercitio nostris

At the time when this involuntary change occurred the sects that caused it were the bitterest enemies of the toleration they demanded. In the same age the Puritans and the Catholics sought a refuge beyond the Atlantic from the persecution which they suffered together under the Stuarts. Flying for the same reason, and from the same oppression, they were enabled respectively to carry out their own views in the colonies which they founded in Massachusetts and Maryland, and the history of those two States exhibits faithfully the contrast between the two Churches. The Catholic emigrants established, for the first time in modern history, a government in which religion was free, and with it the germ of that religious liberty which now prevails in America. The Puritans, on the other hand, revived with greater severity the penal laws of the mother country. In process of time the liberty of conscience in the Catholic colony was forcibly abolished by the neighbouring Protestants of Virginia; while on the borders of Massachusetts the new State of Rhode Island was formed by a party of fugitives from the intolerance of their fellow-colonists.

... si non diversarum religionum exercitia in una eademque provincia toleranda. ... Sic igitur gladio adversus nos armabimus Pontificios, si hanc hypothesin tuebimur, quod exercitium religionis alteri parti nullum prorsus relinqui debeat." — *Scrinium Antiquarium*, I, 335.

Chapter V

SIR ERSKINE MAY'S "DEMOCRACY IN EUROPE"

SCARCELY THIRTY YEARS separate the Europe of Guizot and Metternich from these days of universal suffrage, both in France and in United Germany; when a condemned insurgent of 1848 is the constitutional Minister of Austria; when Italy, from the Alps to the Adriatic, is governed by friends of Mazzini; and statesmen who recoiled from the temerities of Peel have doubled the electoral constituency of England. If the philosopher who proclaimed the law that democratic progress is constant and irrepressible had lived to see old age, he would have been startled by the fulfilment of his prophecy. Throughout these years of revolutionary change Sir Thomas Erskine May has been more closely and constantly connected with the centre of public affairs than any other Englishman, and his place, during most of the time, has been at the table of the House of Commons, where he has sat, like Canute, and watched the rising tide. Few could be better prepared to be the historian of European democracy than one who, having so long studied the mechanism of popular government in the most illustrious of assemblies at the height of its power, has written its history, and taught its methods to the world.

It is not strange that so delicate and laborious a task should have remained unattempted. Democracy is a gigantic current that has been fed by many springs. Physical and spiritual

NOTE: This essay first appeared in *The Quarterly Review*, CXLV, No. 289 (January, 1878), 112-42: reprinted in *The History of Freedom and Other Essays* (London, Macmillan Co., 1907), pp. 61-100.

causes have contributed to swell it. Much has been done by economic theories, and more by economic laws. The propelling force lay sometimes in doctrine and sometimes in fact, and error has been as powerful as truth. Popular progress has been determined at one time by legislation, at others by a book, an invention, or a crime; and we may trace it to the influence of Greek metaphysicians and Roman jurists, of barbarian custom and ecclesiastical law, of the reformers who discarded the canonists, the sectaries who discarded the reformers, and the philosophers who discarded the sects. The scene has changed, as nation succeeded nation, and during the most stagnant epoch of European life the new world stored up the forces that have transformed the old.

A history that should pursue all the subtle threads from end to end might be eminently valuable, but not as a tribute to peace and conciliation. Few discoveries are more irritating than those which expose the pedigree of ideas. Sharp definitions and unsparing analysis would displace the veil beneath which society dissembles its divisions, would make political disputes too violent for compromise and political alliances too precarious for use, and would embitter politics with all the passion of social and religious strife. Sir Erskine May writes for all who take their stand within the broad lines of our constitution. His judgment is averse from extremes. He turns from the discussion of theories, and examines his subject by the daylight of institutions, believing that laws depend much on the condition of society, and little on notions and disputations unsupported by reality. He avows his disbelief even in the influence of Locke, and cares little to inquire how much self-government owes to Independency, or equality to the Quakers; and how democracy was affected by the doctrine that society is founded on contract, that happiness is the end of all government, or labour the only source of wealth; and for this reason, because he always touches ground, and brings to bear, on a vast array of sifted fact, the light of sound sense and tried experience rather than dogmatic precept, all men will read his book with profit, and almost all without offence.

Although he does not insist on inculcating a moral, he has stated in his introductory pages the ideas that guide him; and, indeed, the reader who fails to recognise the lesson of the book in every chapter will read in vain. Sir Erskine May is persuaded that it is the tendency of modern progress to elevate the masses of the people, to increase their part in the work and the fruit of civilisation, in comfort and education, in self-respect and independence, in political knowledge and power. Taken for a universal law of history, this would be as visionary as certain generalisations of Montesquieu and Tocqueville; but with the necessary restrictions of time and place, it cannot fairly be disputed. Another conclusion, supported by a far wider induction, is that democracy, like monarchy, is salutary within limits and fatal in excess; that it is the truest friend of freedom or its most unrelenting foe, according as it is mixed or pure; and this ancient and elementary truth of constitutional government is enforced with every variety of impressive and suggestive illustration from the time of the Patriarchs down to the revolution which, in 1874, converted federal Switzerland into an unqualified democracy governed by the direct voice of the entire people.

The effective distinction between liberty and democracy, which has occupied much of the author's thoughts, cannot be too strongly drawn. Slavery has been so often associated with democracy, that a very able writer pronounced it long ago essential to a democratic state; and the philosophers of the Southern Confederation have urged the theory with extreme fervour. For slavery operates like a restricted franchise, attaches power to property, and hinders Socialism, the infirmity that attends mature democracies. The most intelligent of Greek tyrants, Periander, discouraged the employment of slaves; and Pericles designates the freedom from manual labour as the distinguishing prerogative of Athens. At Rome a tax on manumissions immediately followed the establishment of political equality by Licinius. An impeachment of England for having imposed slavery on America was carefully expunged from the Declaration of Independence; and the French Assembly, having proclaimed the Rights of

Man, declared that they did not extend to the colonies. The abolition controversy has made everybody familiar with Burke's saying, that men learn the price of freedom by being masters of slaves.

From the best days of Athens, the days of Anaxagoras, Protagoras, and Socrates, a strange affinity has subsisted between democracy and religious persecution. The bloodiest deed committed between the wars of religion and the revolution was due to the fanaticism of men living under the primitive republic in the Rhætian Alps; and of six democratic cantons only one tolerated Protestants, and that after a struggle which lasted the better part of two centuries. In 1578 the fifteen Catholic provinces would have joined the revolted Netherlands but for the furious bigotry of Ghent; and the democracy of Friesland was the most intolerant of the States. The aristocratic colonies in America defended toleration against their democratic neighbours, and its triumph in Rhode Island and Pennsylvania was the work not of policy but of religion. The French Republic came to ruin because it found the lesson of religious liberty too hard to learn. Down to the eighteenth century, indeed, it was understood in monarchies more often than in free commonwealths. Richelieu acknowledged the principle whilst he was constructing the despotism of the Bourbons; so did the electors of Brandenburg, at the time when they made themselves absolute; and after the fall of Clarendon, the notion of Indulgence was inseparable from the design of Charles II to subvert the constitution.

A government strong enough to act in defiance of public feeling may disregard the plausible heresy that prevention is better than punishment, for it is able to punish. But a government entirely dependent on opinion looks for some security what that opinion shall be, strives for the control of the forces that shape it, and is fearful of suffering the people to be educated in sentiments hostile to its institutions. When General Grant attempted to grapple with polygamy in Utah, it was found necessary to pack the juries with Gentiles; and the Supreme Court decided that the proceedings were illegal, and that the prisoners must be set free. Even the murderer Lee was absolved, in 1875, by a jury of Mormons.

Modern democracy presents many problems too various and obscure to be solved without a larger range of materials than Tocqueville obtained from his American authorities or his own observation. To understand why the hopes and the fears that it excites have been always inseparable, to determine under what conditions it advances or retards the progress of the people and the welfare of free states, there is no better course than to follow Sir Erskine May upon the road which he has been the first to open.

In the midst of an invincible despotism, among paternal, military, and sacerdotal monarchies, the dawn rises with the deliverance of Israel out of bondage, and with the covenant which began their political life. The tribes broke up into smaller communities, administering their own affairs under the law they had sworn to observe, but which there was no civil power to enforce. They governed themselves without a central authority, a legislature, or a dominant priesthood; and this polity, which, under the forms of primitive society, realised some aspirations of developed democracy, resisted for above three hundred years the constant peril of anarchy and subjugation. The monarchy itself was limited by the same absence of a legislative power, by the submission of the king to the law that bound his subjects, by the perpetual appeal of prophets to the conscience of the people as its appointed guardian, and by the ready resource of deposition. Later still, in the decay of the religious and national constitution, the same ideas appeared with intense energy, in an extraordinary association of men who lived in austerity and self-denial, rejected slavery, maintained equality, and held their property in common, and who constituted in miniature an almost perfect Republic. But the Essenes perished with the city and the Temple, and for many ages the example of the Hebrews was more serviceable to authority than to freedom. After the Reformation, the sects that broke resolutely with the traditions of Church and State as they came down from Catholic times, and sought for their new institutions a higher authority than custom, reverted to the memory of a commonwealth founded on a voluntary contract, on self-government, federalism, equality, in which election was preferred to inheritance, and monarchy was an emblem of the heathen; and they conceived that there was no better model for themselves than a nation constituted by religion, owning no lawgiver but Moses, and obeying no king but God. Political thought had until then been guided by pagan experience.

Among the Greeks, Athens, the boldest pioneer of republican discovery, was the only democracy that prospered. It underwent the changes that were the common lot of Greek society, but it met them in a way that displayed a singular genius for politics. The struggle of competing classes for supremacy, almost everywhere a cause of oppression and bloodshed, became with them a genuine struggle for freedom; and the Athenian constitution grew, with little pressure from below, under the intelligent action of statesmen who were swayed by political reasoning more than by public opinion. They avoided violent and convulsive change, because the rate of their reforms kept ahead of the popular demand. Solon, whose laws began the reign of mind over force, instituted democracy by making the people, not indeed the administrators, but the source of power. He committed the Government not to rank or birth, but to land; and he regulated the political influence of the landowners by their share in the burdens of the public service. To the lower class, who neither bore arms nor paid taxes, and were excluded from the Government, he granted the privilege of choosing and of calling to account the men by whom they were governed, of confirming or rejecting the acts of the legislature and the judgments of the courts. Although he charged the Areopagus with the preservation of 'his laws, he provided that they might be revised according to need; and the ideal before his mind was government by all free citizens. His concessions to the popular element were narrow, and were carefully guarded. He yielded no more than was necessary to guarantee the attachment of the whole people to the State. But he admitted principles that went further than the claims which he conceded. He took only one step towards democracy, but it was the first of a series.

When the Persian wars, which converted aristocratic Athens into a maritime state, had developed new sources of wealth and a new description of interests, the class which had supplied many of the ships and most of the men that had saved the national independence and founded an empire, could not be excluded from power. Solon's principle, that political influence should be commensurate with political service, broke through the forms in which he had confined it, and the spirit of his constitution was too strong for the letter. The fourth estate was admitted to office, and in order that its candidates might obtain their share, and no more than their share, and that neither interest nor numbers might prevail, many public functionaries were appointed by lot. The Athenian idea of a Republic was to substitute the impersonal supremacy of law for the government of men. Mediocrity was a safeguard against the pretensions of superior capacity, for the established order was in danger, not from the average citizens, but from men, like Miltiades, of exceptional renown. The people of Athens venerated their constitution as a gift of the gods, the source and title of their power, a thing too sacred for wanton change. They had demanded a code, that the unwritten law might no longer be interpreted at will by Archons and Areopagites; and a well-defined and authoritative legislation was a triumph of the democracy.

So well was this conservative spirit understood, that the revolution which abolished the privileges of the aristocracy was promoted by Aristides and completed by Pericles, men free from the reproach of flattering the multitude. They associated all the true Athenians with the interest of the State, and called them, without distinction of class, to administer the powers that belonged to them. Solon had threatened with the loss of citizenship all who showed themselves indifferent in party conflicts, and Pericles declared that every man who neglected his share of public duty was a useless member of the community. That wealth might confer no unfair advantage, that the poor might not take bribes from the rich, he took them into the pay of the State during their attendance as jurors. That their numbers might give them no unjust superiority, he restricted the right of citizenship to those who came from Athenian parents on both sides; and thus he expelled more than 4,000 men of mixed descent from the Assembly. This bold measure, which was made acceptable by a distribution of grain from Egypt among those who proved their full Athenian parentage, reduced the fourth class to an equality with the owners of real property. For Pericles, or Ephialtes — for it would appear that all their reforms had been carried in the year 460, when Ephialtes died — is the first democratic statesman who grasped the notion of political equality. The measures which made all citizens equal might have created a new inequality between classes, and the artificial privilege of land might have been succeeded by the more crushing preponderance of numbers. But Pericles held it to be intolerable that one portion of the people should be required to obey laws which others have the exclusive right of making; and he was able, during thirty years, to preserve the equipoise, governing by the general consent of the community, formed by free debate. He made the undivided people sovereign; but he subjected the popular initiative to a court of revision, and assigned a penalty to the proposer of any measure which should be found to be unconstitutional. Athens, under Pericles, was the most successful Republic that existed before the system of representation; but its splendour ended with his life.

The danger to liberty from the predominance either of privilege or majorities was so manifest, that an idea arose that equality of fortune would be the only way to prevent the conflict of class interests. The philosophers, Phaleas, Plato, Aristotle, suggested various expedients to level the difference between rich and poor. Solon had endeavoured to check the increase of estates; and Pericles had not only strengthened the public resources by bringing the rich under the control of an assembly in which they were not supreme, but he had employed those resources in improving the condition and the capacity of the masses. The grievance of those who were taxed for the benefit of others was easily borne so long as the tribute of the confederates filled the treasury. But the Peloponnesian war increased the strain on the revenue and deprived Athens of its dependencies. The balance was upset; and the policy of making one class give, that another might receive, was recommended not only by the interest of the poor, but by a growing theory, that wealth and poverty make bad citizens, that the middle class is the one most easily led by reason, and that the way to make it predominate is to depress whatever rises above the common level, and to raise whatever falls below it. This theory, which became inseparable from democracy, and contained a force which alone seems able to destroy it, was fatal to Athens, for it drove the minority to treason. The glory of the Athenian democrats is, not that they escaped the worst consequences of their principle, but that, having twice cast out the usurping oligarchy, they set bounds to their own power. They forgave their vanquished enemies; they abolished pay for attendance in the assembly; they established the supremacy of law by making the code superior to the people; they distinguished things that were constitutional from things that were legal, and resolved that no legislative act should pass until it had been pronounced consistent with the constitution.

The causes which ruined the Republic of Athens illustrate the connection of ethics with politics rather than the vices inherent to democracy. A State which has only 30,000 full citizens in a population of 500,000, and is governed, practically, by about 3,000 people at a public meeting, is scarcely democratic. The short triumph of Athenian liberty, and its quick decline, belong to an age which possessed no fixed standard of right and wrong. An unparalleled activity of intellect was shaking the credit of the gods, and the gods were the givers of the law. It was a very short step from the suspicion of Protagoras, that there were no gods, to the assertion of Critias that there is no sanction for laws. If nothing was certain in theology, there was no certainty in ethics and no moral obligation. The will of man, not the will of God, was the rule of life, and every man and body of men had the right to do what they had the means of doing. Tyranny was no wrong, and it was hypocrisy to deny oneself the enjoyment it affords. The doctrine of the Sophists gave no limits to power and no security to freedom; it inspired that cry of the Athenians, that they must not be hindered from doing what they pleased, and the speeches of men like Athenagoras and Euphemus, that the democracy may punish men who have done no wrong, and that nothing that is profitable is amiss. And Socrates perished by the reaction which they provoked.

The disciples of Socrates obtained the ear of posterity. Their testimony against the government that put the best of citizens to death is enshrined in writings that compete with Christianity itself for influence on the opinions of men. Greece has governed the world by her philosophy, and the loudest note in Greek philosophy is the protest against Athenian democracy. But although Socrates derided the practice of leaving the choice of magistrates to chance, and Plato admired the bloodstained tyrant Critias, and Aristotle deemed Theramenes a greater statesman than Pericles, yet these are the men who laid the first stones of a purer system, and became the lawgivers of future commonwealths.

The main point in the method of Socrates was essentially democratic. He urged men to bring all things to the test of incessant inquiry, and not to content themselves with the verdict of authorities, majorities, or custom; to judge of right and wrong, not by the will or sentiment of others, but by the light which God has set in each man's reason and conscience. He proclaimed that authority is often wrong, and has no warrant to silence or to impose conviction. But he gave no warrant to resistance. He emancipated men for thought, but not for action. The sublime history of his death shows that the superstition of the State was undisturbed by his contempt for its rulers.

Plato had not his master's patriotism, nor his reverence for the civil power. He believed that no State can command obedience if it does not deserve respect; and he encouraged citizens to despise their government if they were not governed by wise men. To the aristocracy of philosophers he assigned a boundless prerogative; but as no government satisfied that test, his plea for despotism was hypothetical. When the lapse of years roused him from the fantastic dream of his Republic, his belief in divine government moderated his intolerance of human freedom. Plato would not suffer a democratic polity; but he challenged all existing authorities to justify themselves before a superior tribunal; he desired that all constitutions should be thoroughly remodelled, and he supplied the greatest need of Greek democracy, the conviction that the will of the people is subject to the will of God, and that all civil authority, except that of an imaginary state, is limited and conditional. The prodigious vitality of his writings has kept the glaring perils of popular government constantly before mankind; but it has also preserved the belief in ideal politics and the notion of judging the powers of this world by a standard from heaven. There has been no fiercer enemy of democracy; but there has been no stronger advocate of revolution.

In the *Ethics* Aristotle condemns democracy, even with a property qualification, as the worst of governments. But near the end of his life, when he composed his *Politics,* he was brought, grudgingly, to make a memorable concession. To preserve the sovereignty of law, which is the reason and the custom of generations, and to restrict the realm of choice and change, he conceived it best that no class of society should preponderate, that one man should not be subject to another, that all should command and all obey. He advised that power should be distributed to high and low; to the first according to their property, to the others according to numbers; and that it should centre in the middle class. If aristocracy and democracy were fairly combined and balanced against each other, he thought that none would be interested to disturb the serene majesty of impersonal government. To reconcile the two principles, he would admit even the poorer citizens to office and pay them for the discharge of public duties; but he would compel the rich to take their share, and would appoint magistrates by election and not by lot. In his indignation at the extravagance of Plato, and his sense of the significance of facts, he became, against his will, the prophetic exponent of a limited and regenerated democracy. But the *Politics*, which, to the world of living men, is the most valuable of his works, acquired no influence on antiquity, and is never quoted before the time of Cicero. Again it disappeared for many centuries; it was unknown to the Arabian commentators, and in Western Europe it was first brought to light by St. Thomas Aquinas, at the very time when an infusion of popular elements was modifying feudalism, and it helped to emancipate political philosophy from despotic theories and to confirm it in the ways of freedom.

The three generations of the Socratic school did more for the future reign of the people than all the institutions of the States of Greece. They vindicated conscience against authority and subjected both to a higher law; and they proclaimed that doctrine of a mixed constitution, which has prevailed at last over absolute monarchy, and still has to contend against extreme Republicans and Socialists, and against the masters of a hundred legions. But their views of liberty were based on expediency, not on justice. They legislated for the favoured citizens of Greece, and were conscious of no principle that extended the same rights to the stranger and the slave. That discovery, without which all political science was merely conventional, belongs to the followers of Zeno.

The dimness and poverty of their theological speculation caused the Stoics to attribute the government of the universe less to the uncertain design of gods than to a definite law of nature. By that law, which is superior to religious traditions and national authorities, and which every man can learn from a guardian angel who neither sleeps nor errs, all are governed alike, all are equal, all are bound in charity to each other, as members of one community and children of the same God. The unity of mankind implied the existence of rights and duties common to all men, which legislation neither gives nor takes away. The Stoics held in no esteem the institutions that vary with time and place, and their ideal society resembled a universal Church more than an actual State. In every collision between authority and conscience they preferred the inner to the outer guide; and, in the words of Epictetus, regarded the laws of the gods, not the wretched laws of the dead. Their doctrine of equality, of fraternity, of humanity; their defence of individualism against public authority; their repudiation of slavery, redeemed democracy from the narrowness, the want of principle and of sympathy, which are its reproach among the Greeks. In practical life they preferred a mixed constitution to a purely popular government. Chrysippus thought it impossible to please both gods and men; and Seneca declared that the people is corrupt and incapable, and that nothing was wanting, under Nero, to the fullness of liberty, except the possibility of destroying it. But their lofty conception of freedom, as no exceptional privilege but the birthright of mankind, survived in the law of nations and purified the equity of Rome.

Whilst Dorian oligarchs and Macedonian kings crushed the liberties of Greece, the Roman Republic was ruined, not by its enemies, for there was no enemy it did not conquer, but by its own vices. It was free from many causes of instability and dissolution that were active in Greece — the eager quickness, the philosophic thought, the independent belief, the pursuit of unsubstantial grace and beauty. It was protected by many subtle contrivances against the sovereignty of numbers and against legislation by surprise. Constitutional battles had to be fought over and over again; and progress was so slow, that reforms were often voted many years before they could be carried into effect. The authority allowed to fathers, to masters, to creditors, was as incompatible with the spirit of freedom as the practice of the servile East. The Roman citizen revelled in the luxury of power; and his jealous dread of every change that might impair its enjoyment portended a gloomy oligarchy. The cause which transformed the domination of rigid and exclusive patricians into the model Republic, and which out of the decomposed Republic built up the archetype of all despotism, was the fact that the Roman Commonwealth consisted of two States in one. The constitution was made up of compromises between independent bodies, and the obligation of observing contracts was the standing security for freedom. The plebs obtained self-government and an equal sovereignty, by the aid of the tribunes of the people, the peculiar, salient, and decisive invention of Roman statecraft. The powers conferred on the tribunes, that they might be the guardians of the weak, were ill defined, but practically were irresistible. They could not govern, but they could arrest all government. The first and the last step of plebeian progress was gained neither by violence nor persuasion, but by seceding; and, in like manner, the tribunes overcame all the authorities of the State by the weapon of obstruction. It was by stopping public business for five years that Licinius established democratic equality. The safeguard against abuse was the right of each tribune to veto the acts of his colleagues. As they were independent of their electors, and as there could hardly fail to be one wise and honest man among the ten, this was the most effective instrument for the defence of minorities ever devised by man. After the Hortensian law, which in the year 286 gave to the plebeian assembly co-ordinate legislative authority, the tribunes ceased to represent the cause of a minority, and their work was done.

A scheme less plausible or less hopeful than one which created two sovereign legislatures side by side in the same community would be hard to find. Yet it effectually closed the conflict of centuries, and gave to Rome an epoch of constant prosperity and greatness. No real division subsisted in the people, corresponding to the artificial division in the State. Fifty years passed away before the popular assembly made use of its prerogative, and passed a law in opposition to the senate. Polybius could not detect a flaw in the structure as it stood. The harmony seemed to be complete, and he judged that a more perfect example of composite government could not exist. But during those happy years the cause which wrought the ruin of Roman freedom was in full activity; for it was the condition of perpetual war that brought about the three great changes which were the beginning of the end — the reforms of the Gracchi, the arming of the paupers, and the gift of the Roman suffrage to the people of Italy.

Before the Romans began their career of foreign conquest they possessed an army of 770,000 men; and from that time the consumption of citizens in war was incessant. Regions once crowded with the small freeholds of four or five acres, which were the ideal unit of Roman society and the sinew of the army and the State, were covered with herds of cattle and herds of slaves, and the substance of the governing democracy was drained. The policy of the agrarian reform was to reconstitute this peasant class out of the public domains, that is, out of lands which the ruling families had possessed for generations, which they had bought and sold, inherited, divided, cultivated, and improved. The conflict of interests that had so long slumbered revived with a fury unknown in the controversy between the patricians and the plebs. For it was now a question not of equal rights but of subjugation. The social restoration of democratic elements could not be accomplished without demolishing the senate; and this crisis at last exposed the defect of the machinery and the peril of divided powers that were not to be controlled or reconciled. The popular assembly, led by Gracchus, had the power of making laws; and the only constitutional check was, that one of the tribunes should be induced to bar the proceedings. Accordingly, the tribune Octavius interposed his veto. The tribunician power, the most sacred of powers, which could not be questioned because it was founded on a covenant between the two parts of the community and formed the keystone of their union, was employed, in opposition to the will of the people, to prevent a reform on which the preservation of the democracy depended. Gracchus caused Octavius to be deposed. Though not illegal, this was a thing unheard of, and it seemed to the Romans a sacrilegious act that shook the pillars of the State, for it was the first significant revelation of democratic sovereignty. A tribune might burn the arsenal and betray the city, yet he could not be called to account until his year of office had expired. But when he employed against the people the authority with which they had invested him, the spell was dissolved. The tribunes had been instituted as the champions of the oppressed, when the plebs feared oppression. It was resolved that they should not interfere on the weaker side when the democracy were the strongest. They were chosen by the people as their defence against the aristocracy. It was not to be borne that they should become the agents of the aristocracy to make them once more supreme. Against a popular tribune, whom no colleague was suffered to oppose, the wealthy classes were defenceless. It is true that he held office, and was inviolable, only for a year. But the younger Gracchus was re-elected. The nobles accused him of aiming at the crown. A tribune who should be practically irremovable, as well as legally irresistible, was little less than an emperor. The senate carried on the conflict as men do who fight, not for public interests but for their own existence. They rescinded the agrarian laws. They murdered the popular leaders. They abandoned the constitution to save themselves, and invested Sylla with a power beyond all monarchs, to exterminate their foes. The ghastly conception of a magistrate legally proclaimed superior to all the laws was familiar to the stern spirit of the Romans. The decemvirs had enjoyed that arbitrary authority; but practically they were restrained by the two provisions which alone were deemed efficacious in Rome, the short duration of office and its distribution among several colleagues. But the appointment of Sylla was neither limited nor divided. It was to last as long as he chose. Whatever he might do was right; and he was empowered to put whomsoever he pleased to death, without trial or accusation. All the victims who were butchered by his satellites suffered with the full sanction of the law.

When at last the democracy conquered, the Augustan monarchy, by which they perpetuated their triumph, was moderate in comparison with the licensed tyranny of the aristocratic chief. The Emperor was the constitutional head of the Republic, armed with all the powers requisite to master the senate. The instrument which had served to cast down the patricians was efficient against the new aristocracy of wealth and office. The tribunician power, conferred in perpetuity, made it unnecessary to create a king or a dictator. Thrice the senate proposed to Augustus the supreme power of making laws. He declared that the power of the tribunes already supplied him with all that he required. It enabled him to preserve the forms of a simulated republic. The most popular of all the magistracies of Rome furnished the marrow of imperialism. For the Empire was created, not by usurpation, but by the legal act of a jubilant people, eager to close the era of bloodshed and to secure the largess of grain and coin, which amounted, at last, to 900,000 pounds a year. The people transferred to the Emperor the plenitude of their own sovereignty. To limit his delegated power was to challenge their omnipotence, to renew the issue between the many and the few which had been decided at Pharsalus and Philippi. The Romans upheld the absolutism of the Empire because it was their own. The elementary antagonism between liberty and democracy, between the welfare of minorities and the supremacy of masses, became manifest. The friend of the one was a traitor to the other. The dogma, that absolute power may, by the hypothesis of a popular origin, be as legitimate as constitutional freedom, began, by the combined support of the people and the throne, to darken the air.

Legitimate, in the technical sense of modern politics, the Empire was not meant to be. It had no right or claim to subsist apart from the will of the people. To limit the Emperor's authority was to renounce their own; but to take it away was to assert their own. They gave the Empire as they chose. They took it away as they chose. The Revolution was as lawful and as irresponsible as the Empire. Democratic institutions continued to develop. The provinces were no longer subject to an assembly meeting in a distant capital. They obtained the privileges of Roman citizens. Long after Tiberius had stripped the inhabitants of Rome of their electoral function, the provincials continued in undisturbed enjoyment of the right of choosing their own magistrates. They governed themselves like a vast confederation of municipal republics; and, even after Diocletian had brought in the forms as well as the reality of despotism, provincial assemblies, the obscure germ of representative institutions, exercised some control over the Imperial officers.

But the Empire owed the intensity of its force to the popular fiction. The principle, that the Emperor is not subject to laws from which he can dispense others, *princeps legibus solutus,* was interpreted to imply that he was above all legal restraint. There was no appeal from his sentence. He was the living law. The Roman jurists, whilst they adorned their writings with the exalted philosophy of the Stoics, consecrated every excess of imperial prerogative with those famous maxims which have been balm to so many consciences and have sanctioned so much wrong; and the code of Justinian became the greatest obstacle, next to feudalism, with which liberty had to contend.

Ancient democracy, as it was in Athens in the best days of Pericles, or in Rome when Polybius described it, or even as it is idealised by Aristotle in the Sixth Book of his *Politics,* and by Cicero in the beginning of the Republic, was never more than a partial and insincere solution of the problem of popular government. The ancient politicians aimed no higher than to diffuse power among a numerous class. Their liberty was bound up with slavery. They never attempted to found a free State on the thrift and energy of free labour. They never divined the harder but more grateful task that constitutes the political life of Christian nations.

By humbling the supremacy of rank and wealth; by forbidding the State to encroach on the domain which belongs to God; by teaching man to love his neighbour as himself; by promoting the sense of equality; by condemning the pride of race, which was a stimulus of conquest, and the doctrine of separate descent, which formed the philosopher's defence of slavery; and by addressing not the rulers but the masses of mankind, and making opinion superior to authority, the Church that preached the Gospel to the poor had visible points of contact with democracy. And yet Christianity did not directly influence political progress. The ancient watchword of the Republic was translated by Papinian into the language of the Church: "Summa est ratio quæ pro religione fiat:" and for eleven hundred years, from the first to the last of the Constantines, the Christian Empire was as despotic as the pagan.

Meanwhile Western Europe was overrun by men who in their early home had been Republicans. The primitive constitution of the German communities was based on association rather than on subordination. They were accustomed to govern their affairs by common deliberation, and to obey authorities that were temporary and defined. It is one of the desperate enterprises of historical science to trace the free institutions of Europe and America, and Australia, to the life that was led in the forests of Germany. But the new States were founded on conquest, and in war the Germans were commanded by kings. The doctrine of self-government, applied to Gaul and Spain, would have made Frank and Goth disappear in the mass of the conquered people. It needed all the resources of a vigorous monarchy, of a military aristocracy, and of a territorial clergy, to construct States that were able to last. The result was the feudal system, the most absolute contradiction of democracy that has coexisted with civilisation.

The revival of democracy was due neither to the Christian Church nor to the Teutonic State, but to the quarrel between them. The effect followed the cause instantaneously. As soon as Gregory VII made the Papacy independent of the Empire, the great conflict began; and the same pontificate gave birth to the theory of the sovereignty of the people. The Gregorian party argued that the Emperor derived his crown from the nation, and that the nation could take away what it had bestowed. The Imperialists replied that nobody could take away what the nation had given. It is idle to look for the spark either in flint or steel. The object of both parties was unqualified supremacy. Fitznigel has no more idea of ecclesiastical liberty than John of Salisbury of political. Innocent IV is as perfect an absolutist as Peter de Vineis. But each party encouraged democracy in turn, by seeking the aid of the towns; each party in turn appealed to the people, and gave strength to the constitutional theory. In the fourteenth century English Parliaments judged and deposed their kings, as a matter of right; the Estates governed France without king or noble; and the wealth and liberties of the towns, which had worked out their independence from the centre of Italy to the North Sea, promised for a moment to transform European society. Even in the capitals of great princes, in Rome, in Paris, and, for two terrible days, in London, the commons obtained sway. But the curse of instability was on the municipal republics. Strasburg, according to Erasmus and Bodin, the best governed of all, suffered from perpetual commotions. An ingenious historian has reckoned seven thousand revolutions in the Italian cities. The democracies succeeded no better than feudalism in regulating the balance between rich and poor. The atrocities of the Jacquerie, and of Wat Tyler's rebellion, hardened the hearts of men against the common people. Church and State combined to put them down. And the last memorable struggles of mediæval liberty — the insurrection of the Comuneros in Castile, the Peasants' War in Germany, the Republic of Florence, and the Revolt of Ghent — were suppressed by Charles V in the early years of the Reformation.

The middle ages had forged a complete arsenal of constitutional maxims; trial by jury, taxation by representation, local self-government, ecclesiastical independence, responsible authority. But they were not secured by institutions, and the Reformation began by making the dry bones more dry. Luther claimed to be the first divine who did justice to the civil power. He made the Lutheran Church the bulwark of political stability, and bequeathed to his disciples the doctrine of divine right and passive obedience. Zwingli, who was a staunch republican, desired that all magistrates should be elected, and should be liable to be dismissed by the electors; but he died too soon for his influence, and the permanent action of the Reformation on democracy was exercised through the Presbyterian constitution of Calvin.

It was long before the democratic element in Presbyterianism began to tell. The Netherlands resisted Philip II for fifteen years before they took courage to depose him, and the scheme of the ultra-Calvinist Deventer, to subvert the ascendency of the leading States by the sovereign action of the whole people, was foiled by Leicester's incapacity, and by the consummate policy of Barnevelt. The Huguenots, having lost their leaders in 1572, reconstituted themselves on a democratic footing, and learned to think that a king who murders his subjects forfeits his divine right to be obeyed. But Junius Brutus and Buchanan damaged their credit by advocating regicide; and Hotman, whose *Franco-Gallia* is the most serious work of the group, deserted his liberal opinions when the chief of his own party became king. The most violent explosion of democracy in that age proceeded from the opposite quarter. When Henry of Navarre became the next heir to the throne of France, the theory of the deposing power, which had proved ineffectual for more than a century, awoke with a new and more vigorous life. One-half of the nation accepted the view, that they were not bound to submit to a king they would not have chosen. A Committee of Sixteen made itself master of Paris, and, with the aid of Spain, succeeded for years in excluding Henry from his capital. The impulse thus given endured in literature for a whole generation, and produced a library of treatises on the right of Catholics to choose, to control, and to cashier their magistrates. They were on the losing side. Most of them were bloodthirsty, and were soon forgotten. But the greater part of the political ideas of Milton, Locke, and Rousseau, may be found in the ponderous Latin of Jesuits who were subjects of the Spanish Crown, of Lessius, Molina, Mariana, and Suarez.

The ideas were there, and were taken up when it suited them by extreme adherents of Rome and of Geneva; but they produced no lasting fruit until, a century after the Reformation, they became incorporated in new religious systems. Five years of civil war could not exhaust the royalism of the Presbyterians, and it required the expulsion of the majority to make the Long Parliament abandon monarchy. It had defended the constitution against the crown with legal arts, defending precedent against innovation, and setting up an ideal in the past which, with all the learning of Selden and of Prynne, was less certain than the Puritan statesmen supposed. The Independents brought in a new principle. Tradition had no authority for them, and the past no virtue. Liberty of conscience, a thing not to be found in the constitution, was more prized by many of them than all the statutes of the Plantagenets. Their idea that each congregation should govern itself abolished the force which is needed to preserve unity, and deprived monarchy of the weapon which made it injurious to freedom. An immense revolutionary energy resided in their doctrine, and it took root in America, and deeply coloured political thought in later times. But in England the sectarian democracy was strong only to destroy. Cromwell refused to be bound by it; and John Lilburne, the boldest thinker among English democrats, declared that it would be better for liberty to bring back Charles Stuart than to live under the sword of the Protector.

Lilburne was among the first to understand the real conditions of democracy, and the obstacle to its success in England. Equality of power could not be preserved, except by violence, together with an extreme inequality of possessions. There would always be danger, if power was not made to wait on property, that property would go to those who had the power. This idea of the necessary balance of property, developed by Harrington, and adopted by Milton in his later pamphlets, appeared to Toland, and even to John Adams, as important as the invention of printing, or the discovery of the circulation of the blood. At least it indicates the true explanation of the strange completeness with which the Republican party had vanished, a dozen years after the solemn trial and execution of the King. No extremity of misgovernment was able to revive it. When the treason of Charles II against the constitution was divulged, and the Whigs plotted to expel the incorrigible dynasty, their aspirations went no farther than a Venetian oligarchy, with Monmouth for Doge. The Revolution of 1688 confined power to the aristocracy of freeholders. The conservatism of the age was unconquerable.

Republicanism was distorted even in Switzerland, and became in the eighteenth century as oppressive and as intolerant as its neighbours.

In 1769, when Paoli fled from Corsica, it seemed that, in Europe at least, democracy was dead. It had, indeed, lately been defended in books by a man of bad reputation, whom the leaders of public opinion treated with contumely, and whose declamations excited so little alarm that George III offered him a pension. What gave to Rousseau a power far exceeding that which any political writer had ever attained was the progress of events in America. The Stuarts had been willing that the colonies should serve as a refuge from their system of Church and State, and of all their colonies the one most favoured was the territory granted to William Penn. By the principles of the Society to which he belonged, it was necessary that the new State should be founded on liberty and equality. But Penn was further noted among Quakers as a follower of the new doctrine of Toleration. Thus it came to pass that Pennsylvania enjoyed the most democratic constitution in the world, and held up to the admiration of the eighteenth century an almost solitary example of freedom. It was principally through Franklin and the Quaker State that America influenced political opinion in Europe, and that the fanaticism of one revolutionary epoch was converted into the rationalism of another. American independence was the beginning of a new era, not merely as a revival of Revolution, but because no other Revolution ever proceeded from so slight a cause, or was ever conducted with so much moderation. The European monarchies supported it. The greatest statesmen in England averred that it was just. It established a pure democracy; but it was democracy in its highest perfection, armed and vigilant, less against aristocracy and monarchy than against its own weakness and excess. Whilst England was admired for the safeguards with which, in the course of many centuries, it had fortified liberty against the power of the crown, America appeared still more worthy of admiration for the safeguards which, in the deliberations of a single memorable year, it had set up against the power of its own sovereign people. It resembled no other known democracy, for it respected freedom, authority, and law. It resembled no other constitution, for it was contained in half a dozen intelligible articles. Ancient Europe opened its mind to two new ideas — that Revolution with very little provocation may be just; and that democracy in very large dimensions may be safe.

Whilst America was making itself independent, the spirit of reform had been abroad in Europe. Intelligent ministers, like Campomanes and Struensee, and well-meaning monarchs, of whom the most liberal was Leopold of Tuscany, were trying what could be done to make men happy by command. Centuries of absolute and intolerant rule had bequeathed abuses which nothing but the most vigorous use of power could remove. The age preferred the reign of intellect to the reign of liberty. Turgot, the ablest and most far-seeing reformer then living, attempted to do for France what less gifted men were doing with success in Lombardy, and Tuscany, and Parma. He attempted to employ the royal power for the good of the people, at the expense of the higher classes. The higher classes proved too strong for the crown alone; and Louis XVI abandoned internal reforms in despair, and turned for compensation to a war with England for the deliverance of her American Colonies. When the increasing debt obliged him to seek heroic remedies, and he was again repulsed by the privileged orders, he appealed at last to the nation. When the States-General met, the power had already passed to the middle class, for it was by them alone that the country could be saved. They were strong enough to triumph by waiting. Neither the Court, nor the nobles, nor the army, could do anything against them. During the six months from January, 1789, to the fall of the Bastille in July, France travelled as far as England in the six hundred years between the Earl of Leicester and Lord Beaconsfield. Ten years after the American alliance, the Rights of Man, which had been proclaimed at Philadelphia, were repeated at Versailles. The alliance had borne fruit on both sides of the Atlantic, and for France, the fruit was the triumph of American ideas over

English. They were more popular, more simple, more effective against privilege, and, strange to say, more acceptable to the King. The new French constitution allowed no privileged orders, no parliamentary ministry, no power of dissolution, and only a suspensive veto. But the characteristic safeguards of the American government were rejected: Federalism, separation of Church and State, the Second Chamber, the political arbitration of the supreme judicial body. That which weakened the Executive was taken: that which restrained the Legislature was left. Checks on the crown abounded; but should the crown be vacant, the powers that remained would be without a check. The precautions were all in one direction. Nobody would contemplate the contingency that there might be no king. The constitution was inspired by a profound disbelief in Louis XVI and a pertinacious belief in monarchy. The assembly voted without debate, by acclamation, a Civil List three times as large as that of Queen Victoria. When Louis fled, and the throne was actually vacant, they brought him back to it, preferring the phantom of a king who was a prisoner to the reality of no king at all.

Next to this misapplication of American examples, which was the fault of nearly all the leading statesmen, excepting Mounier, Mirabeau, and Siéyès, the cause of the Revolution was injured by its religious policy. The most novel and impressive lesson taught by the fathers of the American Republic was that the people, and not the administration, should govern. Men in office were salaried agents, by whom the nation wrought its will. Authority submitted to public opinion, and left to it not only the control, but the initiative of government. Patience in waiting for a wind, alacrity in catching it, the dread of exerting unnecessary influence, characterise the early presidents. Some of the French politicians shared this view, though with less exaggeration than Washington. They wished to decentralise the government, and to obtain, for good or evil, the genuine expression of popular sentiment. Necker himself, and Buzot, the most thoughtful of the Girondins, dreamed of federalising France.

In the United States there was no current of opinion, and no combination of forces, to be seriously feared. The government needed no security against being propelled in a wrong direction. But the French Revolution was accomplished at the expense of powerful classes. Besides the nobles, the Assembly, which had been made supreme by the accession of the clergy, and had been led at first by popular ecclesiastics, by Siéyès, Talleyrand, Cicé, La Luzerne, made an enemy of the clergy. The prerogative could not be destroyed without touching the Church. Ecclesiastical patronage had helped to make the crown absolute. To leave it in the hands of Louis and his ministers was to renounce the entire policy of the constitution. To disestablish, was to make it over to the Pope. It was consistent with the democratic principle to introduce election into the Church. It involved a breach with Rome; but so, indeed, did the laws of Joseph II, Charles III, and Leopold. The Pope was not likely to cast away the friendship of France, if he could help it; and the French clergy were not likely to give trouble by their attachment to Rome. Therefore, amid the indifference of many, and against the urgent, and probably sincere, remonstrances of Robespierre and Marat, the Jansenists, who had a century of persecution to avenge, carried the Civil Constitution. The coercive measures which enforced it led to the breach with the King, and the fall of the monarchy; to the revolt of the provinces, and the fall of liberty. The Jacobins determined that public opinion should not reign, that the State should not remain at the mercy of powerful combinations. They held the representatives of the people under control, by the people itself. They attributed higher authority to the direct than to the indirect voice of the democratic oracle. They armed themselves with power to crush every adverse, every independent force, and especially to put down the Church, in whose cause the provinces had risen against the capital. They met the centrifugal federalism of the friends of the Gironde by the most resolute centralisation. France was governed by Paris; and Paris by its municipality and its mob. Obeying Rousseau's maxim, that the people cannot delegate its power, they raised the elementary constituency above its representatives. As the greatest constituent body, the most numerous accumulation of primary electors, the largest portion of sovereignty, was in the people of Paris, they designed that the people of Paris should rule over France, as the people of Rome, the mob as well as the senate, had ruled, not ingloriously, over Italy, and over half the nations that surround the Mediterranean. Although the Jacobins were scarcely more irreligious than the Abbé Siéyès or Madame Roland, although Robespierre wanted to force men to believe in God, although Danton went to confession and Barère was a professing Christian, they imparted to modern democracy that implacable hatred of religion which contrasts so strangely with the example of its Puritan prototype.

The deepest cause which made the French Revolution so disastrous to liberty was its theory of equality. Liberty was the watchword of the middle class, equality of the lower. It was the lower class that won the battles of the third estate; that took the Bastille, and made France a constitutional monarchy; that took the Tuileries, and made France a Republic. They claimed their reward. The middle class, having cast down the upper orders with the aid of the lower, instituted a new inequality and a privilege for itself. By means of a taxpaying qualification it deprived its confederates of their vote. To those, therefore, who had accomplished the Revolution, its promise was not fulfilled. Equality did nothing for them. The opinion, at that time, was almost universal, that society is founded on an agreement which is voluntary and conditional, and that the links which bind men to it are terminable, for sufficient reason, like those which subject them to authority. From these popular premises the logic of Marat drew his sanguinary conclusions. He told the famished people that the conditions on which they had consented to bear their evil lot, and had refrained from violence, had not been kept to them. It was suicide, it was murder, to submit to starve and to see one's children starving, by the fault of the rich. The bonds of society were dissolved by the wrong it inflicted. The state of nature had come back, in which every man had a right to what he could take. The time had come for the rich to make way for the poor. With this theory of equality, liberty was quenched in blood, and Frenchmen became ready to sacrifice all other things to save life and fortune.

Twenty years after the splendid opportunity that opened in 1789, the reaction had triumphed everywhere in Europe; ancient constitutions had perished as well as new; and even England afforded them neither protection nor sympathy. The liberal, at least the democratic revival, came from Spain. The Spaniards fought against the French for a king, who was a prisoner in France. They gave themselves a constitution, and placed his name at the head of it. They had a monarchy, without a king. It required to be so contrived that it would work in the absence, possibly the permanent absence, of the monarch. It became, therefore, a monarchy only in name, composed, in fact, of democratic forces. The constitution of 1812 was the attempt of inexperienced men to accomplish the most difficult task in politics. It was smitten with sterility. For many years it was the standard of abortive revolutions among the so-called Latin nations. It promulgated the notion of a king who should flourish only in name, and should not even discharge the humble function which Hegel assigns to royalty, of dotting i's for the people.

The overthrow of the Cadiz constitution, in 1823, was the supreme triumph of the restored monarchy of France. Five years later, under a wise and liberal minister, the Restoration was advancing fairly on the constitutional paths, when the incurable distrust of the Liberal party defeated Martignac, and brought in the ministry of extreme royalists that ruined the monarchy. In labouring to transfer power from the class which the Revolution had enfranchised to those which it had overthrown, Polignac and La Bourdonnaie would gladly have made terms with the working men. To break the influence of intellect and capital by means of universal suffrage, was an idea long and zealously advocated by some of their supporters. They had not foresight or ability to divide their adversaries, and they were vanquished in 1830 by the united democracy.

The promise of the Revolution of July was to reconcile royalists and democrats. The King assured Lafayette that he was a republican at heart; and Lafayette assured France that Louis Philippe was the best of republics. The shock of the great event was felt in Poland, and Belgium, and even in England. It gave a direct impulse to democratic movements in Switzerland.

Swiss democracy had been in abeyance since 1815. The national will had no organ. The cantons were supreme; and governed as inefficiently as other governments under the protecting shade of the Holy Alliance. There was no dispute that Switzerland called for extensive reforms, and no doubt of the direction they would take. The number of the cantons was the great obstacle to all improvement. It was useless to have twenty-five governments in a country equal to one American State, and inferior in population to one great city. It was impossible that they should be good governments. A central power was the manifest need of the country. In the absence of an efficient federal power, seven cantons formed a separate league for the protection of their own interests. Whilst democratic ideas were making way in Switzerland, the Papacy was travelling in the opposite direction, and showing an inflexible hostility for ideas which are the breath of democratic life. The growing democracy and the growing Ultramontanism came into collision. The Sonderbund could aver with truth that there was no safety for its rights under the Federal Constitution. The others could reply, with equal truth, that there was no safety for the constitution with the Sonderbund. In 1847, it came to a war between national sovereignty and cantonal sovereignty. The Sonderbund was dissolved, and a new Federal Constitution was adopted, avowedly and ostensibly charged with the duty of carrying out democracy, and repressing the adverse influence of Rome. It was a delusive imitation of the American system. The President was powerless. The Senate was powerless. The Supreme Court was powerless. The sovereignty of the cantons was undermined, and their power centred in the House of Representatives. The Constitution of 1848 was a first step towards the destruction of Federalism. Another and almost a final step in the direction of centralisation was taken in 1874. The railways, and the vast interests they created, made the position of the cantonal governments untenable. The conflict with the Ultramontanes increased the demand for vigorous action; and the destruction of State Rights in the American war strengthened the hands of the Centralists. The Constitution of 1874 is one of the most significant works of modern democracy. It is the triumph of democratic force over democratic freedom. It overrules not only the Federal principle, but the representative principle. It carries important measures away from the Federal Legislature to submit them to the votes of the entire people, separating decision from deliberation. The operation is so cumbrous as to be generally ineffective. But it constitutes a power such as exists, we believe, under the laws of no other country. A Swiss jurist has frankly expressed the spirit of the reigning system by saying, that the State is the appointed conscience of the nation.

The moving force in Switzerland has been democracy relieved of all constraint, the principle of putting in action the greatest force of the greatest number. The prosperity of the country has prevented complications such as arose in France. The ministers of Louis Philippe, able and enlightened men, believed that they would make the people prosper if they could have their own way, and could shut out public opinion. They acted as if the intelligent middle class was destined by heaven to govern. The upper class had proved its unfitness before 1789; the lower class, since 1789. Government by professional men, by manufacturers and scholars, was sure to be safe, and almost sure to be reasonable and practical. Money became the object of a political superstition, such as had formerly attached to land, and afterwards attached to labour. The masses of the people, who had fought against Marmont, became aware that they had not fought for their own benefit. They were still governed by their employers.

When the King parted with Lafayette, and it was found that he would not only reign but govern, the indignation of the republicans found a vent in street fighting. In 1836, when the horrors of the infernal machine had armed the crown with ampler powers, and had silenced the republican party, the term Socialism made its appearance in literature. Tocqueville, who was writing the philosophic chapters that conclude his work, failed to discover the power which the new system was destined to exercise on democracy. Until then, democrats and communists had stood apart. Although the socialist doctrines were defended by the best intellects of France, by Thierry, Comte, Chevalier, and Georges Sand, they excited more attention as a literary curiosity than as the cause of future revolutions. Towards 1840, in the recesses of secret societies, republicans and socialists coalesced. Whilst the Liberal leaders, Lamartine and Barrot, discoursed on the surface concerning reform, Ledru Rollin and Louis Blanc were quietly digging a grave for the monarchy, the Liberal party, and the reign of wealth. They worked so well, and the vanquished republicans recovered so thoroughly, by this coalition, the influence they had lost by a long series of crimes and follies, that, in 1848, they were able to conquer without fighting. The fruit of their victory was universal suffrage.

From that time the promises of socialism have supplied the best energy of democracy. Their coalition has been the ruling fact in French politics. It created the "saviour of society," and the Commune; and it still entangles the footsteps of the Republic. It is the only shape in which democracy has found an entrance into Germany. Liberty has lost its spell; and democracy maintains itself by the promise of substantial gifts to the masses of the people.

Since the Revolution of July and the Presidency of Jackson gave the impulse which has made democracy preponderate, the ablest political writers, Tocqueville, Calhoun, Mill, and Laboulaye, have drawn, in the name of freedom, a formidable indictment against it. They have shown democracy without respect for the past or care for the future, regardless of public faith and of national honour, extravagant and inconstant, jealous of talent and of knowledge, indifferent to justice but servile towards opinion, incapable of organisation, impatient of authority, averse from obedience, hostile to religion and to established law. Evidence indeed abounds, even if the true cause be not proved. But it is not to these symptoms that we must impute the permanent danger and the irrepressible conflict. As much might be made good against monarchy, and an unsympathising reasoner might in the same way argue that religion is intolerant, that conscience makes cowards, that piety rejoices in fraud. Recent experience has added little to the observations of those who witnessed the decline after Pericles, of Thucydides, Aristophanes, Plato, and of the writer whose brilliant tract against the Athenian Republic is printed among the works of Xenophon. The manifest, the avowed difficulty is that democracy, no less than monarchy or aristocracy, sacrifices everything to maintain itself and strives, with an energy and a plausibility that kings and nobles cannot attain, to override representation, to annul all the forces of resistance and deviation, and to secure, by Plebiscite, Referendum, or Caucus, free play for the will of the majority. The true democratic principle, that none shall have power over the people, is taken to mean that none shall be able to restrain or to elude its power. The true democratic principle, that the people shall not be made to do what it does not like, is taken to mean that it shall never be required to tolerate what it does not like. The true democratic principle, that every man's free will shall be as unfettered as possible, is taken to mean that the free will of the collective people shall be fettered in nothing. Religious toleration, judicial independence, dread of centralisation, jealousy of State interference, become obstacles to freedom instead of safeguards, when the centralised force of the State is wielded by the hands of the people. Democracy claims to be not only supreme, without authority above, but absolute, without independence below; to be its own master, not a trustee. The old sovereigns of the world are exchanged for a new one, who may be flattered and deceived but whom it is impossible to corrupt or to resist, and to whom must be rendered the things that are Cæsar's and also the things that are God's. The enemy to be overcome is no longer the absolutism of the State, but the liberty of the subject. Nothing is more significant than the relish with which Ferrari, the most powerful democratic writer since Rousseau, enumerates the merits of tyrants, and prefers devils to saints in the interest of the community.

For the old notions of civil liberty and of social order did not benefit the masses of the people. Wealth increased, without relieving their wants. The progress of knowledge left them in abject ignorance. Religion flourished, but failed to reach them. Society, whose laws were made by the upper class alone, announced that the best thing for the poor is not to be born, and the next best, to die in childhood, and suffered them to live in misery and crime and pain. As surely as the long reign of the rich has been employed in promoting the accumulation of wealth, the advent of the poor to power will be followed by schemes for diffusing it. Seeing how little was done by the wisdom of former times for education and public health, for insurance, association, and savings, for the protection of labour against the law of self-interest, and how much has been accomplished in this generation, there is reason in the fixed belief that a great change was needed, and that democracy has not striven in vain. Liberty, for the mass, is not happiness; and institutions are not an end but a means. The thing they seek is a force sufficient to sweep away scruples and the obstacles of rival interests, and, in some degree, to better their condition. They mean that the strong hand that heretofore has formed great States, protected religions, and defended the independence of nations, shall help them by preserving life, and endowing it for them with some, at least, of the things men live for. That is the notorious danger of modern democracy. That is also its purpose and its strength. And against this threatening power the weapons that struck down other despots do not avail. The greatest happiness principle positively confirms it. The principle of equality, besides being as easily applied to property as to power, opposes the existence of persons or groups of persons exempt from the common law, and independent of the common will; and the principle, that authority is a matter of contract, may hold good against kings, but not against the sovereign people, because a contract implies two parties.

If we have not done more than the ancients to develop and to examine the disease, we have far surpassed them in studying the remedy. Besides the French Constitution of the year III, and that of the American Confederates, — the most remarkable attempts that have been made since the archonship of Euclides to meet democratic evils with the antidotes which democracy itself supplies, — our age has been prolific in this branch of experimental politics.

Many expedients have been tried, that have been evaded or defeated. A divided executive, which was an important phase in the transformation of ancient monarchies into republics, and which, through the advocacy of Condorcet, took root in France, has proved to be weakness itself.

The Constitution of 1795, the work of a learned priest, confined the franchise to those who should know how to read and write; and in 1849 this provision was rejected by men who intended that the ignorant voter should help them to overturn the Republic. In our time no democracy could long subsist without educating the masses; and the scheme of Daunou is simply an indirect encouragement to elementary instruction.

In 1799 Siéyès suggested to Bonaparte the idea of a great Council, whose function it should be to keep the acts of the Legislature in harmony with the constitution — a function which the *Nomophylakes* discharged at Athens, and the Supreme Court in the United States, and which produced the Sénat Conservateur, one of the favourite implements of Imperialism. Siéyès meant that his Council should also serve the purpose of a gilded ostracism, having power to absorb any obnoxious politician, and to silence him with a thousand a year.

Napoleon the Third's plan of depriving unmarried men of their votes would have disfranchised the two greatest Conservative classes in France, the priest and the soldier.

In the American Constitution it was intended that the chief of the executive should be chosen by a body of carefully selected electors. But since, in 1825, the popular candidate succumbed to one who had only a minority of votes, it has become the practice to elect the President by the pledged delegates of universal suffrage.

The exclusion of ministers from Congress has been one of the severest strains on the American system; and the law which required a majority of three to one enabled Louis Napoleon to make himself Emperor. Large constituencies make independent deputies; but experience proves that small assemblies, the consequence of large constituencies, can be managed by government.

The composite vote and the cumulative vote have been almost universally rejected as schemes for baffling the majority. But the principle of dividing the representatives equally between population and property has never had fair play. It was introduced by Thouret into the Constitution of 1791. The Revolution made it inoperative; and it was so manipulated from 1817 to 1848 by the fatal dexterity of Guizot as to make opinion ripe for universal suffrage.

Constitutions which forbid the payment of deputies and the system of imperative instructions, which deny the power of dissolution, and make the Legislature last for a fixed term, or renew it by partial re-elections, and which require an interval between the several debates on the same measure, evidently strengthen the independence of the representative assembly. The Swiss veto has the same effect, as it suspends legislation only when opposed by a majority of the whole electoral body, not by a majority of those who actually vote upon it.

Indirect elections are scarcely anywhere in use out of Germany, but they have been a favourite corrective of democracy with many thoughtful politicians. Where the extent of the electoral district obliges constituents to vote for candidates who are unknown to them, the election is not free. It is managed by wire-pullers, and by party machinery, beyond the control of the electors. Indirect election puts the choice of the managers into their hands. The objection is that the intermediate electors are generally too few to span the interval between voters and candidates, and that they choose representatives not of better quality, but of different politics. If the intermediate body consisted of one in ten of the whole constituency, the contact would be preserved, the people would be really represented, and the ticket system would be broken down.

The one pervading evil of democracy is the tyranny of the majority, or rather of that party, not always the majority, that succeeds, by force or fraud, in carrying elections. To break off that point is to avert the danger. The common system of representation perpetuates the danger. Unequal electorates afford no security to majorities. Equal electorates give none to minorities. Thirty-five years ago it was pointed out that the remedy is proportional representation. It is profoundly democratic, for it increases the influence of thousands who would otherwise have no voice in the government; and it brings men more near an equality by so contriving that no vote shall be wasted, and that every voter shall contribute to bring into Parliament a member of his own opinions. The origin of the idea is variously claimed for Lord Grey and for Considérant. The successful example of Denmark and the earnest advocacy of Mill gave it prominence in the world of politics. It has gained popularity with the growth of democracy, and we are informed by M. Naville that in Switzerland Conservatives and Radicals combined to promote it.

Of all checks on democracy, federalism has been the most efficacious and the most congenial; but, becoming associated with the Red Republic, with feudalism, with the Jesuits, and with slavery, it has fallen into disrepute, and is giving way to centralism. The federal system limits and restrains the sovereign power by dividing it, and by assigning to government only certain defined rights. It is the only method of curbing not only the majority but the power of the whole people, and it affords the strongest basis for a second chamber, which has been found the essential security for freedom in every genuine democracy.

The fall of Guizot discredited the famous maxim of the Doctrinaires, that Reason is sovereign, and not king or people; and it was further exposed to the scoffer by the promise of Comte that Positivist philosophers shall manufacture political ideas, which no man shall be permitted to dispute. But putting aside international and criminal law, in which there is some approach to uniformity, the domain of political economy seems destined to admit the rigorous certainty of science. Whenever that shall be attained, when the battle between economists and socialists is ended, the evil force which socialism imparts to democracy will be spent. The battle is raging more violently than ever, but it has entered into a new phase, by the rise of a middle party. Whether that remarkable movement, which is promoted by some of the first economists in Europe, is destined to shake the authority of their science, or to conquer socialism, by robbing it of that which is the secret of its strength, it must be recorded here as the latest and the most serious effort that has been made to disprove the weighty sentence of Rousseau, that democracy is a government for gods, but unfit for man.

We have been able to touch on only a few of the topics that crowd Sir Erskine May's volumes. Although he has perceived more clearly than Tocqueville the contact of democracy with socialism, his judgment is untinged with Tocqueville's despondency, and he contemplates the direction of progress with a confidence that approaches optimism. The notion of an inflexible logic in history does not depress him, for he concerns himself with facts and with men more than with doctrines, and his book is a history of several democracies, not of democracy. There are links in the argument, there are phases of development which he leaves unnoticed, because his object has not been to trace out the properties and the connection of ideas, but to explain the results of experience. We should consult his pages, probably, without effect, if we wished to follow the origin and sequence of the democratic dogmas, that all men are equal; that speech and thought are free; that each generation is a law to itself only; that there shall be no endowments, no entails, no primogeniture; that the people are sovereign; that the people can do no wrong. The great mass of those who, of necessity, are interested in practical politics have no such antiquarian curiosity. They want to know what can be learned from the countries where the democratic experiments have been tried; but they do not care to be told how M. Waddington has emended the *Monumentum Ancyranum,* what connection there was between Mariana and Milton, or between Penn and Rousseau, or who invented the proverb *Vox Populi Vox Dei.* Sir Erskine May's reluctance to deal with matters speculative and doctrinal, and to devote his space to the mere literary history of politics, has made his touch somewhat uncertain in treating of the political action of Christianity, perhaps the most complex and comprehensive question that can embarrass a historian. He disparages the influence of the mediæval Church on nations just emerging from a barbarous paganism, and he exalts it when it had become associated with despotism and persecution. He insists on the liberating action of the Reformation in the sixteenth century, when it gave a stimulus to absolutism; and he is slow to recognise, in the enthusiasm and violence of the sects in the seventeenth, the most potent agency ever brought to bear on democratic history. The omission of America creates a void between 1660 and 1789, and leaves much unexplained in the revolutionary movement of the last hundred years, which is the central problem of the book. But if some things are missed from the design, if the execution is not equal in every part, the praise remains to Sir Erskine May, that he is the only writer who has ever brought together the materials for a comparative study of democracy, that he has avoided the temper of party, that he has shown a hearty sympathy for the progress and improvement of mankind, and a steadfast faith in the wisdom and the power that guide it.

CHAPTER VI

NATIONALITY

WHENEVER GREAT INTELLECTUAL cultivation has been combined with that suffering which is inseparable from extensive changes in the condition of the people, men of speculative or imaginative genius have sought in the contemplation of an ideal society a remedy, or at least a consolation, for evils which they were practically unable to remove. Poetry has always preserved the idea, that at some distant time or place, in the Western islands or the Arcadian region, an innocent and contented people, free from the corruption and restraint of civilised life, have realised the legends of the golden age. The office of the poets is always nearly the same, and there is little variation in the features of their ideal world; but when philosophers attempt to admonish or reform mankind by devising an imaginary state, their motive is more definite and immediate, and their commonwealth is a satire as well as a model. Plato and Plotinus, More and Campanella, constructed their fanciful societies with those materials which were omitted from the fabric of the actual communities, by the defects of which they were inspired. The Republic, the Utopia, and the City of the Sun were protests against a state of things which the experience of their authors taught them to condemn, and from the faults of which they took refuge in the opposite extremes. They remained without influence, and have never passed from literary into political history, be-

NOTE: This essay first appeared in *The Home and Foreign Review*, I (July, 1862), 146-74; reprinted in *The History of Freedom and Other Essays* (London, Macmillan Co., 1907), pp. 270-300.

cause something more than discontent and speculative ingenuity is needed in order to invest a political idea with power over the masses of mankind. The scheme of a philosopher can command the practical allegiance of fanatics only, not of nations; and though oppression may give rise to violent and repeated outbreaks, like the convulsions of a man in pain, it cannot mature a settled purpose and plan of regeneration, unless a new notion of happiness is joined to the sense of present evil.

The history of religion furnishes a complete illustration. Between the later mediæval sects and Protestantism there is an essential difference, that outweighs the points of analogy found in those systems which are regarded as heralds of the Reformation, and is enough to explain the vitality of the last in comparison with the others. Whilst Wyclif and Hus contradicted certain particulars of the Catholic teaching, Luther rejected the authority of the Church, and gave to the individual conscience an independence which was sure to lead to an incessant resistance. There is a similar difference between the Revolt of the Netherlands, the Great Rebellion, the War of Independence, or the rising of Brabant, on the one hand, and the French Revolution on the other. Before 1789, insurrections were provoked by particular wrongs, and were justified by definite complaints and by an appeal to principles which all men acknowledged. New theories were sometimes advanced in the cause of controversy, but they were accidental, and the great argument against tyranny was fidelity to the ancient laws. Since the change produced by the French Revolution, those aspirations which are awakened by the evils and defects of the social state have come to act as permanent and energetic forces throughout the civilised world. They are spontaneous and aggressive, needing no prophet to proclaim, no champion to defend them, but popular, unreasoning, and almost irresistible. The Revolution effected this change, partly by its doctrines, partly by the indirect influence of events. It taught the people to regard their wishes and wants as the supreme criterion of right. The rapid vicissitudes of power, in which each party successively appealed to the favour of the masses as the arbiter of success, accustomed the masses to be arbitrary as well as insubordinate. The fall of many governments, and the frequent redistribution of territory, deprived all settlements of the dignity of permanence. Tradition and prescription ceased to be guardians of authority; and the arrangements which proceeded from revolutions, from the triumphs of war, and from treaties of peace, were equally regardless of established rights. Duty cannot be dissociated from right, and nations refuse to be controlled by laws which are no protection.

In this condition of the world, theory and action follow close upon each other, and practical evils easily give birth to opposite systems. In the realms of free-will, the regularity of natural progress is preserved by the conflict of extremes. The impulse of the reaction carries men from one extremity towards another. The pursuit of a remote and ideal object, which captivates the imagination by its splendour and the reason by its simplicity, evokes an energy which would not be inspired by a rational, possible end, limited by many antagonistic claims, and confined to what is reasonable, practicable, and just. One excess or exaggeration is the corrective of the other, and error promotes truth, where the masses are concerned, by counterbalancing a contrary error. The few have not strength to achieve great changes unaided; the many have not wisdom to be moved by truth unmixed. Where the disease is various, no particular definite remedy can meet the wants of all. Only the attraction of an abstract idea, or of an ideal state, can unite in a common action multitudes who seek a universal cure for many special evils, and a common restorative applicable to many different conditions. And hence false principles, which correspond with the bad as well as with the just aspirations of mankind, are a normal and necessary element in the social life of nations.

Theories of this kind are just, inasmuch as they are provoked by definite ascertained evils, and undertake their removal. They are useful in opposition, as a warning or a threat, to modify existing things, and keep awake the consciousness of wrong. They cannot serve as a basis for the reconstruction of civil society, as medicine cannot serve for food; but they may influence it with advantage, because they point out the direction, though not the measure, in which reform is needed. They oppose an order of things which is the result of a selfish and violent abuse of power by the ruling classes, and of artificial restriction on the natural progress of the world, destitute of an ideal element or a moral purpose. Practical extremes differ from the theoretical extremes they provoke, because the first are both arbitrary and violent, whilst the last, though also revolutionary, are at the same time remedial. In one case the wrong is voluntary, in the other it is inevitable. This is the general character of the contest between the existing order and the subversive theories that deny its legitimacy. There are three principal theories of this kind, impugning the present distribution of power, of property, and of territory, and attacking respectively the aristocracy, the middle class, and the sovereignty. They are the theories of equality, communism, and nationality. Though sprung from a common origin, opposing cognate evils, and connected by many links, they did not appear simultaneously. Rousseau proclaimed the first, Babœuf the second, Mazzini the third; and the third is the most recent in its appearance, the most attractive at the present time, and the richest in promise of future power.

In the old European system, the rights of nationalities were neither recognised by governments nor asserted by the people. The interest of the reigning families, not those of the nations, regulated the frontiers; and the administration was conducted generally without any reference to popular desires. Where all liberties were suppressed, the claims of national independence were necessarily ignored, and a princess, in the words of Fénelon, carried a monarchy in her wedding portion. The eighteenth century acquiesced in this oblivion of corporate rights on the Continent, for the absolutists cared only for the State, and the liberals only for the individual. The Church, the nobles, and the nation had no place in the popular theories of the age; and they devised none in their own defence, for they were not openly attacked. The aristocracy retained its privileges, and the Church her property; and the dynastic interest, which overruled the natural inclination of the nations, and destroyed their independence, nevertheless maintained their integrity. The national sentiment was not wounded in its most sensitive part. To dispossess a sovereign of his hereditary crown, and to annex his dominions, would have been held to inflict an injury upon all monarchies, and to furnish their subjects with a dangerous example, by depriving royalty of its inviolable character. In time of war, as there was no national cause at stake, there was no attempt to rouse national feeling. The courtesy of the rulers towards each other was proportionate to the contempt for the lower orders. Compliments passed between the commanders of hostile armies; there was no bitterness, and no excitement; battles were fought with the pomp and pride of a parade. The art of war became a slow and learned game. The monarchies were united not only by a natural community of interests, but by family alliances. A marriage contract sometimes became the signal for an interminable war, whilst family connections often set a barrier to ambition. After the wars of religion came to an end in 1648, the only wars were those which were waged for an inheritance or a dependency, or against countries whose system of government exempted them from the common law of dynastic States, and made them not only unprotected but obnoxious. These countries were England and Holland, until Holland ceased to be a republic, and until, in England, the defeat of the Jacobites in the forty-five terminated the struggle for the Crown. There was one country, however, which still continued to be an exception; one monarch whose place was not admitted in the comity of kings.

Poland did not possess those securities for stability which were supplied by dynastic connections and the theory of legitimacy, wherever a crown could be obtained by marriage or inheritance. A monarch without royal blood, a crown bestowed by the nation, were an anomaly and an outrage in that age of dynastic absolutism. The country was excluded from the European system by the nature of its institutions. It excited a cupidity which could not be satisfied. It gave the reigning families of Europe no hope of permanently strengthening themselves by intermarriage with its rulers, or of obtaining it by request or by inheritance. The Hapsburgs had contested the possession of Spain and the Indies with the French Bourbons, of Italy with the Spanish Bourbons, of the empire with the house of Wittelsbach, of Silesia with the house of Hohenzollern. There had been wars between rival houses for half the territories of Italy and Germany. But none could hope to redeem their losses or increase their power in a country to which marriage and descent gave no claim. Where they could not permanently inherit they endeavoured, by intrigues, to prevail at each election, and after contending in support of candidates who were their partisans, the neighbours at last appointed an instrument for the final demolition of the Polish State. Till then no nation had been deprived of its political existence by the Christian Powers, and whatever disregard had been shown for national interests and sympathies, some care had been taken to conceal the wrong by a hypocritical perversion of law. But the partition of Poland was an act of wanton violence, committed in open defiance not only of popular feeling but of public law. For the first time in modern history a great State was suppressed, and a whole nation divided among its enemies.

This famous measure, the most revolutionary act of the old absolutism, awakened the theory of nationality in Europe, converting a dormant right into an aspiration, and a sentiment into a political claim. "No wise or honest man," wrote Edmund Burke, "can approve of that partition, or can contemplate it without prognosticating great mischief from it to all countries at some future time." [1] Thenceforward there was a nation demanding to be united in a State, — a soul, as it were, wandering in search of a body in which to begin life over again; and, for the first time, a cry was heard that the arrangement of States was unjust — that their limits were unnatural, and that a whole people was deprived of its right to constitute an independent community. Before that claim could be efficiently asserted against the overwhelming power

[1] "Observations on the Conduct of the Minority," *Works*, V, 112.

of its opponents, — before it gained energy, after the last partition, to overcome the influence of long habits of submission, and of the contempt which previous disorders had brought upon Poland, — the ancient European system was in ruins, and a new world was rising in its place.

The old despotic policy which made the Poles its prey had two adversaries, — the spirit of English liberty, and the doctrines of that revolution which destroyed the French monarchy with its own weapons; and these two contradicted in contrary ways the theory that nations have no collective rights. At the present day, the theory of nationality is not only the most powerful auxiliary of revolution, but its actual substance in the movements of the last three years. This, however, is a recent alliance, unknown to the first French Revolution. The modern theory of nationality arose partly as a legitimate consequence, partly as a reaction against it. As the system which overlooked national division was opposed by liberalism in two forms, the French and the English, so the system which insists upon them proceeds from two distinct sources, and exhibits the character either of 1688 or of 1789. When the French people abolished the authorities under which it lived, and became its own master, France was in danger of dissolution: for the common will is difficult to ascertain, and does not readily agree. "The laws," said Vergniaud, in the debate on the sentence of the king, "are obligatory only as the presumptive will of the people, which retains the right of approving or condemning them. The instant it manifests its wish the work of the national representation, the law, must disappear." This doctrine resolved society into its natural elements, and threatened to break up the country into as many republics as there were communes. For true republicanism is the principle of self-government in the whole and in all the parts. In an extensive country, it can prevail only by the union of several independent communities in a single confederacy, as in Greece, in Switzerland, in the Netherlands, and in America; so that a large republic not founded on the federal principle must result in the government of a single city, like Rome and Paris, and, in a less degree, Athens, Berne, and Amsterdam; or, in other words, a great democracy must either sacrifice self-government to unity, or preserve it by federalism.

The France of history fell together with the French State, which was the growth of centuries. The old sovereignty was destroyed. The local authorities were looked upon with aversion and alarm. The new central authority needed to be established on a new principle of unity. The state of nature, which was the ideal of society, was made the basis of the nation; descent was put in the place of tradition, and the French people was regarded as a physical product: an ethnological, not historic, unit. It was assumed that a unity existed separate from the representation and the government, wholly independent of the past, and capable at any moment of expressing or of changing its mind. In the words of Siéyès, it was no longer France, but some unknown country to which the nation was transported. The central power possessed authority, inasmuch as it obeyed the whole, and no divergence was permitted from the universal sentiment. This power, endowed with volition, was personified in the Republic One and Indivisible. The title signified that a part could not speak or act for the whole, — that there was a power supreme over the State, distinct from, and independent of, its members; and it expressed, for the first time in history, the notion of an abstract nationality. In this manner the idea of the sovereignty of the people, uncontrolled by the past, gave birth to the idea of nationality independent of the political influence of history. It sprang from the rejection of the two authorities, — of the State and of the past. The kingdom of France was, geographically as well as politically, the product of a long series of events, and the same influences which built up the State formed the territory. The Revolution repudiated alike the agencies to which France owed her boundaries and those to which she owed her government. Every effaceable trace and relic of national history was carefully wiped away, — the system of administration, the physical divisions of the country, the classes of society, the corporations, the weights and measures, the calendar. France was no longer bounded by the limits she had received from the condemned influence of her history; she could recognise only those which were set by nature. The definition of the nation was borrowed from the material world, and, in order to avoid a loss of territory, it became not only an abstraction but a fiction.

There was a principle of nationality in the ethnological character of the movement, which is the source of the common observation that revolution is more frequent in Catholic than in Protestant countries. It is, in fact, more frequent in the Latin than in the Teutonic world, because it depends partly on a national impulse, which is only awakened where there is an alien element, the vestige of a foreign dominion, to expel. Western Europe has undergone two conquests — one by the Romans and one by the Germans, and twice received laws from the invaders. Each time it rose again against the victorious race; and the two great reactions, while they differ according to the different characters of the two conquests, have the phenomenon of imperialism in common. The Roman republic laboured to crush the subjugated nations into a homogeneous and obedient mass; but the increase which the proconsular authority obtained in the process subverted the republican government, and the reaction of the provinces against Rome assisted in establishing the empire. The Cæsarean system gave an unprecedented freedom to the dependencies, and raised them to a civil equality which put an end to the dominion of race over race and of class over class. The monarchy was hailed as a refuge from the pride and cupidity of the Roman people; and the love of equality, the hatred of nobility, and the tolerance of despotism implanted by Rome became, at least in Gaul, the chief feature of the national character. But among the nations whose vitality had been broken down by the stern republic, not one retained the materials necessary to enjoy independence, or to develop a new history. The political faculty which organises states and finds society in a moral order was exhausted, and the Christian doctors looked in vain over the waste of ruins for a people by whose aid the Church might survive the decay of Rome. A new element of national life was brought to that declining world by the enemies who destroyed it. The flood of barbarians settled over it for a season, and then subsided; and when the landmarks of civilisation appeared once more, it was found that the soil had been impregnated with a fertilising and regenerating influence, and that the inundation had laid the germs of future states and of a new society. The political sense and energy came with the new blood, and was exhibited in the power exercised by the younger race upon the old, and in the establishment of a graduated freedom. Instead of universal equal rights, the actual enjoyment of which is necessarily contingent on, and commensurate with, power, the rights of the people were made dependent on a variety of conditions, the first of which was the distribution of property. Civil society became a classified organism instead of a formless combination of atoms, and the feudal system gradually arose.

Roman Gaul had so thoroughly adopted the ideas of absolute authority and undistinguished equality during the five centuries between Cæsar and Clovis, that the people could never be reconciled to the new system. Feudalism remained a foreign importation, and the feudal aristocracy an alien race, and the common people of France sought protection against both in the Roman jurisprudence and the power of the crown. The development of absolute monarchy by the help of democracy is the one constant character of French history. The royal power, feudal at first, and limited by the immunities and the great vassals, became more popular as it grew more absolute; while the suppression of aristocracy, the removal of the intermediate authorities, was so particularly the object of the nation, that it was more energetically accomplished after the fall of the throne. The monarchy which had been engaged from the thirteenth century in curbing the nobles, was at last thrust aside by the democracy, because it was too dilatory in the work, and was unable to deny its own origin and effectually ruin the class from which it sprang. All those things which constitute the peculiar character of the French Revolution, — the demand for equality, the hatred of nobility and feudalism, and of the Church which was connected with them, the constant reference to pagan examples, the suppression of monarchy, the new code of law, the breach with tradition, and the substitution of an ideal system for everything that had proceeded from the mixture and mutual action of the races, — all these exhibit the common type of a reaction against the effects of the Frankish invasion. The hatred of royalty was less than the hatred of aristocracy; privileges were more detested than tyranny; and the king perished because of the origin of his authority rather than because of its abuse. Monarchy unconnected with aristocracy became popular in France, even when most uncontrolled; whilst the attempt to reconstitute the throne, and to limit and fence it with its peers, broke down, because the old Teutonic elements on which it relied — hereditary nobility, primogeniture, and privilege — were no longer tolerated. The substance of the ideas of 1789 is not the limitation of the sovereign power, but the abrogation of intermediate powers. These powers, and the classes which enjoyed them, come in Latin Europe from a barbarian origin; and the movement which calls itself liberal is essentially national. If liberty were its object, its means would be the establishment of great independent authorities not derived from the State, and its model would be England. But its object is equality; and it seeks, like France in 1789, to cast out the elements of inequality which were introduced by the Teutonic race. This is the object which Italy and Spain have had in common with France, and herein consists the natural league of the Latin nations.

This national element in the movement was not understood by the revolutionary leaders. At first, their doctrine appeared entirely contrary to the idea of nationality. They taught that certain general principles of government were absolutely right in all States; and they asserted in theory the unrestricted freedom of the individual, and the supremacy of the will over every external necessity or obligation. This is in apparent contradiction to the national theory, that certain natural forces ought to determine the character, the form, and the policy of the State, by which a kind of fate is put in the place of freedom. Accordingly the national sentiment was not developed directly out of the revolution in which it was involved, but was exhibited first in resistance to it, when the attempt to emancipate had been absorbed in the desire to subjugate, and the republic had been succeeded by the empire. Napoleon called a new power into existence by attacking nationality in Russia, by delivering it in Italy, by governing in defiance of it in Germany and Spain. The sovereigns of these countries were deposed or degraded; and a system of administration was introduced which was French in its origin, its spirit, and its instruments. The people resisted the change. The movement against it was popular and spontaneous, because the rulers were absent or helpless; and it was national, because it was directed against foreign institutions. In Tyrol, in Spain, and afterwards in Prussia, the people did not receive the impulse from the government, but undertook of their own accord to cast out the armies and the ideas of revolutionised France. Men were made conscious of the national element of the revolution by its conquests, not in its rise. The three things which the Empire most openly oppressed — religion, national independence, and political liberty — united in a short-lived league to animate the great uprising by which Napoleon fell. Under the influence of that memorable alliance a political spirit was called forth on the Continent, which clung to freedom and abhorred revolution, and sought to restore, to develop, and to reform the decayed national institutions. The men who proclaimed these ideas, Stein and Görres, Humboldt, Müller, and De Maistre,[2] were as hostile to Bonapartism as to the

[2] There are some remarkable thoughts on nationality in the State Papers of the Count de Maistre: "En premier lieu les nations sont quelque chose dans le monde, il n'est pas permis de les compter pour rien, de les affliger dans leurs convenances, dans leurs affections, dans leurs intérêts les plus chers . . . Or le traité du 30 mai anéantit complétement la Savoie; il divise l'indivisible; il partage en trois portions une malheureuse nation de 400,000 hommes, une par la langue, une par la religion, une par le caractère, une par l'habitude invétérée, une enfin par les limites naturelles. . . . L'union des nations ne souffre pas de difficultés sur la carte géographique; mais dans la réalité, c'est autre chose; il y a des nations *immiscibles*. . . . Je lui parlai

absolutism of the old governments, and insisted on the national rights, which had been invaded equally by both, and which they hoped to restore by the destruction of the French supremacy. With the cause that triumphed at Waterloo the friends of the Revolution had no sympathy, for they had learned to identify their doctrine with the cause of France. The Holland House Whigs in England, the Afrancesados in Spain, the Muratists in Italy, and the partisans of the Confederation of the Rhine, merging patriotism in their revolutionary affections, regretted the fall of the French power, and looked with alarm at those new and unknown forces which the War of Deliverance had evoked, and which were as menacing to French liberalism as to French supremacy.

But the new aspirations for national and popular rights were crushed at the restoration. The liberals of those days cared for freedom, not in the shape of national independence, but of French institutions; and they combined against the nations with the ambition of the governments. They were as ready to sacrifice nationality to their ideal as the Holy Alliance was to the interests of absolutism. Talleyrand indeed declared at Vienna that the Polish question ought to have precedence over all other questions, because the partition of Poland had been one of the first and greatest causes of the evils which Europe had suffered; but dynastic interests prevailed. All the sovereigns represented at Vienna recovered their dominions, except the King of Saxony, who was punished for his fidelity to Napoleon; but the States that were unrepresented in the reigning families — Poland, Venice, and Genoa — were not revived, and even the Pope had great difficulty in recovering the Legations from the grasp of Aus-

par occasion de l'esprit italien qui s'agite dans ce moment; il (Count Nesselrode) me répondit 'Oui, Monsieur; mais cet esprit est un grand mal, car il peut gêner les arrangements de l'Italie.' " — *Correspondance Diplomatique de J. de Maistre*, II, 7, 8, 21, 25 In the same year, 1815, Gorres wrote: "In Italien wie allerwarts ist das Volk gewecht; es will etwas grossartiges, es will Ideen haben, die, wenn es sie auch nicht ganz begreift, doch einen freien unendlichen Gesichtskreis seiner Einbildung eroffnen. . . . Es ist reiner Naturtrieb, dass ein Volk, also scharf und deutlich in seine naturlichen Granzen eingeschlossen, aus der Zerstreuung in die Einheit sich zu sammeln sucht." — *Werke*, II, 20.

tria. Nationality, which the old *régime* had ignored, which had been outraged by the revolution and the empire, received, after its first open demonstration, the hardest blow at the Congress of Vienna. The principle which the first partition had generated, to which the revolution had given a basis of theory, which had been lashed by the empire into a momentary convulsive effort, was matured by the long error of the restoration into a consistent doctrine, nourished and justified by the situation of Europe.

The governments of the Holy Alliance devoted themselves to suppress with equal care the revolutionary spirit by which they had been threatened, and the national spirit by which they had been restored. Austria, which owed nothing to the national movement, and had prevented its revival after 1809, naturally took the lead in repressing it. Every disturbance of the final settlements of 1815, every aspiration for changes or reforms, was condemned as sedition. This system repressed the good with the evil tendencies of the age; and the resistance which it provoked, during the generation that passed away from the restoration to the fall of Metternich, and again under the reaction which commenced with Schwarzenberg and ended with the administrations of Bach and Manteuffel, proceeded from various combinations of the opposite forms of liberalism. In the successive phases of that struggle, the idea that national claims are above all other rights gradually rose to the supremacy which it now possesses among the revolutionary agencies.

The first liberal movement, that of the Carbonari in the south of Europe, had no specific national character, but was supported by the Bonapartists both in Spain and Italy. In the following years the opposite ideas of 1813 came to the front, and a revolutionary movement, in many respects hostile to the principles of revolution, began in defence of liberty, religion, and nationality. All these causes were united in the Irish agitation, and in the Greek, Belgian, and Polish revolutionists. Those sentiments which had been insulted by Napoleon, and had risen against him, rose against the governments of the restoration. They had been oppressed by the sword, and then by the treaties. The national principle added force, but not justice, to this movement, which, in every case but Poland, was successful. A period followed in which it degenerated into a purely national idea, as the agitation for repeal succeeded emancipation, and Panslavism and Panhellenism arose under the auspices of the Eastern Church. This was the third phase of the resistance to the settlement of Vienna, which was weak, because it failed to satisfy national or constitutional aspirations, either of which would have been a safeguard against the other, by a moral if not by a popular justification. At first, in 1813, the people rose against their conquerors, in defence of their legitimate rulers. They refused to be governed by usurpers. In the period between 1825 and 1831, they resolved that they would not be misgoverned by strangers. The French administration was often better than that which it displaced, but there were prior claimants for the authority exercised by the French, and at first the national contest was a contest for legitimacy. In the second period this element was wanting. No dispossessed princes led the Greeks, the Belgians, or the Poles. The Turks, the Dutch, and the Russians were attacked, not as usurpers, but as oppressors, — because they misgoverned, not because they were of a different race. Then began a time when the text simply was, that nations would not be governed by foreigners. Power legitimately obtained, and exercised with moderation, was declared invalid. National rights, like religion, had borne part in the previous combinations, and had been auxiliaries in the struggles for freedom, but now nationality became a paramount claim, which was to assert itself alone, which might put forward as pretexts the rights of rulers, the liberties of the people, the safety of religion, but which, if no such union could be formed, was to prevail at the expense of every other cause for which nations make sacrifices.

Metternich is, next to Napoleon, the chief promoter of this theory; for the anti-national character of the restoration was most distinct in Austria, and it is in opposition to the Austrian Government that nationality grew into a system. Napoleon, who, trusting to his armies, despised moral forces in politics, was overthrown by their rising. Austria committed the same fault in the government of her Italian provinces. The kingdom of Italy had united all the northern part of the Peninsula in a single State; and the national feelings, which the French repressed elsewhere, were encouraged as a safeguard of their power in Italy and in Poland. When the tide of victory turned, Austria invoked against the French the aid of the new sentiment they had fostered. Nugent announced, in his proclamation to the Italians, that they should become an independent nation. The same spirit served different masters, and contributed first to the destruction of the old States, then to the expulsion of the French, and again, under Charles Albert, to a new revolution. It was appealed to in the name of the most contradictory principles of government, and served all parties in succession, because it was one in which all could unite. Beginning by a protest against the dominion of race over race, its mildest and least-developed form, it grew into a condemnation of every State that included different races, and finally became the complete and consistent theory, that the State and the nation must be co-extensive. "It is," says Mr. Mill, "in general a necessary condition of free institutions, that the boundaries of governments should coincide in the main with those of nationalities." [3]

The outward historical progress of this idea from an indefinite aspiration to be the keystone of a political system, may be traced in the life of the man who gave to it the element in which its strength resides, — Giuseppe Mazzini. He found Carbonarism impotent against the measures of the governments, and resolved to give new life to the liberal movement by transferring it to the ground of nationality. Exile is the nursery of nationality, as oppression is the school of liberalism; and Mazzini conceived the idea of Young Italy when he was a refugee at Marseilles. In the same way, the Polish exiles are the champions of every national movement; for to them all political rights are absorbed in the idea of independence, which, however they may differ with each other, is

[3] Mill's *Considerations on Representative Government*, p. 298.

the one aspiration common to them all. Towards the year 1830 literature also contributed to the national idea. "It was the time," says Mazzini, "of the great conflict between the romantic and the classical school, which might with equal truth be called a conflict between the partisans of freedom and of authority." The romantic school was infidel in Italy, and Catholic in Germany; but in both it had the common effect of encouraging national history and literature, and Dante was as great an authority with the Italian democrats as with the leaders of the mediæval revival at Vienna, Munich, and Berlin. But neither the influence of the exiles, nor that of the poets and critics of the new party, extended over the masses. It was a sect without popular sympathy or encouragement, a conspiracy founded not on a grievance, but on a doctrine; and when the attempt to rise was made in Savoy, in 1834, under a banner with the motto "Unity, Independence, God and Humanity," the people were puzzled at its object, and indifferent to its failure. But Mazzini continued his propaganda, developed his *Giovine Italia* into a *Giovine Europa*, and established in 1847 the international league of nations. "The people," he said, in his opening address, "is penetrated with only one idea, that of unity and nationality. . . . There is no international question as to forms of government, but only a national question."

The revolution of 1848, unsuccessful in its national purpose, prepared the subsequent victories of nationality in two ways. The first of these was the restoration of the Austrian power in Italy, with a new and more energetic centralisation, which gave no promise of freedom. Whilst that system prevailed, the right was on the side of the national aspirations, and they were revived in a more complete and cultivated form by Manin. The policy of the Austrian Government, which failed during the ten years of the reaction to convert the tenure by force into a tenure by right, and to establish with free institutions the condition of allegiance, gave a negative encouragement to the theory. It deprived Francis Joseph of all active support and sympathy in 1859, for he was more clearly wrong in his conduct than his enemies in their doctrines. The real cause of the energy which the national theory has acquired is, however, the triumph of the democratic principle in France, and its recognition by the European Powers. The theory of nationality is involved in the democratic theory of the sovereignty of the general will. "One hardly knows what any division of the human race should be free to do, if not to determine with which of the various collective bodies of human beings they choose to associate themselves." [4] It is by this act that a nation constitutes itself. To have a collective will, unity is necessary, and independence is requisite in order to assert it. Unity and nationality are still more essential to the notion of the sovereignty of the people than the cashiering of monarchs, or the revocation of laws. Arbitrary acts of this kind may be prevented by the happiness of the people or the popularity of the king, but a nation inspired by the democratic idea cannot with consistency allow a part of itself to belong to a foreign State, or the whole to be divided into several native States. The theory of nationality therefore proceeds from both the principles which divide the political world, — from legitimacy, which ignores its claims, and from the revolution, which assumes them; and for the same reason it is the chief weapon of the last against the first.

In pursuing the outward and visible growth of the national theory we are prepared for an examination of its political character and value. The absolutism which has created it denies equally that absolute right of national unity which is a product of democracy, and that claim of national liberty which belongs to the theory of freedom. These two views of nationality, corresponding to the French and to the English systems, are connected in name only, and are in reality the opposite extremes of political thought. In one case, nationality is founded on the perpetual supremacy of the collective will, of which the unity of the nation is the necessary condition, to which every other influence must defer, and against which no obligation enjoys authority, and all resistance is tyrannical. The nation is here an ideal unit founded on the

---
[4] Mill's *Considerations*, p. 296.

race, in defiance of the modifying action of external causes, of tradition, and of existing rights. It overrules the rights and wishes of the inhabitants, absorbing their divergent interests in a fictitious unity; sacrifices their several inclinations and duties to the higher claim of nationality, and crushes all natural rights and all established liberties for the purpose of vindicating itself.[5] Whenever a single definite object is made the supreme end of the State, be it the advantage of a class, the safety or the power of the country, the greatest happiness of the greatest number, or the support of any speculative idea, the State becomes for the time inevitably absolute. Liberty alone demands for its realisation the limitation of the public authority, for liberty is the only object which benefits all alike, and provokes no sincere opposition. In supporting the claims of national unity, governments must be subverted in whose title there is no flaw, and whose policy is beneficent and equitable, and subjects must be compelled to transfer their allegiance to an authority for which they have no attachment, and which may be practically a foreign domination. Connected with this theory in nothing except in the common enmity of the absolute state, is the theory which represents nationality as an essential, but not a supreme element in determining the forms of the State. It is distinguished from the other, because it tends to diversity and not to uniformity, to harmony and not to unity; because it aims not at an arbitrary change, but at careful respect for the existing conditions of political life, and because it obeys the laws and results of history, not the aspirations of an ideal future. While the theory of unity makes the nation a source of despotism and revolution, the theory of liberty regards it as the bulwark of self-government, and the foremost limit to the excessive power of the State. Private rights, which are sacrificed to the unity, are preserved by the union of nations.

---

[5] "Le sentiment d'indépendance nationale est encore plus général et plus profondément gravé dans le cœur des peuples que l'amour d'une liberté constitutionnelle. Les nations les plus soumises au despotisme éprouvent ce sentiment avec autant de vivacité que les nations libres; les peuples les plus barbares le sentent même encore plus vivement que les nations policées." — *L'Italie au Dixneuvième Siècle*, p. 148, Paris, 1821.

No power can so efficiently resist the tendencies of centralisation, of corruption, and of absolutism, as that community which is the vastest that can be included in a State, which imposes on its members a consistent similarity of character, interest, and opinion, and which arrests the action of the sovereign by the influence of a divided patriotism. The presence of different nations under the same sovereignty is similar in its effect to the independence of the Church in the State. It provides against the servility which flourishes under the shadow of a single authority, by balancing interests, multiplying associations, and giving to the subject the restraint and support of a combined opinion. In the same way it promotes independence by forming definite groups of public opinion, and by affording a great source and centre of political sentiments, and of notions of duty not derived from the sovereign will. Liberty provokes diversity, and diversity preserves liberty by supplying the means of organisation. All those portions of law which govern the relations of men with each other, and regulate social life, are the varying result of national custom and the creation of private society. In these things, therefore, the several nations will differ from each other; for they themselves have produced them, and they do not owe them to the State which rules them all. This diversity in the same State is a firm barrier against the intrusion of the government beyond the political sphere which is common to all into the social department which escapes legislation and is ruled by spontaneous làws. This sort of interference is characteristic of an absolute government, and is sure to provoke a reaction, and finally a remedy. That intolerance of social freedom which is natural to absolutism is sure to find a corrective in the national diversities, which no other force could so efficiently provide. The co-existence of several nations under the same State is a test, as well as the best security of its freedom. It is also one of the chief instruments of civilisation; and, as such, it is in the natural and providential order, and indicates a state of greater advancement than the national unity which is the ideal of modern liberalism.

The combination of different nations in one State is as necessary a condition of civilised life as the combination of men in society. Inferior races are raised by living in political union with races intellectually superior. Exhausted and decaying nations are revived by the contact of a younger vitality. Nations in which the elements of organisation and the capacity for government have been lost, either through the demoralising influence of despotism, or the disintegrating action of democracy, are restored and educated anew under the discipline of a stronger and less corrrupted race. This fertilising and regenerating process can only be obtained by living under one government. It is in the cauldron of the State that the fusion takes place by which the vigour, the knowledge, and the capacity of one portion of mankind may be communicated to another. Where political and national boundaries coincide, society ceases to advance, and nations relapse into a condition corresponding to that of men who renounce intercourse with their fellow-men. The difference between the two unites mankind not only by the benefits it confers on those who live together, but because it connects society either by a political or a national bond, gives to every people an interest in its neighbours, either because they are under the same government or because they are of the same race, and thus promotes the interests of humanity, of civilisation, and of religion.

Christianity rejoices at the mixture of races, as paganism identifies itself with their differences, because truth is universal, and errors various and particular. In the ancient world idolatry and nationality went together, and the same term is applied in Scripture to both. It was the mission of the Church to overcome national differences. The period of her undisputed supremacy was that in which all Western Europe obeyed the same laws, all literature was contained in one language, and the political unit of Christendom was personified in a single potentate, while its intellectual unity was represented in one university. As the ancient Romans concluded their conquests by carrying away the gods of the conquered people, Charlemagne overcame the national resistance of the Saxons only by the forcible destruction of their pagan rites. Out of the mediæval period, and the combined action of the German race and the Church, came forth a new system of nations and a new conception of nationality. Nature was overcome in the nation as well as in the individual. In pagan and uncultivated times, nations were distinguished from each other by the widest diversity, not only in religion, but in customs, language, and character. Under the new law they had many things in common; the old barriers which separated them were removed, and the new principle of self-government, which Christianity imposed, enabled them to live together under the same authority, without necessarily losing their cherished habits, their customs, or their laws. The new idea of freedom made room for different races in one State. A nation was no longer what it had been to the ancient world, — the progeny of a common ancestor, or the aboriginal product of a particular region, — a result of merely physical and material causes, — but a moral and political being; not the creation of geographical or physiological unity, but developed in the course of history by the action of the State. It is derived from the State, not supreme over it. A State may in course of time produce a nationality; but that a nationality should constitute a State is contrary to the nature of modern civilisation. The nation derives its rights and its power from the memory of a former independence.

The Church has agreed in this respect with the tendency of political progress, and discouraged wherever she could the isolation of nations; admonishing them of their duties to each other, and regarding conquest and feudal investitude as the' natural means of raising barbarous or sunken nations to a higher level. But though she has never attributed to national independence an immunity from the accidental consequences of feudal law, of hereditary claims, or of testamentary arrangements, she defends national liberty against uniformity and centralisation with an energy inspired by perfect community of interests. For the same enemy threatens both; and the State which is reluctant to tolerate differences, and to do justice to the peculiar character of various races, must from the same cause interfere in the internal government of religion. The connection of religious liberty with the emancipation of Poland or Ireland is not merely the accidental result of local causes; and the failure of the Concordat to unite the subjects of Austria is the natural consequence of a policy which did not desire to protect the provinces in their diversity and autonomy, and sought to bribe the Church by favours instead of strengthening her by independence. From this influence of religion in modern history has proceeded a new definition of patriotism.

The difference between nationality and the State is exhibited in the nature of patriotic attachment. Our connection with the race is merely natural or physical, whilst our duties to the political nation are ethical. One is a community of affections and instincts infinitely important and powerful in savage life, but pertaining more to the animal than to the civilised man; the other is an authority governing by laws, imposing obligations, and giving a moral sanction and character to the natural relations of society. Patriotism is in political life what faith is in religion, and it stands to the domestic feelings and to homesickness as faith to fanaticism and to superstition. It has one aspect derived from private life and nature, for it is an extension of the family affections, as the tribe is an extension of the family. But in its real political character, patriotism consists in the development of the instinct of self-preservation into a moral duty which may involve self-sacrifice. Self-preservation is both an instinct and a duty, natural and involuntary in one respect, and at the same time a moral obligation. By the first it produces the family; by the last the State. If the nation could exist without the State, subject only to the instinct of self-preservation, it would be incapable of denying, controlling, or sacrificing itself; it would be an end and a rule to itself. But in the political order moral purposes are realised and public ends are pursued to which private interests and even existence must be sacrificed. The great sign of true patriotism, the development of selfishness into sacrifice, is the product of political life. That sense of duty which is supplied by race is not entirely separated from its selfish and instinctive basis; and the love of country, like married love, stands at the same time on a material and a moral foundation. The patriot must distinguish between the two causes or objects of his devotion. The attachment which is given only to the country is like obedience given only to the State — a submission to physical influences. The man who prefers his country before every other duty shows the same spirit as the man who surrenders every right to the State. They both deny that right is superior to authority.

There is a moral and political country, in the language of Burke, distinct from the geographical, which may be possibly in collision with it. The Frenchmen who bore arms against the Convention were as patriotic as the Englishmen who bore arms against King Charles, for they recognised a higher duty than that of obedience to the actual sovereign. "In an address to France," said Burke, "in an attempt to treat with it, or in considering any scheme at all relative to it, it is impossible we should mean the geographical, we must always mean the moral and political, country. . . . The truth is, that France is out of itself—the moral France is separated from the geographical. The master of the house is expelled, and the robbers are in possession. If we look for the corporate people of France, existing as corporate in the eye and intention of public law (that corporate people, I mean, who are free to deliberate and to decide, and who have a capacity to treat and conclude), they are in Flanders and Germany, in Switzerland, Spain, Italy, and England. There are all the princes of the blood, there are all the orders of the State, there are all the parliaments of the kingdom. . . . I am sure that if half that number of the same description were taken out of this country, it would leave hardly anything that I should call the people of England."[6] Rousseau draws nearly the same distinction between the country to which we happen to belong and that which fulfils towards us the political functions of the State. In the *Emile* he has a sentence of which it is not easy in a translation to convey the point: "Qui n'a pas une patrie

---
[6] Burke's "Remarks on the Policy of the Allies," *Works*, V. 26, 29, 30.

a du moins un pays." And in his tract on Political Economy he writes: "How shall men love their country if it is nothing more for them than for strangers, and bestows on them only that which it can refuse to none?" It is in the same sense he says, further on, "La patrie ne peut subsister sans la liberté."[7]

The nationality formed by the State, then, is the only one to which we owe political duties, and it is, therefore, the only one which has political rights. The Swiss are ethnologically either French, Italian, or German; but no nationality has the slightest claim upon them, except the purely political nationality of Switzerland. The Tuscan or the Neapolitan State has formed a nationality, but the citizens of Florence and of Naples have no political community with each other. There are other States which have neither succeeded in absorbing distinct races in a political nationality, nor in separating a particular district from a larger nation. Austria and Mexico are instances on the one hand, Parma and Baden on the other. The progress of civilisation deals hardly with the last description of States. In order to maintain their integrity they must attach themselves by confederations, or family alliances, to greater Powers, and thus lose something of their independence. Their tendency is to isolate and shut off their inhabitants, to narrow the horizon of their views, and to dwarf in some degree the proportions of their ideas. Public opinion cannot maintain its liberty and purity in such small dimensions, and the currents that come from larger communities sweep over a contracted territory. In a small and homogeneous population there is hardly room for a natural classification of society, or for inner groups of interests that set bounds to sovereign power. The government and the subjects contend with borrowed weapons. The resources of the one and the aspirations of the other are derived from some external

---

[7] *Œuvres*, I, 593, 595; 11, 717. Bossuet, in a passage of great beauty on the love of country, does not attain to the political definition of the word: "La société humaine demande qu'on aime la terre où l'on habite ensemble, ou la regarde comme une mère et une nourrice commune. . . Les hommes en effet se sentent liés par quelque chose de fort, lorsqu'ils songent, que la même terre qui les a portés et nourris étant vivants, les recevra dans son sein quand ils seront morts." "Politique tirée de l'Ecriture Sainte," *Œuvres*, X, 317.

source, and the consequence is that the country becomes the instrument and the scene of contests in which it is not interested. These States, like the minuter communities of the Middle Ages, serve a purpose, by constituting partitions and securities of self-government in the larger States; but they are impediments to the progress of society, which depends on the mixture of races under the same governments.

The vanity and peril of national claims founded on no political tradition, but on race alone, appear in Mexico. There the races are divided by blood, without being grouped together in different regions. It is, therefore, neither possible to unite them nor to convert them into the elements of an organised State. They are fluid, shapeless, and unconnected, and cannot be precipitated, or formed into the basis of political institutions. As they cannot be used by the State, they cannot be recognised by it; and their peculiar qualities, capabilities, passions, and attachments are of no service, and therefore obtain no regard. They are necessarily ignored, and are therefore perpetually outraged. From this difficulty of races with political pretensions, but without political position, the Eastern world escaped by the institution of castes. Where there are only two races there is the resource of slavery; but when different races inhabit the different territories of one Empire composed of several smaller States, it is of all possible combinations the most favourable to the establishment of a highly developed system of freedom. In Austria there are two circumstances which add to the difficulty of the problem, but also increase its importance. The several nationalities are at very unequal degrees of advancement, and there is no single nation which is so predominant as to overwhelm or absorb the others. These are the conditions necessary for the very highest degree of organisation which government is capable of receiving. They supply the greatest variety of intellectual resource; the perpetual incentive to progress which is afforded not merely by competition, but by the spectacle of a more advanced people; the most abundant elements of self-government, combined with the impossibility for the State to rule all by its own will; and the fullest security for the preservation of local customs and ancient rights. In such a country as this, liberty would achieve its most glorious results, while centralisation and absolutism would be destruction.

The problem presented to the government of Austria is higher than that which is solved in England, because of the necessity of admitting the national claims. The parliamentary system fails to provide for them, as it presupposes the unity of the people. Hence in those countries in which different races dwell together, it has not satisfied their desires, and is regarded as an imperfect form of freedom. It brings out more clearly than before the differences it does not recognise, and thus continues the work of the old absolutism, and appears as a new phase of centralisation. In those countries, therefore, the power of the imperial parliament must be limited as jealously as the power of the crown, and many of its functions must be discharged by provincial diets, and a descending series of local authorities.

The great importance of nationality in the State consists in the fact that it is the basis of political capacity. The character of a nation determines in great measure the form and vitality of the State. Certain political habits and ideas belong to particular nations, and they vary with the course of the national history. A people just emerging from barbarism, a people effete from the excesses of a luxurious civilisation, cannot possess the means of governing itself; a people devoted to equality, or to absolute monarchy, is incapable of producing an aristocracy; a people averse to the institution of private property is without the first element of freedom. Each of these can be converted into efficient members of a free community only by the contact of a superior race, in whose power will lie the future prospects of the State. A system which ignores these things, and does not rely for its support on the character and aptitude of the people, does not intend that they should administer their own affairs, but that they should simply be obedient to the supreme command. The denial of nationality, therefore, implies the denial of political liberty.

The greatest adversary of the rights of nationality is the modern theory of nationality. By making the State and the nation commensurate with each other in theory, it reduces practically to a subject condition all other nationalities that may be within the boundary. It cannot admit them to an equality with the ruling nation which constitutes the State, because the State would then cease to be national, which would be a contradiction of the principle of its existence. According, therefore, to the degree of humanity and civilisation in that dominant body which claims all the rights of the community, the inferior races are exterminated, or reduced to servitude, or outlawed, or put in a condition of dependence.

If we take the establishment of liberty for the realisation of moral duties to be the end of civil society, we must conclude that those states are substantially the most perfect which, like the British and Austrian Empires, include various distinct nationalities without oppressing them. Those in which no mixture of races has occurred are imperfect; and those in which its effects have disappeared are decrepit. A State which is incompetent to satisfy different races condemns itself; a State which labours to neutralise, to absorb, or to expel them, destroys its own vitality; a State which does not include them is destitute of the chief basis of self-government. The theory of nationality, therefore, is a retrograde step in history. It is the most advanced form of the revolution, and must retain its power to the end of the revolutionary period, of which it announces the approach. Its great historical importance depends on two chief causes.

First, it is a chimera. The settlement at which it aims is impossible. As it can never be satisfied and exhausted, and always continues to assert itself, it prevents the government from ever relapsing into the condition which provoked its rise. The danger is too threatening, and the power over men's minds too great, to allow any system to endure which justifies the resistance of nationality. It must contribute, therefore, to obtain that which in theory it condemns,— the liberty of different nationalities as members of one sovereign community. This is a service which no other force could accomplish; for it is a corrective alike of absolute monarchy, of democracy, and of constitutionalism, as well as of the centralisation which is common to all three. Neither the monarchical nor the revolutionary, nor the parliamentary system can do this; and all the ideas which have excited enthusiasm in past times are impotent for the purpose except nationality alone.

And secondly, the national theory marks the end of the revolutionary doctrine and its logical exhaustion. In proclaiming the supremacy of the rights of nationality, the system of democratic equality goes beyond its own extreme boundary, and falls into contradiction with itself. Between the democratic and the national phase of the revolution, socialism had intervened, and had already carried the consequences of the principle to an absurdity. But that phase was passed. The revolution survived its offspring, and produced another further result. Nationality is more advanced than socialism, because it is a more arbitrary system. The social theory endeavours to provide for the existence of the individual beneath the terrible burdens which modern society heaps upon labour. It is not merely a development of the notion of equality, but a refuge from real misery and starvation. However false the solution, it was a reasonable demand that the poor should be saved from destruction; and if the freedom of the State was sacrificed to the safety of the individual, the more immediate object was, at least in theory, attained. But nationality does not aim either at liberty or prosperity, both of which it sacrifices to the imperative necessity of making the nation the mould and measure of the State. Its course will be marked with material as well as moral ruin, in order that a new invention may prevail over the works of God and the interests of mankind. There is no principle of change, no phase of political speculation conceivable, more comprehensive, more subversive, or more arbitrary than this. It is a confutation of democracy, because it sets limits to the exercise of the popular will, and substitutes for it a higher principle. It prevents not only the division, but the extension of the State, and forbids to terminate war by conquest, and to obtain a security for peace. Thus, after surrendering the individual to the collective will, the revolutionary system makes the collective will subject to conditions which are independent of it, and rejects all law, only to be controlled by an accident.

Although, therefore, the theory of nationality is more absurd and more criminal than the theory of socialism, it has an important mission in the world, and marks the final conflict, and therefore the end, of two forces which are the worst enemies of civil freedom,— the absolute monarchy and the revolution.

CHAPTER VII

POLITICAL CAUSES OF THE AMERICAN REVOLUTION

AT THE TIME of the utmost degradation of the Athenian democracy, when the commanders at Arginusæ were condemned by an unconstitutional decree, and Socrates alone upheld the sanctity of the law, the people, says Xenophon, cried out that it was monstrous to prevent them from doing whatever they pleased.[1] A few years later the archonship of Euclides witnessed the restoration of the old constitution, by which the liberty, though not the power, of Athens was revived and prolonged for ages; and the palladium of the new settlement was the provision that no decree of the council or of the people should be permitted to overrule any existing law.[2]

The fate of every democracy, of every government based on the sovereignty of the people, depends on the choice it makes between these opposite principles, absolute power on the one hand, and on the other, the restraints of legality and the authority of tradition. It must stand or fall according to its choice, whether to give the supremacy to the law or to the will of the people; whether to constitute a moral association maintained by duty, or a physical one kept together

---

NOTE: This essay first appeared in *The Rambler, New Series*, V, Part XIII (May, 1861) 17-61: it is reprinted here for the first time since its original publication.

[1] Τὸ δὲ πλῆθος ἐβόα δεινὸν εἶναι εἰ μή τις ἐάσει τὸν δῆμον πράττειν ὃ ἂν βούληται. *Hellen.* i. 7, 12.

[2] Ψήφισμα δὲ μηδὲν μήτε βουλῆς μήτε δήμου νόμου κυριώτερον εἶναι. Andocides de Myst. Or. Att., ed. Dobson i. 259.

by force. Republics offer, in this respect, a strict analogy with monarchies, which are also either absolute or organic, either governed by law, and therefore constitutional, or by a will which, being the source, cannot be the object of laws, and is therefore despotic. But in their mode of growth, in the direction in which they gravitate, they are directly contrary to each other. Democracy tends naturally to realise its principle, the sovereignty of the people, and to remove all limits and conditions of its exercise; whilst monarchy tends to surround itself with such conditions. In one instance force yields to right; in the other might prevails over law. The resistance of the king is gradually overcome by those who resist and seek to share his power; in a democracy the power is already in the hands of those who seek to subvert and to abolish the law. The process of subversion is consequently irresistible, and far more rapid.

They differ, therefore, not only in the direction, but in the principle of their development. The organisation of a constitutional monarchy is the work of opposing powers, interests, and opinions, by which the monarch is deprived of his exclusive authority, and the throne is surrounded with and guarded by political institutions. In a purely popular government this antagonism of forces does not exist, for all power is united in the same sovereign; subject and citizen are one, and there is no external power that can enforce the surrender of a part of the supreme authority, or establish a security against its abuse. The elements of organisation are wanting. If not obtained at starting, they will not naturally spring up. They have no germs in the system. Hence monarchy grows more free, in obedience to the laws of its existence, whilst democracy becomes more arbitrary. The people is induced less easily than the king to abdicate the plenitude of its power, because it has not only the right of might on its side, but that which comes from possession, and the absence of a prior claimant. The only antagonism that can arise is that of contending parties and interests in the sovereign community, the condition of whose existence is that it should be homogeneous. These separate interests can protect themselves only by setting bounds to the power of the majority; and to this the majority cannot be compelled, or consistently persuaded, to consent. It would be a surrender of the direct authority of the people, and of the principle that in every political community authority must be commensurate with power.

"Infirma minoris
Vox cedat numeri, parvaque in parte quiescat."

"La pluralité," says Pascal, "est la meilleure voie, parcequ'elle est visible, et qu'elle a la force pour se faire obéir; cependant c'est l'avis des moins habiles." The minority can have no permanent security against the oppression of preponderating numbers, or against the government which these numbers control, and the moment will inevitably come when separation will be preferred to submission. When the classes which compose the majority and the minority are not defined with local distinctness, but are mingled together throughout the country, the remedy is found in emigration; and it was thus that many of the ancient Mediterranean states, and some of the chief American colonies, took their rise. But when the opposite interests are grouped together, so as to be separated not only politically but geographically, there will ensue a territorial disruption of the state, developed with a rapidity and certainty proportioned to the degree of local corporate organisation that exists in the community. It cannot, in the long run, be prevented by the majority, which is made up of many future, contingent minorities, all secretly sympathising with the seceders because they foresee a similar danger for themselves, and unwilling to compel them to remain, because they dread to perpetuate the tyranny of majorities. The strict principle of popular sovereignty must therefore lead to the destruction of the state that adopts it, unless it sacrifices itself by concession.

The greatest of all modern republics has given the most complete example of the truth of this law. The dispute between absolute and limited power, between centralisation and self-government, has been, like that between privilege and prerogative in England, the substance of the constitutional history of the United States. This is the argument which confers on the whole period that intervenes between the convention of 1787 and the election of Mr. Davis in 1861 an almost epic unity. It is this problem that has supplied the impulse to the political progress of the United States, that underlies all the great questions that have agitated the Union, and bestows on them all their constitutional importance. It has recurred in many forms, but on each occasion the solution has failed, and the decision has been avoided. Hence the American government is justly termed a system of compromises, that is to say, an inconsistent system. It is not founded, like the old governments of Europe, on tradition, nor on principles, like those which have followed the French Revolution; but on a series of mutual concessions, and momentary suspensions of war between opposite principles, neither of which could prevail. Necessarily, as the country grew more populous, and the population more extended, as the various interests grew in importance, and the various parties in internal strength, as new regions, contrasting with each other in all things in which the influence of nature and the condition of society bear upon political life, were formed into states, the conflict grew into vaster proportions and greater intensity, each opinion became more stubborn and unyielding, compromise was more difficult, and the peril to the Union increased.

Viewed in the light of recent events, the history of the American Republic is intelligible and singularly instructive. For the dissolution of the Union is no accidental or hasty or violent proceeding, but the normal and inevitable result of a long course of events, which trace their origin to the rise of the constitution itself. There we find the germs of the disunion that have taken seventy years to ripen, the beginning of an antagonism which constantly asserted itself and could never be reconciled, until the differences widened into a breach.

The convention which sat at Philadelphia in 1787, for the purpose of substituting a permanent constitution in the place of the confederacy, which had been formed to resist the arms of England, but which had broken down in the first years of peace, was not a very numerous body, but it included the most eminent men of America. It is astounding to observe the political wisdom, and still more the political foresight, which their deliberations exhibit. Franklin, indeed, appears to have been the only very foolish man among them, and his colleagues seem to have been aware of it. Washington presided, but he exercised very little influence upon the assembly, in which there were men who far exceeded him in intellectual power. Adams and Jefferson were in Europe, and the absence of the latter is conspicuous in the debates and in the remarkable work which issued from them. For it is a most striking thing that the views of pure democracy, which we are accustomed to associate with American politics, were almost entirely unrepresented in that convention. Far from being the product of a democratic revolution, and of an opposition to English institutions, the Constitution of the United States was the result of a powerful reaction against democracy, and in favour of the traditions of the mother country. On this point nearly all the leading statesmen were agreed, and no contradiction was given to such speeches as the following. Madison said: "In all cases where a majority are united by a common interest or passion, the rights of the minority are in danger. What motives are to restrain them? A prudent regard to the maxim, that honesty is the best policy, is found by experience to be as little regarded by bodies of men as by individuals. Respect for character is always diminished in proportion to the number among whom the blame or praise is to be divided. Conscience, the only remaining tie, is known to be inadequate in individuals; in large numbers little is to be expected from it." [3]

Mr. Sherman opposed the election by the people, "insisting that it ought to be by the State legislatures. The people immediately should have as little to do as may be about the government."

---
[3] Madison's *Reports*, 162.

Mr. Gerry said: "The evils we experience flow from the excess of democracy. The people do not want virtue, but are the dupes of pretended patriots. . . . . He had been too republican heretofore; he was still, however, republican, but had been taught by experience the danger of the levelling spirit." Mr. Mason "admitted that we had been too democratic, but was afraid we should incautiously run into the opposite extreme." Mr. Randolph observed "that the general object was to provide a cure for the evils under which the United States laboured; that, in tracing these evils to their origin, every man had found it in the turbulence and follies of democracy; that some check, therefore, was to be sought for against this tendency of our governments." [4]

Mr. Wilson, speaking in 1787, as if with the experience of the seventy years that followed, said, "Despotism comes on mankind in different shapes; sometimes in an executive, sometimes in a military one. Is there no danger of a legislative despotism? Theory and practice both proclaim it. If the legislative authority be not restrained, there can be neither liberty nor stability." [5] "However the legislative power may be formed," said Gouverneur Morris, the most conservative man in the convention, "it will, if disposed, be able to ruin the country." [6]

Still stronger was the language of Alexander Hamilton: "If government is in the hands of the few, they will tyrannise over the many; if in the hands of the many, they will tyrannise over the few. It ought to be in the hands of both, and they should be separated. This separation must be permanent. Representation alone will not do; demagogues will generally prevail; and, if separated, they will need a mutual check. This check is a monarch. . . . The monarch must have proportional strength. He ought to be hereditary, and to have so much power that it will not be his interest to risk much to acquire more. . . . Those who mean to form a solid republican government ought to proceed to the confines

---
[4] *Ibid.*, 135, 138.
[5] *Ibid.*, 196.
[6] *Ibid.*, 433.

of another government. . . . But if we incline too much to democracy, we shall soon shoot into a monarchy." [7] "He acknowledged himself not to think favourably of republican government, but addressed his remarks to those who did think favourably of it, in order to prevail on them to tone their government as high as possible." [8] Soon after, in the New York convention, for the adoption of the constitution, he said, "It has been observed that a pure democracy, if it were practicable, would be the most perfect government. Experience has proved that no position in politics is more false than this. The ancient democracies, in which the people themselves deliberated, never possessed one feature of good government. Their very character was tyranny." [9]

Hamilton's opinions were in favour of monarchy, though he despaired of introducing it into America. He constantly held up the British constitution as the only guide and model; and Jefferson has recorded his conversations, which show how strong his convictions were. Adams had said that the English government might, if reformed, be made excellent; Hamilton paused and said: "Purge it of its corruption, and give to its popular branch equality of representation, and it would become an impracticable government; as it stands at present, with all its supposed defects, it is the most perfect government which ever existed." And on another occasion he declared to Jefferson, "I own it is my own opinion . . . that the present government is not that which will answer the ends of society, by giving stability and protection to its rights; and that it will probably be found expedient to go into the British form." [10]

In his great speech on the constitution, he spoke with equal decision: "He had no scruple in declaring, supported as he was by the opinion of so many of the wise and good, that the British government was the best in the world, and

---

[7] Hamilton's *Works*, II, 413-417.
[8] Madison's *Reports*, 244.
[9] Hamilton's *Works*, II, 440.
[10] Rayner's *Life of Jefferson*, 268, 169.

that he doubted much whether anything short of it would do in America. .... As to the executive, it seemed to be admitted that no good one could be established on republican principles. Was not this giving up the merits of the question? for can there be a good government without a good executive? The English model was the only good one on this subject..... We ought to go as far, in order to attain stability and permanency, as republican principles will admit." [11]

Mr. Dickinson "wished the Senate to consist of the most distinguished characters, — distinguished for their rank in life and their weight of property, and bearing as strong a likeness to the British House of Lords as possible." [12]

Mr. Pinckney, of South Carolina, said, "Much has been said of the constitution of Great Britain. I will confess that I believe it to be the best constitution in existence; but, at the same time, I am confident it is one that will not or cannot be introduced into this country for many centuries." [13]

The question on which the founders of the constitution really differed, and which has ever since divided, and at last dissolved the Union, was to determine how far the rights of the States were merged in the federal power, and how far they retained their independence. The problem arose chiefly upon the mode in which the central Congress was to be elected. If the people voted by numbers or by electoral districts, the less populous States must entirely disappear. If the States, and not the population, were represented, the necessary unity could never be obtained, and all the evils of the old confederation would be perpetuated. "The knot," wrote Madison in 1831, "felt as the Gordian one, was the question between the larger and the smaller States, on the rule of voting."

There was a general apprehension on the part of the smaller States that they would be reduced to subjection by the rest. Not that any great specific differences separated the different States; for though the questions of the regula-

---

[11] Madison's *Reports*, 202.
[12] *Ibid.*, 166.
[13] *Ibid.*, 234.

tion of commerce and of slavery afterwards renewed the dispute, yet interests were so different from what they have since become, and so differently distributed, that there is little analogy, excepting in principle, with later contests; what was then a dispute on a general principle, has since been envenomed by the great interests and great passions which have become involved in it. South Carolina, which at that time looked forward to a rapid increase by immigration, took part with the large States on behalf of the central power; and Charles Pinckney presented a plan of a constitution which nearly resembled that which was ultimately adopted. The chief subject of discussion was the Virginia plan, presented by Edmund Randolph, in opposition to which the small State of New Jersey introduced another plan founded on the centrifugal or State-rights principle. The object of this party was to confirm the sovereignty of the several States, and to surrender as little as possible to the federal government. This feeling was expressed by Mr. Bedford: "Is there no difference of interests, no rivalship of commerce, of manufacture? Will not these large States crush the small ones, whenever they stand in the way of their ambitions or interested views?" [14]

"The State legislatures," said Colonel Mason, "ought to have some means of defending themselves against encroachments of the national government. In every other department we have studiously endeavoured to provide for its self-defence. Shall we leave the States alone unprovided with means for this purpose?" [15]

These speakers may have been good or bad politicians, they were certainly good prophets. They were nearly balanced in numbers, and surpassed in ability, by the centralising party. Madison, at that time under the powerful influence of Hamilton, and a federalist, but who afterwards was carried by Jefferson into the democratic camp, occupied an uncertain intermediate position. A note preserved in Washington's handwriting records: "Mr. Madison thinks an

---
[14] *Ibid.*, 173.
[15] *Ibid.*, 170.

individual independence of the States utterly irreconcilable with their aggregate sovereignty, and that a consolidation of the whole into one simple republic would be as inexpedient as it is unattainable." [16]

In convention he said: "Any government for the United States formed on the supposed practicability of using force against the unconstitutional proceedings of the States, would prove as visionary and fallacious as the government of Congress." [17]

The consistent Federalists went farther: "Too much attachment," said Mr. Read, "is betrayed to the State governments. We must look beyond their continuance; a national government must soon, of necessity, swallow them all up." [18]

Two years before the meeting of the convention, in 1785, Jay, the very type of a federalist, wrote: "It is my first wish to see the United States assume and merit the character of one great nation, whose territory is divided into different States merely for more convenient government."

Alexander Hamilton went further than all his colleagues. He had taken no part in the early debates, when he brought forward an elaborate plan of his own; the most characteristic features of which are, that the State governments are to be altogether superseded; their governors to be appointed by the general government, with a veto on all State laws, and the president is to hold office on good behaviour. An executive, elected for life, but personally responsible, made the nearest possible approach to an elective monarchy; and it was with a view to this all but monarchical constitution that he designed to destroy the independence of the States. This scheme was not adopted as the basis of discussion. "He has been praised," said Mr. Johnson, "by all, but supported by none." Hamilton's speech is very imperfectly reported, but his own sketch, the notes from which he spoke, are preserved, and outweigh, in depth and in originality of thought, all that we have ever heard or read of American oratory.

---
[16] Williams's *Statesman's Manual*, 268.
[17] *Reports*, 171.
[18] *Ibid.*, 163.

He left Philadelphia shortly after, and continued absent many weeks; but there can be no doubt that the spirit of his speech greatly influenced the subsequent deliberations. "He was convinced," he said, "that no amendment of the confederation, leaving the States in possession of their sovereignty, could answer the purpose. . . . The general power, whatever be its form, if it preserves itself, must swallow up the State powers. . . . . They are not necessary for any of the great purposes of commerce, revenue, or agriculture. Subordinate authorities, he was aware, would be necessary. There must be distinct tribunals; corporations for local purposes. . . . . By an abolition of the States, he meant that no boundary could be drawn between the national and State legislatures; that the former must therefore have indefinite authority. If it were limited at all, the rivalship of the States would gradually subvert it. . . . . As States, he thought they ought to be abolished. But he admitted the necessity of leaving in them subordinate jurisdictions." [19]

This policy could be justified only on the presumption that when all State authorities should disappear before a great central power, the democratic principles, against which the founders of the Constitution were contending, would be entirely overcome. But in this Hamilton's hopes were not fulfilled. The democratic principles acquired new force, the spirit of the convention did not long survive, and then a strong federal authority became the greatest of all dangers to the opinions and institutions which he advocated. It became the instrument of the popular will instead of its barrier; the organ of arbitrary power instead of a security against it. There was a fundamental error and contradiction in Hamilton's system. The end at which he aimed was the best, but he sought it by means radically wrong, and necessarily ruinous to the cause they were meant to serve. In order to give to the Union the best government it could enjoy, it was necessary to destroy, or rather to ignore, the existing authorities. The people was compelled to return to a political state of nature, irrespective of the governments it

---
[19] *Ibid.*, 201, 212.

already possessed, and to assume to itself powers of which there were constituted administrators. No adaptation of existing facts to the ideal was possible. They required to be entirely sacrificed to the new design. All political rights, authorities, and powers must be restored to the masses, before such a scheme could be carried into effect. For the most conservative and anti-democratic government the most revolutionary basis was sought. These objections were urged against all plans inconsistent with the independence of the several States by Luther Martin, Attorney General for Maryland.

"He conceived," he said, "that the people of the States, having already vested their powers in their respective legislatures, could not resume them without a dissolution of their governments. . . . . To resort to the citizens at large for their sanction to a new government, will be throwing them back into a state of nature; the dissolution of the State governments is involved in the nature of the process; — the people have no right to do this without the consent of those to whom they have delegated their power for State purposes." [20] And in his report to the convention of Maryland of the proceedings out of which the constitution arose, he said: "If we, contrary to the purpose for which we were intrusted, considering ourselves as master-builders, too proud to amend our original government, should demolish it entirely, and erect a new system of our own, a short time might show the new system as defective as the old, perhaps more so. Should a convention be found necessary again, if the members thereof, acting upon the same principles, instead of amending and correcting its defects, should demolish that entirely, and bring forward a third system, that also might soon be found no better than either of the former; and thus we might always remain young in government, and always suffering the inconveniences of an incorrect imperfect system." [21]

It is very remarkable that, while the Federalists, headed

[20] *Ibid.*, 218, 248.
[21] Elliot's *Debates*, I, 350.

by Hamilton and Madison; advocated, for the soundest and wisest object, opinions which have since been fatal to the Union, by furnishing the democratic party with an irresistible instrument, and consequently an irresistible temptation, Martin supported a policy in reality far more conservative, although his opinions were more revolutionary, and although he quoted as political authorities writers such as Price and Priestley. The controversy, although identical in substance with that which has at last destroyed the Union, was so different in form, and consequently in its bearings, that the position of the contending parties became inverted as their interests or their principles predominated. The result of this great constitutional debate was, that the States were represented as units in the Senate, and the people according to numbers in the House. This was the first of the three great compromises. The others were the laws by which the regulation of commerce was made over to the central power, and the slave-trade was tolerated for only twenty years. On these two questions, the regulation of commerce and the extension of slavery, the interests afterwards grew more divided, and it is by them that the preservation of the Union has been constantly called in question. This was not felt at first, when Jay wrote "that Providence has been pleased to give this one connected country to one united people; a people descended from the same ancestors, speaking the same language, professing the same religion, attached to the same principles of government, very similar in their manners and customs." [22] The weakening of all these bonds of union gradually brought on the calamities which are described by Madison in another number of the same publication: "A landed interest, a manufacturing interest, a mercantile interest, a moneyed interest, with many lesser interests, grow up of necessity in civilised nations, and divide them into different classes, actuated by different sentiments and views. The regulation of these various and interfering interests forms the principal task of modern legislation, and involves the spirit of party and faction in the

---

[22] *Federalist*, 2.

necessary and ordinary operations of the government. . . . . When a majority is included in a faction, the form of popular government enables it to sacrifice to its ruling passion or interest both the public good and the rights of other citizens. . . . . It is of great importance in a republic not only to guard the society against the oppression of its rulers, but to guard one part of the society against the injustice of the other part. Different interests necessarily exist in different classes of citizens. If a majority be united by common interests, the rights of the minority will be insecure. There are but two methods of providing against this evil: the one by creating a will in the community independent of the majority, that is, of the society itself; the other, by comprehending in the society so many separate descriptions of citizens as will render one unjust combination of a majority of the whole very improbable, if not impracticable. . . . . In a free government the security for civil rights must be the same as that for religious rights. It consists, in the one case, in the multiplicity of interests, and in the other in the multiplicity of sects." [23] That Madison should have given so absurd a reason for security in the new Constitution, can be explained only by the fact that he was writing to recommend it as it was, and had to make the best of his case. It had been Hamilton's earnest endeavour to establish that security for right which Madison considers peculiar to monarchy, an authority which should not be the organ of the majority. " 'Tis essential there should be a permanent will in a community. . . . . The principle chiefly intended to be established is this, that there must be a permanent will. . . . . There ought to be a principle in government capable of resisting the popular current." [24]

This is precisely what Judge Story means when he says: "I would say in a republican government the fundamental truth, that the minority have indisputable and inalienable rights; that the majority are not everything, and the minority nothing; that the people may not do what they please."

---
[23] *Ibid.*, 10, 51.
[24] *Works*, II, 414, 415.

Webster thought the same, but he took a sanguine view of actual facts when he said: "It is another principle, equally true and certain, and, according to my judgment of things, equally important, that the people often limit themselves. They set bounds to their own power. They have chosen to secure the institutions which they establish against the sudden impulses of mere majorities." [25]

Channing was nearer the truth when he wrote: "The doctrine that the majority ought to govern passes with the multitude as an intuition, and they have never thought how far it is to be modified in practice, and how far the application of it ought to be controlled by other principles." [26]

In reality, the total absence of a provision of this kind, which should raise up a law above the arbitrary will of the people, and prevent it from being sovereign, led the greatest of the statesmen who sat in the convention to despair of the success and permanence of their work. Jefferson informs us that it was so with Washington: "Washington had not a firm confidence in the durability of our government. Washington was influenced by the belief that we must at length end in something like a British constitution."

Hamilton, who by his writings contributed more than any other man to the adoption of the Constitution, declared in the convention that "no man's ideas were more remote from the plan than his own," and he explained what he thought of the kind of security that had been obtained: "Gentlemen say that we need to be rescued from the democracy. But what the means proposed? A democratic Assembly is to be checked by a democratic Senate, and both these by a democratic chief magistrate." [27]

"A large and well-organised republic," he said, "can scarcely lose its liberty from any other cause than that of anarchy, to which a contempt of the laws is the high-road. . . . . A sacred respect for the constitutional law is the vital principle, the sustaining energy of a free government.

---
[25] *Works*, VI, 225.
[26] *Memoir*, 417.
[27] *Works*, II, 415.

.... The instruments by which it must act are either the authority of the laws, or force. If the first be destroyed, the last must be substituted; and where this becomes the ordinary instrument of government, there is an end to liberty." [28]

His anticipations may be gathered from the following passages: "A good administration will conciliate the confidence and affection of the people, and perhaps enable the government to acquire more consistency than the proposed constitution seems to promise for so great a country. It may then triumph altogether over the State governments, and reduce them to an entire subordination, dividing the larger States into smaller districts. .... If this should not be the case, in the course of a few years it is probable that the contests about the boundaries of power between the particular governments and the general government, and the momentum of the larger States in such contests, will produce a dissolution of the Union. This, after all, seems to be the most likely result. .... The probable evil is, that the general government will be too dependent on the State legislatures, too much governed by their prejudices, and too obsequious to their humours; that the States, with every power in their hands, will make encroachments on the national authority, till the Union is weakened and dissolved." [29]

The result has justified the fears of Hamilton, and the course of events has been that which he predicted. Democratic opinions, which he had so earnestly combated, gained ground rapidly during the French revolutionary period. Jefferson, who, even at the time of the Declaration of Independence, which was his work, entertained views resembling those of Rousseau and Paine, and sought the source of freedom in the abstract rights of man, returned from France with his mind full of the doctrines of equality and popular sovereignty. By the defeat of Adams in the contest for the presidency, he carried these principles to power, and altered the nature of the American government. As the Federalists

---
[28] *Ibid.,* VII, 164.
[29] *Ibid.,* II, 421, 450.

> The governments she gave are more fragile, it is true, but a hundred times more powerful than any of those she reversed; fragile and powerful by the same causes.

interpreted and administered the constitution, under Washington and Adams, the executive was, what Hamilton intended it to be, supreme in great measure over the popular will. Against this predominance the State legislatures were the only counterpoise, and accordingly the democratic party, which was the creature of Jefferson, vehemently defended their rights as a means of giving power to the people. In apparent contradiction, but in real accordance with this, and upon the same theory of the direct sovereignty of the people, Jefferson, when he was elected president, denied the right of the States to control the action of the executive. Regarding the President as the representative and agent of a power wholly arbitrary, he admitted no limits to its exercise. He held himself bound to obey the popular will even against his own opinions, and to allow of no resistance to it. He acted as the helpless tool of the majority, and the absolute ruler of the minority, as endowed with despotic power, but without free-will.

It is of this principle of the revolution that Tocqueville says: "Les gouvernements qu'elle a fondés sont plus fragiles, il est vrai, mais cent fois plus puissants qu'aucun de ceux qu'elle a renversés; fragiles et puissants par les mêmes causes." [30]

Hence Jefferson's determined aversion to every authority which could oppose or restrain the will of the sovereign people, especially to the State legislatures and to the judiciary. Speaking of an occasion in which the judges had acted with independence, Hildreth says: "Jefferson was not a little vexed at this proceeding, which served, indeed, to confirm his strong prejudices against judges and courts. To him, indeed, they were doubly objects of hatred, as instruments of tyranny in the hands of the Federalists, and as obstacles to himself in exercises of power." [31]

His views of government are contained in a paper which is printed in Rayner's life of him, p. 378: "Governments are republican only in proportion as they embody the will of

---
[30] *L'Ancien Régime et La Révolution*, p. 13.
[31] *History of the United States*, VI, 70.

their people, and execute it. . . . Each generation is as independent of the one preceding as that was of all which had gone before. It has, then, like them, a right to choose for itself the form of government it believes most promotive of its own happiness . . . . it is for the peace and good of mankind, that a solemn opportunity of doing this, every nineteen or twenty years, should be provided by the constitution. . . . . The dead have no rights. . . . . This corporeal globe and everything upon it belong to its present corporeal inhabitants during their generation. . . . . That majority, then, has a right to depute representatives to a convention, and to make the constitution which they think will be best for themselves. . . . . Independence can be trusted nowhere but with the people in mass." With these doctrines Jefferson subverted the republicanism of America, and consequently the Republic itself.

Hildreth describes as follows the contest between the two systems, at the time of the accession of Jefferson to power, in 1801: "From the first moment that party lines had been distinctly drawn, the opposition had possessed a numerical majority, against which nothing but the superior energy, intelligence, and practical skill of the Federalists, backed by the great and venerable name and towering influence of Washington, had enabled them to maintain for eight years past an arduous and doubtful struggle. The Federal party, with Washington and Hamilton at its head, represented the experience, the prudence, the practical wisdom, the discipline, the conservative reason and instincts of the country. The opposition, headed by Jefferson, expressed its hopes, wishes, theories, many of them enthusiastic and impracticable, more especially its passions, its sympathies and antipathies, its impatience of restraint. The Federalists had their strength in those narrow districts where a concentrated population had produced and contributed to maintain that complexity of institutions, and that reverence for social order, which, in proportion as men are brought into contiguity, become more absolutely necessaries of existence. The ultrademocratical ideas of the opposition prevailed in all that more extensive region in which the dispersion of population, and the despotic authority vested in individuals over families of slaves, kept society in a state of immaturity." [82]

Upon the principle that the majority have no duties, and the minority no rights, that it is lawful to do whatever it is possible to do, measures were to be expected which would oppress most tyrannically the rights and interests of portions of the Union, for whom there was no security and no redress. The apprehension was so great among the Federalists, that Hamilton wrote in 1804: "The ill opinion of Jefferson, and jealousy of the ambition of Virginia, is no inconsiderable prop of good principles in that country (New England). But these causes are leading to an opinion, that a dismemberment of the Union is expedient." [33]

Jefferson had given the example of such threats, and owed his election to them during his contest for the presidency with Colonel Burr. He wrote to Monroe, 15 February, 1801: "If they could have been permitted to pass a law for putting the government into the hands of an officer, they would certainly have prevented an election. But we thought it best to declare openly and firmly, one and all, that the day such an act passed the middle States would arm, and that no such usurpation, even for a single day, should be submitted to."

Shortly afterwards, a conjuncture arose in which Jefferson put his principles into practice in such a way as greatly to increase the alarm of the North-Eastern States. In consequence of Napoleon's Berlin decree and of the British orders in council, he determined to lay an embargo on all American vessels. He sent a pressing message to Congress, and the Senate passed the measure after a four hours' debate with closed doors. In the House the debate was also secret, but it lasted several days, and was often prolonged far into the night, in the hope of obtaining a division. The Bill was passed December 22, 1807. The public had no voice in the matter; those whom the measure touched most nearly were taken by surprise, and a conspicuous example was given of secrecy

---
[82] *Ibid.,* V, 414.
[33] *Works,* VII, 852.

and promptitude in a species of government which is not commonly remarkable for these qualities.

The embargo was a heavy blow to the ship-owning states of New England. The others were less affected by it. "The natural situation of this country," says Hamilton, "seems to divide its interests into different classes. There are navigating and non-navigating States. The Northern are properly the navigating states; the Southern appear to possess neither the means nor the spirit of navigation. This difference in situation naturally produces a dissimilarity of interests and views respecting foreign commerce." [34]

Accordingly the law was received in those States with a storm of indignation. Quincy, of Massachusetts, declared in the House: "It would be as unreasonable to undertake to stop the rivers from running into the sea, as to keep the people of New England from the ocean. They did not believe in the constitutionality of any such law. He might be told that the courts had already settled that question. But it was one thing to decide a question before a court of law, and another to decide it before the people." [35]

Even in a juridical point of view the right to make such a law was very doubtful. Story, who first took part in public affairs on this occasion, says: "I have ever considered the embargo a measure which went to the extreme limit of constructive power under the constitution. It stands upon the extreme verge of the constitution." [36]

The doctrine of State-rights, or nullification, which afterwards became so prominent in the hands of the Southern party, was distinctly enunciated on behalf of the North on this occasion. Governor Trumbull, of Connecticut, summoned the legislature to meet, and in his opening address to them he took the ground that, on great emergencies, when the national legislature had been led to overstep its constitutional power, it became the right and duty of the State legislatures "to interpose their protecting shield between the

---
[34] *Ibid.*, II, 433.
[35] Hildreth, VI, 100.
[36] *Life*, I, 185.

rights and liberties of the people, and the assumed power of the general government." [37]

They went further, and prepared to secede from the Union, and thus gave the example which has been followed, on exactly analogous grounds, by the opposite party. Randolph warned the administration that they were treading fast in the fatal footsteps of Lord North." [38]

John Quincy Adams declared in Congress that there was a determination to secede. "He urged that a continuance of the embargo much longer would certainly be met by forcible resistance, supported by the legislature, and probably by the judiciary of the State. . . . . Their object was, and had been for several years, a dissolution of the Union, and the establishment of a separate confederation." Twenty years later, when Adams was President, the truth of this statement was impugned. At that time the tables had been turned, and the South was denying the right of Congress to legislate for the exclusive benefit of the North-Eastern States, whilst these were vigorously and profitably supporting the federal authorities. It was important that they should not be convicted out of their own mouths, and that the doctrine they were opposing should not be shown to have been inaugurated by themselves. Adams therefore published a statement, October 21, 1828, reiterating his original declaration. "The people were constantly instigated to forcible resistance against it, and juries after juries acquitted the violators of it, upon the ground that it was unconstitutional, assumed in the face of a solemn decision of the District Court of the United States. A separation of the Union was openly stimulated in the public prints, and a convention of delegates of the New England States, to meet at New Haven, was intended and proposed." That this was true is proved by the letters of Story, written at the time. "I was well satisfied," he says, "that such a course would not and could not be borne by New England, and would bring on a direct rebellion. . . . . The stories here of rebellion in Massachusetts are continu-

---

[37] Hildreth, VI, 120.
[38] *Ibid.*, VI, 117.

ally circulating. My own impressions are, that the Junto would awaken it, if they dared; but it will not do. . . . . A division of the States has been meditated, but I suspect that the public pulse was not sufficiently inflamed. . . . . I am sorry to perceive the spirit of disaffection in Massachusetts increasing to so high a degree; and I fear that it is stimulated by a desire, in a very few ambitious men, to dissolve the Union. . . . . I have my fears when I perceive that the public prints openly advocate a resort to arms to sweep away the present embarrassments of commerce." [39]

It was chiefly due to the influence of Story that the embargo was at length removed, with great reluctance and disgust on the part of the President. "I ascribe all this," he says, "to one pseudo-republican, Story." [40] On which Story, who was justly proud of his achievement, remarks, "Pseudo-republican of course I must be, as everyone was, in Mr. Jefferson's opinion, who dared to venture upon a doubt of his infallibility." [41] In reality Jefferson meant that a man was not a republican who made the interests of the minority prevail against the wish of the majority. His enthusiastic admirer, Professor Tucker, describes very justly and openly his policy in this affair. "If his perseverance in the embargo policy so long, against the wishes and interests of New England, and the mercantile community generally, may seem to afford some contradiction to the self-denying merit here claimed, the answer is, that he therein fulfilled the wishes of a large majority of the people. . . . . A portion of the community here suffered an evil necessarily incident to the great merit of a republican government, that the will of the majority must prevail." [42]

We have seen that in the case of the embargo, as soon as this democratic theory was acted upon, it called up a corresponding claim of the right of the minority to secede, and that the democratic principle was forced to yield. But seces-

---
[39] *Life*, I, 182, 187, 191, 243.
[40] *Correspondence*, IV, 148.
[41] *Life*, I, 185.
[42] *Life*, II, 322.

sion was not a theory of the Constitution, but a remedy against a vicious theory of the Constitution. A sounder theory would have avoided the absolutism of the democrats and the necessity for secession. The next great controversy was fought upon this ground. It exhibits an attempt to set up a law against the arbitrary will of the government, and to escape the tyranny of the majority, and the remedy, which was worse than the disease. An ideal of this kind had already been sketched by Hamilton. "This balance between the national and state governments ought to be dwelt on with peculiar attention, as it is of the utmost importance. It forms a double security to the people. If one encroaches on their rights, they will find a powerful protection in the other. Indeed, they will both be prevented from overpassing their constitutional limits, by a certain rivalship which will ever subsist between them."[43] This was also what Mr. Dickinson looked forward to when he said in the Convention of 1787: "One source of stability is the double branch of the legislature. The division of the country into distinct States forms the other principal source of stability." [44]

The war with England, and the long suspension of commerce which preceded it, laid the foundations of a manufacturing interest in the United States. Manufactories began to spring up in Pennsylvania, and more slowly in New England. In 1816 a tariff was introduced, bearing a slightly protective character, as it was necessary to accommodate the war prohibitions to peaceful times. It was rather intended to facilitate the period of transition than to protect the new industry; and that interest was still so feeble, and so little affected by the tariff, that Webster, who was already a representative of Massachusetts in Congress, voted against it. It was carried by the coalition of Clay with the South-Carolina statesmen, Lowndes and Calhoun, against whom this vote was afterwards a favourite weapon of attack. In the following years the increasing importance of the cultivation of cotton, and the growth of manufactures, placed the Northern

---
[43] *Works*, II, 444.
[44] Madison's *Debates*, 148.

and Southern interests in a new position of great divergency. Hamilton had said long before: "The difference of property is already great amongst us. Commerce and industry will still increase the disparity. Your government must meet this state of things, or combinations will, in process of time, undermine your system."[45]

The New England manufacturers were awakened to the advantage of protection for their wares. In a memorial of the merchants of Salem, written by Story in 1820, he says: "Nothing can be more obvious than that many of the manufacturers and their friends are attempting, by fallacious statements, founded on an interested policy, or a misguided zeal, or very short-sighted views, to uproot some of the fundamental principles of our revenue policy. .... If we are unwilling to receive foreign manufacturers, we cannot reasonably suppose that foreign nations will receive our raw materials. .... We cannot force them to become buyers when they are not sellers, or to consume our cotton when they cannot pay the price in their own fabrics. We may compel them to use the cotton of the West Indies, or of the Brazils, or of the East Indies." About the same time, May 20, 1820, he writes to Lord Stowell on the same subject: "We are beginning also to become a manufacturing nation; but I am not much pleased, I am free to confess, with the efforts made to give an artificial stimulus to these establishments in our country. .... The example of your great manufacturing cities, apparently the seats of great vices, and great political fermentations, affords no very agreeable contemplation to the statesman or the patriot, or the friend of liberty."[46] The manufacturers obtained a new tariff in 1824, another was carried by great majorities in 1828, and another in 1832 by a majority of two to one. It is the measure of 1828, which raised the duties on an average to nearly fifty per cent on the value of the imports, that possesses the greatest importance in a constitutional point of view. "To it," says the biographer of Mr. Calhoun, "may be traced almost

---
[45] Elliot's *Debates*, 1, 450.
[46] *Life*, I, 385.

every important incident in our political history since that time, as far as our internal affairs are concerned." [47] At this time the interests of North and South were perfectly distinct. The South was teeming with agricultural produce, for which there was a great European demand; whilst the industry of the North, unable to compete with European manufacturers, tried to secure the monopoly of the home market. Unlike the course of the same controversy in England, the agriculturists (at least the cotton-growers) desired free trade, because they were exporters; the manufacturers protection because they could not meet competition. "The question," said Calhoun, "is in reality one between the exporting and non-exporting interests of the country." The exporting interest required the utmost freedom of imports, in order not to barter at a disadvantage. "He must be ignorant of the first principles of commerce, and the policy of Europe, particularly England, who does not see that it is impossible to carry on a trade of such vast extent on any other basis than barter; and that if it were not so carried on, it would not long be tolerated. . . . The last remains of our great and once flourishing agriculture must be annihilated in the conflict. In the first place, we will be thrown on the home market, which cannot consume a fourth of our products; and instead of supplying the world, as we would with a free trade, we would be compelled to abandon the cultivation of three-fourths of what we now raise, and receive for the residue whatever the manufacturers—who would then have their policy consummated by the entire possession of our market —might choose to give." [48] It seemed a fulfilment of the prophecy of Mr. Lowndes, who, in resisting the adoption of the constitution in South Carolina forty years before, declared, that "when this new constitution should be adopted, the sun of the Southern States would set, never to rise again..... The interest of the Northern States would so

---
[47] *Life of Calhoun*, p. 34.
[48] Exposition of South-Carolina Committee on the Tariff, 1828, in Calhoun's *Works*, VI, 12.

predominate as to divest us of any pretensions to the title of a republic." [49] Cobbett, who knew America better than any Englishman of that day, described, in his *Political Register* for 1833, the position of these hostile interests in a way which is very much to the point. "All these Southern and Western States are, commercially speaking, closely connected with Birmingham, Sheffield, Manchester and Leeds; . . . . they have no such connection with the Northern States, and there is no tie whatsoever to bind them together, except that which is of a mere political nature. . . . . Here is a natural division of interests, and of interests so powerful, too, as not to be counteracted by anything that man can do. The heavy duties imposed by the Congress upon British manufactured goods is neither more nor less than so many millions a year taken from the Southern and Western States, and given to the Northern States." [50]

Whilst in England protection benefited one class of the population at the expense of another, in America it was for the advantage of one part of the country at the expense of another. "Government," said Calhoun, "is to descend from its high appointed duty, and become the agent of a portion of the community to extort, under the guise of protection, tribute from the rest of the community." [51]

Where such a controversy is carried on between opposite classes in the same State, the violence of factions may endanger the government, but they cannot divide the State. But the violence is much greater, the wrong is more keenly felt, the means of resistance are more legitimate and constitutional, where the oppressed party is a sovereign State.

The South had every reason to resist to the utmost a measure which would be so injurious to them. It was opposed to their political as well as to their financial interests. For the tariff, while it impoverished them, enriched the government, and filled the treasury with superfluous gold. Now the Southern statesmen were always opposed to the predom-

---
[49] Elliot's *Debates*, IV, 272.
[50] *Political Works*, VI, 662.
[51] *Works*, IV, 181.

inance of the central authority, especially since it lent itself to a policy by which they suffered. They had practical and theoretical objections to it. The increase of the revenue beyond the ordinary wants of the government placed in its hands a tempting and dangerous instrument of influence. Means must be devised for the disposal of these sums, and the means adopted by the advocates of restriction was the execution of public works, by which the people of the different States were bribed to favour the central power. A protective tariff therefore, and internal improvement, were the chief points in the policy of the party, which, headed by Henry Clay, sought to strengthen the Union at the expense of the States, and which the South opposed, as both hostile to their interests and as unconstitutional. "It would be in vain to attempt to conceal," wrote Calhoun of the tariff in 1831, "that it has divided the country into two great geographical divisions, and arrayed them against each other, in opinion at least, if not interests also, on some of the most vital of political subjects—on its finance, its commerce, and its industry. . . . . Nor has the effect of this dangerous conflict ended here. It has not only divided the two sections on the important point already stated, but on the deeper and more dangerous questions, the constitutionality of a protective tariff, and the general principles and theory of the constitution itself: the stronger, in order to maintain their superiority, giving a construction to the instrument which the other believes would convert the general government into a consolidated irresponsible government, with the total destruction of liberty."[52] "On the great and vital point—the industry of the country, which comprehends almost every interest—the interest of the two great sections is opposed. We want free trade, they restrictions; we want moderate taxes, frugality in the government, economy, accountability, and a rigid application of the public money to the payment of the debt, and to the objects authorised by the constitution. In all these particulars, if we may judge by experience, their views of their in-

---

[52] *Works*, VI, 77, 78.

terest are precisely the opposite." [53] In 1828 he said of the protective system: "No system can be more efficient to rear up a moneyed aristocracy;" wherein he is again supported by Cobbett, in the well-known saying, uttered five years later, concerning the United States: "It is there the aristocracy of money, the most damned of all aristocracies." South Carolina took the lead in resisting the introduction of the protective system, and being defeated by many votes on the question itself, took its stand on the constitutional right of each sovereign State to arrest by its veto any general legislation of a kind which would be injurious to its particular interests. "The country," said Calhoun, "is now more divided than in 1824, and then more than in 1816. The majority may have increased, but the opposite sides are, beyond dispute, more determined and excited than at any preceding period. Formerly the system was resisted mainly as inexpedient, but now as unconstitutional, unequal, unjust, and oppressive. Then relief was sought exclusively from the general government; but now many, driven to despair, are raising their eyes to the reserved sovereignty of the States as the only refuge."[54] Calhoun was at that time Vice-President of the United States, and without a seat in Congress. The defence of his theory of the Constitution devolved therefore upon the senator from South Carolina, General Hayne; and a debate ensued between Hayne and Webster, in January 1830, which is reckoned by Americans the most memorable in the parliamentary history of their country. Hayne declared that he did not contend for the mere right of revolution, but for the right of constitutional resistance; and in reply to Webster's defence of the supreme power, he said: "This I know is a popular notion, and it is founded on the idea that as all the States are represented here, nothing can prevail which is not in conformity with the will of the majority; and it is supposed to be a republican maxim, 'that the majority must govern.' .... If the will of a majority of congress is to be the supreme law of the land, it is clear the Constitution is a dead

---
[53] *Ibid.*, VI, 31.
[54] *Ibid.*, VI, 80.

letter, and has utterly failed of the very object for which it was designed — the protection of the rights of the minority. .... The whole difference between us consists in this — the gentleman would make force the only arbiter in all cases of collision between the States and the federal government; I would resort to a peaceful remedy."[55]

Two years later Mr. Calhoun succeeded Hayne as senator for South Carolina, and the contest was renewed. After the tariff of 1828 Virginia, Georgia, and North Carolina joined in the recognition of the principle of nullification. When the tariff of 1832 was carried, South Carolina announced that the levying of dues would be resisted in the State. Calhoun defended the nullifying ordinance in the Senate, and in speeches and writings, with arguments which are the very perfection of political truth, and which combine with the realities of modern democracy the theory and the securities of mediaeval freedom. "The essence of liberty," he said, "comprehends the idea of responsible power,—that those who make and execute the laws should be controlled by those on whom they operate,—that the governed should govern. . . . . . No government based on the naked principle that the majority ought to govern, however true the maxim in its proper sense, and under proper restrictions, can preserve its liberty even for a single generation. The history of all has been the same,—violence, injustice, and anarchy, succeeded by the government of one, or a few, under which the people seek refuge from the more oppressive despotism of the many. . . . . Stripped of all its covering, the naked question is, whether ours is a federal or a consolidated government; a constitutional or absolute one; a government resting ultimately on the solid basis of the sovereignty of the States, or on the unrestrained will of a majority; a form of government, as in all other unlimited ones, in which injustice and violence and force must finally prevail. Let it never be forgotten that, where the majority rules without restriction, the minority is the subject. . . . . . Nor is the right of suffrage more indispensable to enforce the responsibility of the rulers to the

---
[55] Elliot's *Debates*, IV, 498.

ruled, than a federal organisation to compel the parts to respect the rights of each other. It requires the united action of both to prevent the abuse of power and oppression, and to constitute really and truly a constitutional government. To supersede either is to convert it in fact, whatever may be its theory, into an absolute government." [56]

In his disquisition on government Calhoun has expounded his theory of a constitution in a manner so profound, and so extremely applicable to the politics of the present day, that we regret that we can only give a very feeble notion of the argument by the few extracts for which we can make room.

"The powers which it is necessary for government to possess, in order to repress violence and preserve order, cannot execute themselves. They must be administered by men in whom, like others, the individual are stronger than the social feelings. And hence the powers vested in them to prevent injustice and oppression on the part of others, will, if left unguarded, be by them converted into instruments to oppress the rest of the community. That by which this is prevented, by whatever name called, is what is meant by constitution, in its most comprehensive sense, when applied to government. Having its origin in the same principle of our nature, constitution stands to government as government stands to society; and, as the end for which society is ordained would be defeated without government, so that for which government is ordained would, in a great measure, be defeated without constitution. . . . . Constitution is the contrivance of man, while government is of divine ordination. . . . . Power can only be resisted by power, and tendency by tendency. . . . . I call the right of suffrage the indispensable and primary principle; for it would be a great and dangerous mistake to suppose, as many do, that it is of itself sufficient to form constitutional governments. To this erroneous opinion may be traced one of the causes why so few attempts to form constitutional governments have succeeded; and why, of the few which have, so small a number have had durable existence. . . . . So far from being of itself sufficient,—however well-

[56] *Works*, VI, 32, 33, 75.

guarded it might be, and however enlightened the people, —it would, unaided by other provisions, leave the government as absolute as it would be in the hands of irresponsible rulers, and with a tendency at least as strong towards oppression and abuse of its powers. . . . The process may be slow, and much time may be required before a compact, organised majority can be formed; but formed it will be in time, even without preconcert or design, by the sure workings of that principle or constitution of our nature in which government itself originates. . . . . The dominant majority, for the time, would have the same tendency to oppression and abuse of power which, without the right of suffrage, irresponsible rulers would have. No reason, indeed, can be assigned why the latter would abuse their power, which would not apply with equal force to the former. . . . . The minority, for the time, will be as much the governed or subject portion as are the people in an aristocracy, or the subject in a monarchy. . . . . The duration or uncertainty of the tenure by which power is held cannot of itself counteract the tendency inherent in government to oppression and abuse of power. On the contrary, the very uncertainty of the tenure, combined with the violent party warfare which must ever precede a change of parties under such governments, would rather tend to increase than diminish the tendency to oppression. . . . . It is manifest that this provision must be of a character calculated to prevent any one interest, or combination of interests, from using the powers of government to aggrandise itself at the expense of the others. . . . . This too can be accomplished only in one way, and that is, by such an organism of the government—and, if necessary for the purpose, of the community also—as will, by dividing and distributing the powers of government, give to each division or interest, through its appropriate organ, either a concurrent voice in making and executing the laws, or a veto on their execution. . . . . Such an organism as this, combined with the right of suffrage, constitutes, in fact, the elements of constitutional government. The one, by rendering those who make and execute the laws responsible to those on whom they operate, prevents the rulers from oppressing the ruled; and the other, by making it impossible for any one interest or combination of interests, or class, or order, or portion of the community, to obtain exclusive control, prevents any one of them from oppressing the other. . . . It is this negative power,—the power of preventing or arresting the action of the government,—be it called by what term it may, veto, interposition, nullification, check, or balance of power,—which in fact forms the constitution. . . . . It is, indeed, the negative power which makes the constitution, and the positive which makes the government. . . . . It follows necessarily that where the numerical majority has the sole control of the government, there can be no constitution; as constitution implies limitation or restriction; . . . . and hence, the numerical, unmixed with the concurrent majority, necessarily forms in all cases absolute government. . . . . Constitutional governments, of whatever form, are, indeed, much more similar to each other in their structure and character than they are, respectively, to the absolute governments even of their own class; . . . . and hence the great and broad distinction between governments is, — not that of the one, the few, or the many, — but of the constitutional and the absolute. . . . . Among the other advantages which governments of the concurrent have over those of the numerical majority,—and which strongly illustrates their more popular character,—is, that they admit, with safety, a much greater extension of the right of suffrage. It may be safely extended in such governments to universal suffrage, that is, to every male citizen of mature age, with few ordinary exceptions; but it cannot be so far extended in those of the numerical majority, without placing them ultimately under the control of the more ignorant and dependent portions of the community. For, as the community becomes populous, wealthy, refined, and highly civilised, the difference between the rich and the poor will become more strongly marked, and the number of the ignorant and dependent greater in proportion to the rest of the community. . . . . The tendency of the concurrent government is to unite the community, let its interests be ever so diversified or opposed; while that of the numerical is to divide it into two conflicting portions, let its interest be naturally ever so united and identified. . . . . The numerical majority, by regarding the community as a unit, and having as such the same interests throughout all its parts, must, by its necessary operation, divide it into two hostile parts, waging, under the forms of law, incessant hostilities against each other. . . . . To make equality of condition essential to liberty, would be to destroy liberty and progress. The reason is both that inequality of condition, while it is a necessary consequence of liberty, is at the same time indispensable to progress. . . . It is, indeed, this inequality of condition between the front and rear ranks, in the march of progress, which gives so strong an impulse to the former to maintain their position, and to the latter to press forward into their files. This gives to progress its greatest impulse. . . . . These great and dangerous errors have their origin in the prevalent opinion, that all men are born free and equal, than which nothing can be more unfounded and false. . . . . In an absolute democracy party conflicts between the majority and minority . . . . can hardly ever terminate in compromise. The object of the opposing minority is to expel the majority from power, and of the majority to maintain their hold upon it. It is on both sides a struggle for the whole; a struggle that must determine which shall be the governing and which the subject party. . . . . Hence, among other reasons, aristocracies and monarchies more readily assume the constitutional form than absolute popular governments." [57]

This was written in the last years of Calhoun's life, and published after his death; but the ideas, though he matured them in the subsequent contest on slavery, guided him in the earlier stage of the dispute which developed nullification into secession, during the tariff controversy of the years 1828 to 1833. Many of those who differed from him most widely deemed that his resistance was justified by the selfish and unscrupulous policy of the North. Legaré, the most accomplished scholar among American statesmen, afterwards attorney-general, made a Fourth-of-July oration in South Carolina,

[57] *Ibid.*, I, 7-83.

during the height of the excitement of 1831, in which he said: "The authors of this policy are indirectly responsible for this deplorable state of things, and for all the consequences that may grow out of it. They have been guilty of an inexpiable offence against their country. They found us a united, they have made us a distracted people. They found the union of these States an object of fervent love and religious veneration; they have made even its utility a subject of controversy among very enlightened men. .... I do not wonder at the indignation which the imposition of such a burden of taxation has excited in our people, in the present unprosperous state of their affairs. .... Great nations cannot be held together under a united government by any thing short of despotic power, if any one part of the country is to be arrayed against another in a perpetual scramble for privilege and protection, under any system of protection." [58]

Brownson, at that time the most influential journalist of America, and a strong partisan of Calhoun, advocated in 1844 his claims to the Presidency, and would, we believe, have held office in his cabinet if he had been elected. In one of the earliest numbers of his well-known Review he wrote: "Even Mr. Calhoun's theory, though unquestionably the true theory of the federal constitution, is yet insufficient. .... It does not, as a matter of fact, arrest the unequal, unjust, and oppressive measures of the federal government. South Carolina in 1833 forced a compromise; but in 1842 the obnoxious policy was revived, is pursued now successfully, and there is no State to attempt again the virtue of State interposition. .... The State, if she judged proper, had the sovereign right to set aside this obnoxious tariff enactment in her own dominions, and prohibit her subjects or citizens from obeying it. .... The parties to the compact being equal, and there being no common umpire, each, as a matter of course, is its own judge of the infraction of the compact, and of the mode and measure of redress." [59]

The President, General Jackson, had a strong aversion for

---
[58] *Writings of Legaré*, I, 272.
[59] *Quarterly Review*, II, 522, I, 124.

the theory and for the person of Calhoun. He swore that he would have him impeached for treason, and that he should hang on a gallows higher than Haman's. One of the nullifying declarations of his Vice-President reached him late at night; in a fit of exultation he had the law officers of the government called out of their beds, to say whether at last here was not hanging matter. He issued a manifesto condemning the doctrine of nullification and the acts of South Carolina, which was very ably drawn up by Livingston, the Secretary of State, famous in the history of legislation as the author of the Louisiana code. Webster, the first orator of the day, though not a supporter of the administration, undertook to answer Calhoun in the Senate, and he was fetched from his lodging, when the time came, in the President's carriage. His speech, considered the greatest he ever delivered, was regarded by the friends of the Union as conclusive against State-rights. Madison, who was approaching the term of his long career, wrote to congratulate the speaker in words which ought to have been a warning: "It crushes nullification, and must hasten an abandonment of secession. But this dodges the blow by confounding the claim to secede at will with the right of seceding from intolerable oppression."

Secession is but the alternative of interposition. The defeat of the latter doctrine on the ground of the Constitution, deprived the South of the only possible protection from the increasing tyranny of the majority, for the defeat of nullification coincided in time with the final triumph of the pure democratic views; and at the same time that it was resolved that the rights of the minority had no security, it was established that the power of the majority had no bounds. Calhoun's elaborate theory was an earnest attempt to save the Union from the defects of its Constitution. It is useless to inquire whether it is legally right, according to the letter of the Constitution, for it is certain that it is in contradiction with its spirit as it has grown up since Jefferson. Webster may have been the truest interpreter of the law; Calhoun was the real defender of the Union. Even the Unionists made the dangerous admission, that there were cases in which, as there was no redress known to the law, secession was fully justified. Livingston gave the opinion, that "if the act be one of the few which, in its operation, cannot be submitted to the Supreme Court, and be one that will, in the opinion of the State, justify the risk of a withdrawal from the Union, this last extremity may at once be resorted to." [60]

The intimate connection between nullification and secession is shown by the biographer of Clay, though he fails to see that one is not the consequence, but the surrogate, of the other: "The first idea of nullification was doubtless limited to the action of a State in making null and void a federal law or laws within the circle of its own jurisdiction, without contemplating the absolute independence of a secession. Seeing, however, that nullification, in its practical operation, could hardly stop short of secession, the propounders of the doctrine in its first and limited signification, afterwards came boldly up to the claim of the right of secession." [61]

Practically, South Carolina triumphed, though her claims were repudiated. The tariff was withdrawn, and a measure of compromise was introduced by Clay, the leading protectionist, which was felt to be so great a concession that Calhoun accepted, whilst Webster opposed it, and it was carried. But the evil day, the final crisis, was only postponed. The spirit of the country had taken a course in which it could not be permanently checked; and it was certain that new opportunities would be made to assert the omnipotence of the popular will, and to exhibit the total subservience of the executive to it.[62] Already a new controversy had begun, which has since overshadowed that which shook the Union from 1828 to 1833. The commercial question was not settled; the economical antagonism, and the determination on the part of the North to extend its advantages, did not slumber from Clay's Compromise Act to the Morrill Tariff in 1861; and in his farewell address, in 1837, Jackson drew a gloomy and desponding picture of the period which is filled

---
[60] Elliot's *Debates,* IV, 519.
[61] Colton's *Life and Speeches of Clay,* V, 392.
[62] Ὁ γὰρ δῆμος οὐ βούλεται εὐνομουμένης τῆς πόλεως αὐτὸς δουλεύειν, ἀλλ' ἐλεύθερος εἶναι καὶ ἄρχειν, τῆς δὲ κακονομίας αὐτῷ ὀλίγον μέλει ὃ γὰρ σὺ νομίζεις οὐκ εὐνομεῖσθαι, αὐτὸς ἀπὸ τούτου ἰσχύει ὁ δῆμος καὶ ἐλεύθερός ἐστιν. Xenophon, *Athen. Repub.* i 8.

with his name. "Many powerful interests are continually at work to procure heavy duties on commerce, and to swell the revenue beyond the real necessities of the public service; and the country has already felt the injurious effects of their combined influence. They succeeded in obtaining a tariff of duties bearing most oppressively on the agricultural and labouring classes of society, and producing a revenue that could not be usefully employed within the range of the powers conferred upon Congress; and in order to fasten upon the people this unjust and unequal system of taxation, extravagant schemes of internal improvement were got up in various quarters to squander the money and to purchase support. . . . . Rely upon it, the design to collect an extravagant revenue, and to burden you with taxes beyond the economical wants of the government, is not yet abandoned. The various interests which have combined together to impose a heavy tariff, and to produce an overflowing treasury, are too strong, and have too much at stake, to surrender the contest. The corporations and wealthy individuals who are engaged in large manufacturing establishments, desire a high tariff to increase their gains. Designing politicians will support it to conciliate their favour, and to obtain the means of profuse expenditure, for the purpose of purchasing influence in other quarters. . . . . It is from within, among yourselves—from cupidity, from corruption, from disappointed ambition, and inordinate thirst for power,—that factions will be formed and liberty endangered." [63]

Jackson was himself answerable for much of what was most deplorable in the political state of the country. The democratic tendency, which began under Jefferson, attained in Jackson's presidency its culminating point. The immense change in this respect may be shown in a single example. Pure democracy demands quick rotation of office, in order that, as all men have an equal claim to official power and profit, and must be supposed nearly equally qualified for it, and require no long experience (so that at Athens offices were distributed by lot), the greatest possible number of citizens should successively take part in the administration. It

[63] *Statesman's Manual*, 953-960.

diminishes the distinction between the rulers and the ruled, between the State and the community, and increases the dependence of the first upon the last. At first such changes were not contemplated. Washington dismissed only nine officials in eight years, Adams removed only ten, Madison five, Monroe nine, John Quincy Adams only two, both on specific disqualifying grounds. Jefferson was naturally in favour of rotation in office, and caused a storm of anger when he displaced 39 official men in order to supply vacancies for supporters. Jackson, on succeeding the younger Adams, instantly made 176 alterations, and in the course of the first year 491 postmasters lost their places. Mr. Everett says very truly: "It may be stated as the general characteristic of the political tendencies of this period, that there was a decided weakening of respect for constitutional restraint. Vague ideas of executive discretion prevailed on the one hand in the interpretation of the constitution, and of popular sovereignty on the other, as represented by a President elevated to office by overwhelming majorities of the people." [64]

This was the period of Tocqueville's visit to America, when he passed the following judgment: "When a man, or a party, suffers an injustice in the United States, to whom can he have recourse? To public opinion? It is that which forms the majority. To the legislative body? It represents the majority, and obeys it blindly. To the executive power? It is appointed by the majority, and serves as its passive instrument. To public force? It is nothing but the majority under arms. To the jury? It is the majority invested with the right of finding verdicts. The judges themselves, in some States, are elected by the majority. However iniquitous, therefore, or unreasonable the measure from which you suffer, you must submit." [65] Very eminent Americans [66] quite agreed with him in his censure of the course things had taken, and which had been seen long beforehand. In 1818 Story

---
[64] *Memoir of Webster*, p. 101.
[65] Vol. II, cap. 7.
[66] There is a remarkable passage in Story's letters on Tocqueville's celebrated book: "The work of De Tocqueville has had great reputation abroad, partly founded on their ignorance that he has borrowed the greater part of his

writes: "A new race of men is springing up to govern the nation; they are the hunters after popularity; men ambitious, not of the honour so much as of the profits of office,—the demagogues whose principles hang laxly upon them, and who follow, not so much what is right as what leads to a temporary vulgar applause. There is great, very great danger that these men will usurp so much of popular favour that they will rule the nation; and if so, we may yet live to see many of our best institutions crumble in the dust." [67]

The following passages are from the conclusion of his commentary on the Constitution: "The influence of the disturbing causes, which, more than once in the convention, were on the point of breaking up the Union, have since immeasurably increased in concentration and vigour. . . . If, under these circumstances, the Union should once be broken up, it is impossible that a new constitution should ever be formed, embracing the whole territory. We shall be divided into several nations or confederacies, rivals in power and interest, too proud to brook injury, and too close to make retaliation distant or ineffectual." On the 18th February, 1834, he writes of Jackson's administration: "I feel humiliated at the truth, which cannot be disguised, that though we live under the form of a republic, we are in fact under the absolute rule of a single man." And a few years later, 3d November, 1837, he tells Miss Martineau that she has judged too favourably of his country: "You have overlooked the terrible influence of a corrupting patronage, and the system of exclusiveness in official appointments, which have already wrought such extensive mischiefs among us, and threaten to destroy all the safeguards of our civil liberties. . . . . You would have learned, I think, that there may be a despotism exercised in a republic, as irresistible and as ruinous as in any form of monarchy."

The foremost of the Southern statesmen thought exactly

---

reflections from American works, and little from his own observations. The main body of his materials will be found in the *Federalist* and in Story's *Commentaries*." *Life of Story*, II, 330.

[67] *Life*, I, 311.

like the New England judge. "I care not," said Calhoun, "what the form of the government is; it is nothing, if the government be despotic, whether it be in the hands of one, or a few, or of many men, without limitation. . . . While these measures were destroying the equilibrium between the two sections, the action of the government was leading to a radical change in its character, by concentrating all the power of the system in itself. . . . . What was once a constitutional federal republic is now converted, in reality, into one as absolute as that of the autocrat of Russia, and as despotic in its tendency as any absolute government that ever existed. . . . The increasing power of this government, and of the control of the Northern section over all its departments, furnished the cause. It was this which made an impression on the minds of many, that there was little or no restraint to prevent the government from doing whatever it might choose to do." [68] At the same period, though reverting to a much earlier date, Cobbett wrote: "I lived eight years under the republican government of Pennsylvania; and I declare that I believe that to have been the most corrupt and tyrannical government that the world ever knew. . . . . I have seen enough of republican government to convince me that the mere name is not worth a straw." [69] Channing touches on a very important point, the influence of European liberalism on the republicanism of America: "Ever since our revolution we have had a number of men who have wanted faith in our free institutions, and have seen in our almost unlimited extension of the elective franchise the germ of convulsion and ruin. When the demagogues succeed in inflaming the ignorant 'multitude, and get office and power, this anti-popular party increases; in better times it declines. It has been built up in a measure by the errors and crimes of the liberals of Europe. . . . I have endeavoured on all occasions to disprove the notion that the labouring classes are unfit depositaries of political power. I owe it, however, to truth to say that I believe that the elective franchise is extended too far in this

---
[68] *Works*, IV, 351, 550, 553.
[69] *Political Register*, November 1833; *Works*, VI, 683.

country."[70] In 1841 he described very accurately the perils which have since proved fatal: "The great danger to our institutions, which alarms our conservatives most, has not perhaps entered Mr. Smith's mind. It is the danger of a party organisation, so subtle and strong as to make the government the monopoly of a few leaders, and to insure the transmission of the executive power from hand to hand almost as regularly as in a monarchy. . . . . That this danger is real cannot be doubted. So that we have to watch against despotism as well as, or more than, anarchy."[71] On this topic it is impossible to speak more strongly, and nobody could speak with greater authority than Dr. Brownson: "Our own government, in its origin and constitutional form, is not a democracy, but, if we may use the expression, a limited elective aristocracy. . . . But practically the government framed by our fathers no longer exists, save in name. Its original character has disappeared, or is rapidly disappearing. The constitution is a dead letter, except so far as it serves to prescribe the modes of election, the rule of the majority, the distribution and tenure of offices, and the union and separation of the functions of government. Since 1828 it has been becoming in practice, and is now substantially, a pure democracy, with no effective constitution but the will of the majority for the time being. . . . The constitution is practically abolished, and our government is virtually, to all intents and purposes, as we have said, a pure democracy, with nothing to prevent it from obeying the interest or interests which for the time being can succeed in commanding it."[72] Shortly before his conversion he wrote: "Looking at what we were in the beginning, and what we now are, it may well be doubted whether another country in Christendom has so rapidly declined as we have, in the stern and rigid virtues, in the high-toned and manly principles of conduct essential to the stability and wise administration of popular government. . . . The established political order in this country is not

---
[70] *Memoir of Channing*, 418, 419.
[71] *Ibid.*, 421.
[72] Brownson's *Quarterly Review*, 1844, II, 515, 523.

the democratic; and every attempt to apply the democratic theory as the principle of its interpretation is an attempt at revolution, and to be resisted. By a democracy I understand a political order,—if that may be called order which is none, —in which the people, primarily and without reference to any authority constituting them a body politic, are held to be the source of all the legitimate power in the state." [73]

The partisans of democratic absolutism who opposed State-rights in the affair of the tariff, and led to the unhappy consequences and lamentations we have seen, were already supplied with another topic to test the power of their principle. The question of abolition, subordinate at first, though auxiliary to the question of protection, came into the front when the other had lost its interest, and had been suspended for a season by the Compromise Act. It served to enlist higher sympathies on the side of revolution than could be won by considerations of mere profit. It adorned cupidity with the appearance of philanthropy, but the two motives were not quite distinct, and one is something of a pretext, and serves to disguise the other. They were equally available as means of establishing the supremacy of the absolute democracy, only one was its own reward; the other was not so clearly a matter of pecuniary interest, but of not inferior political advantage. A power which is questioned, however real it may be, must assert and manifest itself if it is to last. When the right of the States to resist the Union was rejected, although the question which occasioned the dispute was amicably arranged, it was certain to be succeeded by another, in order that so doubtful a victory might be commemorated by a trophy.

The question of slavery first exhibited itself as a constitutional difficulty about 1820, in the dispute which was settled by the Missouri compromise. Even at this early period the whole gravity of its consequences was understood by discerning men. Jefferson wrote: "This momentous question, like a fire-bell in the night, awakened and filled me with terror. I considered it at once as the knell of the Union. It is

[73] *Ibid.*, I, 84, 19.

hushed, indeed, for the moment. But this is a reprieve only, not a final sentence."

In 1828, when South Carolina was proclaiming the right of veto, and was followed by several of the Southern States, abolition was taken up in the North as a means of coercion against them, by way of reprisal, and as a very powerful instrument of party warfare. Channing writes to Webster, 14th May, 1828: "A little while ago, Mr. Lundy of Baltimore, the editor of a paper called *The Genius of Universal Emancipation*, visited this part of the country, to stir us up to the work of abolishing slavery at the South; and the intention is to organise societies for this purpose. . . . My fear in regard to our efforts against slavery is, that we shall make the case worse by rousing sectional pride and passion for its support, and that we shall only break the country into two great parties, which may shake the foundations of government."

In the heat of the great controversies of Jackson's administration, on the Bank question and the Veto question, slavery was not brought prominently forward; but when the democratic central power had triumphed, when the Bank question was settled, and there was no longer an immediate occasion for discussing State-rights, the party whose opinions had prevailed in the Constitution resolved to make use of their predominance for its extinction. Thenceforward, from about the year 1835, it became the leading question, and the form in which the antagonism between the principles of arbitrary power and of self-government displayed itself. At every acquisition of territory, at the formation of new States, the same question caused a crisis; then in the Fugitive-Slave Act, and finally in the formation of the republican party, and its triumph in 1860. The first effect of making abolition a political party question, and embodying in it the great constitutional quarrel which had already threatened the existence of the Union in the question of taxation, was to verify the prophecy of Channing. Webster, who had been the foremost antagonist of nullification in the affair of the tariff, lived to acknowledge that even secession was being provoked by the insane aggression of the North. In one of his latest speeches, in that which is known as his speech for the Union, 7th March, 1850, he denounced the policy of the abolitionists: "I do not mean to impute gross motives even to the leaders of these societies, but I am not blind to the consequences of their proceedings. I cannot but see what mischiefs their interference with the South has produced. And is it not plain to every man? Let any gentleman who entertains doubts on this point recur to the debates in the Virginia House of Delegates in 1832, and he will see with what freedom a proposition made by Mr. J. Randolph for the gradual abolition of slavery was discussed in that body. . . . Public opinion, which in Virginia had begun to be exhibited against slavery, and was opening out for the discussion of the question, drew back and shut itself up in its castle. . . . We all know the fact, and we all know the cause; and everything that these agitating people have done has been, not to enlarge, but to restrain, not to set free, but to bind faster, the slave-population of the South." [74]

Howe, the Virginian historian, in principle though not in policy an abolitionist, says: "That a question so vitally important would have been renewed with more success at an early subsequent period, seems more than probable, if the current opinions of the day can be relied on; but there were obvious causes in operation which paralysed the friends of abolition, and have had the effect of silencing all agitation on the subject. The abolitionists in the Northern and Eastern States, gradually increasing their strength as a party, became louder in their denunciations of slavery, and more and more reckless in the means adopted for assailing the constitutional rights of the South." [75]

Story writes, 19th January, 1839: "The question of slavery is becoming more and more an absorbing one, and will, if it continues to extend its influence, lead to a dissolution of the Union. At least there are many of our soundest statesmen who look to this as a highly probable event." [76]

---
[74] *Works*, V, 357.
[75] *Historical Collections of Virginia*, p. 128,
[76] *Life*, II, 307.

At that time the abolitionist party was yet in its infancy, and had not succeeded in combining together in a single party all the interests that were hostile to the slave States. Lord Carlisle, describing a conversation he had in 1841 with the present Secretary of State, Mr. Seward, says, "I find that I noted at the time that he was the first person I had met who did not speak slightingly of the abolitionists; he thought they were gradually gaining ground." [77]

But in the following year the abolitionist policy rapidly grew up into a great danger to the Union, which the great rivals, Webster and Calhoun, united to resist at the close of their lives. Commercially speaking, it is not certain that the North would gain by the abolition of slavery. It would increase the Southern market by encouraging white emigration from the North; but the commerce of New England depends largely on the cotton crop, and the New England merchants are not for abolition. Calhoun did not attribute the movement to a desire of gain: "The crusade against our domestic institution does not originate in hostility of interests. . . . . The rabid fanatics regard slavery as a sin, and thus regarding it deem it their highest duty to destroy it, even should it involve the destruction of the constitution and the Union." [78]

In this view he is fully supported by Webster: "Under the cry of universal freedom, and that other cry that there is a rule for the government of public men and private men which is of superior obligation to the constitution of the country, several of the States have enacted laws to hinder, obstruct, and defeat the enactments in this act of Congress to the utmost of their power. . . . . I suspect all this to be the effect of that wandering and vagrant philanthropy which disturbs and annoys all that is present, in time or place, by heating the imagination on subjects distant, remote, and uncertain." [79]

Webster justly considered that the real enemies of the

---
[77] *Lecture on America*, p. 27.
[78] *Works*, IV, 386.
[79] *Ibid.*, VI, 556, 561.

Constitution were the abolitionists, not the slave-owners, who threatened to secede. To appeal from the Constitution to a higher law, to denounce as sinful and contrary to natural right an institution expressly recognized by it, is manifestly an assault upon the Union itself. The South have the letter and the spirit of the law in their favour. The consistent abolitionists must be ready to sacrifice the Union to their theory. If the objection to slavery is on moral grounds, paramount to all political rights and interests, abolition is a peremptory duty, to which the Union itself, whose law is opposed to compulsory abolition, must succumb. It was therefore perfectly just to remind Mr. Seward, that in attacking slavery, and denying that it could be tolerated, he was assailing the law to which he owed his seat in Congress. "No man," said Webster, "is at liberty to set up, or affect to set up, his own conscience as above the law, in a matter which respects the rights of others, and the obligations, civil, social, and political, due to others from him." [80]

Dr. Brownson says, with great truth, as only a Catholic can, "No civil government can exist, none is conceivable even, where every individual is free to disobey its orders, whenever they do not happen to square with his private convictions of what is the law of God. . . . To appeal from the government to private judgment, is to place private judgment above public authority, the individual above the state." [81]

Calhoun was entirely justified in saying that, in the presence of these tendencies, "the conservative power is in the slave-holding States. They are the conservative portion of the country." [82]

His own political doctrines, as we have described them, fully bear out this view. But the conservative, anti-revolutionary character of the South depended on other causes than the influence of its master mind. Slavery is itself in contradiction with the equal rights of man, as they are laid

[80] *Ibid.*, VI, 578.
[81] *Essays and Reviews*, pp. 357, 359.
[82] *Works*, IV, 360.

down in the Declaration of Independence. Slave-owners are incapacitated from interpreting that instrument with literal consistency, for it would contradict both their interests and their daily experience. But as there are advanced democrats at the South as well as at the North, and as, indeed, they succeeded in resisting so long the Northern politicians, by using the jealousy of the Northern people against the wealthy capitalists, and the appearance of aristocracy, they find means of escaping from this dilemma. This is supplied by the theory of the original inferiority of the African race to the rest of mankind, for which the authority of the greatest naturalist in America is quoted: "The result of my researches," says Agassiz, "is, that Negroes are intellectually children; physically one of the lowest races; inclining with the other blacks, especially the South-Sea Negroes, most of all to the monkey type, though with a tendency, even in the extremes, towards the real human form. This opinion I have repeatedly expressed, without drawing from it any objectionable consequence, unless, perhaps, that no coloured race, least of all the Negroes, can have a common origin with ourselves." If this theory were not the property of the infidel science of Europe, one would suppose it must have been invented for the Americans, whom it suits so well.

Webster spoke with great power against the projects of the North: "There is kept up a general cry of one-party against the other, that its rights are invaded, its honour insulted, its character assailed, and its just participation in political power denied. Sagacious men cannot but suspect from all this, that more is intended than is avowed; and that there lies at the bottom a purpose of the separation of the States, for reasons avowed or disavowed, or for grievances redressed or unredressed.

"In the South, the separation of the States is openly professed, discussed, and recommended, absolutely or conditionally, in legislative halls, and in conventions called together by the authority of the law.

"In the North, the State governments have not run into such excess, and the purpose of overturning the government shows itself more clearly in resolutions agreed to in voluntary assemblies of individuals, denouncing the laws of the land, and declaring a fixed intent to disobey them. . . . . It is evident that, if this spirit be not checked, it will endanger the government; if it spread far and wide, it will overthrow the government." [83]

The language of Calhoun about the same period is almost identical with Webster's. "The danger is of a character— whether we regard our safety or the preservation of the Union—which cannot be safely tampered with. If not met promptly and decidedly, the two portions of the Union will become thoroughly alienated, when no alternative will be left to us, as the weaker of the two, but to sever all political ties, or sink down into abject submission." [84]

His last great speech, delivered March 4, 1850, a few days before his death, opened with the words, "I have believed from the first that the agitation of the subject of slavery would, if not prevented by some timely and effective measure, end in disunion." And he went on to say: "If something is not done to avert it, the South will be forced to choose between abolition and secession. Indeed, as events are now moving, it will not require the South to secede in order to dissolve the Union." [85]

The calamity which these eminent men agreed in apprehending and in endeavouring to avert, was brought on after their death by the rise of the republican party—a party in its aims and principles quite revolutionary, and not only inconsistent with the existence of the Union, but ready from the first to give it up. "I do not see," said the New England philosopher Emerson, "how a barbarous community and a civilised community can constitute one State." In order to estimate the extravagance of this party declaration, we will only quote two unexceptionable witnesses, who visited the South at an interval of about forty years from each other; one a Boston divine, the other an eager abolitionist. "How

[83] *Speech of 17th June,* 1850; *Works, VI,* 567, 582.
[84] *Works,* IV, 395.
[85] *Ibid.,* 542, 556.

different from our Northern manners! There, avarice and ceremony, at the age of twenty, graft the coldness and unfeelingness of age on the disinterested ardour of youth. I blush for my own people when I compare the selfish prudence of the Yankee with the generous confidence of a Virginian. Here I find great vices, but greater virtues than I left behind me. There is one single trait which attaches me to the people I live with more than all the virtues of New England,—they love money less than we do." [86] Lord Carlisle says, in the lecture already referred to, "It would be uncandid to deny that the planter in the Southern States has much more in his manner and mode of intercourse that resembles the English country gentleman than any other class of his countrymen." [87]

Emerson's saying is a sign of the extent to which rapid abolitionists were ready to go. Declaring that the Federal Government was devoted to Southern interests, against Northern doctrines, they openly defied it. Disunion societies started up at the North for the purpose of bringing about separation. Several States passed laws against the South and against the Constitution, and there were loud demands for separation. This was the disposition of the North at the presidential election of a successor to Pierce. The North threatened to part company, and if it carried its candidate, it threatened the Southern institutions. The South proclaimed the intention of seceding if Fremont should be elected, and threatened to march upon Washington and burn the archives of the Union. Buchanan's election pacified the South; but it was evident, from the growing strength of the republican party, that it was their last victory. They accordingly made use of their friends in office to take advantage of the time that remained to them to be in readiness when the next election came. Secession was resolved upon and prepared from the time when the strength of the republicans was exhibited in 1856. In spite of all the horrors of American slavery, it is impossible for us to have any sympathy with the party of

---

[86] *Memoir of Channing*, p. 43.
[87] P. 35.

which Mr. Seward is the chief. His politics are not only revolutionary, but aggressive; he is not only for absolutism but for annexation. In a speech on January 26, 1853, he spoke as follows: "The tendency of commercial and political events invites the United States to assume and exercise a paramount influence in the affairs of the nations situated in this hemisphere; that is, to become and remain a great Western continental power, balancing itself against the possible combinations of Europe. The advance of the country toward that position constitutes what, in the language of many, is called 'progress,' and the position itself is what, by the same class, is called 'manifest destiny.' " [88]

When Cass moved a resolution affirming the Monroe Doctrine with regard to Cuba, Seward supported it, together with another resolution perfectly consistent with it, of which he said: "It is not well expressed; but it implies the same policy in regard to Canada which the main resolutions assert concerning Cuba." [89] Nor is this the limit of his ambition. "You are already," he says to his countrymen, "the great continental power of America. But does that content you? I trust it does not. You want the commerce of the world, which is the empire of the world." [90]

When Kossuth was received in the Senate, he was introduced by Mr. Seward, whose European policy is as definite and about as respectable as his American. Speaking of Hungary, he writes, in December, 1851: "I trust that some measure may be adopted by the government which, while it will not at all hazard the peace or prosperity of the country, may serve to promote a cause that appeals so strongly to our interests and our sympathies, viz. the establishment of republicanism, in the countries prepared for it, in Europe." [91] And again, two days later: "Every nation may, and every nation ought, to make its position distinctly known in every case of conflict between despots and States struggling for the inalien-

---
[88] *Works*, III, 606.
[89] *Ibid.*, 609.
[90] *Ibid.*, 618.
[91] *Ibid.*, 505.

able and indefeasible rights of independence and self-government, that when despots combine, free States may lawfully unite."

It is as impossible to sympathise on religious grounds with the categorical prohibition of slavery as, on political grounds, with the opinions of the abolitionists. In this, as in all other things, they exhibit the same abstract, ideal absolutism, which is equally hostile with the Catholic and with the English spirit. Their democratic system poisons everything it touches. All constitutional questions are referred to the one fundamental principle of popular sovereignty, without consideration of policy or expediency. In the Massachusetts convention of 1853, it was argued by one of the most famous Americans, that the election of the judiciary could not be discussed on the grounds of its influence on the administration of justice, as it was clearly consonant with the constitutional theory. "What greater right," says the *North American Review* (LXXXVI, 477), "has government to deprive the people of their representation in the executive and judicial, than in the legislative department?" In claiming absolute freedom, they have created absolute powers, whilst we have inherited from the middle ages the notion that both liberty and authority must be subject to limits and conditions. The same intolerance of restraints and obligations, the same aversion to recognise the existence of popular duty, and of the divine right which is its correlative, disturb their notions of government and of freedom. The influence of these habits of abstract reasoning, to which we owe the revolution in Europe, is to make all things questions of principle and of abstract law. A principle is always appealed to in all cases, either of interest or necessity, and the consequence is, that a false and arbitrary political system produces a false and arbitrary code of ethics, and the theory of abolition is as erroneous as the theory of freedom.

Very different is the mode in which the Church labours to reform mankind by assimilating realities with ideals, and accommodating herself to times and circumstances. Her system of Christian liberty is essentially incompatible with slavery; and the power of masters over their slaves was one of the bulwarks of corruption and vice which most seriously impeded her progress. Yet the Apostles never condemned slavery even within the Christian fold. The sort of civil liberty which came with Christianity into the world, and was one of her postulates, did not require the abolition of slavery. If men were free by virtue of their being formed after the image of God, the proportion in which they realised that image would be the measure of their freedom. Accordingly, St. Paul prescribed to the Christian slave to remain content with his condition.[92]

We have gone at inordinate length into the causes and peculiarities of the revolution in the United States, because of the constant analogy they present to the theories and the events which are at the same time disturbing Europe. It is too late to touch upon more than one further point, which is extremely suggestive. The Secession movement was not provoked merely by the alarm of the slave-owners for their property, when the election of Lincoln sent down the price of slaves from twenty-five to fifty per cent, but by the political danger of Northern preponderance; and the mean whites of the Southern States are just as eager for separation as those who have property in slaves. For they fear lest the republicans, in carrying emancipation, should abolish the barriers which separate the Negroes from their own caste. At the same time, the slaves show no disposition to help the republicans, and be raised to the level of the whites. There is a just reason for this fear, which lies in the simple fact that the United States are a republic. The population of a republic must be homogeneous. Civil equality must be founded on social equality, and on national and physiological unity. This has been the strength of the American republic. Pure democracy is that form of government in which the community is sovereign, in which, therefore, the State is most nearly identified with society. But society exists for the

---

[92] *I Cor.*, VII, 21. The opposite interpretation, common among Protestant commentators, is inconsistent with the verses 20 and 24, and with the tradition of the Greek Fathers.

·protection of interests; the State for the realisation of right —concilia cœtusque hominum *jure* sociati, quae civitates appellantur.[93] The State sets up a moral, objective law, and pursues a common object distinct from the ends and purposes of society. This is essentially repugnant to democracy, which recognises only the interests and rights of the community, and is therefore inconsistent with the consolidation of authority which is implied in the notion of the State. It resists the development of the social into the moral community. If, therefore, a democracy includes persons with separate interests or an inferior nature, it tyrannises over them. There is no mediator between the part and the whole; there is no room, therefore, for differences of class, of wealth, of race; equality is necessary to the liberty which is sought by a pure democracy.

Where society is constituted without equality of condition or unity of race, where there are different classes and national varieties, they require a protector in a form of government which shall be distinct from and superior to every class, and not the instrument of one of them, in an authority representing the State, not any portion of society. This can be supplied only by monarchy; and in this sense it is fair to say that constitutional government, that is, the authority of law as distinguished from interest, can exist only under a king. This is also the reason why even absolute monarchies have been better governors of dependencies than popular governments. In one case they are governed for the benefit of a ruling class; in the other, there is no ruling class, and they are governed in the name of the State. Rome under the Republic and under the Empire is the most striking instance of this contrast. But the tyranny of republics is greatest when differences of races are combined with distinctions of class. Hence South America was a flourishing and prosperous country so long as the Spanish crown served as moderator between the various races, and is still prosperous where monarchy has been retained; whilst the establishment of republics in countries with classes divided by blood has led to hopeless

---
[93] Cicero, *Somnium Scipionis,* 3.

misery and disorder, and constant recourse to dictatorships as a refuge from anarchy and tyranny. Democracy inevitably takes the tone of the lower portions of society, and, if there are great diversities, degrades the higher. Slavery is the only protection that has ever been known against this tendency, and it is so far true that slavery is essential to democracy. For where there are great incongruities in the constitution of society, if the Americans were to admit the Indians, the Chinese, the Negroes, to the rights to which they are justly jealous of admitting European emigrants, the country would be thrown into disorder, and if not, would be degraded to the level of the barbarous races. Accordingly, the Know-nothings rose up as the reaction of the democratic principle against the influx of an alien population. The Red Indian is gradually retreating before the pioneer, and will perish before many generations, or dwindle away in the desert. The Chinese in California inspire great alarm for the same reason, and plans have been proposed of shipping them all off again. This is a good argument too, in the interest of all parties, against the emancipation of the blacks.

The necessity for social equality and national unity has been felt in all democracies where the mass as a unit governs itself. Above all, it is felt as a necessity in France, since the downfall of the old society, and the recognition, under republic, charter, and despotism, of the sovereignty of the people. Those principles with which France revolutionises Europe are perfectly right in her own case. They are detestable in other countries where they cause revolutions, but they are a true and just consequence of the French Revolution. Men easily lose sight of the substance in the form, and suppose that because France is not a republic she is not a democracy, and that her principles therefore will apply elsewhere. This is the reason of the power of the national principle in Europe. It is essential as a consequence of equality to the notion of the people as the source of power. Where there is an aristocracy it has generally more sympathy and connection with foreign aristocracies than with the rest of the nation. The bonds of class are stronger than those of nationality. A democracy, in abolishing classes, renders national unity imperative.

These are some of the political lessons we have learnt from the consideration of the vast process of which we are witnessing the consummation. We may consult the history of the American Union to understand the true theory of republicanism, and the danger of mistaking it. It is simply the spurious democracy of the French Revolution that has destroyed the Union, by disintegrating the remnants of English traditions and institutions. All the great controversies—on the embargo, restriction, internal improvement, the Bank-Charter Act, the formation of new States, the acquisition of new territory, abolition—are phases of this mighty change, steps in the passage from a constitution framed on an English model to a system imitating that of France. The secession of the Southern States—pregnant with infinite consequences to the African race by altering the condition of slavery, to America by awakening an intenser thirst for conquest, to Europe by its reaction on European democracy, to England, above all, by threatening for a moment one of the pillars of her social existence, but still more by the enormous augmentation of her power, on which the United States were always a most formidable restraint—is chiefly important in a political light as a protest and reaction against revolutionary doctrines, and as a move in the opposite direction to that which prevails in Europe.

CHAPTER VIII

THE BACKGROUND OF THE FRENCH REVOLUTION

THE REVENUE OF France was near twenty millions when Louis XVI, finding it inadequate, called upon the nation for supply. In a single lifetime it rose to far more than one hundred millions, while the national income grew still more rapidly; and this increase was wrought by a class to whom the ancient monarchy denied its best rewards, and whom it deprived of power in the country they enriched. As their industry effected change in the distribution of property, and wealth ceased to be the prerogative of a few, the excluded majority perceived that their disabilities rested on no foundation of right and justice, and were unsupported by reasons of State. They proposed that the prizes in the Government, the Army, and the Church should be given to merit among the active and necessary portion of the people, and that no privilege injurious to them should be reserved for the unprofitable minority. Being nearly an hundred to one, they deemed that they were virtually the substance of the nation, and they claimed to govern themselves with a power proportioned to their numbers. They demanded that the State should be reformed, that the ruler should be their agent, not their master.

That is the French Revolution. To see that it is not a meteor from the unknown, but the product of historic in-

NOTE: This lecture first appeared in *Lectures on the French Revolution* as delivered by Lord Acton at Cambridge in the academical years 1895-96, 1896-97, 1897-98, 1898-99 in view of the history tripos of those years (London, Macmillan Co., 1910), pp. 1-19, under the title, "The Heralds of the Revolution."

fluences which by their union were efficient to destroy, and by their division powerless to construct, we must follow for a moment the procession of ideas that went before, and bind it to the law of continuity and the operation of constant forces.

If France failed where other nations have succeeded, and if the passage from the feudal and aristocratic forms of society to the industrial and democratic was attended by convulsions, the cause was not in the men of that day, but in the ground on which they stood. As long as the despotic kings were victorious abroad, they were accepted at home. The first signals of revolutionary thinking lurk dimly among the oppressed minorities during intervals of disaster. The Jansenists were loyal and patient; but their famous jurist Domat was a philosopher, and is remembered as the writer who restored the supremacy of reason in the chaotic jurisprudence of the time. He had learnt from St. Thomas, a great name in the school he belonged to, that legislation ought to be for the people and by the people, that the cashiering of bad kings may be not only a right but a duty. He insisted that law shall proceed from common sense, not from custom, and shall draw its precepts from an eternal code. The principle of the higher law signified Revolution. No government founded on positive enactments only can stand before it, and it points the way to that system of primitive, universal and indefeasible rights which the lawyers of the Assembly, descending from Domat, prefixed to their constitution.

Under the edict of Nantes the Protestants were decided royalists; so that, even after the Revocation, Bayle, the apostle of Toleration, retained his loyalty in exile at Rotterdam. His enemy, Jurieu, though intolerant as a divine, was liberal in his politics, and contracted in the neighbourhood of W. 'liam of Orange the temper of a continental Whig. He taught that sovereignty comes from the people and reverts to the people. The Crown forfeits powers it has made ill use of. The rights of the nation cannot be forfeited. The people alone possess an authority which is legitimate without conditions, and their acts are valid even when they are wrong. The most telling of Jurieu's seditious propositions, preserved in the transparent amber of Bossuet's reply, shared the immortality of a classic, and in time contributed to the doctrine that the democracy is irresponsible and must have its way.

Maultrot, the best ecclesiastical lawyer of the day, published three volumes in 1790 on the power of the people over kings, in which, with accurate research among sources very familiar to him and to nobody else, he explained how the Canon Law approves the principles of 1688 and rejects the modern invention of divine right. His book explains still better the attitude of the clergy in the Revolution, and their brief season of popularity.

The true originator of the opposition in literature was Fénelon. He was neither an innovating reformer nor a discoverer of new truth; but as a singularly independent and most intelligent witness, he was the first who saw through the majestic hypocrisy of the court, and knew that France was on the road to ruin. The revolt of conscience began with him before the glory of the monarchy was clouded over. His views grew from an extraordinary perspicacity and refinement in the estimate of men. He learnt to refer the problem of government, like the conduct of private life, to the mere standard of morals, and extended further than anyone the plain but hazardous practice of deciding all things by the exclusive precepts of enlightened virtue. If he did not know all about policy and international science, he could always tell what would be expected of a hypothetically perfect man. Fénelon feels like a citizen of Christian Europe, but he pursues his thoughts apart from his country or his church, and his deepest utterances are in the mouth of pagans. He desired to be alike true to his own beliefs, and gracious towards those who dispute them. He approved neither the deposing power nor the punishment of error, and declared that the highest need of the Church was not victory but liberty. Through his friends, Fleury and Chevreuse, he favoured the recall of the Protestants, and he advised a general toleration. He would have the secular power kept aloof from ecclesiastical concerns, because protection leads to religious servitude and persecution to religious hypocrisy. There were moments when his steps seemed to approach the border of the undiscovered land where Church and State are parted.

He has written that a historian ought to be neutral between other countries and his own, and he expected the same discipline in politicians, as patriotism cannot absolve a man from his duty to mankind. Therefore no war can be just, unless a war to which we are compelled in the sole cause of freedom. Fénelon wished that France should surrender the ill-gotten conquests of which she was so proud, and especially that she should withdraw from Spain. He declared that the Spaniards were degenerate and imbecile, but that nothing could make that right which was contrary to the balance of power and the security of nations. Holland seemed to him the hope of Europe, and he thought the allies justified in excluding the French dynasty from Spain for the same reason that no claim of law could have made it right that Philip II should occupy England. He hoped that his country would be thoroughly humbled, for he dreaded the effects of success on the temperament of the victorious French. He deemed it only fair that Louis should be compelled to dethrone his grandson with his own guilty hand.

In the judgment of Fénelon, power is poison; and as kings are nearly always bad, they ought not to govern, but only to execute the law. For it is the mark of barbarians to obey precedent and custom. Civilised society must be regulated by a solid code. Nothing but a constitution can avert arbitrary power. The despotism of Louis XIV renders him odious and contemptible, and is the cause of all the evils which the country suffers. If the governing power which rightfully belonged to the nation was restored, it would save itself by its own exertion; but absolute authority irreparably saps its foundations, and is bringing on a revolution by which it will not be moderated, but utterly destroyed. Although Fénelon has no wish to sacrifice either the monarchy or the aristocracy, he betrays sympathy with several tendencies of the movement which he foresaw with so much alarm. He admits the state of nature, and thinks civil society not the primitive condition of man, but a result of the passage from savage life to husbandry. He would transfer the duties of government to local and central assemblies; and he demands entire freedom of trade, and education provided by law, because children belong to the State first and to the family afterwards. He does not resign the hope of making men good by act of parliament, and his belief in public institutions as a means of moulding individual character brings him nearly into touch with a distant future.

He is the Platonic founder of revolutionary thinking. Whilst his real views were little known, he became a popular memory; but some complained that his force was centrifugal, and that a church can no more be preserved by suavity and distinction than a state by liberty and justice. Louis XVI, we are often told, perished in expiation of the sins of his forefathers. He perished, not because the power he inherited from them had been carried to excess, but because it had been discredited and undermined. One author of this discredit was Fénelon. Until he came, the ablest men, Bossuet and even Bayle, revered the monarchy. Fénelon struck it at the zenith, and treated Louis XIV in all his grandeur more severely than the disciples of Voltaire treated Louis XV in all his degradation. The season of scorn and shame begins with him. The best of his later contemporaries followed his example, and laid the basis of opposing criticism on motives of religion. They were the men whom Cardinal Dubois describes as dreamers of the same dreams as the chimerical archbishop of Cambray. Their influence fades away before the great change that came over France about the middle of the century.

From that time unbelief so far prevailed that even men who were not professed assailants, as Montesquieu, Condillac, Turgot, were estranged from Christianity. Politically, the consequence was this: men who did not attribute any deep significance to church questions never acquired definite notions on Church and State, never seriously examined under what conditions religion may be established or disestablished, endowed or disendowed, never even knew whether there exists any general solution, or any principle by which problems of that kind are decided. This defect of knowledge became a fact of importance at a turning point in the Revolution. The theory of the relations between states and churches is bound up with the theory of Toleration, and on that subject the eighteenth century scarcely rose above an intermittent, embarrassed, and unscientific view. For religious liberty is composed of the properties both of religion and liberty, and one of its factors never became an object of disinterested observation among actual leaders of opinion. They preferred the argument of doubt to the argument of certitude, and sought to defeat intolerance by casting out revelation as they had defeated the persecution of witches by casting out the devil. There remained a flaw in their liberalism, for liberty apart from belief is liberty with a good deal of the substance taken out of it. The problem is less complicated and the solution less radical and less profound. Already, then, there were writers who held somewhat superficially the conviction, which Tocqueville made a cornerstone, that nations that have not the self-governing force of religion within them are unprepared for freedom.

The early notions of reform moved on French lines, striving to utilise the existing form of society, to employ the parliamentary aristocracy, to revive the States-General and the provincial assemblies. But the scheme of standing on the ancient ways, and raising a new France on the substructure of the old, brought out the fact that whatever growth of institutions there once had been had been stunted and stood still. If the mediaeval polity had been fitted to prosper, its fruit must be gathered from other countries, where the early notions had been pursued far ahead. The first thing to do was to cultivate the foreign example; and with that what we call the eighteenth century began. The English superiority, proclaimed first by Voltaire, was further demonstrated by Montesquieu. For England had recently created a government which was stronger than the institutions that had stood on antiquity. Founded upon fraud and treason, it had yet established the security of law more firmly than it had ever existed under the system of legitimacy, of prolonged inheritance, and of religious sanction. It flourished on the unaccustomed belief that theological dissensions need not detract from the power of the State, while political dissensions are the very secret of its prosperity. The men of questionable character who accomplished the change and had governed for the better part of sixty years had successfully maintained public order, in spite of conspiracy and rebellion; they had built up an enormous system of national credit, and had been victorious in continental war. The Jacobite doctrine, which was the basis of European monarchy, had been backed by the arms of France, and had failed to shake the newly planted throne. A great experiment had been crowned by a great discovery. A novelty that defied the wisdom of centuries had made good its footing, and revolution had become a principle of stability more sure than tradition.

Montesquieu undertook to make the disturbing fact avail in political science. He valued it because it reconciled him with monarchy. He had started with the belief that kings are an evil, and not a necessary evil, and that their time was running short. His visit to Walpolean England taught him a plan by which they might be reprieved. He still confessed that a republic is the reign of virtue; and by virtue he meant love of equality and renunciation of self. But he had seen a monarchy that throve by corruption. He said that the distinctive principle of monarchy is not virtue but honour, which he once described as a contrivance to enable men of the world to commit almost every offence with impunity. The praise of England was made less injurious to French patriotism by the famous theory that explains institutions and character by the barometer and the latitude. Montesquieu looked about him, and abroad, but not far ahead. His admirable skill in supplying reason for every positive fact sometimes confounds the cause that produces with the argument that defends. He knows so many pleas for privilege that he almost overlooks the class that has none; and having no friendship for the clergy, he approves their immunities. He thinks that aristocracy alone can preserve monarchies, and makes England more free than any commonwealth. He lays down the great conservative maxim, that success generally depends on knowing the time it will take; and the most purely Whig maxim in his works, that the duty of a citizen is a crime when it obscures the duty of man, is Fénelon's. His liberty is of a Gothic type, and not insatiable. But the motto of his work, *Prolem sine matre creatam*, was intended to signify that the one thing wanting was liberty; and he had views on taxation, equality, and the division of powers that gave him a momentary influence in 1789. His warning that a legislature may be more dangerous than the executive remained unheard. The *Esprit des lois* had lost ground in 1767, during the ascendancy of Rousseau. The mind of the author moved within the conditions of society familiar to him, and he did not heed the coming democracy. He assured Hume that there would be no revolution, because the nobles were without civic courage.

There was more divination in d'Argenson, who was Minister of Foreign Affairs in 1745, and knew politics from the inside. Less acquiescent than his brilliant contemporary, he was perpetually contriving schemes of fundamental change, and is the earliest writer from whom we can extract the system of 1789. Others before him had perceived the impending revolution; but d'Argenson foretold that it would open with the slaughter of priests in the streets of Paris. Thirty-eight years later these words came true at the gate of St. Germain's Abbey. As the supporter of the Pretender he was quite uninfluenced by admiration for England, and imputed, not to the English Deists and Whigs but to the Church and her divisions and intolerance, the unbelieving spirit that threatened both Church and State. It was conventionally understood on the Continent that 1688 had been an uprising of Nonconformists, and a Whig was assumed to be a Presbyterian down to the death of Anne. It was easy to infer that a more violent theological conflict would lead to a more violent convulsion. As early as 1743 his terrible foresight discerns that the State is going to pieces, and its doom was so certain that he began to think of a refuge under other masters. He would have deposed the noble, the priest, and the lawyer, and given their power to the masses. Although the science of politics was in its infancy, he relied on the dawning enlightenment to establish rational liberty, and the equality between classes and religions which is the perfection of politics. The world ought to be governed not by parchment and vested rights, but by plain reason, which proceeds from the complex to the simple, and will sweep away all that interposes between the State and the democracy, giving to each part of the nation the management of its own affairs. He is eager to change everything, except the monarchy which alone can change all else. A deliberative assembly does not rise above the level of its average members. It is neither very foolish nor very wise. All might be well if the king made himself the irresistible instrument of philosophy and justice, and wrought the reform. But his king was Louis XV. D'Argenson saw so little that was worthy to be preserved that he did not shrink from sweeping judgments and abstract propositions. By his rationalism, and his indifference to the prejudice of custom and the claim of possession; by his maxim that every man may be presumed to understand the things in which his own interest and responsibility are involved; by his zeal for democracy, equality, and simplicity, and his dislike of intermediate authorities, he belongs to a generation later than his own. He heralded events without preparing them, for the best of all he wrote only became known in our time.

Whilst Montesquieu, at the height of his fame as the foremost of living writers, was content to contemplate the past, there was a student in the Paris seminary who taught men to fix hope and endeavour on the future, and led the world at twenty-three. Turgot, when he proclaimed that upward growth and progress is the law of human life, was studying to become a priest. To us, in any age of science, it has become difficult to imagine Christianity without the attribute of development and the faculty of improving society as well as souls. But the idea was acquired slowly. Under the burden of sin, men accustomed themselves to the consciousness of degeneracy; each generation confessed that they were unworthy children of their parents, and awaited with impatience the approaching end. From Lucretius and Seneca to Pascal and Leibniz we encounter a few dispersed and unsupported passages, suggesting advance towards perfection, and the flame that brightens as it moves from hand to hand; but they were without mastery or radiance. Turgot at once made the idea habitual and familiar, and it became a pervading force in thoughtful minds, whilst the new sciences arose to confirm it. He imparted a deeper significance to history, giving it unity of tendency and direction, constancy where there had been motion, and development instead of change. The progress he meant was moral as much as intellectual; and as he professed to think that the rogues of his day would have seemed sanctified models to an earlier century, he made his calculations without counting the wickedness of men. His analysis left unfathomed depths for future explorers, for Lessing and still more for Hegel; but he taught mankind to expect that the future would be unlike the past, that it would be better, and that the experience of ages may instruct and warn, but cannot guide or control. He is eminently a benefactor to historical study; but he forged a weapon charged with power to abolish the product of history and the existing order. By the hypothesis of progress, the new is always gaining on the old; history is the embodiment of imperfection, and escape from history became the watchword of the coming day. Condorcet, the master's pupil, thought that the world might be emancipated by burning its records.

Turgot was too discreet for such an excess, and he looked to history for the demonstration of his law. He had come upon it in his theological studies. He renounced them soon after, saying that he could not wear a mask. When Guizot called Lamennais a malefactor, because he threw off his cassock and became a freethinker, Scherer, whose course had been some way parallel, observed: "He little knows how much it costs." The abrupt transition seems to have been accomplished by Turgot without a struggle. The *Encyclopaedia*, which was the largest undertaking since the invention of printing, came out at that time, and Turgot wrote for it. But he broke off, refusing to be connected with a party professedly hostile to revealed religion; and he rejected the declamatory paradoxes of Diderot and Raynal. He found his home among the Physiocrats, of all the groups the one that possessed the most compact body of consistent views, and who already knew most of the accepted doctrines of political economy, although they ended by making way for Adam Smith. They are of supreme importance to us, because they founded political science on the economic science which was coming into existence. Harrington, a century before, had seen that the art of government can be reduced to system; but the French economists precede all men in this, that, holding a vast collection of combined and verified truths on matters contiguous to politics and belonging to their domain, they extended it to the whole, and governed the constitution by the same fixed principles that governed the purse. They said: A man's most sacred property is his labour. It is anterior even to the right of property, for it is the possession of those who own nothing else. Therefore he must be free to make the best use of it he can. The interference of one man with another, of society with its members, of the state with the subject, must be brought down to the lowest dimension. Power intervenes only to restrict intervention, to guard the individual from oppression, that is from regulation in an interest not his own. Free labour and its derivative free trade are the first conditions of legitimate government. Let things fall into their natural order, let society govern itself, and the sovereign function of the State will be to protect nature in the execution of her own law. Government must not be arbitrary, but it must be powerful enough to repress arbitrary action in others. If the supreme power is needlessly limited, the secondary powers will run riot and oppress. Its supremacy will bear no check. The problem is to enlighten the ruler, not to restrain him; and one man is more easily enlightened than many. Government by opposition, by balance and control, is contrary to principle; whereas absolutism might be requisite to the attainment of their higher purpose. Nothing less than concentrated power could overcome the obstacles to such beneficent reforms as they meditated. Men who sought only the general good must wound every distinct and separate interest of class, and would be mad to break up the only force that they could count upon, and thus to throw away the means of preventing the evils that must follow if things were left to the working of opinion and the feeling of masses. They had no love for absolute power in itself, but they computed that, if they had the use of it for five years, France would be free. They distinguish an arbitrary monarch and the irresistible but impersonal state.

It was the era of repentant monarchy. Kings had become the first of public servants, executing, for the good of the people, what the people were unable to do for themselves; and there was a reforming movement on foot which led to many instances of prosperous and intelligent administration. To men who knew what unutterable suffering and wrong was inflicted by bad laws, and who lived in terror of the uneducated and inorganic masses, the idea of reform from above seemed preferable to parliamentary government managed by Newcastle and North, in the interest of the British landlord. The economists are outwardly and avowedly less liberal than Montesquieu, because they are incomparably more impressed by the evils of the time, and the need of immense and fundamental changes. They prepared to undo the work of absolutism by the hand of absolutism. They were not its opponents, but its advisers, and hoped to convert it by their advice. The indispensable liberties are those which constitute the wealth of nations; the rest will follow. The disease had lasted too long for the sufferer to heal himself: the relief must come from the author of his sufferings. The power that had done the wrong was still efficient to undo the wrong. Transformation, infinitely more difficult in itself than preservation, was not more formidable to the economists because it consisted mainly in revoking the godless work of a darker age. They deemed it their mission not to devise new laws, for that is a task which God has not committed to man, but only to declare the inherent laws of the existence of society and enable them to prevail.

The defects of the social and political organisation were as distinctly pointed out by the economists as by the electors of of the National Assembly, twenty years later, and in nearly all things they proposed the remedy. But they were persuaded that the only thing to regenerate France was a convulsion which the national character would make a dreadful one. They desired a large scheme of popular education, because commands take no root in soil that is not prepared. Political truths can be made so evident that the opinion of an instructed public will be invincible, and will banish the abuse of power. To resist oppression is to make a league with heaven, and all things are oppressive that resist the natural order of freedom. For society secures rights; it neither bestows nor restricts them. They are the direct consequence of duties. As truth can only convince by the exposure of errors and the defeat of objections, liberty is the essential guard of truth. Society is founded, not on the will of man, but on the nature of man and the will of God; and conformity to the divinely appointed order is followed by inevitable reward. Relief of those who suffer is the duty of all men, and the affair of all.

Such was the spirit of that remarkable group of men, especially of Mercier de la Rivière, of whom Diderot said that he alone possessed the true and everlasting secret of the security and the happiness of empires. Turgot indeed had failed in office; but his reputation was not diminished, and the power of his name exceeded all others at the outbreak of the Revolution. His policy of employing the Crown to reform the State was at once rejected in favour of other counsels; but his influence may be traced in many acts of the Assembly, and on two very memorable occasions it was not auspicious. It was a central dogma of the party that land is the true source of wealth, or, as Asgill said, that man deals in nothing but earth. When a great part of France became national property, men were the more easily persuaded that land can serve as the basis of public credit and of unlimited *assignats*. According to a weighty opinion which we shall have to consider before long, the parting of the ways in the Revolution was on the day when, rejecting the example both of England and America, the French resolved to institute a single undivided legislature. It was the Pennsylvanian model; and Voltaire had pronounced Pennsylvania the best government in the world. Franklin gave the sanction of an oracle to the constitution of his state, and Turgot was its vehement protagonist in Europe.

A king ruling over a level democracy, and a democracy ruling itself through the agency of a king, were long contending notions in the first Assembly. One was monarchy according to Turgot, the other was monarchy adapted to Rousseau; and the latter, for a time, prevailed. Rousseau was the citizen of a small republic, consisting of a single town, and he professed to have applied its example to the government of the world. It was Geneva, not as he saw it, but as he extracted its essential principle, and as it has since become — Geneva illustrated by the Forest Cantons and the Landesgemeinde more than by its own charters. The idea was that the grown men met in the market place, like the peasants of Glarus under their trees, to manage their affairs, making and unmaking officials, conferring and revoking powers. They were equal, because every man had exactly the same right to defend his interest by the guarantee of his vote. The welfare of all was safe in the hands of all, for they had not the separate interests that are bred by the egotism of wealth, nor the exclusive views that come from a distorted education. All being equal in power and similar in purpose, there can be no just cause why some should move apart and break into minorities. There is an implied contract that no part shall ever be preferred to the whole, and minorities shall always obey. Clever men are not wanted for the making of laws, because clever men and their laws are at the root of all mischief. Nature is a better guide than civilisation, because nature comes from God, and His works are good; culture from man, whose works are bad in proportion as he is remoter from natural innocence, as his desires increase upon him, as he seeks more refined pleasures, and stores up more superfluity. It promotes inequality, selfishness, and the ruin of public spirit.

By plausible and easy stages the social ideas latent in parts of Switzerland produced the theory that men come innocent from the hands of the Creator, that they are originally equal, that progress from equality to civilisation is the passage from virtue to vice and from freedom to tyranny, that the people are sovereign, and govern by powers given and taken away; that an individual or a class may be mistaken and may desert the common cause and the general interest, but the people, necessarily sincere, and true, and incorrupt, cannot go wrong; that there is a right of resistance to all governments that are fallible, because they are partial, but none against government of the people by the people, because it has no master and no judge, and decides in the last instance and alone; that insurrection is the law of all unpopular societies founded on a false principle and a broken contract, and submission that of the only legitimate societies, based on the popular will; that there is no privilege against the law of nature, and no right against the power of all. By this chain of reasoning, with little infusion of other ingredients, Rousseau applied the sequence of the ideas of pure democracy to the government of nations.

Now the most glaring and familiar fact in history shows that the direct self-government of a town cannot be extended over an empire. It is a plan that scarcely reaches beyond the next parish. Either one district will be governed by another, or both by somebody else chosen for the purpose. Either plan contradicts first principles. Subjection is the direct negation of democracy; representation is the indirect. So that an Englishman underwent bondage to parliament as much as Lausanne to Berne or as America to England if it had submitted to taxation, and by law recovered his liberty but once in seven years. Consequently Rousseau, still faithful to Swiss precedent as well as to the logic of his own theory, was a federalist. In Switzerland, when one half of a canton disagrees with the other, or the country with the town, it is deemed natural that they should break into two, that the general will may not oppress minorities. This multiplication of self-governing communities was admitted by Rousseau as a preservative of unanimity on one hand, and of liberty on the other. Helvétius came to his support with the idea that men are not only equal by nature but alike, and that society is the cause of variation; from which it would follow that everything may be done by laws and by education.

Rousseau is the author of the strongest political theory that had appeared amongst men. We cannot say that he reasons well, but he knew how to make his argument seem convincing, satisfying, inevitable, and he wrote with an eloquence and a fervour that had never been seen in prose, even in Bolingbroke or Milton. His books gave the first signal of a universal subversion, and were as fatal to the Republic as to the Monarchy. Although he lives by the social contract and the law of resistance, and owes his influence to what was extreme and systematic, his later writings are loaded with sound political wisdom. He owes nothing to the novelty or the originality of his thoughts. Taken jointly or severally, they are old friends, and you will find them in the school of Wolf that just preceded, in the dogmatists of the Great Rebellion and the Jesuit casuists who were dear to Algernon Sidney, in their Protestant opponents, Duplessis Mornay, and the Scots who had heard the last of our schoolmen, Major of St. Andrews, renew the speculations of the time of schism, which decomposed and dissected the Church and rebuilt it on a model very propitious to political revolution, and even in the early interpreters of the Aristotelian Politics which appeared just at the era of the first parliament.

Rousseau's most advanced point was the doctrine that the people are infallible. Jurieu had taught that they can do no wrong: Rousseau added that they are positively in the right. The idea, like most others, was not new, and goes back to the Middle Ages. When the question arose what security there is for the preservation of traditional truth if the episcopate was divided and the papacy vacant, it was answered that the faith would be safely retained by the masses. The maxim that the voice of the people is the voice of God is as old as Alcuin; it was renewed by some of the greatest writers anterior to democracy, by Hooker and Bossuet, and it was employed in our day by Newman to prop his theory of development. Rousseau applied it to the State.

The sovereignty of public opinion was just then coming in through the rise of national debts and the increasing importance of the public creditor. It meant more than the noble savage and the blameless South Sea islander, and distinguished the instinct that guides large masses of men from the calculating wisdom of the few. It was destined to prove the most serious of all obstacles to representative government. Equality of power readily suggests equality of property; but the movement of Socialism began earlier, and was not assisted by Rousseau. There were solemn theorists, such as Mably and Morelly, who were sometimes quoted in the Revolution, but the change in the distribution of property was independent of them.

A more effective influence was imported from Italy; for the Italians, through Vico, Giannone, Genovesi, had an eighteenth century of their own. Sardinia preceded France in solving the problem of feudalism. Arthur Young affirms that the measures of the Grand Duke Leopold had, in ten years, doubled the produce of Tuscany; at Milan, Count Firmian was accounted one of the best administrators in Europe. It was a Milanese, Beccaria, who, by his reform of criminal law, became a leader of French opinion. Continental jurisprudence had long been overshadowed by two ideas: that torture is the surest method of discovering truth, and that punishment deters not by its justice, its celerity, or its certainty, but in proportion to its severity. Even in the eighteenth century the penal system of Maria Theresa and Joseph II was barbarous. Therefore, no attack was more surely aimed at the heart of established usage than that which dealt with courts of justice. It forced men to conclude that authority was odiously stupid and still more odiously ferocious, that existing governments were accursed, that the guardians and ministers of law, divine and human, were more guilty than their culprits. The past was branded as the reign of infernal powers, and charged with long arrears of unpunished wrong.

As there was no sanctity left in law, there was no mercy for its merciless defenders; and if they fell into avenging hands, their doom would not exceed their desert. Men afterwards conspicuous by their violence, Brissot and Marat, were engaged in this campaign of humanity, which raised a demand for authorities that were not vitiated by the accumulation of infamy, for new laws, new powers, a new dynasty.

As religion was associated with cruelty, it is at this point that the movement of new ideas became a crusade against Christianity. A book by the Curé Meslier, partially known at that time, but first printed by Strauss in 1864, is the clarion of vindictive unbelief; and another abbé, Raynal, hoped that the clergy would be crushed beneath the ruins of their altars.

Thus the movement which began, in Fénelon's time, with warnings and remonstrance and the zealous endeavour to preserve, which produced one great scheme of change by the Crown and another at the expense of the Crown, ended in the wild cry for vengeance and a passionate appeal to fire and sword. So many lines of thought converging on destruction explain the agreement that existed when the States-General began, and the explosion that followed the reforms of '89 and the ruins of '93. No conflict can be more irreconcilable than that between a constitution and an enlightened absolutism, between abrogation of old laws and multiplication of new, between representation and direct democracy, the people controlling, and the people governing, kings by contract and kings by mandate.

Yet all these fractions of opinion were called Liberal: Montesquieu, because he was an intelligent Tory; Voltaire, because he attacked the clergy; Turgot, as a reformer; Rousseau, as a democrat; Diderot, as a freethinker. The one thing common to them all is the disregard for liberty.

CHAPTER IX

CONFLICTS WITH ROME

AMONG THE CAUSES which have brought dishonour on the Church in recent years, none have had a more fatal operation than those conflicts with science and literature which have led men to dispute the competence, or the justice, or the wisdom, of her authorities. Rare as such conflicts have been, they have awakened a special hostility which the defenders of Catholicism have not succeeded in allaying. They have induced a suspicion that the Church, in her zeal for the prevention of error, represses that intellectual freedom which is essential to the progress of truth; that she allows an administrative interference with convictions to which she cannot attach the stigma of falsehood; and that she claims a right to restrain the growth of knowledge, to justify an acquiescence in ignorance, to promote error, and even to alter at her arbitrary will the dogmas that are proposed to faith. There are few faults or errors imputed to Catholicism which individual Catholics have not committed or held, and the instances on which these particular accusations are founded have sometimes been supplied by the acts of authority itself. Dishonest controversy loves to confound the personal with the spiritual element in the Church — to ignore the distinction between the sinful agents and the divine institution. And this confusion makes it easy to deny, what otherwise would be too evident to question, that knowledge has a freedom in the Catholic Church which it can

NOTE: This essay first appeared in *The Rambler, New Series*, IV (January, 1864), 209-44: reprinted in *The History of Freedom and Other Essays* (London, Macmillan Co., 1907), pp. 461-91.

find in no other religion; though there, as elsewhere, freedom degenerates unless it has to struggle in its own defence.

Nothing can better illustrate this truth than the actual course of events in the cases of Lamennais and Frohschammer. They are two of the most conspicuous instances in point; and they exemplify the opposite mistakes through which a haze of obscurity has gathered over the true notions of authority and freedom in the Church. The correspondence of Lamennais and the later writings of Frohschammer furnish a revelation which ought to warn all those who, through ignorance, or timidity, or weakness of faith, are tempted to despair of the reconciliation between science and religion, and to acquiesce either in the subordination of one to the other, or in their complete segregation and estrangement. Of these alternatives Lamennais chose the first, Frohschammer the second; and the exaggeration of the claims of authority by the one and the extreme assertion of independence by the other have led them, by contrary paths, to nearly the same end.

When Lamennais surveyed the fluctuations of science, the multitude of opinions, the confusion and conflict of theories, he was led to doubt the efficacy of all human tests of truth. Science seemed to him essentially tainted with hopeless uncertainty. In his ignorance of its methods he fancied them incapable of attaining to anything more than a greater or less degree of probability, and powerless to afford a strict demonstration, or to distinguish the deposit of real knowledge amidst the turbid current of opinion. He refused to admit that there is a sphere within which metaphysical philosophy speaks with absolute certainty, or that the landmarks set up by history and natural science may be such as neither authority nor prescription, neither the doctrine of the schools nor the interest of the Church, has the power to disturb or the right to evade. These sciences presented to his eyes a chaos incapable of falling into order and harmony by any internal self-development, and requiring the action of an external director to clear up its darkness and remove its uncertainty. He thought that no research, however rigorous, could make sure of any fragment of knowledge worthy the name. He admitted no certainty but that which relied on the general tradition of mankind, recorded and sanctioned by the infallible judgment of the Holy See. He would have all power committed, and every question referred, to that supreme and universal authority. By its means he would supply all the gaps in the horizon of the human intellect, settle every controversy, solve the problems of science, and regulate the policy of states.

The extreme Ultramontanism which seeks the safeguard of faith in the absolutism of Rome he believed to be the keystone of the Catholic system. In his eyes all who rejected it, the Jesuits among them, were Gallicans; and Gallicanism was the corruption of the Christian idea.[1] "If my principles are rejected," he wrote on the 1st of November 1820, "I see no means of defending religion effectually, no decisive answer to the objections of the unbelievers of our time. How could these principles be favourable to them? They are simply the development of the great Catholic maxim, *quod semper, quod ubique, quod ab omnibus.*" Joubert said of him, with perfect justice, that when he destroyed all the bases of human certainty, in order to retain no foundation but authority, he destroyed authority itself. The confidence which led him to confound the human element with the divine in the Holy See was destined to be tried by the severest of all tests; and his exaggeration of the infallibility of the Pope proved fatal to his religious faith.

In 1831 the Roman Breviary was not to be bought in Paris. We may hence measure the amount of opposition with which Lamennais' endeavours to exalt Rome would be met by the majority of the French bishops and clergy, and by the school of St. Sulpice. For him, on the other hand, no terms were too strong to express his animosity against those who rejected his teaching and thwarted his designs. The bishops he railed at as idiotic devotees, incredibly blind, supernaturally foolish. "The Jesuits," he said, "were *grenadiers de la folie,* and united imbecility with the vilest passions."[2] He fancied that in many

---
[1] Lamennais, *Correspondence,* Nouvelle édition (Paris: Didier).
[2] April 12 and June 25, 1830.

dioceses there was a conspiracy to destroy religion, that a schism was at hand, and that the resistance of the clergy to his principles threatened to destroy Catholicism in France. Rome, he was sure, would help him in his struggle against her faithless assailants, on behalf of her authority, and in his endeavour to make the clergy refer their disputes to her, so as to receive from the Pope's mouth the infallible oracles of eternal truth.[3] Whatever the Pope might decide would, he said, be right, for the Pope alone was infallible. Bishops might be sometimes resisted, but the Pope never.[4] It was both absurd and blasphemous even to advise him. "I have read in the *Diario di Roma*," he said, "the advice of M. de Chateaubriand to the Holy Ghost. At any rate, the Holy Ghost is fully warned; and if he makes a mistake this time, it will not be the ambassador's fault."

Three Popes passed away, and still nothing was done against the traitors he was for ever denouncing. This reserve astounded him. Was Rome herself tainted with Gallicanism, and in league with those who had conspired for her destruction? What but a schism could ensue from this inexplicable apathy? The silence was a grievous trial to his faith. "Let us shut our eyes," he said, "let us invoke the Holy Spirit, let us collect all the powers of our soul, that our faith may not be shaken."[5] In his perplexity he began to make distinctions between the Pope and the Roman Court. The advisers of the Pope were traitors, dwellers in the outer darkness, blind and deaf; the Pope himself and he alone was infallible, and would never act so as to injure the faith, though meanwhile he was not aware of the real state of things, and was evidently deceived by false reports.[6] A few months later came the necessity for a further distinction between the Pontiff and the Sovereign. If the doctrines of the *Avenir* had caused displeasure at Rome, it was only on political grounds. If the Pope was offended, he was offended not as Vicar of Christ, but as a

---
[3] Feb. 27, 1831.
[4] March 30, 1831.
[5] May 8 and June 15, 1829.
[6] Feb. 8, 1830.

temporal monarch implicated in the political system of Europe. In his capacity of spiritual head of the Church he could not condemn writers for sacrificing all human and political considerations to the supreme interests of the Church, but must in reality agree with them.[7] As the Polish Revolution brought the political questions into greater prominence, Lamennais became more and more convinced of the wickedness of those who surrounded Gregory XVI, and of the political incompetence of the Pope himself. He described him as weeping and praying, motionless, amidst the darkness which the ambitious, corrupt, and frantic idiots around him were ever striving to thicken.[8] Still he felt secure. When the foundations of the Church were threatened, when an essential doctrine was at stake, though, for the first time in eighteen centuries, the supreme authority might refuse to speak,[9] at least it could not speak out against the truth. In this belief he made his last journey to Rome. Then came his condemnation. The staff on which he leaned with all his weight broke in his hands; the authority he had so grossly exaggerated turned against him, and his faith was left without support. His system supplied no resource for such an emergency. He submitted, not because he was in error, but because Catholics had no right to defend the Church against the supreme will even of an erring Pontiff.[10] He was persuaded that his silence would injure religion, yet he deemed it his duty to be silent and to abandon theology. He had ceased to believe that the Pope could not err, but he still believed that he could not lawfully be disobeyed. In the two years during which he still remained in the Church his faith in her system fell rapidly to pieces. Within two months after the publication of the Encyclical he wrote that the Pope, like the other princes, seemed careful not to omit any blunder that could secure his annihilation.[11] Three weeks afterwards he denounced in the fiercest terms the corruption of Rome. He predicted that the eccle-

[7] Aug. 15, 1831.
[8] Feb. 10, 1832.
[9] July 6, 1829.
[10] Sept. 15, 1832.
[11] Oct. 9, 1832.

siastical hierarchy was about to depart with the old monarchies; and, though the Church could not die, he would not undertake to say that she would revive in her old forms.[12] The Pope, he said, had so zealously embraced the cause of antichristian despotism as to sacrifice to it the religion of which he was the chief. He no longer felt it possible to distinguish what was immutable in the external organisation of the Church. He admitted the personal fallibility of the Pope, and declared that, though it was impossible, without Rome, to defend Catholicism successfully, yet nothing could be hoped for from her, and that she seemed to have condemned Catholicism to die.[13] The Pope, he soon afterwards said, was in league with the kings in opposition to the eternal truths of religion, the hierarchy was out of court, and a transformation like that from which the Church and Papacy had sprung was about to bring them both to an end, after eighteen centuries, in Gregory XVI.[14] Before the following year was over he had ceased to be in communion with the Catholic Church.

The fall of Lamennais, however impressive as a warning, is of no great historical importance; for he carried no one with him, and his favourite disciples became the ablest defenders of Catholicism in France. But it exemplifies one of the natural consequences of dissociating secular from religious truth, and denying that they hold in solution all the elements necessary for their reconciliation and union. In more recent times, the same error has led, by a contrary path, to still more lamentable results, and scepticism on the possibility of harmonising reason and faith has once more driven a philosopher into heresy. Between the fall of Lamennais and the conflict with Frohschammer many metaphysical writers among the Catholic clergy had incurred the censures of Rome. It is enough to cite Bautain in France, Rosmini in Italy, and Günther in Austria. But in these cases no scandal ensued, and the decrees were received with prompt and hearty submission. In the cases of Lamennais and Frohschammer no speculative

---
[12] Jan. 25, 1833.
[13] Feb. 5, 1833.
[14] March 25, 1833.

question was originally at issue, but only the question of authority. A comparison between their theories will explain the similarity in the courses of the two men, and at the same time will account for the contrast between the isolation of Lamennais and the influence of Frohschammer, though the one was the most eloquent writer in France, and the head of a great school, and the other, before the late controversy, was not a writer of much name. This contrast is the more remarkable since religion had not revived in France when the French philosopher wrote, while for the last quarter of a century Bavaria has been distinguished among Catholic nations for the faith of her people. Yet Lamennais was powerless to injure a generation of comparatively ill-instructed Catholics, while Frohschammer, with inferior gifts of persuasion, has won educated followers even in the home of Ultramontanism.

The first obvious explanation of this difficulty is the narrowness of Lamennais' philosophy. At the time of his dispute with the Holy See he had somewhat lost sight of his traditionalist theory; and his attention, concentrated upon politics, was directed to the problem of reconciling religion with liberty—a question with which the best minds in France are still occupied. But how can a view of policy constitute a philosophy? He began by thinking that it was expedient for the Church to obtain the safeguards of freedom, and that she should renounce the losing cause of the old *régime*. But this was no more philosophy than the similar argument which had previously won her to the side of despotism when it was the stronger cause. As Bonald, however, had erected absolute monarchy into a dogma, so Lamennais proceeded to do with freedom. The Church, he said, was on the side of freedom, because it was the just side, not because it was the stronger. As De Maistre had seen the victory of Catholic principles in the Restoration, so Lamennais saw it in the revolution of 1830.

This was obviously too narrow and temporary a basis for a philosophy. The Church is interested, not in the triumph of a principle or cause which may be dated as that of 1789, or of 1815, or of 1830, but in the triumph of justice and the just cause, whether it be that of the people or of the Crown, of a Catholic party or of its opponents. She admits the tests of public law and political science. When these proclaim the existence of the conditions which justify an insurrection or a war, she cannot condemn that insurrection or that war. She is guided in her judgment on these causes by criteria which are not her own, but are borrowed from departments over which she has no supreme control. This is as true of science as it is of law and politics. Other truths are as certain as those which natural or positive law embraces, and other obligations as imperative as those which regulate the relations of subjects and authorities. The principle which places right above expedience in the political action of the Church has an equal application in history or in astronomy. The Church can no more identify her cause with scientific error than with political wrong. Her interests may be impaired by some measure of political justice, or by the admission of some fact or document. But in neither case can she guard her interests at the cost of denying the truth.

This is the principle which has so much difficulty in obtaining recognition in an age when science is more or less irreligious, and when Catholics more or less neglect its study. Political and intellectual liberty have the same claims and the same conditions in the eyes of the Church. The Catholic judges the measures of governments and the discoveries of science in exactly the same manner. Public law may make it imperative to overthrow a Catholic monarch, like James II, or to uphold a Protestant monarch, like the King of Prussia. The demonstrations of science may oblige us to believe that the earth revolves round the sun, or that the *Donation of Constantine* is spurious. The apparent interests of religion have much to say against all this; but religion itself prevents those considerations from prevailing. This has not been seen by those writers who have done most in defence of the principle. They have usually considered it from the standing ground of their own practical aims, and have therefore failed to attain that general view which might have been suggested to them by the pursuit of truth as a whole. French writers have done much for political liberty, and Germans for intellectual liberty; but the defenders of the one cause have generally had so little sympathy with the other, that they have neglected to defend their own on the grounds common to both. There is hardly a Catholic writer who has penetrated to the common source from which they spring. And this is the greatest defect in Catholic literature, even to the present day.

In the majority of those who have afforded the chief examples of this error, and particularly in Lamennais, the weakness of faith which it implies has been united with that looseness of thought which resolves all knowledge into opinion, and fails to appreciate methodical investigation or scientific evidence. But it is less easy to explain how a priest, fortified with the armour of German science, should have failed as completely in the same inquiry. In order to solve the difficulty, we must go back to the time when the theory of Frohschammer arose, and review some of the circumstances out of which it sprang.

For adjusting the relations between science and authority, the method of Rome had long been that of economy and accommodation. In dealing with literature, her paramount consideration was the fear of scandal. Books were forbidden, not merely because their statements were denied, but because they seemed injurious to morals, derogatory to authority, or dangerous to faith. To be so, it was not necessary that they should be untrue. For isolated truths separated from other known truths by an interval of conjecture, in which error might find room to construct its works, may offer perilous occasions to unprepared and unstable minds. The policy was therefore to allow such truths to be put forward only hypothetically, or altogether to suppress them. The latter alternative was especially appropriated to historical investigations, because they contained most elements of danger. In them the progress of knowledge has been for centuries constant, rapid, and sure; every generation has brought to light masses of information previously unknown, the successive publication of which furnished ever new incentives, and more and more ample means of inquiry into ecclesiastical history.

This inquiry has gradually laid bare the whole policy and process of ecclesiastical authority, and has removed from the past that veil of mystery wherewith, like all other authorities, it tries to surround the present. The human element in ecclesiastical administration endeavours to keep itself out of sight, and to deny its own existence, in order that it may secure the unquestioning submission which authority naturally desires, and may preserve that halo of infallibility which the twilight of opinion enables it to assume. Now the most severe exposure of the part played by this human element is found in histories which show the undeniable existence of sin, error, or fraud in the high places of the Church. Not, indeed, that any history furnishes, or can furnish, materials for undermining the authority which the dogmas of the Church proclaim to be necessary for her existence. But the true limits of legitimate authority are one thing, and the area which authority may find it expedient to attempt to occupy is another. The interests of the Church are not necessarily identical with those of the ecclesiastical government. A government does not desire its powers to be strictly defined, but the subjects require the line to be drawn with increasing precision. Authority may be protected by its subjects being kept in ignorance of its faults, and by their holding it in superstitious admiration. But religion has no communion with any manner of error: and the conscience can only be injured by such arts, which, in reality, give a far more formidable measure of the influence of the human element in ecclesiastical government than any collection of attached cases of scandal can do. For these arts are simply those of all human governments which possess legislative power, fear attack, deny responsibility, and therefore shrink from scrutiny.

One of the great instruments for preventing historical scrutiny had long been the Index of prohibited books, which was accordingly directed, not against falsehood only, but particularly against certain departments of truth. Through it an effort had been made to keep the knowledge of ecclesiastical history from the faithful, and to give currency to a fabulous and fictitious picture of the progress and action of the Church.

The means would have been found quite inadequate to the end, if it had not been for the fact that while society was absorbed by controversy, knowledge was only valued so far as it served a controversial purpose. Every party in those days virtually had its own prohibitive Index, to brand all inconvenient truths with the note of falsehood. No party cared for knowledge that could not be made available for argument. Neutral and ambiguous science had no attractions for men engaged in perpetual combat. Its spirit first won the naturalists, the mathematicians, and the philologists; then it vivified the otherwise aimless erudition of the Benedictines; and at last it was carried into history, to give new life to those sciences which deal with the tradition, the law, and the action of the Church.

The home of this transformation was in the universities of Germany, for there the Catholic teacher was placed in circumstances altogether novel. He had to address men who had every opportunity of becoming familiar with the arguments of the enemies of the Church, and with the discoveries and conclusions of those whose studies were without the bias of any religious object. Whilst he lectured in one room, the next might be occupied by a pantheist, a rationalist, or a Lutheran, descanting on the same topics. When he left the desk his place might be taken by some great original thinker or scholar, who would display all the results of his meditations without regard for their tendency, and without considering what effects they might have on the weak. He was obliged often to draw attention to books lacking the Catholic spirit, but indispensable to the deeper student. Here, therefore, the system of secrecy, economy, and accommodation was rendered impossible by the competition of knowledge, in which the most thorough exposition of the truth was sure of the victory, and the system itself became inapplicable as the scientific spirit penetrated ecclesiastical literature in Germany.

In Rome, however, where the influences of competition were not felt, the reasons of the change could not be understood, nor its benefits experienced; and it was thought absurd that the Germans of the nineteenth century should discard weapons which had been found efficacious with the Germans of the sixteenth. While in Rome it was still held that the truths of science need not be told, and ought not to be told, if, in the judgment of Roman theologians, they were of a nature to offend faith, in Germany Catholics vied with Protestants in publishing matter without being diverted by the consideration whether it might serve or injure their cause in controversy, or whether it was adverse or favourable to the views which it was the object of the Index to protect. But though this great antagonism existed, there was no collision. A moderation was exhibited which contrasted remarkably with the aggressive spirit prevailing in France and Italy. Publications were suffered to pass unnoted in Germany which would have been immediately censured if they had come forth beyond the Alps or the Rhine. In this way a certain laxity grew up side by side with an unmeasured distrust, and German theologians and historians escaped censure.

This toleration gains significance from its contrast to the severity with which Rome smote the German philosophers like Hermes and Günther when they erred. Here, indeed, the case was very different. If Rome had insisted upon suppressing documents, perverting facts, and resisting criticism, she would have been only opposing truth, and opposing it consciously, for fear of its inconveniences. But if she had refrained from denouncing a philosophy which denied creation or the personality of God, she would have failed to assert her own doctrines against her own children who contradicted them. The philosopher cannot claim the same exemption as the historian. God's handwriting exists in history independently of the Church, and no ecclesiastical exigence can alter a fact. The divine lesson has been read, and it is the historian's duty to copy it faithfully without bias and without ulterior views. The Catholic may be sure that as the Church has lived in spite of the fact, she will also survive its publication. But philosophy has to deal with some facts which, although as absolute and objective in themselves, are not and cannot be known to us except through revelation, of which the Church is the organ. A philosophy which requires the alteration of these facts is in patent contradiction against the Church. Both cannot coexist. One must destroy the other.

Two circumstances very naturally arose to disturb this equilibrium. There were divines who wished to extend to Germany the old authority of the Index, and to censure or prohibit books which, though not heretical, contained matter injurious to the reputation of ecclesiastical authority, or contrary to the common opinions of Catholic theologians. On the other hand, there were philosophers of the schools of Hermes and Günther who would not retract the doctrines which the Church condemned. One movement tended to repress even the knowledge of demonstrable truth, and the other aimed at destroying the dogmatic authority of the Holy See. In this way a collision was prepared, which was eventually brought about by the writings of Dr. Frohschammer.

Ten years ago, when he was a very young lecturer on philosophy in the university of Munich, he published a work on the origin of the soul, in which he argued against the theory of pre-existence, and against the common opinion that each soul is created directly by Almighty God, defending the theory of Generationism by the authority of several Fathers, and quoting, among other modern divines, Klee, the author of the most esteemed treatise of dogmatic theology in the German language. It was decided at Rome that his book should be condemned, and he was informed of the intention, in order that he might announce his submission before the publication of the decree.

His position was a difficult one, and it appears to be admitted that his conduct at this stage was not prompted by those opinions on the authority of the Church in which he afterwards took refuge, but must be explained by the known facts of the case. His doctrine had been lately taught in a book generally read and approved. He was convinced that he had at least refuted the opposite theories, and yet it was apparently in behalf of one of these that he was condemned. Whatever errors his book contained, he might fear that an act of submission would seem to imply his acceptance of an opinion he heartily believed to be wrong, and would therefore be an act of treason to truth. The decree conveyed no conviction to his mind. It is only the utterances of an infallible authority that men can believe without argument and explanation, and here was an authority not infallible, giving no reasons, and yet claiming a submission of the reason. Dr. Frohschammer found himself in a dilemma. To submit absolutely would either be a virtual acknowledgment of the infallibility of the authority, or a confession that an ecclesiastical decision necessarily bound the mind irrespective of its truth or justice. In either case he would have contradicted the law of religion and of the Church. To submit, while retaining his own opinion, to a disciplinary decree, in order to preserve peace and avoid scandal, and to make a general acknowledgment that his work contained various ill-considered and equivocal statements which might bear a bad construction,— such a conditional submission either would not have been that which the Roman Court desired and intended, or, if made without explicit statement of its meaning, would have been in some measure deceitful and hypocritical. In the first case it would not have been received, in the second case it could not have been made without loss of self-respect. Moreover, as the writer was a public professor, bound to instruct his hearers according to his best knowledge, he could not change his teaching while his opinion remained unchanged. These considerations, and not any desire to defy authority, or introduce new opinions by a process more or less revolutionary, appear to have guided his conduct. At this period it might have been possible to arrive at an understanding, or to obtain satisfactory explanations, if the Roman Court would have told him what points were at issue, what passages in his book were impugned, and what were the grounds for suspecting them. If there was on both sides a peaceful and conciliatory spirit, and a desire to settle the problem, there was certainly a chance of effecting it by a candid interchange of explanations. It was a course which had proved efficacious on other occasions, and in the then recent discussion of Günther's system it had been pursued with great patience and decided success.

Before giving a definite reply, therefore, Dr. Frohschammer asked for information about the incriminated articles. This would have given him an opportunity of seeing his error, and making a submission *in foro interno*. But the request was refused. It was a favour, he was told, sometimes extended to men whose great services to the Church deserved such consideration, but not to one who was hardly known except by the very book which had incurred the censure. This answer instantly aroused a suspicion that the Roman Court was more anxious to assert its authority than to correct an alleged error, or to prevent a scandal. It was well known that the mistrust of German philosophy was very deep at Rome; and it seemed far from impossible that an intention existed to put it under all possible restraint.

This mistrust on the part of the Roman divines was fully equalled, and so far justified, by a corresponding literary contempt on the part of many German Catholic scholars. It is easy to understand the grounds of this feeling. The German writers were engaged in an arduous struggle, in which their antagonists were sustained by intellectual power, solid learning, and deep thought, such as the defenders of the Church in Catholic countries have never had to encounter. In this conflict the Italian divines could render no assistance. They had shown themselves altogether incompetent to cope with modern science. The Germans, therefore, unable to recognise them as auxiliaries, soon ceased to regard them as equals, or as scientific divines at all. Without impeaching their orthodoxy, they learned to look on them as men incapable of understanding and mastering the ideas of a literature so very remote from their own, and to attach no more value to the unreasoned decrees of their organ than to the undefended *ipse dixit* of a theologian of secondary rank. This opinion sprang, not from national prejudice or from the self-appreciation of individuals comparing their own works with those of the Roman divines, but from a general view of the relation of these divines, among whom there are several distinguished Germans, to the literature of Germany. It was thus a corporate feeling, which might be shared even by one who was conscious of his own inferiority, or who had written nothing at all. Such a man, weighing the opinion of the theologians of the Gesù and the Minerva, not in the scale of his own performance, but in that of the great achievements of his age, might well be reluctant to accept their verdict upon them without some aid of argument and explanation.

On the other hand, it appeared that a blow which struck the Catholic scholars of Germany would assure to the victorious congregation of Roman divines an easy supremacy over the writers of all other countries. The case of Dr. Frohschammer might be made to test what degree of control it would be possible to exercise over his countrymen, the only body of writers at whom alarm was felt, and who insisted, more than others, on their freedom. But the suspicion of such a possibility was likely only to confirm him in the idea that he was chosen to be the experimental body on which an important principle was to be decided, and that it was his duty, till his dogmatic error was proved, to resist a questionable encroachment of authority upon the rights of freedom. He therefore refused to make the preliminary submission which was required of him, and allowed the decree to go forth against him in the usual way. Hereupon it was intimated to him — though not by Rome — that he had incurred excommunication. This was the measure which raised the momentous question of the liberties of Catholic science, and gave the impulse to that new theory on the limits of authority with which his name has become associated.

In the civil affairs of mankind it is necessary to assume that the knowledge of the moral code and the traditions of law cannot perish in a Christian nation. Particular authorities may fall into error; decisions may be appealed against; laws may be repealed, but the political conscience of the whole people cannot be irrecoverably lost. The Church possesses the same privilege, but in a much higher degree, for she exists expressly for the purpose of preserving a definite body of truths, the knowledge of which she can never lose. Whatever authority, therefore, expresses that knowledge of which she is the keeper must be obeyed. But there is no institution from which this knowledge can be obtained with immediate certainty. A council is not à priori œcumenical; the Holy See is not separately infallible. The one has to await a sanction, the other has repeatedly erred. Every decree, therefore, requires a preliminary examination.

A writer who is censured may, in the first place, yield an external submission, either for the sake of discipline, or because his conviction is too weak to support him against the weight of authority. But if the question at issue is more important than the preservation of peace, and if his conviction is strong, he inquires whether the authority which condemns him utters the voice of the Church. If he finds that it does, he yields to it, or ceases to profess the faith of Catholics. If he finds that it does not, but is only the voice of authority, he owes it to his conscience, and to the supreme claims of truth, to remain constant to that which he believes, in spite of opposition. No authority has power to impose error, and, if it resists the truth, the truth must be upheld until it is admitted. Now the adversaries of Dr. Frohschammer had fallen into the monstrous error of attributing to the congregation of the Index a share in the infallibility of the Church. He was placed in the position of a persecuted man, and the general sympathy was with him. In his defence he proceeded to state his theory of the rights of science, in order to vindicate the Church from the imputation of restricting its freedom. Hitherto his works had been written in defence of a Christian philosophy against materialism and infidelity. Their object had been thoroughly religious, and although he was not deeply read in ecclesiastical literature, and was often loose and incautious in the use of theological terms, his writings had not been wanting in catholicity of spirit; but after his condemnation by Rome he undertook to pull down the power which had dealt the blow, and to make himself safe for the future. In this spirit of personal antagonism he commenced a long series of writings in defence of freedom and in defiance of authority.

The following abstract marks, not so much the outline of his system, as the logical steps which carried him to the point where he passed beyond the limit of Catholicism. Religion, he taught, supplies materials but no criterion for philosophy; philosophy has nothing to rely on, in the last resort, but the unfailing veracity of our nature, which is not corrupt or weak, but normally healthy, and unable to deceive us.[15] There is not greater diversion or uncertainty in matters of speculation than on questions of faith.[16] If at any time error or doubt should arise, the science possesses in itself the means of correcting or removing it, and no other remedy is efficacious but that which it applies to itself.[17] There can be no free philosophy if we must always remember dogma.[18] Philosophy includes in its sphere all the dogmas of revelation, as well as those of natural religion. It examines by its own independent light the substance of every Christian doctrine, and determines in each case whether it be divine truth.[19] The conclusions and judgments at which it thus arrives must be maintained even when they contradict articles of faith.[20] As we accept the evidence of astronomy in opposition to the once settled opinion of divines, so we should not shrink from the evidence of chemistry if it should be adverse to transubstantiation.[21] The Church, on the other hand, examines these conclusions by her standard of faith, and decides whether they can be taught in theology.[22] But she has no means of ascertaining the philosophical truth of an opinion, and cannot convict the philosopher of error. The two domains are as distinct as reason and faith; and we must not identify what we know with what we believe, but must separate the philosopher from his philosophy. The system may be utterly at variance with the whole teaching of Christianity, and yet the philosopher, while he holds it to be philosophically true and certain, may continue to believe all Catholic doctrine, and

---

[15] *Naturphilosophie,* p. 115; *Einleitung in die Philosophie,* pp. 40, 54; *Freiheit der Wissenschaft,* pp 4, 89; *Athenäum,* I, 17.
[16] *Athenäum,* I, 92.
[17] *Freiheit der Wissenschaft,* p. 32.
[18] *Athenäum,* I, 167.
[19] *Einleitung,* pp. 305, 317, 397.
[20] *Athenäum,* I, 208.
[21] *Ibid.,* II, 655.
[22] *Ibid.,* II, 676.

to perform all the spiritual duties of a layman or a priest. For discord cannot exist between the certain results of scientific investigation and the real doctrines of the Church. Both are true, and there is no conflict of truths. But while the teaching of science is distinct and definite, that of the Church is subject to alteration. Theology is at no time absolutely complete, but always liable to be modified, and cannot, therefore, be made a fixed test of truth.[23] Consequently there is no reason against the union of the Churches. For the liberty of private judgment, which is the formal principle of Protestantism, belongs to Catholics; and there is no actual Catholic dogma which may not lose all that is objectionable to Protestants by the transforming process of development.[24]

The errors of Dr. Frohschammer in these passages are not exclusively his own. He has only drawn certain conclusions from premises which are very commonly received. Nothing is more usual than to confound religious truth with the voice of ecclesiastical authority. Dr. Frohschammer, having fallen into this vulgar mistake, argues that because the authority is fallible the truth must be uncertain. Many Catholics attribute to theological opinions which have prevailed for centuries without reproach a sacredness nearly approaching that which belongs to articles of faith: Dr. Frohschammer extends to defined dogmas the liability to change which belongs to opinions that yet await a final and conclusive investigation. Thousands of zealous men are persuaded that a conflict may arise between defined doctrines of the Church and conclusions which are certain according to all the tests of science: Dr. Frohschammer adopts this view, and argues that none of the decisions of the Church are final, and that consequently in such a case they must give way. Lastly, uninstructed men commonly impute to historical and natural science the uncertainty which is inseparable from pure speculation: Dr. Frohschammer accepts the equality, but claims for metaphysics the same certainty and independence which those sciences possess.

[23] *Ibid.*, II, 661.
[24] *Wiedervereinigung der Katholiken und Protestanten*, pp. 26, 35.

Having begun his course in company with many who have exactly opposite ends in view, Dr. Frohschammer, in a recent tract on the union of the Churches, entirely separates himself from the Catholic Church in his theory of development. He had received the impulse to his new system from the opposition of those whom he considered the advocates of an excessive uniformity and the enemies of progress, and their contradiction has driven him to a point where he entirely sacrifices unity to change. He now affirms that our Lord desired no unity or perfect conformity among His followers, except in morals and charity;[25] that He gave no definite system of doctrine; and that the form which Christian faith may have assumed in a particular age has no validity for all future time, but is subject to continual modification.[26] The definitions, he says, which the Church has made from time to time are not to be obstinately adhered to; and the advancement of religious knowledge is obtained by genius, not by learning, and is not regulated by traditions and fixed rules.[27] He maintains that not only the form but the substance varies; that the belief of one age may be not only extended but abandoned in another; and that it is impossible to draw the line which separates immutable dogma from undecided opinions.[28]

The causes which drove Dr. Frohschammer into heresy would scarcely have deserved great attention from the mere merit of the man, for he cannot be acquitted of having, in the first instance, exhibited very superficial notions of theology. Their instructiveness consists in the conspicuous example they afford of the effect of certain errors which at the present day are commonly held and rarely contradicted. When he found himself censured unjustly, as he thought, by the Holy See, it should have been enough for him to believe in his conscience that he was in agreement with the true faith of the Church. He would not then have proceeded to consider the whole Church infected with the liability to err from

---

[25] *Wiedervereinigung*, pp. 8, 10.
[26] *Ibid.*, p. 15.
[27] *Ibid.*, p. 21.
[28] *Ibid.*, pp. 25, 26.

which her rulers are not exempt, or to degrade the fundamental truths of Christianity to the level of mere school opinions. Authority appeared in his eyes to stand for the whole Church: and therefore, in endeavouring to shield himself from its influence, he abandoned the first principles of the ecclesiastical system. Far from having aided the cause of freedom, his errors have provoked a reaction against it, which must be looked upon with deep anxiety, and of which the first significant symptom remains to be described.

On the 21st of December 1863, the Pope addressed a Brief to the Archbishop of Munich, which was published on the 5th of March. This document explains that the Holy Father had originally been led to suspect the recent Congress at Munich of a tendency similar to that of Frohschammer, and had consequently viewed it with great distrust; but that these feelings were removed by the address which was adopted at the meeting, and by the report of the Archbishop. And he expresses the consolation he has derived from the principles which prevailed in the assembly, and applauds the design of those by whom it was convened. He asked for the opinion of the German prelates, in order to be able to determine whether, in the present circumstances of their Church, it is right that the Congress should be renewed.

Besides the censure of the doctrines of Frohschammer, and the approbation given to the acts of the Munich Congress, the Brief contains passages of deeper and more general import, not directly touching the action of the German divines, but having an important bearing on the position of this *Review*. The substance of these passages is as follows: In the present condition of society the supreme authority in the Church is more than ever necessary, and must not surrender in the smallest degree the exclusive direction of ecclesiastical knowledge. An entire obedience to the decrees of the Holy See and the Roman congregations cannot be inconsistent with the freedom and progress of science. The disposition to find fault with the scholastic theology, and to dispute the conclusions and the method of its teachers, threatens the authority of the Church, because the Church has not only allowed theology to remain for centuries faithful to their system, but has urgently recommended it as the safest bulwark of the faith, and an efficient weapon against her enemies. Catholic writers are not bound only by those decisions of the infallible Church which regard articles of faith. They must also submit to the theological decisions of the Roman congregations, and to the opinions which are commonly received in the schools. And it is wrong, though not heretical, to reject those decisions or opinions.

In a word, therefore, the Brief affirms that the common opinions and explanations of Catholic divines ought not to yield to the progress of secular science, and that the course of theological knowledge ought to be controlled by the decrees of the Index.

There is no doubt that the letter of this document might be interpreted in a sense consistent with the habitual language of the *Home and Foreign Review*. On the one hand, the censure is evidently aimed at that exaggerated claim of independence which would deny to the Pope and the Episcopate any right of interfering in literature, and would transfer the whole weight heretofore belonging to the traditions of the schools of theology to the incomplete, and therefore uncertain, conclusions of modern science. On the other hand, the *Review* has always maintained, in common with all Catholics, that if the one Church has an organ it is through that organ that she must speak; that her authority is not limited to the precise sphere of her infallibility; and that opinions which she has long tolerated or approved, and has 'for centuries found compatible with the secular as well as religious knowledge of the age, cannot be lightly supplanted by new hypotheses of scientific men, which have not yet had time to prove their consistency with dogmatic truth. But such a plausible accommodation, even if it were honest or dignified, would only disguise and obscure those ideas which it has been the chief object of the *Review* to proclaim. It is, therefore, not only more respectful to the Holy See, but more serviceable to the principles of the *Review* itself, and more in accordance with the spirit in which it has been conducted, to interpret the words of the Pope as they were really meant, than to elude their consequences by subtle distinctions, and to profess a formal adoption of maxims which no man who holds the principles of the *Review* can accept in their intended signification.

One of these maxims is that theological and other opinions long held and allowed in the Church gather truth from time, and an authority in some sort binding from the implied sanction of the Holy See, so that they cannot be rejected without rashness; and that the decrees of the congregation of the Index possess an authority quite independent of the acquirements of the men composing it. This is no new opinion; it is only expressed on the present occasion with unusual solemnity and distinctness. But one of the essential principles of this *Review* consists in a clear recognition, first, of the infinite gulf which in theology separates what is of faith from what is not of faith, — revealed dogmas from opinions unconnected with them by logical necessity, and therefore incapable of anything higher than a natural certainty — and next, of the practical difference which exists in ecclesiastical discipline between the acts of infallible authority and those which possess no higher sanction than that of canonical legality. That which is not decided with dogmatic infallibility is for the time susceptible only of a scientific determination, which advances with the progress of science, and becomes absolute only where science has attained its final results. On the one hand, this scientific progress is beneficial, and even necessary, to the Church; on the other, it must inevitably be opposed by the guardians of traditional opinion, to whom, as such, no share in it belongs, and who, by their own acts and those of their predecessors, are committed to views which it menaces or destroys. The same principle which, in certain conjunctures, imposes the duty of surrendering received opinions imposes in equal extent, and under like conditions, the duty of disregarding the fallible authorities that uphold them.

It is the design of the Holy See not, of course, to deny the distinction between dogma and opinion, upon which this duty is founded, but to reduce the practical recognition of it among Catholics to the smallest possible limits. A grave question therefore arises as to the position of a *Review* founded in great part for the purpose of exemplifying this distinction.[29] In considering the solution of this question two circumstances must be borne in mind: first, that the antagonism now so forcibly expressed has always been known and acknowledged; and secondly, that no part of the Brief applies directly to the *Review*. The *Review* was as distinctly opposed to the Roman sentiment before the Brief as since, and it is still as free from censure as before. It was at no time in virtual sympathy with authority on the points in question, and it is not now in formal conflict with authority.

But the definiteness with which the Holy See has pronounced its will, and the fact that it has taken the initiative, seem positively to invite adhesion, and to convey a special warning to all who have expressed opinions contrary to the maxims of the Brief. A periodical which not only has done so, but exists in a measure for the purpose of doing so, cannot with propriety refuse to survey the new position in which it is placed by this important act. For the conduct of a *Review* involves more delicate relations with the government of the Church than the authorship of an isolated book. When opinions which the author defends are rejected at Rome, he either makes his submission, or, if his mind remains unaltered, silently leaves his book to take its chance, and to influence men according to its merits. But such passivity, however right and seemly in the author of a book, is inapplicable to the case of a *Review*. The periodical iteration of rejected propositions would amount to insult and defiance,

---

[29] The prospectus of the *Review* contained these words "It will abstain from direct theological discussion, as far as external circumstances will allow, and in dealing with those mixed questions into which theology indirectly enters, its aim will be to combine devotion to the Church with discrimination and candour in the treatment of her opponents; to reconcile freedom of inquiry with implicit faith, and to discountenance what is untenable and unreal, without forgetting the tenderness due to the weak, or the reverence rightly claimed for what is sacred. Submitting without reserve to infallible authority, it will encourage a habit of manly investigation on subjects of scientific interest."

and would probably provoke more definite measures; and thus the result would be to commit authority yet more irrevocably to an opinion which otherwise might take no deep root, and might yield ultimately to the influence of time. For it is hard to surrender a cause on behalf of which a struggle has been sustained, and spiritual evils have been inflicted. In an isolated book, the author need discuss no more topics than he likes, and any want of agreement with ecclesiastical authority may receive so little prominence as to excite no attention. But a continuous *Review*, which adopted this kind of reserve, would give a negative prominence to the topics it persistently avoided, and by thus keeping before the world the position it occupied would hold out a perpetual invitation to its readers to judge between the Church and itself. Whatever it gained of approbation and assent would be so much lost to the authority and dignity of the Holy See. It could only hope to succeed by trading on the scandal it caused.

But in reality its success could no longer advance the cause of truth. For what is the Holy See in its relation to the masses of Catholics, and where does its strength lie? It is the organ, the mouth, the head of the Church. Its strength consists in its agreement with the general conviction of the faithful. When it expresses the common knowledge and sense of the age, or of a large majority of Catholics, its position is impregnable. The force it derives from this general support makes direct opposition hopeless, and therefore disedifying, tending only to division and promoting reaction rather than reform. The influence by which it is to be moved must be directed first on that which gives it strength, and must pervade the members in order that it may reach the head. While the general sentiment of Catholics is unaltered, the course of the Holy See remains unaltered too. As soon as that sentiment is modified, Rome sympathises with the change. The ecclesiastical government, based upon the public opinion of the Church, and acting through it, cannot separate itself from the mass of the faithful, and keep pace with the progress of the instructed minority. It follows slowly and warily, and sometimes begins by resisting and denouncing what in the end it thoroughly adopts. Hence a direct controversy with Rome holds out the prospect of great evils, and at best a barren and unprofitable victory. The victory that is fruitful springs from that gradual change in the knowledge, the ideas, and the convictions of the Catholic body, which, in due time, overcomes the natural reluctance to forsake a beaten path, and by insensible degrees constrains the mouthpiece of tradition to conform itself to the new atmosphere with which it is surrounded. The slow, silent, indirect action of public opinion bears the Holy See along, without any demoralising conflict or dishonourable capitulation. This action belongs essentially to the graver scientific literature to direct: and the inquiry what form that literature should assume at any given moment involves no question which affects its substance, though it may often involve questions of moral fitness sufficiently decisive for a particular occasion.

It was never pretended that the *Home and Foreign Review* represented the opinions of the majority of Catholics. The Holy See has had their support in maintaining a view of the obligations of Catholic literature very different from the one which has been upheld in these pages; nor could it explicitly abandon that view without taking up a new position in the Church. All that could be hoped for on the other side was silence and forbearance, and for a time they have been conceded. But this is the case no longer. The toleration has now been pointedly withdrawn; and the adversaries of the Roman theory have been challenged with the summons to submit.

If the opinions for which submission is claimed were new, or if the opposition now signalised were one of which there had hitherto been any doubt, a question might have arisen as to the limits of the authority of the Holy See over the conscience, and the necessity or possibility of accepting the view which it propounds. But no problem of this kind has in fact presented itself for consideration. The differences which are now proclaimed have all along been acknowledged to exist; and the conductors of this *Review* are unable to yield their assent to the opinions put forward in the Brief.

In these circumstances there are two courses which it is

impossible to take. It would be wrong to abandon principles which have been well considered and are sincerely held, and it would also be wrong to assail the authority which contradicts them. The principles have not ceased to be true, nor the authority to be legitimate, because the two are in contradiction. To submit the intellect and conscience without examining the reasonableness and justice of this decree, or to reject the authority on the ground of its having been abused, would equally be a sin, on one side against morals, on the other against faith. The conscience cannot be relieved by casting on the administrators of ecclesiastical discipline the whole responsibility of preserving religious truth; nor can it be emancipated by a virtual apostasy. For the Church is neither a despotism in which the convictions of the faithful possess no power of expressing themselves and no means of exercising legitimate control, nor is it an organised anarchy where the judicial and administrative powers are destitute of that authority which is conceded to them in civil society — the authority which commands submission even where it cannot impose a conviction of the righteousness of its acts.

No Catholic can contemplate without alarm the evil that would be caused by a Catholic journal persistently labouring to thwart the published will of the Holy See, and continously defying its authority. The conductors of this *Review* refuse to take upon themselves the responsibility of such a position. And if it were accepted, the *Review* would represent no section of Catholics. But the representative character is as essential to it as the opinions it professes, or the literary resources it commands. There is no lack of periodical publications representing science apart from religion, or religion apart from science. The distinctive feature of the *Home and Foreign Review* has been that it has attempted to exhibit the two in union; and the interest which has been attached to its views proceeded from the fact that they were put forward as essentially Catholic in proportion to their scientific truth, and as expressing more faithfully than even the voice of authority the genuine spirit of the Church in relation to intellect. Its object has been to elucidate the harmony which exists between religion and the established conclusions of secular knowledge, and to exhibit the real amity and sympathy between the methods of science and the methods employed by the Church. That amity and sympathy the enemies of the Church refuse to admit, and her friends have not learned to understand. Long disowned by a large part of our Episcopate, they are now rejected by the Holy See; and the issue is vital to a *Review* which, in ceasing to uphold them, would surrender the whole reason of its existence.

Warned, therefore, by the language of the Brief, I will not provoke ecclesiastical authority to a more explicit repudiation of doctrines which are necessary to secure its influence upon the advance of modern science. I will not challenge a conflict which would only deceive the world into a belief that religion cannot be harmonised with all that is right and true in the progress of the present age. But I will sacrifice the existence of the *Review* to the defence of its principles, in order that I may combine the obedience which is due to legitimate ecclesiastical authority, with an equally conscientious maintenance of the rightful and necessary liberty of thought. A conjuncture like the present does not perplex the conscience of a Catholic; for his obligation to refrain from wounding the peace of the Church is neither more nor less real than that of professing nothing beside or against his convictions. If these duties have not been always understood, at least the *Home and Foreign Review* will not betray them; and the cause it has imperfectly expounded can be more efficiently served in future by means which will neither weaken the position of authority nor depend for their influence on its approval.

If, as I have heard, but now am scarcely anxious to believe, there are those, both in the communion of the Church and out of it, who have found comfort in the existence of this *Review*, and have watched its straight short course with hopeful interest, trusting it as a sign that the knowledge deposited in their minds by study, and transformed by conscience into inviolable convictions, was not only tolerated among Catholics, but might be reasonably held to be of the very essence of their system; who were willing to accept its principles as a possible solution of the difficulties they saw in Catholicism, and were even prepared to make its fate the touchstone of the real spirit of our hierarchy; or who deemed that while it lasted it promised them some immunity from the overwhelming pressure of uniformity, some safeguard against resistance to the growth of knowledge and of freedom, and some protection for themselves, since, however weak its influence as an auxiliary, it would, by its position, encounter the first shock, and so divert from others the censures which they apprehended; who have found a welcome encouragement in its confidence, a satisfaction in its sincerity when they shrank from revealing their own thoughts, or a salutary restraint when its moderation failed to satisfy their ardour; whom, not being Catholics, it has induced to think less hardly of the Church, or, being Catholics, has bound more strongly to her; — to all these I would say that the principles it has upheld will not die with it, but will find their destined advocates, and triumph in their appointed time. From the beginning of the Church it has been a law of her nature, that the truths which eventually proved themselves the legitimate products of her doctrine, have had to make their slow way upwards through a phalanx of hostile habits and traditions, and to be rescued, not only from open enemies, but also from friendly hands that were not worthy to defend them. It is right that in every arduous enterprise someone who stakes no influence on the issue should make the first essay, whilst the true champions, like the Triarii of the Roman legions, are behind, and wait, without wavering, until the crisis calls them forward.

And already it seems to have arrived. All that is being done for ecclesiastical learning by the priesthood of the Continent bears testimony to the truths which are now called in question; and every work of real science written by a Catholic adds to their force. The example of great writers aids their cause more powerfully than many theoretical discussions. Indeed, when the principles of the antagonism which divides Catholics have been brought clearly out, the part of theory is accomplished, and most of the work of a *Review* is done.

It remains that the principles which have been made intelligible should be translated into practice, and should pass from the arena of discussion into the ethical code of literature. In that shape their efficacy will be acknowledged, and they will cease to be the object of alarm. Those who have been indignant at hearing that their methods are obsolete and their labours vain, will be taught by experience to recognise in the works of another school services to religion more momentous than those which they themselves have aspired to perform; practice will compel the assent which is denied to theory; and men will learn to value in the fruit what the germ did not reveal to them. Therefore it is to the prospect of that development of Catholic learning which is too powerful to be arrested or repressed that I would direct the thoughts of those who are tempted to yield either to a malignant joy or an unjust despondency at the language of the Holy See. If the spirit of the *Home and Foreign Review* really animates those whose sympathy it enjoyed, neither their principles, nor their confidence, nor their hopes will be shaken by its extinction. It was but a partial and temporary embodiment of an imperishable idea — the faint reflection of a light which still lives and burns in the hearts of the silent thinkers of the Church.

CHAPTER X

THE VATICAN COUNCIL

THE INTENTION OF Pius IX to convene a General Council became known in the autumn of 1864, shortly before the appearance of the Syllabus. They were the two principal measures which were designed to restore the spiritual and temporal power of the Holy See. When the idea of the Council was first put forward it met with no favour. The French bishops discouraged it; and the French bishops holding the talisman of the occupying army, spoke with authority. Later on, when the position had been altered by the impulse which the Syllabus gave to the ultramontane opinions, they revived the scheme they had first opposed. Those who felt their influence injured by the change persuaded themselves that the Court of Rome was more prudent than some of its partisans, and that the Episcopate was less given to extremes than the priesthood and laity. They conceived the hope that an assembly of bishops would curb the intemperance of a zeal which was largely directed against their own order, and would authentically sanction such an exposition of Catholic ideas as would reconcile the animosity that feeds on things spoken in the heat of controversy, and on the errors of incompetent apologists. They had accepted the Syllabus; but they wished to obtain canonicity for their own interpretation of it. If those who had succeeded in assigning an acceptable meaning to its censures could appear in a body to plead their

NOTE: This essay first appeared in *The North British Review*, LIII, No. 105 (October, 1870), 183-229: reprinted in *The History of Freedom and Other Essays* (London: Macmillan Co., 1907), pp. 492-550.

cause before the Pope, the pretensions which compromised the Church might be permanently repressed.

Once, during the struggle for the temporal power, the question was pertinently asked, how it was that men so perspicacious and so enlightened as those who were its most conspicuous champions, could bring themselves to justify a system of government which their own principles condemned. The explanation then given was, that they were making a sacrifice which would be compensated hereafter, that those who succoured the Pope in his utmost need were establishing a claim which would make them irresistible in better times, when they should demand great acts of conciliation and reform. It appeared to these men that the time had come to reap the harvest they had arduously sown.

The Council did not originate in the desire to exalt beyond measure the cause of Rome. It was proposed in the interest of moderation; and the Bishop of Orleans was one of those who took the lead in promoting it. The Cardinals were consulted, and pronounced against it. The Pope overruled their resistance. Whatever embarrassments might be in store, and however difficult the enterprise, it was clear that it would evoke a force capable of accomplishing infinite good for religion. It was an instrument of unknown power that inspired little confidence, but awakened vague hopes of relief for the ills of society and the divisions of Christendom. The guardians of immovable traditions, and the leaders of progress in religious knowledge, were not to share in the work. The schism of the East was widened by the angry quarrel between Russia and the Pope; and the letter to the Protestants, whose orders are not recognised at Rome, could not be more than a ceremonious challenge. There was no promise of sympathy in these invitations or in the answers they provoked; but the belief spread to many schools of thought, and was held by Dr. Pusey and by Dean Stanley, by Professor Hase and by M. Guizot, that the auspicious issue of the Council was an object of vital care to all denominations of Christian men.

The Council of Trent impressed on the Church the stamp of an intolerant age, and perpetuated by its decrees the spirit of an austere immorality. The ideas embodied in the Roman Inquisition became characteristic of a system which obeyed expediency by submitting to indefinite modification, but underwent no change of principle. Three centuries have so changed the world that the maxims with which the Church resisted the Reformation have become her weakness and her reproach, and that which arrested her decline now arrests her progress. To break effectually with that tradition and eradicate its influence, nothing less is required than an authority equal to that by which it was imposed. The Vatican Council was the first sufficient occasion which Catholicism had enjoyed to reform, remodel, and adapt the work of Trent. This idea was present among the motives which caused it to be summoned. It was apparent that two systems which cannot be reconciled were about to contend at the Council; but the extent and force of the reforming spirit were unknown.

Seventeen questions submitted by the Holy See to the bishops in 1867 concerned matters of discipline, the regulation of marriage and education, the policy of encouraging new monastic orders, and the means of making the parochial clergy more dependent on the bishops. They gave no indication of the deeper motives of the time. In the midst of many trivial proposals, the leading objects of reform grew more defined as the time approached, and men became conscious of distinct purposes based on a consistent notion of the Church. They received systematic expression from a Bohemian priest, whose work, *The Reform of the Church in its Head and Members*, is founded on practical experience, not only on literary theory, and is the most important manifesto of these ideas. The author exhorts the Council to restrict centralisation, to reduce the office of the Holy See to the ancient limits of its primacy, to restore to the Episcopate the prerogatives which have been confiscated by Rome, to abolish the temporal government, which is the prop of hierarchical despotism, to revise the matrimonial discipline, to suppress many religious orders and the solemn vows for all, to modify the absolute rule of celibacy for the clergy, to admit the use of the vernacular in the Liturgy, to allow a larger share to the laity in the management of ecclesiastical affairs, to encourage the education of the clergy at universities, and to renounce the claims of mediæval theocracy, which are fruitful of suspicion between Church and State.

Many Catholics in many countries concurred in great part of this programme; but it was not the symbol of a connected party. Few agreed with the author in all parts of his ideal church, or did not think that he had omitted essential points. Among the inveterate abuses which the Council of Trent failed to extirpate was the very one which gave the first impulse to Lutheranism. The belief is still retained in the superficial Catholicism of Southern Europe that the Pope can release the dead from Purgatory; and money is obtained at Rome on the assurance that every mass said at a particular altar opens heaven to the soul for which it is offered up. On the other hand, the Index of prohibited books is an institution of Tridentine origin, which has become so unwieldly and opprobrious that even men of strong Roman sympathies, like the bishops of Würzburg and St. Pölten, recommended its reform. In France it was thought that the Government would surrender the organic articles, if the rights of the bishops and the clergy were made secure under the canon law, if national and diocesan synods were introduced, and if a proportionate share was given to Catholic countries in the Sacred College and the Roman congregations. The aspiration in which all the advocates of reform seemed to unite was that those customs should be changed which are connected with arbitrary power in the Church. And all the interests threatened by this movement combined in the endeavour to maintain intact the papal prerogative. To proclaim the Pope infallible was their compendious security against hostile States and Churches, against human liberty and authority, against disintegrating tolerance and rationalising science, against error and sin. It became the common refuge of those who shunned what was called the liberal influence in Catholicism.

Pius IX constantly asserted that the desire of obtaining the recognition of papal infallibility was not originally his motive in convoking the Council. He did not require that a privilege which was practically undisputed should be further defined. The bishops, especially those of the minority, were never tired of saying that the Catholic world honoured and obeyed the Pope as it had never done before. Virtually he had exerted all the authority which the dogma could confer on him. In his first important utterance, the Encyclical of November 1846, he announced that he was infallible; and the claim raised no commotion. Later on he applied a more decisive test, and gained a more complete success, when the bishops summoned to Rome, not as a Council but as an audience, received from him an additional article of their faith. But apart from the dogma of infallibility he had a strong desire to establish certain cherished opinions of his own on a basis firm enough to outlast his time. They were collected in the Syllabus, which contained the essence of what he had written during many years, and was an abridgment of the lessons which his life had taught him. He was anxious that they should not be lost. They were part of a coherent system. The Syllabus was not rejected; but its edge was blunted and its point broken by the zeal which was spent in explaining it away; and the Pope feared that it would be contested if he repudiated the soothing interpretations. In private he said that he wished to have no interpreter but himself. While the Jesuit preachers proclaimed that the Syllabus bore the full sanction of infallibility, higher functionaries of the Court pointed out that it was an informal document, without definite official value. Probably the Pope would have been content that these his favourite ideas should be rescued from evasion by being incorporated in the canons of the Council. Papal infallibility was implied rather than included among them. Whilst the authority of his acts was not resisted, he was not eager to disparage his right by exposing the need of a more exact definition. The opinions which Pius IX was anxiously promoting were not the mere fruit of his private meditations; they belonged to the doctrines of a great party, which was busily pursuing its own objects, and had not been always the party of the Pope. In the days of his trouble he had employed an advocate; and the advocate had absorbed the client. During his exile a Jesuit had asked his approbation for a Review, to be conducted by the best talents of the Order, and to be devoted to the papal cause; and he had warmly embraced the idea, less, it should seem, as a prince than as a divine. There were his sovereign rights to maintain; but there was also a doctrinaire interest, there were reminiscences of study as well as practical objects that recommended the project. In these personal views the Pope was not quite consistent. He had made himself the idol of Italian patriots, and of the liberal French Catholics; he had set Theiner to vindicate the suppresser of the Jesuits; and Rosmini, the most enlightened priest in Italy, had been his trusted friend. After his restoration he submitted to other influences; and the writers of the *Civiltà Cattolica*, which followed him to Rome and became his acknowledged organ, acquired power over his mind. These men were not identified with their Order. Their General, Roothan, had disliked the plan of the Review, foreseeing that the Society would be held responsible for writings which it did not approve, and would forfeit the flexibility in adapting itself to the moods of different countries, which is one of the secrets of its prosperity. The Pope arranged the matter by taking the writers under his own protection, and giving to them a sort of exemption and partial immunity under the rule of their Order. They are set apart from other Jesuits; they are assisted and supplied from the literary resources of the Order, and are animated more than any of its other writers by its genuine and characteristic spirit; but they act on their own judgment under the guidance of the Pope, and are a bodyguard, told off from the army, for the personal protection of the Sovereign. It is their easy function to fuse into one system the interests and ideas of the Pope and those of their Society. The result has been, not to weaken by compromise and accommodation, but to intensify both. The prudence and sagacity which are sustained in the government of the Jesuits by their complicated checks on power, and their consideration for the interests of the Order under many various conditions, do not always restrain men who are partially emancipated from its rigorous discipline and subject to a more capricious rule. They were chosen in their capacity as Jesuits, for the sake of the peculiar spirit which their system develops. The Pope appointed them on account of that devotion to himself which is a quality of the Order, and relieved them from some of the restraints which it imposes. He wished for something more papal than other Jesuits; and he himself became more subject to the Jesuits than other pontiffs. He made them a channel of his influence, and became an instrument of their own.

The Jesuits had continued to gain ground in Rome ever since the Pope's return. They had suffered more than others in the revolution that dethroned him; and they had their reward in the restoration. They had long been held in check by the Dominicans; but the theology of the Dominicans had been discountenanced and their spirit broken in 1854, when a doctrine which they had contested for centuries was proclaimed a dogma of faith. In the strife for the Pope's temporal dominion the Jesuits were most zealous; and they were busy in the preparation and in the defence of the Syllabus. They were connected with every measure for which the Pope most cared; and their divines became the oracles of the Roman congregations. The papal infallibility had been always their favourite doctrine. Its adoption by the Council promised to give to their theology official warrant, and to their Order the supremacy in the Church. They were now in power; and they snatched their opportunity when the Council was convoked.

Efforts to establish this doctrine had been going on for years. The dogmatic decree of 1854 involved it so distinctly that its formal recognition seemed to be only a question of time and zeal. People even said that it was the real object of that decree to create a precedent which should make it impossible afterwards to deny papal infallibility. The Catechisms were altered, or new ones were substituted, in which it was taught. After 1852 the doctrine began to show itself in the Acts of provincial synods, and it was afterwards supposed that the bishops of those provinces were committed to it. One of these synods was held at Cologne; and three surviving members were in the Council at Rome, of whom two were in the minority, and the third had continued in his writings to oppose the doctrine of infallibility, after it had found its way into the Cologne decree. The suspicion that the Acts had been tampered with is suggested by what passed at the synod of Baltimore in 1866. The Archbishop of St. Louis signed the Acts of that synod under protest, and after obtaining a pledge that his protest would be inserted by the apostolic delegate. The pledge was not kept. "I complain," writes the archbishop, "that the promise which had been given was broken. The Acts ought to have been published in their integrity, or not at all."[1] This process was carried on so boldly that men understood what was to come. Protestants foretold that the Catholics would not rest until the Pope was formally declared infallible; and a prelate returning from the meeting of bishops at Rome in 1862 was startled at being asked by a clear-sighted friend whether infallibility had not been brought forward.

It was produced not then, but at the next great meeting, in 1867. The Council had been announced; and the bishops wished to present an address to the Pope. Haynald, Archbishop of Colocza, held the pen, assisted by Franchi, one of the clever Roman prelates and by some bishops, among whom were the Archbishop of Westminster and the Bishop of Orleans. An attempt was made to get the papal infallibility acknowledged in the address. Several bishops declared that they could not show themselves in their dioceses if they came back without having done anything for that doctrine. They were resisted in a way which made them complain that its very name irritated the French. Haynald refused their demand, but agreed to insert the well-known words of the Council of Florence; and the bishops did not go away empty-handed.

A few days before this attempt was made, the *Civiltà Cattolica* had begun to agitate, by proposing that Catholics

---

[1] Fidem mihi datam non servatam fuisse queror. Acta supprimere, aut integra dare oportebat. He says also: Omnia ad nutum delegati Apostolici fiebant.

should bind themselves to die, if need be, for the truth of the doctrine; and the article was printed on a separate sheet, bearing the papal *imprimatur*, and distributed widely. The check administered by Haynald and his colleagues brought about a lull in the movement; but the French bishops had taken alarm, and Maret, the most learned of them, set about the preparation of his book.

During the winter of 1868-69 several commissions were created in Rome to make ready the materials for the Council. The dogmatic commission included the Jesuits Perrone, Schrader, and Franzelin. The question of infallibility was proposed to it by Cardoni, Archbishop of Edessa, in a dissertation which, having been revised, was afterwards published, and accepted by the leading Roman divines as an adequate exposition of their case. The dogma was approved unanimously, with the exception of one vote, Alzog of Freiberg being the only dissentient. When the other German divines who were in Rome learned the scheme that was on foot in the Dogmatic Commission, they resolved to protest, but were prevented by some of their colleagues. They gave the alarm in Germany. The intention to proclaim infallibility at the Council was no longer a secret. The first bishop who made the wish public was Fessler of St. Pölten. His language was guarded, and he only prepared his readers for a probable contingency; but he was soon followed by the Bishop of Nîmes, who thought the discussion of the dogma superfluous, and foreshadowed a vote by acclamation. The *Civiltà* on the 6th of February gave utterance to the hope that the Council would not hesitate to proclaim the dogma and confirm the Syllabus in less than a month. Five days later the Pope wrote to some Venetians who had taken a vow to uphold his infallibility, encouraging their noble resolution to defend his supreme authority and all his rights. Until the month of May Cardinal Antonelli's confidential language to diplomatists was that the dogma was to be proclaimed, and that it would encounter no difficulty.

Cardinal Reisach was to have been the President of the Council. As Archbishop of Munich he had allowed himself and his diocese to be governed by the ablest of all the ultramontane divines. During his long residence in Rome he rose to high estimation, because he was reputed to possess the secret, and to have discovered the vanity, of German science. He had amused himself with Christian antiquities; and his friendship for the great explorer De' Rossi brought him for a time under suspicion of liberality. But later he became unrelenting in his ardour for the objects of the *Civiltà*, and regained the confidence of the Pope. The German bishops complained that he betrayed their interests, and that their church had suffered mischief from his paramount influence. But in Rome his easy temper and affable manners made him friends; and the Court knew that there was no cardinal on whom it was so safe to rely.

Fessler, the first bishop who gave the signal of the intended definition, was appointed Secretary. He was esteemed a learned man in Austria, and he was wisely chosen to dispel the suspicion that the conduct of the Council was to be jealously retained in Roman hands, and to prove that there are qualities by which the confidence of the Court could be won by men of a less favoured nation. Besides the President and Secretary, the most conspicuous of the Pope's theological advisers was a German. At the time when Passaglia's reputation was great in Rome, his companion Clement Schrader shared the fame of his solid erudition. When Passaglia fell into disgrace, his friend smote him with reproaches and intimated the belief that he would follow the footsteps of Luther and debauch a nun. Schrader is the most candid and consistent asserter of the papal claims. He does not shrink from the consequences of the persecuting theory; and he has given the most authentic and unvarnished exposition of the Syllabus. He was the first who spoke out openly what others were variously attempting to compromise or to conceal. While the Paris Jesuits got into trouble for extenuating the Roman doctrine, and had to be kept up to the mark by an abbé who reminded them that the Pope, as a physical person, and without co-operation of the Episcopate, is infallible, Schrader proclaimed that his will is supreme even against the joint and several opinions of the bishops.[2]

When the proceedings of the dogmatic commission, the acts of the Pope, and the language of French and Austrian bishops, and of the press serving the interests of Rome, announced that the proclamation of infallibility had ceased to be merely the aspiration of a party and was the object of a design deliberately set on foot by those to whom the preparation and management of the Council pertained, men became aware that an extraordinary crisis was impending, and that they needed to make themselves familiar with an unforeseen problem. The sense of its gravity made slow progress. The persuasion was strong among divines that the episcopate would not surrender to a party which was odious to many of them; and politicians were reluctant to believe that schemes were ripening such as Fessler described, schemes intended to alter the relations between Church and State. When the entire plan was made public by the *Allgemeine Zeitung* in March 1869, many refused to be convinced.

It happened that a statesman was in office who had occasion to know that the information was accurate. The Prime Minister of Bavaria, Prince Hohenlohe, was the brother of a cardinal; the University of Munich was represented on the Roman commissions by an illustrious scholar; and the news of the thing that was preparing came through trustworthy channels. On the 9th of April Prince Hohenlohe sent out a diplomatic circular on the subject to the Council. He pointed out that it was not called into existence by any purely theological emergency, and that the one dogma which was to be brought before it involved all those claims which cause collisions between Church and State, and threaten the liberty and the security of governments. Of the five Roman Commissions, one was appointed for the express purpose of dealing with the mixed topics common to religion and to politics. Besides infallibility and politics, the Council was

---

[2] Citra et contra singulorum suffragia, imo praeter et supra omnium vota pontificis solius declarationi atque sententiae validam vim atque irreformabilem adesse potestatem.

to be occupied with the Syllabus, which is in part directed against maxims of State. The avowed purpose of the Council being so largely political, the governments could not remain indifferent to its action; lest they should be driven afterwards to adopt measures which would be hostile, it would be better at once to seek an understanding by friendly means and to obtain assurance that all irritating deliberations should be avoided, and no business touching the State transacted except in presence of its representatives. He proposed that the governments should hold a conference to arrange a plan for the protection of their common interest.

Important measures proposed by small States are subject to suspicion of being prompted by a greater Power. Prince Hohenlohe, as a friend of the Prussian alliance, was supposed to be acting in this matter in concert with Berlin. This good understanding was suspected at Vienna; for the Austrian Chancellor was more conspicuous as an enemy of Prussia than Hohenlohe as a friend. Count Beust traced the influence of Count Bismarck in the Bavarian circular. He replied, on behalf of the Catholic empire of Austria, that there were no grounds to impute political objects to the Council, and that repression and not prevention was the only policy compatible with free institutions. After the refusal of Austria, the idea of a conference was dismissed by the other Powers; and the first of the storm clouds that darkened the horizon of infallibility passed without breaking.

Although united action was abandoned, the idea of sending ambassadors to the Council still offered the most inoffensive and amicable means of preventing the danger of subsequent conflict. Its policy or impolicy was a question to be decided by France. Several bishops, and Cardinal Bonnechose among the rest, urged the Government to resume its ancient privilege, and send a representative. But two powerful parties, united in nothing else, agreed in demanding absolute neutrality. The democracy wished that no impediment should be put in the way of an enterprise which promised to sever the connection of the State with the Church. M. Ollivier set forth this opinion in July 1868, in a speech which was to serve him in his candidature for office; and in the autumn of 1869 it was certain that he would soon be in power. The ministers could not insist on being admitted to the Council, where they were not invited, without making a violent demonstration in a direction they knew would not be followed. The ultramontanes were even more eager than their enemies to exclude an influence that might embarrass their policy. The Archbishop of Paris, by giving the same advice, settled the question. He probably reckoned on his own power of mediating between France and Rome. The French Court long imagined that the dogma would be set aside, and that the mass of the French bishops opposed it. At last they perceived that they were mistaken, and the Emperor said to Cardinal Bonnechose, "You are going to give your signature to decrees already made." He ascertained the names of the bishops who would resist; and it was known that he was anxious for their success. But he was resolved that it should be gained by them, and not by the pressure of his diplomacy at the cost of displeasing the Pope. The Minister of Foreign Affairs and his chief secretary were counted by the Court of Rome among its friends; and the ordinary ambassador started for his post with instructions to conciliate, and to run no risk of a quarrel. He arrived at Rome believing that there would be a speculative conflict between the extremes of Roman and German theology, which would admit of being reconciled by the safer and more sober wisdom of the French bishops, backed by an impartial embassy. His credulity was an encumbrance to the cause which it was his mission and his wish to serve.

In Germany the plan of penetrating the Council with lay influence took strange form. It was proposed that the German Catholics should be represented by King John of Saxony. As a Catholic and a scholar, who had shown, in his Commentary on Dante, that he had read St. Thomas, and as a prince personally esteemed by the Pope, it was conceived that his presence would be a salutary restraint. It was an impracticable idea; but letters which reached Rome during the winter raised an impression that the King regretted that he could not be there. The opinion of Germany would still have some weight if the North and South, which included more than thirteen millions of Catholics, worker together. It was the policy of Hohenlohe to use this united force, and the ultramontanes learned to regard him as a very formidable antagonist. When their first great triumph, in the election of the Commission on Doctrine, was accomplished, the commentary of a Roman prelate was, "Che colpo per il Principe Hohenlohe!" The Bavarian envoy in Rome did not share the views of his chief, and he was recalled in November. His successor had capacity to carry out the known policy of the prince; but early in the winter the ultramontanes drove Hohenlohe from office, and their victory, though it was exercised with moderation, and was not followed by a total change of policy, neutralised the influence of Bavaria in the Council.

The fall of Hohenlohe and the abstention of France hampered the Federal Government of Northern Germany. For its Catholic subjects, and ultimately in view of the rivalry with France, to retain the friendship of the papacy is a fixed maxim at Berlin. Count Bismarck laid down the rule that Prussia should display no definite purpose in a cause which was not her own, but should studiously keep abreast of the North German bishops. Those bishops neither invoked, nor by their conduct invited, the co-operation of the State; and its influence would have been banished from the Council but for the minister who represented it in Rome. The vicissitudes of a General Council are so far removed from the normal experience of statesmen that they could not well be studied or acted upon from a distance. A government that strictly controlled and dictated the conduct of its envoy was sure to go wrong, and to frustrate action by theory. A government that trusted the advice of its minister present on the spot enjoyed a great advantage. Baron Arnim was favourably situated. A Catholic belonging to any but the ultramontane school would have been less willingly listened to in Rome than a Protestant who was a conservative in politics, and whose regard for the interests of religion was so undamaged by the sectarian taint that he was known to be sincere in the wish that Catholics should have cause to rejoice in the prosperity of their Church. The apathy of Austria and the vacillation of France contributed to his influence, for he enjoyed the confidence of bishops from both countries; and he was able to guide his own government in its course towards the Council.

The English Government was content to learn more and to speak less than the other Powers at Rome. The usual distrust of the Roman Court towards a Liberal ministry in England was increased at the moment by the measure which the Catholics had desired and applauded. It seemed improbable to men more solicitous for acquired rights than for general political principle, that Protestant statesmen who disestablished their own Church could feel a very sincere interest in the welfare of another. Ministers so utopian as to give up solid goods for an imaginary righteousness seemed, as practical advisers, open to grave suspicion. Mr. Gladstone was feared as the apostle of those doctrines to which Rome owes many losses. Public opinion in England was not prepared to look on papal infallibility as a matter of national concern, more than other dogmas which make enemies to Catholicism. Even if the Government could have admitted the Prussian maxim of keeping in line with the bishops, it would have accomplished nothing. The English bishops were divided; but the Irish bishops, who are the natural foes of the Fenian plot, were by an immense majority on the ultramontane side. There was almost an ostentation of care on the part of the Government to avoid the appearance of wishing to influence the bishops or the Court of Rome, When at length England publicly concurred in the remonstrances of France, events had happened which showed that the Council was raising up dangers for both Catholic and liberal interests. It was a result so easy to foresee, that the Government had made it clear from the beginning that its extreme reserve was not due to indifference.

The lesser Catholic Powers were almost unrepresented in Rome. The government of the Regent of Spain possessed no moral authority over bishops appointed by the Queen; and the revolution had proved so hostile to the clergy that they were forced to depend on the Pope. Diplomatic relations being interrupted, there was nothing to restrain them from seeking favour by unqualified obedience.

Portugal had appointed the Count de Lavradio ambassador to the Council; but when he found that he was alone he retained only the character of envoy to the Holy See. He had weight with the small group of Portuguese bishops; but he died before he could be of use, and they drifted into submission.

Belgium was governed by M. Frère Orban, one of the most anxious and laborious enemies of the hierarchy, who had no inducement to interfere with an event which justified his enmity, and was, moreover, the unanimous wish of the Belgium Episcopate. When Protestant and Catholic Powers joined in exhorting Rome to moderation, Belgium was left out. Russia was the only Power that treated the Church with actual hostility during the Council, and calculated the advantage to be derived from decrees which would intensify the schism.

Italy was more deeply interested in the events at Rome than any other nation. The hostility of the clergy was felt both in the political and financial difficulties of the kingdom; and the prospect of conciliation would suffer equally from decrees confirming the Roman claims, or from an invidious interposition of the State. Public opinion watched the preparations for the Council with frivolous disdain; but the course to be taken was carefully considered by the Menabrea Cabinet. The laws still subsisted which enabled the State to interfere in religious affairs; and the government was legally entitled to prohibit the attendance of the bishops at the Council, or to recall them from it. The confiscated church property was retained by the State, and the claims of the episcopate were not yet settled. More than one hundred votes on which Rome counted belonged to Italian subjects. The means of applying administrative pressure were therefore great, though diplomatic action was impossible.

The Piedmontese wished that the resources of their ecclesiastical jurisprudence should be set in motion. But Minghetti, who had lately joined the Ministry, warmly advocated the opinion that the supreme principle of the liberty of the Church ought to override the remains of the older legislation, in a State consistently free; and, with the disposition of the Italians to confound Catholicism with the hierarchy, the policy of abstention was a triumph of liberality. The idea of Prince Hohenlohe, that religion ought to be maintained in its integrity and not only in its independence, that society is interested in protecting the Church even against herself, and that the enemies of her liberty are ecclesiastical as well as political, could find no favour in Italy. During the session of 1869, Menabrea gave no pledge to Parliament as to the Council; and the bishops who inquired whether they would be allowed to attend it were left unanswered until October. Menabrea then explained in a circular that the right of the bishops to go to the Council proceeded from the liberty of conscience, and was not conceded under the old privileges of the crown, or as a favour that could imply responsibility for what was to be done. If the Church was molested in her freedom, excuse would be given for resisting the incorporation of Rome. It the Council came to decisions injurious to the safety of States, it would be attributed to the unnatural conditions created by the French occupation, and might be left to the enlightened judgment of Catholics.

It was proposed that the fund realised by the sale of the real property of the religious corporations should be administered for religious purposes by local boards of trustees representing the Catholic population, and that the State should abdicate in their favour its ecclesiastical patronage, and proceed to discharge the unsettled claims of the clergy. So great a change in the plans by which Sella and Rattazzi had impoverished the Church in 1866 and 1867 would, if frankly carried into execution, have encouraged an independent spirit among the Italian bishops; and the reports of the prefects represented about thirty of them as being favourable to conciliation. But the Ministry fell in November, and was succeeded by an administration whose leading members, Lanza and Sella, were enemies of religion. The Court of Rome was relieved from a serious peril.

The only European country whose influence was felt in the attitude of its bishops was one whose government sent out no diplomatists. While the Austrian Chancellor regarded the issue of the Council with a profane and supercilious eye, and so much indifference prevailed at Vienna that it was said that the ambassador at Rome did not read the decrees, and that Count Beust did not read his despatches, the Catholic statesmen in Hungary were intent on effecting a revolution in the Church. The system which was about to culminate in the proclamation of infallibility, and which tended to absorb all power from the circumference into the centre, and to substitute authority for autonomy, had begun at the lower extremities of the hierarchical scale. The laity, which once had its share in the administration of Church property and in the deliberations of the clergy, had been gradually compelled to give up its rights to the priesthood, the priests to the bishops, and the bishops to the Pope. Hungary undertook to redress the process, and to correct centralised absolutism by self-government. In a memorandum drawn up in April 1848, the bishops imputed the decay of religion to the exclusion of the people from the management of all Church affairs, and proposed that whatever is not purely spiritual should be conducted by mixed boards, including lay representatives elected by the congregations. The war of the revolution and the reaction checked this design; and the Concordat threw things more than ever into clerical hands. The triumph of the liberal party after the peace of Prague revived the movements; and Eötvös called on the bishops to devise means of giving to the laity a share and an interest in religious concerns. The bishops agreed unanimously to the proposal of Deák, that the laity should have the majority in the boards of administration; and the new constitution of the Hungarian Church was adopted by the Catholic Congress on the 17th of October 1869, and approved by the King on the 25th. The ruling idea of this great measure was to make the laity supreme in all that is not liturgy and dogma, in patronage, property, and education; to break down clerical exclusiveness and government control; to deliver the people from the usurpations of the hierarchy, and the Church from the usurpations of the State. It was an attempt to reform the Church by constitutional principles, and to crush ultramontanism by crushing Gallicanism. The Government, which had originated the scheme, was ready to surrender its privileges to the newly-constituted authorities; and the bishops acted in harmony with the ministers and with public opinion. Whilst this good understanding lasted, and while the bishops were engaged in applying the impartial principles of self-government at home, there was a strong security that they would not accept decrees that would undo their work. Infallibility would not only condemn their system, but destroy their position. As the winter advanced the influence of these things became apparent. The ascendency which the Hungarian bishops acquired from the beginning was due to other causes.

The political auspices under which the Council opened were very favourable to the papal cause. The promoters of infallibility were able to coin resources of the enmity which was shown to the Church. The danger which came to them from within was averted. The policy of Hohenlohe, which was afterwards revived by Daru, had been, for a time, completely abandoned by Europe. The battle between the papal and the episcopal principle could come off undisturbed, in closed lists. Political opposition there was none; but the Council had to be governed under the glare of inevitable publicity, with a free press in Europe, and hostile views prevalent in Catholic theology. The causes which made religious science utterly powerless in the strife, and kept it from grappling with the forces arrayed against it, are of deeper import than the issue of the contest itself.

While the voice of the bishops grew louder in praise of the Roman designs, the Bavarian Government consulted the universities, and elicted from the majority of the Munich faculty an opinion that the dogma of infallibility would be attended with serious danger to society. The author of the Bohemian pamphlet affirmed that it had not the conditions which would enable it ever to become the object of a valid definition. Janus compared the primacy, as it was known to the Fathers of the Church, with the ultramontane ideal, and traced the process of transformation through a long series of forgeries. Maret published his book some weeks after Janus and the Reform. It had been revised by several French bishops and divines, and was to serve as a vindication of the Sorbonne and the Gallicans, and as the manifesto of men who were to be present at the Council. It had not the merit of novelty or the fault of innovation, but renewed with as little offence as possible the language of the old French school.[3] While Janus treated infallibility as the critical symptom of an ancient disease, Maret restricted his argument to what was directly involved in the defence of the Gallican position. Janus held that the doctrine was so firmly rooted and so widely supported in the existing constitution of the Church, that much must be modified before a genuine Œcumenical Council could be celebrated. Maret clung to the belief that the real voice of the Church would make itself heard at the Vatican. In direct contradiction with Janus, he kept before him the one practical object, to gain assent by making his views acceptable even to the unlearned.

At the last moment a tract appeared which has been universally attributed to Döllinger, which examined the evidences relied on by the infallibilists, and stated briefly the case against them. It pointed to the inference that their theory is not merely founded on an illogical and uncritical habit, but on unremitting dishonesty in the use of texts. This

---

[3] Nous restons dans les doctrines de Bossuet parce que nous les croyons généralement vraies; nous les défendons parce qu'elles sont attaquées, et qu'un parti puissant veut les faire condamner Ces doctrines de l'épiscopat français, de l'école de Paris, de notre vieille Sorbonne, se ramènent pour nous á trois propositions, à trois vérités fondamentales· 1° l'Eglise est une monarchie efficacement tempérée d'aristocracie, 2° la souveraineté spirituelle est essentiellement composée de ces deux éléments quoique le second soit subordonné au premier; 3° le concours de ces éléments est nécessaire pour établir la règle absolue de la foi, c'est-à-dire, pour constituer l'acte par excellence de la souveraineté spirituelle.

was coming near the secret of the whole controversy, and the point that made the interference of the Powers appear the only availing resource. For the sentiment on which infallibility is founded could not be reached by argument, the weapon of human reason, but resided in conclusions transcending evidence, and was the inaccessible postulate rather than demonstrable consequence of a system of religious faith. The two doctrines opposed, but never met each other. It was as much an instinct of the ultramontane theory to elude the tests of science as to resist the control of States. Its opponents, baffled and perplexed by the serene vitality of a view which was impervious to proof, saw want of principle where there was really a consistent principle, and blamed the ultramontane divines for that which was of the essence of ultramontane divinity. How it came that no appeal to revelation or tradition, to reason or conscience, appeared to have any bearing whatever on the issue is a mystery which Janus and Maret and Döllinger's reflections left unexplained.

The resources of mediæval learning were too slender to preserve an authentic record of the growth and settlement of Catholic doctrine. Many writings of the Fathers were interpolated; others were unknown, and spurious matter was accepted in their place. Books bearing venerable names — Clement, Dionysius, Isidore — were forged for the purpose of supplying authorities for opinions that lacked the sanction of antiquity. When detection came, and it was found that fraud had been employed in sustaining doctrines bound up with the peculiar interests of Rome and of the religious Orders, there was an inducement to depreciate the evidences of antiquity, and to silence a voice that bore obnoxious testimony. The notion of tradition underwent a change; it was required to produce what it had not preserved. The Fathers had spoken of the unwritten teaching of the apostles, which was to be sought in the churches they had founded, of esoteric doctrines, and views which must be of apostolic origin because they are universal, of the inspiration of general Councils, and a revelation continued beyond the New Testament. But the Council of Trent resisted the conclusions which this language seemed to countenance, and they were left to be pursued by private speculation. One divine deprecated the vain pretence of arguing from Scripture, by which Luther could not be confuted, and the Catholics were losing ground; [4] and at Trent a speaker averred that Christian doctrine had been so completely determined by the Schoolmen that there was no further need to recur to Scripture. This idea is not extinct, and Perrone uses it to explain the inferiority of Catholics as Biblical critics.[5] If the Bible is inspired, says Peresius, still more must its interpretation be inspired. It must be interpreted variously, says the Cardinal of Cusa, according to necessity; a change in the opinion of the Church implies a change in the will of God.[6] One of the greatest Tridentine divines declares that a doctrine must be true if the Church believes it, without any warrant from Scripture. According to Petavius, the general belief of Catholics at a given time is the work of God, and of higher authority than all antiquity and all the Fathers. Scripture may be silent, and tradition contradictory, but the Church is independent of both. Any doctrine which Catholic divines commonly assert, without proof, to be revealed, must be taken as revealed. The testimony of Rome, as the only remaining apostolic Church, is equivalent to an unbroken chain of tradition.[7] In this way, after Scripture had been subjugated, tradition itself was deposed; and the constant

---

[4] Si hujus doctrinae memores fuissemus, haereticos scil cet non esse infirmandos vel convincendos ex Scripturis, meliore sane loco essent res nostrae; sed dum ostentandi ingenii et eruditionis gratia cum Luthero in certamen descenditur Scripturarum, excitatum est hoc, quod, proh dolor! nunc videmus, incendium (Pighius).
[5] Catholici non admondum solliciti sunt de critica et hermeneutica biblica . . . Ipsi, ut verbo dicam, jam habent aedificium absolutum sane ac perfectum, in cujus possessione firme ac secure consistant.
[6] Praxis Ecclesiae uno tempore interpretatur Scripturam uno modo et alio tempore alio modo, nam intellectus currit cum praxi. — Mutato judicio Ecclesiae mutatum est Dei judicium.
[7] Si viri ecclesiastici, sive in concilio oecumenico congregati, sive seorsim scribentes, aliquod dogma vel unamquamque consuetudinem uno ore ac diserte testantur ex traditione divina haberi, sine dubio certum argumentum est, uti ita esse credamus. — Ex testimonio hujus solius Ecclesiae sumi potest certum argumentum ad probandas apostolicas traditiones (Bellarmine).

belief of the past yielded to the general conviction of the present. And, as antiquity had given way to universality, universality made way for authority. The Word of God and the authority of the Church came to be declared the two sources of religious knowledge. Divines of this school, after preferring the Church to the Bible, preferred the modern Church to the ancient, and ended by sacrificing both to the Pope. "We have not the authority of Scripture," wrote Prierias in his defence of Indulgences, "but we have the higher authority of the Roman pontiffs."[8] A bishop who had been present at Trent confesses that in matters of faith he would believe a single Pope rather than a thousand Fathers, saints, and doctors.[9] The divine training develops an orthodox instinct in the Church, which shows itself in the lives of devout but ignorant men more than in the researches of the learned, and teaches authority not to need the help of science, and not to heed its opposition. All the arguments by which theology supports a doctrine may prove to be false, without diminishing the certainty of its truth. The Church has not obtained, and is not bound to sustain it, by proof. She is supreme over fact as over doctrine, as Fénelon argues, because she is the supreme expounder of tradition, which is a chain of facts.[10] Accordingly, the organ of one ultramontane bishop lately declared that infallibility could be defined without arguments; and the Bishop of Nîmes thought

---

[8] Veniae sive indulgentiae autoritate Scripturae nobis non innotuere, sed autoritate ecclesiae Romanae Romanorumque Pontificum, quae major est.

[9] Ego, ut ingenue fatear, plus uni summo pontifici crederem, in his, quae fidei mysteria tangunt, quam mille Augustinis, Hieronymis, Gregoriis (Cornelius Mussus).

[10] The two views contradict each other; but they are equally characteristic of the endeavour to emancipate the Church from the obligation of proof. Fénelon says: "Oseroit-on soutenir que l'Église après avoir mal raisonné sur tous les textes, et les avoir pris à contre-sens, est tout à coup saisie par un enthousiasme aveugle, pour juger bien, en raisonnant mal?" And Mohler: "Die altesten okumenischen Synoden fuhrten daher fur ihre dogmatischen Beschlusse nicht einmal bestimmte biblische Stellen an; und die katholischen Theologen lehren mit allgemeiner Uebereinstimmung und ganz aus dem Geiste der Kirche heraus, dass selbst die biblische Beweisfuhrung eines fur untruglich gehaltenen Beschlusses nicht untruglich sei, sondern eben nur das ausgesprochene Dogma selbst."

that the decision need not be preceded by long and careful discussion. The Dogmatic Commission of the Council proclaims that the existence of tradition has nothing to do with evidence, and that objections taken from history are not valid when contradicted by ecclesiastical decrees.[11] Authority must conquer history.

This inclination to get rid of evidence was specially associated with the doctrine of papal infallibility, because it is necessary that the Popes themselves should not testify against their own claim. They may be declared superior to all other authorities, but not to that of their own see. Their history is not irrelevant to the question of their rights. It could not be disregarded; and the provocation to alter or to deny its testimony was so urgent that men of piety and learning became a prey to the temptation of deceit. When it was discovered in the manuscript of the *Liber Diurnus* that the Popes had for centuries condemned Honorius in their profession of faith, Cardinal Bona, the most eminent man in Rome, advised that the book should be suppressed if the difficulty could not be got over; and it was suppressed accordingly.[12] Men guilty of this kind of fraud would justify it by saying that their religion transcends the wisdom of philosophers, and cannot submit to the criticism of historians. If any fact manifestly contradicts a dogma, that is a warning to science to revise the evidence. There must be some defect in the materials or in the method. Pending its discovery, the true believer is constrained humbly but confidently to deny the fact.

The protest of conscience against this fraudulent piety grew loud and strong as the art of criticism became more certain. The use made of it by Catholics in the literature

---

[11] Cujuscumque ergo scientiae, etiam historiae ecclesiasticae conclusiones, Romanorum Pontificum infallibilitati adversantes, quo manifestius haec ex revelationis fontibus infertur, eo certius veluti totidem errores habendas esse consequitur.

[12] Cum in professione fidei electi pontificis damnetur Honorius Papa, ideo quia pravis haereticorum assertionibus fomentum impendit, si verba delineata sint vere in autographo, nec ex notis apparere possit, quomodo huic vulneri medelam offerat, praestat non divulgari opus.

of the present age, and their acceptance of the conditions of scientific controversy, seemed to ecclesiastical authorities a sacrifice of principle. A jealousy arose that ripened into antipathy. Almost every writer who really served Catholicism fell sooner or later under the disgrace or the suspicion of Rome. But its censures had lost efficacy; and it was found that the progress of literature could only be brought under control by an increase of authority. This could be obtained if a general council declared the decisions of the Roman congregations absolute, and the Pope infallible.

The division between the Roman and the Catholic elements in the Church made it hopeless to mediate between them; and it is strange that men who must have regarded each other as insincere Christians or as insincere Catholics, should not have perceived that the meeting in Council was an imposture. It may be that a portion, though only a small portion, of those who failed to attend, stayed away from that motive. But the view proscribed at Rome was not largely represented in the episcopate; and it was doubtful whether it would be manifested at all. The opposition did not spring from it, but maintained itself by reducing to the utmost the distance that separated it from the strictly Roman opinions, and striving to prevent the open conflict of principles. It was composed of ultramontanes in the mask of liberals, and of liberals in the mask of ultramontanes. Therefore the victory or defeat of the minority was not the supreme issue of the Council. Besides and above the definition of infallibility arose the question how far the experience of the actual encounter would open the eyes and search the hearts of the reluctant bishops, and how far their language and their attitude would contribute to the impulse of future reform. There was a point of view from which the failure of all attempts to avert the result by false issues and foreign intrusion, and the success of the measures which repelled conciliation and brought on an open struggle and an overwhelming triumph, were means to another and a more importunate end.

Two events occurred in the autumn which portended

trouble for the winter. On the 6th of September nineteen German bishops, assembled at Fulda, published a pastoral letter in which they affirmed that the whole episcopate was perfectly unanimous, that the Council would neither introduce new dogmas nor invade the civil province, and that the Pope intended its deliberations to be free. The patent and direct meaning of this declaration was that the bishops repudiated the design announced by the *Civiltà* and the *Allgemeine Zeitung*, and it was received at Rome with indignation. But it soon appeared that it was worded with studied ambiguity, to be signed by men of opposite opinions, and to conceal the truth. The Bishop of Mentz read a paper, written by a professor of Würzburg, against the wisdom of raising the question, but expressed his own belief in the dogma of papal infallibility; and when another bishop stated his disbelief in it, the Bishop of Paderborn assured him that Rome would soon strip him of his heretical skin. The majority wished to prevent the definition, if possible, without disputing the doctrine; and they wrote a private letter to the Pope warning him of the danger, and entreating him to desist. Several bishops who had signed the pastoral refused their signatures to the private letter. It caused so much dismay at Rome that its nature was carefully concealed; and a diplomatist was able to report, on the authority of Cardinal Antonelli, that it did not exist.

In the middle of November, the Bishop of Orleans took leave of his diocese in a letter which touched lightly on the learned questions connected with papal infallibility, but described the objections to the definition as of such a kind that they could not be removed. Coming from a prelate who was so conspicuous as a champion of the papacy, who had saved the temporal power and justified the Syllabus, this declaration unexpectedly altered the situation at Rome. It was clear that the definition would be opposed, and that the opposition would have the support of illustrious names.

The bishops who began to arrive early in November were received with the assurance that the alarm which had been raised was founded on phantoms. It appeared that nobody had dreamed of defining infallibility, or that, if the idea had been entertained at all, it had been abandoned. Cardinals Antonelli, Berardi, and De Luca, and the Secretary Fessler disavowed the *Civiltà*. The ardent indiscretion that was displayed beyond the Alps contrasted strangely with the moderation, the friendly candour, the majestic and impartial wisdom, which were found to reign in the higher sphere of the hierarchy. A bishop, afterwards noted among the opponents of the dogma, wrote home that the idea that infallibility was to be defined was entirely unfounded. It was represented as a mere fancy, got up in Bavarian newspapers, with evil intent; and the Bishop of Sura had been its dupe. The insidious report would have deserved contempt if it had caused a revival of obsolete opinions. It was a challenge to the Council to herald it with such demonstrations, and it unfortunately became difficult to leave it unnoticed. The decision must be left to the bishops. The Holy See could not restrain their legitimate ardour, if they chose to express it; but it would take no initiative. Whatever was done would require to be done with so much moderation as to satisfy everybody, and to avoid the offence of a party triumph. Some suggested that there should be no anathema for those who questioned the doctrine; and one prelate imagined that a formula could be contrived which even Janus could not dispute, and which yet would be found in reality to signify that the Pope is infallible. There was a general assumption that no materials existed for contention among the bishops, and that they stood united against the world.

Cardinal Antonelli openly refrained from connecting himself with the preparation of the Council, and surrounded himself with divines who were not of the ruling party. He had never learned to doubt the dogma itself; but he was keenly alive to the troubles it would bring upon him, and thought that the Pope was preparing a repetition of the difficulties which followed the beginning of his pontificate. He was not trusted as a divine, or consulted on questions of theology; but he was expected to ward off unflinching skill.

The Pope exhorted the diplomatic corps to aid him in allaying the alarm of the infatuated Germans. He assured one diplomatist that the *Civiltà* did not speak in his name. He told another that he would sanction no proposition that could sow dissension among the bishops. He said to a third, "You come to be present at a scene of pacification." He described his object in summoning the Council to be to obtain a remedy for old abuses and for recent errors. More than once, addressing a group of bishops, he said that he would do nothing to raise disputes among them, and would be content with a declaration in favour of intolerance. He wished of course that Catholicism should have the benefit of toleration in England and Russia, but the principle must be repudiated by a Church holding the doctrine of exclusive salvation. The meaning of this intimation, that persecution would do as a substitute for infallibility, was that the most glaring obstacle to the definition would be removed if the Inquisition was recognised as consistent with Catholicism. Indeed it seemed that infallibility was a means to an end which could be obtained in other ways, and that he would have been satisfied with a decree confirming the twenty-third article of the Syllabus, and declaring that no Pope has ever exceeded the just bounds of his authority in faith, in politics, or in morals.[13]

Most of the bishops had allowed themselves to be reassured, when the Bull *Multiplices inter,* regulating the procedure at the Council, was put into circulation in the first days of December. The Pope assumed to himself the sole initiative in proposing topics, and the exclusive nomination of the officers of the Council. He invited the bishops to bring forward their own proposals, but required that they should submit them first of all to a Commission which was appointed by himself, and consisted half of Italians. If any proposal was allowed to pass by this Commission, it had still to obtain the sanction of the Pope, who could therefore exclude at

---

[13] That article condemns the following proposition: "Romani Pontifices et Concilia oecumenica a limitibus suae potestati recesserunt, jura Principum usurparunt, atque etiam in rebus fidei et morum definiendis errarunt."

will any topic, even if the whole Council wished to discuss it. Four elective Commissions were to mediate between the Council and the Pope. When a decree had been discussed and opposed, it was to be referred, together with the amendments, to one of these Commissions, where it was to be reconsidered, with the aid of divines. When it came back from the Commission with corrections and remarks, it was to be put to the vote without further debate. What the Council discussed was to be the work of unknown divines: what it voted was to be the work of a majority in a Commission of twenty-four. It was in the election of these Commissions that the episcopate obtained the chance of influencing the formation of its decrees. But the papal theologians retained their predominance, for they might be summoned to defend or alter their work in the Commission, from which the bishops who had spoken or proposed amendments were excluded. Practically, the right of initiative was the deciding point. Even if the first regulation had remained in force, the bishops could never have recovered the surprises, and the difficulty of preparing for unforeseen debates. The regulation ultimately broke down under the mistake of allowing the decree to be debated only once, and that in its crude state, as it came from the hands of the divines. The authors of the measure had not contemplated any real discussion. It was so unlike the way in which business was conducted at Trent, where the right of the episcopate was formally asserted, where the envoys were consulted, and the bishops discussed the questions in several groups before the general congregations, that the printed text of the Tridentine Regulation was rigidly suppressed. It was further provided that the reports of the speeches should not be communicated to the bishops; and the strictest secrecy was enjoined on all concerning the business of the Council. The bishops, being under no obligation to observe this rule, were afterwards informed that it bound them under grievous sin.

This important precept did not succeed in excluding the action of public opinion. It could be applied only to the debates; and many bishops spoke with greater energy and freedom before an assembly of their own order than they would have done if their words had been taken down by Protestants, to be quoted against them at home. But printed documents, distributed in seven hundred copies, could not be kept secret. The rule was subject to exceptions which destroyed its efficacy; and the Roman cause was discredited by systematic concealment, and advocacy that abounded in explanation and colour, but abstained from the substance of fact. Documents couched in the usual official language, being dragged into the forbidden light of day, were supposed to reveal dark mysteries. The secrecy of the debates had a bad effect in exaggerating reports and giving wide scope to fancy. Rome was not vividly interested in the discussions; but its cosmopolitan society was thronged with the several adherents of leading bishops, whose partiality compromised their dignity and envenomed their disputes. Everything that was said was repeated, inflated, and distorted. Whoever had a sharp word for an adversary, which could not be spoken in Council, knew of an audience that would enjoy and carry the matter. The battles of the Aula were fought over again, with anecdote, epigram, and fiction. A distinguished courtesy and nobleness of tone prevailed at the beginning. When the Archbishop of Halifax went down to his place on the 28th of December, after delivering the speech which taught the reality of the opposition, the Presidents bowed to him as he passed them. The denunciations of the Roman system by Strossmayer and Darboy were listened to in January without a murmur. Adversaries paid exorbitant compliments to each other, like men whose disagreements were insignificant, and who were one at heart. As the plot thickened, fatigue, excitement, friends who fetched and carried, made the tone more bitter. In February the Bishop of Laval described Dupanloup publicly as the centre of a conspiracy too shameful to be expressed in words, and professed that he would rather die than be associated with such iniquity. One of the minority described his opponents as having disported themselves on a certain occasion like a herd of cattle. By that time the whole temper of the Council had been changed; the Pope himself had gone into the arena; and violence of language and gesture had become an artifice adopted to hasten the end.

When the Council opened, many bishops were bewildered and dispirited by the Bull *Multiplices.* They feared that a struggle could not be averted, as, even if no dogmatic question was raised, their rights were cancelled in a way that would make the Pope absolute in dogma. One of the Cardinals caused him to be informed that the Regulation would be resisted. But Pius IX knew that in all that procession of 750 bishops one idea prevailed. Men whose word is powerful in the centres of civilisation, men who three months before were confronting martyrdom among barbarians, preachers at Notre Dame, professors from Germany, Republicans from Western America, men with every sort of training and every sort of experience, had come together as confident and as eager as the prelates of Rome itself, to hail the Pope infallible. Resistance was improbable, for it was hopeless. It was improbable that bishops who had refused no token of submission for twenty years would now combine to inflict dishonour on the Pope. In their address of 1867 they had confessed that he is the father and teacher of all Christians; that all the things he has spoken were spoken by St. Peter through him; that they would believe and teach all that he believed and taught. In 1854 they had allowed him to proclaim a dogma, which some of them dreaded and some opposed, but to which all submitted when he had decreed without the intervention of a Council. The recent display of opposition did not justify serious alarm. The Fulda bishops feared the consequences in Germany; but they affirmed that all were united, and that there would be no new dogma. They were perfectly informed of all that was being got ready in Rome. The words of their pastoral meant nothing if they did not mean that infallibility was no new dogma, and that all the bishops believed in it. Even the Bishop of Orleans avoided a direct attack on the doctrine, proclaimed his own devotion to the Pope, and promised that the Council would be a scene of concord.[14] It was certain that any real attempt that might be made to prevent the definition could be overwhelmed by the preponderance of those bishops whom the modern constitution of the Church places in dependence on Rome.

The only bishops whose position made them capable of resisting were the Germans and the French; and all that Rome would have to contend with was the modern liberalism and decrepit Gallicanism of France, and the science of Germany. The Gallican school was nearly extinct; it had no footing in other countries, and it was essentially odious to the liberals. The most serious minds of the liberal party were conscious that Rome was as dangerous to ecclesiastical liberty as Paris. But, since the Syllabus made it impossible to pursue the liberal doctrines consistently without collision with Rome, they had ceased to be professed with a robust and earnest confidence, and the party was disorganised. They set up the pretence that the real adversary of their opinions was not the Pope, but a French newspaper; and they fought the King's troops in the King's name. When the Bishop of Orleans made his declaration, they fell back, and left him to mount the breach alone. Montalembert, the most vigorous spirit among them, became isolated from his former friends, and accused them, with increasing vehemence, of being traitors to their principles. During the last disheartening year of his life he turned away from the clergy of his country, which was sunk in Romanism, and felt that the real abode of his opinions was on the Rhine.[15] It was only lately that the ideas

---

[14] J'en suis convaincu; à peine aurai-je touché la terre sacrée, à peine aurai-je baisé le tombeau des Apôtres, que je me sentirai dans la paix, hors de la bataille, au sein d'une assemblée présidée par un Père et composée de Frères. Là, tous les bruits expireront, toutes les ingérences téméraires cesseront, toutes les imprudences disparaîtront, les flots et les vents seront apaisés.

[15] Vous admirez sans doute beaucoup l'évêque d'Orléans, mais vous l'admireriez bien plus encore, si vous pouviez vous figurer l'abîme d'idolatrie où est tombé le clergé français. Cela dépasse tout ce que l'on aurait jamais pu l'imaginer aux jours de ma jeunesse, au temps de Frayssinous et de La Mennais. Le pauvre Mgr. Maret, pour avoir exposé des idées très modérées dans un langage plein d'urbanité et de charité, est traité publiquement dans les journaux soi-disant religieux d'hérésiarque et d'apostat, par les derniers de nos curés. De tous les mystères que présente en si grand nombre l'histoire de l'Église je n'en connais pas qui égale ou dépasse cette transformation si

of the Coblentz address, which had so deeply touched the sympathies of Montalembert, had spread widely in Germany. They had their seat in the universities; and their transit from the interior of lecture rooms to the outer world was laborious and slow. The invasion of Roman doctrines had given vigour and popularity to those which opposed them, but the growing influence of the universities brought them into direct antagonism with the episcopate. The Austrian bishops were generally beyond its reach, and the German bishops were generally at war with it. In December, one of the most illustrious of them said: "We bishops are absorbed in our work, and are not scholars. We sadly need the help of those that are. It is to be hoped that the Council will raise only such questions as can be dealt with competently by practical experience and common sense." The force that Germany wields in theology was only partially represented in its episcopate.

At the opening of the Council the known opposition consisted of four men. Cardinal Schwarzenberg had not published his opinion, but he made it known as soon as he came to Rome. He brought with him a printed paper, entitled *Desideria patribus Concilii oecumenici proponenda,* in which he adopted the ideas of the divines and canonists who are the teachers of his Bohemian clergy. He entreated the Council not to multiply unnecessary articles of faith, and in particular to abstain from defining papal infallibility, which was beset with difficulties, and would make the foundations of faith to tremble even in the devoutest souls. He pointed out that the Index could not continue on its present footing, and urged that the Church should seek her strength in the cultivation of liberty and learning, not in privilege and coercion; that she should rely on popular institutions, and

---

prompte et si complète de la France Catholique en une basse-cour de *l'anticamera du Vatican.* J'en serais encore plus désesperé qu'humilié, si là, comme partout dans les régions illuminées par la foi, la miséricorde et l'esperance ne se laissaient entrevoir à travers les ténèbres. "C'est du Rhin aujourd'hui que nous vient la lumière." L'Allemagne a été choisie pour opposer une digue à ce torrent de fanatisme servile que menaçait de tout engloutir (Nov. 7, 1869).

obtain popular support. He warmly advocated the system of autonomy that was springing up in Hungary.[16] Unlike Schwarzenberg, Dupanloup, and Maret, the Archbishop of Paris had taken no hostile step in reference to the Council, but he was feared the most of all the men expected at Rome. The Pope had refused to make him a cardinal, and had written to him a letter of reproof such as has seldom been received by a bishop. It was felt that he was hostile, not episodically, to a single measure, but to the peculiar spirit of this pontificate. He had none of the conventional prejudices and assumed antipathies which are congenial to the hierarchical mind. He was without passion or pathos or affectation; and he had good sense, a perfect temper, and an intolerable wit. It was characteristic of him that he made the Syllabus an occasion to impress moderation on the Pope: "Your blame has power, O Vicar of Jesus Christ; but your blessing is more potent still. God has raised you to the apostolic See between the two halves of this century, that you may absolve the one and inaugurate the other. Be it yours to reconcile reason with faith, liberty with authority, politics with the Church. From the height of that triple majesty with which religion, age, and misfortune adorn you, all that you do and all that you say reaches far, to disconcert or to encourage the nations. Give them from your large priestly

---

[16] Non solum ea quae ad scholas theologicas pertinent scholis relinquantur, sed etiam doctrinae quae a fidelibus pie tenentur et coluntur, sine gravi causa in codicem dogmatum ne inferantur In specie ne Concilium declaret vel definiat infallibilitatem Summi Pontificis, a doctissimis et prudentissimis fidelibus Sanctae sedi intime addictis, vehementer optatur. Gravia enim mala exinde oritura timent tum fidelibus tum infidelibus. Fideles enim, qui Primatum magisterii et jurisdictionis in Summo Pontifice ultro agnoscunt, quorum pietas et obedientia erga Sanctam Sedem nullo certe tempore major fuit, corde turbarentur magis quam erigerentur, ac si nunc demum fundamentum Ecclesiae et verae doctrinae stabiliendum sit; infideles vero novam calumniarum et derisionum materiam lucrarentur. Neque desunt, qui ejusmodi definitionem logice impossibilem vocant. . . . Nostris diebus defensio veritatis ac religionis tum praesertim efficax et fructuosa est, si sacerdotes a lege caeterorum civium minus recedunt, sed communibus omnium juribus utuntur, ita ut vis defensionis sit in veritate interna non per tutelam externae exemtionis. . . . Praesertim Ecclesia se scientiarum, quae hominem ornant perficiuntque, amicam et patronam exhibeat, probe noscens, omne verum a Deo esse, et profunda ac seria literarum studia opitulari fidei.

heart one word to amnesty the past, to reassure the present, and to open the horizons of the future."

The security into which many unsuspecting bishops had been lulled quickly disappeared; and they understood that they were in presence of a conspiracy which would succeed at once if they did not provide against acclamation, and must succeed at last if they allowed themselves to be caught in the toils of the Bull *Multiplices*. It was necessary to make sure that no decree should be passed without reasonable discussion, and to make a stand against the regulation. The first congregation, held on the 10th of December, was a scene of confusion; but it appeared that a bishop from the Turkish frontier had risen against the order of proceeding, and that the President had stopped him, saying that this was a matter decided by the Pope, and not submitted to the Council. The bishops perceived that they were in a snare. Some began to think of going home. Others argued that questions of Divine right were affected by the regulation, and that they were bound to stake the existence of the Council upon them. Many were more eager on this point of law than on the point of dogma, and were brought under the influence of the more clear-sighted men, with whom they would not have come in contact through any sympathy on the question of infallibility. The desire of protesting against the violation of privileges was an imperfect bond. The bishops had not yet learned to know each other; and they had so strongly impressed upon their flocks at home the idea that Rome ought to be trusted, that they were going to manifest the unity of the Church and to confound the insinuations of her enemies, that they were not quick to admit all the significance of the facts they found. Nothing vigorous was possible in a body of so loose a texture. The softer materials had to be eliminated, the stronger welded together by severe and constant pressure, before an opposition could be made capable of effective action. They signed protests that were of no effect. They petitioned; they did not resist.

It was seen how much Rome had gained by excluding the ambassadors; for this question of forms and regulations would have admitted the action of diplomacy. The idea of being represented at the Council was revived in France; and a weary negotiation began, which lasted several months, and accomplished nothing but delay. It was not till the policy of intervention had ignominiously failed, and till its failure had left the Roman court to cope with the bishops alone, that the real question was brought on for discussion. And as long as the chance remained that political considerations might keep infallibility out of the Council, the opposition abstained from declaring its real sentiments. Its union was precarious and delusive, but it lasted in this state long enough to enable secondary influences to do much towards supplying the place of principles.

While the protesting bishops were not committed against infallibility, it would have been possible to prevent resistance to the bull from becoming resistance to the dogma. The Bishop of Grenoble, who was reputed a good divine among his countrymen, was sounded in order to discover how far he would go; and it was ascertained that he admitted the doctrine substantially. At the same time, the friends of the Bishop of Orleans were insisting that he had questioned not the dogma but the definition; and Maret, in the defence of his book, declared that he attributed no infallibility to the episcopate apart from the Pope. If the bishops had been consulted separately, without the terror of a decree, it is probable that the number of those who absolutely rejected the doctrine would have been extremely small. There were many who had never thought seriously about it, or imagined that it was true in a pious sense, though not capable of proof in controversy. The possibility of an understanding seemed so near that the archbishop of Westminster, who held the Pope infallible apart from the episcopate, required that the words should be translated into French in the sense of independence, and not of exclusion. An ambiguous formula embodying the view common to both parties, or founded on mutual concession, would have done more for the liberty than the unity of opinion, and would not have strengthened the authority of the Pope. It was resolved to proceed with caution, putting in motion the strong machinery of Rome, and exhausting the advantages of organisation and foreknowledge.

The first act of the Council was to elect the Commission on Dogma. A proposal was made on very high authority that the list should be drawn up so as to represent the different opinions fairly, and to include some of the chief opponents. They would have been subjected to other influences than those which sustain party leaders; they would have been separated from their friends and brought into frequent contact with adversaries; they would have felt the strain of official responsibility; and the opposition would have been decapitated. If these sagacious counsels had been followed, the harvest of July might have been gathered in January, and the reaction that was excited in the long struggle that ensued might have been prevented. Cardinal de Angelis, who ostensibly managed the elections, and was advised by Archbishop Manning, preferred the opposite and more prudent course. He caused a lithographed list to be sent to all the bishops open to influence, from which every name was excluded that was not on the side of infallibility.

Meantime the bishops of several nations selected those among their countrymen whom they recommended as candidates. The Germans and Hungarians, above forty in number, assembled for this purpose under the presidency of Cardinal Schwarzenberg; and their meetings were continued, and became more and more important, as those who did not sympathise with the opposition dropped away. The French were divided into two groups, and met partly at Cardinal Mathieu's, partly at Cardinal Bonnechose's. A fusion was proposed, but was resisted, in the Roman interest, by Bonnechose. He consulted Cardinal Antonelli, and reported that the Pope disliked large meetings of bishops. Moreover, if all the French had met in one place, the opposition would have had the majority, and would have determined the choice of the candidates. They voted separately; and the Bonnechose list was represented to foreign bishops as the united choice of the French episcopate. The Mathieu group believed that this had been done fraudulently, and resolved to make their complaint to the Pope; but Cardinal Mathieu, seeing that a storm was rising, and that he would be called on to be the spokesman of his friends, hurried away to spend Christmas at Besançon. All the votes of his group were thrown away. Even the bishop of Grenoble, who had obtained twenty-nine votes at one meeting, and thirteen at the other, was excluded from the Commission. It was constituted as the managers of the election desired, and the first trial of strength appeared to have annihilated the opposition. The force under entire control of the court could be estimated from the number of votes cast blindly for candidates not put forward by their own countrymen, and unknown to others, who had therefore no recommendation but that of the official list. According to this test Rome could dispose of 550 votes.

The moment of this triumph was chosen for the production of an act already two months old, by which many ancient censures were revoked, and many were renewed. The legislation of the Middle Ages and of the sixteenth century appointed nearly two hundred cases by which excommunication was incurred *ipso facto*, without inquiry or sentence. They had generally fallen into oblivion, or were remembered as instances of former extravagance; but they had not been abrogated. and, as they were in part defensible, they were a trouble to timorous consciences. There was reason to expect that this question, which had often occupied the attention of the bishops, would be brought before the Council; and the demand for a reform could not have been withstood. The difficulty was anticipated by sweeping away as many censures as it was thought safe to abandon, and deciding, independently of the bishops, what must be retained. The Pope reserved to himself alone the faculty of absolving from the sin of harbouring or defending the members of any sect, of causing priests to be tried by secular courts, of violating asylum or alienating the real property of the Church. The prohibition of anonymous writing was restricted to works on theology, and the excommunication hitherto incurred by reading books which are on the Index was confined to readers of heretical books. This Constitution had no other immediate effect than to indicate the prevailing spirit, and to increase the difficulties of the partisans of Rome. The organ of the Archbishop of Cologne justified the last provision by saying, that it does not forbid the works of Jews, for Jews are not heretics; nor the heretical tracts and newspapers, for they are not books; nor listening to heretical books read aloud, for hearing is not reading.

At the same time, the serious work of the Council was begun. A long dogmatic decree was distributed, in which the special theological, biblical, and philosophical opinions of the school now dominant in Rome were proposed for ratification. It was so weak a composition that it was as severely criticised by the Romans as by the foreigners; and there were Germans whose attention was first called to its defects by an Italian cardinal. The disgust with which the text of the first decree was received had not been foreseen. No real discussion had been expected. The Council hall, admirable for occasions of ceremony, was extremely ill adapted for speaking, and nothing would induce the Pope to give it up. A public session was fixed for the 6th of January, and the election of Commissions was to last till Christmas. It was evident that nothing would be ready for the session, unless the decree was accepted without debate, or infallibility adopted by acclamation.

Before the Council had been assembled a fortnight, a store of discontent had accumulated which it would have been easy to avoid. Every act of the Pope, the Bull *Multiplices,* the declaration of censures, the text of the proposed decree, even the announcement that the Council should be dissolved in case of his death, had seemed an injury or an insult to the episcopate. These measures undid the favourable effect of the caution with which the bishops had been received. They did what the dislike of infallibility alone would not have done. They broke the spell of veneration for Pius IX which fascinated the Catholic Episcopate. The jealousy with which he guarded his prerogative in the appointment of officers, and of the great Commission, the pressure during the elections, the prohibition of national meetings, the refusal to hold debates in a hall where they could be heard, irritated and alarmed many bishops. They suspected that they had been summoned for the very purpose they had indignantly denied, to make the papacy more absolute by abdicating in favour of the official prelature of Rome. Confidence gave way to a great despondency, and a state of feeling was aroused which prepared the way for actual opposition when the time should come.

Before Christmas the Germans and the French were grouped nearly as they remained to the end. After the flight of Cardinal Mathieu, and the refusal of Cardinal Bonnechose to coalesce, the friends of the latter gravitated towards the Roman centre, and the friends of the former held their meetings at the house of the Archbishop of Paris. They became, with the Austro-German meeting under Cardinal Schwarzenberg, the strength and substance of the party that opposed the new dogma; but there was little intercourse between the two, and their exclusive nationality made them useless as a nucleus for the few scattered American, English, and Italian bishops whose sympathies were with them. To meet this object, and to centralise the deliberations, about a dozen of the leading men constituted an international meeting, which included the best talents, but also the most discordant views. They were too little united to act with vigour, and too few to exercise control. Some months later they increased their numbers. They were the brain but not the will of the opposition. Cardinal Rauscher presided. Rome honoured him as the author of the Austrian Concordat; but he feared that infallibility would bring destruction on his work, and he was the most constant, the most copious, and the most emphatic of its opponents.

When the debate opened, on the 28th of December, the idea of proclaiming the dogma by acclamation had not been abandoned. The Archbishop of Paris exacted a promise that it should not be attempted. But he was warned that the promise held good for the first day only, and that there was no engagement for the future. Then he made it known that one hundred bishops were ready, if a surprise was attempted, to depart from Rome, and to carry away the Council, as he said, in the soles of their shoes. The plan of carrying the measure by a sudden resolution was given up, and it was determined to introduce it with a demonstration of overwhelming effect. The debate on the dogmatic decree was begun by Cardinal Rauscher. The Archbishop of St. Louis spoke on the same day so briefly as not to reveal the force and the fire within him. The Archbishop of Halifax concluded a long speech by saying that the proposal laid before the Council was only fit to be put decorously underground. Much praise was lavished on the bishops who had courage, knowledge, and Latin enough to address the assembled Fathers; and the Council rose instantly in dignity and in esteem when it was seen that there was to be real discussion. On the 30th, Rome was excited by the success of two speakers. One was the Bishop of Grenoble, the other was Strossmayer, the bishop from the Turkish frontier, who had again assailed the regulation, and had again been stopped by the presiding Cardinal. The fame of his spirit and eloquence began to spread over the city and over the world. The ideas that animated these men in their attack on the proposed measure were most clearly shown a few days later in the speech of a Swiss prelate. "What boots it," he exclaimed, "to condemn errors that have been long condemned, and tempt no Catholic? The false beliefs of mankind are beyond the reach of your decrees. The best defence of Catholicism is religious science. Give to the pursuit of sound learning every encouragement and the widest field; and prove by deeds as well as words that the progress of nations in liberty and light is the mission of the Church."[17]

---
[17] Quid enim expedit damnare quae damnata jam sunt, quidve juvat errores proscribere quos novimus jam esse proscriptos? . . . Falsa sophistarum dogmata, veluti cineres a turbine venti evanuerunt, corrupuerunt, fateor, permultos, infecerunt genium saeculi hujus, sed numquid credendum est, corruptionis contaginem non contigisse, si ejusmodi errores decretorum anathemate prostrati fuissent? . . . Pro tuenda et tute servanda religione Catholica praeter gemitus et preces ad Deum aliud medium praesidiumque nobis datum non est nisi Catholica scientia, cum recta fide per omnia concors. Excolitur summopere apud heterodoxos fidei inimica scientia, excolatur ergo oportet et omni opere augeatur apud Catholicos vera scientia, Ecclesiae amica.

The tempest of criticism was weakly met; and the opponents established at once a superiority in debate. At the end of the first month nothing had been done; and the Session imprudently fixed for the 6th of January had to be filled up with tedious ceremonies. Everybody saw that there had been a great miscalculation. The Council was slipping out of the grasp of the Court, and the regulation was a manifest hindrance to the despatch of business. New resources were required.

A new president was appointed. Cardinal Reisach had died at the end of December without having been able to take his seat, and Cardinal De Luca had presided in his stead. De Angelis was now put into the place made vacant by the death of Reisach. He had suffered imprisonment at Turin, and the glory of his confessorship was enhanced by his services in the election of the Commissions. He was not suited otherwise to be the moderator of a great assembly; and the effect of his elevation was to dethrone the accomplished and astute De Luca, who had been found deficient in thoroughness, and to throw the management of the Council into the hands of the Junior Presidents, Capalti and Bilio. Bilio was a Barnabite monk, innocent of court intrigues, a friend of the most enlightened scholars in Rome, and a favourite of the Pope. Cardinal Capalti had been distinguished as a canonist. Like Cardinal Bilio, he was not reckoned among men of extreme party; and they were not always in harmony with their colleagues, De Angelis and Bizarri. But they did not waver when the policy they had to execute was not their own.

The first decree was withdrawn, and referred to the Commission on Doctrine. Another, on the duties of the episcopate, was substituted; and that again was followed by others, of which the most important was on the Catechism. While

... Obmutescere faciamus ora obtrectantium qui falso nobis imputare non desistunt, Catholicam Ecclesiam opprimere scientiam, et quemcumque liberum cogitandi modum ita cohibere, ut neque scientia, nec ulla alia animi libertas in ea subsistere vel florescere possit. ... Propterea monstrandum hoc est, et scriptis et factis manifestandum, in Catholica Ecclesia veram pro populis esse libertatem, verum profectum, verum lumen, veramque prosperitatem.

they were being discussed, a petition was prepared, demanding that the infallibility of the Pope should be made the object of a decree. The majority undertook to put a strain on the prudence or the reluctance of the Vatican. Their zeal in the cause was warmer than that of the official advisers. Among those who had the responsibility of conducting the spiritual and temporal government of the Pope, the belief was strong that his infallibility did not need defining, and that the definition could not be obtained without needless obstruction to other papal interests. Several Cardinals were inopportunists at first, and afterwards promoted intermediate and conciliatory proposals. But the business of the Council was not left to the ordinary advisers of the Pope, and they were visibly compelled and driven by those who represented the majority. At times this pressure was no doubt convenient. But there were also times when there was no collusion, and the majority really led the authorities. The initiative was not taken by the great mass whose zeal was stimulated by personal allegiance to the Pope. They added to the momentum, but the impulse came from men who were as independent as the chiefs of the opposition. The great Petition, supported by others pointing to the same end, was kept back for several weeks, and was presented at the end of January.

At that time the opposition had attained its full strength, and presented a counter-petition, praying that the question might not be introduced. It was written by Cardinal Rauscher, and was signed, with variations, by 137 bishops. To obtain that number the address avoided the doctrine itself, and spoke only of the difficulty and danger in defining it; so that this, their most imposing act, was a confession of inherent weakness, and a signal to the majority that they might force on the dogmatic discussion. The bishops stood on the negative. They showed no sense of their mission to renovate Catholicism; and it seemed that they would compound for the concession they wanted, by yielding in all other matters, even those which would be a practical substitute for infallibility. That this was not to be, that the forces needed for a great revival were really present, was made manifest by the speech of Strossmayer on the 24th of January, when he demanded the reformation of the Court of Rome, decentralisation in the government of the Church, and decennial Councils. That earnest spirit did not animate the bulk of the party. They were content to leave things as they were, to gain nothing if they lost nothing, to renounce all premature striving for reform if they could succeed in avoiding a doctrine which they were as unwilling to discuss as to define. The words of Ginoulhiac to Strossmayer, "You terrify me with your pitiless logic," expressed the inmost feelings of many who gloried in the grace and the splendour of his eloquence. No words were too strong for them if they prevented the necessity of action, and spared the bishops the distressing prospect of being brought to bay, and having to resist openly the wishes and the claims of Rome.

Infallibility never ceased to overshadow every step of the Council,[18] but it had already given birth to a deeper question. The Church had less to fear from the violence of the majority than from the inertness of their opponents. No proclamation of false doctrines could be so great a disaster as the weakness of faith which would prove that the power of recovery, the vital force of Catholicism, was extinct in the episcopate. It was better to be overcome after openly attesting their belief than to strangle both discussion and definition, and to disperse without having uttered a single word that could reinstate the authorities of the Church in the respect of men. The future depended less on the outward struggle between two parties than on the process by which the stronger spirit within the minority leavened the mass. The opposition was as averse to the actual dogmatic discussion among themselves as in the Council. They feared an inquiry which would divide them. At first the bishops who understood and resolutely contemplated their real mission in the Council were exceedingly few. Their influence was strengthened

---

[18] Il n'y a au fond qu'une question devenue urgente et inévitable, dont la décision faciliterait le cours et la décision de toutes les autres, dont le retard paralyse tout. Sans cela rien n'est commencé ni même abordable (*Univers*, February 9).

by the force of events, by the incessant pressure of the majority, and by the action of literary opinion.

Early in December the Archbishop of Mechlin brought out a reply to the letter of the Bishop of Orleans, who immediately prepared a rejoinder, but could not obtain permission to print it in Rome. It appeared two months later at Naples. Whilst the minority were under the shock of this prohibition, Gratry published at Paris the first of four letters to the Archbishop of Mechlin, in which the case of Honorius was discussed with so much perspicuity and effect that the profane public was interested, and the pamphlets were read with avidity in Rome. They contained no new research, but they went deep into the causes which divided Catholics. Gratry showed that the Roman theory is still propped by fables which were innocent once, but have become deliberate untruths since the excuse of mediæval ignorance was dispelled; and he declared that this school of lies was the cause of the weakness of the Church, and called on Catholics to look the scandal in the face, and cast out the religious forgers. His letters did much to clear the ground and to correct the confusion of ideas among the French. The bishop of St. Brieuc wrote that the exposure was an excellent service to religion, for the evil had gone so far that silence would be complicity.[19] Gratry was no sooner approved by one bishop than he was condemned by a great number of others. He had brought home to his countrymen the question whether they could be accomplices of a dishonest system, or would fairly attempt to root it out.

While Gratry's letters were disturbing the French, Döllinger published some observations on the petition for infallibility, directing his attack clearly against the doctrine

---

[19] Gratry had written: "Cette apologétique sans franchise est l'une des causes de notre décadence religieuse depuis des siècles . . Sommes-nous les prédicateurs du mensonge ou les apôtres de la vérité? Le temps n'est-il pas venu de rejeter avec dégoût les fraudes, les interpolations, et les mutilations que les menteurs et les faussaires, nos plus cruels ennemis, ont pu introduire parmi nous?" The bishop wrote: "Jamais parole plus puissante, inspirée par la conscience et le savoir, n'est arrivée plus à propos que la vôtre. . . . Le mal est tel et le danger si effrayant que le silence deviendrait de la complicité."

itself. During the excitement that ensued, he answered demonstrations of sympathy by saying that he had only defended the faith which was professed, substantially, by the majority of the episcopate in Germany. These words dropped like an acid on the German bishops. They were writhing to escape the dire necessity of a conflict with the Pope; and it was very painful to them to be called as compurgators by a man who was esteemed the foremost opponent of the Roman system, whose hand was suspected in everything that had been done against it, and who had written many things on the sovereign obligations of truth and faith which seemed an unmerciful satire on the tactics to which they clung. The notion that the bishops were opposing the dogma itself was founded on their address against the regulation; but the petition against the definition of infallibility was so worded as to avoid that inference, and had accordingly obtained nearly twice as many German and Hungarian signatures as the other. The Bishop of Mentz vehemently repudiated the supposition for himself, and invited his colleagues to do the same. Some followed his example, others refused; and it became apparent that the German opposition was divided, and included men who accepted the doctrines of Rome. The precarious alliance between incompatible elements was prevented from breaking up by the next act of the Papal Government.

The defects in the mode of carrying on the business of the Council were admitted on both sides. Two months had been lost; and the demand for a radical change was publicly made in behalf of the minority by a letter communicated to the *Moniteur.* On the 22nd of February a new regulation was introduced, with the avowed purpose of quickening progress. It gave the Presidents power to cut short any speech, and provided that debate might be cut short at any moment when the majority pleased. It also declared that the decrees should be carried by majority — *id decernetur quod majori Patrum numero placuerit.* The policy of leaving the decisive power in the hands of the Council itself had this advantage, that its exercise would not raise the question of liberty and coercion in the same way as the interference of authority. By the Bull *Multiplices,* no bishop could introduce any matter not approved by the Pope. By the new regulation he could not speak on any question before the Council, if the majority chose to close the discussion, or if the Presidents chose to abridge his speech. He could print nothing in Rome, and what was printed elsewhere was liable to be treated as contraband. His written observations on any measure were submitted to the Commission, without any security that they would be made known to the other bishops in their integrity. There was no longer an obstacle to the immediate definition of papal infallibility. The majority was omnipotent.

The minority could not accept this regulation without admitting that the Pope is infallible. Their thesis was, that his decrees are not free from the risk of error unless they express the universal belief of the episcopate. The idea that particular virtue attaches to a certain number of bishops, or that infallibility depends on a few votes more or less, was defended by nobody. If the act of a majority of bishops in the Council, possibly not representing a majority in the Church, is infallible, it derives its infallibility from the Pope. Nobody held that the Pope was bound to proclaim a dogma carried by a majority. The minority contested the principle of the new Regulation, and declared that a dogmatic decree required virtual unanimity. The chief protest was drawn up by a French bishop. Some of the Hungarians added a paragraph asserting that the authority and œcumenicity of the Council depended on the settlement of this question; and they proposed to add that they could not continue to act as though it were legitimate unless this point was given up. The author of the address declined this passage, urging that the time for actual menace was not yet come. From that day the minority agreed in rejecting as invalid any doctrine which should not be passed by unanimous consent. On this point the difference between the thorough and the simulated opposition was effaced, for Ginoulhiac and Ketteler were as positive as Kenrick or Hefele. But it was a point which Rome could not surrender without giving up its whole position. To wait for unanimity was to wait forever, and to admit that a minority could prevent or nullify the dogmatic action of the papacy was to renounce infallibility. No alternative remained to the opposing bishops but to break up the Council. The most eminent among them accepted this conclusion, and stated it in a paper declaring that the absolute and indisputable law of the Church had been violated by the Regulation allowing articles of faith to be decreed on which the episcopate was not morally unanimous; and that the Council, no longer possessing in the eyes of the bishops and of the world the indispensable condition of liberty and legality, would be inevitably rejected. To avert a public scandal, and to save the honour of the Holy See, it was proposed that some unopposed decrees should be proclaimed in solemn session, and the Council immediately prorogued.

At the end of March a breach seemed unavoidable. The first part of the dogmatic decree had come back from the Commission so profoundly altered that it was generally accepted by the bishops, but with a crudely expressed sentence in the preamble, which was intended to rebuke the notion of the reunion of Protestant Churches. Several bishops looked upon this passage as an uncalled-for insult to Protestants, and wished it changed; but there was danger that if they then joined in voting the decree they would commit themselves to the lawfulness of the Regulation against which they had protested. On the 22nd of March Strossmayer raised both questions. He said that it was neither just nor charitable to impute the progress of religious error to the Protestants. The germ of modern unbelief existed among the Catholics before the Reformation, and afterwards bore its worst fruits in Catholic countries. Many of the ablest defenders of Christian truth were Protestants, and the day of reconciliation would have come already but for the violence and uncharitableness of the Catholics. These words were greeted with execrations, and the remainder of the speech was delivered in the midst of a furious tumult. At length, when Strossmayer declared that the Council had forfeited its authority by the rule which abolished the necessity of unanimity, the Presidents and the multitude refused to let him go on.[20] On the following day

---

[20] Pace eruditissimorum virorum dictum esto: mihi haecce nec veritati congrua esse videntur, nec caritati. Non veritati; verum quidem est Protestantes

THE VATICAN COUNCIL 347

he drew up a protest, declaring that he could not acknowledge the validity of the Council if dogmas were to be decided

gravissimam commisisse culpam, dum spreta et insuperhabita divina Ecclesiae auctoritate, aeternas et immutabiles fidei veritates subjectivae rationis judicio et arbitrio subjecissent. Hoc superbiae humanae fomentum gravissimis certe malis, rationalismo, criticismo, etc occasionem dedit. Ast hoc quoque respectu dici debet, protestantismi ejus qui cum eodem in nexu existit rationalismi germen saeculo xvi praeextitisse in sic dicto humanismo et classicismo, quem in sanctuario ipso quidam summae auctoritatis viri incauto consilio fovebant et nutriebant; et nisi hoc germen praeextitisset concipi non posset quomodo tam parva scintilla tantum in medio Europae excitare potuisset incendium, ut illud ad hodiernum usque diem restingui non potuerit Accedit et illud, fidei et religionis, Ecclesiae et omnis auctoritatis contemptum absque ulla cum Protestantismo cognatione et parentela in medio Catholicae gentis saeculo xviii temporibus Voltarii et encyclopaedistarum enatum fuisse. . . . Quidquid interim sit de rationalismo, puto venerabilem deputationem omnino falli dum texendo genealogiam naturalismi, materialismi, pantheismi, atheismi, etc, omnes omnino hos errores foetus Protestantismi esse asserit. . . . Errores superius enumerati non tantum nobis verum et ipsis Protestantibus horrori sunt et abominationi, ut adeo Ecclesiae et nobis Catholicis in iis oppugnandis et refellendis auxilio sint et adjumento Ita Leibnitius erat certe vir eruditus et omni sub respectu praestans; vir in dijudicandis Ecclesiae Catholicae institutis aequus; vir in debellandis sui temporis erroribus strenuus; vir in revehenda inter Christianas communitates concordia optime animatus et meritus. [Loud cries of "Oh! Oh!" The President de Angelis rang the bell and said, "Non est hicce locus laudandi Protestantes."] . . . Hos viros quorum magna copia existit in Germania, in Anglia, item et in America septentrionali, magna hominum turba inter Protestantes sequitur, quibus omnibus applicari potest illud magni Augustini· "Errant, sed bona fide errant; haeretici sunt, sed illi nos haereticos tenent Ipsi errorem non invenerunt, sed a perversis et in errorem inductis parentibus haereditaverunt, parati errorem deponere quamprimum convicti fuerint." [Here there was a long interruption and ringing of the bell, with cries of "Shame! shame!" "Down with the heretic!"] Hi omnes etiamsi non spectent ad Ecclesiae corpus, spectant tamen ad ejus animam, et de muneribus Redemptioris aliquatenus participant. Hi omnes in amore quo erga Iesum Christum Dominum nostrum feruntur, atque in illis positivis veritatibus quas ex fidei naufragio salvarunt, totidem gratiae divinae momenta possident, quibus misericordia Dei utetur, ut eos ad priscam fidem et Ecclesiam reducat, nisi nos exaggerationibus nostris et improvidis charitatis ipsis debitae laesionibus tempus misericordiae divinae elongaverimus. Quantum autem ad charitatem, ei certe contrarium est vulnera aliena alio fine tangere quam ut ipsa sanentur; puto autem hac enumeratione errorum, quibus Protestantismus occasionem dedisset, id non fieri. . . . Decreto, quod in supplementum ordinis interioris nobis nuper communicatum est, statuitur res in Concilio hocce suffragiorum majoritate decidendas fore. Contra hoc principium, quod omnem praecedentium Conciliorum praxim funditus evertit, multi episcopi reclamarunt, quin tamen aliquod responsum obtinuerint. Responsum autem in re tanti momenti dari debuisset clarum, by a majority,[21] and sent it to the Presidents after it had been approved at the meeting of the Germans, and by bishops of other nations. The preamble was withdrawn, and another was inserted in its place, which had been written in great haste by the German Jesuit Kleutgen, and was received with general applause. Several of the Jesuits obtained credit for the ability and moderation with which the decree was drawn up. It was no less than a victory over extreme counsels. A unanimous vote was insured for the public session of 24th April; and harmony was restored. But the text proposed originally in the Pope's name had undergone so many changes as to make it appear that his intentions had been thwarted. There was a supplement to the decree, which the bishops had understood would be withdrawn, in order that the festive concord and good feeling might not be disturbed. They were informed at the last moment that it would be put to the vote, as its withdrawal would be a confession of defeat for Rome. The supplement was an admonition that the constitutions and decrees of the Holy See must be observed even when they proscribe opinions not actually heretical.[22] Ex-

---

perspicuum et omnis ambiguitatis expers. Hoc ad summas Concilii hujus calamitates spectat, nam hoc certe et praesenti generationi et posteris praebebit ansam dicendi: huic concilio libertatem et veritatem defuisse. Ego ipse convictus sum, aeternam ac immutabilem fidei et traditionis regulam semper fuisse semperque mansuram communem, adminus moraliter unanimem consensum. Concilium, quod hac regula insuperhabita, fidei et morum dogmata majoritate numerica definire intenderet, juxta meam intimam convictionem eo ipso excideret jure conscientiam orbis Catholici sub sanctione vitae ac mortis aeternae obligandi.

[21] Dum autem ipse die hesterno ex suggestu hanc quaestionem posuissem et verba de consensu moraliter unanimi in rebus fidei definiendis necessario protulissem, interruptus fui, mihique inter maximum tumultum et graves comminationes possibilitas sermonis continuandi adempta est. Atque haec gravissima sane circumstantia magis adhuc comprobat necessitatem habendi responsi, quod clarum sit omnisque ambiguitatis expers. Peto itaque humillime, ut hujusmodi responsum in proxima congregatione generali detur. Nisi enim haec fierent anceps haererem an manere possem in Concilio, ubi libertas Episcoporum ita opprimitur, quemadmodum heri in me oppressa fuit, et ubi dogmata fidei definientur novo et in Ecclesia Dei adusque inaudito modo.

[22] Quoniam vero satis non est, haereticam pravitatem devitare, nisi ii quoque errores diligenter fugiantur, qui ad illam plus minusve accedunt, omnes

traordinary efforts were made in public and in private to prevent any open expression of dissent from this paragraph. The Bishop of Brixen assured his brethren, in the name of the Commission, that it did not refer to questions of doctrine, and they could not dispute the general principle that obedience is due to lawful authority. The converse proposition, that the papal acts have no claim to be obeyed, was obviously untenable. The decree was adopted unanimously. There were some who gave their vote with a heavy heart, conscious of the snare.[23] Strossmayer alone stayed away.

The opposition was at an end. Archbishop Manning afterwards reminded them that by this vote they had implicitly

---

officii monemus, servandi etiam Constitutiones et Decreta quibus pravae eiusmodi opiniones, quae isthic diserte non enumerantur, ab hac Sancta Sede proscriptae et prohibitae sunt.

[23] In the speech on infallibility which he prepared, but never delivered, Archbishop Kenrick thus expressed himself: "Inter alia quae mihi stuporem injecerunt dixit Westmonasteriensis, nos additamento facto sub finem Decreti de Fide, tertia Sessione lati, ipsam Pontificiam Infallibilitatem, saltem implicite, jam agnovisse, nec ab ea recedere nunc nobis licere. Si bene intellexerim R^m Relatorem, qui in Congregatione generali hoc additamentum, prius oblatum, deinde abstractum, nobis mirantibus quid rei esset, illud iterum inopinato commendavit — dixit, verbis clarioribus, per illud nullam omnino doctrinam edoceri; sed eam quatuor capitibus ex quibus istud decretum compositum est imponi tanquam eis coronidem convientem; eamque disciplinarem magis quam doctrinalem characterem habere. Aut deceptus est ipse, si vera dixit Westmonasteriensis; aut nos sciens in errorem induxit, quod de viro tam ingenuo minime supponere licet. Utcumque fuerit, ejus declarationi fidentes, plures suffragia sua isti decreto haud deneganda censuerunt ob istam clausulam; aliis, inter quos egomet, dolos parari metuentibus, et aliorum voluntati hac in re aegre cedentibus. In his omnibus non est mens mea aliquem ex Reverendissimis Patribus malae fidei incusare, quos omnes, ut par est, veneratione debita prosequor. Sed extra concilium adesse dicuntur viri religiosi — forsan et pii — qui maxime in illud influunt; qui calliditati potius quam bonis artibus confisi, rem Ecclesiae in maximum ex quo orta sit discrimen adduxerunt; qui ab inito concilio effecerunt ut in Deputationes conciliares ii soli eligerentur qui eorum placitis fovere aut noscerentur aut crederentur; qui nonnullorum ex eorum praedecessoribus vestigia prementes in schematibus nobis propositis, et ex eorum officina prodeuntibus, nihil magis cordi habuisse videntur quam Episcopalem auctoritatem deprimere, Pontificiam autem extollere, et verborum ambagibus incautos decipere velle videntur, dum alia ab aliis in eorum explicationem dicantur. Isti grave hoc incendium in Ecclesia excitarunt, et in illud insufflare non desinunt, scriptis eorum, pietatis speciem prae se ferentibus sed veritate ejus vacuis, in populos spargentibus.

accepted infallibility. They had done even more. They might conceivably contrive to bind and limit dogmatic infallibility with conditions so stringent as to evade many of the objections taken from the examples of history; but, in requiring submission to papal decrees on matters not articles of faith, they were approving that of which they knew the character, they were confirming without let or question a power they saw in daily exercise, they were investing with new authority the existing Bulls, and giving unqualified sanction to the Inquisition and the Index, to the murder of heretics and the deposing of kings. They approved what they were called on to reform, and solemnly blessed with their lips what their hearts knew to be accursed. The Court of Rome became thenceforth reckless in its scorn of the opposition, and proceeded in the belief that there was no protest they would not forget, no principle they would not betray, rather than defy the Pope in his wrath. It was at once determined to bring on the discussion of the dogma of infallibility. At first, when the minority knew that their prayers and their sacrifices had been vain, and that they must rely on their own resources, they took courage in extremity. Rauscher, Schwarzenberg, Hefele, Ketteler, Kenrick, wrote pamphlets, or caused them to be written, against the dogma, and circulated them in the Council. Several English bishops protested that the denial of infallibility by the Catholic episcopate had been an essential condition of emancipation, and that they could not revoke that assurance after it had served their purpose, without being dishonoured in the eyes of their countrymen.[24] The Archbishop of St. Louis, ad-

---

[24] The author of the protest afterwards gave the substance of his argument as follows: "Episcopi et theologi publice a Parlamento interrogati fuerunt, utrum Catholici Angliae tenerent Papam posse definitiones relativas ad fidem et mores populis imponere absque omni consensu expresso vel tacito Ecclesiae. Omnes Episcopi et theologi responderunt Catholicos hoc non tenere. Hisce responsionibus confisum Parlamentum Angliae Catholicos admisit ad participationem iurium civilium. Quis Protestantibus persuadebit Catholicos contra honorem et bonam fidem non agere, qui quando agebatur de iuribus sibi acquirendis publice professi sunt ad fidem Catholicam non pertinere doctrinam infallibilitatis Romani Pontificis, statim autem ac obtinuerint quod volebant, a professione publice facta recedunt et contrarium affirmant?"

mitting the force of the argument, derived from the fact that a dogma was promulgated in 1854 which had long been disputed and denied, confessed that he could not prove the Immaculate Conception to be really an article of faith.[25]

An incident occurred in June which showed that the experience of the Council was working a change in the fundamental convictions of the bishops. Döllinger had written in March that an article of faith required not only to be approved and accepted unanimously by the Council, but that the bishops united with the Pope are not infallible, and that the œcumenicity of their acts must be acknowledged and ratified by the whole Church. Father Hötzl, a Franciscan friar, having published a pamphlet in defence of this proposition, was summoned to Rome, and required to sign a paper declaring that the confirmation of a Council by the Pope alone makes it œcumenical. He put his case into the hands of German bishops who were eminent in the opposition, asking first their opinion on the proposed declaration, and, secondly, their advice on his own conduct. The bishops whom he consulted replied that they believed the declaration to be erroneous; but they added that they had only lately arrived at the conviction, and had been shocked at first by Döllinger's doctrine. They could not require him to suffer the consequences of being condemned at Rome as a rebellious friar and obstinate heretic for a view which they themselves had doubted only three months before. He followed the advice, but he perceived that his advisers had considerately betrayed him.

When the observations on infallibility which the bishops had sent in to the Commission appeared in print it seemed that the minority had burnt their ships. They affirmed that the dogma would put an end to the conversion of Protestants,

---

[25] Archbishop Kenrick's remarkable statement is not reproduced accurately in his pamphlet *De Pontificia infallibilitate*. It is given in full in the last pages of the *Observationes*, and is abridged in his *Concio habenda sed non habita*, where he concludes: "Eam fidei doctrinam esse neganti, non video quomodo responderi possit, cum objiceret Ecclesiam errorem contra fidem divinitus revelatam diu tolerare non potuisse, quin, aut quod ad fidei depositum pertineret non scivisse, aut errorem manifestum tolerasse videretur."

that it would drive devout men out of the Church and make Catholicism indefensible in controversy, that it would give governments apparent reason to doubt the fidelity of Catholics, and would give new authority to the theory of persecution and of the deposing power. They testified that it was unknown in many parts of the Church, and was denied by the Fathers, so that neither perpetuity nor universality could be pleaded in its favour; and they declared it an absurd contradiction, founded on ignoble deceit, and incapable of being made an article of faith by Pope or Council.[26] One bishop protested that he would die rather than proclaim it. Another thought it would be an act of suicide for the Church.

What was said, during the two months' debate, by men perpetually liable to be interrupted by a majority acting less from conviction than by command,[27] could be of no practical

---

[26] Certissimum ipsi esse fore ut infallibilitate ista dogmatice definita, in dioecesi sua, in qua ne vestigium quidem traditionis de infallibilitate S. P. hucusque inveniatur, et in aliis regionibus multi, et quidem non solum minoris, sed etiam optimae notae, a fide deficiant — Si edatur, omnis progressus conversionum in Provinciis Foederatis Americae funditus extinguetur. Episcopi et sacerdotes in disputationibus cum Protestantibus quid respondere possent non haberent. — Per eiusmodi definitionem acatholicis, inter quos haud pauci iique optimi hisce praesertim temporibus firmum fidei fundamentum desiderant, ad Ecclesiam reditus redditur difficilis, imo impossibilis. — Qui Concilii decretis obsequi vellent, invenient se maximis in difficultatibus versari. Gubernia civilia eos tanquam subditos minus fidos, haud sine verisimilitudinis specie, habebunt. Hostes Ecclesiae eos lacessere non verebuntur, nunc eis objicientes errores quos Pontifices aut docuisse, aut sua agendi ratione probasse, dicuntur et risu excipient responsa quae sola afferri possint. — Eo ipso definitur in globo quidquid per diplomata apostolica huc usque definitum est. . . . Poterit, admissa tali definitione, statuere de dominio temporali, de eius mensura, de potestate deponendi reges, de usu coercendi haereticos. — Doctrina de Infallibilitate Romani Pontificis nec in Scriptura Sacra, nec in traditione ecclesiastica fundata mihi videtur. Immo contrariam, ni fallor, Christiana antiquitas tenuit doctrinam. — Modus dicendi Schematis supponit existere in Ecclesia duplicem infallibilitatem, ipsius Ecclesiae et Romani Pontificis, quod est absurdum et inauditum. — Subterfugiis quibus theologi non pauci in Honorii causa usi sunt, derisui me exponerem. Sophismata adhibere et munere episcopali et natura rei, quae in timore Domini pertractanda est, indignum mihi videtur. — Plerique textus quibus eam comprobant etiam melioris notae theologi, quos Ultramontanos vocant, mutilati sunt, falsificati, interpolati, circumtruncati, spurii, in sensum alienum detorti. — Asserere audeo eam sententiam, ut in schemate jacet, non esse fidei doctrinam, nec talem devenire posse per quamcumque definitionem etiam conciliarem.

[27] This, at least, was the discouraging impression of Archbishop Kenrick:

account, and served for protest, not for persuasion. Apart from the immediate purpose of the discussion, two speeches were memorable — that of Archbishop Conolly of Halifax, for the uncompromising clearness with which he appealed to Scripture and repudiated all dogmas extracted from the speculations of divines, and not distinctly founded on the recorded Word of God,[28] and that of Archbishop Darboy, who foretold that a decree which increased authority without increasing power, and claimed for one man, whose infallibility was only now defined, the obedience which the world refused to the whole Episcopate, whose right had been unquestioned in the Church for 1800 years, would raise up new hatred and new suspicion, weaken the influence of religion over society, and wreak swift ruin on the temporal power.[29]

Semper contigit ut Patres surgendo assensum sententiae deputationis praebuerint. Primo quidem die suffragiorum, cum quaestio esset de tertia parte primae emendationis, nondum adhibita indicatione a subsecretario, deinde semper facta, plures surrexerunt adeo ut necesse foret numerum surgentium capere, ut constaret de suffragiis. Magna deinde confusio exorta est, et ista emendatio, quamvis majore forsan numero sic accepta, in crastinum diem dilata est. Postero die R^{ms} Relator ex ambone Patres monuit, deputationem emendationem istam admittere nolle Omnes fere eam rejiciendam surgendo statim dixerunt.

[28] Quodcumque Dominus Noster non dixerit etiam si metaphysice aut physice certissimum nunquam basis esse poterit dogmatis divinae fidei. Fides enim per auditum, auditus autem non per scientiam sed per verba Christi. . . . Non ipsa verba S Scripturae igitur, sed genuinus sensus, sive litteralis, sive metaphoricus, prout in mente Dei revelantis fuit, atque ab Ecclesiae patribus semper atque ubique concorditer expositus, et quem nos omnes juramento sequi abstringimur, hic tantummodo sensus Vera Dei revelatio dicendus est. . . . Tota antiquitas silet vel contraria est. . . . Verbum Dei volo et hoc solum, quaeso et quidem indubitatum, ut dogma fiat.

[29] Hanc de infallibilitate his conditionibus ortam et isto modo introductam aggredi et definire non possumus, ut arbitror, quin eo ipso tristem viam sternamus tum cavillationibus impiorum, tum etiam objectionibus moralem hujus Concilii auctoritatem minuentibus. Et hoc quidem eo magis cavendum est, quod jam prostent et pervulgentur scripta et acta quae vim ejus et rationem labefactare attentant; ita ut nedum animos sedare queat et quae pascis sunt afferre, e contra nova dissensionis et discordiarum semina inter Christianos spargere videatur. . . . Porro, quod in tantis Ecclesiae angustiis laboranti mundo remedium affertur? Iis omnibus qui ab humero indocili excutiunt onera antiquitus imposita, et consuetudine Patrum veneranda, novum ideoque grave et odiosum onus imponi postulant schematis auctores. Eos omnes qui infirmae fidei sunt novo et non satis opportuno dogmate quasi obruunt, doctrina scilicet hucusque nondum definita, praesentis discussionis vulnere non-

The general debate had lasted three weeks, and forty-nine bishops were still to speak, when it was brought to a close by an abrupt division on the 3rd of June. For twenty-four hours the indignation of the minority was strong. It was the last decisive opportunity for them to reject the legitimacy of the Council. There were some who had despaired of it from the beginning, and held that the Bull *Multiplices* deprived it of legal validity. But it had not been possible to make a stand at a time when no man knew whether he could trust his neighbour, and when there was fair ground to hope that the worst rules would be relaxed. When the second regulation, interpreted according to the interruptors of Strossmayer, claimed the right of proclaiming dogmas which part of the Episcopate did not believe, it became doubtful whether the bishops could continue to sit without implicit submission. They restricted themselves to a protest, thinking that it was sufficient to meet words with words, and that it would be time to act when the new principle was actually applied. By the vote of the 3rd of June the obnoxious regulation was enforced in a way evidently injurious to the minority and their cause. The chiefs of the opposition were now convinced of the invalidity of the Council, and advised that they should all abstain from speaking, and attend at St. Peter's

---

nihil sauciata, et a Concilio cujus liberatem minus aequo apparere plurimi autumant et dicunt pronuntianda. . . . Mundus aut aeger est aut perit, non quod ignorat veritatem vel veritatis doctores, sed quod ab ea refugit eamque sibi non vult imperari. Igitur, si eam respuit, quum a toto docentis Ecclesiae corpore, id est ab 800 episcopis per totum orbem sparsis et simul cum S. Pontifice infallibilibus praedicatur, quanto magis quum ab unico Doctore infallibili, et quidem ut tali recenter declarato praedicabitur? Ex altera parte, ut valeat et efficaciter agat auctoritas necesse est non tantum eam affirmari, sed insuper admitti. . . . Syllabus totam Europam pervasit at cui malo mederi potuit etiam ubi tanquam oraculum infallibile susceptus est? Duo tantum restabant regna in quibus religio florebat, non de facto tantum, sed et de jure dominans: Austria scilicet et Hispania. Atqui in his duobus regnis ruit iste Catholicus ordo, quamvis ab infallibili auctoritate commendatus, imo forsan saltem in Austria eo praecise quod ab hac commendatus. Audeamus igitur res uti sunt considerare. Nedum Sanctissimi Pontificis independens infallibilitas praejudicia et objectiones destruat quae permultos a fide avertunt, ea potius auget et aggravat. . . . Nemo non videt si politicae gnarus, quae semina dissensionum schema nostrum contineat et quibus periculis exponatur ipsa temporalis Sanctae sedis potestas.

only to negative by their vote the decree which they disapproved. In this way they thought that the claim to œcumenicity would be abolished without breach or violence. The greater number were averse to so vigorous a demonstration; and Hefele threw the great weight of his authority into their scale. He contended that they would be worse than their word if they proceeded to extremities on this occasion. They had announced that they would do it only to prevent the promulgation of a dogma which was opposed. If that were done the Council would be revolutionary and tyrannical; and they ought to keep their strongest measure in reserve for that last contingency. The principle of unanimity was fundamental. It admitted no ambiguity, and was so clear, simple, and decisive, that there was no risk in fixing on it. The Archbishops of Paris, Milan, Halifax, the Bishops of Djakovar, Orleans, Marseilles, and most of the Hungarians, yielded to these arguments, and accepted the policy of less strenuous colleagues, while retaining the opinion that the Council was of no authority. But there were some who deemed it unworthy and inconsistent to attend an assembly which they had ceased to respect.

The debate on the several paragraphs lasted till the beginning of July, and the decree passed at length with eighty-eight dissentient votes. It was made known that the infallibility of the Pope would be promulgated in solemn session on the 18th, and that all who were present would be required to sign an act of submission. Some bishops of the minority thereupon proposed that they should all attend, repeat their vote, and refuse their signature. They exhorted their brethren to set a conspicuous example of courage and fidelity, as the Catholic world would not remain true to the faith if the bishops were believed to have faltered. But it was certain that there were men amongst them who would renounce their belief rather than incur the penalty of excommunication, who preferred authority to proof, and accepted the Pope's declaration, "La tradizione son' io." It was resolved by a small majority that the opposition should renew its negative vote in writing, and should leave Rome in a body before the session. Some of the most conscientious and resolute adversaries of the dogma advised this course. Looking to the immediate future, they were persuaded that an irresistible reaction was at hand, and that the decrees of the Vatican Council would fade away and be dissolved by a power mightier than the Episcopate and a process less perilous than schism. Their disbelief in the validity of its work was so profound that they were convinced that it would perish without violence, and they resolved to spare the Pope and themselves the indignity of a rupture. Their last manifesto, *La dernière Heure,* is an appeal for patience, an exhortation to rely on the guiding, healing hand of God.[30] They deemed that they had assigned the course which was to save the Church, by teaching the Catholics to reject a Council which was neither legitimate in constitution, free in action, nor unanimous in doctrine, but to observe moderation in contesting an authority over which great catastrophes impend. They conceived that it would thus be possible to save the peace and unity of the Church without sacrifice of faith and reason.

---

[30] Espérons que l'excès du mal provoquera le retour du bien. Ce Concile n'aura eu qu'un heureux résultat, celui d'en appeler un autre, réuni dans la liberté. . . . Le Concile du Vatican demeurera stérile, comme tout ce qui n'est pas éclos sous le souffle de l'Esprit Saint. Cependant il aura révélé non seulement jusqu'à quel point l'absolutisme peut abuser des meilleures institutions et des meilleurs instincts, mais aussi ce que vaut encore le droit, alors même qu'il n'a plus que le petit nombre pour le défendre. . . . Si la multitude passe quand même nous lui prédisons qu'elle n'ira pas loin. Les Spartiates, qui étaient tombés aux Thermopyles pour défendre les terres de la liberté, avaient préparé au flot impitoyable au déspotisme la défaite de Salamis.

ACTON-CREIGHTON CORRESPONDENCE

Mandell Creighton, later a Bishop in the Church of England, was the author of the five-volume *History of the Papacy during the Reformation*. The first two volumes appeared in 1882, and Creighton suggested to the editor of the *Academy* that Acton review the book, "as I wanted to be told my shortcomings by the one Englishman whom I considered capable of doing so." Acton's review was not at all diffident; the main shortcoming of which he complained was the familiar one of excessive moral leniency. Creighton thanked him, frankly admiring his probity and earnestness. Five years later, as editor of the newly founded *English Historical Review*, he offered the next two volumes to Acton for review. This time Acton more than lived up to his reputation as a severe critic. The first draft of his review was so harsh it lacked even the conventional courtesies of academic polemics. Creighton, prepared to publish it, wrote to R. L. Poole, professor at Oxford and an associate on the journal, of this "ill-natured, passionate and almost incoherent" piece of writing, and of the absurd situation of an editor "inviting and publishing a savage onslaught on himself." Finally, after the exchange of a series of letters between Acton and Creighton, the most important of which is printed below, Acton volunteered to recast the review. In the final version, as it appeared in the *English Historical Review* of 1887 (and as it was reprinted in the *Historical Essays and Studies*), his criticism, although not essentially modified, is couched in more amiable terms.

The originals of the two letters printed here are among the manuscripts in the Cambridge University Library (Add. MSS, 6871). About a fourth of Acton's letter, plus the postscript, has been carelessly edited in the appendix to the *Historical Essays and Studies*. ("Gams" appears as "Gauss," "Penn" as "Perrin," etc.) Brief — and more accurate — excerpts have also appeared, together with Creighton's reply, in *Life and Letters of Mandell Creighton* (London, 1904). The juxtaposition of the complete letters (only one irrelevant passage in Creighton's letter has been omitted) provides an interesting contrast of temperament and philosophy. Acton's is particularly revealing because it is distinctly sharper in tone and thought than most of his formal essays; it is also a good example of the elliptical style of writing with which his correspondents were favored. — G.H.

Cannes, April 5, 1887

Dear Mr. Creighton,

I thank you very sincerely for your letter, which, though dated April 1, is as frank as my review was artful and reserved. The postponement gives me time to correct several errors besides those you point out, if you will let me have my manuscript out here. The other will also be the better for leisurely revision. Forgive me if I answer you with a diffuseness degenerating into garrulity.

The criticism of those who complained that I attacked the Germans without suggesting a better method seems to me undeserved. I was trying to indicate the progress and—partial—improvement of their historical writing; and when I disagreed I seldom said so, but rather tried to make out a possible case in favour of views I don't share. Nobody can be more remote than I am from the Berlin and the Tübingen schools; but I tried to mark my disagreement by the lightest touch. From the Heidelberg school I think there is nothing to learn, and I said so. Perhaps I have been ambiguous sometimes, for you say that appreciation such as yours for the essentials of the Roman system is no recommendation in my eyes. If that conclusion is drawn from my own words I am much in fault. But that has nothing of importance to do with a critique in the H. R. [*English Historical Review*].

And when you say that I am desirous to show how the disruption might have been avoided, I only half recognise myself. The disruption took place over one particular, well-defined point of controversy; and when they went asunder upon that, the logic of things followed. But they needed not to part company on that particular. It was a new view that Luther attacked. Theological authority in its favour there was very little. It was not approved by Hadrian VI, or by many Tridentine divines, or by many later divines, even among the Jesuits. Supposing, therefore, there had been men of influence at Rome such as certain fathers of Constance formerly, or such as Erasmus or Gropper, it might well have been that they would have preferred the opinion of Luther to the opinion of Tetzel, and would have effected straightway the desired reform of the indulgences for the Dead.

But that is what set the stone rolling, and the consequences were derived from that one special doctrine or practice. *Cessante causa cessat effectus.* Introduce, in 1517, the reforms desired six years later, by the next Pope, demanded by many later divines, adopt, a century and a half before it was written, the Exposition de la Foi, and then the particular series of events which ensued would have been cut off.

For the Reformation is not like the Renaissance or the Revolution, a spontaneous movement springing up in many places, produced by similar though not identical causes. It all derives, more or less directly, from Luther, from the consequences he gradually drew from the resistance of Rome on that one disputed point.

I must, therefore, cast the responsibility on those who refused to say, in 1517, what everybody had said two centuries before, and many said a century later. And the motive of these people was not a religious idea, one system of salvation set up against another; but an ecclesiastical one. They said, Prierias says quite distinctly, that the whole fabric of authority would crumble if a thing permitted, indirectly or implicitly sanctioned by the supreme authority responsible for souls should be given up.

(The English disruption proceeded along other lines, but nearly parallel. Nearly the same argument applies to it, and it is not just now the question.)

Of course, an adversary, a philosophical historian, a *Dogmengeschichtslehrer,* may say that, even admitting that things arose and went on as I say, yet there was so much gunpowder about that any spark would have produced much the same explosion. I cannot disprove it. I do not wish to disprove it. But I know nothing about it. We must take things as they really occurred. What occurred is that Luther raised a just objection, that the authority of tradition and the spiritual interest of man were on his side, and that the Catholic divines refused to yield to him for a reason not founded on tradition or on charity.

Therefore I lay the burden of separation on the shoulders of two sets of men—those who, during the Vice chancellorship and the pontificate of Borgia, promoted the theory of the Privileged Altars (and indirectly the theory of the Dispensing Power); and those who, from 1517 to 1520, sacrificed the tradition of the Church to the credit of the Papacy.

Whether the many reforming rills, partly springing in different regions—Wyclif, the Bohemians before Hus, Hus, the Bohemians after him, the Fratres Communis Vitae, the divines described by Ullmann, and more than twenty other symptoms of somewhat like kind, would have gathered into one vast torrent, even if Luther had been silenced by knife or pen, is a speculative question not to be confounded with the one here discussed. Perhaps America would have gone, without the help of Grenville or North.

My object is not to show how disruption might have been avoided, but how it was brought on. It was brought on, *secundo me,* by the higher view of the papal monarchy in spirituals that grew with the papal monarchy in temporals (and with much other monarchy). The root, I think, is there, while the Italian prince is the branch. To the growth of those ideas after the fall of the Councils I attribute what followed, and into that workshop or nursery I want to pry. If Rovere or Borgia had never sought or won territorial sovereignty, the breach must have come just the same, with the Saxons if not with the English.

I was disappointed at not learning from you what I never could find out, how that peculiar discipline established itself at Rome between the days of Kempis and of Erasmus. It would not have appeared mysterious or esoteric to your readers if I had said a little more about it. Nor is this a point of serious difference. When you come to talk of the crisis I do not doubt you will say how it came about. Probably you will not give quite the same reasons that occur to me, because you are more sure than I am that the breach was inevitable. But I did think myself justified in saying that these two volumes do not contain an account of some of the principal things pertaining to the Papacy during the Reformation, and in indicating the sort of explanation I desiderate in Vol. V.

What is not at all a question of opportunity or degree is our difference about the Inquisition. Here again I do not admit that there is anything esoteric in my objection. The point is not whether you like the Inquisition—I mean that is a point which the H.R. may mark, but ought not to discuss—but whether you can, without reproach to historical accuracy, speak of the later mediæval papacy as having been tolerant and enlightened. What you say on that point struck me exactly as it would strike me to read that the French Terrorists were tolerant and enlightened, and avoided the guilt of blood. Bear with me whilst I try to make my meaning quite clear.

We are not speaking of the Papacy towards the end of the fifteenth or early sixteenth century, when, for a couple of generations, and down to 1542, there was a decided lull in the persecuting spirit. Nor are we speaking of the Spanish Inquisition, which is as distinct from the Roman as the Portuguese, the Maltese, or the Venetian. I mean the Popes of the thirteenth and fourteenth centuries, from Innocent III down to the time of Hus. These men instituted a system of Persecution, with a special tribunal, special functionaries, special laws. They carefully elaborated, and developed, and applied it. They protected it with every sanction, spiritual and temporal. They inflicted, as far as they could, the penalties of death and damnation on everybody who resisted it. They constructed quite a new system of procedure, with unheard of cruelties, for its maintenance. They devoted to it a whole code of legislation, pursued for several generations, and not to be found in [?].

But although not to be found there it is to be found in books just as common; it is perfectly familiar to every Roman Catholic student initiated in canon law and papal affairs; it has been worn threadbare in a thousand controversies; it has been constantly attacked, constantly defended, and never disputed or denied, by any Catholic authority. There are some dozens of books, some of them official, containing the particulars.

Indeed it is the most conspicuous fact in the history of the mediæval papacy, just as the later Inquisition, with what followed, is the most conspicuous and characteristic fact in the history and record of the modern papacy. A man is hanged not because he can or cannot prove his claim to virtues, but because it can be proved that he has committed a particular crime. That one action overshadows the rest of his career. It is useless to argue that he is a good husband or a good poet. The one crime swells out of proportion to the rest. We all agree that Calvin was one of the greatest writers, many think him the best religious teacher, in the world. But that one affair of Servetus outweighs the nine folios, and settles, by itself, the reputation he deserves. So with the medieval Inquisition and the Popes that founded it and worked it. That is the breaking point, the article of their system by which they stand or fall.

Therefore it is better known than any other part of their government, and not only determines the judgment but fills the imagination, and rouses the passions of mankind. I do not complain that it does not influence your judgment. Indeed I see clearly how a mild and conciliatory view of Persecution will enable you to speak pleasantly and inoffensively of almost all the performers in your list, except More and Socinius; whilst a man with a good word for More and Socinius would have to treat the other actors in the drama of the Reformation as we treat the successive figures on the inclined plane of the French Revolution, from Dumouriez to Barras. But what amazes and disables me is that you speak of the Papacy not as exercising a just severity, but as not exercising any severity. You do not say, these misbelievers deserved to fall into the hands of these torturers and Fire-the-faggots; but you ignore, you even deny, at least implicitly, the existence of the torture-chamber and the stake.

I cannot imagine a more inexplicable error, and I thought I had contrived the gentlest formula of disagreement in coupling you with Cardinal Newman.

The same thing is the case with Sixtus IV and the Spanish Inquisition. What you say has been said by Hefele and Gams and others. They, at least, were in a sort, avowed defenders of the Spanish Inquisition. Hefele speaks of Ximenes as one might speak of Andrewes or Taylor or Leighton. But in what sense is the Pope not responsible for the constitution by which he established the new tribunal? If we passed a law giving Dufferin powers of that sort, when asked for, we should surely be responsible. No doubt, the responsibility in such a case is shared by those who ask for a thing. But if the thing is criminal, if, for instance, it is a license to commit adultery, the person who authorises the act shares the guilt of the person who commits it. Now the Liberals think Persecution a crime of a worse order than adultery, and the acts done by Ximenes considerably worse than the entertainment of Roman courtesans by Alexander VI. The responsibility exists whether the thing permitted be good or bad. If the thing be criminal, then the authority permitting it bears the guilt. Whether Sixtus is infamous or not depends on our view of persecution and absolutism. Whether he is responsible or not depends simply on the ordinary evidence of history.

Here, again, what I said is not in any way mysterious or esoteric. It appeals to no hidden code. It aims at no secret moral. It supposes nothing and implies nothing but what is universally current and familiar. It is the common, even the vulgar, code I appeal to.

Upon these two points we differ widely; still more widely with regard to the principle by which you undertake to judge men. You say that people in authority are not [to] be snubbed or sneezed at from our pinnacle of conscious rectitude. I really don't know whether you exempt them because of their rank, or of their success and power, or of their date. The chronological plea may have some little value in a limited sphere of instances. It does not allow of our saying that such a man did not know right from wrong, unless we are able to say that he lived before Columbus, before Copernicus, and could not know right from wrong. It can scarcely apply to the centre of Christendom, 1500 after the birth of our Lord. That would imply that Christianity is a mere system of metaphysics, which borrowed some ethics from elsewhere. It is rather a system of ethics which borrowed its metaphysics elsewhere. Progress in ethics means a constant turning of white into black and burning what one has adored. There is little of that between St. John and the Victorian era.

But if we might discuss this point until we found that we nearly agreed, and if we do argue thoroughly about the impropriety of Carlylese denunciations, and Pharisaism in history, I cannot accept your canon that we are to judge Pope and King unlike other men, with a favourable presumption that they did no wrong. If there is any presumption it is the other way against holders of power, increasing as the power increases. Historic responsibility has to make up for the want of legal responsibility. Power tends to corrupt and absolute power corrupts absolutely. Great men are almost always bad men, even when they exercise influence and not authority: still more when you superadd the tendency or the certainty of corruption by authority. There is no worse heresy than that the office sanctifies the holder of it. That is the point at which the negation of Catholicism and the negation of Liberalism meet and keep high festival, and the end learns to justify the means. You would hang a man of no position, like Ravaillac; but if what one hears is true, then Elizabeth asked the gaoler to murder Mary, and William III ordered his Scots minister to extirpate a clan. Here are the greater names coupled with the greater crimes. You would spare these criminals, for some mysterious reason. I would hang them, higher than Haman, for reasons of quite obvious justice; still more, still higher, for the sake of historical science.

The standard having been lowered in consideration of

date, is to be still further lowered out of deference to station. Whilst the heroes of history become examples of morality, the historians who praise them, Froude, Macauley, Carlyle, become teachers of morality and honest men. Quite frankly, I think there is no greater error. The inflexible integrity of the moral code is, to me, the secret of the authority, the dignity, the utility of history. If we may debase the currency for the sake of genius, or success, or rank, or reputation, we may debase it for the sake of a man's influence, of his religion, of his party, of the good cause which prospers by his credit and suffers by his disgrace. Then history ceases to be a science, an arbiter of controversy, a guide of the wanderer, the upholder of that moral standard which the powers of earth, and religion itself, tend constantly to depress. It serves where it ought to reign; and it serves the worst cause better than the purest.

Let me propose a crux whereby to part apologetic history from what I should like to call conscientious history:—an Italian government was induced by the Pope to set a good round price on the heads of certain of its subjects, presumably Protestants, who had got away. Nobody came to claim the reward. A papal minister wrote to the government in question to say that the Holy Father was getting impatient, and hoped to hear soon of some brave deed of authentic and remunerated homicide. The writer of that letter lies in the most splendid mausoleum that exists on earth; he has been canonized by the lawful, the grateful, the congenial authority of Rome; his statue, in the attitude of blessing, looks down from the Alps upon the plain of Lombardy; his likeness is in our churches; his name is upon our altars; his works are in our schools. His editor specially commends the letter I have quoted; and Newman celebrates him as a glorious Saint.

Here is all you want, and more. He lived many a year ago; he occupied the highest stations, with success and honour; he is held in high, in enthusiastic reverence by the most intelligent Catholics, by converts, by men who, in their time, have drunk in the convictions, haply the prejudices, of Protestant England; the Church that holds him up as a mirror of sanctity stands and falls with his good name; thousands of devout men and women would be wounded and pained if you call him an infamous assassin.

What shall we call him? *In foro conscientiae,* what do you think of the man or of his admirers? What should you think of Charlotte Corday if, instead of Marat, she had stabbed Borromeo? At what stage of Dante's pilgrimage should you expect to meet him?

And whereas you say that it is no recommendation in my eyes to have sympathy with the Roman system in its essentials, though you did not choose those terms quite seriously, one might wonder what these essentials are. Is it essential—for salvation within the communion of Rome—that we should accept what the canonization of such a saint implies, or that we should reject it? Does Newman or Manning, when he invokes St. Charles [Borromeo], act in the essential spirit of the Roman system, or in direct contradiction with it? To put it in a walnutshell: could a man be saved who allowed himself to be persuaded by such a chain of argument, by such a cloud of witnesses, by such a concourse of authorities, to live up to the example of St. Charles?

Of course I know that you do sometimes censure great men severely. But the doctrine I am contesting appears in your preface, and in such places as where you can hardly think that a pope can be a poisoner. This is a far larger question of method in history than what you mean when you say that I think you are afraid to be impartial; as if you were writing with purposes of conciliation and in opposition to somebody who thinks that the old man of the Seven Mountains is worse than the old man of one. I do not mean that, because your language about the Inquisition really baffles and bewilders me. Moreover, you are far more severe on Sixtus about the Pazzi than others; more, for instance, than Capponi or Reumont. And my dogma is not the special wickedness of my own spiritual superiors, but the general wickedness of men in authority—of Luther and Zwingli and Calvin and Cranmer and Knox, of Mary Stuart and Henry VIII, of Philip II and Elizabeth, of Cromwell and Louis XIV, James and Charles and William, Bossuet and Ken. Before this, it is a mere detail that imperfect sincerity is a greater reproach in divines than in laymen, and that, in our Church, priests are generally sacrilegious; and sacrilege is a serious thing. Let me add one word to explain my objection to your use of materials. Here is Pastor, boasting that he knows much that you do not. He does not stand on a very high level, and even his religion seems to be chiefly ecclesiastical. But I do apprehend that his massive information will give him an advantage over you when he gets farther. In that light I regret whatever does not tend to increase the authority of a work written on such *Culturstufe* as yours. I did not mean to overlook what may be urged *per contra*. When you began there was no rival more jealous than Gregorovius. That is not the case now. I should have wished your fortification to be strengthened against a new danger.

I am sure you will take this long and contentious letter more as a testimony of heart confidence and respect than of hostility—although as far as I grasp your method I don't agree with it. Mine seems to me plainer and safer; but it has never been enough to make me try to write a history, from mere want of knowledge. I will put it into canons, leaving their explanation and development to you.

I remain, yours most sincerely
Acton

Advice to persons about to write History:—Don't. Visit the Monte Purgatorio, as Austin called the Magnesian rock that yields Epsom Salts; or: Get rid of Hole and Corner Buffery.

In the Moral Sciences Prejudice is Dishonesty.

A Historian has to fight against temptations special to his mode of life, temptations from Country, Class, Church, College, Party, authority of talents, solicitation of friends.

The most respectable of these influences are the most dangerous.

The historian who neglects to root them out is exactly like a juror who votes according to his personal likes or dislikes.

In judging men and things, Ethics go before Dogma, Politics or Nationality.

The Ethics of History cannot be denominational.

Judge not according to the orthodox standard of a system, religious, philosophical, political, but according as things promote or fail to promote the delicacy, integrity and authority of Conscience.

Put Conscience above both System and Success.

History provides neither compensation for suffering nor penalties for wrong.

The moral code, in its main lines, is not new; it has long been known; it is not universally accepted in Europe, even now. The difference in moral insight between past and present is not very large.

But the notion and analysis of Conscience is scarcely older than 1700; and the notion and analysis of veracity is scarcely older than our time—barring Sacred Writings of East and West.

In Christendom, time and place do not excuse—if the Apostle's Code sufficed for Salvation.

Strong minds think things out, complete the circle of their thinking, and must not be interpreted by types.

Good men and great men are *ex vi termini,* aloof from the action of surroundings.

But goodness generally appeared in unison with authority, sustained by environment, and rarely manifested the force and sufficiency of the isolated will and conscience.

The Reign of Sin is more universal, the influence of unconscious error is less, than historians tell us. Good and evil lie close together. Seek no artistic unity in character.

History teaches a Psychology which is not that of private experience and domestic biography.

The principles of public morality are as definite as those of the morality of private life; but they are not identical.

A good cause proves less in a man's favour than a bad cause against him.

The final judgment depends on the worst action.

Character is tested by true sentiments more than by conduct. A man is seldom better than his word.

History is better written from letters than from histories: let a man criminate himself.

No public character has ever stood the revelation of private utterance and correspondence.

Be prepared to find that the best repute gives way under closer scrutiny.

In public life, the domain of History, vice is less than crime.

Active, transitive sins count for more than others.

The greatest crime is Homicide.

The accomplice is no better than the assassin; the theorist is worse.

Of killing from private motives or from public, from political or from religious, *eadem est ratio*. Morally, the worst is the last. The source of crime is *pars melior nostri*. What ought to save, destroys. The sinner is hardened and proof against Repentance.

Faith must be sincere. When defended by sin it is not sincere; theologically, it is not Faith. God's grace does not operate by sin.

Transpose the nominative and the accusative and see how things look then.

History deals with Life; Religion with Death. Much of its work and spirit escapes our ken.

The systems of Barrow, Baxter, Bossuet higher, spiritually, constructively, scientifically, than Penn's. In our scales his high morality outweighs them.

Crimes by constituted authorities worse than crimes by Madame Tussaud's private malefactors. Murder may be done by legal means, by plausible and profitable war, by calumny, as well as by dose or dagger.

The College,
Worcester
[April 9, 1887]

My dear Lord Acton,

Your letter is an act of true friendliness, and I am very grateful to you for it, more grateful than I can say. It is a rare encouragement to have such a standard set up as you have put before me. Judged by it I have nothing to say except to submit: *efficaci do manus scientiae*. Before such an ideal I can only confess that I am shallow and frivolous, limited alike in my views and in my knowledge. You conceive of History as an Architectonic, for the writing of which a man needs the severest and largest training. And it is impossible not to agree with you: so it ought to be.

I can only admit that I fall far short of the equipment necessary for the task that I have undertaken. I was engaged in reading quietly for the purpose, and the beginning of writing lay in the remote distance in my mind, when I received a letter asking me to look through the papers of an old gentleman whom I slightly knew, who on his deathbed had made me his literary executor. I came across him at Oxford in the Bodleian, where he came to read for a history of the rise of Universities. He died at the age of seventy-four, possessor of a vast number of notes, out of which all that I could piece together was an article on Wyclif's Oxford life. This filled me with a horror of notebooks and urged me to begin definitely to write. I thought that I had best frankly do what I could; anything would serve as a step for my successors. So I wrote.

I entirely agree with your principles of historical judgments: but apparently I admit casuistry to a larger extent than you approve. I remember that in 1880 I met John Bright at dinner: he was very cross, apparently a cabinet meeting had disagreed with him. Amongst other things he said: "If the people knew what sort of men statesmen were, they would rise and hang the whole lot of them." Next day I met a young man who had been talking to Gladstone, who urged him to parliamentary life, saying: "Statesmanship is the noblest way to serve mankind."

I am sufficient of a Hegelian to be able to combine both judgments; but the results of my combination cannot be expressed in the terms of the logic of Aristotle. In studying history the question of the salvability of an archdeacon becomes indefinitely extended to all officials, kings and popes included. What I meant in my offending sentence in my preface was that anyone engaged in great affairs occupied a representative position, which required special consideration. Selfishness, even wrongdoing, for an idea, an institution, the maintenance of an accepted view of the basis of society, does not cease to be wrongdoing: but it is not quite the same as personal wrongdoing. It is more difficult to prove, and it does not equally shock the moral sense of others or disturb the moral sense of the doer. The acts of men in power are determined by the effective force behind them of which they are the exponents: their morality is almost always lower than the morality of the mass of men: but there is generally a point fixed below which they cannot sink with impunity. Homicide is always homicide: but there is a difference between that of a murderer for his own gain, and that of a careless doctor called in to see a patient who would probably have died anyhow; and the carelessness of the doctor is a difficult thing to prove.

What is tolerance nowadays? Is it a moral virtue in the possessor, or is it a recognition of a necessity arising from an equilibrium of parties? It often seems to me that we speak as if it was the first, when actually it is the second. My liberalism admits to everyone the right to his own opinion and imposes on me the duty of teaching him what is best; but I am by no means sure that that is the genuine conviction of all my liberal friends. French liberalism does not convince me that it is universal. I am not quite sure how Frederick Harrison or Cotter Morrison would deal with me if they were in a majority. The possession of a clear and definite ideal of society seems to me dangerous to its possessors. The Mediæval Church had such an ideal: the result was the Inquisition, which was generally approved by the common consciousness. In the period of the end of the fifteenth century the Papacy seemed to me to have wearied of the Inquisition which was not much supported. The Popes were comparatively tolerant to Jews, Marrani, Turks; they did not attack the humanists; they did not furbish up the old weapons and apply them to new cases—except in the recognition of the Spanish Inquisition by Sixtus IV, about whom I have probably expressed myself loosely, but I have not my volumes here and I do not exactly [recall] what I said. What I meant was that to Sixtus IV this recognition was a matter of official routine. To have refused it he would have had to enunciate a new principle and make a new departure in ecclesiastical jurisdiction. I should have honoured him if he had done so; but I do not think him exceptionally persecuting because he did not do so. He accepted what he found. My purpose was not to justify him, but to put him in rank with the rest. I think, however, that I was wrong, and that you are right: his responsibility was graver than I have admitted. I think he knew better.

You judge the whole question of persecution more rigorously than I do. Society is an organism and its laws are an expression of the conditions which it considers necessary for its own preservation. When men were hanged in England for sheep stealing it was because people thought that sheep stealing was a crime and ought to be severely put down. We still think it a crime, but we think it can be checked more effectively by less stringent punishments. Nowadays people are not agreed about what heresy is; they do not think it a menace to society; hence they do not ask for its punishment. But the men who conscientiously thought heresy a crime may be accused of an intellectual mistake, not necessarily of a moral crime. The immediate results of the Reformation were not to favour free thought, and the error of Calvin, who knew that ecclesiastical unity was abolished, was a far greater one than that of Innocent III who struggled to maintain it. I am hopelessly tempted to admit degrees of criminality, otherwise history becomes a dreary record of wickedness.

I go so far with you that it supplies me with few heroes, and records few good actions; but the actors were men like myself, sorely tempted by the possession of power, trammeled by holding a representative position (none were more trammeled than popes), and in the sixteenth century especially looking at things in a very abstract way. I suppose statesmen rarely regard questions in the concrete. I cannot follow the actions of contemporary statesmen with much moral satisfaction. In the past I find myself regarding them with pity—who am I that I should condemn them? Surely they knew not what they did.

This is no reason for not saying what they did; but what they did was not always what they tried to do or thought that they were doing.

Moral progress has indeed been slow; it still is powerless to affect international relations. If Bright's remedy were adopted and every statesman in Europe were hanged, would that mend matters?

In return for your wisdom I have written enough to show my foolishness. Your letter will give me much food for meditation, and may in time lead to an amendment of my ways. That you should have written shows that you think me capable of doing better. I will only promise that if I can I will; but the labours of practical life multiply, and I have less time for work at my subject now then I had in the country. For a period coming on I ought to spend years in Archives: which is impossible. . . . .

My jottings bear traces of the incoherence of one who has preached five sermons this week, and has two more to preach tomorrow. I have not had time to think over your letter: but I wanted to thank you. Perhaps the effort to rid myself of prejudice has left me cold and abstract in my mode of expression and thinking. If so it is an error to be amended and corrected.

Will you not someday write an article in the *Historical Review* on the Ethics of History? I have no objection to find my place among the shocking examples. Believe me that I am genuinely grateful to you.

Yours most sincerely
M. Creighton

BIBLIOGRAPHY

Compiled by Bert F. Hoselitz

In the compilation of this bibliography several already available bibliographical studies of Lord Acton's work have been consulted. Of greatest use was the bibliography of Lord Acton's works compiled by W. A. Shaw, and published in his work *A Bibliography of the Historical Works of Dr. Creighton..., Dr. Stubbs, Dr. S. R. Gardiner and The Late Lord Acton*, London, Royal Historical Society, 1903. In addition to this work the information provided by Cardinal Gasquet in his work, *Lord Acton and His Circle*, and the items furnished by him to the editors of Acton's *History of Freedom and Other Essays* (p. 597) was very helpful. Finally, use has been made of the bibliography compiled by F. E. Lally, published in his work, *As Lord Acton Says*, Remington Ward, Publisher, Newport, Rhode Island, 1942. In several cases Acton's manuscripts in the Cambridge University Library have been helpful in corroborating or correcting information derived from other sources. The published works of Lord Acton have been subdivided in six groups. An attempt has been made to arrange his publications chronologically in each group according to the date of composition or publication.

Books

A Lecture on the Study of History (Inaugural Lecture delivered at Cambridge, June 11, 1895), (London, 1895). Pp. 142. Reprinted in *Lectures on Modern History* (London, 1906) under the title, "An Inaugural Lecture on 'The Study of History'." Text, pp. 1-30, footnotes, pp. 319-42.

Lectures on Modern History (delivered by Lord Acton in his ordinary course at Cambridge in the academical years 1899-1900, and 1900-1901). Published from MS. "exactly in the form in which they were delivered." Edited by J. N. Figgis and R. V. Laurence (London, 1906) Pp. xix and 362.

Historical Essays and Studies, edited by J. N. Figgis and R. V. Laurence (London, 1907) Pp. 544.*

The History of Freedom and Other Essays, edited by J. N. Figgis and R. V. Laurence (London, 1907) Pp. xxxix and 638.**

---
* In the later part of this bibliography this work will be referred to as *HES*.
** In the later part of this bibliography this work will be referred to as *HOF*.

Lectures on the French Revolution (as delivered by Lord Acton at Cambridge in the academical years 1895-96, 1896-97, 1897-98, 1898-99 in view of the history tripos of those years), edited by J. N. Figgis and R. V. Laurence (London, 1910) Pp. 379.

ARTICLES, LECTURES AND MISCELLANEOUS MATERIALS

"Lord Acton's American Diaries," *The Fortnightly Review*, Vol. CX, New Series, No. DCLIX (November, 1921), pp. 727-42, Vol. CX, New Series, No. DCLX (December, 1921), pp. 917-34, and Vol. CXI, New Series, No. DCLXI (January, 1922), pp. 63-83.

THE FOLLOWING ARTICLES APPEARED IN *The Rambler, New Series:*

"Mr. Buckle's Thesis and Method," Vol. X, part 55 (July, 1858), pp. 27-42. Acton's co-editor, Richard Simpson, probably wrote the major part of this article. Republished in *HES*, pp. 305-23.

"Mr. Buckle's Philosophy of History," Vol. X, part 56 (August, 1858), pp. 88-104. Republished in *HES*, pp. 324-43.

"The Count de Montalembert," Vol. X, part 60 (December, 1858), pp. 421-28.

"Political Thoughts on the Church," Vol. XI, part 61 (January, 1859), pp. 30-49. Republished in *HOF*, pp. 188-211.

"The Catholic Press," Vol. XI, part 62 (February, 1859), pp. 73-90.

THE FOLLOWING ARTICLES APPEARED IN *The Rambler, New Series* (i.e., *Third Series*).*

"Historical Annotations to the Foregoing Article" ("The Abbé

---
* The Shaw bibliography attributes to Acton an additional article: "Mill on Liberty," *The Rambler, New Series* (i.e. *Third Series*), Vol. II, part IV (November, 1859), pp. 62-76, and Vol. II, part VI (March, 1860), pp 376-85. Among the Acton manuscripts in the University of Cambridge Library is a letter from T. Arnold (son of the famous Thomas Arnold of Rugby and brother of Matthew Arnold) to John Newman, dated June 7, 1859, offering a paper on Mill's *On Liberty* Newman forwarded it to Acton, adding the note: "I suspect Arnold would not write without pay His name would be good. I declined his offer, as being too late [for this issue]." Subsequently, it was apparently decided to print it; in three letters of Acton to Richard Simpson, his collaborator on *The Rambler*, dated August 24, 28, and 30, 1859, he mentioned the article by Arnold on Mill (Gasquet [ed.], *Lord Acton and his Circle*, pp. 81, 83, 85). Dr. Shaw may have been misled by the fact that the article was signed "A."

de Lamennais," by the Baron d'Eskstein), Vol. I, part I (May, 1859), pp. 70-77.

"The Roman Question," Vol. II, part V (January, 1860), pp. 136-54.

"The Political System of the Popes," Vol. II, part V (January, 1860), pp. 154-65; Vol. III, part VII (May, 1860), pp. 27-38; Vol. IV, part XI (January, 1861), pp. 183-93.

"The States of the Church," Vol. II, part VI (March, 1860), pp. 291-323.

"Hefele's Life of Ximenes," Vol. III, part VIII (July, 1860), pp. 159-70.

"National Defense," Vol. III, part IX (September, 1860), pp. 289-300.

"Irish Education," Vol. III, part IX (September, 1860), pp. 418-19.

"Döllinger's History of Christianity," Vol. IV, part XI (January, 1861), pp. 145-75.

"Notes on the Present State of Austria," Vol. IV, part XI (January, 1861), pp. 193-205.

"Political Causes of the American Revolution," Vol. V, part XIII (May, 1861), pp. 17-61.

"Cavour," Vol. V, part XIV (July, 1861), pp. 141-65. Republished in *HES*, pp. 174-203.

"The Catholic Academy," Vol. V, part XV (September, 1861), pp. 291-302.

"Döllinger on the Temporal Power," Vol. VI, part XVI (November, 1861), pp. 1-62. Republished in *HOF*, pp. 301-74.

"Mr. Goldwin Smith's Irish History," Vol. VI, part XVII (January, 1862), pp. 190-220. Republished in *HOF*, pp. 232-69.

"The Protestant Theory of Persecution," Vol. VI, part XVIII (March, 1862), pp. 318-51. Republished in *HOF*, pp. 150-87.

"Note on Events in Italy, Mexico, and Russia," in the section on Foreign Events, Vol. VI, part XIX (May, 1862), pp. 526-34.

THE FOLLOWING ARTICLES APPEARED IN *The Home and Foreign Review:*

"Nationality," Vol. I, No. 1 (July, 1862), pp. 1-25. Republished in *HOF*, pp. 270-300.

"Secret History of Charles II," Vol. I, No. 1 (July, 1862), pp. 146-74. Republished in *HES*, pp. 85-122.

"Cardinal Wiseman and the *Home and Foreign Review*," Vol.

I, No. 2 (October, 1862), pp. 501-20. Republished in HOF, pp. 436-60.

"Confessions of Frederick the Great," Vol. II, No. 3 (January, 1863), pp. 152-71.

"The Waldensian Forgeries," Vol. II, No. 4 (April, 1863), pp. 504-30. This was a contribution of Döllinger. Acton translated and edited it.

"Ultramontanism," Vol. III, No. 5 (July, 1863), pp. 162-206.

"Mediaeval Fables of the Popes," Vol. III, No. 6 (October, 1863), pp. 610-37.

"The Munich Congress," Vol. IV, No. 7 (January, 1864), pp. 209-44.

"Conflicts with Rome," Vol. IV, No. 8 (April, 1864), pp. 667-96. Republished in *HOF*, pp. 461-91.

Human Sacrifice, a pamphlet privately printed by Robson, Levey, and Franklyn, at London (probably 1863).

"The Civil War in America, its Place in History," *Bridgnorth Journal* (January 20, 1866). Republished in *HES*, pp. 123-42.

"The Rise and Fall of the Mexican Empire," *Bridgnorth Journal* (March 14, 1868). Republished in *HES*, pp. 143-72.

THE FOLLOWING ARTICLES APPEARED IN *The Chronicle*:

"Material Resources of the Papacy," Vol. I (March 30, 1867), pp. 7-8.

"Fra Paolo Sarpi," *ibid.* (March 30), pp. 14-17.

"The Case of Monte Cassino," *ibid.* (April 6), p. 33.

"Dollinger on Universities," *ibid.* (April 13), pp. 57-59.

"The Ministerial Changes in Italy," *ibid.* (April 20), pp. 81-83.

"Secret History of the Italian Crisis," *ibid.* (April 27), pp. 102-3.

"The Secret Bull," *ibid.* (May 4), pp. 124-25.

"Reminiscences of Massimo d'Azeglio," *ibid.* (May 11), pp. 158-59.

"The Next General Council," *ibid.* (July 13), pp. 368-70.

"Ranke" (on Ranke's 'Englische Geschichte'), *ibid.* (July 20), pp. 393-95.

"The Situation at Florence," *ibid.* (July 27), pp. 415-16.

"Professor Hergenröther's 'Life of Photius'," *ibid.* (July 27), pp. 419-21.

"M. Littré on the Middle Ages," *ibid.* (August 3), pp. 443-44.

"The Early Years of H. R. H. The Prince Consort," *ibid.* (August 10), pp. 470-71.

"Mr. Goldwin Smith on the Political History of England," *ibid.* (August 31), pp. 543-44.

"Nicholas of Cusa," *ibid.* (September 7), pp. 565-67.

"Mr. Bergenroth's Introduction" (to Vol. II of the "Calendar of State Papers, Spanish"), *ibid.* (September 14), pp. 587-89.

"Essays in Academical Literature" ("Essays in Religion and Literature" edited by Archbishop Manning), *ibid.* (October 5), pp. 664-67.

"Maurice of Saxony," *ibid.* (October 19), pp. 710-11.

"The Acta Sanctorum," *ibid.* (November 2), pp. 756-58.

"Mr. Grant Duff's 'Glance Over Europe'," Vol. II (January 11, 1868), pp. 31-32.

"The Queen's Journal," *ibid.* (January 18), pp. 65-66.

"Ozanam on the Fifth Century," *ibid.* (February 1), pp. 106-8.

"The Massacre of St. Bartholomew," *ibid.* (February 15), pp. 158-60.

Under the head of "Current Events" *The Chronicle* also contained a succession of notes and comments by Lord Acton on the political situation in Italy and the Papal State from March 1867 to February 1868 as follows:

1867, March 30, p. 2, from "Decentralisation checked" to p. 3, "called on to support".

April 6, p. 27, from "The Roman papers of the 23rd of March" to p. 28, "not easily overcome".

May 11, p. 148, Rome and Italy.
May 18, p. 171, Rome and Italy.
June 15, pp. 266-67, Italy and Rome.
June 29, pp. 314-15, Rome.
July 6, pp. 339-40, Rome.
July 13, p. 362, Rome.
July 20, pp. 386-87, Italy.
August 3, p. 435, The Revolution in Rome.
September 28, pp. 625-26, Rome and Italy.
October 5, p. 650, Rome and Italy.
October 12, p. 673, Rome.
October 19, pp. 697-98, Rome.
October 26, p. 721, The Roman Question.
November 2, pp. 745-46, The Roman Question.

November 9, pp. 769-70, Italy and France.
November 16, pp. 793-94, Italy and Rome.
November 23, p. 819, Italy and Rome.
November 30, pp. 841-2, Rome.
December 7, pp. 865-66, The Roman Question and the Conference.
December 14, p. 889, The Roman Question.
December 21, p. 914, The Roman Question.
December 29, p. 937, The Roman Question.
1868, January 4, p. 2, Italy.
January 11, p. 25, Italy.
January 18, p. 50, Italy.
January 25, p. 73, The Italian Budget.
February 8, p. 122, Letter of General della Marmora.

"The Massacre of St. Bartholomew," *North British Review*, Vol. LI, No. 101 (October, 1869), pp. 30-70. Republished in *HOF*, pp. 101-49.

"The Pope and the Council," *North British Review*, Vol. LI, No. 101 (October, 1869), pp. 127-35.

"The Vatican Council," *North British Review*, Vol. LIII, No. 105 (October, 1870), pp. 183-229. Republished in *HOF*, pp. 492-550.

"The Borgias and Their Latest Historian," *North British Review*, Vol. LIII, No. 106 (January, 1871), pp. 351-67. Republished in *HES*, pp. 65-84.

The War of 1870, A lecture, London, 1871. Republished in *HES*, pp. 226-72.

"Letters and Papers, Foreign and Domestic, of the Reign of Henry VIII," *The Quarterly Review*, Vol. CXLIII, No. 285 (January, 1877), pp. 1-51. Republished under the title, "Wolsey and the Divorce of Henry VIII," in *HES*, pp. 1-64.

The History of Freedom in Antiquity, an address delivered February 26, 1877 (Bridgnorth, 1877). Pp. 11. Republished in *HOF*, pp. 1-29.

The History of Freedom in Christianity, an address delivered May 28, 1877 (Bridgnorth, 1877). Pp. 12. Republished in *HOF*, pp. 30-60.

"Sir Erskine May's 'Democracy in Europe'," *The Quarterly Review,* Vol. CXLV, No. 289 (January, 1878), pp. 112-42. Republished in *HOF,* pp. 61-100.

"J. W. Cross's 'Life of George Eliot'," *The Nineteenth Century,* Vol. XVII, No. 97 (March, 1885), pp. 464-85. Republished in *HES* under the title "George Eliot's Life," pp. 273-304.

"German Schools of History," *English Historical Review,* Vol. I, No. 1 (June, 1886), pp. 7-42. Republished in *HES,* pp. 344-92.

"Wilhelm von Giesebrecht," *English Historical Review,* Vol. V, No. 18 (April, 1890), pp. 306-10. Republished in *HES,* pp. 496-502.

"Döllinger's Historical Work," *English Historical Review,* Vol. V, No. 20 (October, 1890), pp. 700-44. Republished in *HOF,* pp. 375-435.

Introductory note to L. A. Burd's edition of *Il Principe* by Niccolo Machiavelli (Oxford, 1891). The Introductory Note covers pp. xix-xl. Reprinted in *HOF,* 212-31.

The Causes of the Franco-German War, an essay read before the Trinity Historical Society at Cambridge, the "Eranus" society at Cambridge, and the S. Catharine's College Historical Society at Cambridge in 1899. Republished under the title, "The Causes of the Franco-Prussian War," in *HES,* pp. 204-25.

Record Experiences, an essay read before the Trinity Historical Society at Cambridge and the "Eranus" Society at Cambridge, 1899 [unpublished?].

Introduction to *Annals of Politics and Culture,* by G. P. Gooch (Cambridge, 1901). The Introduction covers p. v.

Correspondence

(This section includes the private correspondence of Lord Acton, as far as it has been published as well as his open letters, letters to editors, circulars, etc.)

Selections from the Correspondence of the First Lord Acton, edited with an introduction by J. N. Figgis and R. V. Laurence (London, 1917), Vol. I [all published], pp. xx and 324. The correspondence covers the period from 1844 to 1900.

Lord Acton and His Circle, edited with an introduction by Abbot (later Cardinal) Gasquet (London and New York, 1906), pp. lxxxviii and 372. The correspondence covers the period from 16 February, 1858 to 16 January, 1875.

Letter on "Our Public Schools and Universities before the Reformation" (signed A.), *The Rambler, New Series* (i.e. Third Series), Vol. VI, part XVI (November, 1861), pp. 119-24.

Letter on "The Danger of Physical Science" (signed N. N.), *The Rambler, New Series* (i.e. Third Series), Vol. VI, part XIX (May, 1862), pp. 526-34.

Letter of Sir John Acton to General Robert E. Lee (dated Bologna, November 4, 1866), reprinted in D. S. Freeman, *Robert E. Lee* (New York and London, 1935), Vol. IV, pp. 515-17.

Römische Briefe vom Concil, by Quirinus, four parts (Munich, 1870). Pp. 710. English translation, *Letters from Rome on the Council,* three series (London, 1870). Pp. 856. These letters appeared originally in the *Augsburger Allgemeine Zeitung* during December 1869 and the first part of 1870.

Sendschreiben an einen deutschen Bischof des vaticanischen Concils (Nördlingen, September, 1870). Pp. 19 (dated Tegernsee, August 30, 1870).

Letters to the *Times* on the Vatican Degrees. *Times,* November 9, 1874, November 24, 1874, November 30, 1874, and December 12, 1874. Reprinted in *Selections from the Correspondence of the First Lord Acton,* edited by J. N. Figgis and R. V. Laurence (London, 1917), pp. 119-44.

"Harpsfield's 'Narrative of the Divorce'," *The Academy,* Vol. IX, No. 216, New Series (June 24, 1876), pp. 609-10.

Letters of Lord Acton to Mary Gladstone (Mrs. Drew), edited with an introductory memoir by Herbert Paul (London and New York, 1904), p. 353. The correspondence covers the period from October, 1874 to January, 1886.

The same, second edition (London, 1913). The correspondence covers the period from October 1874 to the end of 1898.

Letter to Mary Gladstone (Mrs. Drew) on the Hundred Best Books. Published in Clement Shorter, "Lord Acton's Hundred Best Books," *Pall Mall Magazine,* Vol. XXXVI, No. 147 (July, 1905), pp. 4-7. The letter was written apparently in the year 1882 or 1883.

"Briefe Lord Acton's über George Eliot," contributed by Rudolf Imelmann, published in *Probleme der englischen Sprache und Kultur* (edited by Wolfgang Keller) (Heidelberg, 1925), pp. 195-207. The letters were written between October 19, 1885 and March 11, 1886.

Extracts from letters to Mandell Creighton on the latter's work

on the *History of the Papacy.* Published in *HES,* pp. 503-7. The letters were written probably in 1887.

Letters to the Syndicate of the Cambridge University Press on the plan of its proposed Universal History. Published in a booklet of the Cambridge University Press, *The Cambridge Modern History, etc.* (Cambridge, 1907). The letters were written in the late 1890's.

Printed circular to the contributors "From the Editor of the Cambridge Modern History," dated at Cambridge, March 12, 1898. Published in *Lectures on Modern History* (London, 1907). Pp. 315-18.

Edited Matter

Les matinés royales, ou l'art de régner, opuscule inédit de Frédéric II, dit le Grand, Roi de Prusse. Edited by Lord Acton (London and Edinburgh, 1863). P. 35.

Introduction to *Letters of James II, to the Abbot of La Trappe,* edited by Lord Acton, Miscellanies of the Philobiblion Society, Vol. XIV (London, 1872-76). The Introduction by Lord Acton covers pp. iii-xv.

The second book containing all the historical portions of Dr. Harpsfield, *Narrative of the Divorce* (privately printed by Whittingham and Wilkins, London, 1877). Pp. 124.

Speech in the House of Commons

"The Roman Government Question," Sir John Acton's speech in Parliament as reported in Hansard, *Parliamentary Debates,* Vol. CLVIII (Third Series), cols. 679-81 [23 Victoria], 1860.

Book Reviews

In *The Rambler, New Series*

Thomas Macknight, "History of the Life and Times of Edmund Burke," Vol. IX, part 53 (April, 1858), pp. 268-73.

R. P. Félix, "Le progrès par le Christianisme: Conférences de Notre Dame de Paris," Vol. X, part 55 (July, 1858), pp. 70-72.

M. Villemain, La Tribune Moderne, Vol. X, part 56 (August, 1858), pp. 140-42.

A. Theiner, "Documents inédits relatifs aux affaires réligieuses de France," Vol. X, part 58 (October, 1858), pp. 265-67.

Thomas Carlyle, "History of Frederick II of Prussia, called Frederick the Great," Vol. X, part 60 (December, 1858), p. 429.

In *The Rambler, New Series* (i.e., *Third Series*):

Schmidt–Weissenfels, "Geschichte der französischen Revolutions–Literatur." Vol. II, part IV (November, 1859), pp. 104-7.

J. B. Robertson, "Lectures on Ancient and Modern History" Vol. II, part VI (March, 1860), pp. 396-98.

P. Charles of St. Aloysius, "Statistisches Jahrbuch der Kirche," Vol. III, part VIII (July, 1860), pp. 262-64.

"The Tyrolese Patriots of 1809" by the Author of "Du Guesclin," Vol. IV, part X (November, 1860), pp. 126-28.

J. F. A. Peyré, "Histoire de la Première Croisade," Vol. V, part XV (September, 1861), pp. 403-6.

F. Guizot, "The Christian Church and Society in 1861," Vol. VI, part XVII (January, 1862), pp. 265-68.

G. Finlay, "History of the Greek Revolution," Vol. VI, part XVIII (March, 1862), pp. 404-8.

E. Arnold, "The Marquis of Dalhousie's Administration of British India," Vol. VI, part XIX (May, 1862), pp. 534-36.

In *The Home and Foreign Review*:

F. Beckman, "Zur Geschichte des Kopernikanischen Systems," Vol. I, No. 1 (July, 1862), pp. 240-41.

Alex. Teulet, "Relations politiques de la France et de l'Espagne avec l'Écosse au XVIme siècle," *ibid.*, p. 241.

J. Spedding, "Letters and Life of Francis Bacon," *ibid.*, pp. 241-42.

Le Père J. M. Prat, "Histoire du père Ribadeneyra," *ibid.*, pp. 242-43.

H. d'Arbois de Jubainville, "Histoire des ducs de Champagne," Vol. I, No. II (October, 1862), pp. 538-40.

Le Baron Kervyn de Lettenhove, "Commentaires de Charles Quint," *ibid.*, pp. 540-42.

V. Fournel, "La Littérature indépendante," *ibid.*, pp. 542-43.

A. F. DeCareil, "Œuvres de Leibniz," *ibid.*, pp. 543-45.

M. Matter, "Saint Martin, le philosophe inconnu," *ibid.*, pp. 545-47.

M. Mortimer-Ternaux, "Histoire de la Terreur," *ibid.*, pp. 547-48.

"Mémoires sur Carnot, par son fils," *ibid.*, pp. 548-50.

"Mémoires de M. Dupin," *ibid.*, pp. 550-51.

P. Gagarin, "Œuvres choisies de Pierre Tchadaïef," *ibid.*, pp. 551-52.

F. Hülskamp and H. Rump, "Literarischer Handweiser für das katholische Deutschland," *ibid.*, pp. 561-62.

H. Formby, "Pictorial Bible and Church History Stories," Vol. II, No. III (January, 1863), pp. 215-19.

B. Niehues, "Geschichte des Verhältnisses zwischen Kaiserthum und Papstthum im Mittelalter," *ibid.*, pp. 220-21.

H. Holland, "Geschichte der altdeutschen Dichtkunst in Bayern," *ibid.*, pp. 221-23.

G. A. Bergenroth, "Calendar of State Papers, Spanish," *ibid.*, pp. 227-30.

E. H. J. Reusens, "Anecdota Adriani Sexti," *ibid.*, pp. 230-31.

Hugo Laemmer, "Monumenta vaticana historiam ecclesiasticam saeculi XVI illustrantia," *ibid.*, pp. 231-33.

W. Roscher, "Die deutsche Nationalökonomie," *ibid.*, pp. 233-5.

A. Gindely, "Meine Forschungen in fremden und einheimischen Archiven," *ibid.*, pp. 235-36.

M. Napier, "Memorials of Graham of Claverhouse, Viscount Dundee," *ibid.*, pp. 236-37.

"Recueil de documents sur l'histoire de Lorraine," *ibid.*, pp. 237-38.

L. Dussieux and E. Soulié, "Mémoires du Duc de Luynes, 1735-58," *ibid.*, pp. 238-39.

L. Schauer and Alp Chuquet, "La correspondance inédite de L. C. Saint Martin et Kirchberger baron de Liebistorf, 1792-7," *ibid.*, pp. 240-42.

C. von Martens, "Vor fünfzig Jahren. Tagebuch meines Feldzugs in Russland, 1812," *ibid.*, pp. 242-43.

M. Bogdanowitsch, "Geschichte des Feldzugs im Jahre 1812," *ibid.*, pp. 243-44.

A. Thiers, "Histoire du Consulat et de l'Empire," *ibid.*, pp. 244-48.

Jos. Beck, "Freiherr I. Heinrich von Wessenberg," *ibid.*, pp. 248-50.

T. Arnold, "A Manual of English Literature," *ibid.*, pp. 250-54.

C. Knight, "The Popular History of England," *ibid.*, pp. 254-57.

F. Arnold, "The Public Life of Lord Macaulay," *ibid.*, pp. 257-60.

J. J. Thonissen, "Vie du Comte Félix de Mérode," *ibid.*, pp. 268-70.

"Zeitgenossen . . . von A. von Reumont," *ibid.*, pp. 270-72.

Dr. Hoefer, "Nouvelle Biographie Générale, Vol. XL," *ibid.*, pp. 274-76.

"Mémoires de Canler, ancien chef du service de la Sûreté," *ibid.*, pp. 276-77.

J. A. Gerth von Wijk, "Specimen historico-theologicum exhibens historiam ecclesiae ultrajectinae Romano-Catholicae male Jansenisticae dictae," *ibid.*, pp. 277-78.

"Die kirchliche Frage und ihre protestantische Lösung . . mit Beziehung auf die Schriften J. J. I. von Döllinger's und Bischof von Ketteler's," *ibid.*, pp. 281-83.

F. J. Buss, "Oesterreichs Umbau im Verhältniss des Reichs zur Kirche," *ibid.*, pp. 283-84.

F. Bodenstedt, "Russische Fragmente," *ibid.*, pp. 284-86.

E. A. Freeman, "History of Federal Government," Vol. II, No. IV (April, 1863), pp. 587-89.

C. Merivale, "History of the Romans under the Empire," *ibid.*, pp. 589-93.

J. C. Morison, "The Life and Times of St. Bernard, Abbot of Clairvaux," *ibid.*, pp. 608-12.

T. L. Kington, "History of Frederick II," *ibid.*, pp. 613-14.

J. C. Kopp, "Geschichte der eidgenössischen Bünde," *ibid.*, pp. 615-16.

P. Villari, "History of Girolamo Savonarola," *ibid.*, pp. 616-17.

W. N. Sainsbury, "Calendar of Colonial State Papers, 1513-16," *ibid.*, pp. 617-19.

Armand Baschet, "La diplomatie Vénitienne. Les princes de l'Europe au XVIième siècle," *ibid.*, pp. 622-23.

C. de Moüy, "Don Carlos et Philippe II," *ibid.*, pp. 623-25.

J. J. I. von Döllinger, "Beiträge zur politischen, kirchlichen und Cultur-Geschichte der sechs letzten Jahrhunderte," *ibid.*, pp. 625-29.

F. von Hurter, "Wallenstein's vier letzte Lebensjahre," *ibid.*, pp. 629-31.

Honoré Bonhomme, "Madame de Maintenon et sa famille," *ibid.*, pp. 631-32.

Edmund et Jules de Goncourt, "La femme au dix-huitième siècle," *ibid.*, pp. 632-34.

T. Macknight, "Life of Henry St. John, Viscount Bolingbroke," *ibid.*, pp. 634-37.

L. Häusser, "Deutsche Geschichte, *Vols. II and III*," *ibid.*, pp. 642-45.

N. W. Senior, "Biographical Sketches," *ibid.*, pp. 645-47.
M. Guizot, "Histoire parlementaire de France," *ibid.*, pp. 650-51.
Sir G. C. Lewis, "A Dialogue on the best Form of Government," *ibid.*, pp. 651-52.
H. W. J. Thiersch, "Griechenlands Schicksale," *ibid.*, pp. 652-55.
B. Carneri, "Demokratie, Nationalität und Napoleonismus," *ibid.*, pp. 655-56.
E. M. Hudson, "The Second War of Independence in America," *ibid.*, pp. 656-59.
E. Augier, "Le fils de Giboyer," *ibid.*, pp. 666-69.
Edward Vaughan Kenealy, "A New Pantomime," *ibid.*, pp. 669-74.
H. Brockhaus (Ersch und Grüber), "Allgemeine Encyclopädie," Vol. III, No. V (July, 1863), pp. 269-70.
M. C. Debombourg, "Atlas chronologique des Etats de l'Eglise," *ibid.*, p. 279.
G. F. Maclear, "A History of Christian Missions during the Middle Ages," *ibid.*, pp. 279-82.
(?) M. l'Abbé Alliez, "Histoire du Monastère de Lérins," *ibid.*, pp. 282-83.
M. A. Huguenin, "Histoire du royaume Mérovingien," *ibid.*, pp. 283-84.
A. de Brimont, "Un Pape au Moyen Age," *ibid.*, pp. 284-85.
L'Abbé Magnan, "Histoire d'Urbain V," *ibid.*, pp. 285-86.
L'Abbé J. B. Christophe, "Histoire de la Papauté pendant le XVme Siècle," *ibid.*, pp. 287-89.
J. Janssen, "Frankfurt's Reichscorrespondenz, 1376-1439," *ibid.*, pp. 289-90.
E. H. J. Reussens, "Syntagma Doctrinae Theologicae," *ibid.*, p. 290.
E. Stähelin, "Johannes Calvin: Leben und ausgewählte Schriften," *ibid.*, pp. 290-91.
Jakob Maehly, "Sebastian Castellio," *ibid.*, pp. 291-92.
F. Brandes, "John Knox," *ibid.*, p. 292.
E. Benoist, "Guichardin," *ibid.*, pp. 292-93.
A. Reumont d'Aquisgrana, "Bibliografia dei lavori pubblicati in Germania sulla Storia d'Italia," *ibid.*, pp. 293-95.
R. R. Madden, "Galileo and the Inquisition," *ibid.*, p. 295.
S. R. Gardiner, "History of England, 1603-16," *ibid.*, pp. 296-97.

M. C. Hippeau, "Mémoires inédits du Comte Leveneur de Tillières," *ibid.,* pp. 297-98.

H. Woodhead, "Memoirs of Christina, Queen of Sweden," *ibid.,* p. 300.

Count Macdonnel, "Diary of an Austrian Secretary of Legation at the Court of Czar Peter the Great," *ibid.,* p. 300.

M. Roux, "Mémoires de l'Abbé Le Gendre," *ibid.,* pp. 303-5.

A. Coquerel fils, "Voltaire, lettres inédites sur la tolérance," *ibid.,* pp. 305-6.

C. Desmaze, "Le Châtelet de Paris," *ibid.,* p. 306.

Dom Devienne, "Histoire de la ville de Bordeaux," *ibid.,* p. 307.

M. Kayserling, "Moses Mendelssohn," *ibid.,* 307-9.

W. Herbst, "Matthias Claudius der Wandsbecker Bote," *ibid.,* p. 309.

Silvestre de Sacy, "Dacier: tableau historique de l'Erudition française depuis 1789," *ibid.,* pp. 309-10.

F. Colincamp and M. Naudet, "J. F. Boissonade, critique littéraire sous le premier Empire," *ibid.,* pp. 310-11.

Alexandre Sorel, "Le Couvent des Carmes et le Séminaire de Saint-Sulpice pendant la Terreur," *ibid.,* pp. 311-12.

W. Massey, "History of England during the Reign of George III," *ibid.,* pp. 312-14.

Maximilian Ritter von Thielen, "Erinnerungen aus dem Kriegerleben &c," *ibid.,* pp. 314-15.

A. Nettement, "Histoire de la Restauration," *ibid.,* pp. 316-18.

C. A. Sainte-Beuve, "Nouveaux Lundis," *ibid.,* pp. 318-19.

A. M. du Gratry, "La République de Paraguay," *ibid.,* pp. 319-20.

Charles Calvo, "Recueil complet de Traités de tous les états de l'Amérique Latine," *ibid.,* pp. 320-21.

Bonamy Price, "Venetia and the Quadrilateral," *ibid.,* pp. 321-22.

"Thirteen Months in the Rebel Army: by an impressed New Yorker," *ibid.,* pp. 325-26.

"Two months in the Confederate States: by an English Merchant," *ibid.,* pp. 326-37.

F. D. Gerlach, "Vorgeschichte, &c., des Römischen Staats," Vol. III, No. VI (October, 1863), pp. 679-81.

A. Potthast, "Bibliotheca Historica Medii Aevi," *ibid.,* pp. 681-82.

J. Carnaudet, "Acta Sanctorum," *ibid.,* pp. 682-85.

M. Joël, "Verhältniss Albert des Grossen zu Moses Maimonides," *ibid.*, pp. 689-90.

W. A. Hollenberg, "Studien zu Bonaventura," *ibid.*, p. 690.

S. Sugenheim, "Geschichte der Aufhebung der Leibeigenschaft in Europa," *ibid.*, pp. 691-92.

Mgr. Jager, "Histoire de l'Eglise Catholique en France," *ibid.*, pp. 693-94.

F. Gregorovius, "Geschichte der Stadt Rom im Mittelalter," *ibid.*, pp. 694-95.

J. Friedrich, "Johann Wessel," *ibid.*, pp. 696-97.

V. Fournel, "Les contemporains de Molière," *ibid.*, pp. 697-98.

Ch. Marty-Laveaux, "Œuvres de P. Corneille," *ibid.*, pp. 698-99.

F. Lachat, "Œuvres complètes de Bossuet," *ibid.*, pp. 699-701.

M. le Cte. de Seilhac, "L'Abbé Dubois," *ibid.*, pp. 701-2.

Alfred Ritter von Arneth, "Maria Theresia's erste Regierungsjahre," *ibid.*, pp. 702-3.

C. H. Gildemeister, "Johann Georg Hamann's des 'Magus in Norden' Autorschaft," *ibid.*, pp. 703-4.

H. Nadault de Buffon, "Buffon; sa Famille, &c.," *ibid.*, pp. 704-11.

A. Springer, "Geschichte Oesterreichs seit 1809," *ibid.*, pp. 711-13.

O. Klopp, "Kleindeutsche Geschichtsbaumeister," *ibid.*, p. 713.

J. G. Phillimore, "History of England during the Reign of George III," *ibid.*, pp. 713-15.

T. E. May, "Constitutional History of England," *ibid.*, pp. 715-18.

E. Scherer, "Etudes critiques sur la littérature contemporaine," *ibid.*, pp. 718-20.

F. Wolf, "Histoire de la littérature Brésilienne," *ibid.*, pp. 722-24.

C. Nitsch, "Die evangelische Bewegung in Italien," *ibid.*, pp. 724-26.

Adolf Stahr, "Tiberius," Vol. IV, No. VII (January, 1864), pp. 276-81.

J. E. Doyle, "A Chronicle of England, B.C. 55-A.D. 1485," *ibid.*, pp. 289-90.

J. F. Maguire, "Father Matthew — A Biography," *ibid.*, pp. 305-8.

H. E. Manning, "Sermons on Ecclesiastical Subjects," *ibid.*, pp. 310-12.

G. de Molinari, "Cours d'économie politique," *ibid.,* pp. 313-15.

W. Forsyth, "Life of M. T. Cicero," Vol. IV, No. VIII (April, 1864), p. 705.

J. W. Jones, "The Travels of Ludovico di Varthema," *ibid.,* pp. 707-8.

Sylvester Malone, "A Church History of Ireland," *ibid.,* pp. 708-15.

Baum, Cunitz, &c., "Corpus Reformatorum, Vol. XXIX," *ibid.,* p. 715.

F. Laurent, "Etudes sur l'histoire de l'Humanité," *loc. cit.*

L. von Ranke, "Englische Geschichte, Vol. IV," *ibid.,* pp. 715-16.

M. Matter, "Swedenborg," *ibid.,* p. 717.

C. J. Riethmüller, "Alexander Hamilton and his Contemporaries," *ibid.,* pp. 718-19.

Max von Eelking, "Die deutschen Hülfstruppen im Nordamerikanischen Befreiungskriege," *ibid.,* pp. 719-20.

H. Richelot, "Goethe, ses mémoires, &c.," *ibid.,* pp. 720-21.

W. Reymond, "Corneille, Shakespeare et Goethe," *ibid.,* p. 721.

"Kleine historische Schriften von H. von Sybel," *ibid.,* p. 722.

Léon Verdier, "Histoire politique et littéraire de la Restauration," *ibid.,* pp. 722-23.

M. Guizot, "Mémoires pour servir à l'histoire de mon temps," *ibid.,* pp. 723-24.

Ed. Laboulaye, "Le parti libéral, son programme, et son avenir," *ibid.,* pp. 724-25.

G. Ticknor, "Life of W. H. Prescott," *ibid.,* pp. 725-26.

"Pensées et fragments divers de Charles Neuhaus," *ibid.,* pp. 733-34.

In *The Chronicle*

"Instruzione del Duca di Savoia Carlo Emmanuele I. al Marchese Fr. Villa inviato alla Maestà del Re d' Inghilterra," Vol. I (March 30, 1867), pp. 18-19.

L. Chodzko, "Le Métropolitain K. G. C. Cieciszowski et son temps," *ibid.,* p. 19.

A. Nettement, "Histoire de la Restauration," *ibid.,* p. 19.

G. Sander, "Geschichte des vierjährigen Bürgerkrieges in den Vereinigten Staaten von Amerika," *ibid.,* p. 19.

C. Martha, "Les Moralistes sous l'Empire Romain," *ibid.,* p. 43.

F. de Saulcy, "Les derniers jours de Jérusalem," (April 6, 1867), p. 43.
A. Cappelli, "Lettere di Ludovico Ariosto," ibid., pp. 43-44.
H. Taine, "Philosophie de l'art en Italie," ibid., p. 44.
Ch. A. Dauban, "Précis d'histoire contemporaine," ibid., p. 44.
E. Geruzez, "Mélanges et Pensées," ibid., p. 44.
G. Perrot, "L'Ile de Crète, souvenirs de voyage," ibid., p. 44.
S. Sugenheim, "Geschichte des deutschen Volkes," (April 13, 1867), pp. 64-5.
P. Clément, "Jacques Coeur et Charles VII," ibid., p. 65.
G. de Leva, "Storia documentata di Carlo V," ibid., pp. 65-66.
E. Ricotti, "Storia della Monarchia Piemontese," ibid., p. 66.
"Œuvres complètes de P. Rossi," ibid., pp. 66-67.
Pietro de Donato Giannini, "Della vita e delle opere di Massimo d'Azeglio," ibid., p. 67.
M. Deutinger, "Der gegenwärtige Zustand der deutschen Philosphie," ibid., p. 67.
Cesare Cantù, "Storia della Letterature Italiana," (April 20, 1867), pp. 89-90.
M. le Marquis de Sainte-Aulaire, "Correspondance complète de Madame du Deffand," ibid., p. 90.
"Mémoires du Comte Beugnot, ancien ministre (1783-1815)," ibid., pp. 90-91.
A. Desplanque, "Projet d'assassinat de Philippe le Bon par les Anglais," (April 27, 1867), p. 115.
P. Clément, "Lettres, instructions et mémoires de Colbert," ibid., pp. 115-16.
G. Campori, "Lettere artistiche inedite," (May 4, 1867), p. 138.
C. Milanesi, "Il sacco di Roma del 1527," ibid., pp. 138-39.
M. Gachard, "Don Carlos et Philippe II," ibid., pp. 139-40.
J. E. Erdmann, "Grundriss der Geschichte der Philosophie," ibid., p. 140.
C. A. Sainte-Beuve, "Nouveaux Lundis," ibid., pp. 140-41.
K. Werner, "Geschichte der katholischen Theologie in Deutschland," (May 11, 1867), pp. 164-65.
M. Amari, "La Guerra del Vespro Siciliano," ibid., p. 165.
J. Crétineau-Joly, "Histoire des trois derniers Princes de la Maison de Condé," ibid., pp. 165-66.
A. von Reumont, "Geschichte der Stadt Rom," (May 18, 1867), pp. 187-88.
P. Emiliani-Giudici, "Storia dei Comuni Italiani," p. 188.

Le Comte de Christen, "Journal de ma Captivité," *ibid.,* p. 189.
A. Mickiewicz, "Histoire populaire de la Pologne," *ibid.* (June 1st, 1867), p. 233.
J. Vapereau, "L'année littéraire et dramatique," *ibid.,* p. 234.
J. G. Courcelle-Seneuil, "Traité théorique et pratique d'économie politique," *ibid.,* p. 235.
A. Bardonnet, "Procès-verbal de délivrance à Jean Chandos, Commissaire du Roi d'Angleterre, des places françaises abandonnées par le traité de Bretigny," *ibid.* (June 8, 1867), pp. 258-59.
M. W. Freer, "The Regency of Anne of Austria, mother of Louis XIV," *ibid.,* p. 259.
A. Coppi, "Annali d'Italia dal 1750," *ibid.,* pp. 259-60.
Dr. von H . . st, "Das Attentat vom 4 April, 1866," *ibid.* (June 15, 1867), p. 284.
G. Rosa, "Storia generale delle Storie," *ibid.* (June 22, 1867), p. 306.
Lizzie S. Eden, "A Lady's Glimpse of the late War in Bohemia," *ibid.,* p. 307.
E. Hatin, "Bibliographie historique et critique de la presse périodique," *ibid.* (June 29, 1867), p. 332.
C. Kingsley, "Three lectures on the Ancien Régime," *ibid.* (July 13, 1867), pp. 379-80.
M. Guizot, "Mémoires pour servir à l'histoire de mon temps," *ibid.,* p. 380.
M. Saint-Marc Girardin, "La Fontaine et les Fabulistes," *ibid.,* p. 380.
J. G. Magnabal's translation of le Marquis de Pidal's "Philippe II, Antonio Perez, et le royaume d'Aragon," *ibid.* (July 20, 1867), pp. 402-3.
H. Mendelssohn-Bartholdy, "Friedrich von Gentz," *ibid.,* p. 403.
W. L. Gage, "Life of Professor Carl Ritter," *ibid.,* pp. 403-4.
"Guide de Paris, par les principaux Ecrivains et Artistes de la France," *ibid.,* p. 405.
P. Clément, "L'Italie en 1671," *ibid.* (July 27, 1867), p. 426.
O. Hamst, "A Martyr to Bibliography," *ibid.,* p. 426.
A. de Pontmartin, "Nouveaux Samedis," *ibid.,* p. 426.
E. E. Marcy, "Christianity and its Conflicts, Ancient and Modern," *ibid.* (August 3, 1867), p. 450.
E. Chasles, "Michel de Cervantes," *ibid.,* pp. 450-51.
E. Quinet, "Histoire de la Campagne de 1815," *ibid.,* p. 451.

M. Kayserling, "Geschichte der Juden in Portugal," *ibid.,* (August 10, 1867), p. 475.

M. Lenient, "La Satire en France au XVIme Siècle," *ibid.,* p. 475.

A. Geffroy, "Gustave III et la cour de France," *ibid.,* pp. 475-76.

B. Hubler, "Die Constanzer Reformation und die Concordate von 1418," *ibid.* (August 24, 1867), p. 523.

A. Moreau de Jonnès, Etat économique et social de la France depuis Henri IV," *ibid.,* pp. 523-24.

J. G. Droysen, "Geschichte der preussischen Politik-Friedrich I, König von Preussen," *ibid.* (September 7, 1867), p. 572.

T. Juste, "Le Comte le Hon," *ibid.,* pp. 572-73.

M. Nourrisson, "La politique de Bossuet," *ibid.* (September 14, 1867), p. 596.

J. B. Mullinger, "Cambridge Characteristics in the 17th Century," *ibid.,* pp. 596-97.

L. Ratisbonne, "Alfred de Vigny: Journal d'un poète," *ibid.,* p. 597.

O. Klopp, "Die preussische Politik des Fridericianismus nach Friedrich II," *ibid.* (October 5, 1867), p. 692.

"Notizie intorno alla vita ed alle opere di Monsignor Celestino Cavedoni," *ibid.* (October 12, 1867), p. 692.

W. Wattenbach, "Algier," *ibid.,* pp. 692-93.

M. Ritter, "Geschichte der deutschen Union .... 1598-1612," *ibid.* (October 19, 1867), p. 716.

W. L. Holland, "Briefe der Herzogin Elisabeth Charlotte von Orléans, 1676-1706," *ibid.,* pp. 716-17.

M. Wohl, "Mahnruf zur Bewahrung Suddeutschlands," *ibid.,* p. 717.

E. H. Meyer, "J. M. Lappenberg," *ibid.* (October 26, 1867), p. 740.

J. R. Browne, "The Land of Thor," *ibid.,* pp. 740-41.

T. Toeche, "Kaiser Heinrich VI," (November 2, 1867), pp. 764-65.

"Die vorgebliche Tochter der Kaiserin Elisabeth Petrowna," *ibid.,* p. 765.

Lucia Norman, "A Youth's History of California," *ibid.* (November 9, 1867), pp. 787-88.

L. Passy, "Histoire Administrative, 1789-1815," *ibid.,* p. 788.

G. Peacock, "Handbook of Abyssinia," *ibid.,* p. 788.

M. Guizot, "M. de Barante" (English Translation) *ibid.* (November 16, 1867), pp. 810-11.

T. Martin, "Memoir of W. E. Aytoun," *ibid.,* p. 811.

A. Schwegler, "Handbook of the History of Philosophy,' *ibid.* (November 30, 1867), pp. 858-59.

Sir H. L. Bulwer, "Historical Characters," *ibid.* p. 860.

Emma Sophia, Countess Brownlow, "Slight Reminiscences of a Septuagenarian," (December 7, 1867), p. 883.

Th. von Karajan, "Abraham à Sancta Clara," *ibid.* (December 14, 1867), p. 906.

H. Rüttimann, "Das nordamerikanische Bundesstaatsrecht," *ibid.* (December 21, 1867), p. 929.

S. Smiles, "The Huguenots," *ibid.* (December 28, 1867), pp. 953-54.

Maistre de Roger de la Lande, "Histoire de la Prusse, 1815-67," Vol. II (January 4, 1868), p. 18.

"Officieller Ausstellungs-Bericht des Oesterreichischen Central-Comités," *ibid.,* p. 20.

T. Bernhardt, "Preussens moderne Entwickelung," *ibid.* (January 11, 1868), pp. 41-42.

W. H. Riehl, "Neues Novellenbuch," *ibid.* (January 18, 1868), p. 68.

C. von Schätzler, "Neue Aufersuchungen über das Dogma von der Gnade und das Wesen des christlichen Glaubens," *ibid.,* pp. 68-69.

Le Marquis de Noailles, "Henri de Valois et la Pologne en 1572," *ibid.* (January 25, 1868), p. 90.

A. Bisset, "History of the Commonwealth of England," *ibid.* (February 8, 1868), pp. 139-40.

Major B. B. Malleson, "History of the French in India, 1674-1761," *ibid.* (February 15, 1868), pp. 163-64.

In *The North British Review*

G. Martha, "Le poème de Lucrèce; morale, religion, science," Vol. LI, No. 101 (October, 1869), pp. 215-16.

Carl Peter, "Geschichte Roms," *ibid.,* pp. 217-18.

Paul Gaffarel, "Etude sur les rapports de l'Amérique et de l'ancien continent avant Christophe Colomb," *ibid.,* pp. 232-33.

Paul Friedmann, "Les dépêches di Giovanni Michiel, 1554-7," *ibid.,* pp. 233-35.

F. P. Perrens, "Les Mariages Espagnols, 1602-15," *ibid.,* pp. 237-38.

Arabella G. Campbell, "The Life of Fra Paolo Sarpi," *ibid.,* pp. 238-39.

L. von Ranke, "Zur deutschen Geschichte vom Religionsfrieden bis zum dreissigjährigen Krieg," *ibid.,* pp. 239-40.

S. R. Gardiner, "Prince Charles and the Spanish Marriage," *ibid.,* pp. 240-46.

F. Williams, "Memoirs and correspondence of Bishop Atterbury," *ibid.,* pp. 247-49.

W. Lee, "Life and newly discovered Writings of Daniel De Foe," *ibid.,* pp. 249-51.

Alphonse Jobez, "La France sous Louis XV," *ibid.,* pp. 252-53.

E. Reimann, "Geschichte des Bayrischen Erbfolgekrieges," *ibid.,* pp. 253-55.

A. von Arneth, "Joseph II, und Katharina von Russland," *ibid.,* p. 255.

E. von Cosel, "Geschichte des preussischen Staats und Volkes," *ibid.,* pp. 255-56.

Le Comte de la Boutetière, "Le Chevalier de Sapinaud et les chefs Vendéens," *ibid.,* pp. 256-57.

Augustus Theiner, "Histoire des deux Concordats," *ibid.,* pp. 262-63.

J. Crétineau-Joly, "Bonaparte, le concordat de 1801, &c.," *ibid.,* pp. 263-64.

C. D. Yonge, "Life and Administration of the 6th Earl of Liverpool," *ibid.,* pp. 264-65.

M. Büdinger, "Wellington," *ibid.,* pp. 265-66.

Horace Greeley, "Recollections of a Busy Life," *ibid.,* pp. 268-69.

G. von S. N., "Geschichte Oesterreichs," *ibid.,* pp. 269-70.

R. H. Gillett, "Democracy in the United States," *ibid.,* pp. 273-74.

H. Blankenburg, "Die innern Kämpfe der nordamerikanischen Union," *ibid.,* p. 274.

H. Ewald, "Die zwei Wege in Deutschland," *ibid.,* p. 275.

W. Wattenbach, "Eine Ferienreise nach Spanien und Portugal," *ibid.,* pp. 275-76.

P. Le Page Renouf, "The Case of the Pope Honorius," Vol. LI, No. 102 (January, 1870), pp. 525-26.

C. de Cherrier, "Histoire de Charles VIII, roi de France," *ibid.,* pp. 541-44.

"Trois documents de l'église du 15me siècle," *ibid.,* p. 544.

M. Gachard, "La Bibliothèque des Princes Corsini à Rome," *ibid.,* pp. 544-45.

"Dispacci di Giovanni Michiel," *ibid.,* pp. 545-46.

F. Sclopis, "Le Cardinal Jean Morone," *ibid.*, pp. 546-47.

S. R. Gardiner, "Narrative of the Spanish Marriage Treaty," *ibid.*, pp. 549-50.

G. Droysen, "Gustaf Adolf," *ibid.*, pp. 550-51.

L. Von Ranke, "Geschichte Wallensteins," *ibid.*, pp. 551-53.

B. Erdmannsdorfer, "Graf Georg Friedrich von Waldeck," *ibid.*, pp. 553-54.

J. G. Droysen, "Friedrich Wilhelm I., König von Preussen," *ibid.*, pp. 556-58.

P. A. Carayon, "Le Père Ricci, Général des Jésuites," *ibid.*, pp. 558-62.

The Baron Carl de Ketschendorf, "Archives Judicaires . . . des grands procès politiques en France, 1792-1840," *ibid.*, pp. 565-66.

R. Lavollée, "Portalis, sa vie et ses œuvres," *ibid.*, pp. 566-67.

G. H. Klippel, "Das Leben des Generals von Scharnhorst," *ibid.*, pp. 568-69.

L. Hymans, "Histoire de la Belgique, 1814-30," *ibid.*, pp. 570-71.

"Aus den Memoiren eines Russischen Dekabristen," *ibid.*, pp. 570-71.

J. J. Honegger, "Grundsteine einer allgemeinen Kulturgeschichte der neuesten Zeit," *ibid.*, p. 575.

"Briefe von Alexander von Humboldt an Bunsen," *ibid.*, pp. 577-78.

C. Asselineau, "Charles Baudelaire, sa vie et son œuvre," *ibid.*, p. 578.

A. Cucheval-Clarigny, "Histoire de la Constitution de 1852," *ibid.*, pp. 582-83.

C. Schirren, "Livländische Antwort an Herrn Juri Samarin," *ibid.*, pp. 584-85.

W. H. Riehl, "Wanderbuch," *ibid.*, p. 589.

C. A. Sainte-Beuve, "Nouveaux Lundis," *ibid.*, pp. 594-95.

J. Waddington, "Congregational History," Vol. LII, No. 103 (April, 1870), p. 245.

"Cinco Cartas de D. Diego Sarmiento de Acuna, primer Conde de Gondomar," *ibid.*, pp. 253-54.

E. Pfleiderer, "Gottfried Wilhelm Leibniz," *ibid.*, pp. 255-58.

L. von Ranke, "Briefwechsel Friedrich des Grossen mit dem Prinzen Wilhelm IV von Oranien," *ibid.*, pp. 258-59.

T. Feuillet de Conches, "Louis XVI, Marie-Antoinette et Madame Elisabeth," *ibid.*, pp. 259-62.

Jules de Vroil, "Etude sur Cliquot-Blervache, économiste du 18me siècle," *ibid.*, pp. 262-63.

F. von Ompteda, "Politischer Nachlass des Ludwig von Ompteda, 1804-13," *ibid.*, pp. 263-65.

G. H. Pertz, "Das Leben des Feldmarschalls Grafen Neithardt von Gneisenau," *ibid.*, pp. 265-67.

G. T. Curtis, "Life of Daniel Webster," *ibid.*, pp. 268-71.

E. Kelchner and K. Mendelssohn-Bartholdy, "Briefe des K. F. Friedrich von Nagler," *ibid.*, pp. 271-72.

G. Freitag, "Karl Mathy; Geschichte seines Lebens," *ibid.*, pp. 277-78.

K. Goedeke, "Emanual Geibel," *ibid.*, pp. 279-80.

W. Wattenbach, "Peter Luder," Vol. LII, No. 104 (July, 1870), pp. 536-37.

G. Baguenault de Purchèse, "Jean de Morvillier évêque d'Orléans," *ibid.*, pp. 537-40.

A. Desjardins, "Les moralistes français du seizième siècle," *ibid.*, pp. 540-41.

"The pontifical decrees against the motion of the earth," *ibid.*, pp. 546-47.

J. Stroughton, "Ecclesiastical History of England," *ibid.*, pp. 550-51.

A. Pichler, "Die Theologie des Leibniz," *ibid.*, pp. 551-52.

Lord Stanhope, "Reign of Queen Anne," *ibid.*, pp. 553-56.

L. de Lavergne, "Les économistes français du 18me siècle," *ibid.*, pp. 556-58.

Le Baron de la Morinerie, "Souvenirs d'émigration de Madame la Marquise de Lâge de Volude," *ibid.*, pp. 558-60.

H. von Sybel, "Historische Zeitschrift," Bd. XXIII, *ibid.*, pp. 560-62.

A. R. von Vivenot, "Korsakoff," *ibid.*, pp. 562-64.

K. von Klinkowstrom, "Aus der alten Registratur der Staatskanzlei," *ibid.*, pp. 565-66.

T. Juste, "Le soulèvement de la Hollande en 1813," *ibid.*, p. 567.

Anton Springer, "Friedrich Christoph Dahlmann," *ibid.*, pp. 568-69.

"Œuvres de Charles Dunoyer," *ibid.*, pp. 569-70.

G. T. Curtis, "Life of Daniel Webster," *ibid.*, pp. 573-74.

Karl Eugen von Ujfalvy, "Alfred de Musset," *ibid.*, pp. 573-74.

M. Bernard, "A Historical Account of the Neutrality of Great Britain During the American Civil War," *ibid.*, pp. 578-79.

J. van Lennep, "Travels in little-known parts of Asia Minor," *ibid.*, pp. 579-81.

W. H. Dixon, "Free Russia," *ibid.*, pp. 584-89.

"Documents Magistri Johannis Hus vitam illustrania," Vol. LIII, No. 105 (October, 1870), p. 243.

E. de Rozière, "Liber diurnus, ou recueil des formules usitées par la Chancellerie Pontificale du Ve au.XIme siècle," *ibid.*, pp. 252-53.

M. Mortimer-Ternaux, "Histoire de la Terreur," *ibid.*, pp. 259-61.

C. A. Dauban, "Paris en 1794 et en 1795," *ibid.*, pp. 261-63.

A. L. W., "Der Feldzug am Mittelrhein, 1794," *ibid.*, pp. 263-65.

M. Büdinger, "Lafayette," *ibid.*, pp. 271-72.

General C. Mercer, "Journal of the Waterloo Campaign," *ibid.*, pp. 272-73.

Earl of Malmesbury, "Letters of the First Earl of Malmesbury," *ibid.*, pp. 273-75.

"Der Staatsstreich vom 2. December 1851," *ibid.*, pp. 282-84.

G. Carcano, "Lettere di Massimo d'Azeglio," *ibid.*, pp. 284-86.

C. Frantz, "Die Naturlehre des Staats," *ibid.*, pp. 295-96.

J. Stevenson, "Calendar of State Papers, Foreign, Elizabeth," Vol. LIII, No. 106 (January, 1871), p. 561.

"La Strage di San Bartolomeo," *ibid.*, pp. 561-62.

Dr. Philippson, "Heinrich IV und Philipp III," *ibid.*, p. 564.

O. Stobbe, "Hermann Conring," *ibid.*, pp. 564-65.

A. von Arneth, "Maria Theresia," *ibid.*, pp. 575-79.

Sir H. L. Bulwer, "Life of Henry John Temple, Viscount Palmerston," *ibid.*, pp. 586-89.

"Lettres du Marquis A. de Custine à Varnhagen d' Ense," *ibid.*, pp. 591-92.

G. Fischbach, "Die Belagerung von Strassburg," *ibid.*, pp. 595-97.

H. Baumgarter, "Wie wir wieder ein Volk geworden sind," *ibid.*, pp. 597-98.

H. H. Milman, "Savonarola, Erasmus, &c.," *ibid.*, pp. 603-4.

J. Schmidt, "Bilder aus dem geistigen Leben unserer Zeit," *ibid.*, pp. 605-6.

In *The Academy*

Mandell Creighton, "History of the Papacy during the Period of the Reformation, Vols. I and II (1378-1464)," Vol. XXII (1882), pp. 407-9.

In *The Nineteenth Century*

T. W. Reid, "Life, letters, and friendships of R. Monckton Milnes, 1st Lord Houghton," Vol. XXVIII (December, 1890), pp. 993-1000. Reprinted in *HES*, pp. 414-25.

"Talleyrand's Memoirs," Vol. XXIX (April, 1891), pp. 670-84. Reprinted in *HES*, pp. 393-413.

"L. A. Burd's Edition of Macchiavelli's 'Il Principe'," Vol. XXXI, (April, 1892), pp. 696-700.

"Souvenirs d'Alexis de Tocqueville," Vol. XXXIII (May, 1893), pp. 883-86.

In *The English Historical Review*

Creighton's "History of the Papacy, Vols. III and IV," Vol. II (1887), pp. 571-81. Reprinted in the *HES*, pp. 426-41.

J. R. Seeley, "A Short History of Napoleon the First," John C. Ropes, "The First Napoleon," Vol. II (1887), pp. 593-603. Reprinted in *HES*, pp. 442-58.

Emmanuel de Broglie, "Mabillon et la Société de l'Abbaye de Saint-Germain-des-Prés à la fin du XVIIme siècle," Vol. III (1888), pp. 585-92. Reprinted in *HES*, pp. 459-71.

H. C. Lea, "A History of the Inquisition of the Middle Ages," Vol. III (1888), pp. 773-88. Reprinted in *HOF*, pp. 551-74.

J. F. Bright, "History of England, 1837-80," Vol. III (1888), pp. 798-809. Reprinted in *HES*, pp. 472-90.

J. Bryce, "The American Commonwealth," Vol. IV (1889), pp. 388-96. Reprinted in *HOF*, pp. 575-87.

H. M. Stephans, "A History of the French Revolution," Vol. VII (1892), pp. 381-84. Reprinted in *HES*, pp. 491-95.

R. Flint, "Historical Philosophy in France and French Belgium and Switzerland," Vol. X (1895), pp. 108-13. Reprinted in *HOF*, pp. 588-96.

APPENDIX

NOTES TO CHAPTER I — INAUGURAL LECTURE ON THE STUDY OF HISTORY

¹ No political conclusions of any value for practice can be arrived at by direct experience. All true political science is, in one sense of the phrase, *a priori*, being deduced from the tendencies of things, tendencies known either through our general experience of human nature, or as the result of an analysis of the course of history, considered as a progressive evolution. — Mill, *Inaugural Address*, 51.

² Contemporary history is, in Dr. Arnold's opinion, more important than either ancient or modern; and in fact superior to it by all the superiority of the end to the means. — Seeley, *Lectures and Essays*, 306.

³ The law of all progress is one and the same, the evolution of the simple into the complex by successive differentiation. — *Edinburgh Review*, CLVII, 248. Die Entwickelung der Völker vollzieht sich nach zwei Gesetzen. Das erste Gesetz is das der Differenzierung. Die primitiven Einrichtungen sind einfach und einheitlich, die der Civilisation zusammengesetzt und geteilt, und die Arbeitsteilung nimmt beständig zu. — Sickel, *Goettinger Gelehrte Anzeigen*, 1890, 563.

⁴ Nous risquons toujours d'être influencés par les préjugés de notre époque; mais nous sommes libres des préjugés particuliers aux époques antérieures. — E. Naville, *Christianisme de Fénelon*, 9.

⁵ La nature n'est qu'un écho de l'esprit. L'idée est la mère du fait, elle façonne graduellement le monde à son image. — Feuchtersleben, in Caro, *Nouvelles Études Morales*, 132. Il n'est pas d'étude morale qui vaille l'histoire d'une idée. — Laboulaye, *Liberté Religieuse*, 25.

⁶ Il y a des savants qui raillent le sentiment religieux. Ils ne savent pas que c'est à ce sentiment, et par son moyen, que la science historique doit d'avoir pu sortir de l'enfance.... Depuis des siècles les âmes indépendantes discutaient les textes et les traditions de l'église, quand les lettrés n'avaient pas encore eu l'idée de porter un regard critique sur les textes de l'antiquité mondaine. — *La France Protestante*, II, 17.

⁷ In our own history, above all, every step in advance has been at the same time a step backwards. It has often been shown how our latest constitution is, amidst all external differences, essentially the same as our earliest, how every struggle for right and freedom, from the thirteenth century onwards, has simply been a struggle for recovering something old. — Freeman, *Historical Essays*, IV, 253. Nothing but a thorough knowledge of the social system, based upon a regular study of its growth, can give us the power we require to affect it. — Harrison, *Meaning of History*, 19. Eine

399

Sache wird nur völlig auf dem Wege verstanden, wie sie selbst entsteht. — In dem genetischen Verfahren sind die Grunde der Sache, auch die Grunde des Erkennens — Trendelenburg, *Logische Untersuchungen*, II, 395, 388.

[8] Une telle liberté . . . n'a rien de commun avec le savant système de garanties qui fait libres les peuples modernes — Boutmy, *Annales des Sciences Politiques*, I, 157. Les trois grandes réformes qui ont renouvelé l'Angleterre, la liberté religieuse, la réforme parlementaire, et la liberté économique, ont été obtenues sous la pression des organisations extra-constitutionnelles — Ostrogorski, *Revue Historique*, LII, 272.

[9] The question which is at the bottom of all constitutional struggles, the question between the national will and the national law — Gardiner, *Documents*, XVIII. Religion, considered simply as the principle which balances the power of human opinion, which takes man out of the grasp of custom and fashion, and teaches him to refer himself to a higher tribunal, is an infinite aid to moral strength and elevation. — Channing, *Works*, IV, 83. Je tiens que le passé ne suffit jamais au présent. Personne n'est plus disposé que moi à profiter de ses leçons; mais en même temps, je le demande, le présent ne fournit-il pas toujours les indications qui lui sont propres? —Molé, in Falloux, *Etudes et Souvenirs*, 130. Admirons la sagesse de nos pères, et tachons de l'imiter, en faisant ce qui convient à notre siècle. — Galiani, *Dialogues*, 40.

[10] Ceterum in legendis Historiis malim te ductum animi, quam anxias leges sequi. Nullae sunt, quae non magnas habeant utilitates; et melius haerent, quae libenter legimus. In universum tamen, non incipere ab antiquissimis, sed ab his, quae nostris temporibus nostraeque notitiae propius cohaerent, ac paulatim deinde in remotiora eniti, magis è re arbitror. — Grotius, *Epistolae*, 18.

[11] The older idea of a law of degeneracy, of a "fatal drift towards the worse," is as obsolete as astrology or the belief in witchcraft. The human race has become hopeful, sanguine. — Seeley, *Rede Lecture*, 1887. *Fortnightly Review*, July, 1887, 124.

[12] Formuler des idées générales, c'est changer le salpêtre en poudre. — A. DeMusset, *Confessions d'un Enfant du Siècle*, 15. Les révolutions c'est l'avènement des idées libérales. C'est presque toujours par les révolutions quelles prévalent et se fondent, et quand les idées libérales en sont véritablement le principe et le but, quand elles leur ont donné naissance, et quand elles les couronnet à leur dernier jour, alors ces révolutions sont légitimes. — Rémusat, 1839, in *Revue des Deux Mondes*, 1875, VI, 335. Il y a même des personnes de piété qui prouvent par raison qu'il faut renoncer à la raison; que ce n'est point la lumière, mais la foi seule qui doit nous conduire, et que l'obéissance aveugle est la principale vertu des chrétiens. La paresse des inférieurs et leur esprit flatteur s'accommode souvent de cette vertu prétendue, et l'orgueil de ceux qui commandent en est toujours très content. De sorte qu'il se trouvera peut'être des gens qui seront scandalisés que je fasse cet honneur à la raison, de l'élever au dessus de toutes les puissances, et qui s'imagineront que je me révolte contre les autorités légitimes à cause que je prends son parti et que je soutiens que c'est à elle à décider et à regner. — Malebranche, *Morale*, I, 2, 13. That great statesman (Mr. Pitt) distinctly avowed that the application of philosophy to politics was at that time an innovation, and that it was an innovation worthy to be

adopted. He was ready to make the same avowal in the present day which Mr. Pitt had made in 1792. — Canning, 1st June, 1827. *Parliamentary Review*, 1828, 71. American history knows but one avenue of success in American legislation, freedom from ancient prejudice. The best law givers in our colonies first became as little children. — Bancroft, *History of the United States*, I, 494. Every American, from Jefferson and Gallatin down to the poorest squatter, seemed to nourish an idea that he was doing what he could to overthrow the tyranny which the past had fastened on the human mind. — Adams, *History of the United States*, I, 175.

[13] The greatest changes of which we have had experience as yet are due to our increasing knowledge of history and nature. They have been produced by a few minds appearing in three or four favoured nations, in comparatively a short period of time. May we be allowed to imagine the minds of men everywhere working together during many ages for the completion of our knowledge? May not the increase of knowledge transfigure the world? —Jowett, *Plato*, I, 414. Nothing, I believe, is so likely to beget in us a spirit of enlightened liberality, of christian forbearance, of large-hearted moderation, as the careful study of the history of doctrine and the history of interpretation —Perowne, *Psalms*, I, p. xxxi.

[14] Ce n'est guère avant la seconde moitié du XVIIe siècle qu'il devient impossible de soutenir l'authenticité des fausses décrétales, des Constitutions apostoliques, des Récognitions Clémentines, du faux Ignace, du pseudonymes qui grossissait souvent du tiers ou de la moitié l'héritage littéraire des auteurs les plus considérables.— Duchesne, *Témoins anténicéens de la Trinité*, 1883, 36.

[15] A man who does not know what has been thought by those who have gone before him is sure to set an undue value upon his own ideas.—M. Pattison, *Memoirs*, 78.

[16] Travailler à discerner, dans cette discipline, le solide d'avec l'opinion, ce qui forme le jugment d'avec ce qui ne fait que charger la mémoire. — Lamy, *Connoissance de soi-même*, V, 459.

[17] All our hopes of the future depend on a sound understanding of the past.—Harrison, *The Meaning of History*, 6.

[18] The real history of mankind is that of the slow advance of resolved deed following laboriously just thought; and all the greatest men live in their purpose and effort more than it is possible for them to live in reality.—The things that actually happened were of small consequence — the thoughts that were developed are of infinite consequence.—Ruskin. Facts are the mere dross of history. It is from the abstract truth which interpenetrates them, and lies latent among them like gold in the ore, that the mass derives its value.—Macaulay, *Works*, V, 131.

[19] Die Gesetze der Geschichte sind eben die Gesetze der ganzen Menschheit, gehen nicht in die Geschicke eines Volkes, einer Generation oder gar eines Einzelnen auf. Individuen und Geschlechter, Staaten und Nationen, konnen zerstauben, die Menschheit bleibt.—A Schmidt, *Zuricher Monatsschrift*, i, 45.

[20] Le grand péril des âges démocratiques, soyez-en sûr, c'est la destruction ou l'affiblissement excessif des parties du corps social en présence du tout. Tout ce qui relàve de nos jours l'idée de l'individu est sain. — Tocqueville, 3rd January, 1840, *Œuvres*, VII, 97. En France, il n'y a plus d'hommes. On a systématiquement tué l'homme au profit du peuple, des masses, comme

disent nos législateurs écervelés. Puis un beau jour, on s'est apercu que ce peuple n'avait jamais existé qu'en projet, que ces masses étaient un troupeau mi-partie de moutons et de tigres. C'est une triste histoire. Nous avons à rélèver l'âme humaine contre l'aveugle, et brutale tyrannie des multitudes.— Lanfrey, 23rd March, 1855. M. duCamp, *Souvenirs Littéraires*, II, 273. C'est le propre de la vertu d'être invisible, même dans l'histoire à tout autre œil que celui de la conscience.—Vachesat, *Comptes Rendus de l'Institut*, LXIX, 319. Dans l'histoire où la bonté est la perle rare, qui a été bon passe presque avant qui a été grand. — V. Hugo, *Les Misérables*, VII, 46. Grosser Maenner Leben und Tod der Wahrheit gemaess mit Liebe zu schildern, ist zu allen Zeiten herzerhebend; am meisten aber dann, wenn in Kreislauf der irdischen Dinge die Sterne wieder aehnlich stehen wie damals als sie unter uns lebten. —Lasaulx, *Sokrates*, 3. Instead of saying that the history of mankind is the history of the masses, it would be much more true to say that the history of mankind is the history of its great men.—Kingsley, *Lectures*, 329.

[21] Le génie n'est que la plus complète émancipation de toutes les influences de temps, de mœurs et de pays.—Nisand, *Souvenirs*, II, 43.

[22] Meine kritische Richtung zieht mich in der Wissenschaft durchaus zur Kritik meiner eigenen Gedanken hin, nicht zu der Gedanken Anderer.— Rothe, *Ethik*, I, p. xi.

[23] When you are in young years the whole mind is, as it were, fluid, and is capable of forming itself into any shape that the owner of the mind pleases to order it to form itself into.—Carlyle, *On the Choice of Books*, 131. Nach allem ersheint es somit unzweifelhaft als eine der psychologischen Voraussetzungen des Strafrechts, ohne welche der Zurechnungsbegriff nicht haltbar ware, dass der Mensch fur seinen Charakter verantwortlich ist und ihn muss abandern konnen.—Rumelin, *Reden und Aufsatze*, II, 60. An der tiefen und verborgenen Quelle, worhaus der Wille entspringt, an diesem Punkt, nur hier steht die Freiheit, und fuhrt das Steuer und lenkt den Willen. Wer nicht bis zu dieser Tiefe in sich einkehren und seinen natürlichen Charakter von hier aus bemeistern kann, der hat nicht den Gebrauch seiner Freiheit, der ist nicht frei, sondern unterworfen dem Triebwerk seiner Interessen, und dadurch in der Gewalt des Weltlaufs, worin jede Begebenheit und jede Handlung eine notwendige Folge ist aller vorhergehenden.—Fischer, *Problem der Freiheit*, 27.

[24] I must regard the main duty of a Professor to consist, not simply in communicating information, but in doing this in such a manner, and with such an accompaniment of subsidiary means, that the information he conveys may be the occasion of awakening his pupils to a vigorous and varied exertion of their faculties.—Sir W. Hamilton, *Lectures*, I, 14. No great man really does his work by imposing his maxims on his disciples, he evokes their life. The pupil may become much wiser than his instructor, he may not accept his conclusions, but he will own, "You awakened me to be myself; for that I thank you."—Maurice, *The Conscience*, 7, 8.

[25] Ich sehe die Zeit kommen, wo wir die neuere Geschichte nicht mehr auf die Berichte selbst nicht der gleichzeitigen Historiker, ausser in so weit ihnen neue originale Kenntniss beiwohnte, geschweige denn auf die weiter abgeleiteten Bearbeitungen zu grunden haben, sondern aus den Relationen der Augenzeugen und der ächten und unmittelbarsten Urkunden aufbauen werden.—Ranke, *Reformation*, Preface, 1838. Ce qu'on a trouvé et mis en

APPENDIX 403

œuvre est considérable en soi: c'est peu de chose au prix de ce qui reste à trouver et à mettre en œuvre.—Aulard, *Etudes sur la Révolution,* 21.

[26] N'attendez donc pas les leçons de l'expérience; elles coûtent trop cher aux nations.—O. Barrot, *Mémoire,* II, 435. Il y a des leçons dans tous les temps, pour tous le temps; et celles qu'on emprunte à des ennemis ne sont pas les moins précieuses.—Lanfrey, *Napoléon,* v. p II Old facts may always be fresh, and may give out a fresh meaning for each generation—Maurice, *Lectures,* 62. The object is to lead the student to attend to them; to make him take interest in history not as a mere narrative, but as a chain of causes and effects still unwinding itself before our eyes, and full of momentous consequences to himself and his descendants — an unremitting conflict between good and evil powers, of which every act done by anyone of us, insignificant as we are, forms one of the incidents; a conflict in which even the smallest of us cannot escape from taking part, in which whoever does not help the right side is helping the wrong.—Mill, *Inaugural Address,* 59.

[27] I hold that the degree in which Poets dwell in sympathy with the Past, marks exactly the degree of their poetical faculty.—Wadsworth, in C. Fox, *Memoirs,* June 1842. In all political, all social, all human questions whatever, history is the main resource of the inquirer.—Harrison, *Meaning of History,* 15. There are no truths which more readily gain the assent of mankind, or are more firmly retained by them, than those of an historical nature, depending upon the testimony of others. — Priestley, *Letters to French Philosophers,* 9. Improvement consists in bringing our opinions into nearer agreement with facts; and we shall not be likely to do this while we look at facts only through glasses coloured by those very opinions.—Mill, *Inaugural Address,* 25.

[28] He who has learnt to understand the true character and tendency of many succeeding ages is not likely to go very far wrong in estimating his own.—Lecky, *Value of History,* 21. C'est à l'histoire qu'il faut se prendre, c'est le fait que nous devons interroger, quand l'idée vacille et fuit à nos yeux.—Michelet, *Disc. d'Ouverture,* 263. C'est la loi des faits tell qu'elle se manifeste dans leur succession. C'est la règle de conduite donnée par la nature humaine et indiquée par l'histoire. C'est la logique, mais cette logique qui ne fait qu'un avec l'enchaînement des choses. C'est l'enseignement de l'expérience.—Scherer, *Mélanges,* 558. Wer seine Vergangenheit nicht als seine Geschichte hat und weiss wird und ist characterlos Wem ein Ereigniss sein Sonst plotzlich abreisst von seinem Jetzt wird leicht wurzellos.—Kliefoth, *Rheinwalds Repertorium,* XLIV, 20. La politique est une des meilleures écoles pour l'esprit. Elle force à chercher la raison de toutes choses, et ne permet pas cependant de la chercher hors des faits.—Rémusat, *Le Temps Passé,* I, 31. It is an unsafe partition that divides opinions without principle from unprincipled opinions.—Coleridge, *Lay Sermons,* 373.

Wer nicht von drei tausend Jahren sich weiss Rechenschaft zu geben,
Bleib' im Dunkeln unerfahren, mag von Tag zu Tage leben!
Goethe.

What can be rationally required of the student of philosophy is not a preliminary and absolute, but a gradual and progressive, abrogation of prejudices. — Sir W. Hamilton, *Lectures,* IV, 92.

[29] Die Schlacht bei Leuthen ist wohl die letzte, in welcher diese religiösen

Gegensätze entscheidend eingewirkt haben.—Ranke, *Allgemeine Deutsche Biographie*, VII, 70.

[30] The only real cry in the country is the proper and just old No Popery cry.—*Major Beresford*, July 1847. Unfortunately the strongest bond of union amongst them is an apprehension of Popery.—*Stanley*, 12th September 1847. The great Protestionist party having degenerated into a No Popery, No Jew Party, I am still more unfit now than I was in 1846 to lead it.—G. *Bentinck*, 26th December 1847; *Croker's Memoirs*, III, 116, 132, 157.

[31] In the case of Protestantism, this constitutional instability is now a simple matter of fact, which has become too plain to be denied. The system is not fixed, but in motion; and the motion is for the time in the direction of complete self-dissolution.— We take it for a transitory scheme, whose breaking up is to make room in due time for another and far more perfect state of the Church.— The new order in which Protestantism is to become thus complete cannot be reached without the co-operation and help of Romanism.—Nevin, *Mercersburg Review*, IV, 48.

[32] Diese Heiligen waren es, die aus dem unmittelbaren Glaubensleben und den Grundgedanken der christlichen Freiheit zuerst die Idee allgemeiner Menschenrechte abgeleitet und rein von Selbstsucht vertheidigt haben.— Weingarten, *Revolutionskirchen*, 447. Wie selbst die Idee allgemeiner Menschenrechte, die in dem gemeinsamen Character der Ebenbildlichkeit Gottes gegründet sind, erst durch das Christenthum zum Bewusstsein gebracht werden, während jeder andere Eifer fur politische Freiheit als ein mehr oder weniger selbstsuchtiger und beschränkter sich erwiesen hat.—Neander, *Pref. to Uhden's Wilberforce*, p.v. The rights of individuals and the justice due to them are as dear and precious as those of states; indeed the latter are founded on the former, and the great end and object of them must be to secure and support the rights of individuals, or else vain is government.— Cushing, in Conway, *Life of Paine*, I, 217. At it is owned the whole scheme of Scripture is not yet understood; so, if it ever comes to be understood, before the restitution of all things, and without miraculous interpositions, it must be in the same way as natural knowledge is come at — by the continuance and progress of learning and liberty.—Butler, *Analogy*, II, 3.

[33] Comme les lois elles-mêmes sont faillibles, et qu'il peut y avoir une autre justice que la justice écrite, les sociétés modernes ont voulu garantir les droits de la conscience à la poursuite d'une justice meilleure que celle qui existe; et là est le fondement de ce qu'on appelle liberté de conscience, liberté d'écrire, liberté de pensée.—Janet, *Philosophie Contemporaine*, 308. Si la force matérielle a toujours fini par céder à l'opinion, combien plus ne seraet-elle pas contrainte de céder à la conscience? Car la conscience, c'est l'opinion renforcée par le sentiment de l'obligation.—Vinet, *Liberté Religieuse*, 3.

[34] Après la volonté d'un homme, la raison d'état; apres la raison d'état, la religion; après la religion, la liberté. Voilà toute la philosophie de l'histoire.—Flottes, *La Souveraineté du Peuple*, 1851, 192. La répartition plus égale des biens et des droits dans ce monde est le plus grand objet que doivent se proposer ceux qui mènent les affaires humaines. Je veux seulement que l'égalité en politique consiste à être également libre.—Tocqueville, 10th September 1856. *Mme. Swetchine*, I, 455. On peut concevoir une législation très simple, lorsqu'on voudra en écarter tout ce qui est arbitraire, ne

consulter que les deux premières lois de la liberté et de la propriété, et ne point admettre de lois positives qui ne tirent leur raison de ces deux lois souveraines de la justice essentielle et absolue.—Letrosne, *Vues sur la Justice Criminelle*, 16. Summa enim libertas est, ad optimum recta ratione cogi.— Nemo optat sibi hanc libertatem, volendi quae velit, sed potius volendi optima —Leibniz, *De Facto*. Trendelenburg, *Beitrage zur Philosophie*, II, 190.

[85] All the world is, by the very law of its creation, in eternal progress; and the cause of all the evils of the world may be traced to that natural, but most deadly error of human indolence and corruption, that our business is to preserve and not to improve.—Arnold, *Life*, I, 259. In whatever state of knowledge we may conceive man to be placed, his progress towards a yet higher state need never fear a check, but must continue till the last existence of society.—Herschel, *Prel. Dis.*, 360. It is in the development of thought as in every other development; the present suffers from the past, and the future struggles hard in escaping from the present —Max Muller, *Science of Thought*, 617. Most of the great positive evils of the world are in themselves removable, and will, if human affairs continue to improve, be in the end reduced within narrow limits. Poverty in any of society combined with the good sense and providence of individuals.— All the grand sources, in short, of human suffering are in a great degree, many of them almost entirely, conquerable by human care and effort.—J. S. Mill, *Utilitarianism*, 21, 22. The ultimate standard of worth is personal worth, and the only progress that is worth striving after, the only acquisition that is truly good and enduring, is the growth of the soul.—Bixby, *Crisis of Morals*, 210. La science, et l'industrie qu'elle produit, ont, parmi tous les autres enfants du génie de l'homme, ce privilège particulier, que leur vol non-seulement ne peut pas s'interrompre, mais qu'il s'accélère sans cesse.—Cuvier, *Discours sur la Marche des Sciences*, 24 Avril, 1816. Aucune idée parmi celles qui se réfèrent à l'ordre des faits naturels, ne tient de plus près à la famille des idées religieuses que l'idée du progrès, et n'est plus propre à devenir le principe d'une sorte de foi religieuse pour ceux qui n'en ont pas d'autres. Elle a, comme la foi religieuse, la vertu de relever les âmes et les caractères —Cournot, *Marche des Idées*, II, 425. Dans le spectacle de l'humanité errante, souffrante et travaillant toujours à mieux voir, à mieux penser, a mieux agir, à diminuer l'infirmité de l être humain, à apaiser l'inquiétude de son cœur, la science découvre une direction et un progrès.—A. Sorel, *Discours de Réception*, 14. Le jeune homme qui commence son éducation quinze ans après son père, à une époque où celui-ci, engagé dans une profession spéciale et active, ne peut que suivre les anciens principes, acquiert une supériorité théorique dont on doit tenir compte dans la hiérarchie sociale. Le plus souvent le père n'est-il pas pénétré de l'esprit de routine, tandis que le fils représente et défend la science progressive? En diminuant l'écart qui existait entre l'influence des jeunes générations et celle de la vieillesse ou de l'âge mûr, les peuples modernes n'auraient donc fait que reproduire dans leur ordre social un changement de rapports qui s'était déjà accompli dans la nature intime des choses.—Boutmy, *Revue Nationale*, XXI, 393. Il y a dans l'homme individuel des principes de progrès viager; il y a, en toute société, des causes constantes qui transforment ce progrès viager en progrès héréditaire. Une société quelconque tend à progresser tant que les circonstances ne touchent pas aux causes de progrès que nous avons reconnues, l'imitation des dévan-

ciers par les successeurs, des étrangers par les indigènes.—Lacombe, *L'Histoire comme Science*, 292. Veram creatae mentis beatitudinem consistere in non impedito progressu ad bona majora.—Leibniz to Wolf, 21st February 1705. In cumulum etiam pulchritudinis perfectionisque universalis operum divinorum progressus quidam perpetuus liberrimusque totius universi est agnoscendus, ita ut ad majorem semper cultum procedat.—Liebniz ed. Erdmann, 150*a*. Der Creaturen und auch unsere Vollkommenheit bestehet in einen ungehinderten starken Forttrieb zu neuen und neuen Vollkommenheiten — Leibniz, *Deutsche Schriften*, II, 36 Hegel, welcher annahm, der Fortschritt der Neuzeit gegen das Mittelalter sei dieser, dass die Principien der Tugend und des Christenthums, welche im Mittelalter sich allein im Privatleben und der Kirche zur Geltung gebracht hatten, nun auch anfingen, das politische Leben zu durchdringen.—Fortlage, *Allg. Monatsschrift*, 1853, 777. Wir Slawen wissen, dass die Geister einzelner Menschen und ganzer Volker sich nur durch die Stufe ihrer Entwicklung unterscheiden.—Mickiewicz, *Slawische Literatur*, II, 436. Le progrès ne disparait jamais, mais il se déplace souvent. Il va des gouvernants aux gouvernés. La tendance des révolutions est de le ramener toujours parmi les gouvernants. Lorsqu'il est à la tête des sociétés, il marche hardiment, car il conduit. Lorsqu'il est dans la masse, il marche à pas lents, car il lutte.—Napoléon III, *Des Idées Napoléoniennes*. La loi du progrès avait jadis l'inexorable rigueur du destin; elle prend maintenant de jour en jour la douce puissance de la Providence. C'est l'erreur, c'est l'iniquité, c'est le vice, que la civilisation tend à emporter dans sa marche irrésistible; mais la vie des individus et des peuples est devenue pour elle une chose sacrée. Elle transforme plutôt qu'elle ne détruit les choses qui s'opposent a son développement, elle procède par absorption graduelle plutôt que par brusque exécution; elle aime à conquérir par l'influence des idées plutôt que par la force des armes, un peuple, une classe, une institution qui résiste au progrès.—Vacherot, *Essais de Philosophie Critique*, 443. Peu à peu l'homme intellectuel finit par effacer l'homme physique.—Quetelet, *De l'Homme*, II, 285. In dem Fortschritt der ethischen Anschauungen liegt daher der Kern des geschichtlichen Fortschritts überhaupt.—Schafer, *Arbeitsgebiet der Geschichte*, 24. Si l'homme a plus de devoirs à mesure qu'il avance en âge, ce qui est mélancolique, mais ce qui est vrai, de même aussi l'humanité est tenue d'avoir une morale plus sévère à mesure qu'elle prend plus de siècles.—Faguet, *Revue des Deux Mondes*, 1894, III, 871. Si donc il y a une loi de progrès, elle se confond avec la loi morale, et la condition fondamentale du progrès, c'est la pratique de cette loi.—Carrau, *Ib.* 1875, V, 585. L'idée du progrès, du développement, me parait être l'idée fondamentale contenue sous le mot de civilisation.—Guizot, *Cours d'Histoire*, 1828, 15. Le progrès social est continu. Il a ses périodes de fièvre ou d'atonie, de surexcitation ou de léthargie; il a ses soubresauts et ses haltes, mais il avance toujours.—De Decker, *La Providence*, 174. Ce n'est pas au bonheur seul, c'est au perfectionnement que notre destin nous appelle; et la liberté politique est le plus puissant, le plus énergique moyen de perfectionnement que le ciel nous ait donné.—B. Constant, *Cours de Politique*, II, 559. To explode error, on whichever side it lies, is certainly to secure progress.—Martineau, *Essays*, I, 114. Die sammtlichen Freiheitsrechte, welche der heutigen Menschheit so theuer sind, sind in Grunde nur Anwendungen des Rechts der Entwickelung.—Bluntschli, *Kleine Schriften*,

I, 51. Geistiges Leben ist auf Freiheit beruhende Entwicklung, mit Freiheit vollzogene That und geschichtlicher Fortschritt.—*Münchner Gel. Anzeigen,* 1849, II, 83. Wie das Denken erst nach und nach reift, so wird auch der freie Wille nicht fertig geboren, sondern in der Entwickelung erworben.— Trendelenburg, *Logische Untersuchungen,* II, 94. Das Liberum Arbitrium im vollen Sinne (die vollstandig aktuelle Macht der Selbstbestimmung) lässt sich seinem Begriff zufolge schlechterdings nicht unmittelbar geben; es kann nur erworben werden durch das Subjekt selbst, in sich moralisch hervorgebracht werden kraft seiner eigenen Entwickelung.—Rothe, *Ethik,* I, 360. So gewaltig sei der Andrang der Erfindungen und Entdeckungen, dass "Entwicklungsperioden, die in früheren Zeiten erst in Jahrhunderten durchlaufen wurden, die im Beginn unserer Zeitperiode noch der Jahrzehnte bedurften, sich heute in Jahren vollenden, haufig schon in voller Ausbildung ins Dasein treten." — Philippovich, *Fortschritt und Kulturentwicklung,* 1892, I, quoting Siemens, 1886. Wir erkennen dass dem Menschen die schwere körperliche Arbeit, von der er in seinem Kampfe um's Dasein stets schwer niedergedruckt war und grossenteils noch ist, mehr und mehr durch die wachsende Benutzung der Naturkrafte zur mechanischen Arbeitsleistung abgenommen wird, dass die ihm zufallende Arbeit immer mehr eine intellektuelle wird.—Siemens, 1886, *Ib.* 6.

[86] Once, however, he wrote:— Darin konnte man den idealen Kern der Geschichte des menschlichen Geschlechtes uberhaupt sehen, dass in den Kämpfen, die sich in den gegenseitigen Interessen der Staaten und Volker vollziehen, doch immer hohere Potenzen emporkommen, die das Allgemeine demgemäss umgestalten und ihm wieder einen anderen Charakter verleihen. —Ranke, *Weltgeschichte,* III, I, 6.

[87] Toujours et partout, les hommes furent de plus en plus dominés par l'ensemble de leurs prédécesseurs, dont ils purent seulement modifier l'empire nécessaire.—Comte, *Politique Positive,* III, 621.

[88] La liberté est l'âme du commerce.— Il faut laisser faire les hommes qui s'appliquent sans peine à ce qui convient le mieux; c'est ce qui apporte le plus d'advantage. — Colbert, in *Comptes Rendus de l'Institut,* XXXIX, 93.

[39] Il n'y a que les choses humaines exposées dans leur vérité, c'est-à-dire avec leur grandeur, leur variété, leur inépuisable fécondité, qui aient le droit de retenir le lecteur et qui le retiennent en effet Si l'écrivain paraît une fois, il ennuie ou fait sourire de pitié les lecteurs sérieux — Thiers to Ste Beuve, *Lundis,* III, 195. Comme l'a dit Taine, la disparition du style, c'est la perfection du style. — Faguet, *Revue Politique,* LIII, 67.

[40] Ne m'applaudissez pas; ce n'est pas moi qui vous parle; c'est l'histoire qui parle par ma bouche. — *Revue Historique,* XLI, 278

[41] Das Evangelium trat als Geschichte in die Welt, nicht als Dogma — wurde als Geschichte in der christlichen Kirche deponirt — Rothe, *Kirchengeschichte,* II, p. x. Das Christenthum ist nicht der Herr Christus, sondern dieser macht es. Es ist sein Werk, und zwar ein Werk, das er stets unter der Arbeit hat — Er selbst, Christus der Herr, bleibt der er ist in alle Zukunft, dagegen liegt es ausdrucklich im Begriffe seines Werks, des Christenthums, dass es nicht so bleibt, wie es anhebt. — Rothe, *Allgemeine kirchliche Zeitschrift,* 1864, 299. Diess Werk, weil es dem Wesen der Geschichte zufolge eine Entwickelung ist, muss uber Stufen hinweggehen, die einander ablosen, und von denen jede folgende neue immer nur unter der Zertrummerung der ihr

vorangehenden Platz greifen kann. — Rothe, *Ib.* 19th April, 1865. Je grösser ein geschichtliches Princip ist, desto langsamer und über mehr Stufen hinweg entfaltet es seinen Gehalt; desto langlebiger ist es aber ebendeshalb auch in diesen seinen unaufhorlichen Abwandelungen. — Rothe, *Stille Stunden,* 301. Der christliche Glaube geht nicht von der Anerkennung abstracter Lehrwahrheiten aus, sondern von der Anerkennung einer Reihe von Thatsachen, die in der Erscheinung Jesu ihren Mittelpunkt haben. — Nitzsch, *Dogmengeschichte,* I, 17. Der Gedankengang der evangelischen Erzahlung gibt darum auch eine vollstandige Darstellung der christlichen Lehre in ihren wesentlichen Grundzugen; aber er gibt sie im allseitigen lebendigen Zusammenhange mit der Geschichte der christlichen Offenbarung, und nicht in einer theoretisch zusammenhangenden Folgenreihe von ethischen und dogmatischen Lehrsatzen. — Deutinger, *Reich Gottes,* I, p v.

[42] L'Univers ne doit pas être considéré seulement dans ce qu'il est; pour le bien connoître, il faut le voir aussi dans ce qu'il doit estre. C'est cet avenir surtout qui a été le grand objet de Dieu dans la création, et c'est pour cet avenir seul que le présent existe — D'Houteville, *Essai sur la Providence,* 273. La Providence emploie les siècles à élever toujours un plus grand nombre de familles et d'individus à ces biens de la liberté et de l'égalité légitimes que, dans l'enfance des sociétés, la force avait rendus le privilège de quelques-uns. — Guizot, *Gouvernement de la France,* 1820, 9. La marche de la Providence n'est pas assujettie à d'étroites limites; elle ne s'inquiète pas de tirer aujourd'hui la conséquence du principe qu'elle a posé hier, elle la tirera dans des siècles, quand l'heure sera venue, et pour raisonner lentement selon nous, sa logique n'est pas moins sûre — Guizot, *Histoire de la Civilisation,* 20 Der Keim fortschreitender Entwicklung ist, auch auf gottlichem Geheisse, der Menschheit eingepflanzt. Die Weltgeschichte ist der blosse Ausdruck einer vorbestimmten Entwicklung. — A. Humboldt, 2nd January, 1842, *Im Neuen Reich,* 1872, I, 197. Das historisch grosse ist religios gross; es ist die Gottheit selbst, die sich offenbart. — Raumer, April, 1807, *Erinnerungen,* I, 85.

[43] Je suis arrivé à l'âge où je suis, à travers bien des évènements différents, mais avec une seule cause, celle de la liberté régulière. — Tocqueville, 1st May 1852, *Œuvres Inédites,* II, 185. Me trouvant dans un pays où la religion et le libéralisme sont d'accord, j'avais respiré. — J'exprimais ce sentiment, il y a plus de vingt ans, dans l'avant-propos de la *Démocratie.* Je l'éprouve aujourd'hui aussi vivement que si j'étais encore jeune, et je ne sais s'il y a une seule pensée qui ait été plus constamment présente à mon esprit. — 5th August 1857, *Œuvres,* VI, 395. Il n'y a que la liberté (j'entends la modérée et la régulière) et la religion, qui, par un effort combiné, puissent soulever les hommes au-dessus du bourbier où l'égalité démocratique les plonge naturellement — 1st December 1852, *Œuvres,* VII, 295. L'un de mes rêves, le principal en entrant dans la vie politique, était de travailler à concilier l'esprit libéral et l'esprit de religion, la société nouvelle et l'église. — 15th November 1843, *Œuvres Inédites,* II, 121. La véritable grandeur de l'homme n'est que dans l'accord du sentiment libéral et du sentiment religieux. — 17 September 1853, *Œuvres Inédites,* II, 228. Qui cherche dans la liberté autre chose qu'elle-même est fait pour servir. — *Ancien Régime,* 248. Je regarde, ainsi que je l'ai toujours fait, la liberté comme le premier des biens; je vois toujours en elle l'une des sources les plus fécondes des vertus mâles et des actions grandes. Il n'y a pas de tranquillité ni de bien-

être qui puisse me tenir lieu d'elle. — 7th January 1856, M*me* Swetchine, I, 452. La liberté a un faux air d'aristocratie; en donnant pleine carrière aux facultés humaines, en encourageant le travail et l'économie, elle fait ressortir les supériorités naturelles ou acquises. — Laboulaye, *L'Etat et ses Limites*, 154. Dire que la liberté n'est point par elle-même, qu'elle dépend d'une situation, d'une opportunité, c'est lui assigner une valeur négative La liberté n'est pas dès qu'on la subordonne. Elle n'est pas un principe purement négatif, un simple élément de contrôle et de critique Elle est le principe actif, créateur organisateur par excellence. Elle est le moteur et la règle, la source de toute vie, et le principe de l'ordre Elle est, en un mot, le nom que prend la conscience souveraine, lorsque, se posant en face du monde social et politique, elle émerge du moi pour modeler les sociétés sur les données de la raison. — Brisson, *Revue Nationale*, XXIII, 214. Le droit, dans l'histoire, est le développement progressif de la liberté, sous la loi de la raison — Lerminier, *Philosophie du Droit*, I, 211. En prouvant par les leçons de l'histoire que la liberté fait vivre les peuples et que le despotisme les tue, en montrant que l'expiation suit la faute et que la fortune finit d'ordinaire par se ranger du côté de la vertu, Montesquieu n'est ni moins moral ni moins religieux que Bossuet. — Laboulaye, *Œuvres de Montesquieu*, II, 109. Je ne comprendrais pas qu'une nation ne praçât pas les libertés politiques au premier rang, parce que c'est des libertés politiques que doivent découler toutes les autres. — Thiers, *Discours*, X, 8, 28th March 1865. Nous sommes arrivés à une époque où la liberté est le but sérieux de tous, où le reste n'est plus qu'une question de moyens. — J. Lebeau, *Observations sur le Pouvoir Royal* Liège, 1830, p. 10. Le libéralisme, ayant la prétention de se fonder uniquement sur les principes de la raison, croit d'ordinaire n'avoir pas besoin de tradition Là est son erreur. L'erreur de l'école libérale est d'avoir trop cru qu'il est facile de créer la liberté par la réflexion, et de n'avoir pas vu qu'un établissement n'est solide que quand il a des racines historiques. — Renan, 1858, *Nouvelle Revue*, LXXIX, 596. Le respect des individus et des droits existants est autant au-dessus du bonheur de tous, qu'un intérêt moral surpasse un intérêt purement temporel. — Renan, 1858, *Ib*. LXXIX, 597. Die Rechte gelten nichts, wo es sich handelt um das Recht, und das Recht der Freiheit kann nie verjahren, weil es die Quelle alles Rechtes selbst ist. — C. Frantz, *Ueber die Freiheit*, 110. Wir erfahren hienieden nie die ganze Wahrheit· wir geniessen nie die ganze Freiheit. — Reuss, *Reden*, 56. Le gouvernement constitutionnel, comme tout gouvernement libre, présente et doit présenter un état de lutte permanent. La liberté est la perpétuité de la lutte — De Serre. Broglie, *Nouvelles Etudes*, 243. The experiment of free government is not one which can be tried once for all. Every generation must try it for itself. As each new generation starts up to the responsibilities of manhood, there is, as it were, a new launch of Liberty, and its voyage of experiment begins afresh. — Winthrop, *Addresses*, 163 L'histoire perd son véritable caractère du moment que la liberté en a disparu; elle devient une sorte de physique sociale. C'est l'élément personnel de l'histoire qui en fait la réalité. — Vacherot, *Revue des Deux Mondes*, 1869, IV, 215. Demander la liberté pour soi et la refuser aux autres, c'est la définition du despotisme. — Laboulaye, 4th December 1874. Les causes justes profitent de tout, des bonnes intentions comme des mauvaises, des calculs personnels comme des dévouements courageux, de la démence, enfin, comme de la raison. — B. Constant, *Les Cent*

Jours, II, 29. Sie ist die Kunst, das Gute der schon weit gediehenen Civilisation zu sichern. — Baltisch, *Politische Freiheit*, 9. In einem Volke, welches sich zur burgerlichen Gesellschaft, uberhaupt zum Bewusstseyn der Unendlichkeit des Freien — entwickelt hat, ist nur die constitutionelle Monarchie moglich — Hegel's *Philosophie des Rechts*, § 137, *Hegel und Preussen*, 1841, 31. Freiheit ist das hochste Gut. Alles andere ist nur das Mittel dazu: gut falls es ein Mittel dazu ist, ubel falls es dieselbe hemmt. — Fichte, *Werke*, IV, 403. You are not to inquire how your trade may be increased, nor how you are to become a great and powerful people, but how your liberties can be secured. For liberty ought to be the direct end of your government. — Patrick Henry, 1788; Wirt, *Life of Henry*, 272.

44 Historiae ipsius praeter delectationem utilitas nulla est, quam ut religionis Christianae veritas demonstretur, quod aliter quam per historiam fieri non potest. — Leibniz, *Opera*, ed. Dutens, VI, 297. The study of Modern History is, next to Theology itself, and only next in so far as Theology rests on a divine revelation, the most thoroughly religious training that the mind can receive. It is no paradox to say that Modern History, including Medieval History in the term, is co-extensive in its field of view, in its habits of criticism, in the persons of its most famous students, with Ecclesiastical History. — Stubbs, *Lectures*, 9. Je regarde donc l'étude de l'histoire comme l'étude de la providence — L'histoire est vraiment une seconde philosophie. — Si Dieu ne parle pas toujours, il agit toujours en Dieu. — D'Aguesseau, *Œuvres*, XV, 34, 31, 35. Fur diejenigen, welche das Wesen der menschlichen Freiheit erkannt haben, bildet die denkende Betrachtung der Weltgeschichte, besonders des christlichen Weltalters, die hochste, und umfassendste Theodicee. — Vatke, *Die Menschliche Freiheit*, 1841, 516. La théologie, que l'on regarde volontiers comme la plus étroite et la plus stérile des sciences, en est, au contraire, la plus étendue et la plus féconde. Elle confine à toutes les études et touche à toutes les questions. Elle renferme tous les éléments d'une instruction libérale. — Scherer, *Mélanges*, 522. The belief that the course of events and the agency of man are subject to the laws of a divine order, which it is alike impossible for any one either fully to comprehend or effectually to resist — this belief is the ground of all our hope for the future destinies of mankind. — Thirlwall, *Remains*, III, 282. A true religion must consist of ideas and facts both; not of ideas alone without facts, for then it would be mere philosophy; nor of facts alone without ideas, of which those facts are the symbols, or out of which they are grounded; for then it would be mere history. — Coleridge, *Table Talk*, 144. It certainly appears strange that the men most conversant with the order of the visible universe should soonest suspect it empty of directing mind; and, on the other hand, that humanistic, moral and historical studies — which first open the terrible problems of suffering and grief, and contain all the reputed provocatives of denial and despair — should confirm, and enlarge rather than disturb, the prepossessions of natural piety. — Martineau, *Essays*, I, 122. Die Religion hat nur dann eine Bedeutung fur den Menschen, wenn er in der Geschichte einen Punkt findet, dem er sich vollig unbedingt hingeben kann. — Steffens, *Christliche Religionsphilosophie*, 440, 1839. Wir erkennen darin nur eine Thatigkeit des zu seinem achten und wahren Leben, zu seinem verlornen, objectiven Selbstverstandnisse sich zurucksehnenden christlichen Geistes unserer Zeit, einen Ausdruck fur das Bedurfnisse desselben, sich aus den unwahren und unachten

Verkleidungen, womit ihn der moderne, subjective Geschmack der letzten Entwickelungsphase des theologischen Bewusstseyns umhüllt hat, zu seiner historischen allein wahren und ursprunglichen Gestalt wiederzugebaren, zu derjenigen Bedeutung zuruckzukehren, die ihm in dem Bewusstseyn der Geschichte allein zukommt und deren Verstandniss in dem wogenden luxuriösen Leben der modernen Theologie langst untergegangen ist. — Georgii, *Zeitschrift fur Hist. Theologie*, IX, 5, 1839.

45 Liberty, in fact, means just so far as it is realised, the right man in the right place. — Seeley, *Lectures and Essays*, 109.

46 In diesem Sinne ist Freiheit und sich entwickelnde moralische Vernunft und Gewissen gleichbedeutend. In diesen Sinne ist der Mensch frei, sobald sich das Gewissen in ihm entwickelt. — Scheidler, *Ersch und Gruber*, XLIX, 20. Aus der unendlichen und ewigen Geltung der menschlichen Personlichkeit vor Gott, aus der Vorstellung von der in Gott freien Personlichkeit, folgt auch der Anspruch auf das Recht derselben in der weltlichen Sphare, auf burgerliche und politische Freiheit, auf Gewissen und Religionsfreiheit, auf freie wissenschaftliche Forschung u.s w., und namentlich die Forderung, dass niemand lediglich zum Mittel fur andere diene. — Martensen, *Christliche Ethik*, I, 50.

47 Es giebt angeborne Menschenrechte, weil es angeborne Menschenpflichten giebt. — Wolff, *Naturrecht*; Loeper, *Einleitung zu Faust*, LVII.

48 La constitution de l'état reste jusqu'à un certain point à notre discrétion. La constitution de la société ne dépend pas de nous; elle est donnée par la force des choses, et si l'on veut élever le langage, elle est l'œuvre de la Providence. — Rémusat, *Revue des Deux Mondes*, 1861, V, 795.

49 Die Freiheit ist bekanntlich kein Geschenk der Gotter, sondern ein Gut das jedes Volk sich selbst verdankt und das nur bei dem erforderlichen Mass moralischer Kraft und Wurdigkeit gedeiht. — Ihering, *Geist des Romischen Rechts*, II, 290. Liberty, in the very nature of it, absolutely requires, and even supposes, that people be able to govern themselves in those respects in which they are free; otherwise their wickedness will be in proportion to their liberty, and this greatest of blessings will become a curse. — Butler, *Sermons*, 331. In each degree and each variety of public development there are corresponding institutions, best answering the public needs; and what is meat to one is poison to another. Freedom is for those who are fit for it. — Parkman, *Canada*, 396. Die Freiheit ist die Wurzel einer neuen Schopfung in der Schopfung. — Sederholm, *Die ewigen Thatsachen*, 86.

50 La liberté politique, qui n'est qu'une complexité plus grande, de plus en plus grande, dans le gouvernement d'un peuple. à mesure que le peuple lui-même contient un plus grand nombre de forces diverses ayant droit et de vivre et de participer à la chose publique, est un fait de civilisation qui s'impose lentement à une société organisée, mais qui n'apparaît point comme un principe à une société qui s'organise. — Faguet, *Revue des Deux Mondes*, 1889, II, 942.

51 Il y a bien un droit du plus sage, mais non pas un droit du plus fort. — La justice est le droit du plus faible. — Joubert, *Pensées*, I, 355, 358.

52 Nicht durch ein pflanzenahnliches Wachsthum, nicht aus den dunklen Gründen der Volksempfindung, sondern durch den männlichen Willen, durch die Ueberzeugung, durch die That, durch den Kampf entsteht, behauptet, entwickelt sich das Recht. Sein historisches Werden ist ein bewusstes,

im hellen Mittagslicht der Erkenntniss und der Gesetzgebung. — *Rundschau,* November, 1893, 13. Nicht das Normale, Zahme, sondern das Abnorme, Wilde, bildet uberall die Grundlage und den Anfang einer neuen Ordnung. — Lasaulx, *Philosophie der Geschichte,* 143.

[53] Um den Sieg zu vervollstandigen, erübrigte das zweite Stadium oder die Aufgabe die Berechtigung der Mehrheit nach allen Seiten hin zur gleichen Berechtigung aller zu erweitern, d.h. bis zur Gleichstellung aller Bekenntnisse im Kirchenrecht, aller Volker im Volkerrecht, aller Staatsburger im Staatsrecht und aller socialen Interessen im Gesellschaftsrecht fortzufuhren — A. Schmidt, *Zuricher Monatschrift,* I, 68.

[54] Notre histoire ne nous enseignait nullement la liberté. Le jour où la France voulut être libre, elle eut tout à créer, tout à inventer dans cet ordre de faits. — Cependant il faut marcher, l'avenir appelle les peuples. Quand on n'a point pour cela l'impulsion du passé, il faut bien se confier à la raison. — Dupont White, *Revue des Deux Mondes,* 1861, VI, 191. Le peuple français a peu de goût pour le développement graduel des institutions. Il ignore son histoire, il ne s'y reconnaît pas, elle n'a pas laissé de trace dans sa conscience. — Scherer, *Etudes Critiques,* I, 100 Durch die Revolution befreiten sich die Franzosen von ihrer Geschichte. — Rosenkranz, *Aus einem Tagebuch,* 199.

[55] The discovery of the comparative method in philology, in mythology — let me add in politics and history and the whole range of human thought — marks a stage in the progress of the human mind at least as great and memorable as the revival of Greek and Latin learning. — Freeman, *Historical Essays,* IV, 301. The diffusion of a critical spirit in history and literature is affecting the criticism of the Bible in our own day in a manner not unlike the burst of intellectual life in the fifteenth and sixteenth centuries. — Jowett, *Essays and Reviews,* 346. As the revival of literature in the sixteenth century produced the Reformation, so the growth of the critical spirit, and the change that has come over mental science, and the mere increase of knowledge of all kinds, threaten now a revolution less external but not less profound. — Haddan, *Replies,* 348.

[56] In his just contempt and detestation of the crimes and follies of the Revolutionists, he suffers himself to forget that the revolution itself is a process of the Divine Providence, and that as the folly of men is the wisdom of God, so are their iniquities instruments of His goodness. — Coleridge, *Biographia Literaria,* II, 240. In other parts of the world, the idea of revolutions in government is, by a mournful and indissoluble association, connected with the idea of wars, and all the calamities attendant on wars. But happy experience teaches us to view such revolutions in a very different light — to consider them only as progressive steps in improving the knowledge of government, and increasing the happiness of society and mankind. — J. Wilson, 26th November, 1787, *Works,* III, 293. La Révolution, c'est-à-dire l'œuvre des siècles, ou, si vous voulez, le renouvellement progressif de la société, ou encore, sa nouvelle constitution. — Rémusat, *Correspondance,* 11th October, 1818. A ses yeux loin d'avoir rompu le cours naturel des évènements, ni la Révolution d'Angleterre, ni la nôtre, n'ont rien dit, rien fait, qui n'eût été dit, souhaité, fait, ou tenté cent fois avant leur explosion. "Il faut en ceci," dit-il, "tout accorder à leurs adversaires, les surpasser même en sévérité, ne regarder à leurs accusations que pour y ajouter, s'ils en oublient; et puis les sommer de dresser, à leur tour, le compte des erreurs, des crimes, et des maux de ces temps et de ces pouvoirs

qu'ils ont pris sous leur garde." — *Revue de Paris,* XVI, 303, on Guizot. Quant aux nouveautés mises en œuvre par la Révolution Française on les retrouve une à une, en remontant d'âge en âge, chez les philosophes du XVIII⁰ siècle, chez les grands penseurs du XVI⁰, chez certains Pères d'Église et jusque dans la République de Platon. — En présence de cette belle continuité de l'histoire, qui ne fait pas plus de sauts que la nature, devant cette solidarité nécessaire des révolutions avec le passé qu'elles brisent.— Krantz, *Revue Politique,* XXXIII, 264. L'esprit du XIX⁰ siècle est de comprendre et de juger les choses du passé. Notre œuvre est d'expliquer ce que le XVIII⁰ siècle avait mission de nier. — Vacherot, *De la Démocratie,* pref , 28.

[57] La commission recherchera, dans toutes les parties des archives pontificales, les pièces relatives à l'abus que les papes ont fait de leur ministère spirituel contre l'autorité des souveraines et la tranquillité des peuples. — Daunou, *Instructions,* 3rd January, 1811. Laborde, *Inventaires,* p cxii.

[58] Aucun des historiens remarquables de cette époque n'avait senti encore le besoin de chercher les faits hors des livres imprimés, aux sources primitives, la plupart inédites alors, aux manuscrits de nos bibliothèques, aux documents de nos archives — Michelet, *Histoire de France,* 1869, I, 2.

[59] Doch besteht eine Grenze, wo die Geschichte aufhort und das Archiv anfangt, und die von der Geschichtschreibung nicht uberschritten werden sollte. *Unsere Zeit,* 1866, II, 635 Il faut avertir nos jeunes historiens à la fois de la nécessité inéluctable du document et, d'autre part, du danger qu'il présente. — M. Hanotaux.

[60] This process consists in determining with documentary proofs, and by minute investigations duly set forth, the literal, precise, and positive inferences to be drawn at the present day from every authentic statement, without regard to commonly received notions, to sweeping generalities, or to possible consequences. — Harrisse, *Discovery of America,* 1892, p. VI. Perhaps the time has not yet come for synthetic labours in the sphere of History. It may be that the student of the Past must still content himself with critical inquiries — *Ib.* p. v. Few scholars are critics, few critics are philosophers, and few philosophers look with equal care on both sides of a question. — W. S. Landor in Holyoake's *Agitator's Life,* II, 15. Introduire dans l'histoire, et sans tenir compte des passions politiques et religieuses, le doute méthodique que Descartes, le premier, appliqua à l'étude de la philosophie, n'est-ce pas là une excellente méthode? N'est-ce pas même la meilleure? — Chantelauze, *Correspondant,* 1883, I, 129. La critique historique ne sera jamais populaire. Comme elle est de toutes les sciences la plus délicate, la plus déliée, elle n'a de crédit qu'auprès des esprits cultivés. — Cherbuliez, *Revue des Deux Mondes,* XCVII, 517. Nun liefert aber die Kritik, wenn sie rechter Art ist, immer nur einzelne Data, gleichsam die Atome des Thatbestandes, und jede Kombination, jede Zusammenfassung und Schlussfolgerung, ohne die es doch einmal nicht abgeht, ist ein subjektiver Akt des Forschers. Demnach blieb Waitz, bei der eigenen Arbeit wie bei jener der anderen, immer hochst misstrauisch gegen jedes Résumé, jede Definition, jedes abschliessende Wort. — Sybel, *Historische Zeitschrift,* LVI, 484. Mit blosser Kritik wird darin nichts ausgerichtet, denn die ist nur eine Vorarbeit, welche da aufhort, wo die echte historische Kunst anfangt. — Lasaulx, *Philosophie der Kunste,* 212.

[61] The only case in which such extraneous matters can be fairly called in is when facts are stated resting on testimony; then it is not only just, but it is

necessary for the sake of truth, to inquire into the habits of mind of him by whom they are adduced. — Babbage, *Bridgewater Treatise*, p. xiv.

[62] There is no part of our knowledge which it is more useful to obtain at first hand — to go to the fountain-head for — than our knowledge of History. — J. S. Mill, *Inaugural Address*, 34. The only sound intellects are those which, in the first instance, set their standard of proof high. — J. S. Mill, *Examination of Hamilton's Philosophy*, 525.

[63] There are so few men mentally capable of seeing both sides of a question; so few with consciences sensitively alive to the obligation of seeing both sides; so few placed under conditions either of circumstance or temper, which admit of their seeing both sides. — Greg, *Political Problems*, 1870, 173. Il n'y a que les Allemands qui sachent être aussi complètement objectifs. Ils se dédoublent, pour ainsi dire, en deux hommes, l'un qui a des principes très arrêtés et des passions très vives, l'autre qui sait voir et observer comme s'il n'en avait point. — Laveleye, *Revue des Deux Mondes*, 1868, I, 431 L'écrivain qui penche trop dans le sens où il incline, et qui ne se défie pas de ses qualités presque autant que ses défauts, cet écrivain tourne à la manière. — Scherer, *Mélanges*, 484. Il faut faire volteface, et vivement, franchement, tourner le dos au moyen âge, à ce passé morbide, qui, même quand il n'agit pas, influe terriblement par la contagion de la mort. Il ne faut ni combattre, ni critiquer, mais oublier. Oublions et marchons! — Michelet, *La Bible de l'Humanité*, 483. It has excited surprise that Thucydides should speak of Antiphon, the traitor to the democracy, and the employer of assassins, as "a man inferior in virtue to none of his contemporaries." But neither here nor elsewhere does Thucydides pass moral judgments. — Jowett, *Thucydides*, II, 501.

[64] Non theologi provinciam suscepimus; scimus enim quantum hoc ingenii nostri tenuitatem superet: ideo sufficit nobis τὸ ὅτι fideliter ex antiquis auctoribus retulisse. — Morinus, *De Poenitentia*, IX, 10. — Il faut avouer que la religion chrétienne a quelque chose d'étonnant! C'est parce que vous y êtes né, dira-t-on. Tant s'en faut, je me roidis contre par cette raison-là même, de peur que cette prévention ne me suborne. — Pascal, *Pensées*, XVI, 7. — I was fond of Fleury for a reason which I express in the advertisement; because it presented a sort of photograph of ecclesiastical history without any comment upon it. In the event, that simple representation of the early centuries had a good deal to do with unsettling me. — Newman, *Apologia*, 152. Nur was sich vor dem Richterstuhl einer achten, unbefangenen, nicht durch die Brille einer philosophischen oder dogmatischen Schule stehenden Wissenschaft als wahr bewahrt, kann zur Erbauung, Belehrung und Warnung tüchtig seyn. — Neander, *Kirchengeschichte*, I, p. vii. Wie weit bei katholischen Publicisten bei der Annahme der Ansicht von der Staatsanstalt apologetische Gesichtspunkte massgebend gewesen sind, mag dahingestellt bleiben. Der Historiker darf sich jedoch nie durch apologetische Zwecke leiten lassen; sein einziges Ziel soll die Ergrundung der Wahrheit sein. — Pastor, *Geschichte der Pabste*, II, 545. Church history falsely written is a school of vainglory, hatred, and uncharitableness; truly written, it is a discipline of humility, of charity, of mutual love. — Sir W. Hamilton, *Discussions*, 506. The more trophies and crowns of honour the Church of former ages can be shown to have won in the service of her adorable head, the more tokens her history can be brought to furnish of his powerful presence in her midst, the more will we be pleased and rejoice, Protestant though we be. — Nevin, *Mercersburg*

Review, 1851, 168. S'il est une chose à laquelle j'ai donné tous mes soins, c'est à ne pas laisser influencer mes jugements par les opinions politiques ou religieuses; que si j'ai quelquefois péché par quelque excès, c'est par la bienveillance pour les œuvres de ceux qui pensent autrement que' moi — Monod, *R. Hist.* XVI, 184. Nous n'avons nul intérêt à faire parler l'histoire en faveur de nos propres opinions. C'est son droit imprescriptible que le narrateur reproduise tous les faits sans aucune réticence et range toutes les évolutions dans leur ordre naturel. Notre récit restera complètement en dehors des préoccupations de la dogmatique et des déclamations de la polémique. Plus les questions auxquelles nous aurons à toucher agitent et passionnent de nos jours les esprits, plus il est du devoir de l'historien de s'effacer devant les faits qu'il veut faire connaître. — Reuss, *Nouvelle Revue de Théologie*, VI, 193, 1860. To love truth for truth's sake is the principal part of human perfection in this world, and the seed-plot of all other virtues — Locke, *Letter to Collins*. Il n'est plus possible aujourd'hui à l'historien d'être national dans le sens étroit du mot. Son patriotisme à lui c'est l'amour de la vérité. Il n'est pas l'homme d'une race ou d'un pays, il est l'homme de tous les pays, il parle au nom de la civilisation générale. — Lanfrey, *Hist. de Nap.* III, 2, 1870. Juger avec les parties de soi-même qui sont le moins des formes du tempérament, et le plus des facultés pénétrées et modelées par l'expérience, par l'étude, par l'investigation, par le non-moi. — Faguet, *R. de Paris*, I, 151. Aucun critique n'est aussi impersonnel que lui, aussi libre de partis pris et d'opinions préconçues, aussi objectif. — Il ne mêle ou parfait mêler à ses appréciations ni inclinations personnelles de goût ou d'humeur, ou théories d'aucune sorte. G. Monod, of Faguet, *Revue Historique*, XLII, 417 On dirait qu'il a peur, et généralisant ses observations, en systématisant ses connaissances, de mêler de lui-même aux choses. — Je lis tout un volume de M. Faguet, sans penser une fois à M. Faguet; je ne vois que les originaux qu'il montre. — J'envisage toujours une réalité objective, jamais l'idée de M. Faguet, jamais la doctrine de M. Faguet. — Lanson, *Revue Politique*, 1894, I, 98.

65 It should teach us to disentangle principles first from parties, and again from one another; first of all as showing how imperfectly all parties represent their own principles, and then how the principles themselves are a mingled tissue. — Arnold, *Modern History*, 184. I find it a good rule, when I am contemplating a person from whom I want to learn, always to look out for his strength, being confident that the weakness will discover itself. — Maurice, *Essays*, 305. We may seek for agreement somewhere with our neighbours, using that as a point of departure for the sake of argument. It is this latter course that I wish here to explain and defend. The method is simple enough, though not yet very familiar. — It aims at conciliation; it proceeds by making the best of our opponent's case, instead of taking him at his worst. — The most interesting part of every disputed question only begins to appear when the rival ideals admit each other's right to exist. — A. Sidgwick, *Distinction and the Criticism of Beliefs*, 1892, 211. That cruel reticence in the breasts of wise men which makes them always hide their deeper thought. — Ruskin, *Sesame and Lilies*, I, 16. Je offener wir die einzelnen Wahrheiten des Sozialismus anerkennen, desto erfolgreicher konnen wir seine fundamentalen Unwahrheiten widerlegen. — Roscher, *Deutsche Vierteljahrschrift*, 1849, I, 177.

66 Dann habe ihn die Wahrnehmung, dass manche Angaben in den histori-

schen Romanen Walter Scott's, mit den gleichzeitigen Quellen im Widerspruch standen, "mit Erstaunen" erfüllt, und ihn zu dem Entschlusse gebracht, auf das Gewissenhafteste an der Ueberlieferung der Quellen festzuhalten. — Sybel, *Gedachtnissrede auf Ranke. Akad. der Wissenschaften,* 1887, p. 6. Sich frei zu halten von allem Widerschein der Gegenwart, sogar, soweit das menschenmöglich, von dem der eignen subjektiven Meinung in den Dingen des Staates, der Kirche und der Gesellschaft. — A. Dove, *Im Neuen Reich,* 1875, II, 967. Wir sind durchaus nicht für die leblose und schemenartige Darstellungsweise der Ranke'schen Schule eingenommen; es wird uns immer kühl bis ans Herz heran, wenn wir derartige Schilderungen der Reformation und der Revolution lesen, welche so ganz im kühlen Element des Pragmatismus sich bewegen und dabei so ganz undinenhaft sind und keine Seele haben. — Wir lassen es uns lieber gefallen, dass die Männer der Geschichte hier und dort gehofmeistert werden, als dass sie uns mit Glasaugen ansehen, so meisterhaft immer die Kunst sein mag, die sie ihnen eingesetzt hat. — Gottschall, *Unsere Zeit,* 1866, II, 636, 637. A vivre avec des diplomates, il leur a pris des qualités qui sont un défaut chez un historien. L'historien n'est pas un témoin, c'est un juge; c'est à lui d'accuser et de condamner au nom du passé opprimé et dans l'intérêt de l'avenir. — Laboulaye on Ranke; *Débats,* 12th January, 1852.

[67] Un théologien qui a composé une éloquente histoire de la Réformation, rencontrant à Berlin un illustre historien qui, lui aussi, a raconté Luther et le XVIe siècle, l'embrassa avec effusion en le traitant de confrère. "Ah! permettez," lui répondit l'autre en se dégageant, "il y a une grande différence entre nous: vous êtes avant tout chrétien, et je suis avant tout historien." — Cherbuliez, *Revue des Deux Mondes,* 1872, I, 537.

[68] Nackte Wahrheit ohne allen Schmuck; gründliche Erforschung des Einzelnen; das Uebrige, Gott befohlen. — *Werke,* XXXIV, 24. Ce ne sont pas les théories qui doivent nous servir de base dans la recherche des faits, mais ce sont les faits qui doivent nous servir de base pour la composition des théories. — Vincent, *Nouvelle Revue de Théologie,* 1859, II, 252.

[69] Die zwanglose Anordnungs — die leichte und leise Andeutungskunst des grossen Historikers voll zu würdigen, hinderte ihn in früherer Zeit sein Bedürfniss nach scharfer begrifflicher Ordnung und Ausführung, später, und in immer zunehmenden Grade, sein Sinn für strenge Sachlichkeit, und genaue Erforschung der ursächlichen Zusammenhange, noch mehr aber regte sich seine geradherzige Offenheit seine männliche Ehrlichkeit, wenn er hinter den fein verstrichenen Farben der Rankeschen Erzahlungsbilder die gedeckte Haltung des klugen Diplomaten zu entdecken glaubte. — Haym, *Duncker's Leben,* 437. The ground of criticism is indeed, in my opinion, nothing else but distinct attention, which every reader should endeavour to be master of. — Hare, December, 1736; *Warburton's Works,* XIV, 98. Wenn die Quellenkritik so verstanden wird, als sei sie der Nachweis, wie ein Autor den andern benutzt hat, so ist das nur ein gelegentliches Mittel — eins unter anderen — ihre Aufgabe, den Nachweis der Richtigkeit zu losen oder vorzubereiten. — Droysen, *Historik,* 18.

[70] L'esprit scientifique n'est autre en soi que l'instinct du travail et de la patience, le sentiment de l'ordre, de la réalité et de la mesure. — Papillon, *R. des Deux Mondes,* 1873, V, 704. Non seulement les sciences, mais toutes les institutions humaines s'organisent de même, et sous l'empire des mêmes

APPENDIX 417

idées régulatrices. — Cournot, *Idées Fondamentales*, I, 4. There is no branch of human work whose constant laws have not close analogy with those which govern every other mode of man's exertion. But more than this, exactly as we reduce to greater simplicity and surety any one group of these practical laws, we shall find them passing the mere condition of connection or analogy, and becoming the actual expression of some ultimate nerve or fibre of the mighty laws which govern the moral world. — Ruskin, *Seven Lamps*, 4. The sum total of all intellectual excellence is good sense and method. When these have passed into the instinctive readiness of habit, when the wheel revolves so rapidly that we cannot see it revolve at all, then we call the combination genius. But in all modes alike, and in all professions, the two sole component parts, even of genius, are good sense and method. — Coleridge, June, 1814, *Mem, of Coleorton*, II, 172. Si l'exercice d'un art nous empêche d'en apprendre un autre, il n'en est pas ainsi dans les sciences: la connoissance d'une vérité nous aide à en découvrir une autre. — Toutes les sciences sont tellement liées ensemble qu'il est bien plus facile de les apprendre toutes à la fois que d'en apprendre une seule en la détachant des autres. — Il ne doit songer qu'à augmenter les lumières naturelles de sa raison, non pour résoudre telle ou telle difficulté de l'école, mais pour que dans chaque circonstance de la vie son intelligence montre d'avance à sa volonté le parti qu'elle doit prendre. — Descartes, *Œuvres Choisies*, 300, 301. *Règles pour la Direction de l'Esprit.* La connaissance de la méthode qui a guidé l'homme de génie n'est pas moins utile au progrès de la science et même à sa propre gloire, que ses découvertes. — Laplace, *Système du Monde*, II, 371. On ne fait rien sans idées préconçues, il faut avoir seulement la sagesse de ne croire à leurs déductions qu'autant que l'expérience les confirme. Les idées préconçues, soumises au contrôle sévère de l'expérimentation, sont la flamme vivante des sciences d'observation; les idées fixes en sont le danger. — Pasteur, in *Histoire d'un Savant*, 284. Douter des vérités humaines, c'est ouvrir la porte aux découvertes; en faire des articles de foi, c'est la fermer. — Dumas, *Discours*, I, 123.

71 We should not only become familiar with the laws of phenomena within our own pursuit, but also with the modes of thought of men engaged in other discussions and researches, and even with the laws of knowledge itself, that highest philosophy. — Above all things, know that we call you not here to run your minds into our moulds. We call you here on an excursion, on an adventure, on a voyage of discovery into space as yet uncharted. — Allbutt, *Introductory Address at St. George's*, October, 1889. Consistency in regard to opinions is the slow poison of intellectual life. — Davy, *Memoirs*, 68.

72 Ce sont vous autres physiologistes des corps vivants, qui avez appris à nous autres physiologistes de la société (qui est aussi un corps vivant) la manière de l'observer et de tirer des conséquences de nos observations. — J. B. Say to De Candolle, 1st June, 1827; De Candolle, *Mémoires*, 567.

73 Success is certain to the pure and true: success to falsehood and corruption, tyranny and aggression, is only the prelude to a greater and an irremediable fall. — Stubbs, *Seventeen Lectures*, 20. The Carlylean faith, that the cause we fight for, so far as it is true, is sure of victory, is the necessary basis of all effective activity for good. — Caird, *Evolution of Religion*, II, 43. It is the property of truth to be fearless, and to prove victorious over every adversary. Sound reasoning and truth, when adequately communicated, must always be victorious over error. — Godwin, *Political Justice* (Conclu-

sion). Vice was obliged to retire and give place to virtue. This will always be the consequence when truth has fair play. Falsehood only dreads the attack, and cries out for auxiliaries. Truth never fears the encounter; she scorns the aid of the secular arm, and triumphs by her natural strength. — Franklin, *Works*, II, 292. It is a condition of our race that we must ever wade through error in our advance towards truth; and it may even be said that in many cases we exhaust almost every variety of error before we attain the desired goal. — Babbage, *Bridgewater Treatise*, 27. Les hommes ne peuvent, en quelque genre que ce soit, arriver à quelque chose de raisonnable qu'après avoir, en ce même genre, épuisé toutes les sottises imaginables. Que de sottises ne dirions-nous pas maintenant, si les anciens ne les avaient pas déjà dites avant nous, et ne nous les avaient, pour ainsi dire, enlevées! — Fontenelle. Without premature generalisations the true generalisation would never be arrived at. — H. Spencer, *Essays*, II, 57. The more important the subject of difference, the greater, not the less, will be the indulgence of him who has learned to trace the sources of human error, — of error, that has its origin not in our weakness and imperfection merely, but often in the most virtuous affections of the heart. — Brown, *Philosophy of the Human Mind*, I, 48, 1824 Parmi les châtiments du crime qui ne lui manquent jamais, à côté de celui que lui inflige la conscience, l'histoire lui en inflige un autre encore, éclatant et manifeste, l'impuissance. — Cousin, *Phil. Mod.*, II, 24. L'avenir de la science est garanti; car dans le grand livre scientifique tout s'ajoute et rien ne se perd. L'erreur ne fonde pas; aucune erreur ne dure très longtemps. — Renan, *Feuilles Détachées*, XIII. Toutes les fois que deux hommes sont d'un avis contraire sur la même chose, à coup sûr, l'un ou l'autre se trompe; bien plus, aucun ne semble posséder la vérité; car si les raisons de l'un étoient certaines et évidentes, il pourroit les exposer à l'autre de telle manière qu'il finiroit par le convaincre également. — Descartes, *Règles; Œuvres Choisies*, 302. Le premier principe de la critique est qu'une doctrine ne captive ses adhérents que par ce qu'elle a de légitime. — Renan, *Essais de Morale*, 184. Was dem Wahn solche Macht giebt ist wirklich nicht er selbst, sondern die ihm zu Grunde liegende und darin nur verzerrte Wahrheit. — Frantz, *Schelling's Philosophie*, I, 62. Quand les hommes ont vu une fois la vérité dans son éclat, ils ne peuvent plus l'oublier. Elle reste debout, et tôt ou tard elle triomphe, parce qu'elle est la pensée de Dieu et le besoin du monde. — Mignet, *Portraits*, II, 295. C'est toujours le sens commun inaperçu qui fait la fortune des hypothèses auxquelles il se mêle. — Cousin, *Fragments Phil.* I, 51, Preface of 1826. Wer da sieht, wie der Irrthum selbst ein Träger mannigfaltigen und bleibenden Fortschritts wird, der wird auch nicht so leicht aus dem thatsächlichen Fortschritt der Gegenwart auf Unumstösslichkeit unserer Hypothesen schliessen. — Das richtigste Resultat der geschichtlichen Betrachtung ist die akademische Ruhe, mit welcher unsere Hypothesen und Theorieen ohne Feindschaft und ohne Glauben als das betrachtet werden, was sie sind; als Stufen in jener unendlichen Annäherung an die Wahrheit, welche die Bestimmung unserer intellectuellen Entwickelung zu sein scheint — Lange, *Geschichte des Materialismus*, 502, 503. Hominum errores divina providentia reguntur, ita ut saepe male jacta bene cadant. — Leibniz, ed Klopp, I, p. lii. Sainte-Beuve n'était même pas de la race des libéraux, c'est-à-dire de ceux qui croient que, tout compte fait, et dans un état de civilisation donné, le bien triomphe du mal à armes égales, et la vérité de l'erreur. — D'Haussonville, *Revue des Deux Mondes,* 1875, I, 567. In the progress of the human mind, a period of controversy amongst the cultivators of any branch of science must necessarily precede the period of unanimity. — Torrens, *Essay on the Production of Wealth,* 1821, p. xiii. Even the spread of an error is part of the wide-world process by which we stumble into mere approximations to truth. — L. Stephen, *Apology of an Agnostic,* 81. Errors, to be dangerous, must have a great deal of truth mingled with them; it is only from this alliance that they can ever obtain an extensive circulation. — S. Smith, *Moral Philosophy,* 7. The admission of the few errors of Newton himself is at least of as much importance to his followers in science as the history of the progress of his real discoveries. — Young, *Works,* III, 621. Error is almost always partial truth, and so consists in the exaggeration or distortion of one verity by the suppression of another, which qualifies and modifies the former. — Mivart, *Genesis of Species,* 3. The attainment of scientific truth has been effected, to a great extent, by the help of scientific errors. — Huxley: Ward, *Reign of Victoria,* II, 337. Jede neue tief eingreifende Wahrheit hat meiner Ansicht nach erst das Stadium der Einseitigkeit durchzumachen. — Ihering, *Geist des R Rechts,* II, 22. The more readily we admit the possibility of our own cherished convictions being mixed with error, the more vital and helpful whatever is right in them will become. — Ruskin, *Ethics of the Dust,* 225. They hardly grasp the plain truth unless they examine the error which it cancels. — Cory, *Modern English History,* 1880, I, 109. Nur durch Irrthum kommen wir, der eine kurzeren und gluckhcheren Schrittes, als der andere, zur Wahrheit; und die Geschichte darf nirgends diese Verirrungen ubergehen, wenn sie Lehrerin und Warnerin fur die nachfolgenden Geschlechter werden will. — *München Gel. Anzeigen,* 1840, I, 737.

74 Wie die Weltgeschichte das Weltgericht ist, so kann in noch allgemeinerem Sinne gesagt werden, dass das gerechte Gericht, d.h. die wahre Kritik einer Sache, nur in ihrer Geschichte liegen kann. Insbesondere in der Hinsicht lehrt die Geschichte denjenigen, der ihr folgt, ihre eigene Methode, dass ihr Fortschritt niemals ein reines Vernichten, sondern nur ein Aufheben im philosophischen Sinne ist. — Strauss, *Hallische Jahrbucher,* 1839, 120.

75 Dans tous les livres qu'il lit, et il en dévore des quantités, Darwin ne note que les passages qui contrarient ses idées systématiques. — Il collectionne les difficultés, les cas épineux, les critiques possibles. — Vernier, *Le Temps,* 6th Décembre, 1887. Je demandais à un savant célèbre où il en était de ses recherches. "Cela ne marche plus," me dit-il, "je ne trouve plus de faits contradictoires." Ainsi le savant cherche à se contredire lui-même pour faire avancer sa pensée — Janet, *Journal des Savants,* 1892, 20. Ein Umstand, der uns die Selbständigkeit des Ganges der Wissenschaft anschaulich machen kann, ist auch der: dass der Irrthum, wenn er nur grundlich behandelt wird, fast ebenso fördernd ist als das Finden der Wahrheit, denn er erzeugt fortgesetzten Widerspruch. — Baer, *Blicke auf die Entwicklung der Wissenschaft,* 120. It is only by virtue of the opposition which it has surmounted that any truth can stand in the human mind. — Archbishop Temple; Kinglake, *Crimea, Winter Troubles,* app. 104. I have for many years found it expedient to lay down a rule for my own practice, to confine my reading mainly to those journals the general line of opinions in which is adverse to my own. — Hare, *Means of Unity,* I, 19. Kant had a harder struggle with himself than he could possibly

have had with any critic or opponent of his philosophy. — Caird, *Philosophy of Kant*, 1889, I, p. ix.

76 The social body is no more liable to arbitrary changes than the individual body. — A full perception of the truth that society is not a mere aggregate, but an organic growth, that it forms a whole, the laws of whose growth can be studied apart from those of the individual atom, supplies the most characteristic postulate of modern speculation. — L. Stephen, *Science of Ethics*, 31. Wie in dem Leben des einzelnen Menschen kein Augenblick eines vollkommenen Stillstandes wahrgenommen wird, sondern stete organische Entwicklung, so verhalt es sich auch in dem Leben der Volker, und in jedem einzelnen Element, woraus dieses Gesammtleben besteht. So finden wir in der Sprache stete Fortbildung und Entwicklung, und auf gleiche Weise in dem Recht. Und auch diese Fortbildung steht unter demselben Gesetz der Erzeugung aus innerer Kraft und Nothwendigkeit, unabhangig von Zufall und individueller Willkur, wie die ursprüngliche Entstehung. — Savigny, *System*, I, 16, 17. Seine eigene Entdeckung, dass auch die geistige Produktion, bis in einem gewissen Punkte wenigstens, unter dem Gesetze der Kausalität steht, dass jedeiner nur geben kann, was er hat, nur hat, was er irgendwoher bekommen, muss auch fur ihn selber gelten. — Bekker, *Das Recht des Besitzes bei den Romern*, 3, 1880. Die geschichtliche Wandlung des Rechts, in welcher vergangene Jahrhunderte halb ein Spiel des Zufalls und halb ein Werk vernunftelnder Willkür sahen, als gesetzmassige Entwickelung zu begreifen, war das unsterbliche Verdienst der von Männern wie Savigny, Eichhorn und Jacob Grimm gefuhrten historischen Rechtsschule. — Gierke, *Rundschau*, XVIII, 205.

77 The only effective way of studying what is called the philosophy of religion, or the philosophical criticism of religion, is to study the history of religion. The true science of war is the history of war, the true science of religion is, I believe, the history of religion. — M. Muller, *Theosophy*, 3, 4. La théologie ne doit plus être que l'histoire des efforts spontanés tentés pour résoudre le problème divin. L'histoire, en effet, est la forme nécessaire de la science de tout ce qui est soumis aux lois de la vie changeante et successive. La science de l'esprit humain, c'est de même, l'histoire de l'esprit humain. — Renan, *Averroes*, Pref. vi.

78 Political economy is not a science, in any strict sense, but a body of systematic knowledge gathered from the study of common processes, which have been practised all down the history of the human race in the production and distribution of wealth. — Bonamy Price, *Social Science Congress*, 1878. Such a study is in harmony with the best intellectual tendencies of our age, which is, more than anything else, characterised by the universal supremacy of the historical spirit. To such a degree has this spirit permeated all our modes of thinking, that with respect to every branch of knowledge, no less than with respect to every institution and every form of human activity, we almost instinctively ask, not merely what is its existing condition, but what were its earliest discoverable germs, and what has been the course of its development. — Ingram, *History of Political Economy*, 2. Wir dagegen stehen keinen Augenblick an, die Nationalokonomie fur eine reine Erfahrungswissenschaft zu erklaren, und die Geschichte ist uns daher nicht Hülfsmittel, sondern Gegenstand selber. — Roscher, *Deutsche Vierteljahrschrift*, 1849, I, 182. Der bei weitem grosste Theil menschlicher Irrthümer beruhet darauf,

dass man zeitlich und örtlich Wahres oder Heilsames für absolut wahr oder heilsam ausgiebt. Für jede Stufe der Volksentwickelung passt eine besondere Staatsverfassung, die mit allen ubrigen Verhaltnissen des Volks als Ursache und Wirkung auf's Innigste verbunden ist; so passt auch fur jede Entwickelungsstufe eine besondere Landwirthschaftsverfassung — Roscher, *Archiv f. p. Oek.*, VIII, 2, Heft, 1845. Seitdem vor allen Roscher, Hildebrand und Knies den Werth, die Berechtigung und die Nothwendigkeit derselben unwiderleglich dargethan, hat sich immer allgemeiner der Gedanke Bahn gebrochen, dass diese Wissenschaft, die bis dahin nur auf die Gegenwart, auf die Erkenntniss der bestehenden Verhaltnisse und die in ihnen sichtbaren Gesetze den Blick gerichtet hatte, auch in die Vergangenheit, in die Erforschung der bereits hinter uns liegenden wirthschaftlichen Entwicklung der Völker sich vertiefen müsse. — Schonberg, *Jahrbucher f. Nationalokonomie und Statistik*, Neue Folge, 1867, I, 1. Schmoller, moins dogmatique et mettant comme une sorte de coquetterie à être incertain, démontre, par les faits, la fausseté ou l'arbitraire de tous ces postulats, et laisse l'économie politique se dissoudre dans l'histoire. — Breton, *R. de Paris*, IX, 67. Wer die politische Oekonomie Feuerlands unter dieselben Gesetze bringen wollte mit der des heutigen Englands, wurde damit augenscheinlich nichts zu Tage fördern als den allerbanalsten Gemeinplatz. Die politische Oekonomie ist somit wesentlich eine historische Wissenschaft. Sie behandelt einen geschichtlichen, das heisst einen stets wechselnden Stoff. Sie untersucht zunächst die besondern Gesetze jeder einzelnen Entwicklungsstufe der Produktion und des Austausches, und wird erst am Schluss dieser Untersuchung die wenigen, für Produktion und Austausch uberhaupt geltenden, ganz allgemeinen Gesetze aufstellen konnen. — Engels, *Duhrings Umwalzung der Wissenschaft*, 1878, 121.

[79] History preserves the student from being led astray by a too servile adherence to any system. — Wolowski. No system can be anything more than a history, not in the order of impression, but in the order of arrangement by analogy. — Davy, *Memoirs*, 68. Avec des matériaux si nombreux et si importants, il fallait bien du courage pour résister à la tentation de faire un système. De Saussure eut ce courage, et nous en ferons le dernier trait et le trait principal de son éloge. — Cuvier, *Eloge de Saussure*, 1810.

[80] C'était, en 1804, une idée heureuse et nouvelle, d'appeler l'histoire au secours de la science, d'interroger les deux grandes écoles rivales au profit de la vérité. — Cousin, *Fragments Littéraires*, 1843, 95, on Dégerando. No branch of philosophical doctrine, indeed, can be fairly investigated or apprehended apart from its history. All our systems of politics, morals, and metaphysics would be different if we knew exactly how they grew up, and what transformations they have undergone; if we knew, in short, the true history of human ideas. — Cliffe Leslie, *Essays in Political and Moral Philosophy*, 1879, 149. The history of philosophy must be rational and philosophic. It must be philosophy itself, with all its elements, in all their relations, and under all their laws represented in striking characters by the hands of time and of history, in the manifested progress of the human mind. — Sir William Hamilton, *Edin. Rev.* I, 200, 1829. Il n'est point d'étude plus instructive, plus utile que l'étude de l'histoire de la philosophie; car on y apprend à se désabuser des philosophes, et l'on y désapprend la fausse science de leurs systèmes. — Royer Collard, *Œuvres de Reid*, IV, 426. On ne peut guère

échapper à la conviction que toutes les solutions des questions philosophiques n'aient été développées ou indiquées avant le commencement du dix-neuvième siècle, et que par conséquent il ne soit très difficile, pour ne pas dire impossible, de tomber, en pareille matière, sur une idée neuve de quelque importance. Or si cette conviction est fondée, il s'ensuit que la science est faite. — Jouffroy, in Damiron, *Philosophie du XIXe Siècle*, 363. Le but dernier de tous mes efforts, l'âme de mes écrits et de tout mon enseignement, c'est l'identité de la philosophie et de son histoire. — Cousin, *Cours de* 1829. Ma route est historique, il est vrai, mais mon but est dogmatique; je tends à une théorie, et cette théorie je la demande à l'histoire. — Cousin, *Ph. du XVIIIe Siècle*, 15. L'histoire de la philosophie est contrainte d'emprunter d'abord à la philosophie la lumière qu'elle doit lui rendre un jour avec usure. — Cousin, *Du Vrai*, 1855, 14. M. Cousin, durant tout son professorat de 1816 à 1829, a pensé que l'histoire de la philosophie était la source de la philosophie même. Nous ne croyons pas exagérer en lui prêtant cette opinion. — B. St. Hilaire, *Victor Cousin*, I, 302. Il se hâta de convertir le fait en loi, et proclama que la philosophie, étant identique à son histoire, ne pouvait avoir une loi différente, et était vouée à jamais à l'évolution fatale des quatre systèmes, se contredisant toujours, mais se limitant, et se modérant, par cela même de manière à maintenir l'équilibre, sinon l'harmonie de la pensée humaine. — Vacherot, *Revue des Deux Mondes*, 1868, III, 957. Er hat uberhaupt das unvergangliche Verdienst, zuerst in Frankreich zu der Erkenntniss gelangt zu sein, dass die menschliche Vernunft nur durch das Studium des Gesetzes ihrer Entwickelungen begriffen werden kann. — Lauser, *Unsere Zeit*, 1868, I, 459. Le philosophe en quête du vrai en soi, n'est plus réduit à ses conceptions individuelles; il est riche du trésor amassé par l'humanité. — Boutroux, *Revue Politique*, XXXVII, 802. L'histoire, je veux dire l'histoire de l'esprit humain, est en ce sens la vraie philosophie de notre temps. — Renan, *Études de Morale*, 83. Die Philosophie wurde eine hochst bedeutende Hülfswissenschaft der Geschichte, sie hat ihre Richtung auf das Allgemeine gefordert, ihren Blick fur dasselbe gescharft, und sie, wenigstens durch ihre Vermittlung, mit Gesichtspuncten, Ideen, bereichert, die sie aus ihrem eigenen Schoosse sobald noch nicht erzeugt haben würde. Weit die fruchtbarste darunter war die aus der Naturwissenschaft geschopfte Idee des organischen Lebens, dieselbe auf der die neueste Philosophie selbst beruht. Die seit zwei bis drei Jahrzehnten in der Behandlung der Geschichte eingetretene durchgreifende Veranderung, wie die völlige Umgestaltung so mancher anderen Wissenschaft . . . ist der Hauptsache nach ihr Werk. — Haug, *Allgemeine Geschichte*, 1841, I, 22. Eine Geschichte der Philosophie in eigentlichen Sinne wurde erst moglich, als man an die Stelle der Philosophen deren Systeme setzte, den inneren Zusammenhang zwischen diesen feststellte und — wie Dilthey sagt — mitten im Wechsel der Philosophien ein siegreiches Fortschreiten zur Wahrheit nachwies. Die Gesammtheit der Philosophie stellt sich also dar als eine geschichtliche Einheit. — Saul, *Rundschau*, February, 1894, 307. Warum die Philosophie eine Geschichte habe und haben musse, blieb unerortert, ja ungeahnt, dass die Philosophie am meisten von allen Wissenschaften historisch sei, denn man hatte in der Geschichte den Begriff der Entwicklung nicht entdeckt. — Marbach, *Griechische Philosophie*, 15. Was bei oberflachlicher Betrachtung nur ein Gewirre einzelner Personen und Meinungen zu sein schien, zeigt sich bei genauerer und grundlicherer Untersuchung als eine

APPENDIX 423

geschichtliche Entwicklung, in der alles, bald näher, bald entfernter, mit allem anderen zusammenhängt. — Zeller, *Rundschau*, February, 1894, 307. Nur die Philosophie, die an die geschichtliche Entwickelung anknupft kann auf bleibenden Erfolg auch fur die Zukunft rechnen und fortschreiten zu dem, was in der bisherigen philosophischen Entwickelung nur erst unvollkommen erreicht oder angestrebt worden ist Kann sich doch die Philosophie überhaupt und insbesondere die Metaphysik ihrer eigenen geschichtlichen Entwickelung nicht entschlagen, sondern hat eine Geschichte der Philosophie als eigene und zwar zugleich historische und spekulative Disziplin, in deren geschichtlichen Entwickelungsphasen und geschichtlich aufeinanderfolgenden Systemen der Philosophen die neuere Spekulation seit Schelling und Hegel zugleich die Philosophie selbst als ein die verschiedenen geschichtlichen Systeme umfassendes ganzes in seiner dialektischen Gliederung erkannt hat — Gloatz, *Spekulative Theologie*, I, 23 Die heutige Philosophie fuhrt uns auf einen Standpunkt von dem aus die philosophische Idee als das innere Wesen der Geschichte selbst erscheint. So trat an die Stelle einer abstrakt philosophischen Richtung, welche das Geschichtliche verneinte, eine abstrakt geschichtliche Richtung, welche das Philosophische verlaugnete. Beide Richtungen sind als uberschrittene und besiegte zu betrachten. — Berner, *Strafrecht*, 75. Die Geschichte der Philosophie hat uns fast schon die Wissenschaft der Philosophie selbst ersetzt. — Hermann, *Phil. Monatshefte*, II, 198, 1889.

[81] Le siècle actuel sera principalement caractérisé par l'irrévocable prépondérance de l'histoire, en philosophie, en politique, et même en poésie. — Comte, *Politique Positive*, III, 1.

[82] The historical or comparative method has revolutionised not only the sciences of law, mythology, and language, of anthropology and sociology, but it has forced its way even into the domain of philosophy and natural science. For what is the theory of evolution itself, with all its far-reaching consequences, but the achievement of the historical method? — Prothero, *Inaugural; National Review*, December, 1894, 461. To facilitate the advancement of all the branches of useful science, two things seem to be principally requisite. The first is, an historical account of their rise, progress, and present state Without the former of these helps, a person every way qualified for extending the bounds of science labours under great disadvantages; wanting the lights which have been struck out by others, and perpetually running the risk of losing his labour, and finding himself anticipated. — Priestley, *History of Vision*, 1772, I, Pref. i. Cuvier se proposait de montrer l'enchaînement scientifique des découvertes, leurs relations avec les grands évènements historiques, et leur influence sur le progrés et le développement de la civilisation. — Dareste, *Biographie, Générale*, XII, 685. Dans ses éloquentes leçons, l'histoire des sciences est devenue l'histoire même de l'esprit humain; car, remontant aux causes de leurs progrès et de leurs erreurs, c'est toujours dans les bonnes ou mauvaises routes suivies par l'esprit humain, qu'il trouve ces causes. — Flourens, *Eloge de Cuvier*, XXXI. Wie keine fortlaufende Entwickelungsreihe von nur Einem Punkte aus vollkommen aufzufassen ist, so wird auch keine lebendige Wissenschaft nur aus der Gegenwart begriffen werden konnen. — Deswegen ist aber eine solche Darstellung doch noch nicht der gesammten Wissenschaft adaquat, und sie birgt, wenn sie damit verwechselt wird, starke Gefahren der Einseitigkeit, des Dogmatismus und damit der

Stagnation in sich. Diesen Gefahren kann wirksam nur begegnet werden durch die verstandige Betrachtung der Geschichte der Wissenschaften, welche diese selbst in stetem Flusse zeigt und die Tendenz ihres Fortschreitens in offenbarer und sicherer Weise klarlegt. — Rosenberger, *Geschichte der Physik*, III, p. vi. Die Continuitat in der Ausbildung aller Auffassungen tritt um so deutlicher hervor, je vollstandiger man sich damit wie sie zu verschiedenen Zeiten waren, vertraut macht. — Kopp, *Entwickelung der Chemie*, 814.

[83] Die Geschichte und die Politik sind Ein und derselbe Janus mit dem Doppelgesicht, das in der Geschichte in die Vergangenheit, in der Politik in die Zukunft hinschaut. — Gugler's *Leben*, II, 59.

[84] The papers inclosed, which give an account of the killing of two men in the county of Londonderry; if they prove to be Tories, 'tis very well they are gone. — I think it will not only be necessary to grant those a pardon who killed them, but also that they have some reward for their own and others' encouragement. — Essex, *Letters*, 10, 10th January, 1675. The author of this happened to be present. There was a meeting of some honest people in the city, upon the occasion of the discovery of some attempt to stifle the evidence of the witnesses. — Bedloe said he had letters from Ireland, that there were some Tories to be brought over hither, who were privately to murder Dr. Oates and the said Bedloe. The doctor, whose zeal was very hot, could never after this hear any man talk against the plot, or against the witnesses, but he thought he was one of these Tories, and called almost every man a Tory that opposed him in discourse; till at last the word Tory became popular. — Defoe, *Edinburgh Review*, I, 403.

[85] La España serà el primer pueblo en donde se encenderá esta guerra patriotica que solo puede libertar á Europa. — Hemos oido esto en Inglaterra á varios de los que estaban alli presentes. Muchas veces ha oido lo mismo al duque de Wellington el general Don Miguel de Alava, y dicho duque refirió el suceso en una comida diplomatica que dió en Paris el duque de Richelieu en 1816. — Toreno, *Historia del Levantamiento de España*, 1838, I, 508.

[86] Nunquam propter auctoritatem illorum, quamvis magni sint nominis (supponimus scilicet semper nos cum eo agere qui scientiam historicam vult consequi), sententias quas secuti sunt ipse tamquam certas admittet, sed solummodo ob vim testimoniorum et argumentorum quibus eas confirmarunt. — De Smedt, *Introductio ad historiam critice tractandam*, 1866, I, 5.

[87] Hundert schwere Verbrechen wiegen nicht so schwer in der Schale der Unsittlichkeit, als ein unsittliches Princip. — *Hallische Jahrbucher*, 1839, 308. Il faut flétrir les crimes; mais il faut aussi, et surtout, flétrir les doctrines et les systèmes qui tendent à les justifier. — Mortimer Ternaux, *Histoire de la Terreur*.

[88] We see how good and evil mingle in the best of men and in the best of causes; we learn to see with patience the men whom we like best often in the wrong, and the repulsive men often in the right; we learn to bear with patience the knowledge that the cause which we love best has suffered, from the awkwardness of its defenders, so great disparagement, as in strict equity to justify the men who were assaulting it. — Stubbs, *Seventeen Lectures*, 97.

[89] *Caeteris paribus*, on trouvera toujours que ceux qui ont plus de puissance sont sujets à pécher davantage; et il n'y a point de théorème de géométrie qui soit plus asseuré que cette proposition. — Leibniz, 1688, ed. Rommel, II, 197.

APPENDIX 425

Il y a toujours eu de la malignité dans la grandeur, et de l'opposition à l'esprit de l'Évangile; mais maintenant il y en a plus que jamais, et il semble que comme le monde va à sa fin, celui qui est dans l'élévation fait tous ses efforts pour dominer avec plus de tyrannie, et pour étouffer les maximes du Christianisme et le règne de Jésus-Christ, voiant qu'il s'approche. — Godeau, *Lettres*, 423, 27th March, 1667. There is, in fact, an unconquerable tendency in all power, save that of knowledge, acting by and through knowledge, to injure the mind of him by whom that power is exercised. — Wordsworth, 22nd June, 1817; *Letters of Lake Poets*, 369.

[90] I cieli han messo sulla terra due giudici delle umane azioni, la coscienza e la storia. — Colletta. Wenn gerade die edelsten Manner um des Nachruhmes willen gearbeitet haben, so soll die Geschichte ihre Belohnung sein, sie auch die Strafe für die Schlechten. — Lasaulx, *Philosophie der Kunste*, 211. Pour juger ce qui est bon et juste dans la vie actuelle ou passée, il faut posséder un criterium, qui ne soit pas tiré du passé ou du présent, mais de la nature humaine. — Ahrens, *Cours de Droit Naturel*, I, 67.

[91] L'homme de notre temps! La conscience moderne! Voilà encore de ces termes qui nous ramènent la pretendue philosophie de l'histoire et la doctrine du progrès, quand il s'agit de la justice, c'est-à-dire de la conscience pure et de l'homme rationnel, que d'autres siècles encore que le nôtre ont connu. — Renouvier, *Crit. Phil.*, 1873, II, 55.

[92] Il faut pardonner aux grands hommes le marchepied de leur grandeur. — Cousin, in J. Simon, *Nos Hommes d'État*, 1887, 55. L'esprit du XVIIIe siècle n'a pas besoin d'apologie: l'apologie d'un siècle est dans son existence. — Cousin, *Fragments*, III, 1826. Suspendus aux lèvres éloquentes de M. Cousin, nous l'entendîmes s'écrier que la meilleure cause l'emportait toujours, que c'était la loi de l'histoire, le rhythme immuable du progrès. — Gasparin, *La Liberté Morale*, II, 63. Cousin verurtheilen heisst darum nichts Anderes als jenen Geist historischer Betrachtung verdammen, durch welchen das 19 Jahrhundert die revolutionäre Kritik des 18 Jahrhunderts ergänzt, durch welchen insbesondere Deutschland die geistigen Wohlthaten vergolten hat, welche es im Zeitalter der Aufklärung von seinen westlichen Nachbarn empfangen. — Iodl, *Gesch. der Ethik*, II, 295. Der Gang der Weltgeschichte steht ausserhalb der Tugend, des Lasters, und der Gerechtigkeit. — Hegel, *Werke*, VIII, 425. Die Vermischung des Zufalligen im Individuum mit dem an ihm Historischen fuhrt zu unzahligen falschen Ansichten und Urtheilen. Hierzu gehort namentlich alles Absprechen uber die moralische Tuchtigkeit der Individuen, und die Verwunderung, welche bis zur Verzweiflung an göttlicher Gerechtigkeit sich steigert, dass historisch grosse Individuen moralisch nichtswurdig erscheinen konnen. Die moralische Tuchtigkeit besteht in der Unterordnung alles dessen, was zufallig am Einzelnen unter das an ihm Allgemeinen Angehorige. — Marbach, *Geschichte der Griechischen Philosophie*, 7. Das Sittliche der Neuseeländer, der Mexikaner ist vielmehr ebenso sittlich, wie das der Griechen, der Romer; und das Sittliche der Christen des Mittelalters ist ebenso sittlich, wie das der Gegenwart. — Kirchmann, *Grundbegriffe des Rechts*, 194. Die Geschichtswissenschaft als solche kennt nur ein zeitliches und mithin auch nur ein relatives Maass der Dinge. Alle Werthbeurtheilung der Geschichte kann daher nur relativ und aus zeitlichen Momenten fliessen, und wer sich nicht selbst täuschen und den Dingen nicht Gewalt anthun will, muss ein für allemal in dieser Wissenschaft

auf absolute Werthe verzichten. — Lorenz, *Schlosser*, 80. Only according to his faith is each man judged. Committed as this deed has been by a pureminded, pious youth, it is a beautiful sign of the time. — De Wette to Sand's Mother; Cheyne, *Founders of Criticism*, 44. The men of each age must be judged by the ideal of their own age and country, and not by the ideal of ours. — Lecky, *Value of History*, 50.

⁹³ La durée ici-bas, c'est le droit, c'est la sanction, de Dieu. — Guiraud, *Philosophie Catholique de l'Histoire*.

⁹⁴ Ceux qui ne sont pas contens de l'ordre des choses ne sçauroient se vanter d'aimer Dieu comme il faut — Il faut toujours estre content de l'ordre du passé, parce qu'il est conforme à la volonté de Dieu absolue, qu'on connoît par l'évènement Il faut tâcher de rendre l'avenir, autant qu'il dépend de nous, conforme à la volonté de Dieu présomptive — Leibniz, *Werke*, ed. Gerhardt, II, 136. Ich habe damals bekannt und bekenne jetzt, dass die politische Wahrheit aus denselben Quellen zu schopfen ist, wie alle anderen, aus dem göttlichen Willen und dessen Kundgebung in der Geschichte des Menschengeschlechts. — Radowitz, *Neue Gesprache*, 65.

⁹⁵ A man is great as he contends best with the circumstances of his age. — Froude, *Short Studies*, I, 388. La persuasion que l'homme est avant tout une personne morale et libre, et qu'ayant conçu seul, dans sa conscience et devant Dieu, la règle de sa conduite, il doit s'employer tout entier à l'appliquer en lui, hors de lui, absolument, obstinément, inflexiblement, par une résistance perpétuelle opposée aux autres; et par une contrainte perpétuelle exercée sur soi, voilà la grande idée anglaise. — Taine; Sorel, *Discours de Réception*, 24. In jeder Zeit des Christenthums hat es einzelne Manner gegeben, die uber ihrer Zeit standen und von ihren Gegensatzen nicht berührt wurden. — Bachmann, *Hengstenberg*, I, 160. Eorum enim qui de iisdem rebus mecum aliquid ediderunt, aut solus insanio ego, aut solus non insanio; tertium enim non est, nisi (quod dicet forte aliquis) insaniamus omnes. — Hobbes, quoted by De Morgan, 3rd June, 1858: *Life of Sir W. R. Hamilton*, III, 552.

⁹⁶ I have now to exhibit a rare combination of good qualities, and a steady perseverance in good conduct, which raised an individual to be an object of admiration and love to all his contemporaries, and have made him to be regarded by succeeding generations as a model of public and private virtue. — The evidence shows that upon this occasion he was not only under the influence of the most vulgar credulity, but that he violated the plainest rules of justice, and that he really was the murderer of two innocent women. — Hale's motives were most laudable. — Campbell's *Lives of the Chief Justices*, I, 512, 561, 566. It was not to be expected of the colonists of New England that they should be the first to see through a delusion which befooled the whole civilised world, and the gravest and most knowing persons in it. — The people of New England believed what the wisest men of the world believed at the end of the seventeenth century. — Palfrey, *New England*, IV, 127, 129 (also speaking of witchcraft). Il est donc bien étrange que sa sévérité tardive s'exerce aujourd'hui sur un homme auquel elle n'a d'autre reproche à faire que d'avoir trop bien servi l'état par des mesures politiques, injustes peut-être, violentes, mais qui, en aucune manière, n'avaient l'intérêt personnel du coupable pour objet. — M. Hastings peut sans doute paraître répréhensible aux yeux des étrangers, des particuliers même, mais il est assez

APPENDIX 427

extraordinaire qu'une nation usurpatrice d'une partie de l'Indostan veuille mêler les règles de la morale à celles d'une administration forcée, injuste et violente par essence, et à laquelle il faudrait renoncer à jamais pour être conséquent. — Mallet Du Pan, *Mémoires*, ed. Sayous, I, 102.

[97] On parle volontiers de la stabilité de la constitution anglaise. La vérité est que cette constitution est toujours en mouvement et en oscillation et qu'elle se prête merveilleusement au jeu de ses différentes parties. Sa solidité vient de sa souplesse; elle plie et ne rompt pas. — Boutmy, *Nouvelle Revue*, 1878, 49.

[98] This is not an age for a man to follow the strict morality of better times, yet sure mankind is not yet so debased but that there will ever be found some few men who will scorn to join concert with the public voice when it is not well grounded. — *Savile Correspondence*, 173.

[99] Cette proposition: L'homme est incomparablement plus porté au mal qu'au bien, et il se fait dans le monde incomparablement plus de mauvaises actions que de bonnes — est aussi certaine qu'aucun principe de métaphysique. Il est donc incomparablement plus probable qu'une action faite par un homme, est mauvaise, qu'il n'est probable qu'elle soit bonne. Il est incomparablement plus probable que ces secrets ressorts qui l'ont produite sont corrompus, qu'il n'est probable qu'ils soient honnêtes. Je vous avertis que je parle d'une action qui n'est point mauvaise extérieurement. — Bayle, *Œuvres*, II, 248.

[100] A Christian is bound by his very creed to suspect evil, and cannot release himself. — His religion has brought evil to light in a way in which it never was before; it has shown its depth, subtlety, ubiquity; and a revelation, full of mercy on the one hand, is terrible in its exposure of the world's real state on the other. The Gospel fastens the sense of evil upon the mind; a Christian is enlightened, hardened, sharpened, as to evil, he sees it where others do not. — Mozley, *Essays*, I, 308. All satirists, of course, work in the direction of Christian doctrine, by the support they give to the doctrine of original sin, making a sort of meanness and badness a law of society. — Mozley, *Letters*, 333. Les critiques, même malveillants, sont plus près de la vérité dernière que les admirateurs. — Nisard, *Lit. fr.*, Conclusion. Les hommes supérieurs doivent nécessairement passer pour méchants. Où les autres ne voient ni un défaut, ni un ridicule, ni un vice, leur implacable œil l'aperçoit. — Barbey d'Aurevilly, *Figaro*, 31st March, 1888.

[101] Prenons garde de ne pas trop expliquer, pour ne pas fournir des arguments à ceux qui veulent tout excuser. — Broglie, *Réception de Sorel*, 46

[102] The eternal truths and rights of things exist, fortunately, independent of our thoughts or wishes, fixed as mathematics, inherent in the nature of man and the world. They are no more to be trifled with than gravitation. — Froude, *Inaugural Lecture at St. Andrews*, 1869, 41. What have men to do with interests? There is a right way and a wrong way. That is all we need think about. — Carlyle to Froude, *Longman's Magazine*, December, 1892, 151. As to History, it is full of indirect but very effective moral teaching. It is not only, as Bolingbroke called it, "Philosophy teaching by examples," but it is morality teaching by examples. — It is essentially the study which best helps the student to conceive large thoughts. — It is impossible to overvalue the moral teaching of History. — Fitch, *Lectures on Teaching*, 432 Judging from the past history of our race, in ninety-nine cases out of a hundred, war

is a folly and a crime. — Where it is so, it is the saddest and the wildest of all follies, and the most heinous of all crimes. — Greg, *Essays on Political and Social Science*, 1853, I, 562. La volonté de tout un peuple ne peut rendre juste ce qui est injuste: les représentants d'une nation n'ont pas le droit de faire ce que la nation n'a pas le droit de faire elle-même. — B. Constant, *Principes de Politique*, I, 15.

103 Think not that morality is ambulatory; that vices in one age are not vices in another, or that virtues, which are under the everlasting seal of right reason, may be stamped by opinion. — Sir Thomas Browne, *Works*, IV, 64.

104 Osons croire qu'il seroit plus à propos de mettre de côté ces traditions, ces usages, et ces coutumes souvent si imparfaites, si contradictoires, si incohérentes, ou de ne les consulter que pour saisir les inconvéniens et les éviter; et qu'il faudroit chercher non-seulement les éléments d'une nouvelle législation, mais même ses derniers détails dans une étude approfondie de la morale. — Letrosne, *Réflexions sur la Législation Criminelle*, 137. M. Renan appartient à cette famille d'esprits qui ne croient pas en réalité la raison, la conscience, le droit applicables à la direction des sociétés humaines, et qui demandent à l'histoire, à la tradition, non à la morale, les règles de la politique. Ces esprits sont atteints de la maladie du siècle, le scepticisme moral. — Pillon, *Critique Philosophique*, I, 49.

105 The subject of modern History is of all others, to my mind, the most interesting, inasmuch as it includes all questions of the deepest interest relating not to human things only, but to divine. — Arnold, *Modern History*, 311.

INDEX

Abolition, 237
  Calhoun on, 240
  Channing on, 238
  Howe on, 239
  Webster on, 239
Absolutism, 68, 170f.
  checks against, 32f.
  and the Church, 68f.
  early, 34f.
  French economists on, 261f.
  Roman, 144
  Royal
    Descartes on, 75
    Hobbes on, 75
    Pascal on, 75
    Spinoza on, 75
  of the state, 32f.
Acropolis, 55
Act of Settlement, 81
Acton, John Emerich Edward Dalberg-, 1st Baron (Lord Acton)
  compared with Maritain, lii
  life of, xvff.
  submission to Rome, xxvi
  and Ultramontanism, xxiiff.
Adams, Henry, xlvii
  on power, xlvi
Adams, John, 149, 200, 202, 211f.
  on Jefferson's embargo, 216
Adams, John Quincy, 32
  on Jefferson's embargo, 216
  on secession, 216
Addison, Joseph, 180
Afrancesados, 178
Agassiz, Louis
  on the Negroes, 242
Albert, Charles, 181
Albigenses, 108
Alcuin
  on the infallibility of the people, 266
Alighieri, Dante, 18, 22, 182
Alzog, Johann Baptist
  opposition to Ultramontanism at Vatican Council, 307

Ambrose, Saint, 79
American Revolution, *see* Revolution
American Civil War, *see* Civil War
Americans
  homogeneity of, Jay on, 208
Amsterdam, 173
Anabaptists, 93, 106
  intolerance of, 110f.
  Luther on, 95
  Œcolampadius on, 115f.
  persecution of, by Lutherans, 110
  Protestant intolerance towards, 108
Anaxagoras, 131
Angelis, Cardinal, 335, 340
Anti-clericalism, 268
Antigone, 5
Antonelli, Cardinal, 335
  support of Ultramontanism at Vatican Council, 307
Antonius, 51
Aquinas, Saint Thomas, 65, 73, 139, 252
  and Burke, 73
  on self-government, 64
Areopagus, 133
Argenson, René Louis de
  political theories of, 558
Arians, 78
Aristides
  political ideas of, 134
Aristocracy
  feudal, 175
  privileges of, 169
Aristophanes, 159
Aristotle, 47, 135, 370
  political ideas of, 138
  Politics, 50, 145
  on power, 138
  on Theramenes, 137
Arnim, Harry Karl, Baron, 312f.
Arnold, Matthew, xxxviii, lviii, lxvi
  on Mill and Macaulay, xxxv
Artevelde, Jacob van, 66

429

Articles ot Faith
  Dollinger on, 351
Asgill, John
  on land, 263
Asia, 33f.
Asoka, 54
Assassination
  for the public good, 76f.
Athenagoras
  on democracy, 137
Athenians
  legal theories of, 136
Athens, 30, 35, 38, 40f., 173
  constitution of, 39, 133f.
  democracy, degradation of, 196
  republic, failure of, 136f.
  republicanism of, 134f.
Athanasius, Saint, 79
Augsburg, 78
  Confession of, 97
Augustine, Saint, 32, 61
  on Seneca, 53
Augustus, Emperor, 51, 56, 144
Austria, 9, 11, 16, 192
  and the Concordat, 188
  and the Congress of Vienna, 179
  Italian provinces of, 181
  and nationalism, 190ff.
Authority
  and liberty, 184
  and Christianity, 61

Babœuf, François
  and communism, 169
Bach, Alexander, 179
Bacon, Sir Francis, 25, 64, 75
Bacon, Sir Nicholas, 71
Bacon, Roger, 72
Baden
  and nationalism, 190
Baer, Karl von, 22
Ball, Sir Robert, 22
Bank-Charter Act, 250
Barbarians
  freedom among, 59f
Barère de Vieuzac, Bertrand, 154
Barras, Paul de, Count, 362
Barillon, Jean, 9
Barnevelt, Jan van Olden, 148
Barrot, Odilon, 158
Bautain, Louis Eugène
  censure of, 274

Bavaria
  persecution of Luther by dukes of, 69
  and the Vatican Council, 312
Baxter, Richard, 79
Bayle, Pierre, 28, 255
  in exile, 252
  toleration of, 252
Beaconsfield, Benjamin Disraeli, Earl of, xlviii, 151
Beccaria, Cesare di, 267
Bedford, Gunning, Jr.
  on State-rights, 204
Belgium, 66, 156
  and nationalism, 179
  and the Vatican Council, 314
Bellarmine, Cardinal, 71
Bentham, Jeremy, 22, 32
Berlin, 8, 182
Bernard, Saint, 72
Berne, 173
Beust, Friedrich, Count
  on the Vatican Council, 310
Beza, Théodore
  defense of Calvin, 122
  on heresy, 123
Bigamy
  of Landgrave Philip, 98
Bilio, Cardinal, 340
Bishops
  French, 299
  Lamennais on, 271
Bismarck, Otto von
  and the Vatican Council, 312
Blanc, Louis, 158
Blue Laws of Connecticut, 82
Bodin, Jean, 147
Bolingbroke, Henry, 266
Bonald, Louis de
  on monarchy, 275
Bonaparte, see Napoleon
Bonapartism
  hostility to, of
    Gorres, 177
    Humboldt, 177
    de Maistre, 177
    Muller, 177
    Stein, 177
Bonnechose, Cardinal, 335
Books
  Catholic attitude on, 277

INDEX 431

Borgia, Cesare, 360
Borromeo, Carlo, Saint, 366
Bossuet, Jacques, 75, 255, 367
　on nationalism, 190
　reply to Jurieu, 252
Boucher, François, 73
Bourbons
　and Divine Right, 74
　French, 171
　Spanish, 171
Brabant, rising of, 167
Bright, John
　on statesmanship, 370
Brissot de Warville, Jean, 268
Broglie, Achille, Duke de, 28
Brougham, Henry, Baron 22
Browne, Sir Thomas, 28
Brownson, Orestes
　on government
　　American, 236f.
　　civil, 241
　on the tariff, 229
Bruce, House of, 63
Bruce, Robert, 63
Brussels, 8
Bucer, Martin
　on persecution, 111f.
Buchanan, James, 71, 73, 244
　on regicide, 148
Bucholtz, Samuel, 16
Bulgaria, 60
Bullinger, Heinrich
　influence of, on Leo Judae, 113f.
　on persecution and heresy, 114
　on Servetus, 114
Burckhardt, Jacob, xlvif.
Burke, Edmund, xxxvii, lvi, lxii, lxv, 25, 50, 80
　and Aquinas, 73
　on the division of Poland, 171
　on historical morality, 29
　on nationalism, 189
　on the rights of men, 82f.
　on slavery, 131
Burnet, Gilbert, Bishop, 17
Burr, Aaron, 214
Butler, Joseph, Bishop, 14
Butterfield, Herbert, xliv
Buzot, François
　on Federalism, 152
Byzantine despotism, 61

Cadiz, 8
　overthrow of constitution in 1823, 155
Caesar, Julius, 43f., 175
Calhoun, John, 158, 219, 224, 228, 230
　on the abolitionists, 240
　aversion of Jackson to, 229f.
　on the Constitution, 225ff.
　on liberty, 224
　on power, 235
　on secession, 243
　on Southern conservatism, 241
　support of tariff by, 218
　on the tariff, 220-223
Calvin, John, 71, 115, 366
　defense of, by Beza, 122
　Institutes, 70
　on the Jews, Mohammedans, Catholics, 118
　on obedience, 120
　political ideas of, 116 ff.
　Presbyterian Constitution of, 147
　on rebellion, 118f.
　and Servetus, death of, 121
　theocracy of, 117f.
　early writing on toleration, 122
Calvinism, lii
Cambray, Archbishop of, 255
Cambridge Modern History, xxxii
Camden, Charles Pratt, Earl of
　on taxation and representation, 82
Campana, Jeanne Louise, 17
Campanella, Tommaso
　City of the Sun, influence of, 166f.
Capalte, Cardinal, 340
Capito, Wolfgang
　influence of, on Leo Judae, 113f.
　tolerance of, 111
Capponi, 366
Carbonari, the, 179
Carbonarism
　and Mazzini, 181
Cardinals of France, 69
Carlisle, George Howard, Earl of
　on Seward, 240
　on Southern planters, 244
Carlstadt (Andrew Bodenstein)
　on polygamy, 98
Carlyle, Thomas, xxxv, 365
　on progress, 13
Carneades, 44
Carnegie, Andrew, xxx

Carthage, 48
Cass, Lewis, 245
Castelar, Emilio
    fall of, 11
Catholicism (see also Church)
    and books, 277
    and slavery, 246
Catholics
    Calvin on, 118
    exclusion of Henry of Navarre from Paris by, 148
    French, reaction of, against Henry III and Henry of Navarre, 72
    intolerance of, 108f., 300f.
    Judae on, 113
    Knox on, 71
    Melanchthon on, 107
    persecution of, li
        by Protestants, Œcolampadius on, 116
    on the scriptures, authority of, 320f.
    theory of absolute toleration, 107
    tolerance by, in Maryland, 127
    toleration of Jews and Mohammedans, 108
Cato, 26
Censorship
    Catholic, 278-298
    of Ultramontanism, 344f.
Centralism, 163
Channing, William Ellery
    on abolition, 238
    on majorities, 210
    on the power of political parties, 236
    on the voting franchise, 235f.
Charlemagne, 61
Charles I, 75
Charles II, 31
    and the Constitution, 131
        treason against, 149
    death of, 78
    support of, by Louis XIV, 80
Charles V, 68f., 147
Charles IX, 77
Charles X, 31
Charron, Pierre, 73
Chateaubriand, François, Count
    Lammenais on, 272
Chatham, William Pitt, Earl of, 81f.
    on the Napoleonic War, 24

Checks and balances
    Dickinson on, 218
Chesterton, G. K., xxxv
Chevalier, Michel, 158
Chevreuse, Marie de, 253
Chinese, 249
Christianity, 46, 48
    and authority, 61
    early influence of, 45
    and liberty, 57
    teachings of, 145
Christians
    early, 55f., 84
        persecution of, 58
Chrysippus, 45, 140
Chuquet, Arthur, 19
Church, the (Roman Catholic)
    and absolutism, 68f.
    as an enemy of nationalism, 186
    Frohschammer on, 268f.
    Ranke on, 10
    reform in its head and members, 301
Church and State, liii, 61, 255, 258
    conflict between
        England, 86
        Teutonic State, 146
    influence of, in Rome, 45
    Luther on, 92, 96
    rise of liberty in collision between, 62
    separation of, 79
        Fénelon on, 253f.
    and Ultramontanism, 309
    Zwingli on, 112
Cicé, 153
Cicero, 32, 44, 53, 61, 139
Citizens
    responsibility of, in Athens, 38
Civil War, 150f.
    political causes of, 196-250
    triumph of idea of, in France, 151f.
Civiltà Cattolica
    and Pius IX, 304
Clarendon, Edward Hyde, Earl of, 131
Classes
    structure and interest of, 248
    Madison on, 208f.
Clay, Henry, 222, 231
Clovis, 61, 175

INDEX 433

Cobbett, William
  on the tariff, 221
  on the tyranny of republicanism, 235
Colbert, Jean Baptiste, 13
Colton, Calvin
  on secession and nullification, 231
Columbus, Christopher, 5, 364
Commerce
  Hamilton on, 219
  regulation of, in America, 208
Commines, Philip de
  on taxation, 67
Commune, 158
Communism, xlix, 45
  and Babœuf, 169
Compagni, Dino, 18
Compomanes, 151
Compromise Act, 231, 237
Comte, Auguste, 23, 158
  on progress, 13
Condillac, Etienne Bonnot de, 255
Condorcet, Marie Jean, Marquis de, 161
Congregationalism
  idea of, 149
Congress of Vienna, 179
Conscience
  Webster on, 241
Conservatism
  in the South, Calhoun on, 241
Constantine the Great 58f., 79
Constantinople, 58
Constitution
  American, 161
    Calhoun on, 225ff.
    convention at Philadelphia, 199f.
    Pinckney presents plan of, 204
  Athenian, 39, 133f.
  British, Dickinson on, 203
    Muller on, 27
    treason of Charles II against, 149
  Cadiz
    overthrow of, in 1823, 155
  French, 152
    civil, 153
  Roman, 141
  Spanish, of 1812, 155
  Swiss
    federal, 156
    of 1848, 156f.
    of 1874, 156

Constitutional government
  British, 15
Constitutional monarchy, 183f.
Constitutions
  Fénelon on, 254
  organic development of, 33
  Sir James Mackintosh on, 85
  written and organic, 8
Conversion
  Luther on use of force for, 101
Copernicus, Nikolaus, 6, 364
  system of, Luther on, 99
Corday, Charlotte, 366
Cordoni, Archbishop
  support of Ultramontanism at Vatican Council, 307
Coulton, G. G., 88n.
Cranmer, Thomas, Archbishop, 366
Creighton, Mandell, xxix, xxxi, lii, 257-273
  on the morals of power, 371
  on the Reformation, 372
  on tolerance, 371
Critias, 46, 137
Cromwell, Oliver, 10, 77, 149, 366
Crucifixion, 58
Crusades, 18, 26, 65
Cuba
  Seward on, 245
Cullen, Paul, 22
Cultural multiplicity, 185f., 190
Cumberland, Richard, 74
Cuvier, Georges, Baron, 23

Dalberg-Acton, *see* Acton
Dante Alighieri, 18, 22, 182
Danton, Georges, 154
Darboy, Georges, Archbishop
  opposition to Ultramontanism at Vatican Council, 328
Darwin, Charles, 22
Daunou, Pierre Claude François, 161
Davis, Jefferson, 199
Declaration of Independence 3, 83, 130, 211, 242
Defoe, Daniel, 24, 80f.
Democracy, 14, 48, 161
  American
    Tocqueville on, 233f.
  Athenagorus on, 137
  Athenian, 36
    degradation of, 196

failure of, 40
restoration of, 41
class interest and, 248
dangers of, 163
definition of, 159
Euphemus on, 137
European, May on, 128
evils of, Gerry on, 201
failure of, 160f.
Hamilton on, 202, 210f.
homogeneity and, 247
Huguenots and, 148
liberty and, distinction between, 130
minorities in, 197ff.
Presbyterianism and, 147f.
and religious persecution, 131
understanding, problem of, 132
Descartes, René
on royal absolutism, 75
Despotism
Asiatic, 33
of Christian empire, 146
of Louis XIV, Fénelon on, 254f.
theories of, in ancient times, 46
Wilson on, 201
Deventer, 148
Dickinson, John
on checks and balances, 218
on the United States Senate, 203
Diderot, Denis, 261, 268
on de la Rivière, 263
Diocletian, 43, 58, 144
Diogenes, 46
Dispensing power, 360
Disraeli, Benjamin, xlviii, 151
Divine Right, 6, 13, 63, 73ff.
and the Bourbons, 74
and the Stuarts, 74
Divines
of the Roman Empire, 61
of the second century, 56
Döllinger, Johann von, xvii-xx, xxii, xxiv, xxvi, xxviiif.
on the Articles of Faith, 351
excommunication of, xxv
on Ultramontanism, 318f, 343f.
Domat, Jean, 252
Dominicans, 305
Dubois, Guillaume, Cardinal, 255
Dufferin and Ava, Frederick Blackwood, Marquis of, 363

Dumouriez, Charles, 362
Dupanloup, Felix, Bishop, xviif, 300
opposition to Ultramontanism at Vatican Council, 328, 330, 332, 343

Economists, 23
French
on absolutism, 261f.
on free labor, 261
on free trade, 261
on government, 261
and Montesquieu, 262
on power, 261
Edict of Nantes, 252
revocation of, 109
Edinburgh, 3
Edward I, 82
Edward II, 65
Edward III, 63
Egypt, 58
Elections
fraudulent, at Vatican Council, 335f.
popular, Sherman on, 200
Eliot, George, xl
Elizabeth, Queen of England, 68, 364, 366
Embargo
Jefferson's, 214f.
Emerson, Ralph Waldo
on slavery, 243
Ends and means, 68, 364
Enghein, Louis, Duke of, 75
England, 11, 18, 51, 69, 83, 156, 170, 192
Constitution of, Dickinson on, 203
government of, Hamilton on, 202
law of, 256f.
parliament of, 63, 147
and the Vatican Council, 313
English Historical Review, 88n., 357
Ephialtes, 135
Epicurus, 46
Equality, 75
political, Licinius on, 130
and Rousseau, 169
theory of, and the French Revolution, 154
Erasmus, Desiderius, 6, 79, 85, 147, 359f.

INDEX

Essenes, 54f., 84
  republicanism of, 132
Estates
  French, 147
Euclides, 196
Euphemus
  on democracy, 137
Europe, 33
  democracy in, 128
    May as historian of, 128ff.
  Teutonic, 34
Everett, Edward
  on the presidency, 233
Excommunication, 336
  Luther on, 96f.
  Œcolampadius on, 116
Exile, 181f
  of Bayle, 252
  of Mazzini, 181
  and nationalism, 181
  Polish, 181
Experimentation
  limitation of, 161

Fascism, xlix
Faraday, Michael, 22
Federalism, 163
  Buzot on, 152
  and the Jeffersonians, Hildreth on, 213f.
Federalists
  Jefferson on, 214
  on the presidency, 211f.
Fénelon, François, Archbishop, 7, 76, 85
  on constitutions, 254
  on the historian, role of, 254f
  on liberty, 253f.
  on Louis XIV, despotism of, 254f.
  on national independence, 169
  on power, 254
  on separation of Church and State, 253f.
  on social institutions, 255
  on the structure of society, 254f.
  on toleration, 253f
  on war, 254
Ferdinand I, 68
Ferdinand II, 68
Ferrari, Giuseppe, 160

Fessler, Joseph, Bishop
  support of Ultramontanism at Vatican Council, 307f.
Feudalism, 62, 175
Figgis, J. N , 88n.
Firmian, Karl von, Count, 267
Fitznigel, Richard, 146
Five Codes of France, 32
Fleury, André de, 253
Florence
  and nationalism, 190
  Republic of, 147
Fox, Charles, 81
France, 4, 9, 16, 83, 263
  Cardinals of, 69
  constitution of
    Civil, 152-153
    of 1791, 162
  Estates of, 147
  nationalism of, 190
  reform in, 151f.
  States-General of, 15, 63
  triumph of idea of American Revolution in, 151f.
  unity of, Siéyès on, 173
  universal suffrage in, 162
  and the Vatican Council, 310f.
  opposition to Ultramontanism at, 338
Francis I
  persecution of Huguenots by, 71
Francis, Joseph, 182f.
Frankfort, 8
Franklin, Benjamin, 200
Franks, 62
Franzelin, Cardelin
  support of Ultramontanism at Vatican Council, 307
Fratres Communis Vitae, 360
Frederick I, 9
Frederick II (the Great), 43, 90
Free cities, 66
Freedom
  among barbarians, 59f
  of conscience, and the Reformation, 92
  history of
    in antiquity, 30-57
    in Christianity, 58-87
  intellectual, and the Catholic Church, 269-298

interpretation of, by Montesquieu, 5
Luther on, 69
of minorities, 30
Madison on, 200
and religion, Tocqueville on, 256
Free Trade, 220
French economists on, 261
Fremont, John, 244
French Assembly, 130
French Revolution, 77, 152ff., 167, 172, 175, 219f., 362
background of, 251-266
and the theory of equality, 154
Freret, Nicolas, 16
Friesland
intolerance of, 131
Frohschammer, Jacob, 270-298
on the Catholic Church, 286f.
censure of, 285ff.
on dogma, 287f.
influence of, 275
on the Protestant and Catholic churches, union of, 287f.
and the Roman Court, 283-285
on the soul, origin of, 281
and submission, 282
Froude, James Anthony, 28, 365
on progress, 13
Fugitive Slave Act, 238
Fustel de Coulanges, Numa, 14

Gallican theory, 63
Lamennais on, 271
Gams, Pius, 363
Gardiner, Samuel Rawson, 9
Gasquet, Francis, Cardinal, 88n.
Geneva, 8, 70, 77, 264f.
Genoa
and the Congress of Vienna, 179
Genovesi, Antonio, 267
George III, 82, 150
Georgia, 223
Germany, 3, 14, 16, 63, 128, 171
and nationalism, 190
primitive communities, republicanism of, 146
and the Vatican Council, 311f.
opposition to Ultramontanism at, 330, 338
Gerry, Elbridge
on the evils of democracy, 201

Ghent, 66
bigotry of, 131
revolt of, 147
Ghibellines, 64
Giannone, Pietro, 267
Gibbon, Edward, 16, 22
Ginoulhiac, Jacques, Bishop, 345
on the Protestants, 346
on Strossmayer, 342
Girondins, 152
Gladstone, Mary, xxvii
Gladstone, William Ewart, xvii, xxi, xxiii, xxv, xxixf., xlvii, lix
on statesmanship, 370
and the Vatican Council, 313
Glencoe
massacre of, 27
Goethe, Johann Wolfgang von, xlvii
Goires, Johann von
on Bonapartism, 177
Goths, 62
Government
civil, Brownson on, 241
English, Hamilton on, 202
federal
Read on, 205
Jay on, 205
French economists on, 261
Harrington on, 261
Hebrew, primitive, 132
representative, 54, 67, 267
Rousseau's theory of, 264f.
United States, Brownson on, 236f.
state, Hamilton on, 205
Gracchi, 43
reforms of, 142
Gracchus, Gaius, 142f.
Grace
Schwenkfeld on, 106
Grant, Ulysses S.
and Mormon polygamy, 131
Granville, George Leveson-Gower, Lord, xviiif., xxi
Gratry, Auguste
and Ultramontanism, 343
Greece, 34, 37, 39, 50
and nationalism, 37, 179
Greek mythology
failure of, 37f.
Gregorovius, Ferdinand, 367
Gregory VII, 146

INDEX

Grenoble, Bishop of
  and the Vatican Council
    support of Ultramontanism at, 334
    opposition to Ultramontanism at, 339
Grenville, George, 360
Grey, Charles Grey, 2nd Earl (Lord Grey), 163
Gropper, Johann, 359
Grote, George, 22
Grotius, Hugo, 32, 73f.
Guelphs, 64, 69
Guizot, François, 31, 128, 162, 163
  on Lamennais, 260
  on Scherer, 260
  on the Vatican Council, 300
Günther, Anton
  censure of, 274, 280

Habeas Corpus Act, 31, 67
Hadrian VI, 359
Hague, The, 9
Halifax, Archbishop of
  opposition to Ultramontanism at Vatican Council, 328, 339
  on the scriptures, 353
Halifax, Charles Wood, Viscount, 27, 80
Hallam, Henry
  on James II, 9
Hamilton, Alexander, 50, 204, 208, 211
  on commerce and industry, 218
  on democracy, 202, 210f.
  on government
    English, 202
    federal, 205
  on Jefferson, 214
    embargo of, 215
  Johnson on, 205
  Madison on, 202f.
  on monarchy, 201f.
  political theories of
    Madison on, 206
    Martin on, 207
  on the will of the people, 209
Hapsburgs, 171
Harrington, James, 27, 77
  on government, 261
  and property, 149

Hase, Karl von
  on the Vatican Council, 300
Hayne, Robert
  debate with Webster, 223
  on majority rule, 223f.
Hefele, Karl van, 363
  and Ultramontanism, 345, 350, 355
Hegel, Georg, 260
  on the function of royalty, 155
Henry II
  persecution of Huguenots by, 71
Henry III (of Navarre), 68
  exclusion from Paris by Catholics, 148
  reaction of French Catholics against, 72
Henry V, 71
Henry VIII, 69, 366
Heraclitus, 49f.
Heresy, 96
  Beza on, 123
  Bullinger on, 114
  Luther on, 102f.
  Swiss Reformers on, 114
Heretics
  punishment of
    Münzer on, 110
    by state, Œcolampadius on, 115
Hermes, Georg
  censure of, 280
Hildebrandine controversy
  and Long Parliament, 73
Hildreth, Richard
  on federalism and the Jeffersonians, 213f.
  on Jefferson, 212
Historian, the
  Acton's advice to, 367ff.
  of European democracy, May as, 128ff.
  impartiality of, 13, 18f., 29
  role of
    Fénelon on, 254f.
    Ranke on, 20
Historical knowledge
  importance of, 21f.
Historical writing
  new method in, 7
  source of, 17f.
  technique of, 17
History
  authority of, Catholics on, 322

documents, use of, 9ff, 16f.
  ecclesiastical, 5
  Historical School of, 16
  influence of, on other disciplines, 22f.
  Liberal School of, 16
  May's theory of, 130
  modern
    definition of, 5
    need for, study of, 4
    progress in, 12ff.
  moral character of, x
  and moral judgment, 25f.
  precepts for, 24f.
  purpose of, 9ff.
  Romantic School of, 16
  study of, 3-29
Hobbes, Thomas, xlvif.
  on royal absolutism, 75
Hohenlohe-Schillingsfurst, Chlodwig, Prince of, 309f.
Hohenzollern, House of, 171
Holland, 170
Home and Foreign Review, xx
  and censorship, 294
  discontinuation of, 295-298
  function of, 290
Homicide, xi
Holy Alliance, 178f.
Holy See, 314ff.
Homogeneity
  democracy and, 247ff.
Hooker, Richard
  Ecclesiastical Polity, 72
Hooker, Thomas
  on the infallibility of the people, 266
Hort, Fenton, 18
Hotman, François
  Franco-Gallia, 148
House of Commons 31
Huguenots
  and democracy, 148
  persecution of, by Francis I and Henry II, 71
Humboldt, Friedrich von
  on Bonapartism, 177
Hume, David, 81, 258
Hungary
  Catholic Church, reform of in, 316f
  Seward on, 245

Hunter, John, 22
Huss, John, 167, 360

Imperialism, 85
  Roman, 6
Independence
  Fénelon on, 169
  War of, 167
Index of Prohibited Books, 278-281, 291, 336f.
  Fessler, Bishop, on, 302
  Wurzburg, Bishop of, on, 302
India, 54
Indians, 249
Indies, 171
Industry
  growth of, 65f.
Infallibilty of the people
  Alcuin on, 266
  Bossuet on, 266
  Hooker on, 266
  Jurieu on, 266
  Newman on, 267
  Rousseau on, 266
Infallibility, Papal, *see* Vatican Council
Innocent III, 372
Innocent IV, 146
Inquisition, 90f., 301
  English rejection of, 86
  Spanish, 69, 90f., 363
Institutions
  social, Fénelon on, 255
Insurrection, 91, 167
  Luther on, 92n.
  right of, 67
  Spanish, 147
Intolerance
  of Anabaptists, 110f.
  Catholic, 180f, 300f.
  of Friesland, 131
  Protestant
    in Massachusetts, 127
    towards Socinians and Anabaptists, 108
  Spanish, 109
  Sweden and, 109
Ireland, 23, 51
  and nationalism, 179
Italy, 9, 16, 35, 63, 128, 171, 181
  and nationalism, 177, 190

Jackson, Andrew
   aversion to Calhoun, 229f.
   condemnation of nullification, 230
   dismissal of officials, 233
   power in government of, Story on, 234
   presidency of, 158
   on the tariff, 231f
Jacobins, 153f.
Jacobites
   defeat of, 170
   doctrine of, and monarchy, 257
Jacquerie, the, 147
James II, 77
   Hallam on, 9
James, Henry, xxvii
Janet, Paul
   on Luther, 92n.
Jansenists, 153, 252
Janus, xxii
   on Ultramontanism, 318, 325
Jay, John
   on the homogeneity of Americans, 208
Jefferson, Thomas, 15, 200, 202, 204, 230
   democratic ideas of, 211
   Embargo of, 214f.
      Adams on, 216
      Hamilton on, 215
      Quincy on, 251
      Story on, 251
   Hamilton on, 214
   Hildreth on, 212
   on majorities, 212f.
   on the presidency, 212
   on slavery, 237f.
   on Washington, 210
Jerusalem, 5, 34, 58
Jesuits, 148, 163, 303f., 359
   Lamennais on, 271
   and Pius IX, 304f
   on Ultramontanism, 305
Jesus, 14, 57
Jews, 5, 26
   Calvin on, 118
   Catholic tolerance of, 108
   early government of, 33, 132
   Luther on, 103
John, King of Saxony, 311f.
John of Salisbury, 72, 146

Johnson, William
   on Hamilton, 205
Joseph II
   penal system of, 267
Joubert, Joseph
   on Lamennais, 271
Judae, Leo
   on the Catholics, 113
   influence on, by Bullinger and Capito, 113f.
Julian, Emperor, 19
"Junius," 148
Jurieu, Pierre
   Bossuet's reply to, 253
   on the infallibilty of the people, 266
   on popular sovereignty, 252
Jurisprudence
   Continental, 267
Justification by faith
   Luther on, 97
   Newman on, 101
Justinian I, 59

Kant, Immanuel, 14
Kempis, Thomas à, 360
Ken, Thomas, 367
Kenrick, Peter, Archbishop, 306
   and Ultramontanism, 339, 345-350
Kettler, Wilhelm von, Bishop
   and Ultramontanism, 345, 350
Klee, Heinrich
   Frohschammer on, 281
Know-nothings, 249
Knox, John, 72, 366
   on the Catholics, 71
Kossuth, Louis, 245

Labor
   free, French economists on, 261
Laboulaye, Edouard, 158
La Bourdonnaie, François de, 155
Lafayette, Marie, Marquis de, 83, 156f.
Laissez faire, 13
La Luzerne, Cézar, 153
Lamartine, Alphonse Marie Louis de, 158
Lamennais, Robert de, xxxvi, 273f.
   on Chateaubriand, 272
   fall of, 274
   on the French bishops, 271

on Gallicanism, 271
Guizot on, 260
influence of, 274f.
on the Jesuits, 271
philosophy of, 275
on the Pope
  infallibility of, 272, 274
on Rome
  corruption of, 273f.
  Court of, 272
on Ultramontanism, 271
Land
  Asgill on, 263
Lanfrey, Pierre, 19
Laud, William, 78
Laurence, R. V., 88n.
Laval, Bishop of
  opposition to Ultramontanism at Vatican Council, 328
Law
  Athenian theories of, 136
  higher, doctrine of, 33
Lecky, William, lix
Legaré, Hugh, 228
  on the tariff, 229
Legitimacy, 85, 183
Leibnitz, Gottfried Wilhelm, 16, 260, 410n.
Leicester, Robert Dudley, Earl of, 148, 151
Leighton, Frederic, 363
Leopold I, Grand Duke of Tuscany, 151
  Arthur Young on, 267
Lessing, Gotthold, 260
Lessius, Leonard, 148
Letters from Rome on the Council, xxiiif.
Leuthen
  Lutherans at, 10
Liberty, 265f.
  and authority, 184ff.
  Burke on, 82f
  Calhoun on, 224f.
  characterizations of, 14f.
  Christian, 246
  and Christianity, 57
  in collision between Church and State, 62
  of conscience, 15, 54, 149
  danger to, from majorities, 135

definition of, 32f.
  religious, 90
  and democracy, distinction between, 130
  Fénelon on, 253f.
  function of, 51
  as the guardian of religion, 33
  Luther's hostility to, 94
  and nationalism, 193
  of opinion, 15
  and property rights, 81
  of prophesying, 12
  religious, 90, 188, 256
  of representation, 15
  rise of, 62
  Socratic School, contribution to, 139
Licinius
  on political equality, 130
Liebig, Justus von
  Organic Chemistry, 22
Lightfoot, Joseph, Bishop, 18
Lilburne, John, 77, 149
Lincoln, Abraham, 247
Lingard, John, 9
Linnaeus, 22
Livingston, Robert, 230
  on secession, 231
Locke, John, 65, 79f., 129, 148
  doctrine of resistance, 81
Lollards, 78
Long Parliament
  and Hildebrandine controversy, 73
Louis XIII, 68
Louis XIV, 75, 151, 366
  despotism of, Fénelon on, 254f.
  support of Charles II, 80
  tyranny of, 76f.
Louis XVI, 75, 84, 151, 251
Louis Philippe, xxxvi, 31, 83, 157
Louisiana, 230
Lowndes, William
  and the tariff, 220
  support of, 218
Luca, de, Cardinal, 340
Lucretius, 260
Lural, Bishop of
  support of Ultramontanism at Vatican Council, 332
Luther, Martin, li, 6, 9, 19, 92, 167, 359, 366
  on the Anabaptists, 95n

INDEX   441

and civil power, 147
on conversion, the use of force for, 92n., 101
on Catholic worship, 102f.
on Christian freedom, 99
as an enemy of freedom, 69
on excommunication, 96f.
on the faithful, 97
on heresy, 102f.
hostility of, to liberty, 94
hostility of, to the Peasants' Rebellion, 95
on his being persecuted, 94
on insurrection, 92n.
on the intervention of the state in religion, 92, 96
Janet on, 92n.
on the Jews, 103
on justification by faith, 97
on the Mosaic law, 98
passive obedience, 100
persecution of, by Charles V and the dukes of Bavaria, 69
political ideas of, 97f., 116f.
influence of, on Catholic countries, 97
Ranke on, 100
ridicule of the Copernican system, 99
on the Scripture, 98
turning to the princes, 94
Lutheran states, 69
Lutheranism, lii
Lutherans
persecution of Anabaptists by 110
salvation of, 97
Lycurgus, 32, 52

Mably, Gabriel, 267
Macaulay, Thomas, xxxiv, xxxvii, xlv, 13, 17, 27, 80, 365
Arnold on, xxxv
Machiavelli, Niccolo di Bernardo, xlvi f., 6, 21, 68, 71
on assassination, 76
Mackintosh, Sir James, 16
on constitutions, the organic development of, 85
Madison, James, 209
on class structure and interest, 208f.

on Hamilton, 202f.
political theories of, 206
on minorities, freedom of, 200
on nullification, Webster's speech against, 230
on voting, the role of, 203
Washington on, 204f.
Magna Carta, 31
Maine, Henry, xlvii
Maistre, Joseph de
on Bonapartism, 177
Majorities
Channing on, 210
danger to liberty from, 135
Jefferson on, 212
as oppressors of minorities, 40
rule of
Hayne on, 223f.
at Vatican Council, 348
Manifest destiny
Seward on, 245
Manin, Daniele, 182
Manning, Henry, Cardinal, xx, xxvi, lv, 335
support of Ultramontanism at Vatican Council, 349f.
Manteuffel, Otto von, 179
Manufacturing
in America, 218
Hamilton on, 219
Marat, Jean, 84, 153f., 268, 366
Marcel, Étienne, 66
Maret, Bishop, 307
on Ultramontanism, 318
opposition to, at Vatican Council, 332ff.
Maria Theresa
penal system of, 267
Mariana, Juan de, 72, 148, 165
Maritain, Jacques, liii ff.
compared with Acton, lii
Marius, Caius, 51
Marlborough, John, Duke of, 80
Marmont, Auguste de, 157
Marsilius of Padua
on freedom, 64f.
Martignac, Jean, Viscount de, 155
Martin, Luther, 208
on Hamilton's political theories, 207
Martineau, Harriet, 234

Mary Stuart, 68, 366
Marxism, xlix
Maryland
  tolerance of Catholics in, 127
Mason, George, Colonel, 201
  on State-rights, 204
Massachusetts
  intolerance of Puritans in, 127
Massacre of St. Bartholomew, 71
Massey, Gerald, lviii
Matthew, Cardinal, 335f.
Maultrot, Gabriel
  on popular sovereignty, 253
May, Sir Thomas Erskine, 128-165
  as historian of European democracy, 128ff.
  as public figure, 128
  theory of history, 130
Mazarin, Jules, Cardinal, 9
Mazzini, Giuseppe, 85, 128
  and Carbonarism, 181
  and nationalism, 169, 181f.
Melanchthon, Philip, 98f.
  on the Catholics, 107
    persecution by, 103f.
  on the dissident sects, 105
  and Servetus, condemnation of, 106f.
  tolerance of his last years, 109
  on the Zwicau prophets, 103
Melito, Bishop, 56
Mémoires d'un Homme d'Etat, 21
Metternich, Klemens, 128, 179
  and nationalism, 180
Mexico
  and nationalism, 190f.
Michaud, Eugène, xxv
Michelet, Jules, 16, 21
Middle Ages, 6, 25, 32, 66f., 75, 191
Mignet, François, 16
Mill, John Stuart, xxxvii, xxxix, 158, 163
  Arnold on, xxxv
  Logic, 22
  on Macaulay, xxxiv f.
  on nationalism, 181, 183
Miltiades, 134
Milton, John, 78f., 148f., 165, 266
Minorities
  in a democracy, 197ff.
  freedom of, 33
    Madison on, 200

  as oppressors of majorities, 40
  Story on, 209
  Webster on, 210
Mirabeau, Victor, Marquis de, 152
Missouri Compromise, 237
Mohammedans
  Calvin on, 118
  Catholic tolerance of, 108
Molina, Luis de, 148
Mommsen, Theodor, 13
Monarchy, 32f., 48, 75, 174, 176
  absolute, 175
  Bonald on, 275
  checks on, 49
  and family alliances, 170
  Jacobite doctrine and, 257
  Montesquieu on, 257f.
  need for, Hamilton on, 200f.
Monroe, James, 83
Monroe Doctrine, 245
Montalembert, Charles de, xxxvi
  opposition to Ultramontanism at Vatican Council, 330
Montesquieu, Charles de Secondat de, 5, 65, 81, 130, 255, 259, 268
  compared with French economists, 262
  on English superiority, 256
  on monarchy, 257f.
Montfort, Simon de, 64
Moral integrity, 4
Morality
  God as the guide to, 5°
  historical, Burke on, 29
  and power, Creighton on 371
  Smith, Goldwin, on, 28
More, Thomas, xii, 79, 85, 362
  Utopia, 72
  influence of, 166f.
Morelly, Abbé, 267
Morley, John, vii, xxxii, xxxvii, xxxix
Mormons
  polygamy, General Grant and, 131
Morris, Gouverneur
  on legislative power, 201
Mosaic Law
  and polygamy, 98
Mounier, Jean Joseph, 152
Mozley, James, xi, xlv, 28

Muller, Johannes
  on Bonapartism, 177
  on the British Constitution, 27
Munich, 182
  Archbishop of, xx
Munzer, Thomas
  on the punishment of heretics, 110
Muratists, 178
Muratori, Ludovico, 16

Nantes, Edict of, 252
  revocation of, 109
Naples, 17
  and nationalism, 190
Napoleon I, 7, 17, 19, 44, 76, 161
  and nationalism, 177-180
Napoleon III, xxxvi, 44
Nationalism, 14, 85, 166-195
  Austria and, 190ff.
  Baden and, 190
  Belgium and, 179
  Bossuet on, 190
  Burke on, 189
  Catholic Church as an enemy of, 186
  and the Congress of Vienna, 178ff.
  and exile, 181
  as an extension of family life, 188
  Florence and, 190
  France and, 190
  Germany and, 190
  Greece and, 37, 179
  growth of, 179ff.
  Ireland and, 179
  Italy and, 177, 190
  and liberty, 193
  Mazzini on, 169, 181f.
  Metternich on, 180
  Mexico and, 190f.
  Mill on, 181, 183
  Naples and, 190
  Napoleon and, 177-180
  Neapolitan States and, 190
  origin of, 172
  Parma and, 190
  Poland and, 179
  political, 188ff.
  Prussia and, 177
  Rousseau on, 189f.
  Russia and, 177
  and slavery, influence on, 191
  socialism, contrasted with, 194f.
  Spain and, 177
  and the State, 192
  Switzerland and, 190
  Tuscany and, 190
  Tyrol and, 177
Naville, Edouard Henri, 163
Neapolitan States
  and nationalism, 190
Necker, Jacques, 152
Negroes, 249
  Agassiz on, 242
Nero, 140
Nerva, Marcus, 43
Netherlands, 77
  rebellion in, 71f.
  resistance to Philip II, 147
  revolt of, 167
New Jersey, 204
Newman, John Henry, Cardinal, xxvi, xxxv, 23, 365
  on the infallibility of the people, 266
  on Luther's theory of justification by faith, 101
  on progress, 13
Niebuhr, Barthold, 21, 85
Normans, 62
North, Frederick, Lord, 216, 360
North British Review, xxii
North Carolina, 224
Nugent, Laval
  proclamation to Italians, 181
Nullification, 215, 236
  Colton on, 231
  Jackson's condemnation of, 230
  principle of, 224
  Webster's speech against, Madison on, 230

Oates, Titus, 24, 80
Obedience
  Calvin on, 120
  passive, Luther on, 100
Octavius
  and the veto, 142
Œcolampadius, John
  on the Anabaptists, 115f.
  on excommunication, 116
  on heresy, state punishment of, 115

on persecution of the Catholics by the Protestants, justification of, 116
Old Catholic churches, xxiv
Ollivier, Olivier, 310f.
Optatus, Saint, 56
Origen
 on tyranny, 56
Orleans, Bishop of, *see* Dupanloup
Osiander, Andreas, 95
Oxford, Bishop of, 14

Paderborn, Bishop of
 support of Ultramontanism at Vatican Council, 324
Paine, Thomas, 211
Pallas, 37
Panhellenism, 180
Pan-Slavism, 180
Paoli, Pasquale, 150
Papacy, 361
 archives of, 16
Paris, 8, 16
Paris, Archbishop of, *see* Darboy
Parliament
 English, 31, 63, 147
 Scottish, 63f.
Parma
 and nationalism, 190
Parnassus, 37
Pascal, Blaise, 198, 260
 on royal absolutism, 75
Pastor, Ludwig von, 367
Patriotism, 188
Paul, Saint
 on slavery, 247
Pazzi Conspiracy, 366
Peasants' War, 93, 147
 Luther's hostility to, 95
Peel, Sir Robert, 11, 128
Peloponnesian War, 39, 136
Penal system
 of Joseph II, 267
 of Maria Theresa, 267
Penn, William, 150, 165
Periander
 on slavery, 130
Pericles, 37ff, 159
 distribution of power by, 38f.
 political ideas of, 134
 on public duty, 134f.
 on slavery, 130

Pericles, 18
Perrone, Giovanni
 support of Ultramontanism at Vatican Council, 307
Persecution
 Bucer on, 111f.
 Bullinger on, 114
 Catholic, li
 Melanchthon on, 103f.
 of early Christians, 58
 of Huguenots, 71
 liberals' view of, 363
 of Luther, 69
 Œcolampadius on, 116
 Protestant theory of, 88-127 *passim*
 religious, democracy and, 131
Persian War, 36
Phaleas, 135
Philadelphia, 8
 Constitutional Convention of, 31, 199f.
Philip II, 71, 77, 366
 resistance of Netherlands to, 147
Philip, Landgrave
 bigamy of, 98
Philo, 53f.
Philosophy
 German, mistrust of, by Rome, 283
Physiocrats, 261
Pierce, Franklin, 244
Pinckney, Charles
 on the British Constitution, 203
 presents plan of a constitution, 204
Pitt, William, *see* Chatham, William Pitt, Earl of
Pius IX, xviii, xx, 299f.
 address of the bishops to, 306f.
 and *Civiltà Cattolica*, 304
 and the Germans, 326
 and the Jesuits, 304f.
 letter of, to the Protestants, 300
 and Russia, 300
 Syllabus of Errors of, 229, 303, 310, 326
 and Ultramontanism, 302f.
 and the Vatican Council, 337ff.
Plantagenet, House of, 63
Plato, 46f., 55, 135, 159
 Laws, 50
 political ideas of, 137f.
 Republic, influence of, 166f.

Plotinus, 166
Plutarch, 18
Pocock, Edward, 17
Poland, 70, 76, 156, 170, 178ff., 188
 and the Congress of Vienna, 178
 division of, 171f.
  Burke on, 171
 and nationalism, 179
 Talleyrand and, 178
Polignac, Melchior de, 155
Political parties
 power of, Channing on, 236
Political science
 the Catholic Church and, 276
Political theories
 of Aristides, 134
 of the Christian sects, 132f.
 of Hamilton
  Madison on, 206
  Martin on, 207
 of Pericles, 134
 of Plato, 137f
 of Solon, 133f.
 of Zwingli, 117
Politics
 lack of principles in, 73
Polity
 ecclesiastical, Hooker on, 72
Polybius, 145
Polygamy
 Carlstadt on, 98
 Mormon, Grant and, 131
 and Mosaic Law, 98
Pompey, 51
Portugal
 and the Vatican Council, 314
Power, 13, 15, 364
 Calhoun on, 235
 civil, Luther on, 99, 147
 decentralization of, 49
 desire for, 30
 distribution of
  and the mixed constitution, 47f.
  by Pericles, 38f.
  by Solon, 35f.
 Fénelon on, 254
 French economists on, 261
 legislative, Morris on, 201
 morals of, Creighton on, 371
 of political parties, Channing on, 236

Presbyterianism
 and democracy, 147f.
Presidency
 of Andrew Jackson, 158
 Everett on, 233
 Federalists on, 211f.
Price, Richard, 208
Prierias, Sylvester
 on the scriptures, 321
Priestley, Joseph, 208
Printing
 invention of, 67
Privileged Altars
 theory of, 360
Progress
 Carlyle on, 13
 Comte on, 13
 Froude on, 13
 Newman on, 13
 Ranke on, 13
 Turgot on, 259f.
Property
 balance of, Harrington on, 149
Protagoras, 49, 131
Protestant, 10
Protestant Reformation, 1
Protestant Reformers
 Servetus and, 123ff.
Protestantism
 influence on state policy of, 88ff.
Protestants
 intolerance towards Socinians and
  Anabaptists, 108
 persecution of, li
  by King of France, 71
 persecution of Catholics, Œcolampadius on, 116
 and Pius IX, 300
 Strossmayer on, 346
 and the suppression of error, Reformers on, 103ff.
 and toleration, 89, 91
Prussia, 9, 11
 and nationalism, 177
Prynne, William, 149
Public duty
 Pericles on, 134f.
Pufendorf, Samuel, 74
Punic War, Second, 5
Pusey, Edward
 on the Vatican Council, 300
Pythagoras, 49

Quakers, 129
　and toleration, 150
Quentin Durward, 20
Quincy, Joseph
　on Jefferson's embargo, 215
"Quirinus," xxiii

The Rambler, xix, 88n.
Randolph, Edmund Jennings, 216, 239
　and the Virginia Plan, 204
　on democracy, 201
Ranke, Leopold von, x, 9, 20f.
　on the Church in politics, 10
　on the historian, role of, 20
　on Luther, 100
　on progress, 13
　on William III, 27
Ravaillac, François, 364
Raynal, Guillaume, 261, 268
Read, George
　on the United States federal government, 205
Reason and faith, 274
Rebellion
　Calvin on, 118f.
　the Great, 167
　right of
　　against tyrants, 71
　　against a king, 77
　Tyler on, 147
Reform
　of the Church, 246
　　in its head and members, 301
　in France, 151
Reformation, 11, 20, 69f., 79, 94, 358f.
　conquests of, 11
　and conscience, freedom of, 92
　Creighton on, 372
　early, 92
　English, 11
　Protestant, 1
　Scotch, 70
Reformers, 360
　Swiss, republicanism of, 112
Regicide
　Buchanan on, 148
Reisach, Cardinal
　support of Ultramontanism at Vatican Council, 307f.

Religion, 10
　as the mother of freedom, 12
　and politics, 11f.
Renaissance, 6, 359
Renan, Ernest, xli, 19
Representation
　American, in the House and Senate, 208
Republican Party, 238, 243ff.
Republicanism
　of Athens, 134f.
　of the Essenes, 132
　Federal, 15
　primitive, 60
　of German communities, 146
　of Rome, 145
　of Swiss Reformers, 112
　tyranny of, Cobbett on, 235
　of Zwingli, 147
Republics
　English, failure of, 77f.
　rise of, 83f.
Resistance
　Locke's doctrine of, 81
Restoration
　French, 9
　of the Stuarts, 11
Reumont, Alfred von, 366
Revolution
　American, 9, 81f., 150f.
　　political causes of, 196-250
　doctrine of, 12
　Dutch, 15
　of 1848, 158
　French, 152, 167, 172, 175
　of Ghent, 147
　historical writing and, 15f.
　idea of, 6
　of 1688, 149
　theory of, 167f.
　Whig, 64
Rhode Island, 127
Richelieu, Armand de, Cardinal, lix, 9, 75, 131
Rienzi, Niccolo, 66
Rights of Man, 12, 82, 130f., 151
Rivière, Mercier de la
　Diderot on, 263
Robespierre, Maximilien, 153f.
Roland, Madame, 154
Rollin, Ledru, 158

Romans
  wars of the, 142
Rome, 9, 11, 42, 48, 58, 78
  absolutism of, 144
  civil law of, 44
  constitution of, 141
  history of, 42ff.
  corruption of, Lamennais on, 273f.
  Court of, 299
    Frohschammer and, 283ff.
    Lamennais on, 272
  Empire of, 43f.
    divines of, 61
    migration of barbarians, 60
  jurisprudence, reform of, 45
  jurists of, 53f., 145
  patricians and plebeians, controversy of, in, 142
  Republic of, 43, 174
    failure of, 140
    republicanism of, 145
  Senate of, 51
  slavery, mitigation of, in, 44
  tribunes of, 142ff.
  triumvirate of, 44
Roothan, Johann, 304
Rope, John, 19
Roscher, Wilhelm, 50
Rosmini-Serbati, Antonio, 304
  censure of, 274
Rothschild, Nathaniel, xxi
Rouscher, Cardinal
  opposition to Ultramontanism at Vatican Council, 338, 341, 350
Rousseau, Jean Jacques, 25, 84, 148, 150, 153, 160, 164f., 211, 258, 267
  and equality, 169
  on the infallibility of the people, 266
  on nationalism, 189
  and the *Social Contract*, 266
  theory of government of, 264f.
Rovere, Guliano della, 360
Royalty
  Hegel on the function of, 155
Ruskin, John, xxxv
Russell, John, Lord, xvii, 80
Russia, 32
  and nationalism, 177
  and Pius IX, 300
  and the Vatican Council, 314

Sacred College, 302
Saint Louis, Archbishop of, see Kenrick
Salvanius, 61
Salvation
  of Lutherans, 97
  Thamer on, 105f.
Samuel, 33
Sand, Georges, 158
Saxons, 62, 187
Saxony, King of
  and Congress of Vienna, 178
Scherer, Edmond
  Guizot on, 260
Schmalkald, Confession of, 97
Scholars
  German, problems of, 279
Scholarship
  German, toleration of, by Rome, 280
Schrader, Clement
  support of Ultramontanism at Vatican Council, 307ff.
Schwarzenberg, Cardinal, 179
  opposition to Ultramontanism at Vatican Council, 331f., 335, 338, 350
Schwegler, Albert, 18
Schwenkfeld, Kaspar von
  on grace, 106
Science
  and Catholicism, 270, 276-298
  of the Greeks, 37f.
Scipio, 44
Scotland, 72
  parliament of, address on Robert Bruce, 63f.
  and Reformation, 70
Scriptures
  authority of
    Catholics on, 320f.
    Luther on, 98
  Halifax on, 353
  Prierias on, 321
Secession, 230, 238, 241, 244, 247
  Adams on, 216
  Calhoun on, 243
  Colton on, 231
  justification of, 231
  Livingston on, 231

Sects
  Christian, political theories of, 132f.
  Melanchthon on, 105
Seeley, John, 3
Selden, John, 149
Self-government, 49, 265
  among the Jews, 33
  Aquinas on, 64
Seneca, 32, 53, 55, 140, 260
Servetus, Michael
  Bullinger on, 114
  condemnation of, 106
    Melanchthon on, 106f.
  death of, and Calvin, 121
  and the Protestant Reformers, 123ff.
Seven Years' War, 10
Seward, William
  Carlisle on, 240
  on Cuba, 245
  on Hungary, 245
  on manifest destiny, 245
Shaftesbury, Anthony, Lord, 80
Sherman, Roger
  on popular election, 200
Sicily, 69
Sidney, Algernon, 80
Siéyès, Abbé, 15, 84, 152ff.
  council, idea of, 161
  on France, unity of, 173
Simpson, Richard, 88n.
Sixtus IV, 363, 366
Slavery, 15, 32, 47, 53f., 56f., 67, 130, 243, 250
  Burke on, 131
  and Catholicism, 246
  Emerson on, 243
  Jefferson on, 237f.
  and nationalism, influence of, on, 191
  Paul on, 247
  Periander on, 130
  Pericles on, 130
  in Rome, 44
  Story on, 239
  in the United States, 208
Smith, Adam, lx, 25, 84, 261
  Wealth of Nations, 56
Smith, Goldwin
  on historical morality, 28
Social Contract, 266

Socialism, 158, 267
Society
  structure of, Fénelon on, 254f.
Socinians
  Protestant intolerance towards, 108
Socinus, Faustus, 12, 79, 362
Socrates, 5, 46, 54, 57, 131, 137, 196
  democratic ideas of, 137
  martyrdom of, 41
Solon, 39, 52, 135
  distribution of power by, 35f.
  political ideas of, 133f.
Sophistry, 46
Sophists, 137
Sophocles, 55
South, the
  conservatism of, Calhoun on, 241
  planters of, 244
South Carolina, 204, 238
Sovereignty
  popular
    Jurieu on, 252
    Maultrot on, 253
Spain, 9, 11, 62, 171
  and the Constitution of 1812, 155
  Inquisition, 69, 363
  insurrection in, 147
  intolerance of, 109
  and nationalism, 177
  and the Vatican Council, 313f.
Spanish Cortes, 31
Sparta, 48
Spinoza, Benedict
  on royal absolutism, 75
Staël, Anne Louise, Madame de, 28
Stanley, Arthur, Bishop
  on the Vatican Council, 300
State-rights, 215, 237f.
  Bedford on, 204
  Mason on, 204
  Trumbull on, 215f.
States-General, 31, 268
Stein, Heinrich, Baron
  on Bonapartism, 177
Stephen, Leslie, xviii
Stoics, 52ff., 57
  political theories of, 139
Story, Joseph
  on Jackson, power in government of, 234
  on Jefferson, embargo of, 215f.

on minorities, 209
on slavery, 239
on the tariff, 219
Strafford, Thomas Wentworth, Earl of, 78
Strossmayer, Joseph
 on majority rule at the Vatican Council, 348
 on the Protestants, 346
 opposition to Ultramontanism at Vatican Council, 328, 339, 342
Struensee, John, 151
Stuarts
 and Divine Right, 74
Stubbs, William, Bishop, 18
Suarez, Francisco, 148
Suffrage, 31
 universal, in America, 162
Sunderland, Robert Spencer, Earl of, 27
Superstitions
 Catholic, 302
Sweden
 and intolerance, 109
Swiss Reformers
 on heresy, 114
 republicanism of, 112
Switzerland, 66
 constitution of
  federal, 156
  of 1848, 156f.
  of 1874, 156.
 democracy in, 156
 nationalism of, 190
Sylla, 143
Syllabus of Errors of Pius IX, xxi, 299, 303, 310, 326

Tacitus, 43, 48
Talleyrand, Périgord de, 153
 on Poland, 178
Tariff, American
 Brownson on, 229
 Calhoun on, 220-223
 Cobbett on, 221
 Jackson on, 231f.
 Legaré on, 229
 Lowndes on, 220
 opposition to
  by South, 221f.
  by Webster, 218
 Story on, 219
 support of, by Lowndes and Calhoun, 218
 withdrawal of, 231
Taxation
 of America by England, 82
 Camden on, 82
 de Commines on, 67
 in France, Vauban on, 75f.
 of incomes, 67
 and representation, 67
Taylor, Jeremy, 79, 363
Temple, Sir William, 27
Tertullian, 56
Tetzel, Johann, 359
Teutonic State
 conflict between Church and, 146
Thamer, Theobald
 on salvation, 105f.
Theiner, Augustin, 304
Theocracy
 of Calvin, 117f.
Theognis, 35
Thierry, Jacques, 158
Thiers, Louis Adolphe, 13, 17
Thirty Years' War, 9
Thomas à Kempis, 360
Thucydides, 41, 159
Tillemont, Sébastien de, 16
Tocqueville, Alexis de, xliii, lvi, lix, 32, 50, 130, 132, 158, 164, 212
 on American democracy, 233f.
 on freedom and religion, 256
Toland, John, 149
Tolerance
 of Capito, 111
 Catholic
  of Jews and Mohammedans, 108
  in Maryland, 127
 Creighton on, 371
 of Melanchthon, 109
 by Moors and Turks, 126
 and the Quakers, 150
Toleration, 12
 of Bayle, 252
 Calvin on, 121
 Fénelon on, 253f.
 sects of, 12
 theory of, 256
  absolute, 107
 of Protestants, 89, 91
Tories, 19, 23f.

Toynbee, Arnold J., ix, xxxi
Trade, free
  French economists on, 261
Tradition
  use of, by English patriots, 78
Trafalgar, 24
Treitschke, Heinrich von, 13
Trent, Council of, xxii, 300, 319f.
Tridentine divines, 359
Trumbull, Jonathan
  on State-rights, 215f.
Turgot, Anne Robert, 151, 255, 263, 268
  on progress, 259f.
Tuscany
  and nationalism, 190
Tyler, Wat, rebellion, 147
Tyranny
  of Louis XIV, 76
  Origen on, 56
  of republicanism, Cobbett on, 235
Tyrants
  murder of, 72f.
  right of rebellion against, 71
Tyrol
  and nationalism, 177

Ullman, Karl, 360
Ulm
  Austrian surrender at, 24
Ultramontanism, xviii, 156, 299-356
  censorship of, 344f
  Church and State and, 309
  and *Civiltà Cattolica*, 306f.
  Dogmatic Commission of, 307, 309
  Dogmatic Decree of 1854, 305
  Dollinger on, 318f., 343f.
  and the encyclical of November, 1846, 303
  failure of, 355f.
  Gratry and, 343
  Hefele and, 345, 350, 355
  Hungarian Church and, 317
  Janus on, 318, 325
  Jesuits on, 305
  Kenrick and, 345, 350
  Kettler and, 345, 350
  Maret on, 318
  opposition to, at Vatican Council, by
    Alzog, 307
    Darboy, 328, 332f., 338
    Dupanloup, 328, 332
    French, 330, 338
    German, 330, 338
    Grenoble, Bishop of, 339
    Halifax, Archbishop of, 328, 339
    Kenrick, 339, 345-350
    Laval, Bishop of, 328
    Maret, 332, 334
    Montalembert, 330
    Rouscher, Cardinal, 338, 341, 350
    Schwarzenberg, Cardinal, 331f., 335, 338, 350
    Strossmayer, 328, 339, 342
  and Pius IX, 302f.
  prohibitions against, 343
  support of, at Vatican Council, by
    Antonelli, Cardinal, 307
    Cardoni, Archbishop, 307
    Fessler, Bishop, 307f.
    Franzelin, 307
    Grenoble, Bishop of, 334
    Laval, Bishop of, 332
    Manning, Archbishop, 349f.
    Mechlin, Archbishop of, 343
    Paderborn, Bishop of, 324
    Perrone, 307
    Reisach, Cardinal, 307f.
    Schrader, 307ff.
    Westminster, Archbishop of, 334
  yielding of, 354ff.
United States, 8, 196-250
  commerce, regulation of, in, 208
  democracy of, Tocqueville on, 223f.
  House of Representatives of, representation in, 208
  manufacturing in, 218
  presidency of
    Federalists on, 211f.
    Jefferson on, 212
  Senate of
    Dickinson on, 202
    representatives in, 208
  slavery in, 208
  suffrage, universal, in, 162
  Supreme Court of, 131, 161
Ussher, James, Archbishop, 75
Utilitarianism, 45

INDEX

Valentinian, 79
Vatican, the
  Archives, 9
Vatican Council, xxii, xxiv, 299-356
  activity at, 377f.
  Bavaria and, 312
  Belgium and, 314
  Beust on, 310
  Bismarck and, 312
  and the Bull *Multiplices,* 329, 333, 337, 345
  Cardinals and, 300
  Commission on Dogma of, 335
  commissions at, 327, 346
  De Angelis, Cardinal, and, 340
  decrees at, 340f.
  elections, fraudulent, at, 335f.
  England and, 313
  forgeries at, 319
  France and, 310f.
    delegation of, 335
  Germany and, 311
    Bishops of, at Fulda, 324
    delegation of, 335, 344
  Gladstone and, 313
  Guizot on, 300
  Hase, 300
  Hohenlohe, Prince, and, 309f.
  Hungarian delegation and, 335
  Italy and, 314ff.
  John, King of Saxony, and, 311
  majority rule at, 348
  and Pius IX, 337ff.
  Portugal and, 314
  procedure at, 327f., 344, 355
  Pusey on, 300
  questions for discussion at, 301f.
  Russia and, 314
  Spain and, 313f.
  Stanley on, 300
Vauban, Sebastien de
  on taxation in France, 75f.
Venice, 17, 76
  and Congress of Vienna, 178
Vergniaud, Pierre
  on the will of the people, 172
Versailles, 8
Veto
  Octavius and, 142
  right of, 238
Vico, Giambattista, 267

Vienna, 182
  Congress of, 178ff.
  and Austria, 179
  and Genoa, 178
  and nationalism, 179
  and Poland, 178
  and Saxony, King of, 178
  and Venice, 178
Vineis, Peter de, 146
Vinet, Alexandre, 14, 32
Virginia, 224
  House of Delegates of, 239
Virginia Plan
  presented by Edmund Randolph, 204
Voltaire, François de, 255, 268
  on English superiority, 256
Voting
  role of, Madison on, 203
Voting franchise
  Channing on, 235f.

Waddington, William, 165
War
  of 1870, 4, 11
  Fénelon on, 254
  Napoleonic, Pitt on, 24
Ward, William George, xx
Washington, George, 19, 31, 200, 211
  Jefferson on, 210
  on Madison, 204f.
Waterloo, 178
Wealth of Nations, 56
Webster, Daniel, 230, 238, 240, 243
  on the abolitionists, 239f.
  on conscience, 241
  debate with Hayne, 233
  on minorities, 209
  nullification, speech against, Madison on, 230
  tariff, opposition to, 218
Wellesley, Richard, 24
Westminster, Archbishop of
  support of Ultramontanism at Vatican Council, 334
Whigs, 25
  Holland House, 178
  theory of revolution of, 64
Will of the people
  Hamilton on, 209
William III, 77, 364
  Ranke on, 27

William the Norman, 61
William of Orange, 72, 77, 80, 252
Wilson, James
 on despotism, 201
Winchester, Bishop of, 71
Wiseman, Nicholas, Bishop, xviif., xx
Wittelsbach, House of, 171
Worship
 Catholic, Luther on, 102
Wyclif, John, 167, 360

Xenophon, 159, 196

Young, Arthur
 on Grand Duke Leopold, 267

Zeno, 45, 53, 139
Zurich, 70
Zwickau prophets
 Melanchthon on, 103
Zwingli, Ulrich, 70, 114, 366
 on the intervention of the State in religion, 112
 political theory of, 117
 republicanism of, 147
Zwinglian schism, 93

CPSIA information can be obtained at www.ICGtesting.com
Printed in the USA
BVOW03s1707140813

328602BV00010B/269/P